Frommer's®
Croatia

My Croatia
by Karen Torme Olson

QUESTIONS INEVITABLY SURFACE WHEN PEOPLE FIND OUT THAT I WRITE about Croatia. Is it safe? Did the war leave anything worth seeing? How do Croatians feel about Americans? I had the same questions (and a healthy dose of motherly concern) in 1999, when my son Greg announced he was moving to Croatia to work on a rebuilding project. Within a few months, Greg had lost his heart to the land, its people, and a beautiful girl named Sanja, and I grudgingly headed for this central European country to see what my kid was up to. What I found was an achingly beautiful land that pulled me into its thrall in a nanosecond.

In just one visit I found myself poking around Istria's hilltop towns, floating off Pag's shore in water so clear I could see sand crabs having lunch 9m (30 ft.) down, relishing the sound of Andrea Bocelli's magnificent voice from a vantage point on an ancient stone bench in Pula's Roman amphitheater, sipping wine in a Striga vineyard, and catching cooling spray from the tumbling waterfalls at Plitvice. But what captivated me even more than gorgeous landscapes and historical sites was the warmth and hospitality of Croatia's people. Check out the photos that follow, and my "Best of Croatia" chapter, and you'll get the idea.

ROVINJ (left) wins my vote for the prettiest town in Croatia. It was founded by Romans, was deeply influenced by Venetians, and is still home to an Italian majority, which is reflected in the food and street signs. Must-see attractions are the hilltop church of St. Euphemia (visible in this photo), the art galleries on Grisia Street, and Balbi's Arch, next to the Town Museum.

Turquoise lakes, rushing water, and a tranquil forest are the setting for **PLITVICE LAKES NATIONAL PARK (above)**. Whether you explore this UNESCO Heritage site for an hour or a day, you'll see spectacular waterfalls of every size and intensity, woodland gardens, and the occasional critter. When your hike is over, nothing tastes better than *janjetina*, lamb roasted on a spit. Get it hot off the fire just outside the park.

Evidence of Croatia's Homeland War has largely disappeared from most of the country, with the exception of the town of **VUKOVAR (left)**. Mortar-ravaged churches, pock-marked houses, and roofless structures still stand as testament to the 1991 destruction that hit this once-robust town on the Danube. Some say politicians have left the damage unrepaired deliberately, as a reminder of the attack.

By day, the **PERISTIL AREA OF DIOCLETIAN'S PALACE (above)** is a popular meeting place, an outdoor cafe, and one of the biggest remaining chunks of the Emperor's former digs. At night, especially during Split's Summer Fest, it becomes an open-air opera house. Tickets are difficult to find. If you can't snag a seat, book Room 302 on the top floor of the adjacent Peristil Hotel and open the window. The music will float up to you as you listen in comfort.

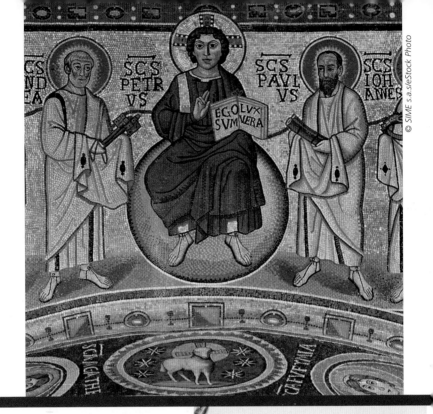

Poreč is home to the fabulous St. Euphrasius Basilica and its eye-popping mosaics, which still glow with gold, gems, and brilliant color after 14 centuries. The **APSE MOSAICS (above)** depict Christ and His Apostles and compare favorably with celebrated mosaics in Ravenna, Italy. My tip: Don't miss the mosaics displayed in outdoor courtyards *in situ*—not as vibrant as the Apse Mosaics but still amazing.

Almost every Croatian church and museum of religious art has a few ornate gold or silver arm, leg, or head sculptures. Each sculpture is a **RELIQUARY (right)** containing human relics from a saint or saintly person. I recommend seeing Zadar's exhibit and, if you have time, Vodjnan's in Istria.

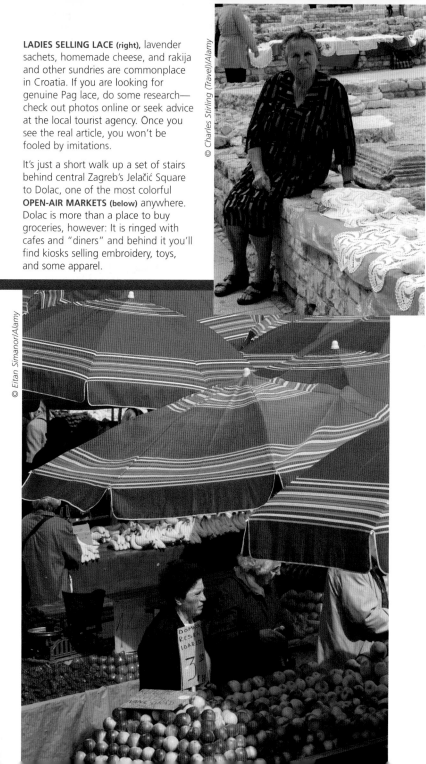

LADIES SELLING LACE (right), lavender sachets, homemade cheese, and rakija and other sundries are commonplace in Croatia. If you are looking for genuine Pag lace, do some research—check out photos online or seek advice at the local tourist agency. Once you see the real article, you won't be fooled by imitations.

It's just a short walk up a set of stairs behind central Zagreb's Jelačić Square to Dolac, one of the most colorful **OPEN-AIR MARKETS (below)** anywhere. Dolac is more than a place to buy groceries, however: It is ringed with cafes and "diners" and behind it you'll find kiosks selling embroidery, toys, and some apparel.

© Charles Stirling (Travel)/Alamy

© Eitan Simanor/Alamy

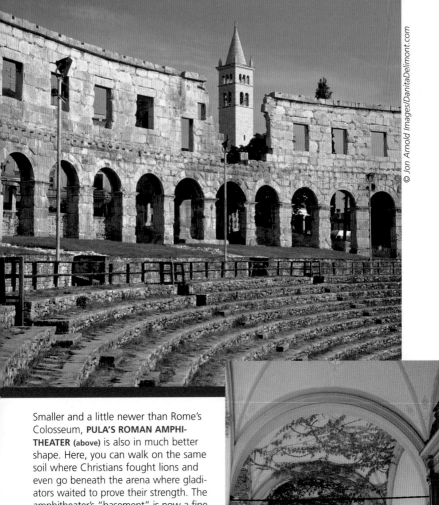

© Jon Arnold Images/DanitaDelimont.com

Smaller and a little newer than Rome's Colosseum, **PULA'S ROMAN AMPHI-THEATER (above)** is also in much better shape. Here, you can walk on the same soil where Christians fought lions and even go beneath the arena where gladiators waited to prove their strength. The amphitheater's "basement" is now a fine museum dedicated to Istrian history. In the summer, you can take in films and concerts by big-name music stars in the coliseum, sometimes at no charge.

Visiting a cemetery on a vacation might seem odd, but **MIROGOJ (right)** is much more than a graveyard. Famous Croatian sculptors created the monuments that mark the graves of notables, soldiers, and common folk alike. Even more unusual: There's no religious segregation here. You'll find Christians, Jews, and Muslims buried side by side. Don't miss the ivy-covered Herman Bollé façade and the Neo-Renaissance arcades (shown here) that lead to the ornate burial chambers of Croatian society.

© AA World Travel Library/Alamy

Frommer's®

Croatia

3rd Edition

by Dr. Karen Tormé Olson

with Sanja Bažulić Olson

WILEY

Wiley Publishing, Inc.

Published by:

WILEY PUBLISHING, INC.

111 River St.
Hoboken, NJ 07030-5774

ISBN 978-0-470-54128-9

Editor: Stephen Bassman
Production Editor: Heather Wilcox
Cartographer: Andrew Dolan
Photo Editor: Richard Fox
Production by Wiley Indianapolis Composition Services
Front cover photo: The walled city of Dubrovnik ©Art Kowalsky/Alamy Images
Back cover photo: The Roman Amphitheater (Pula) on the Istrian peninsula ©Walter Bibikow/AGE Fotostock, Inc.

For information on our other products and services or to obtain technical support, please contact our Customer Care Department within the U.S. at 877/762-2974, outside the U.S. at 317/572-3993 or fax 317/572-4002.

Wiley also publishes its books in a variety of electronic formats. Some content that appears in print may not be available in electronic formats.

Manufactured in the United States of America

5   4   3   2   1

CONTENTS

LIST OF MAPS	**vii**

1 THE BEST OF CROATIA   1

1 The Best Travel Experiences 1

2 The Best Natural Wonders 2

3 The Best Open-Air Markets 3

4 The Best Small Hotels & Inns 3

5 The Best Big Luxury Hotels 4

6 The Best Roman Ruins 5

7 The Best Beaches 5

8 The Most Charming Rustic
Villages 5

9 The Best Cathedrals & Churches 6

10 The Best Castles 6

11 The Best Restaurants 7

2 CROATIA IN DEPTH   9

1 Croatia Today .9

2 Looking Back at Croatia 10

3 Croatia's Art & Architecture 17

4 Croatia in Books, Film & Music 19

5 Eating & Drinking in Croatia 20

3 PLANNING YOUR TRIP TO CROATIA   23

1 When to Go 23

    Calendar of Events 24

2 Entry Requirements 26

3 Getting There & Getting Around 28

4 Money & Costs 33

5 Health 35

6 Safety 36

7 Specialized Travel Resources 36

8 Sustainable Tourism 40

    *General Resources for
Green Travel* 42

9 Staying Connected 43

10 Special-Interest Trips & Tours 44

11 Tips on Accommodations 47

4 CROATIA REGIONS & SUGGESTED ITINERARIES   49

1 The Regions in Brief 49

    Shipwreck Diving 52

2 A Weekend in Zagreb 53

3 Zagreb & Beyond in 1 Week 54

4 Dubrovnik & Beyond in 1 Week 56

5 DUBROVNIK   59

1 Orientation 59
   Fast Facts: Dubrovnik 61
   Nature's Waiting Room 63
   Who Is St. Blaise? 69
   Walking Tour: Dubrovnik's Stradun 70

   Down-Home Dubrovnik 82
   Dalmatia Dish Decoder 84
2 Dubrovnik Day Trips 89
   Wine Road Detour 97
   What Happened at Međugorje? . . . 100

6 LOWER DALMATIA   101

1 Orientation 101
2 Split 101
   Fast Facts: Split 104
   Exploring the Palace 108
   Split Walking Tours 110
3 Salona 118
4 Trogir 120
5 Makarska Riviera 126

   Biokovo Nature Park 127
6 Brač 129
7 Hvar 134
   The Rest of Hvar 141
8 Korčula 143
   Moreška Sword Dance 147
   The Rest of Korčula 148
9 Vis 148

7 UPPER DALMATIA   155

1 Orientation 155
2 Senj & the Velebit 156
3 Pag Island 158
   Pag Patterns 162
4 Zadar 165
   Fast Facts: Zadar 168
5 Zadar Environs 177
6 Paklenica National Park & Nin . . . 177

   Bishop Gregorius of Nin 179
   The Zadar Archipelago 181
7 Biograd Na Moru 182
8 Kornati National Park 183
9 Šibenik 184
   Rest in Peace 185
   Krka National Park 186

8 THE KVARNER GULF   189

1 Rijeka 189
   Rijeka's Morčićl (Moretto, Moro) . . . 190
2 Crikvenica & Novi Vinodolski 195
3 The Opatija Riviera 197
4 Krk Island 206

5 Baška & Environs 210
6 Rab Island 212
   Church Hours 215
7 Cres & Lošinj Islands 217

CROATIA

CONTENTS

1 Orientation 226

2 Pula (Pola)....................... 228

  Church of St. Fosca (Sveti Foška)... 233

3 Brijuni Archipelago (Brioni)...... 235

4 Vodnjan (Dignano).............. 236

5 Rovinj (Rovigno) 237

  Grisia Street Standout........... 239

  The Legend of St. Euphemia 240

  What's Your Wine IQ? 243

  Vrsar (Orsera) & Environs 245

6 Poreč (Parenzo) 245

  The Legend of Baredine Cave 248

7 Novigrad (Cittanova) 253

8 Umag (Umago) &
  Savudrija (Salvore) 256

9 Inland Istria 259

10 Pazin (Pisino)................... 260

11 Grožnjan, Buje & Momjan 262

  On the (Wine & Olive Oil) Road ... 263

12 Motovun, Livade & Oprtalj 265

13 Istarske Toplice, Roc,
  Hum & Buzet 268

  Black (& White) Gold.............269

1 Essentials 271

  The Neighborhoods in Brief....... 273

  Fast Facts: Zagreb................ 275

2 What to See & Do............... 277

  Marija Jurić Zagorka 280

  Lenuci's Horseshoe............... 281

  Ivan Meštrović (1883–1962) 283

  Heart of the Matter 285

  Zagreb Shopping Malls 286

3 Where to Stay................... 287

4 Where to Dine 294

5 Zagreb After Dark............... 302

1 Orientation 304

2 Excursions South of Zagreb 306

3 Samobor to the Žumberak...... 307

  Samobor Castle 308

  View from the Top 310

4 Karlovac 311

5 Plitvice Lakes National Park...... 315

  Waterfall Chemistry............. 317

6 Excursions North of Zagreb 318

7 Marija Bistrica, Kumrovec &
  Veliki Tabor 319

  Veronika of Desinić.............. 321

8 Trakošćan, Krapina,
  Lepoglava & Ludbreg 324

  Hilltop Wonders 325

  Center of the World 326

9 Varaždin 327

10 Međimurje...................... 330

  Dragons & Devils 332

12 INLAND CROATIA 334

1 Orientation 33

2 Sisak & the Lonjsko Polje 335

   What Happened at Jasenovac?... 338

3 Podravina & Bjelovar-Bilogora ... 339

4 Hlebine & Đurđevac............. 340

   A Bird in the Hand 341

5 Čazma, Bjelovar & Daruvar 342

6 Eastern Slavonia................. 345

7 Slavonski Brod, Đakovo &
Nova Gradiška 345

   The Treasure of Nova Gradiška.... 347

8 Osijek.......................... 349

9 Baranja......................... 357

   A Pair of Podrumi *(Wine Cellars)*... 358

10 Vukovar & Ilok.................. 359

   The Vučedol Dove............... 359

   Sv. Ivan Kapistran............... 361

13 FAST FACTS: CROATIA 364

INDEX 367

LIST OF MAPS

Croatia 50

Suggested Croatia Itineraries 55

Old Town Attractions 65

Where to Stay & Dine in
    Dubrovnik 75

Where to Stay & Dine in Old Town . 79

Dubrovnik Day Trips 91

Lower Dalmatia 103

Split 105

Hvar & Korčula 135

Upper Dalmatia 157

Zadar 167

Kvarner Gulf 191

Krk 207

Istria 227

Pula 229

What to See & Do in Zagreb 279

Where to Stay in Zagreb 289

Where to Dine in Zagreb 295

Excursions from Zagreb 305

Inland Croatia 337

Osijek 351

ACKNOWLEDGMENTS

Thanks to Sanda Sokol, Antonija Strilic, Nada and Goran Kožul, Nena Komarica, Marića Matkovic, Danica Plazibat, Mitchell Tocher, and all the wonderful Croatian people who graciously shared their advice, time, and encouragement during our research for this guide. Special thanks (again) to Mirko and Finka Bažulić, who opened their home and hearts to the authors. Thanks, too, to my ASA sorority sister Jeanne Jardine, my son, Greg, and my husband, Randy Weissman, each of whom joined us in Croatia at various times and places along the way. Their company and input were valuable additions and greatly appreciated. Finally, thanks to Wiley editors Linda Barth and Stephen Bassman for their editorial diligence and insights.

HOW TO CONTACT US

In researching this book, we discovered many wonderful places—hotels, restaurants, shops, and more. We're sure you'll find others. Please tell us about them, so we can share the information with your fellow travelers in upcoming editions. If you were disappointed with a recommendation, we'd love to know that, too. Please write to:

Frommer's Croatia, 3rd Edition
Wiley Publishing, Inc. • 111 River St. • Hoboken, NJ 07030

AN ADDITIONAL NOTE

Please be advised that travel information is subject to change at any time—and this is especially true of prices. We therefore suggest that you write or call ahead for confirmation when making your travel plans. The authors, editors, and publisher cannot be held responsible for the experiences of readers while traveling. Your safety is important to us, however, so we encourage you to stay alert and be aware of your surroundings. Keep a close eye on cameras, purses, and wallets, all favorite targets of thieves and pickpockets.

ABOUT THE AUTHORS

Dr. Karen Tormé Olson and her daughter-in-law Sanja Bažulić Olson have spent every summer and holiday since 2003 traveling Croatia as a writer-translator team to gather information for *Frommer's Croatia.* Karen is a photographer, freelance travel writer, and former *Chicago Tribune* editor. She has a doctorate in administration, is a member of the Society of American Travel Writers, and holds a day job as a school counselor, fencing coach, and literary magazine advisor. She lives in a Chicago suburb with her husband, Randy Weissman, their son, Drew, and three large shelter dogs.

Sanja Bažulić Olson was born in Denmark but was reared and educated in Croatia, where she has lived for most of her life. She holds a master's degree in agricultural engineering from Zagreb University, and since 2003 Sanja has lived in Uganda, Washington, D.C., Kabul, Afghanistan, and Pristina, Kosovo, with her husband, Greg, who works in micro development for the U.S. Agency for International Development (USAID).

FROMMER'S STAR RATINGS, ICONS & ABBREVIATIONS

Every hotel, restaurant, and attraction listing in this guide has been ranked for quality, value, service, amenities, and special features using a **star-rating system.** In country, state, and regional guides, we also rate towns and regions to help you narrow down your choices and budget your time accordingly. Hotels and restaurants are rated on a scale of zero (recommended) to three stars (exceptional). Attractions, shopping, nightlife, towns, and regions are rated according to the following scale: zero stars (recommended), one star (highly recommended), two stars (very highly recommended), and three stars (must-see).

In addition to the star-rating system, we also use **eight feature icons** that point you to the great deals, in-the-know advice, and unique experiences that separate travelers from tourists. Throughout the book, look for:

Finds	Special finds—those places only insiders know about
Fun Facts	Fun facts—details that make travelers more informed and their trips more fun
Kids	Best bets for kids, and advice for the whole family
Moments	Special moments—those experiences that memories are made of
Overrated	Places or experiences not worth your time or money
Tips	Insider tips—great ways to save time and money
Value	Great values—where to get the best deals
Warning!	Warning—traveler's advisories are usually in effect

The following **abbreviations** are used for credit cards:

AE	American Express	**DISC**	Discover	**V**	Visa
DC	Diners Club	**MC**	MasterCard		

TRAVEL RESOURCES AT FROMMERS.COM

Frommer's travel resources don't end with this guide. Frommer's website, **www.frommers. com**, has travel information on more than 4,000 destinations. We update features regularly, giving you access to the most current trip-planning information and the best airfare, lodging, and car-rental bargains. You can also listen to podcasts, connect with other Frommers.com members through our active-reader forums, share your travel photos, read blogs from guidebook editors and fellow travelers, and much more.

The Best of Croatia

Until recently, July and August in Croatia belonged to Germans and Italians, who clogged border crossings in their annual migration to the country's endless beaches and clear blue sea. Finally, the rest of the world has discovered Croatia's charms: its wealth of Roman ruins, medieval hilltop castles, and staggering cache of natural wonders. Even though the summer crowds are now larger and more diverse, it still is possible to find a secluded cove or patch of beach where it seems you're the only person on Earth. When all the name-brand hotels are filled, there always is a room waiting in a private home where the landlord welcomes you like a long-lost friend.

Every town and village has at least one restaurant where the locals hang out and where the slice of life you get with your meal is the best dessert there is. In Croatia, each building has a story that adds another facet to this gem of a country.

This chapter is a "road map," directing you to some of our favorites. We know you'll add to the list when you find some of your own.

1 THE BEST TRAVEL EXPERIENCES

- **Listening to the Sea Organ** (Zadar): Waves create music as they move water through this organ's undersea pipes. Add a set of white stone steps leading into the crystal water above the submerged organ and shooting beams of light from sister installation **Greeting to the Sun** on Zadar's Riva. The result is a matchless venue to enjoy a multimedia symphony courtesy of the sea and sky. See p. 171.

- **Viewing Mummies** (Vodjnan): They look a little like skeletons shrink-wrapped in leather, and they are billed as the mortal coils of holy people who died centuries ago but miraculously never decomposed. You can't get too close to these relics because viewing distance is restricted. You can, however, recognize these mummies as former human beings even in the dimly lighted area behind the altar of St. Blaise Church in Vodjnan. Soulful background music and overly dramatic

piped-in commentary make the experience creepy but riveting. See p. 237.

- **Watching the Sunrise over Vis Town Harbor** (Vis): Vis Town and its harbor were the view from our balcony at the Bellevue Apartments in the hills above. It was a perfect vantage point for witnessing a kaleidoscope of color washing over the landscape as the sun moved above the horizon each morning. At night everything was black and gray, then just before dawn, the scene was painted in liquid gold. Pinks and blues were next, and finally the buildings and sea came into focus in silver, turquoise, and red. It was such a glorious sight that we were up before dawn every day just to catch the show.

- **Exploring the Village of Hum** (Istria): It calls itself the smallest town in the world, and population-wise, it might be. But so many people visit this village high in the Istrian interior that it always seems crowded. The village fathers have done a wonderful job of restoring the buildings in town to make it tourist-friendly. See p. 269.

- **Strolling Through Mirogoj Cemetery** (Zagreb): As much sculpture garden as burial ground, this 19th-century cemetery was designed by architect Hermann Bollé. It is home to Croatian patriots, common folk, and people of all faiths and nationalities. The tombstones range from small and simple to enormous and elaborate, but each is a story in itself. Don't miss the black granite slab at the grave of former president Franjo Tuđman

or the sculpture-rich arcades on either side of the entrance. See p. 285.

- **Descending into Iločki Podrumi** (Ilok): You'll get the chills from two sources in this second-oldest wine cellar in Croatia: the temperature and the history. The cellar was looted by the Serbs during the Homeland War, but not before the owners concealed bottles of the best vintages behind a false wall. Today those bottles are out of hiding and on display along with the barrels and vats used to store the winery's newest vintages. See p. 361.

2 THE BEST NATURAL WONDERS

- **Plitvice Lakes National Park** (145km/90 miles southwest of Zagreb): Plitvice is Croatia's best-known natural wonder. The park's 16 crystal-clear, turquoise lakes and countless waterfalls put on a great show. The lakes flow into one another and tumble over deposits of travertine, creating waterfalls that drop a few feet or plunge as much as 64m (210 ft.). All this beauty is set in a dense forest accessed via footpaths and populated by bears and wild boar. See p. 315.

- **Kornati National Park** (part of the Zadar Archipelago): Kornati's 140 islands are really the tops of mountains that were above sea level 20,000 years ago but now are mostly submerged. One side of each island is rocky and lightly blanketed with vegetation (a few grapevines and olive trees). The side facing the sea is a sheer rock wall known as a "crown" that plunges almost 76m (250 ft.) straight into the water. Sixty-nine species of butterflies live here. Perhaps the most interesting part is

Kornati's offshore underwater landscape. Its rock formations support flourishing flora and fauna. See p. 183.

- **Paklenica National Park** (btw. Zadar and Karlobag): Paklenica's raw beauty is best appreciated by hikers and nature lovers. But even motorists respect the imposing Velebit peaks because the limestone cliffs that soar above deep gorges and dense vegetation are visible for miles from nearby highways. Even from afar you can see cave openings and imagine what's inside. See p. 177.

- **Krka National Park** (less than half an hour from Šibenik): The park was formed to protect the Krka River, which runs from its source near Knin to the sea near Šibenik. The river has created a series of spectacular gorges, waterfalls, lakes, and rapids on its trip through the mountains. The jaw-droppingly steep Skradinski Buk and Roški Slapovi are the most impressive. Between the two are Lake Visovac and Visovac Island, home to a Franciscan monastery. See p. 186.

3 THE BEST OPEN-AIR MARKETS

- **Dolac** (Zagreb): The urban market is above the main square at the foot of Old Town, but it is more than just a place to buy fruits and veggies. Dolac is a crossroads where people come to see and be seen; to trade gossip; and to relax with a cup of coffee. Morning is the best time to visit because that's when the bread is freshest, the displays the prettiest, and the people the most interesting. See p. 278.
- **Pazarin** (Split): Pazarin is reminiscent of a Turkish bazaar in looks, sounds, and smells. Booths and tables line both sides of Hrvojeva Street outside the east

wall of Diocletian's Palace from the Riva to the Silver Gate. Pazarin has the usual assortment of produce plus a variety of textiles and the country's most persuasive vendors. See p. 109.
- **Bjelovar** (Bjelovar): This market is quite civilized and partially covered. It is noteworthy as the place where farmers from Croatia's agricultural belt bring their best produce, dairy products, fish, and meat every day. The market is at its busiest from 7am to noon, but a few vendors stay open until 6pm or so. The later it gets, the lower the prices go. See p. 343.

4 THE BEST SMALL HOTELS & INNS

- **Hotel San Rocco** (Brtonigla): San Rocco's location deep in Istria adds to the romance in its lovingly restored stone buildings and grounds. Flowers, olive groves, and an assortment of ruins comprise the hotel's sensual "curb appeal." But it's really the beautifully put together guest rooms with their mélange of antique and modern touches, the inviting pool, and the magnificent gourmet restaurant that seal the deal. See p. 254.
- **Lešič Dimitri Palace** (Korčula): Each of the six *pied-à-terre* in this lavishly renovated urban palace has a personality of its own and each is drenched in luxury. Privacy, elegance, and whimsy are built into each unit, any of which would be a fitting home for royalty in Manhattan or Marrakesh. See p. 146.
- **Villa Kukuljica** (Zaton Mali): Villa K is a modest inn compared to most of the splashy accommodations in the Dubrovnik area, but in a single night its authenticity made a lasting impression. Experience real Croatian hospitality in

the person of Kukuljica's owners. It's a revelation of culture, food, and hospitality. See p. 82.
- **Hotel Waldinger** (Osijek): Waldinger packs a lot of elegance into its 18 rooms, each of which drips with period elegance in the heart of a city that has not altogether recovered from the Homeland War. From here you easily can walk to the banks of the Drava, shop the city market, and explore medieval Tvrđa. See p. 353.
- **Hotel Boškinac** (Novalja, Pag Island): Boškinac is in the middle of nowhere even for Pag, but that's part of its charm. The country-chic hotel is surrounded by gardens, olive groves, vineyards, and forest, far from the madding weekenders who descend on nearby Novalja all summer long. Boškinac's restaurant is one of most food-forward in Croatia, and the wines from its vineyards are prized all over the country. See p. 163.
- **Hotel Palazzo** (Poreč): When the Hotel Riviera opened a century ago, it was

standing on Istria's first landfill. Today the Riviera has been reincarnated in the same spot with all its original charm and elegance. It's the Palazzo now, with the soul of 1910 Italy in a 2010 body, a heady combination of history, romance, and comfort. See p. 249.

- **Hotel Vestibul Palace** (Split): The Roman Empire meets the 21st century at the Palace, where most rooms share at least part of a wall built by Diocletian. History and gourmet delights align to make this one of the best hotel experiences in Croatia. Each room has a

personality of its own, complete with cleverly designed windows carved into the stone walls to reveal views of various aspects of Old Town. See p. 112.

- **Valsabbion** (Pula): This hedonistic experience is not to be missed. The hotel's seven rooms, three suites, and spa are decorated with flair in a breezy, romantic style that carries over to its exquisite restaurant, one of the best in Croatia. You might come here for the beach, but you'll stay for the food and the pampering. See p. 233.

5 THE BEST BIG LUXURY HOTELS

- **The Regent Esplanade** (Zagreb): The most gracious hotel in Croatia compares favorably with luxury hotels in New York and Paris for a fraction of the cost. From rich furnishings in the guest rooms to a concierge who is a gallant repository of Croatian history, a stay at the Esplanade is an experience you'll never forget. See p. 290.
- **Hilton Imperial** (Dubrovnik): This is the U.S. chain's first foray into Croatia. Rather than build a hotel from scratch, Hilton had the wisdom to restore what was salvageable from Dubrovnik's historic 19th-century Imperial and graft a modern hotel onto the base. Every detail has been taken care of, and you'll be treated as an honored guest here. See p. 76.
- **Excelsior** (Dubrovnik): We love the Excelsior for its understated profile and for the way it channels the graceful elegance of the 1930s in style and attitude. Every service is personalized and every visitor is treated as if he or she is the hotel's guest of honor. In Dubrovnik's frenetic tourism environment, that is no small feat. See p. 77.
- **Le Meridien Lav** (Split): Le Meridien's seaside location in Podstrana, 20 minutes from Split's Old Town, gives it a resort feel. Its spacious, well-appointed

rooms, spa, casino, and high-design public areas contribute luxury, and its marina, tennis courts, and pools make it a destination hotel. If you are looking for a place you don't have to leave to have fun, this is it. See p. 112.

- **Monte Mulini** (Rovinj): The Monte Mulini is Rovinj's first true luxury hotel. Even the lowest priced room has a huge glamour bathroom with a shower that is separate from the tub and an array of designer toiletries. MM's world class restaurants, services, and a people-centric staff cater to guests' every whim. The spa is the ultimate in decadence with a floating bath filled with water that has such a high concentration of salt that you stay suspended in water no matter how hard you try to touch bottom. See p. 241.
- **Radisson BLU** (Orašac): Orašac is 12km (7½ miles) from Dubrovnik and an idyllic spot for getting away from it all without going too far. The nice thing about the BLU is that you never have to leave its lavishly landscaped grounds. You can veg out right there and still experience Dalmatia's natural beauty, fine food, and hospitality. Even better, the BLU provides all the above while being environmentally responsible. See p. 78.

6 THE BEST ROMAN RUINS

- **Pula Amphitheater** (Pula): Smaller than Rome's coliseum but in much better shape, the amphitheater is more accessible to tourists than its Rome counterpart. Don't miss the restored underground chambers and their exhibits featuring Istrian history. And if you're in town when a concert is scheduled, get a ticket no matter who is headlining. See p. 230.

- **Salona** (Solin): The grandeur that was Rome still is evident in the crumbling buildings and foundations of this former outpost of the empire. It isn't difficult to imagine what Salona looked like in its prime, but it is tough to imagine why Salona was left to sink into the Earth for a couple of centuries. Do not approach without sturdy walking shoes, sunscreen, and a full water bottle. See p. 118.

- **Diocletian's Palace** (Split): Diocletian built his estate on a scale so grand it was converted into a city after he died, but its landscape has been tinkered with so much during the last 15 centuries that the character of the original complex has been all but obliterated. What remains of the palace and what has been built on its footprint is now Split's Old Town. If you walk around it, through it, and under it enough, you'll begin to understand Diocletian's enormous ego. See p. 107.

7 THE BEST BEACHES

- **Baška** (Krk Island): This is a sun-lover's paradise, with more than 30 beaches of varying size and a promenade that skirts most of them. Baška's beaches once were sand, but now the sand is covered with pebbles that extend a few feet into the water. See p. 210.

- **Novalja** (Pag Island): Any cove off Novalja can be a private beach. The water offshore is so clear you can see the white, sandy bottom 6m (20 ft.) below. If you have a boat, drop anchor for a while, take a dip, and let your stress float away. See p. 161.

- **Zlatni Rat** (Brač Island): Visit this beach just so you can say you did. This is the famous strip that appears in all the Croatia ads, usually in an aerial view. From above, Zlatni Rat resembles a green finger rimmed with sand and tipped with a curling tendril extending into the sapphire sea. From ground level, it is a sun-blasted, pebbled landscape covered with a huge international crowd soaking up the rays and the local culture. See p. 129.

- **Orebić** (Pelješac Peninsula): Orebić is a civilized place where families linger together and, at the end of the day, Mom brings covered bowls full of fruit down to kids who don't want to leave their sand castles and snorkels. The water is warm, the sun constant, and the people as nice as they come. See p. 94.

8 THE MOST CHARMING RUSTIC VILLAGES

- **Kumrovec** in the Zagorje region is like a Croatian Williamsburg, Virginia, with restored cabins and barns furnished as they were when Croatia's most famous son, Josip Broz Tito, was born in the late 19th century. Some of the rustic buildings in this open-air museum contain photos and displays,

THE BEST OF CROATIA

1

THE MOST CHARMING RUSTIC VILLAGES

while others feature docents in traditional costumes who explain weaving, candle making, and some of the crafts of the times. See p. 320.

- **Čigoć** is known as the "Stork Place" because of the long-legged birds that perch atop roofs in this Lonjsko Polje village. The storks are the hook that gets tourists to stop in the middle of the marsh, but the historic cabins and natural surroundings keep them there for hours. See p. 336.

- **Štrigova** isn't exceptionally rustic, but it is a quaint launching pad for a visit to the surrounding Međimurje region. From Štrigova, you can explore the rolling vineyards and wineries of northern Croatia. See chapter 11.

- **Hlebine,** in the north-central part of inland Croatia, is home to a colony of nearly 200 painters and sculptors, the country's naive art movement, and the ateliers of Josip and Ivan Generalić. It is the cradle of the naive art movement in Croatia. Many works from these artists are on display in the town's galleries, one of which is the Generalić home. See p. 340.

9 THE BEST CATHEDRALS & CHURCHES

- **Holy Cross Church** (Nin): Holy Cross is the oldest church in Croatia and also the world's smallest cathedral, according to posted signs. According to one scientist, the little white stone church is also a giant sun dial and was constructed according to mathematical calculations. See p. 179.

- **Euphrasian Basilica Complex** (Poreč): A must-see sight in this city of superlatives, the UNESCO World Heritage church is the last of four that were built on top of each other. One of the basilica's premier attractions is the collection of Byzantine mosaics on display. Euphrasius is not just one church, but a series of church buildings, each with its own story. See p. 247.

- **St. Donatus** (Zadar): Notable for its unusual shape (circular inside), St. Donatus is void of decoration. The church is no longer used for Mass, but its great acoustics make it a hot venue for classical concerts. Like other churches of its time (9th c.), Donatus is one of several buildings in a clerical complex. See p. 171.

- **Church of St. Mary** (Beram): This chapel in the woods is so small and so remote that you would never notice it if it weren't in a guidebook. But St. Mary's remoteness is what protected the eye-popping frescoes that dance on its walls. You'll need to pick up one of the church's keepers in Beram and drive her to the chapel in the woods so she can unlock it. See p. 260.

10 THE BEST CASTLES

- **Pazin Kaštel** (Istria): One of the best-preserved castles in Istria, this is a surprising "must-see" in the Istrian interior. Pazin Kaštel is next to one of the scariest-looking gorges ever, a feature that was conveniently utilized as a dumping ground (literally) for enemies of whoever

controlled the castle at the time. What may be Croatia's best ethnographic museum is inside. See p. 261.

- **Stari Grad** (Varaždin): The Gothic Renaissance defensive complex includes a castle and the Varaždin Town Museum. As a whole, Stari Grad is this

Baroque town's best attraction. The museum is an excellent showcase for artwork and historical items. Multilingual docents are happy to help visitors. See p. 328.

- **Veliki Tabor** (Zagorje Region): North of Zagreb is an imposing, solid brick fortress that looks like the place Rapunzel let down her hair. Veliki Tabor has its own legends, including murder, mayhem, and a ghost. While the exterior of the 12th-century structure looks like it could withstand a nuclear attack, the inside is still in the process of renovation. See p. 322.

- **Trakošćan Castle** (near Varaždin): North of Zagreb is one of Croatia's most visited sites and one of its most impressive castles—from the outside. The grounds are extensive and the structure itself is everything you'd expect a storybook castle to be—stone walls, turrets, a drawbridge—but inside, renovations have been less than meticulous and sometimes border on tacky. However, Trakošćan is worth the trip if for no other reason than to ponder the plastic deer mounted on the walls outside the entrance. See p. 326.

11 THE BEST RESTAURANTS

- **Valsabbion** (Pula): Valsabbion is so avant-garde that it defies categorization. It is innovative yet traditional; stylish yet not overly so; a mecca of haute cuisine but not intimidating. This is a temple to Istrian ingredients and dishes that are a perfect match for its talented chef. Together they make magic. See p. 233.

- **Mala Hiza** (Mačkovec): Mala Hiza is one of the finest restaurants in the country. The building was constructed in 1887 and once stood outside Zagreb—it later was taken apart, plopped in the middle of a gorgeous garden, and reassembled 4km (2½ miles) outside Čakovic. The menu is full of creative interpretations of regional Croatian cuisine, and the chef will prepare any old-time recipe if you call ahead with your request. See p. 333.

- **Klub Gastronomada** (Zagreb): Dining at this upstairs room off Jelačića Square awakened taste buds we didn't know we had. The restaurant's bent clearly is locavore, but its soul is experimental theater. From clear tomato soup to nettle sauce to Istrian beef to a dessert made with black olive jam, we were surprised (and wowed) with every bite (and every sip of IQ wine). See p. 297.

- **Zinfandel's** (Regent Esplanade, Zagreb): We dined at Zinfandel's on several occasions over the years and found it to be a solid, traditional choice. This time (2009), we were blown away by its new attitude, menu, and the deftness of its chef. The old school elegance of the room and impeccable service still are there, but the food is lighter, more contemporary, and the preparations and presentations are as creative as any we encountered. This is a special occasion place and a don't-miss-it for anyone who cares about gourmet dining. See p. 296.

- **Zigante** (Livade): Behold truffle king Giancarlo Zigante's gourmet palace. Almost everything on the extensive menu here utilizes the truffle, the precious fungus with which Zigante made his fortune. The restaurant is not a gimmick: Everything on the menu is expertly prepared and even flirts with creativity. See p. 267.

- **Boškinac** (Novalja, Pag Island): Boškinac has a knack for turning fresh produce and local ingredients like Pag lamb and Pag cheese into dishes that surprise the palate. Whether it's a Saturday lunch on the sunny terrace or a gala dinner in the elegant dining room, Boškinac's creations are sublime. We don't know how the chef did it, but the four cuts of lamb in a single sauce each had a personality all its own. Go out of your way for Boškinac and take home a bottle of its boutique wine. See p. 164.

- **Bitoraj** (Fužine): Bitoraj is a 75-year-old restaurant in a new setting, which only enhances the dining experience. Game dishes available nowhere else are on the menu in company with traditional delicacies. From bear steak and deer ham to Bitoraj's signature dish of young wild boars baked under a lid on an open fire *(peka)*, Bitoraj utilizes the best ingredients the surrounding woods can offer. See p. 191.

- **Riblji Restaurant Foša** (Zadar): Foša has one of the best locations in Croatia. It is at the water outside the Zadar wall, and it has a view and sea breeze that make the food taste that much better. The restaurant is a favorite hangout for locals. See p. 174.

- **Palača Paladini** (Hvar Town): This restaurant appeals to all five senses: It is set in a beautiful garden with blooming lavender and orange trees frequented by songbirds. It has a great list of wines, and it offers superb Dalmatian cuisine that tastes as good as it smells and looks. See p. 142.

Croatia in Depth

"The Mediterranean as It Once Was," "Europe's Summer Home," "Ethnic Battlefield," "War-Torn Nation." Croatia has been labeled all these things, but which is it, and is the country worth visiting when there are so many exciting but less controversial destinations vying for a traveler's time and dollars?

The answer is that Croatia is a little of each but not dominated by any, and that's part of its allure.

Where else can you spend the night in a room on a working farm, then spend the day poking around an intact Roman amphitheater? How many places let you walk atop a massive fortification wall in the steps of a guard on the lookout for invaders from the sea, then sip martinis at midnight watching models strut down a runway in a square surrounded by churches and remnants of the Renaissance? Is there another destination where you can hike through a forest to the tempo of water rushing from falls too numerous to count, then dress for dinner on a candlelit terrace where passengers from the Orient Express once mingled during a layover?

Germans, Italians, Austrians, Hungarians, and other Europeans know Croatia as the sun-drenched playground where their ancestors spent more than a century of August vacations frolicking in the sea and dining on just-caught seafood. Other foreigners know Croatia as the site of one of the most vicious wars in European history. For Croatians, the country is simply home and heritage, and they are proud of who they are, what they have endured, and who they have become.

Contemporary Croatia is a product of its history, its present, and even its future aspirations. It is a country that is embracing progress, but hasn't forgotten its past. That's no different from the histories of Italy, France, Germany, or any other popular destination that entices tourists to leave home. The difference is that Croatia's struggles are more recent and have not yet faded to black.

Our advice is to put aside labels and preconceived notions about Croatia and plan to experience the country "as is." Seek out experiences that appeal to you as you read this book, then be prepared to be surprised, stay open to a change of plans, and don't be afraid to pursue your own discoveries. Head for the coast and bask in the sun, but take a day to explore villages in the inland hills, too. Book a room in a name-brand resort area, but carve out time to have lunch at a family-run inn in the country. You might wander a bit, but you'll never feel lost.

1 CROATIA TODAY

More than 15 years after the end of the Homeland War, Croatia still is rebuilding its image as a tourist destination following a collapse of tourism during the hostilities. It still is determining its structure as an independent nation in anticipation of taking its place at the world table as it clears hurdles necessary for admittance to the European Union, which is expected no later than 2011.

The 2009 world economic crisis changed the country's trajectory toward prosperity, but until then, signs of an economic boom had been everywhere, but most especially in the tourism industry. Since then, the country's luxury hotels on the Adriatic coast have seen fewer guests, stores and malls fewer shoppers, and restaurants have served fewer diners. The downturn in tourism and commerce is understandable in the current economic climate, but it could not have come at a more inopportune time.

Without explanation, Croatia's long-time Prime Minister Ivo Sanader withdrew from politics on July 1, 2009, in a sudden move that shocked the nation. Sanader was in the middle of his second term as prime minister, and he was president of the country's ruling party. Local media had been speculating that Sanader would run for president in elections scheduled for early 2010 and that he would leave his post as prime minister to run for the office. He quashed that rumor when he announced that not only was he resigning his post, but he also was quitting politics altogether.

One of Sanader's key political goals had been to lead the former Yugoslav republic into NATO, and that was realized in April 2009. Another goal was to bring Croatia into the European Union, an initiative that still is in progress.

Upon Sanader's resignation, his deputy, Jadranka Kosor, immediately took over as prime minister and seems to have been left holding the economic bag: In the first 4 months of her term, circumstances forced Kosor to do serious damage control with respect to Croatia's finances. Within weeks of taking office, she had to take unpopular emergency measures to shore up the country's economy to evade bankruptcy, and as a result, Croatia raised its value-added tax (VAT) from 22% to 23% and levied a "crisis tax" of 2% to 4% on anyone making more that 3,000kn per month. Construction projects—including in-progress highway construction—were stopped or slowed because government funding was pulled. There even was talk of the need for requesting an economic rescue from the International Monetary Fund, though Croatia decided to go it alone to handle its debts.

Precise figures for Croatia's economic plight had not been made public at press time, but early reports show that the country's biggest economic engine, tourism, was down more than 30% overall in the first 3 months of 2009 and anticipated to settle into a 15% or more downturn for the year after 4 straight years of growth.

Experts expect the across-the-board economic slide in Croatia to last until at least 2012. How that will affect Croatia's schedule for admittance to the European Union still is unknown. Admission to the E.U. carries economic requirements, but reports say that Croatia's petition still is on track to be completed in 2011.

Economic issues are just one bump in the road delaying Croatia's membership in the E.U., however. Corruption in both the public and private sectors, inefficiency in its legal system and government, and Croatia's cooperation (or lack of cooperation) with the International Criminal Tribunal for the former Yugoslavia all present considerable challenges, though progress is being made.

2 LOOKING BACK AT CROATIA

PREHISTORY

At the turn of the 20th century (1899), the remains of a type of Neanderthal who lived in caves some 30,000 years ago were discovered at Krapina, a tiny town north of Zagreb. These early cave dwellers' bones were dubbed "Krapina Man," and they established a time line that put humans in

Croatia in the middle of the Stone Age. Traces of other prehistoric cultures also have been found in Vukovar in eastern Croatia, but none is more significant than Krapina Man.

ILLYRIANS

Recorded Croatian history begins around 1200 B.C., when the people occupying the region that is now Croatia, Bosnia, Albania, and Serbia began to form a coalition of tribes known as the Illyrians. Illyrian lifestyles had similarities, such as burial customs and dwelling styles, but there is no concrete evidence that any tribe was assimilated by any other. In fact, the tribes were known by different names according to where they settled, and at least some of them became regional powers and established cities that survive today.

THE GREEK COLONISTS

The Greeks began colonizing the Adriatic coast of Croatia in the 4th century B.C., beginning with Issa (Vis), a colony founded by residents of Syracuse (Sicily). Other settlements followed, including Paros (Hvar) and Tragurion (Trogir). The Illyrians traded oil, wine, salt, metals, and other commodities with the Greeks but nonetheless tried to get rid of foreign settlements. In the 3rd century B.C., the Illyrians attempted to form an independent state under the leadership of one of its pirate tribes. In 229 B.C., the Greeks, who were alarmed by this turn of events, asked the Romans for help in containing Illyrian lawlessness. When the Romans sent messengers to negotiate peace with the Illyrian Queen Teuta, she had them executed. This touched off a series of wars that lasted more than 60 years, ending with the defeat of the Illyrians and the creation of the Roman province of Illyricum.

THE ROMAN OCCUPATION

The spread of Roman colonies across Croatia continued until A.D. 9, when the Adriatic coast and interior lands were annexed by the Emperor Tiberius to create three Roman provinces: Dalmatia (Adriatic seacoast), Noricum (northern territory/ Austria), and Pannonia (Hungary). The Romans built fortresses, roads, bridges, aqueducts, and sparkling new cities that overtook Illyrian culture or drove it away. The main Roman cities of that time were Pola (Pula), Jader (Zadar), Salona (Solin) near Split, and Epidaurum (Cavtat). The Roman propensity for building roads linked northeast Italy to Byzantium (Istanbul) and opened lines of communication that facilitated trade and troop movements and the spread of Roman culture.

Those same roads brought Christianity to the area, and with it persecution, primarily by Emperor Diocletian, whose "retirement home" at Split is one of Croatia's best-preserved vestiges of the Roman era, which flourished until the end of the 4th century.

From about A.D. 395 until the 7th century, Croatia suffered a series of invasions by the Ostrogoths, Slavs, and other barbarians. But it was the Avars, a warlike Asian tribe, who allegedly brought the Slavic Croats—ancestors to today's Croatians—to the area.

According to the 10th-century Byzantine emperor Constantine Porphyrogenitus, Emperor Heraclius asked the Croats to get rid of the Avars and to protect Rome's interests, though the Croats didn't stop at saving the Roman occupation.

THE CROAT MIGRATION

Porphyrogenitus's account has been disputed, partly because it was written 300 years after the fact. Other accounts differ about the Croats' appearance in southeastern Europe. Some experts say the Croats came from the Ukraine; others pinpoint Poland; and some say the Croats migrated from Iran because the name "Hvrat" has Persian origins. The trail leading back to the Croats is further clouded because "Hvrat" was used by other Slavic tribes of the times (White Croats in Poland; Croats in the Czech Republic area; and other groups from nearby Slovenia, Slovakia, and Macedonia). It is likely that there were several waves of Croat migration, with the first group settling the part of the Roman province of Pannonia that is now southern Hungary. Later migrations settled land all the way to Dalmatia.

Eventually, the Croat émigrés organized into two dukedoms, and at the same time they began to accept Roman-rite Christianity and Roman culture. But the existence of two distinct centers of culture—Mediterranean (Dalmatia) and central European (Pannonia)—served to form a dueling Croatian psyche, which lingers today. Croats continued to live under a series of foreign and Croatian administrations until A.D. 924, when the country was united under the leadership of Tomislav I, the first king of Croatia.

MEDIEVAL CROATIA

When Tomislav was crowned around A.D. 924, he united the Pannonian and Dalmatian duchies, which included much of present-day Slavonia, Dalmatia, Istria, and Bosnia/Herzegovina. Tomislav died about A.D. 928, and no one disputes that he had a profound effect on Croatia. He was succeeded by a series of monarchs who enjoyed relative stability for almost the next 2 centuries. Among them were King Petar Krešimir IV (1058–74) and King Dmitar Zvonimir (1075–89). Zvonimir's reign is notable because he entrenched Catholicism in Croatia and strengthened the country's relationship with the Roman Church. His reign is immortalized on the Baška Tablet, a kind of Croatian Rosetta stone engraved with the oldest known Croatian text. The tablet is on display in Zagreb's archaeological museum.

HUNGARY & VENICE

After Zvonimir's death in the 11th century, the monarchy withered, and Croatia

and Hungary formed a common kingdom guided by a parliament (Sabor). During this time, the wealth and power of the landed nobility grew, and an increase in the feudal obligations of the agrarian population followed.

Free cities (Dubrovnik, among others) were founded along the coast, increasing trade and political strength in the region. Many made trade agreements with Venice, which by now was a contender for control of Croatia's ports.

Trade increased, and northern Croatian cities also saw rapid development, but a Tatar invasion in 1242 diverted the government's attention to the country's defense as invaders razed Zagreb and everything else in their path. Ultimately, Hungarian King Bela IV outmaneuvered the Tatars and retained control, but the country's growing strength from its alliance with Hungary fueled Venice's determination to control Istria and Dalmatia and ultimately access to the sea.

Venice began a long-term campaign to take over the Croatian coast early in the 13th century: They captured Zadar in 1202 and Dubrovnik in 1205. For the next century, the Venetian influence along the coast increased until they achieved their objective. During the period of Venetian acquisition, the counts of Anjou came to the Croatian throne, and in 1358 they reasserted Hungarian control of Dalmatia thanks to Louis of Anjou. King Louis expelled the Venetians, but disarray in the House of Anjou ultimately resulted in the sale of rights over Dalmatia back to the Venetians in 1409.

OTTOMANS & HAPSBURGS

During the 15th century, the Ottoman Turks advanced on Croatian lands, taking Bulgaria and Bosnia and leaving the rest of Croatia vulnerable. During the battle against the Turks at Mohács, Hungarian King Louis II was killed in action, leaving the Turk Sultan Suleyman the Magnificent in control of much of southern Croatia. Louis did not have an heir, and the throne went to his designated successor, Ferdinand I of Hapsburg, a move that put Croatia in the Hapsburg Empire.

The first Hapsburg rulers were determined to defend Croatia against the Turks, who continued to gobble up Croat land until the mid–17th century despite efforts to contain them. During this time, Croatia lost 75% of its territory and people, but by the mid–17th century, the Hapsburgs had retaken Croatia and pushed the Turks out of the region. Subsequently, Hapsburg armies gradually drove the Turks out of the rest of central Europe (except for Bosnia and Herzegovina).

The decrease in Turk strength opened the door for the Venetians to once again surge in Dalmatia.

In 1671, the Croats made a push for self-rule, but the Hapsburgs would have none of it and quashed the movement. During the next century, the Hapsburgs gradually squeezed out Croatian authority, which further made Croatia a takeover target.

By this time many Orthodox Serbs who were living in Catholic Croatia and Russia began to show an interest in the region. This raised the question of who would take control, Catholic Austria or Orthodox Russia. Thus began the so-called Eastern Question, which was one of the precipitators of World War I.

THE NAPOLEON EFFECT

During the 18th century, Austria, Hungary, and Venice all continued to vie for pieces of Croatia and for imposition of their own cultures. The Hapsburgs pushed to install German customs and language; the Hungarians proposed that Hungarian be accepted as the official language and claimed that Slavonia belonged to Hungary; the Venetians extended their territories to the Dinara mountains and beyond, thanks to the Treaty of Požarevac; and the

Turks retained control of Bosnia and Herzegovina. The Požarevac treaty made it difficult to define Croatia's geography, but in 1808 Napoleon "solved" the problem by capturing coastal towns, uniting Dalmatia with parts of Slovenia and Croatia, and renaming the joint territories the Illyrian Provinces. Napoleon's influence was profound but short-lived. He promoted agriculture and commerce, raised the status of the Orthodox population, and started a reawakening of Croatian nationalism. But with his defeat in 1815 at the hands of the English navy, control of Dalmatia once again reverted to the Hapsburgs, who immediately reasserted authority over Croatia.

ILLYRIANISM

After the fall of Napoleon, Austria created the Kingdom of Illyria, an administrative unit designed to thwart Hungarian nationalism and unification of the South Slavs. Dalmatia, however, was not part of this reorganization, as Austria decided to keep this gold mine as its vacation playground. Eventually, the Hapsburgs' attempts to exert absolute control over every aspect of Croatian life backfired. Croatian leaders began stirring up nationalism by promoting the Croatian language and culture as well as formation of a Slavic kingdom under the Hapsburgs' noses. In 1832, Ljudevit Gaj, a Croatian noble, tried to elbow the Hungarians aside by addressing the Sabor in the Croatian language, which was daring at the time. Gaj, who was a journalist and linguist, pushed a South Slavic literary language, engineered a Latin-based script, and in 1836 founded an anti-Hungarian journal that called for cultural and political unity. The Hungarians were understandably angered by these developments and tried to impose Hungarian as the official language of Slavonia. The Croatians responded by sending any correspondence written in Hungarian back to Hungary unread.

AUSTRO-HUNGARIAN RULE

2

In 1848, Hungary challenged Austria during the revolution that was sweeping across Europe. Croatians, who feared another wave of domination from Hungary and who had hoped for unification, sided with Austria and began to call for self-determination. Austria yielded to Croatian pressure and raised Josip Jelačić to the position of Ban (viceroy) of Croatia. Jelačić immediately convened the Croatian Sabor to consolidate his support. He suspended relations with Hungary and declared war, but his Austrian allies reasserted their authority over Croatia after defeating the Hungarians with Jelačić's help.

Austria ended absolute rule over Croatia in 1860, and in 1866 the Austro-Hungarian empire was near collapse. In order to save it, Emperor Franz Joseph united Austria and Hungary in a dual monarchy. In a Sabor dominated by pro-Hungarian officials, a compromise on Croatia was reached that acknowledged the country as a distinct political entity within the empire.

Croatia increased its autonomy within the empire and in 1868 established a political/cultural base in Zagreb. However, the Croatian leadership was divided between those advocating a South Slav union and those favoring a Greater Croatia. In addition, animosity between the Croats and Serbs was on the rise. Bishop Josip Strossmayer attempted to reduce the religious differences between the Croats and Serbs to defuse the growing tensions.

Ante Starčević represented the opposition to Strossmayer's initiatives and was suspicious of any conciliatory moves directed at the Serbs. Both movements were sabotaged by Ban Károly Khuen-Héderváry when he ignored a compromise that allowed home rule for Croatia and promoted Hungarian language and culture by provoking conflict between Croats and Serbs.

Despite Héderváry's treachery, in 1906, Serbs and Croats again came together to create the Croat-Serb Coalition, which immediately came under attack from Vienna, which feared a loss of Austrian influence.

WORLD WAR I

In 1908, Austria-Hungary annexed Bosnia and its diverse population of Catholic Croats, Orthodox Serbs, and Muslims. This move set back the Serb goal of creating a Serbian state and reignited tensions between Croats and Serbs. Thus, when Hapsburg heir Franz Ferdinand visited the Bosnian capital of Sarajevo in 1914, the mood of the city was hostile.

On June 28, Bosnian Serb Gavrilo Princip assassinated Franz Joseph and his wife, and a month later Austria-Hungary declared war on Serbia. Germany sided with Austria; Russia, France, and Great Britain countered by forming an alliance of their own, thus drawing a line in the sand for World War I.

For a time, the Croats sided with the Hapsburg contingent, but on December 1, 1918, after the Austro-Hungarian empire had been defeated, Serb Prince Aleksandar Karadordević broke rank and created the Kingdom of Serbs, Croats, and Slovenes. The unification seemed reasonable in theory, but it did not allow for autonomy of any of the nations nor did it provide any guidelines to facilitate cooperation among diverse people suddenly thrown together under a single umbrella.

Only one Croat raised an alarm about the ramifications of unification. Stjepan Radić, leader of the Croatian Peasant's Party, urged caution, but his pleas went unheeded. After the new Croatian government failed to move in the direction of autonomy, in 1927 Radić and Serbian Svetozar Pribićević of the Independent Democratic Party joined forces to unite the Serbs and Croats. However, on June 20, 1928, extremists from Belgrade fatally shot Radić and two members of the Peasant's Party while parliament was in session. Fearing that the assassination would incite further ethnic violence, King Aleksandar dissolved parliament, established a dictatorship, and changed the name of the state to the Kingdom of Yugoslavia (South Slavia).

WORLD WAR II

Aleksandar's dictatorship resembled a police state in which 90% of the police and government officials were Serbian, a situation that invited trouble. As a reaction to this state of affairs, in 1929 Croat Ante Pavelić founded the Ustaše, an organization dedicated to the overthrow of Aleksandar's state. Five years later, in 1934, the Ustaše, with Italy's help, assassinated the king in Marseilles, an act that threw Yugoslavia into turmoil and made it vulnerable to Nazi exploitation.

Yugoslavia tried to remain neutral at the start of World War II, but pressure to support the Axis side was great, and on March 25, 1941, Yugoslavia's Prince Pavle aligned the country with the fascists. Within 2 days the prince was overthrown and the pact nullified, but the Nazis would not let the cancellation stand. On April 6, they bombed Belgrade and invaded Yugoslavia. It took the Nazis just 10 days to defeat the Yugoslav army. Shortly after that, the Ustaše formed the Independent State of Croatia (Nezavisna Država Hrvatska, NDH), leaving the rest of Yugoslavia isolated.

The Ustaše at first attempted to drive the Serbs out of Croatia, but when that proved impossible, they set up several concentration camps, the most infamous being the camps at Jasenovac, about 97km (60 miles) south of Zagreb on the Sava River. No one knows how many people died in Jasenovac at the hands of the Ustaše, but reports did chronicle acts of inhumanity and barbarism in the camps. Not all Croats condoned the Ustaše and their methods.

A resistance movement to counter the Ustaše was organized almost immediately after Germany invaded in 1941, but it was divided between the pro-Serbian Četniks and the pro-Communist Partisans led by Josip Broz "Tito." Committed as these groups were, they were not very effective in combating the Ustaše because they were more intent on competing with and killing each other. However, the Allies recognized Tito's Partisans as the official resistance at the Tehran Conference and funneled all aid to the Communist group, which helped liberate Belgrade.

Ironically, the internal conflict between opposing resistance groups in Yugoslavia helped the Allied victory because it tied up hundreds of thousands of Axis troops, who then were unavailable to fight the Allies. Even so, when the war ended in 1944, more than 1.7 million Yugoslavs had died as a result of the fighting, a number that represented 10% of the country's population.

POSTWAR YUGOSLAVIA

After the war, Tito's Communist Party won the Yugoslav election with 90% percent of the vote, but Tito was not in lockstep with Stalin and declared Yugoslav nonalignment in 1948, which allowed him to be a cafeteria Communist.

Nonalignment was a double-edged sword for Yugoslavia. On the one hand, the country had to endure a Soviet blockade in the 1950s as a result of Tito's nonconformity, but on the other, Tito's position helped tourism flourish along the Adriatic coast. His approval of site management allowed competition and created efficiencies in the workplace. He also gave each of Yugoslavia's six republics—Croatia, Serbia, Slovenia, Bosnia/Herzegovina, Macedonia, and Montenegro—control over its own internal affairs.

Tito's largesse had its limits. In 1967 the Croatian economy was booming, which buoyed national sentiment. The first expression of renewed nationalism surfaced in the cultural realm: The Croatian intelligentsia, worried by attempts to create a single Serb-Croat literary language, issued a declaration stating that Croatian was a language distinct from Serbian. Croatia's Serbs issued a retort stating that they had a right to their own language, too, and that they wanted to use the Cyrillic script. Tito quickly suppressed both sides of the argument, which put an end to the nascent nationalist movement dubbed "Croatian Spring."

For a while, other efforts at liberalization—demands for autonomy, student strikes, calls for government reform—were attempted, but in 1971 Tito cracked down on those reformers, too, effectively putting an end to the Croatian Spring once and for all. Tito's hard line had a chilling effect on reform efforts not only in Croatia but also in the rest of Yugoslavia, though his iron hand didn't stop Yugoslavs outside the country from criticizing his style of government.

YUGOSLAVIA IN TURMOIL

On May 4, 1980, after decades of balancing Communist ideology with Western capitalism in Yugoslavia, Josip Broz "Tito" died at the age of 88. His funeral in Belgrade was attended by thousands of Yugoslavs and more than 100 heads of state.

Unfortunately, as with many authoritarian leaders, Tito had not developed a plan of succession, which left the Yugoslav state without a strong leader. To complicate matters, the region's economy was deteriorating in the wake of the 1970s oil crisis, a huge national debt, and the disappearance of foreign credit sources. The republics once again became restless, and old problems resurfaced.

The first hot spot was Kosovo, a region in southwest Serbia with a large Muslim Albanian population that in 1981 aspired to republic status after having enjoyed a modicum of autonomy. Six years later, the emboldened Serb minority in Kosovo took the position that the Albanians there were a threat to them. That inspired Serbs in Croatia to almost simultaneously express the same sentiment about the Croats. A collective angst spread, cracking Yugoslavia along national, religious, and ethnic lines.

In 1987, a relatively unknown Serb politician named Slobodan Milošević began to proclaim Serb superiority while working toward installing a Communist government in Yugoslavia. Two years after Milošević's debut as a champion of Serbs, the Berlin Wall came down, leaving him holding an unpopular position while the rest of Europe raced off in the opposite ideological direction.

WAR IN CROATIA

Despite Milošević's efforts to expand his bloc of followers, Croatia and other Yugoslav republics were trying to make the transition to democracy. In May 1989 the Croatian Democratic Union (HDZ), led by former general and historian Franjo Tuđman, became one of the first non-Communist organizations in Croatia, and in less than a year began campaigning for Croatia's secession from Yugoslavia. By April, free elections were held in Croatia and Tuđman was sworn in as president the next month. He promptly declared Croatian statehood, a preliminary stage before independence. At the same time, Stjepan Mešić was chosen as Croatia's first post-Communist prime minister, and a constitution was written that declared Serbs in Croatia a national minority rather than a nation within the republic.

This classification fomented outrage in the Serb community. In 1991, Milošević, seeing that the breakup of Yugoslavia was inevitable, began gathering support for a Greater Serbia, which would include all the areas of Croatia and Bosnia/Herzegovina where Serbs were in residence. Worse, Milošević developed a plan to "ethnically cleanse" eastern Croatia of any Croats living there. Under such conditions, civil war was imminent.

Hostilities broke out in 1991 with Milošević pulling Serb forces into Croatia from all over Yugoslavia. During the violence, cities such as Dubrovnik, Vukovar, and Osijek suffered heavy damage, thousands of Croatians were forced to leave their homes, and thousands more were killed. The fighting also spread to other republics in Yugoslavia—most notably Bosnia—as Milošević and the Serbs kept advancing and pressuring Croats and Muslims in Bosnia to fight each other.

Finally, hostilities between the Croats and the Muslims in Bosnia were ended by the U.S., and peace was declared in northern Yugoslavia in 1995. But 3 more years passed before the last Serb military units left Croatia. A year later, Tuđman died, paving the way for the election of Stjepan Mesić, who had opposed Tuđman's war policies in Bosnia/Herzegovina, and he has served as president of Croatia since then.

POSTWAR CROATIA

Croatia's economy was a shambles as the war drew to a close: Unemployment was hovering at 20%; industry was almost nonexistent; agricultural output was drastically low; and some companies were unable to pay workers the depressed average monthly wage of $400.

In some business sectors, the country's economy still is struggling, but until the 2009 economic crisis, tourism and service industries were growing as tourists returned to Croatia.

The bad memories from the Croat-Serb civil war haven't completely disappeared, and many people are trying to recover from the horrors of ethnic cleansing, poverty, and loss. In April 2001, Slobodan Milošević, architect of the campaign to "cleanse" certain areas of all but Serbs, was arrested and charged with corruption after a 26-hour armed standoff with police at his Belgrade home. Two months later Milošević was turned over to the United Nations and charged with committing crimes against humanity in Kosovo and Croatia.

In November 2001, the United Nations War Crimes Tribunal charged Milošević with genocide stemming from his alleged activity during the 1992–95 Bosnian war. He is the first head of state to face an international war-crimes court. He died on March 12, 2006, while in custody at The Hague. His trial was in progress, and a verdict was never was reached.

Since then, Croatia has raised its international profile. It is on track for admission to the European Union by 2011, and it has achieved NATO membership. How the global economic crisis will affect Croatia's progress is yet to be determined, but if history is any indicator, Croatia will emerge as a strong, independent player on the world stage.

3 CROATIA'S ART & ARCHITECTURE

Croatian art and literature are largely unknown outside the Balkans. But that's understandable given the country's size and the restrictions imposed by past dictators. Croatia's art phases follow a timeline that is parallel to the nation's past, and much of it is informed by the tastes of serial occupiers who invaded the country in waves through the centuries.

PREHISTORIC TO 1 B.C.

The remains of cave dwellers have been found in Vukovar, on Vis, and most famously in Krapina in the northwestern part of the country where archaeologists found the bones of the 100,000-year-old Krapina Man. Specimens of primitive art—pottery, tools, even jewelry—usually are part of any such find, but the most famous Croatian objet d'art discovered in these ancient time capsules is the ceramic **Dove of Vučedol** (2000 B.C.), which was found during an archaeological dig in Vučedol, 4.8km (3 miles) outside of Vukovar. The Vučedol Dove has become the symbol of Vukovar and is available in many souvenir renditions.

ILLYRIAN, ROMAN & BYZANTINE (1ST–6TH C.)

There is almost nowhere in Croatia that is without a collection of art or architecture from at least one of these cultures, usually items that were found nearby. Vestiges of the Illyrians and Greeks who settled Vis (Issa) are scarce inland, but beautiful examples of sculpture, textiles, metal work and architecture are on display in Vis's archeological museum and *in situ*. Go there just to see a perfect sculpture of the **head of the goddess Aphrodite** (or Artemis) from the 4th century B.C. as well as **the remains of a Roman theater** that held 3,500. There's also the mosaic floor of a **Roman bathhouse** that still is being excavated.

The Romans completely infiltrated Croatia, and there are few places along the country's coast, on its islands, or even inland that are without something the Romans brought or built there. Pula, which was a Roman outpost called Pietas Julias, is home to one of the largest **Roman amphitheaters** still standing. The 1st-century beauty was built to hold more than 20,000 spectators, and though now reduced in size, it's in terrific shape, thanks to restoration. The remains of **Diocletian's Palace** in Split, numerous **Roman summer homes** *(villa rusticate)* on the islands and along the coast, and the remains of **Salona,** the former Roman seat of power outside Split, are just a few examples of the mark the Romans left on Croatia. And of course, smaller, more portable Roman leavings, such as **amphorae, funerary art,** and **statues,** have been found all over Croatia. They are on display in most of the country's museums.

Enter the barbarians and the fall of Rome. Just as Roman influence was receding in its provinces, including Croatia, the influence of Byzantium was creeping in, thanks to the **Emperor Justinian,** who was educated in Constantinople and served as consul there. It is almost impossible to distinguish between Rome as it declined and the Byzantine empire of Constantinople because both were part of the same political institution, the Roman Empire. Byzantium's capitol, Constantinople, had been founded as the capital of Rome by the emperor Constantine, and while it was a solid part of the Roman Empire, it had Greek influences, too. One of the best architectural examples of this transition is the 6th century **Basilica of Euphrasius** in Poreč, with its mosaics set on a gilded background. The basilica is on the UNESCO World Heritage list.

ROMANESQUE TO RENAISSANCE (7TH–17TH C.)

There is some controversy about where the Croats originated, but there is agreement that they arrived in Croatia in the 7th century. Whatever their origins, this migrating group brought its art with it and introduced a signature design *(pleter)* that resembles stylized Celtic knots. The design found its way onto the stone ornamentation of almost every medieval church in Croatia, including the first built by this new group of immigrants, **Nin's Holy Cross Church.**

As with all art movements, this one segued into another style, the Romanesque phase, but not until **St. Donat's in Zadar** was built with three apses, a soaring rotunda, and remnants of Roman architectural ornamentation.

4 CROATIA IN BOOKS, FILM & MUSIC

My favorite read on Croatia is *Travels in Undiscovered Country* (University of Alberta Press, 2003), an account of author Tony Fabijančić's travels through the country in search of his father's roots. The people he meets and the situations he encounters enlighten more than any travelogue ever could.

For the first time, an English-language book puts Croatia's art and architecture in the context of its history. *Croatia: Aspects of Art, Architecture, and Cultural Heritage* (Frances Lincoln, 2009) is a scholarly look at the monuments, grand houses, art collections, Roman influence, and Gothic leavings that embody the story of Croatia. Essays and anecdotes from American, English, and Croatian experts predominate.

Rebecca West's *Black Lamb and Grey Falcon: A Journey Through Yugoslavia* (Penguin Books, 1994) is a classic, a graceful history/travel journal that portrays Croatia in a Balkan context. West, who was a journalist, novelist, and critic, undertook her research in the Balkans with the idea of writing a travel book, but the final product turned out to be a seminal work that illuminates the tangled history of the former Yugoslavia.

Croatia: A Nation Forged in War by Marcus Tanner (Yale University Press, 2001) is also a history of Croatia, but Tanner's book goes from the beginning of Croatia's history in A.D. 800 through the start of the millennium and includes the 1991–95 Homeland War.

Robin Harris's *Dubrovnik: A History* (SAQI, 2003) is an excellent historical overview of the former Republic of Ragusa and helps shed light on how Dubrovnik came to be the "Pearl of the Adriatic."

For a quick tutorial in Croatian folk music, dancing, and costume, get a DVD featuring LADO, Croatia's National Folk Dance Ensemble (www.lado.hr, $20). LADO was founded in 1949 in Zagreb with the aim of researching, artistically interpreting, and presenting examples of traditional Croatian music and dance. The troupe toured North America in October 2009. If you can get tickets when you're in Croatia (they are in high demand), catching a performance is even better.

Harrison's Flowers is a 2007 film available on DVD set in Croatia during the Homeland War. It is the fictional story of a woman searching for her photojournalist husband in Vukovar and elsewhere in the war zone in the middle of battle. While the plot is fiction, the setting is not and the film gives some context to the situation in Croatia during the hostilities.

Dressed in Tradition

LADO owns more than 1,200 authentic, original folk costumes carefully gathered and preserved from all corners of Croatia. Some are so elaborate that it takes the dancers 2 hours to dress.

5 EATING & DRINKING IN CROATIA

Traditional Croatian cuisine reflects widely diverse cultural and geographic influences. Some are a result of Croatia's proximity to the sea and fertile farmland, and some are the result of foreign occupiers who imported their tastes and recipes. Croatians are very proud of their gastronomic traditions, and while there are regional differences, you'll find that freshness, grilling, and daily baking are consistent across the country.

Until recently, there was little menu variety within the region. But in summer 2009, it was clear that a new breed of chefs had infiltrated Croatia's dining scene with food-forward trends and preparations. In large cities and small, menus offering dishes made with local produce, meats, and fish were being prepared using sophisticated methods like *sous-vide,* infusion, and vertical presentation. The new culinary outlook has given new life to Croatia's dining scene, which is now innovative and exciting.

In Istria, the development of the country's first quality rating system for wine and olive oil production has been introduced, opening the way for development of new export possibilities. And in such cities as Dubrovnik and Zagreb, there has been an explosion of ethnic restaurants offering Croatians the opportunity to sample global cuisines including Thai, Mexican, Japanese, and even southern American. These are long overdue accomplishments, and they are making a significant contribution to more interesting dining choices and the development of a new Croatian culinary tradition.

MEALS & DINING CUSTOMS

Croatia's *old* dining tradition still is strong, but it is changing as citizens change their work hours, eating habits, and culinary awareness.

BREAKFAST & GABLEC Western-style breakfast (*doručak;* eggs, pastries, meats, cereals) is served at larger hotels and restaurants throughout Croatia. In smaller towns and in homes, a glass of *rakija* (fruit brandy), a cup of coffee, and bread or a roll hot from the local bakery comprise the usual early-morning meal.

Around 10am Croatians who farm or start work early often stop for *gablec* (*marenda* on the coast), literally "breakfast eaten with cutlery." This meal is a smaller version of lunch, Croatia's main meal, but it sometimes substitutes.

Gablec was common in the former Yugoslavia because back then people started work and school around 6 or 7am, which didn't allow time for breakfast. They were hungry around midmorning and a meal of home-style food like *sarma* (stuffed sour cabbage), *goulash,* or *fis paprikas* customarily was offered in factories, schools, and local restaurants.

LUNCH Lunch (*ručak*) generally is Croatia's main meal. It often begins with a bowl of soup followed by an entree of roasted meat, vegetable or salad, potatoes or noodles, and dessert. Croatians eat lunch anywhere from 10am to late afternoon, and if they eat dinner at all, it usually is a light meal.

DINNER Dinner (*večera*) for Croatians often consists of a very thin-crusted pizza or a shared plate of snacks, such as *čevapi* (spicy grilled sausage), *pršut* (smoked ham) and cheese, or grilled sardines, usually served well after 8pm. If they aren't eating at home, Croatians most frequently dine at **restorans** or **konobas,** both of which serve a wide range of dishes but differ in levels of formality, with *restorans* being the fancier of the two.

COFFEE & ICE CREAM Drinking coffee is a social event in Croatia. People sipping espresso are a common sight on almost every street in every town at any time of day. Sometimes Croatian coffee shops are cafes attached to restaurants or pastry shops, and sometimes they are free-standing shops that serve only drinks (alcoholic or nonalcoholic). Ice-cream shops—almost as ubiquitous as coffee shops—serve coffee and mostly nonalcoholic beverages plus a huge array of frozen concoctions ranging from basic cones to multilayered sundaes, as well as a selection of cakes and pastries.

TIPPING Tipping in Croatia is becoming more commonplace, especially in upscale restaurants. In the past, tipping was welcome but not expected. Today, an extra 10% or 15% is the norm in upscale establishments and in big cities. Tipping is rare and not expected in informal restaurants and in smaller towns, but most people leave any coins they receive in change for the waiter. Croatian waiters do not depend on tips for living wages.

COUVERT Adding a *couvert* to the bill is a relatively new practice in Croatian restaurants and it is not uniformly imposed. The *couvert* is a "cover charge" that is a prima facie charge for bread, which is brought to the table automatically in most places. Menus usually list the couvert and its cost, which can range from 5kn to 70kn or more. You can refuse the bread and escape the couvert, but once the bread basket lands on your table, you have to pay the charge.

REGIONAL SPECIALTIES

Dining is a national sport in Croatia. Generally, food is surprisingly good in all regions of the country. However, besides consistent quality and an ever-present offering of grilled meat and fish and pizza from north to south, each part of the country prides itself on specific traditional dishes.

CONTINENTAL CROATIA (ZAGREB, BILOGORA, ZAGORJE, PODRAVINA, MEÐIMURJE) Food traditions in this region have roots in seasonal climate, fertile farmland, and the rural lifestyle of the common people, plus the lavish gastronomy of the nobility (Austro-Hungarian) who lived in castles dotting the terrain.

Consequently, cuisine in this part of Croatia is more substantial than in other regions. For example, the need to store meat safely inspired *lodrica ili tiblica* (big wooden bowl), baked meats kept in bowls full of lard in cool places for later use. Smoking and drying, also methods used to preserve meats, extended to cheese (*prgica*), still a popular item in regional markets. *Žganci*, a kind of grits topped with cheese, sour cream, yogurt, or bacon, is a common breakfast dish. Turkey or duck with *mlinci* (baked noodles), *sarma* (ground meat in cabbage leaves), and *krvavice* (blood sausage with sauerkraut) are popular mains.

Favorite desserts in this region are *štrukle* (phyllo filled with fresh cheese, apples, cherries, or other fruit) and *palačinke* (crepes filled with honey and walnuts or jam). *Knedle sa šljivama* (potato dumplings stuffed with plums) are on almost every restaurant menu. In Medimurje, *prekomurska gibanica* (yeast cake layered with fresh cheese, apples, walnuts, poppy seeds, and raisins) is a must-try sweet after dinner.

GORSKI KOTAR & LIKA The area southwest of central Croatia (including Plitvice Lakes National Park) is a combination of forests, hills, and pastures where winters are long and summers short. The food is similar to that of continental Croatia, with a few notable additions. You'll see a lot of roadside stalls selling homemade cheeses and fruit brandies as well as spit-roasted lamb and pork. Look for *janjetina* (lamb) or *janjetina* baked under a *peka* (a metal, bell-shaped lid). *Lika*-style sauerkraut is another specialty that consists of marinated cabbage and smoked sausage served with potatoes boiled in their skins. *Pijane pastrve* (drunken trout) is fish cooked in wine sauce and served with potatoes and veggies, while *lički lonac* (Licki pot) is a stew of cabbage, potatoes, root vegetables, and meat.

SLAVONIA & BARANJA Cuisine in the eastern part of continental Croatia has a Hungarian influence: The food is quite heavy and seasoned with a lot of paprika. Specialties include *čobanac* (goulash made from meat and seasoned with hot paprika, garlic, and bay leaves), *ribli paprikaš* (paprika-based stew with a variety of fish), *punjene paprikaš* (paprika peppers stuffed with minced pork, rice, and bacon), and freshwater fish grilled on a spit over an open fire. *Kulen* (spicy paprika sausage), *rezanci* (broad egg noodles topped with sweetened walnuts or poppy seeds), and *breskvice* (dough balls filled with walnuts, sugar, chocolate, and fruit brandy, colored red to resemble peaches) are other regional delights. And the red stuff served with meat is called *ajvar*, a kind of red-pepper tapenade that can be mild or hot.

KVARNER & ISTRIA These two regions offer the most diverse cuisine in Croatia, perhaps because they combine both inland and coastal tastes. Here the *peka* covers food placed on a ceramic slab during cooking. The peka is covered with hot ash during the process. In the Kvarner, try *Creska janjetina* (lamb from the island of Cres) and *škampi* (shrimp cooked under the peka); or try game stews infused with bay leaves that from the mountainous part of Cres island.

In Lovran and along Kvarner Bay, *maruni* (chestnuts) are used in almost everything, including *kroštule* (fried strips of dough made with flour, eggs, lemon zest, and grape brandy). On Pag, try *Paški* *sir* (Pag cheese), lamb, and *pršut* (Dalmatian ham), all infused with a distinct Pag flavor because of the animals' diet of local herbs.

Istria has the most refined cuisine in Croatia, and it is also the source of some of the country's best wines. Try *riblja juha* (fish soup), *riblji složenac* (fish stew), *kuhane kozice* (boiled prawns), *crni rižoto sa plodovima mora* (black and white seafood risotto), and any dish with *tartufe* (truffles), including *Istarski fuži sa tartufima* (Istrian fuzi with truffles). A special *Istarski fuži sa gulasom od divljači* (fuzi with game goulash) is worth trying. Wines from this region are *Malvazija* and *Vrbnička žlahtina* (whites); and *Teran* and *Borgonja* (reds).

DALMATIA Freshness and simplicity are the watchwords that most aptly characterize Dalmatian cuisine. Main meals typically start with *pršut* and *Paški sir,* both often scattered with olives that have different flavors, depending on the Dalmatian village that grows and processes them. Oysters *(kamenice)* from Ston on the Pelješac Peninsula are also prized, as is anything from the sea. *Riba na lešo* (fish grilled with olive oil) and served with *blitva* (boiled Swiss chard and potatoes) is a common main course, as is *školjke i škampi na buzaru* (shellfish and shrimp stew). There are as many recipes and spellings for *buzara* as there are restaurants, but common ingredients in this sauce seem to be oil, garlic, parsley, wine, and shellfish. *Pašticada* (larded beef or pork roasted in wine and spices) is another good choice.

Wines to seek out in this region include *Bogdanuša* and *Postup* (white); and *Kaštelet* and *Plavac* (red).

3

Planning Your Trip to Croatia

Croatia can be unfamiliar territory for even the most seasoned traveler, but it's no more difficult to put together a dream trip to Croatia than it is to organize a visit to any other European destination. Once you understand that there are no direct flights from North America to Croatia and that getting there requires a stop in a city with connecting flights, ferry routes, or land access, planning is easy. However, planning visits to one or more of Croatia's 1,100-plus islands needs more precise logistical planning, if only to make sure you don't waste time on long layovers and missed connections. For specific information on planning your trip and for more on-the-ground resources in Croatia, please turn to individual chapters on your chosen regions and "Fast Facts," on p. 364.

1 WHEN TO GO

Summer, specifically July and August, is the busiest time on Croatia's coast and islands. This is the country's "season," a time when the sun is the hottest, the sea the bluest, and traffic endless. The Croatian coast is at its best—and worst—during midsummer. Hotel room rates top out; restaurant tables are always full, and crowds can be overwhelming. This is the period that makes or breaks many businesses that depend on tourism for a year's income, and it can be tough on unsuspecting travelers.

Much of the madness is due to traditional European vacation schedules which coincide with the coast's glorious summer weather. Boating enthusiasts, tour groups, and independent travelers from all over the world make up the rest of the traffic.

WEATHER

Weather in Croatia generally can be divided into two miniclimates. Northern Croatia has a Continental climate, with average temperatures ranging from near freezing in January to about 77°F (25°C) in August. The coastal areas have a more Mediterranean climate, with average temperatures ranging from the mid-40s in January to 100°F (38°C) or more in August. Spring and autumn are pleasant and mild along the coast; winter inland can be cold and snowy.

The bottom line is that in July and August, good weather is almost a certainty and tourism is in full swing, but prices and availability on the coast can be prohibitive. Conversely, in the interior, summer crowds are minimal and prices can reach their lowest levels. Zagreb and other interior cities can be real bargains then because many residents will be on the coast, leaving the city less crowded than usual. However, that means many Zagreb restaurants and shops may be closed. *A word of warning:* The weather on the coast is usually nice, the sea warm, and prices lower in May, June, September, and October, but some establishments, especially those on the islands, might be shuttered and some ferry routes might be canceled or on reduced schedules.

Croatia's Average Temperatures (°F/°C)

	Jan	Feb	Mar	Apr	May	June	July	Aug	Sept	Oct	Nov	Dec
Interior												
High	38/3	43/6	52/11	61/16	70/21	76/24	79/26	77/25	70/21	59/15	49/9	40/4
Low	29/-2	32/0	38/3	47/8	54/12	58/14	61/16	61/16	56/13	47/8	38/3	31/-1
Coastal												
High	50/10	52/11	56/13	63/17	72/22	79/26	85/29	85/29	77/25	68/20	58/14	52/11
Low	41/5	43/6	45/7	52/11	59/15	65/18	70/21	70/21	65/18	58/14	49/9	43/6

CALENDAR OF EVENTS

The festivals mentioned in this section, unless otherwise specified, fall on different dates every year. Inquire at the Croatian National Tourist Office (www.croatia.hr) or at local tourist offices for event contact information and for an updated calendar. For an exhaustive list of events beyond those listed here, check http://events.frommers.com, where you'll find a searchable, up-to-the-minute roster of what's happening in cities all over the world.

JANUARY

Old Christmas: On January 7, Croatians who follow Eastern Orthodox rules celebrate Christmas; everyone else takes a day off from work.

FEBRUARY

Rijeka Carnival: This pre-Lenten celebration begins in mid-February and ends at midnight on Shrove Tuesday. It is celebrated all over the country, lavishly so in Rijeka and Samobor with parades, masquerades, and merrymaking similar to those of New Orleans's Mardi Gras.

Feast of St. Blaise: Catholics all over the world honor St. Blaise on February 3 with the blessing of throats, but in Croatia, the celebration is much more elaborate. In Dubrovnik, for example, there also is a parade and lots of eating and drinking because St. Blaise is the city's patron saint.

MARCH

Vukovar Puppet Festival: During the last week of March, this eastern Croatia city becomes a venue for puppet shows, workshops, and demonstrations.

APRIL

Biennale: An international festival of contemporary music, Biennale is held in April in odd-numbered years in Zagreb. Contemporary classical musicians are the focus. For more information, go to www.biennale-zagreb.hr.

MAY

Dubrovnik International Film Festival: The annual cinema festival showcases the work of Croatian filmmakers as well as internationally produced films. Showings are in theaters across the city in late May.

One-Minute Film Festival: Požega in east-central Croatia is the setting for these obviously short, usually avant-garde films.

1001 Delights: Split hosts an annual 2-day food festival that includes workshops, tastings, and exhibits related to Croatian cuisine. Go to www.delicija.com for details.

JUNE

International Children's Festival: Šibenik is the setting for the annual festival, which encourages creativity in children. Programs showcasing youthful talents are presented in venues across the city from mid-June to early July.

Contemporary Dance Week: Zagreb is the main stage for this dance and choreography showcase, but parallel events are held in Rijeka and Zadar.

Histria Festival: Pula Amphitheater is a perfect venue for open-air concerts. Big names in pop, opera, and dance sign up for this cultural series, which runs from late June to early September. Go to www.histriafestival.com for dates.

JULY

Rab Festival: Every year at the end of July, the island of Rab goes medieval with a costumed festival celebrating the customs, traditional crafts, and lifestyles of that era. Every day of the week-long festival begins in the afternoon and lasts until after midnight.

Motovun Film Festival: This tiny medieval town in the heart of Istria hosts an annual film festival in late July to celebrate independent films. Go to www.motovunfilmfestival.com for more information.

Split Summer Festival: From mid-July to mid-August, the Split Summer Festival takes over the city's historic core with exhibitions, concerts, dance, theater, and especially opera performed in the Peristil of Diocletian's former palace.

Dubrovnik Summer Festival: Well-known international artists perform during this annual event, which takes place from early July to late August. Dubbed "Libertas," the festival has opened every year since 1950, even during the Homeland War.

International Folklore Festival: For a week in mid-July, Zagreb comes alive with dancing, song, musical performances, workshops, and exhibitions that celebrate Croatia's cultural heritage.

Extreme Sports Festival: Brač is known for its fine windsurfing and that's just one of the competitions held during the island's weeklong Extreme Sports Festival near Supetar. Take the half-hour ferry ride from Split and besides windsurfing, you can see athletes vie for medals in skateboarding, rock climbing, dirt bike riding, and diving. Go to www.sutivan.hr for more information.

Zagreb Baroque Festival: As part of its Summer Nights series, Zagreb includes almost 30 Baroque concerts at venues around the city, including concerts at Zagreb Cathedral. Go to www.kdz.hr for more information.

AUGUST

Street Art Festival Poreč: For 10 days in August, the streets of Poreč become a stage for music and dance performances, and a gallery for clowns, acrobats, and jugglers. The annual event starts the second week of August. Go to www.porec.hr for more information.

International Puppet Festival: European ensembles demonstrate their puppetry skills in venues all over Zagreb during this festival, which occurs at the end of August. Go to www.srce.hr/pif festival for more information.

Grisia Street Art Festival: Rovinj's "art street" becomes an indoor-outdoor gallery for 1 week in August (usually starting the first weekend). Anyone can set up shop at this time and the steep, narrow, cobbled street is crammed with browsers and artists until the wee hours. Go to www.tzgrovinj.hr/eng/home.asp for more information.

Zadar Dreams Festival: The second week of August is a time for whimsy in Zadar. Admission to events is free for anyone into alternative drama or performance art. For more information go to www.zadarsnova.hr.

SEPTEMBER

Varaždin Festival of Baroque Music: Listen to Baroque music in one of Europe's most Baroque cities mid-September through early October. Performances are mostly in Varaždin's churches. Go to www.vbv.hr for more information.

Zagreb International Trade Fair: You won't be able to get into this huge fair without credentials. (You'll also have a tough time getting a hotel room in Zagreb during the second week of Sept when the trade fair is in town.)

OCTOBER

Marunada (Chestnut Festival): For three weekends in October, the tiny town of Lovran near Opatija in the Kvarner region celebrates everything chestnut-related with food, merrymaking, and even cook-offs, all in honor of the chestnut and its many culinary uses.

International Jazz Days: Zagreb is host for this fall jazz festival, usually the first weekend in November. Go to www.jazz.hr for more information.

NOVEMBER

Martinje (St. Martin's Day): Besides being a church feast day, November 11 is also the day when the new wine is blessed and "tested" in unlimited amounts. The ceremony is conducted in almost all grape-growing regions of Croatia and begins with a song in honor of St. Martin. It ends with a prayer for a good year for all. When possible, the blessing is in a vineyard, but wherever it is held, it is followed by a party that includes eating, drinking, and singing well into the night. Most Croatian restaurants mark the occasion by offering special dinners (much as the French do when celebrating the *nouveau Beaujolais*).

Comic Book Festival: Anime and comic book aficionados will enjoy this weekend celebration of cartoons and music in Zagreb. Go to www.crs-festival.com for more information.

DECEMBER

St. Nicholas Day: Komiža on the island of Vis honors the town's patron saint on his feast day December 6 with a huge party that opens with the burning of an old fishing boat in front of St. Nicholas Church in Vis Town. Go to www.dalmatia.hr for more information.

New Year's Regatta: This event from December 28 to December 31 features small-boat races off the island of Hvar.

2 ENTRY REQUIREMENTS

PASSPORTS & VISAS

All foreign nationals (non-Croatians) need a valid passport for entrance to Croatia. Citizens of the U.S., U.K., Australia, Canada, New Zealand, Israel, Ireland, and Singapore do not need visas for tourist/business trips of fewer than 90 days within a 6-month period. A visa is required and should be obtained in advance for stays over 90 days. South Africans do require visas, even for short stays. For more information on visas, go to **www.croatiaemb.org**.

For U.S. citizens: Go to "Passports" in the "Fast Facts: Croatia" chapter, p. 365—the websites listed provide downloadable passport applications as well as the current fees for processing passport applications. For an up-to-date country-by-country listing of passport requirements around the world, go to the "Foreign Entry Requirement" Web page of the U.S. State Department at **http://travel.state.gov**.

CUSTOMS
What You Can Bring into Croatia

Foreign visitors can bring in currency in any amount, but anything above 40,000kn must be declared in writing. Local currency is limited to 15,000kn. Visitors also may bring in 200 cigarettes, 1 liter of spirits, 2 liters of wine, and 2 liters of liqueur duty-free. Foreign visitors can bring in boats without duty or taxes if the vessels are for private use while in Croatia and if they take them home when they leave.

What You Can Take Home from Croatia

U.S. citizens who have been away from the U.S. for at least 48 hours are allowed to bring back, once every 30 days, $800 worth of merchandise duty-free. A flat duty rate is charged on the next $1,000 worth of purchases. Any dollar amount beyond that is dutiable at whatever rates apply. On mailed gifts, the duty-free limit is $200. Citizens returning to the U.S. should have their receipts or purchases handy to expedite the declaration process. *Note:* Anyone who owes duty is required to pay upon arrival in the United States, either by cash, personal check, government or traveler's check, or money order, and in some locations, by Visa or MasterCard.

To avoid paying duty on foreign-made personal items owned before leaving the U.S., bring along a bill of sale, insurance policy, jeweler's appraisal, or receipts of purchase. Or register items that can be readily identified by permanently affixed serial numbers or markings—think laptop computers, cameras, and CD players—with Customs before leaving U.S. soil. Take the items to the nearest Customs office or register them with Customs at the departure airport. You'll receive, at no cost, a certificate of registration, which allows duty-free entry for the life of each item.

With few exceptions, fresh fruits and vegetables cannot be brought into the United States from another country. For specifics on what is and is not allowed, download the invaluable free pamphlet *Know Before You Go* online at **www.cbp. gov.** (Click on "Travel," and then click on "Know Before You Go! Online Brochure.") Or contact the **U.S. Customs & Border**

Protection **(CBP),** 1300 Pennsylvania Ave. NW, Washington, DC 20229 (© **877/ 287-8667)** and request the pamphlet.

For a clear summary of **Canadian** rules, write for the booklet *I Declare,* issued by the **Canada Border Services Agency** (© **800/461-9999** in Canada, or 204/ 983-3500; www.cbsa-asfc.gc.ca). Canada allows its citizens a C$750 exemption, and they are allowed to bring back, duty-free, 1 carton of cigarettes, 1 can of tobacco, 40 imperial ounces of liquor, and 50 cigars. In addition, mailed gifts to Canada valued at less than C$60 a day are allowed, provided they're unsolicited and don't contain alcohol or tobacco. (Write on the package: "Unsolicited gift, under $60 value.") All valuables should be declared on the Y-38 form before departure from Canada, including serial numbers of valuables you already own, such as expensive foreign cameras. *Note:* The C$750 exemption can be used only once a year and only after an absence of 7 days.

U.K. citizens returning from a **non-E.U. country** have a Customs allowance of 200 cigarettes; 50 cigars; 250 grams of smoking tobacco; 2 liters of still table wine; 1 liter of spirits or strong liqueurs (over 22% alcohol by volume); 2 liters of fortified wine, sparkling wine, or other liqueurs; 60cc (ml) perfume; 250cc (ml) toilet water; and £145 worth of all other goods, including gifts and souvenirs. Those under 17 are not entitled to a tobacco or alcohol allowance. For more information, contact HM Customs & Excise at © **0845/010-9000** (or 020/ 8929-0152 from outside the U.K.), or consult its website at **www.hmce.gov.uk**.

The duty-free allowance in **Australia** is A$400 or, for those under 18, A$200. Citizens can bring in 250 cigarettes or 250 grams of loose tobacco, and 1,125 milliliters of alcohol. Anyone returning with previously owned valuables, such as foreign-made cameras, should file form B263. A helpful brochure available from

Australian consulates or Customs offices is *Know Before You Go.* For more information, call the **Australian Customs Service** at ℂ **1300/363-263** or log on to **www.customs.gov.au**.

The duty-free allowance for **New Zealand** is NZ$700. Citizens over 17 can bring in 200 cigarettes, 50 cigars, or 250 grams of tobacco (or a mixture of all three if their combined weight doesn't exceed 250g); plus 4.5 liters of wine and beer, or 1.125 liters of liquor. New Zealand currency does not carry import or export restrictions. Fill out a certificate of export, listing the valuables leaving the country; that way you can bring them back into the country without paying duty. Most questions are answered in a free pamphlet available at New Zealand consulates and Customs offices: *New Zealand Customs Guide for Travelers, Notice no. 4.* For more information, contact **New Zealand Customs,** the Customhouse, 17–21 Whitmore St., Box 2218, Wellington (ℂ **0800/428-786** or 04/473-6099; www.customs.govt.nz).

For information on what you're allowed to bring home, contact one of the following agencies:

U.S. Citizens: U.S. Customs & Border Protection (CBP), 1300 Pennsylvania Ave. NW, Washington, DC 20229 (ℂ **877/287-8667;** www.cbp.gov).

Canadian Citizens: Canada Border Services Agency (ℂ **800/461-9999** in Canada, or 204/983-3500; www.cbsa-asfc.gc.ca).

U.K. Citizens: HM Customs & Excise at ℂ **0845/010-9000** (from outside the U.K., 020/8929-0152), or consult their website at www.hmce.gov.uk.

Australian Citizens: Australian Customs Service at ℂ **1300/363-263,** or log on to www.customs.gov.au.

New Zealand Citizens: New Zealand Customs, the Customhouse, 17–21 Whitmore St., Box 2218, Wellington (ℂ **04/473-6099** or 0800/428-786; www.customs.govt.nz).

For further information on what you can bring into and take out of Croatia, see **"Customs,"** earlier in this chapter.

MEDICAL REQUIREMENTS

For information on medical requirements and recommendations, see "Health," p. 35.

---

3 GETTING THERE & GETTING AROUND

GETTING TO CROATIA
By Plane

Croatia Air (ℂ **385/1487-2727;** www.croatiaairlines.hr) flies routes between Croatia and Europe's major hubs, among them Amsterdam, Berlin, Brussels, Dusseldorf, Frankfurt, Moscow, Munich, Paris, Prague, Rome, Sarajevo, and Vienna. Zagreb (ZAG) and Dubrovnik (DUB) are Croatia's biggest gateways and Lufthansa is the largest international carrier that serves them. Both Lufthansa and Croatia Air are members of the Star Alliance, which includes United Airlines. At publication time, no

U.S. carriers were flying directly into Croatian airports.

Tip: It's wise to book your flight to Croatia on United or a Star Alliance member airline (Austrian, Swiss, SAS, and so on) if only to smooth luggage handling. If your initial carrier is a member, bags will be checked through to your destination, a boon when catching connecting flights. But if you start your trip on a nonmember carrier, you might have to pick up your bag, go through Customs, carry your bags through the airport to the connecting gate, and recheck them with Croatia Air or your connecting airline. It happened to us and we also were hit with an "overweight fee" on our luggage for the second leg of our flight even though we were fine on the first. European weight rules kicked in because we were checking in there. You can avoid that by making sure your luggage is checked through to your destination city in Croatia no matter how many stops you make.

Besides Croatia Air, a number of Europe's discount carriers (**Ryanair, Easyjet,** and **SkyEurope**) serve Croatia via smaller European cities such as Venice. To find out which airlines travel to Croatia, please see specific destination chapters.

Departure Tips

In 2003, the Transportation Security Administration (TSA) phased out **gate check-in** at all U.S. airports. And **e-tickets** have made paper tickets nearly obsolete. Passengers with e-tickets can beat the ticket-counter lines by using airport **electronic kiosks** or even **online check-in** from their home computers. Online check-in involves logging on to your airline's website, accessing your reservation, and printing out your boarding pass—and the airline may even offer you bonus miles to do so! If you're using a kiosk at the airport, bring the credit card with which you booked the ticket, or bring your frequent-flier card. Print out your boarding pass from the kiosk and proceed to the security checkpoint with your pass and a photo ID. If you're checking bags or looking to snag an exit-row seat, you will be able to do so using most airline kiosks. Even the smaller airlines are employing the kiosk system, but always call your airline to make sure these alternatives are available. Security checkpoint lines vary in length from country to country and from airport to airport. If you have trouble standing for long periods of time, tell an airline employee; the airline will provide a wheelchair.

Speed up security by **not wearing metal objects** such as big belt buckles. If you have metallic body parts, a note from your doctor can prevent a long chat with the security screeners. Keep in mind that only **ticketed passengers** are allowed past security, except for folks escorting children or passengers with disabilities.

Federalization has stabilized **what you can carry on** and **what you can't.** The rules keep changing, but in general sharp things such as knives are out, nail clippers are okay, and food and beverages must be purchased *after* you clear security. Liquids are limited to 3-ounce containers that fit in one, 1-quart plastic bag. Keep this bag outside your suitcase to show screeners as you pass through security.

Note: In Croatia, battery-operated devices equipped with working batteries are not allowed in checked luggage, so take out that alarm clock before you check your bag. Bring food in your carry-on rather than check it in, as explosive-detection machines used on checked luggage have been known to mistake food (especially chocolate, for some reason) for bombs. On Croatia Air and most European airlines travelers are allowed one carry-on bag, plus a "personal item" such as a purse, briefcase, or laptop computer bag. Check size and weight requirements for each of the airlines you book. Limits on carry-on weight and dimensions set by Croatia Air and most European airlines are much lower than limits on U.S. airlines.

Airport screeners may decide that your checked luggage needs to be searched by hand. You can purchase luggage locks that allow screeners to open and relock a checked bag if hand searching is necessary. Look for Travel Sentry–certified locks at luggage or travel shops and Brookstone stores (you can buy them online at www. brookstone.com). These locks, approved by the TSA, can be opened by luggage inspectors with a special code or key. For more information on the locks, visit www. travelsentry.org. If you use something other than TSA-approved locks, your lock will be cut off your suitcase if a TSA agent needs to hand-search your luggage.

The TSA has issued a **list of restricted items;** check its website (www.tsa.gov/public/index.jsp) for details.

By Car

The highways that connect Croatia to its neighbors (Slovenia, Hungary, Bosnia, Herzegovina, Serbia, and Montenegro) are good and getting better as miles of new pavement are poured. This is especially true of the span between Ljubljana and Zagreb, a route that takes just 2 hours to complete. The route from Budapest to Zagreb runs across Croatia's northern border and is also popular. It takes about 5 hours to reach Zagreb (362km/225 miles) from the Hungarian capital.

Visitors coming from Italy and Austria must pass through Slovenia to get to Croatia's border, but Slovenia's roads are excellent, too.

Note: If you choose the route through Slovenia, be aware that on July 1, 2009, Slovenia began requiring tariff stickers for cars using Slovenian roads. Weekly stickers for motorcycles are 7.5€, cars 15€. The monthly fee for a motorcycle is 25€ and 30€ for a car. Even if you are just passing through, you'll have to buy the sticker.

In addition, the E.U. countries that abut Croatia (Slovenia, Hungary) anticipate subscribing to the Schengen protocol, under which internal borders among E.U. countries are dissolved. Croatia is in the process of applying for E.U. membership, and once it gains full membership, crossing national lines to and from Croatia should be seamless.

But even if European border checks disappear, travelers always should carry passport, insurance card, and any rental car papers (including the car's registration). This is especially true if you are going through Serbia or Montenegro, countries that are not yet fully in the E.U. membership pipeline.

Car rental: Car rental in Croatia is expensive, and it can be tricky. Even if you use a global agency like Hertz or Avis, it is best to reserve a car by contacting a local agency branch in the city where you plan to rent rather than through the agency's parent company or online.

In our experience, on two occasions, car rental companies at the Zagreb airport had "no record" of our online reservation and we had to rebook on the spot at a higher rate. We also witnessed the "we-have-no-record" scenario played out with a couple from Italy who had prepaid for the car via an Italian travel agency.

It is a good idea to take the "full insurance" package offered with your car rental even though it can add considerable cost to your rental. You will be given a chance to inspect your vehicle with your car rental rep, and you should be certain the rep documents any existing scratches or other damage before you take the keys. Any dings incurred thereafter, not to mention major damage, will be charged to you at full rate. *Note:* Most cars rented in Croatia are stick shift. Vehicles with automatic transmissions are scarce and you will pay extra if you need this feature.

Warning: In most cases, liability coverage from your domestic auto insurance policy **will not** cover you on vehicles rented outside the U.S. That is also true of the auto coverage that comes with most major bank cards. Check with your insurance agent and credit card companies to be sure.

By Train

Trains connect all major Croatian cities north of Split, but there is no train service to cities between Split and Dubrovnik in southern Dalmatia.

Croatia does have convenient railway links with Slovenia, Hungary, Italy, Austria, Switzerland, Slovakia, France, Germany, and Bosnia and Herzegovina, but the railway links to and from other European countries can be extremely time-consuming. The train ride from Paris to Zagreb, for example, takes 18-plus hours, while a rail trip from Frankfurt to Split will take almost 24 hours. If you must get to Croatia by rail from another European city, check schedules, fares and details on rail passes at **Rail Europe,** www.raileurope.com. For trains within Croatia, check **Croatia Railways,** www.hznet.hr.

By Ferry

There are four ferry lines with regular service from Bari, Ancona, Pescara, and Venice in Italy to major ports in Croatia. Several other lines operate seasonal routes. In most cases, you hop on a cruise ship after 9pm and arrive in Croatia just as the sun is rising. Routes, fares, schedules, and booking information for all ferry lines listed below are available at www.cemar.it. Fares and schedules are subject to frequent change.

Jadrolinija: Croatia's national ferry line has three international routes. Jadrolinija ships travel twice a week between Ancona and Zadar and Ancona and Split in central Dalmatia and once a week between Bari and Dubrovnik. Round-trip deck passage for two adults without a vehicle runs from 230€ for the overnight trip between Bari and Dubrovnik, while the fare on the same route for two in an external cabin with toilet plus a vehicle runs 700€.

Prices are the same for Ancona-Split and slightly less for Ancona-Zadar.

Blue Line International: This ferry line has daily overnight service between Ancona and Split. Round-trip deck accommodations for two without a vehicle run from 275€ while a deluxe cabin for two with a vehicle runs 600€ round trip during the summer. Weekend departures from late July through late August are even higher as a 25% surcharge is added to the bill if you travel Friday to Sunday at that time and a 50% surcharge is added if you travel alone in a double cabin.

In addition to the ferry options above, **SNAV** operates several "express" routes between Italy and Croatia and it is the only international connection to popular Hvar Island. The SNAV Hvar "Jet" catamaran service departs from Pescara, Italy, and deposits passengers at Hvar's Stari Grad port. The trip takes about 3½ hours, but service is seasonal (mid-June through early Sept). A round-trip between Pescara and Hvar for two costs 366€. Prices and schedule information are available from April through September at www.cemar.it.

Last, **Venezia Lines** travels between Venice in Italy and such cities as Rovinj, Poreč, and Pula on Istria's western coast. Current schedule and fare information is available at the website listed above or at www.venezialines.com from April through September.

GETTING AROUND
By Plane

Croatia Air has a near monopoly on flights that travel among Croatia's seven airports (Zagreb, Split, Dubrovnik, Rijeka, Pula, Zadar, and Brač), and unless one of these cities is your final destination, you'll have to transfer to some other mode of transportations to finish your trip.

Note: Domestic flights booked on Croatia Air from outside the country can cost nearly twice as much as flights booked at a Croatia Air office in the country, unless they are part of a multicity international ticket. Online prices are uniform.

By Bus

Almost every town in Croatia has a bus station, and the network of bus routes makes this form of transportation an excellent, economical option for travel within Croatia. Express routes on updated highways facilitate travel among major cities and buses stop at almost every village in the country, though schedules might be inconvenient for those with limited time.

By Ferry

Ferry/catamaran travel is a way of life on Croatia's coast. There is no other way to get to the islands (except Pag and Krk, which are linked to the mainland via bridges). Jadrolinija, Sem Marina, and SNAV are the major ferry operators. In summer, ferry schedules are beefed up to handle the increased traffic, but not necessarily aligned to make multiple connections needed for island hopping convenient. Some lines reduce their winter schedules, which further hampers efficient travel. Weather is another trip buster: Whenever the *bura* blows (the fierce northwestern wind that regularly hammers the area), ferries may be delayed or sidelined altogether.

Note: When planning your trip, do not underestimate the time it takes to travel by ferry. Besides calculating time for the water crossing, build in time to get to the ferry port, time to wait in line (which can be hours), and time to get from the port to your final destination. Check ferry schedules carefully, as not all routes operate every day.

By Car

Driving is the best method for seeing the real Croatia—even the islands. However, car rental and fuel, with a subcompact starting at 50€ per day and gas selling at unprecedented high prices (7.5kn per liter in the summer of 2009) can be expensive. During July and August, it is important to reserve a rental car before you arrive.

You will pay extra for each driver authorized to drive the car besides the primary renter, and every driver must be 25 or older to rent a car in Croatia.

We used local agency M.A.C.K. in Dubrovnik to rent our car. Besides Dubrovnik, M.A.C.K. also has offices in Rijeka, Zagreb, Split, and Cavtat and offers excellent rates. Reps speak English, provide maps and directions, and are very helpful. Go to www.mack-concord.hr/english.shtml for information. Global agencies Hertz, Avis, Thrifty, and Budget all have offices at the Dubrovnik and Zagreb Airports plus other locations in the city.

Croatia's main highways *(autocestas)* are well marked and well maintained. Secondary roads vary in quality and can range from excellent to unmarked dirt tracts. Gas stations are readily available on the autocestas, along main highways, and outside smaller towns. These usually are hyper gas stations in that most have attached restaurants, convenience markets, picnic areas, and liquor stores. Gas station restrooms are generally immaculate in Croatia, and some even offer shower facilities. They usually are open from 7am to 7pm every day and until 10pm in summer.

Maps that locate gas stations across the country are available and a wise investment if you plan on driving long distances. They usually are available at gas stations. See www.ina.hr and www.hak.hr for details.

Note: Almost every city and town in Croatia seems to be converting intersections with traffic lights to roundabouts with varying rules for entering and exiting, so proceed with caution.

Warning: Police are strictly enforcing Croatia's drinking/driving laws and posted speed limits. If you are a driver under 24 years of age, zero tolerance (0.0% blood alcohol) applies. For those 24 and over, a limit of 0.5% is the rule.

The speed limit in urban areas is 50kmph (31 mph) unless otherwise marked, 80kmph (50 mph) on secondary roads, and 130kmph (81 mph) on highways. You'll have to pay fines on the spot. If you are stopped for any reason, you will be expected to produce a valid driver's license, car registration papers and rental contract, and an insurance certificate. Watch for speed traps along the coastal highway and in rural towns and villages.

By Train

Croatian Railways (www.hznet.hr) is an efficient way to travel between Zagreb and

4 MONEY & COSTS

This guide lists prices in the local currency. The currency conversions quoted above were correct at press time. However, rates fluctuate, so before departing consult a currency exchange website such as **www. xe.com** or **www.oanda.com/convert/ classic** to check up-to-the-minute rates.

CURRENCY

The Croatian national currency is the **kuna (kn),** which comes in notes of 5, 10, 20, 50, 100, 200, 500, and 1,000. One kuna equals 100 lipa, and coins with values of 1, 2, 5, 10, 20, and 50 lipa and 1, 2, 5, and 25 kuna are in circulation. To convert prices in kunas to current prices in U.S. dollars, go to www.xe.com/ucc.

With Croatia's anticipated E.U. membership in process, many Croatian businesses are beginning to express their prices in euros and kuna, though euros are not yet widely accepted. Foreign currency can be exchanged at post offices, banks, and exchange offices. Numerous hotels and travel agencies also will exchange currency, but beware of the service charges, which can be as high as 3%. To convert prices in kunas to prices in U.S. dollars, go to www. xe.com/ucc.

Warning: Kunas and euros are very similar in look but dissimilar in value: One euro is worth seven times as much as one kuna. Be sure you separate the two and keep the currencies in separate compartments of your wallet.

ATMS

The easiest and best way to get cash in Croatia is from an ATM (automated teller machine, aka Bankomat in Croatia). The **Cirrus** (© **800/424-7787;** www.master card.com) and **PLUS** (© **800/843-7587;** www.visa.com) networks span the globe; look at the back of your bank card to see which network you're on, then call or check online for ATM locations at your destination. Be sure you know your personal identification number (PIN) before you leave home, and be sure to find out your daily withdrawal limit before you depart. Also keep in mind that many banks impose a fee every time a card is used at another bank's ATM, and that fee can be higher for international transactions ($5 or more) than for domestic ones (where they're rarely more than $3). On top of this, the bank from which you withdraw cash may charge its own fee. To compare banks' ATM fees within the U.S., use www.bankrate.com. For international withdrawal fees, ask your bank.

TRAVELER'S CHECKS

You can get traveler's checks at almost any bank. **American Express** offers denominations of $20, $50, $100, $500, and (for cardholders only) $1,000. You'll pay a service charge ranging from 1% to 4%. You can also get American Express traveler's checks over the phone by calling © **800/ 221-7282;** Amex gold and platinum

The Value of the Kuna vs. Other Popular Currencies

Cro kn	US$	Can$	UK£	Euro (€)	Aus$	NZ$
1	21¢	22¢	13p	0.14€	23¢	28¢

cardholders who use this number are exempt from the 1% fee.

Visa offers traveler's checks at Citibank locations nationwide, as well as at several other banks. The service charge ranges between 1.5% and 2%; checks come in denominations of $20, $50, $100, $500, and $1,000. Call ℭ **800/732-1322** for information. American Automobile Association (AAA) members can obtain Visa checks for a $9.95 fee (for checks up to $1,500) at most AAA offices or by calling ℭ **866/339-3378. MasterCard** also offers traveler's checks. Call ℭ **800/223-9920** for a location near you.

Foreign currency traveler's checks are useful if you're traveling to one country, or to the euro zone; they're accepted at locations such as bed-and-breakfasts where dollar checks may not be, and they minimize the amount of math you have to do at your destination. **American Express, Thomas Cook, Visa,** and **MasterCard** offer foreign currency traveler's checks. You'll pay the rate of exchange at the time of your purchase (so it's a good idea to monitor the rate before you take the plunge), and most companies charge a transaction fee per check order (and a shipping fee if you order online).

Another option is the new prepaid traveler's check cards, reloadable cards that work much like debit cards but aren't linked to your checking account. The

American Express Travelers Cheque Card, for example, requires a minimum deposit, sets a maximum balance, and has a one-time issuance fee of $15. You can withdraw money from an ATM (for a fee of $2.50 per transaction, not including bank fees), and the funds can be purchased in dollars, euros, or pounds. If you lose the card, your available funds will be refunded within 24 hours.

CREDIT CARDS

Credit cards are a safe way to carry money: They provide a convenient record of all your expenses, and they generally offer relatively good exchange rates. In Croatia, credit cards are accepted by most hotels and restaurants in larger cities, but they generally are not accepted for private accommodations or in rural areas. In addition, some establishments that accept credit cards will offer a discount if you pay in cash.

You can withdraw cash advances from your credit cards at banks or ATMs, provided you know your PIN. If you've forgotten your PIN, or didn't even know you had one, call the number on the back of your credit card and ask the bank to send it to you. It usually takes 5 to 7 business days, though some banks will provide the number over the phone if you tell them your mother's maiden name or some other personal information.

What Things Cost in Croatia

Pizza	30kn–40kn
Pasta dish	30kn–40kn
Half-liter beer	20kn
Cappuccino	6kn–10kn
Coca-Cola	15kn–25kn
Ice-cream cone	5kn per scoop
Airport taxi	150kn
Three-course dinner	65kn

Prices outside metropolitan areas in general will be 20% to 40% lower.

Keep in mind that when you use your credit card abroad, most banks assess a 2% fee above the 1% fee charged by Visa or MasterCard or American Express for currency conversion on credit charges.

In addition, when I called Visa and MasterCard to alert them I would be using my credit cards abroad, I was warned that I would be charged a 3% service charge on every foreign transaction. Even so, credit cards still may be the smart way to go when you factor in things like exorbitant ATM fees and higher traveler's-check exchange rates (and service fees).

Visa, MasterCard, Diners Club, and American Express credit cards are accepted in most Croatian establishments that accept plastic. The Maestro debit card is also widely accepted.

Croatia is an affordable country compared to other European destinations. Hotel rooms and rental cars will be your highest expenditures, but food, entertainment, and public transportation costs are well below those of nearby E.U. countries, such as Austria and Italy.

5 HEALTH

STAYING HEALTHY
Health Care Availability

Croatia provides its citizens with excellent, all-inclusive health care. Foreign tourists do not have to pay for medical services if there is a signed health insurance convention between Croatia and their home country. Healthcare costs for tourists from a country that does not have a signed convention with Croatia are paid directly by the user at the time of service.

No special vaccinations are required to enter Croatia. Contact the **International Association for Medical Assistance to Travelers (IAMAT; © 716/754-4883,** or 416/652-0137 in Canada; www.iamat. org) for tips on travel and health concerns in the countries you're visiting, and for lists of local, English-speaking doctors. The United States **Centers for Disease Control and Prevention (© 800/311-3435;** www.cdc.gov) provides up-to-date information on health hazards by region or country and offers tips on food safety. **Travel Health Online** (www.tripprep. com), sponsored by a consortium of travel medicine practitioners, may offer helpful advice on traveling abroad. You can find listings of reliable medical clinics overseas at the **International Society of Travel Medicine** (www.istm.org).

COMMON AILMENTS

BITES & STINGS Mosquitoes found in most parts of Croatia generally do not carry malaria. Use an insect repellent containing DEET. Bees and wasps are commonplace, especially on some islands and where beekeeping is an industry. Be especially aware of this if you are allergic to bee venom, and always carry an Epi-pen for emergencies.

DIETARY RED FLAGS Croatian food generally is not spicy, so gastric sensitivities are rarely triggered by the national cuisine. However, if you have fish or shellfish allergies, be sure to ask about ingredients, especially when dining on the coast. Restaurants serving vegetarian choices are becoming more commonplace, especially in larger cities, but you can find cheese *burek* or plain pasta almost anywhere.

SEA URCHINS & OTHER WILDLIFE CONCERNS Sea urchin needles and sharp rocks pose the greatest health hazards to swimmers in Croatia, especially around rockier beaches. It is best to wear rubber swim shoes both on the beach and in the water. These are available in most resort areas and in towns near the sea. Snake sightings are rare but can occur in wooded areas. If you are bitten, immobilize the site and get medical help as quickly as possible.

SUN/ELEMENTS/EXTREME WEATHER EXPOSURE Visitors should be aware that summer in Croatia can be very hot, especially in the southern regions. Air-conditioning is not prevalent in private accommodations or outside of the larger cities. Sunstroke and heat exhaustion can overtake the unwary quickly. Be sure to drink lots of water and get to a shady area or into air-conditioning if you feel dizzy and tired or if you develop a severe headache. These may be signs of heat exhaustion. Sunstroke is more serious and may require emergency medical attention. Symptoms can include fainting and/or agitation. Always carry enough sunscreen

with an SPF of at least 15 for all members of your party.

WHAT TO DO IF YOU GET SICK AWAY FROM HOME

Pack **prescription medications** in your carry-on luggage and carry them in their original containers, with pharmacy labels—otherwise they won't make it through airport security. Bring along copies of your prescriptions in case you lose your pills or run out. Don't forget an extra pair of contact lenses or prescription glasses. Carry the generic names of prescription medicines, in case a local doctor is unfamiliar with the brand name. ***Note:*** In Croatia, *all* medicines, even over-the-counter medications like aspirin, are sold only at pharmacies; other drugs require a Croatian doctor's prescription.

Additional **emergency numbers** are in "Fast Facts: Croatia" on p. 364.

6 SAFETY

Croatia generally is very safe for travelers. Theft and crimes against persons are not commonplace. However, you should exercise caution anytime you're out and about in an unfamiliar area after dark wherever you are.

In some areas, land mines left over from the 1991 war can pose hazards to unsuspecting travelers. According to www.landmines. org, more than 700,000 land mines were buried in Croatia, mostly in eastern Slavonia, around Zadar in northern Dalmatia, and some near Dubrovnik in southern

Dalmatia. The government has been demining the country since the end of the Homeland War in 1995, but finding and destroying the ordnance is a slow process. Usually, suspected land-mine areas are marked with red-and-white skull-and-crossbones signs (in Croatian), but you shouldn't tramp around any part of the countryside unless you have a local guide, especially in the above areas. Land mines kill a few Croatians every year. These are mostly hunters who disregard posted signs, or farmers who are impatient to till unswept fields.

7 SPECIALIZED TRAVEL RESOURCES

In addition to the destination-specific resources listed below, please visit Frommers.com for additional specialized travel resources.

GAY & LESBIAN TRAVELERS

In Roman Catholic Croatia, gays are tolerated but not celebrated. The country legalized homosexuality in 1977, but overt homosexual behavior is frowned upon in general and may be met with hostility in rural areas. Except for a few places in Zagreb, gay clubs are almost nonexistent, though some nightclubs and discos are patronized almost exclusively by homosexuals. During the summer, many gays frequent FKK (nudist) beaches (p. 164.), the larger cities (Dubrovnik, Split), and the island of Hvar. As in many other cities worldwide, the last Saturday in June is Gay Pride Day in Zagreb.

Many agencies offer tours and travel itineraries specifically for gay and lesbian travelers. **The International Gay and Lesbian Travel Association (IGLTA;** ✆ **800/448-8550** or 954/776-2626; www.iglta.org) is the trade association for the gay and lesbian travel industry, and it offers an online directory of gay- and lesbian-friendly travel businesses and tour operators. For Croatia-specific tips, check out http://travel.gay.hr/en, which posts a real-time special-interest guide for gays. If you are traveling to Zagreb, you can find arts and entertainment information geared to gays at www.queerzagreb.org.

Many agencies offer tours and travel itineraries specifically for gay and lesbian travelers. **Above and Beyond Tours** (✆ **800/397-2681;** www.abovebeyond tours.com) are gay Australia tour specialists. San Francisco–based **Now, Voyager** (✆ **800/255-6951;** www.nowvoyager. com) offers worldwide trips and cruises, and **Olivia** (✆ **800/631-6277;** www. olivia.com) offers lesbian cruises and resort vacations.

Gay.com Travel (✆ 800/929-2268 or 415/644-8044; www.gay.com/travel or www.outandabout.com) is an excellent online successor to the popular *Out & About* print magazine. It provides regularly updated information about gay-owned, gay-oriented, and gay-friendly lodging, dining, sightseeing, nightlife, and shopping establishments in every important destination worldwide. British travelers should click on the "Travel" link at www.uk.gay.com for advice and gay-friendly trip ideas.

The Canadian website **GayTraveler** (**www.gaytraveler.ca**) offers ideas and advice for gay travel all over the world.

The following travel guides are available at many bookstores, or you can order them from any online bookseller: *Spartacus International Gay Guide, 35th Edition* (Bruno Gmünder Verlag; www. spartacusworld.com/gayguide) and *Odysseus: The International Gay Travel Planner, 17th Edition* (www.odyusa. com); and the *Damron* guides (www. damron.com), with separate, annual books for gay men and lesbians.

TRAVELERS WITH DISABILITIES

Most disabilities shouldn't stop anyone from traveling. There are more options and resources out there than ever before.

In Croatia, as in other parts of Europe, many hotels, restaurants, and sites are not equipped to provide easy access for visitors with disabilities. However, public restroom facilities in train and bus stations, airports, and some hotels usually have been modified to accommodate wheelchairs. In general, museums, churches, private accommodations, ferries, shuttle boats, and local trams have not. There are a few exceptions and those are noted throughout this book.

Organizations that offer a vast range of resources and assistance to travelers with disabilities include **MossRehab** (✆ **800/ CALL-MOSS;** www.mossresourcenet. org); the **American Foundation for the Blind (AFB;** ✆ **800/232-5463;** www.afb. org); and **SATH** (Society for Accessible Travel & Hospitality; ✆ **212/447-7284;** www.sath.org). **AirAmbulanceCard.com** is now partnered with SATH and allows you to preselect top-notch hospitals in case of an emergency.

Access-Able Travel Source (✆ **303/ 232-2979;** www.access-able.com) offers a comprehensive database on travel agents from around the world with experience in accessible travel; destination-specific access information; and links to such resources as service animals, equipment rentals, and access guides.

Many travel agencies offer customized tours and itineraries for travelers with disabilities. Among them are **Flying Wheels Travel** (© 507/451-5005; www.flying wheelstravel.com); and **Accessible Journeys** (© 800/846-4537 or 610/521-0339; www.disabilitytravel.com).

Flying with Disability (www.flying-with-disability.org) is a comprehensive information source on airplane travel. **Avis Rent a Car** (© 888/879-4273) has an "Avis Access" program that offers services for customers with special travel needs. These include specially outfitted vehicles with swivel seats, spinner knobs, and hand controls; mobility scooter rentals; and accessible bus service. Be sure to reserve well in advance.

Also check out the quarterly magazine *Emerging Horizons* (www.emerging horizons.com), available by subscription ($16.95 year U.S.; $21.95 outside U.S.).

The "Accessible Travel" link at **Mobility-Advisor.com** (www.mobility-advisor. com) offers a variety of travel resources to travelers with disabilities.

British travelers should contact **Holiday Care** (© 0845-124-9971 in the U.K. only; www.holidaycare.org.uk) to access a wide range of travel information and resources for elderly people and people with disabilities.

FAMILY TRAVEL

If you have trouble getting your kids out of the house in the morning, dragging them thousands of miles away may seem like an insurmountable challenge. But family travel can be immensely rewarding, giving you new ways of seeing the world through younger eyes.

To locate those accommodations, restaurants, and attractions that are particularly kid-friendly, refer to the "Kids" icon throughout this guide.

Recommended family travel websites include **Family Travel Forum** (www.family travelforum.com), a comprehensive site that offers customized trip planning; **Family Travel Network** (www.familytravel network.com), an online magazine providing travel tips; **TravelWithYourKids.com** (www.travelwithyourkids.com), a comprehensive site written by parents for parents offering sound advice for long-distance and international travel with children.

Frommer's Croatia with Your Family is written with kids in mind and gives insider tips for traveling with children in Croatia.

WOMEN TRAVELERS

Women do not face any particular travel difficulties in Croatia They are treated with courtesy and respect in both big cities and small towns. However, female visitors who go out in public looking unkempt might earn a few disapproving looks because Croatian women take great pride in their appearance and what they wear. Women should leave the sloppy PJ bottoms and flip-flops at home and opt for a put-together look to fit in. If any church visits are planned, remember that women are expected to wear tops with sleeves and bottoms that fall beneath the knees. Churches and some museums post their dress codes and they will turn you away if you are not in compliance.

Check out the award-winning website **Journeywoman** (www.journeywoman. com), a "real life" women's travel-information network where you can sign up for a free e-mail newsletter and get advice on everything from etiquette and dress to safety. The travel guide *Safety and Security for Women Who Travel* by Sheila Swan and Peter Laufer (Travelers' Tales Guides, 2004), offering common-sense tips on safe travel.

For general travel resources for women, go to www.frommers.com/planning.

SENIOR TRAVEL

In most Croatian cities, reduced-price admission to theaters, museums, and other attractions is available for "retired persons," though no age requirement usually is given. Otherwise, there are no breaks for seniors, perhaps because Croatia's senior population is so active and vibrant.

Members of **AARP,** 601 E. St. NW, Washington, DC 20049 (© 888/687-2277; www.aarp.org), get discounts on hotels, airfares, and car rentals at select locations. AARP offers members a wide range of benefits, including *AARP The Magazine* and a monthly newsletter. Anyone over 50 can join.

Many reliable agencies and organizations target the 50-plus market. **Elderhostel** (© 800/454-5768; www.elderhostel. org) arranges worldwide study programs for those aged 55 and over. **ElderTreks** (© 800/741-7956, or 416/558-5000 outside North America; www.eldertreks. com) offers small-group tours to off-the-beaten-path or adventure-travel locations, restricted to travelers 50 and older.

STUDENT TRAVEL

The **International Student Travel Confederation** (**ISTC;** www.istc.org) was formed in 1949 to make travel around the world more affordable for students. Check out its website for comprehensive travel services information and details on how to get an **International Student Identity Card** (**ISIC**), which qualifies students for substantial savings on rail passes, plane tickets, entrance fees, and more. It also provides students with basic health and life insurance and a 24-hour help line. The card is valid for a maximum of 18 months. You can apply for the card online or in person at **STA Travel** (© 800/781-4040 in the U.S. and Canada; www.statravel. com), the biggest student travel agency in

the world; check out the website to locate STA Travel offices worldwide. If you're no longer a student but are still under 26, you can get an **International Youth Travel Card** (**IYTC**) from the same people. It entitles you to some discounts. **Travel CUTS** (© 800/592-2887; www.travel cuts.com) offers similar services for both Canadians and U.S. residents. Irish students may prefer to turn to **USIT** (© 01/602-1904; www.usit.ie), an Ireland-based specialist in student, youth, and independent travel.

SINGLE TRAVELERS

On package vacations, single travelers often are hit with a "single supplement" in addition to the base price. To avoid it, you can agree to room with other single travelers or find a compatible roommate from one of the many roommate-locator agencies.

Travel Buddies Singles Travel Club (© 800/998-9099; www.travelbuddies worldwide.com), based in Canada, runs small, intimate, single-friendly group trips and will match you with a roommate free of charge. **TravelChums** (© 212/787-2621; www.travelchums.com) is an Internet-only travel-companion matching service with elements of an online personals-type site, hosted by the respected New York–based Shaw Guides travel service.

Many reputable tour companies offer singles-only trips. **Backroads** (© 800/462-2848; www.backroads.com) offers "Singles + Solos" active-travel trips to destinations worldwide.

For more information, check out Eleanor Berman's classic *Traveling Solo: Advice and Ideas for More Than 250 Great Vacations, 5th Edition* (Globe Pequot), updated in 2005.

For more information on traveling single, go to www.frommers.com/planning.

8 SUSTAINABLE TOURISM

In May 2009, *Forbes* magazine named Croatia the 20th cleanest country in the world and the cleanest overall in eastern Europe and central Asia. That determination was made using an instrument called the Environmental Performance Index (EPI). The EPI was developed by Columbia and Yale Universities and it measures the effects of pollution on human health, ecosystem vitality, health of fisheries, the amount of greenhouse gas released into the air, and how well the country preserves its diversity of plants and animals. Those factors probably aren't high on anyone's list of considerations when planning a vacation, but the steps Croatia takes to keep its air and water clean and its flora and fauna healthy are remarkable and should be noted.

BOTTLE COLLECTION

In 2006, Croatia's Ministry for Environmental Protection introduced a policy that has eliminated virtually 100% of glass and plastic bottle litter in the country. Under the plan, people can bring every glass or plastic beverage bottle to any market larger than 200 sq. m (2,153 sq. ft.) and they'll receive 5 lipa, or half a kuna (approximately 6kn to the U.S. dollar) for each bottle returned even if they purchased the drink at some other store.

We saw the system in action at a Kaufland supermarket in Bjelovar. People place bottles one at a time on a conveyer belt in the store's lobby. As the belt moves under an infrared light each bottle's bar code is scanned and the number of bottles turned in is tallied. A receipt with the amount earned is then issued to the customer. That can be exchanged for cash or used against the grocery bill.

We witnessed people lined up out the door with plastic garbage bags full of bottles to return. In fact, that line was longer than any of the store's cashier lines. We saw the same scenario repeated over and over in different stores on different days.

The success of the program has been dramatic. Croatia estimates that more than two billion bottles have been collected since the return policy went into effect and that's virtually every bottle sold in the country. We didn't see a single glass or plastic bottle marring the landscape anywhere in Croatia—not on the beach, in the rivers, on the streets. Bonus: The government estimates that 1,300 jobs have been created in the recycling industry thanks to the program.

BLUE FLAG BEACHES

The Blue Flag is an exclusive eco-award given to beaches and marinas that meet strict criteria for both water quality and environmental management. It was introduced in 1987 and sets common standards of good management across Europe. Croatia prides itself on the number and quality of its Blue Flag beaches and marinas, which numbered 114 in 2009.

To earn a Blue Flag, a facility has to pass several tests. Water quality is sampled 20 times in summer and must reach the higher of two standards set in the organization's Bathing Water Directive. Beach management criteria include beach cleanliness, wheelchair access, dog control, first aid, safety, and environmental information. Marina management criteria includes provisions for information about the environment, adequate containers for trash and special waste, clean toilets and washing facilities, and safety equipment. Beaches and marinas are monitored both before and during the award year to ensure that all criteria are being fulfilled and that high standards are being maintained. For more information go to www.blueflag.org.

SMOKING BAN

In May 2009, Croatia issued a total smoking ban in all public places, including cafes, restaurants, bars, and clubs. The government backpedaled on the directive 4 months later after small business owners complained they were being ruined en masse. The ban is now optional for smaller establishments and others can accommodate smokers as long as they provide a private, separately ventilated space for them. But in a country where almost everyone smoked just 5 years ago, this is progress.

BIRDS & BEES

Croatia fiercely protects its natural resources and wildlife. It maintains eight national parks, and countless arboretums, botanical gardens, wetlands, and animal habitats. Bird-watchers in Croatia delight in multiple opportunities to observe a variety of feathered phenoms. **Caput Insulae Ecology Center** on the island of Cres long has been a haven and educational center devoted to protecting the rare griffon vulture. The center also sponsors volunteer trips to support its efforts.

The **Lonjsko Polje Nature Park** in north central Croatia is home to numerous wetlands and bird sanctuaries. The village of **Čigoć** and villages in the surrounding area not only comprise habitats for hundreds of species of insects, fish, frogs, and birds, including Čigoć's famous storks, these historic settlements also protect collections of ethnographic artifacts, including chimney-free houses made of centuries-old timbers.

The **Kopački Rit Nature Reserve** in Slavonia on Croatia's eastern border is the country's most fascinating wetland. Besides huge bird populations, the area is beginning to attract cyclists, hikers, and wine lovers thanks to redevelopment of bike trails, removal of land mines, and a rebirth of the region's vast vineyards.

The **Adriatic Dolphin Project** with research centers on the islands of Lošinj and Vis is working to study and protect the population ecology, genetics, acoustics, and habitats of bottlenose dolphins and other Cetacean species of the Adriatic. This is an E.U. PHARE project, and it includes a marine education center on Lošinj with permanent and temporary exhibits, interactive multimedia presentations, lectures, and education programs for visitors. Go to www.blue-world.org for more information.

ECO-CONSCIOUS HOTELS

As we crisscrossed Croatia in the summer of 2009, we found many hotels taking steps to protect the environment.

The **Radisson BLU** in Dubrovnik was built with a green roof and an HVAC system that is cooled by the ocean. The **Novi** in Novi Vinodolski also has a green roof, uses electric trams to move people around its vast property, and it recycles.

The **Kempinski Adriatic** uses nothing but stored rainwater to keep the only 18-hole golf course in Croatia green. The hotel also grows its own culinary herbs for use in its restaurants. Almost all hotels in Croatia have installed smart rooms with on-demand electricity that works only if a guest inserts his or her key card in a central slot.

WIND FARMS

From southern Dalmatia to Pag Island to Slavonia you'll see windmills dotting the horizon. Croatia is embracing wind power to produce energy. Croatians are frugal and conserving fuel, energy, and water is second nature for them.

The sustainable travel industry in Croatia is in its infancy, but conservation and environmental management are not. Croatia always has taken care of its land, water, and air, and all indications are that it will continue to do so.

General Resources for Green Travel

In addition to the resources for Croatia listed above, the following websites provide valuable wide-ranging information on sustainable travel. For a list of even more sustainable resources, as well as tips and explanations on how to travel greener, visit www.frommers.com/planning.

- **Responsible Travel** (www.responsibletravel.com) is a great source of sustainable travel ideas; the site is run by a spokesperson for ethical tourism in the travel industry. **Sustainable Travel International** (www.sustainable travelinternational.org) promotes ethical tourism practices, and manages an extensive directory of sustainable properties and tour operators around the world.

- In the U.K., **Tourism Concern** (www.tourismconcern.org.uk) works to reduce social and environmental problems connected to tourism. The **Association of Independent Tour Operators** (AITO; www.aito.co.uk) is a group of specialist operators leading the field in making vacations sustainable.

- In Canada, **www.greenlivingonline.com** offers extensive content on how to travel sustainably, including a travel and transport section and profiles of the best green shops and services in Toronto, Vancouver, and Calgary.

- In Australia, the national body that sets guidelines and standards for ecotourism is **Ecotourism Australia** (www.ecotourism.org.au). **The Green Directory** (www.thegreendirectory.com.au), **Green Pages** (www.thegreen pages.com.au), and **Eco Directory** (www.ecodirectory.com.au) offer sustainable travel tips and directories of green businesses.

- **Carbonfund** (www.carbonfund.org), **TerraPass** (www.terrapass.org), and **Carbon Neutral** (www.carbonneutral.org) provide info on "carbon offsetting," or offsetting the greenhouse gas emitted during flights.

- **Greenhotels** (www.greenhotels.com) recommends green-rated member hotels around the world that fulfill the company's stringent environmental requirements. **Environmentally Friendly Hotels** (www.environmentally friendlyhotels.com) offers more green accommodations ratings. The **Hotel Association of Canada** (www.hacgreenhotels.com) has a Green Key Eco-Rating Program, which audits the environmental performance of Canadian hotels, motels, and resorts.

- **Sustain Lane** (www.sustainlane.com) lists sustainable eating and drinking choices around the U.S.; also visit **www.eatwellguide.org** for tips on eating sustainably in the U.S. and Canada.

- For information on animal-friendly issues throughout the world, visit **Tread Lightly** (www.treadlightly.org). For information about the ethics of swimming with dolphins, visit the **Whale and Dolphin Conservation Society** (www.wdcs.org).

- **Volunteer International** (www.volunteerinternational.org) has a list of questions to help you determine the intentions and the nature of a volunteer program. For general info on volunteer travel, visit **www.volunteer abroad.org** and **www.idealist.org**.

9 STAYING CONNECTED

Staying connected with the folks back home is easier than ever thanks to innovations in telecommunications. No matter what kind of hardware you use, you'll need to know (initially) which numbers to punch in and their proper sequence.

1. Dial the international access code: 011 from the U.S.; 00 from the U.K., Ireland, or New Zealand; or 0011 from Australia
2. Dial Croatia's country code, 385.
3. Dial the city code. For Zagreb, for example, that is 1.
4. Dial the phone number.

To make international calls from Croatia:

1. Dial the access code 00.
2. Dial the country code (U.S. or Canada 1, U.K. 44, Ireland 353, Australia 61, New Zealand 64).
3. Dial the area code.
4. Dial the number.

For example, if you wanted to call the British Embassy in Washington, D.C., from Croatia you would dial 00-1-202-588-7800.

To call from one city code to another within Croatia: Dial the Croatian city code, including the zero, followed by the phone number.

To make a local call within a Croatian city: Dial the phone number. No codes necessary. Local calls cost about 5kn per minute.

For directory assistance: Dial 988 if you're looking for a number inside Croatia, and dial 902 for numbers to all other countries.

For operator assistance: If you need operator assistance in making a call, dial 901 if you're trying to make either an international call or if you want to call a number in Croatia.

Toll-free numbers: Toll-free numbers in Croatia start with 0800. *Warning:* Calling a 1-800 number in the United States from Croatia is *not* toll-free. In fact, it costs the same as an overseas call.

Prepaid Phone Cards: To use a prepaid phone card, call the service, key in the code on the back of the card, and call the number. It's a good idea to have a prepaid phone card for emergencies because Croatian pay phones don't take coins and you'll need a card to use them. You can buy prepaid cards in denominations of 50, 100, 200, and 500 units at most newspaper kiosks, at post offices, and at some tobacconists. Calls are based on unit-per-minute rates, and the farther away you call, the more each unit costs and the faster you use units.

In Zagreb, you can buy prepaid cards at **Nexcom,** Zavrtnica 17 (📞 **01/606-03-33**); or at **Voicecom,** Ilica 109 (📞 **01/376-01-23;** www.voicecom.hr). There is free 0800 access.

SMART PHONES

Advances in smart phone technology, affordable devices and service plans, and a dizzying array of applications have fueled a boom in the use and ownership of these one-stop communication-media wonders. Smart phones blend cellphone, Internet, GPS, still and movie camera, and more in one device. You can download news, read messages, take and send photos, play video games, and amuse yourself with countless other applications, but these services come at a price. Whether your phone of choice is a BlackBerry, an iPhone, or some other brand, knowing what these phones can and cannot do, how they work with European carriers, and how much their functionality will cost you abroad can help avoid nasty surprises when the bill comes in. Follow the steps below to avoid phone bill shock.

- Before you go, contact your carrier to purchase the biggest international data package you think you'll need during your trip. If you don't know how much that is, note that downloading a 3-minute YouTube video or sending one e-mail with a photo attached can use 2MB for each function. That will cost you $2 per 2MB action with a prearranged plan versus $40 per 2MB without one. Buying a plan that allows unlimited data transfer is safest, but it's also the most expensive as most carriers require you to sign a 1-year service contract.
- Turn your smart phone's international data roaming off when abroad. Leaving it on risks charges that can amount to $100 a day and more even if you don't make a single phone call. Limits on roaming charges now apply to European carriers serving European clients, but there are no limits on what they can charge foreign users.
- Whenever possible, use Wi-Fi instead of your phone network to access e-mail and the Web. Data downloads are free with Wi-Fi, but not through the network.
- Download e-mail manually instead of setting your phone to automatically fetch it from the Internet. That way *you* control the data flow. Remember that with a smart phone you pay for every megabyte of data that comes in or goes out.
- Keep track of your megabyte usage with the phone's tracker feature and turn off the phone when you get close to your limit.
- When you do use the phone to send or receive data, be aware of what's coming in and going out.
- Finally, keep your service provider's number handy.

That's a lot to remember and following the protocol takes some of the euphoria out of having a smart phone that can do so many things, but it's a routine you should master. I learned about my iPhone the hard way. Even though I had purchased a data plan before leaving for Croatia, it wasn't big enough. In 6 weeks, I had accrued a $6,000 cellphone bill without making a single phone call.

10 SPECIAL-INTEREST TRIPS & TOURS

SPECIAL-INTEREST TRIPS
Special-interest tours abound in Croatia. Tour operators in and outside the country can arrange tours to suit almost any specification.

Classic Journeys, 7855 Ivanhoe Ave., Ste. 220, La Jolla, CA 92037 (© **800/200-3887;** www.classicjourneys.com), is a California-based operator that specializes in customized itineraries for small groups. The focus is culinary, family, or cultural walking tours. Accommodations, meals, and transport are first-rate and each tour is led by a local English-speaking guide, who accompanies the group through the entire trip. Currently, Classic Journeys offers two Croatian itineraries, one to Dubrovnik and Hvar, and another through Istria.

Smithsonian Journeys (© **877/338-8687;** www.smithsonianjourneys.org) runs a 12-day Mediterranean boat adventure down the Dalmatian coast from Venice, Italy. The tour includes lectures on the area's culture and history.

Adriatica.net (www.adriatical.net) is a general tour operator based in Zagreb that puts together stays in many of Croatia's lighthouses and farmhouses and arranges sailing vacations.

ADVENTURE & WELLNESS TRIPS

With 1,185 islands and miles of coastline, Croatia attracts a huge number of boating and water sports enthusiasts. Croatia has a large number of charter companies that can put sailors in the captain's chair.

Sunsail (www.sunsail.com) runs charters with (skippered) or without (bareboat) crews that let you set your own course. If you have the required boating certifications, you can captain your own ship. If you don't, you can rent a fully crewed ship and kick back while embracing the role of pampered passenger. Sunsail has offices in Dubrovnik, Biograd (Kornati), and Kremik near Primošten.

Sail Croatia (www.sailcroatia.net) puts together customized floating holidays for experienced sailors and novices alike. Its offices are in Split, Pula, and Dubrovnik.

Dalmatia Charter (www.dalmatiacharter.com), a family-run company, operates boating vacations out of Trogir and Kremik.

The remains of the passenger ferry Baron Gautsch off Rovinj is one of the most popular diving sites in Croatia. **Diving Petra** (☎ 052/812-880; www.divingpetra.hr) in Rovinj organizes excursions to the 1914 wreck.

Biokovo Active Holidays (☎ 021/679-655; www.biokovo.net) runs guided hikes and mountain biking on the Biokovo massif and sea kayaking near Brela.

Investigator tours (☎ 021/321-698) lists rafting, canyoning, mountain biking, free climbing and paintball among its services.

Adventure Dalmatia (☎ 021/540-642; www.adventuredalmatia.com) runs rafting and canyoning trips on the river Cetina and sea kayaking around Hvar.

Check out the **Issa Diving Center** on the island of Vis (☎ 021/713-651; www.scubadiving.hr) to book a dive to the World War II U.S. B-17G bomber off the island's coast. Issa can arrange dives to other wrecks and it can put beginners through an elementary diving course or take them on explorations of Vis's many underwater caves.

Diving at Kornati National Park is strictly regulated. Most excursions to Kornati originate at Murter. Check with the **Murter Tourist Office** (☎ 022/434-995; www.tzo-murter.hr) for advice on diving trips to Kornati.

WINDSURFING

Bol on the island of Brač and Viganj near Orebić on the Pelješac peninsula draw the most windsurfing fans. In Bol, go to **Big Blue Sport** (☎ 021/635-614; www.big-blue-sport.hr) for scuba and diving lessons and equipment, or check out **Orca Sport** (☎ 021/740-625; www.orca-sport.com) on Potočine Beach less than a mile out of town. Check with the **Orebić Tourist Office** (☎ 020/754-452; www.tz-orebic.com) for information on where to rent boards and where to get lessons in Vigani.

CYCLING

Bicycling for tourists is growing in Croatia. To date, bike trails are regional and not well advertised. However, if you are interested in cross-country or mountain biking, check out www.findcroatia.com. The site lists agencies and links to other websites that can direct you to bike information.

One exception is biking up to 1,035m-high (3,395-ft.) Sljeme on "Bear Mountain" outside Zagreb. To rent bikes and cycling equipment and arrange an itinerary, go to **Sport Diomed** in Zagreb. Get info at www.sport-diomed.hr. It's also possible to use bikes in Zagreb proper. Look for red-painted bike lanes on streets in the city center.

FOOD & WINE TOURS

Increasingly, Croatian entrepreneurs are marketing local products by developing wine and olive roads as well as special excursions for truffle hunting and wine dinners. Istria, Međimurje, Korčula, Vis, and Slavonia all have mapped out winery routes where you can stop and taste and even get a meal in some instances. For maps and information on Istria's wine roads go to www.istra.com/zupan/eng/v1.html. For Međimurje wine tours, check out the **Tourist Board of Međimurje County** in Cakovec at R. Boskovica 3 (© **040/390-191;** www.tzm.hr). They can provide you with a well-done map tracing Međimurje's wine road and wineries where you can stop to taste or buy local vintages. You can get similar information at the **Cakovec Tourist Office** at Trg Kralja Tomislava 2 (© **040/313-319;** www. tourism-cakovec.hr). Slavonia/Baranja wine road information can be found at www. tzosbarzup.hr. General information on Croatian wine is at www.vinocroatia.com.

ESCORTED GENERAL-INTEREST TOURS

Escorted tours are structured group tours, with a group leader. The price usually includes everything from airfare to hotels, meals, tours, admission costs, and local transportation.

Despite the fact that escorted tours require big deposits and they predetermine hotels, restaurants, and itineraries, many travelers derive security and peace of mind from the structure they offer. Escorted tours—whether they're navigated by bus, motorcoach, train, or boat—let travelers sit back and enjoy the trip without having to drive or worry about details. They take you to the maximum number of attractions in the minimum amount of time with the least amount of hassle. They're particularly convenient for people with limited mobility, and they can be a great way to make new friends.

On the downside, you'll have little opportunity for serendipitous interactions with locals. The tours can be jampacked with activities, leaving little room for individual sightseeing, whim, or adventure. They often focus on the heavily traveled sites, so you miss out on many a lesser-known gem.

More than 50 U.S. tour operators offer packages to Croatia. Try **Adriatic Tours,** 777 W. 9th St., San Pedro, CA 90731 (© **800/262-1718;** fax 310/831-8382; www.adriatictours.com), or **Homeric Tours,** 55 E. 59th St., New York, NY 10022 (© **800/223-5570;** fax 212/753-0319; www.homerictours.com).

Adriatic specializes in Croatia and offers both escorted and hosted tours to almost all regions of the country. Adriatic also puts together religious tours and cruises. **Homeric** offers one hosted tour with a Croatian component and a "Dalmatian Sunshine" escorted tour that visits Dubrovnik, Split, Plitvice Lakes, Zagreb, and more. The New York–based **Croatia Travel Agency** (© **800/554-7016;** www. croatiatravel.com) offers a full complement of itineraries for Croatia.

Private guides: If you have the resources, consider booking a private English-speaking guide who not only can plan a custom itinerary for you but also can arrange transport, transfers, and admittance to otherwise inaccessible sites. **Jelena Delić** (© **91-531-8782;** damale3@ hotmail.com) is one of the best. **Nada Kozul** (© **098/373-167;** OS571643@ yahoo.com) is another accomplished English-speaking guide who can take you "behind the scenes" at vineyards, kulen and cheese factories, national parks, and other venues where tourists rarely venture on their own. She will customize your Croatia tour to fit your specifications as well as accompany you along the route.

For more information on escorted general-interest tours, including questions to ask before booking your trip, see www. frommers.com/planning.

Hotel room prices in Croatia vary considerably with location and time of year. Generally, hotel prices in larger inland cities and towns are the most stable, while hotels in major tourist areas along the coast sometimes publish as many as seven rate schedules based on time of year, as well as price variations based on amenities. Croatian hotel rates almost always include breakfast, while private accommodations almost always do not. Private accommodations rented through individuals are the least expensive and can cost as little as $10 per night. In one word: *bargain.*

For example, 1 night in a double room at a hotel in central Zagreb (Sheraton) costs $150 and up with breakfast, while a similar room in New York would go for $200 or more without breakfast. In London, the same Sheraton room without breakfast costs $265. These are Internet rates, which tend to be lower than rack rates.

Croatia has more than 400 star-rated hotels that are a combination of '60s and '70s high-rises; stately, ornate, turn-of-the-20th-century buildings; and, more recently, family-run boutique hotels. Currently, the country seems to be in a "renovate and rebuild" mode, and many establishments have completed or are undergoing updating.

HOTELS Most hotels in Croatia carry international star ratings from one to five stars, which seem to relate to amenities only and don't consider service, atmosphere, or quality of accommodations. In addition, the star ratings can seem arbitrary: In some cases a room in a one-star hotel might offer rooms with private bathroom, TV, and restaurant, while another one-star hotel might offer rooms with the bathroom down the hall, no TV, and breakfast in the lobby for the same price. In general, a one-star hotel offers a bare-bones room with a shared bathroom; a two-star hotel room has a private bathroom and usually a TV. A three-star room has a private bathroom (usually with a shower, not a tub), TV, and perhaps other amenities, though this category is unpredictable and can be a value or a rip-off depending on management. Four-star hotels will offer a room with a larger bathroom, possibly with tub; good-quality furnishings; little extras, such as toiletries; and other facilities like a fitness center, several restaurants, and a pool. Five-star hotels are few but increasing in number and mostly in larger cities and resort towns, though some of the smaller hotels are earning their fifth star by adding a pool, an elevator, or some other amenity to meet the requirement. They offer the highest level of luxury and in some cases rival the best the U.S. has to offer.

Croatian chains tend to be local: Arenaturist in Pula, Liburnia in Opatija, Hoteli Borik in Zadar. These generally manage either package hotels in resort areas or former grande dames in various stages of repair that range from crumbling to completely refurbished. Many establishments

---

Tips   BB, Don't Forget My Number

BB it means *bez broja* (without number). This is quite common in Croatia, particularly if the place is a well-known church or restaurant. If you see an address listed with a street name followed by bb, and you are having trouble finding it, ask a local for directions.

are single-site houses, usually owned by a family or group of friends who live on-site or nearby.

PRIVATE ACCOMMODATIONS Private rooms and apartments are by far the most common accommodations (and the best deals) in Croatia. These are divided into three categories: An A-level room has a private bathroom, perhaps a TV, and good quality furnishings. A B-level room has a private bathroom. A C-level room will have a bed, a place to hang clothes, and a shared bathroom. What you get in any given category can vary wildly, so it is always a good idea to inspect the rooms before you plunk down any money. Private accommodations often are little more than unused apartments or rooms that generate extra income for the owner. Frequently proprietors will refuse to rent for fewer than 4 nights, and if they do, they will charge extra. Licensed private accommodations are best booked through local tourist agencies, but you can find and book private villas and rooms via www. adriatica.net, too.

SOBES Another tier of accommodations in Croatia is the *sobe*, or room in a private home. These generally are cheaper than those procured through agencies, but they are unregulated and can be anything from a suite of rooms with private bathroom to a bed in an attic. Sobe signs often are found outside houses in smaller towns, but sometimes they are "advertised," usually by older men and women who whisper, "Need a room?" to new arrivals at ferry, bus, and train stations.

CAMPGROUNDS Camping is very popular in Croatia, especially on the coast. Most auto camps are small cities with campsites, markets, restaurants, laundries, and sports facilities. Frequently, campgrounds will be located on prime real estate close to the beach or near a large resort facility.

FKK CAMPGROUNDS Croatia has more FKK campgrounds (nudist camps) than any other European country. Many regular campgrounds have sections set aside for clothing-free campers. Most of these camps are outside cities in the northern Adriatic resort areas (Vrsar, Rovinj, Pag, Poreč, Krk) and are similar in size and scope to the larger general-interest auto camps.

YOUTH HOSTELS Croatia doesn't have a strong network of youth hostels, but these establishments do exist in Zagreb, Zadar, Dubrovnik, Pula, and a few other locations. Most of the time they are quite reasonable, though they usually have check-in and checkout times and rules similar to those enforced in college dorms.

Croatia Regions & Suggested Itineraries

Croatia is such a diverse country that it is difficult to standardize any touring plan of action to cover all its important places without leaving out many "must-sees." Consequently, we've divided our itineraries into two parts: routes for those who enter the country at Zagreb, and routes for those who start in Dubrovnik. These include our favorite places and allow for time frames of varying lengths.

Note: If you plan to spend 2 weeks in Croatia, simply follow two 1-week itineraries, in whatever order you prefer.

1 THE REGIONS IN BRIEF

There are many ways to designate Croatia's regions—coastal and inland, islands and mainland, northern and southern—and the best way to get a feel for the diverse charms of its geography is to look at each from a variety of perspectives.

DALMATIAN COAST Croatia's **Dalmatian Coast** is characterized by extremes. From Zadar in the north to **Dubrovnik** in the south, the terrain that extends westward from the dramatic backdrop of the rugged Dinaric mountain range becomes a sun-washed 3-D mosaic of red-tiled roofs, graceful bell towers, lush vegetation, and shimmering beaches as the land rolls toward the sea. The coast also is a repository of history with very visible Roman and Venetian influences. Add to that a mild Mediterranean climate that supports a thriving fishing industry and an agricultural economy rich in olives and grapes, and you have the formula for tourism gold. Offshore, Croatia's many islands (1,168) lure boating and watersports enthusiasts, sun worshipers, Europeans on vacation, and celebrities trying to get away from it all. They are part of Dalmatia's mystique and some of its most valuable assets.

The picture isn't so rosy on the Dinaric's eastern side. There the sun's rays become harsh spotlights that emphasize the landscape's stark and rocky personality, its struggling economy, and the effects of war.

INLAND CROATIA The area resembles a melting pot of cultures, each distinct, but all Croatian. The country's largest city, **Zagreb,** is there, a thriving metropolis of more than one million people. Zagreb is the economic and political center of this part of Croatia, which is a gateway to the spectacular natural wonders in the south and to the hilly, winegrowing regions to the north. The extreme northern part of the country is home to many Hapsburg-inspired towns and castles set at regular intervals across the rolling farmland east of Zagreb and all the way to the Danube. The countryside flattens out into farmland and historic towns and villages that have been the subject of battles for centuries. This area was severely affected by the 1991 war.

Shipwreck Diving

Croatia's 5,830km-long (3,625-mile) coastline and the waters around its 1,185 islands are a diver's paradise. Marine life, reefs, parts of sunken cities, and rock formations abound, but sunken ships often are the biggest lure for these deep sea explorers. For complete information on diving opportunities in Croatia, go to www.croprodiv.info and download their catalogue in English. Some of Croatia's most popular submerged wrecks and their locations are listed below.

VIS

USAF Boeing B-17: This World War II military plane settled on the ocean floor off the island's south coast in 1943 at a depth of almost 75m (250 ft.). The aircraft's fuselage and engines were damaged in a bombing raid on Maribor, and it sank while attempting a landing on Vis. For experienced divers.

Vassilios T: The Greek cargo ship went down in storm in 1939 and is at rest at depths of 66 to 180 feet off the coast of Komiza. The ship's coal cargo still is visible in the cargo holds and around the vessel. Underwater lamps are plus for viewing the vessel's interior. For intermediate divers.

BRAČ

Meja: This wreck is located in 39m (131 ft.) of water off Brač east of the isle of Mrduja. Diving is possible in the cabin section, and there is a sunken wall that can be visited on the return from the wreck. For experienced divers.

PULA

Baron Guatsch: A torpedo took out this Austro-Hungarian passenger ship in 1914 just north of the Brijuni Islands. It has four decks and is at rest 39m (131 ft.) down on a sandy bottom. Only two of the decks are available for exploration, but the ship has become a habitat for a variety of fish, shells, and plants. For experienced divers.

CAVTAT

Greek cargo ship flotsam and jetsam: The 2,000-year-old shipwrecks are long gone, but their cargo is strewn over a large area off Cavtat. Amphorae are plentiful and marine life is rich and diverse. There is a "newer" cargo ship from A.D. 400, 29m (98 ft.) down, but it is protected by a steel cage. For beginners diving with a registered club.

ISTRIA Istria is a peninsula that hangs off the northwestern end of Croatia into the northern Adriatic. Istria is Croatia's de facto league of nations: It is the part of the country that abuts western Europe, and it has a complex identity thanks to cultural osmosis and a long history of occupation by Romans, Venetians, Austro-Hungarians, Italians, and Yugoslavs prior to becoming part of independent Croatia. Part of Istria's charm is due to its foresight in letting the region's coastal towns and interior medieval settlements retain their personalities through the centuries. These places still possess unique architecture and customs that are a strong draw for people both outside and within Croatia. Istria knows how to be an excellent host to visitors, who have been flocking to the region's seaside resorts and Roman ruins from western Europe—and now from everywhere—for more than a century. Istria also is known as one of Croatia's food and wine capitals thanks to the excellent wines produced in its vineyards, the rich supply of truffles found in its forests, and the refined cuisine served in its restaurants, a mix that reflects the region's cultural past and future.

KVARNER GULF The **Kvarner Gulf** is home to some of Croatia's largest islands and biggest resorts. Croatia's largest port and one of the country's biggest transportation hubs (Rijeka) is here, as is one of its most developed holiday cities (Opatija). The entire area skirts the Kvarner Gulf, which lies between Istria and Dalmatia. It is a mélange of stark island landscapes, sophisticated resorts, excellent beaches, and some of the most forbidding mountains in Croatia. The islands of Krk, Cres, Losinj, Pag, and Rab are easily accessed from Rijeka and other points on the mainland and they are especially busy with tourists during the summer months. Croatia's wild and wooly northeastern wind *(bura)* is the only deterrent to enjoying this part of the country. When the *bura* blows, tourism goes.

---

2 A WEEKEND IN ZAGREB

If you find yourself in Zagreb over a weekend during a business trip or other visit, there's no reason to spend the time in your hotel room. Take a hike in Mount Medvednica's (the Bear Mountain's) forests; book a tour or drive to Plitvice National Park; or head north of the city to castle country. We've put together a 3-day itinerary that is short in duration but long on discovery.

Day ❶: Bear Mountain & Medvedgrad

You don't need a car or a tour to see **Sljeme,** the highest peak in the Zagrebačka highlands, or to poke around **Medvedgrad,** a 13th-century castle 4km (2½ miles) south of Sljeme. You can catch the no. 14 tram at Trg Jelačić to the end of the line at Mihaljevac and transfer to the no. 15 to Dolje. From there it's a 10-minute walk to the cable car that will take you to the top of the mountain for 11kn (17kn for the ride down). The cable cars run from 8am to 8pm daily in summer with shortened hours other times, but you won't need more than half a day to walk the wooded trails, snap a panoramic photo of Zagreb, or stop for lunch at the **Tomislavov Dom** hotel—unless you take the

trail below the hotel toward medieval Medvedgrad. *Note:* If you drive, be aware that the road up to Sljeme is one way up and one way down and that there is another road that leads to the backside of the mountain, where the Zagorje region begins. You'll have plenty of time when you get back to Zagreb to stroll **Tkalčićeva Street** and have dinner at **Klub Gastronomada** to celebrate your achievement.

Day ❷: Plitvice National Park

Plitvice (Plitvička Jezera; www.np-plitvicka-jezera.hr) is second only to the Adriatic coast when it comes to tourist visits in Croatia. Once you get there, you can choose sightseeing loops that take from 2 to 8 hours to complete and that vary in difficulty. The **park** comprises 16 lakes, countless waterfalls, and a wide array of flora and fauna. Hiking is the usual way to see everything, but Plitvice also uses environmentally friendly hiker assists like small ferries and electric buses to move people through the park, which is open from 8am to 7pm daily in summer with shorter hours other times. Park entry costs 90kn and includes a map on the back of your ticket. Get there via a day trip booked in Zagreb at the **Plitvice tourism office** at Trg Kralja Komislava 19 (✆ **01/461-35-86**), at other tourist agencies, or at most large hotels. You also can rent a car and drive there. The trip from Zagreb takes about 2 hours each way. *Tip:* If you drive, you can stop for authentic Lička cuisine at **Lička Kuča,** a fine traditional restaurant opposite the park's Ulaz 1 (entrance 1).

Day ❸: Castle Country

The Zagorje region northwest of Zagreb is Hansel and Gretel country. In a single day you can visit **Kumrovec** and the open-air ethno museum that was **Josip Broz Tito's birthplace,** investigate the imposing 12th-century **Veliki Tabor Castle** and its resident ghost, and have lunch at **Grešna Gorica** restaurant, a homey restaurant that's appears to have been plopped down in the middle of a farmyard. Daily buses run from Zagreb to Kumrovec, but if you want to also see Veliki Tabor and anything else, you can book a tour at the Zagreb Tourist Bureau or rent a car and set your own course. This is a day trip that can be either a half- or full-day adventure. If you like what you see and have time for an overnight, the castles at **Varaždin** and **Trackošćan** are a little farther north but well worth a visit.

3 ZAGREB & BEYOND IN 1 WEEK

If you are flying to Croatia directly from North America, chances are you will land in Zagreb. That means that even if your plan is to move on to somewhere else, you will have at least half a day to explore the Croatian capital—just enough time to scratch the surface. You may want to consider giving yourself more time to explore.

Day ❶: Zagreb

Pick up your rental car or catch the shuttle to town at the Zagreb airport. Settle into your hotel, then catch the tram to **Jelačić Trg,** the central square at the foot of Old Town. Explore Zagreb's historic **Old Town**—discover trendy bars, a rustic *klet* (a restaurant serving local cuisine), a jeweler's atelier, and a museum full of sculpted masterpieces.

Days ❷ & ❸: Rijeka & Pula

Drive to **Samobor,** where you can stop for a midmorning *kremešnite* (the custard-filled pastry this town is famous for) and explore the quaint town square. Get back on the highway and take the **Karlovac** exit where **Karlovačko Brewery,** historic buildings, and a lovely river walk await you. Spend the night at the **Korana Hotel.** Continue on toward **Rijeka** (p. 189) but make a stop at **Trsat** (p. 194) just outside town and explore the castle-museum and Marian shrine there. From **Rijeka,** you'll cross into Istria. Follow the road that goes south along Istria's eastern coast to **Pula.** If you haven't reserved a room at **Valsabbion,** stop at any tourist agency to book private accommodations—preferably a place that advertises agritourism. Or, if you want to sample a small family-run hotel, arrange to stay at the **Scaletta,** just a few blocks from Pula's 2nd-century **amphitheater** and the sea.

On **Day 3,** spend the morning exploring the amphitheater and the rest of Pula's cache of Roman ruins. Then head toward **Rovinj** (p. 237) around 2pm. That should give you plenty of time to stop in **Vodnjan** to see its mummies (p. 236) and still get to Rovinj for dinner. If you haven't booked a room at the **Monte Mulini** or **Angelo d'Oro,** stop at any tourist agency and secure private accommodations. Spend the evening having dinner at **Monte** at the foot of the hill leading **St. Euphemia Church.** Then walk off the calories by walking down **Grisia Street.** Don't forget to poke your head into the street's ateliers as you stroll.

Days ❹ & ❺: Poreč

Take a morning walk to Rovinj's market near the dock and stop at any cafe for coffee and a roll. Be sure to photograph this part of town in the morning light. Collect your things and head north to **Poreč** (p. 245). Once you settle into **the Hotel Palazzo** at the harbor or in the private accommodations that you booked on the way into town, head for the city's walled Old Town, which is laid out in a geometric design popular with the Romans. Poreč is very attuned to tourists' needs; there are multilingual signs and captions in front of every important building. **Trg Marafor** used to be the site of the Poreč's Forum and a temple dedicated to Jupiter, Juno, and Minerva. You still can see the ruins of that ancient house of worship. You'll want to reserve a couple of hours to view the **Basilica of Euphrasius,** its art, and its fabulous mosaics. Once you're finished, take a predinner promenade through Old Town, which probably has more jewelry shops per capita than any other place in Croatia (followed closely by the number of gelaterias). You'll have to resist their siren's song if you want to see anything historic.

Plan to spend **Day 5** out of town. Poreč is an excellent jumping-off point for a trip to **Pazin** and its **castle-museum and chasm.** From there, you can meet up with the local woman who guides visitors to the frescoes at **St. Mary's in Beram** as well as the **Church of St. Nicholas.** If you didn't catch the **Vodnjan mummies** on the way into Poreč, now is the time. Spend the night in Poreč.

Days ❻ & ❼: Motovun & Opatija

Leave Poreč after breakfast for Istria's medieval hilltop towns. These are fairly close together, but the roads are narrow, steep, and winding, so the trip through this part of Istria takes longer than you might think. You'll start by going toward **Pazin,** but about halfway there you'll veer north to **Motovun,** which is about 16km (10 miles) northwest of Pazin. You'll have to leave your car at the bottom of the hill that leads to Motovun and walk. Be warned that walking around this walled enclave is like lurching on a cobbled roller-coaster framework, but the effort is worth it because the views of the valley are stunning. From Motovun, go north through seemingly endless vineyards to **Livade,** and stop for lunch at **Zigante,** one of Croatia's best restaurants. Lunch will be pricey, but you'll get an education about truffles. From Livade, head a few more miles north to **Grožnjan** and take time to soak up its heady atmosphere. If you're lucky, there will be music in the air. Finally, start back to Zagreb via **Glagolitic Alley** and its sculpture garden displaying ancient Croatian symbols; Roč and its very low fortification wall; and **Hum,** supposedly the world's smallest town. You can stop at any agrihotel displaying a sign or get back on the main road and drive through the **Učka Tunnel** toward **Opatija** (p. 197) and spend the night there.

Start **Day 7** with a swim off one of Opatija's concrete beaches and then drive to **Lovran** to inspect the countryside and **Mount Učka.** Return to Opatija for a 2.4km (1½-mile) walk along the waterfront promenade to **Volosko,** where **Amfora** restaurant serves a fabulous lunch (you can drive there, too). You'll know at this point that you haven't had enough time in Opatija, but to keep to your schedule, you must now head toward Zagreb. You should be back in time for dinner.

4 DUBROVNIK & BEYOND IN 1 WEEK

If you are visiting Dubrovnik, chances are you changed planes in Zagreb and landed in Dubrovnik, Or, you deplaned in Zagreb, took the overnight train to Split, and drove to Dubrovnik. Perhaps you took a ferry from Rijeka or Italy to reach the walled city. Whichever way you arrived at this spectacular city in southern Dalmatia, you'll want to make the most of every moment inside—and outside—its walls.

Days ❶ & ❷ Dubrovnik

Settle into your hotel, take a swim, and catch the bus to the **Pile Gate** (or walk there if you happen to be staying at the **Hilton Imperial.** Before you get to the gate, stop at the tourist office across the street from the Hilton and pick up a map of Dubrovnik's Old Town and any other publications available. You can sign onto one of their computers and let everyone at home know that you've arrived safely. Next, check the time. If it is between 11am and 5pm, kill time by strolling the Stradun: Explore the **Old Town's** churches and museums; stop for lunch, perhaps at **Rozarij;** and wait until the sun is low in the sky before you start your walk on the walls. Then grab a bottle of water and head for the **Pile Gate** entrance to the stairs leading to the top of the stone fortification. Doing the entire 2km (1¼-mile) circuit atop the walls is a nonnegotiable must-do if you are physically able. After all, you've traveled all the way to Dubrovnik and this is the ultimate Dubrovnik experience. Allow a minimum of an hour for this trek, more if you are prone to ooh-ing and ahh-ing at spectacular scenery or if you decide to join other intrepid tourists in the sea off the walls before or after you start your trek. When you've come down to earth, you'll be ready for a break, a swim, or a glass of wine, and by this time, the promenade on the Stradun will have begun.

Spend **Day 2** in Dubrovnik exploring everything Old Town has to offer, including all the places up and down the streets that radiate from the **Stradun.** You'll find some interesting surprises there, including the second-oldest synagogue in Europe, galleries, restaurants, and a shop or two. This is the day to "do" the churches, museums, and palaces in Old Town. Perhaps check out **Lokrum** via the water taxis; or swim in the Adriatic off the rocks next to the wall. Have dinner in **Lapad** or at any place overlooking the sea, but make it an early night because Day 3 will be busy.

Days ❸ & ❹: A Day Trip from Dubrovnik

An ideal side trip will take you to the **Pelješac Peninsula** (p. 94). You can take a self-guided tour or sign up at Atlas or another agency for an escorted tour of the Pelješac vineyards and wineries. If you drive yourself, take the coastal highway north.

The next stop is **Ston** (p. 97), the Pelješac town closest to the mainland. Ston's obvious draw is the 5km (3-mile) **14th-century defensive wall** that stretches above the town from both sides and forms a horseshoe above it in the hills. You'll want to climb this mini–Great Wall of China with a friend just so he or she can take your picture with the wall behind you. This is not an easy climb (think climbing the stairs in a skyscraper), and not all the wall is navigable, though renovation is under way. Ston and its twin city **Mali Ston** up the road are both known for their oyster and mussel beds, and both have restaurants that serve fabulous versions of these shellfish. You can walk the salt pans outside town to see how this ancient salt collection method works (and you'll probably have the place to yourself). Stop at the ticket kiosk at the entrance and buy a few bags of souvenir sea salt from Ston.

The Pelješac Peninsula runs for about 64km (40 miles) from Ston to Lovišće and measures from 2.4 to 6.8km (1½–4¼ miles) wide at various points. However, those parameters are deceptive because Pelješac is quite mountainous, and the end-to-end drive usually takes more than 2 hours. It will be midafternoon by the time you finish with Ston, and you'll want to visit some of Pelješac's wineries, which are scattered all over the peninsula.

Day ❺: Orebić

From Ston, you'll head to low-key **Orebić** (p. 94) toward the far end of the peninsula, where you'll spend the night in private accommodations you arranged in Dubrovnik.

Orebić is a lively town from dawn to dusk; people stay on the beach and in the sea well into dark. At night the promenade along the waterfront is alive with families walking to and from restaurants, the sound of live entertainment pouring out of tavernas, and glowing lights from little galleries where art shows are in progress.

Days ❻ & ❼: Korčula

From Orebić, it is a half-hour's boat ride to the island of **Korčula** (p. 143) and the walled city of **Korčula Town** where Marco Polo supposedly was born. You can book Atlas-led excursions to Korčula at the main tourist office on the promenade and through other agencies in Orebić. Korčula Town is a nice, relaxing day trip, and while its beach isn't the best, there are plenty of museums, restaurants, and other sites to explore here. If you have a car or rent a scooter when you land, you can venture farther afield and see more of the island. You'll return to **Orebić** to spend the night and prepare for the trip back to **Dubrovnik.**

The trip back to Dubrovnik will take about 3 hours if you drive straight through, but you'll undoubtedly stop at more wineries along the road, investigate more quaint towns, and stop to take photos or go for a swim. Once back in Dubrovnik, you can reprise your favorite experiences or see the things you missed when you arrived.

Dubrovnik

Hollywood's most creative designers would struggle to build a set as perfect as Dubrovnik. This "city made of stone and light" is as dazzling as the sunlight and moonbeams that ricochet off its 14th-century ramparts.

Serb shells devastated this UNESCO World Heritage Site during the 1991–92 sieges, but the walled city is remarkably whole. One of the few telltale reminders of those violent days is the brighter shade of orange sported by new terracotta roof tiles on buildings blasted in the war. You might find a tiny bullet scar if you are looking for marks of hostility, but by and large the "Pearl of the Adriatic" is as lustrous as it was 5 centuries ago when Dubrovnik was a major sea power bustling with prosperous merchants and dripping with Renaissance grandeur.

Dubrovnik (née Ragusa) began as a Roman settlement. From the Middle Ages on it was a prize sought by Venice, Hungary, Turkey, and others who recognized the city's logistical value as a maritime port. But *Libertas* (Liberty), the city's motto, has always been uppermost in the minds of Dubrovnik's citizens, and through the ages their thirst for independence repeatedly trumped other nations' plans for domination.

In 1667, another kind of assault leveled Dubrovnik when an earthquake destroyed almost everything except a few palaces and church buildings in Old Town. The city was quickly rebuilt in the Baroque style of the time, only to be shattered again during the 1991–92 sieges. Croatia's war with Serbia destroyed the tourism industry throughout Croatia, but Dubrovnik was especially hard hit. Not only was the city physically scarred, but it also was economically crushed. Happily, crowds are once again flocking to this charming city nestled between the Adriatic and the Dinaric Alps, and Dubrovnik has regained its status as a vacation destination par excellence.

Inside protective walls, the pedestrian-only Old Town is bustling with an international crowd. Here you will find almost all the area's sights worth seeing—historic churches and public buildings; designer shops and homey restaurants; ancient sculptures and modern galleries; fountains and bell towers; monasteries and gardens; and the ancient city wall itself.

Outside the Old Town walls, Dubrovnik's suburban districts are packed with hotels, restaurants, parks, and campgrounds, all focused on the hordes of tourists clamoring to bask in the city's Mediterranean magic and revel in its citizens' devotion to Libertas.

1 ORIENTATION

Reaching Dubrovnik by any means except air can be inconvenient and expensive. Even driving there from elsewhere in Croatia is challenging because of the city's position between the mountains and sea and the lack of modern roads in the area. Ferry routes to Dubrovnik often include multiple stops at various islands, and train service is nonexistent. Build in extra travel time when you plan a visit to Dubrovnik.

ARRIVING BY PLANE **Croatia Airlines** (✆ **385/1487-2727;** www.croatiaairlines. hr) operates daily flights to and from Zagreb and select European cities. Planes land at Dubrovnik International Airport (Zračna Luka), located at Čilipi, 18km (11miles) from the city center (www.airport-dubrovnik.hr).

Croatia Airlines operates shuttle buses to and from Dubrovnik Airport, and they are coordinated with incoming flights, even late ones. Buses supposedly leave the main terminal in Dubrovnik near Gruž Port 90 minutes before each Croatia Airlines flight, but there is no posted schedule. You don't have to be a Croatia Airlines passenger to ride, however. The fare is 35kn one-way; the trip takes about 25 minutes.

There is also taxi service to and from the airport. Taxi cost is metered at 25kn plus 8kn per kilometer, 2kn for each piece of luggage, and 80kn per hour for waiting. Twenty-four kilometers (15 miles) from the airport to Dubrovnik costs about 250kn, and it could be more if you don't settle on the price and terms before you get in the cab. The taxi company's website (www.taxiservicedubrovnik.com) tells you not to pay if the driver doesn't turn on the meter, but that could get ugly.

BY BUS Daily buses operate between the Dubrovnik ferry port at Gruž and Zagreb, Zadar, Split, Šibenik, Rijeka, Orebić, and Korčula in Croatia, as well as Mostar and Sarajevo in Bosnia and Međugorje in Hercegovina. For more on bus service within Croatia, see p. 31. The main Dubrovnik bus terminal is in a temporary location near Gruž but it is expected to be moved again (✆ **020/357-020**).

BY FERRY Jadrolinija operates ferries that connect Dubrovnik with the islands and cities up the coast, including the island of Hvar and the cities of Split and Zadar. Local ferries run to the Elafiti Islands and Mljet. Buy tickets and obtain schedule information at the Dubrovnik Jadrolinija office in Gruž (✆ **020/418-000**) or at Jadroagent at Radića 32 (✆ **020/419-000**).

BY CAR The A1 autocesta between Zagreb and Split opened in June 2005 and was extended another 27km (16 miles) to Omiš in 2007, reducing travel time between the two cities to about 3 hours. In summer 2009 the highway had progressed to Ravča, shaving even more time off the trip, but the rest of the highway that continues to Dubrovnik 92km (57 miles) is still under construction as we go to print. If you choose the coastal route to Dubrovnik, you will have to take the much slower E-65. If you drive from Zagreb to Dubrovnik, even using the new highway, it will take approximately 7 hours, more during summer gridlock, so plan accordingly. *Warning:* Do not try to drive into Dubrovnik at night. Besides narrow lanes and tight turns on hilly roads leading into town, the city's streets can be confusing. There are few street signs in the city, and those are not lighted and impossible to see in the dark.

VISITOR INFORMATION

You'll find the Dubrovnik-Neretva County Tourist Board office at Vukovarska 24 (✆ **020/324-999;** www.visitdubrovnik.com). It is open from 8am to 4pm Monday to Friday, and closed Saturday and Sunday. The Dubrovnik Tourist Board office, Sv. Dominika 7 (✆ **020/323-887;** www.tzdubrovnik.com), is open 8am to 4pm Monday to Friday and from 9am to 1pm Saturday. Closed Sunday. Private tourist offices abound in Dubrovnik. There is one very accessible office across the street from the Hilton Imperial on the road leading to the Pile Gate (✆ **020/427-591**) as well as at several other locations in Old Town. The Pile Gate location is also an Internet center where you can check your e-mail or connect with home via Skype.

Another **Tourist Information Center** inside the walls at Placa 1, across from the Franciscan monastery in Old Town (© 020/323-350; fax 020/323-351), can help with maps, brochures, and information on local concerts, events, and some excursions. Private tourist agencies can be helpful, too—the following represents a partial list. **Atlas Travel Agency** has several locations in Dubrovnik: at the Pile Gate, in Old Town, and at the harbor. Atlas operates many excursions out of Dubrovnik and can help you find private accommodations. **Elite Travel** at Vukovarska 17 (© 020/358-200) runs specialized tours such as the UNESCO World Heritage Croatia Tour, which visits the country's protected cultural and natural sites, a horseback tour of Konavle, and a canoe safari on the Trebezit River, among others. **Generalturist** can book sailboat and car rentals as well as excursions and accommodations (Obala Stjepana Radića 24; © 020/432-974; www. generalturist.com). **Gulliver Travel** offers a broad range of excursions to Dubrovnik's offshore islands and towns up and down the southern Adriatic coast (Obala Stjepana Radića 32; © 020/313-313; www.gulliver.hr). **Huck Finn** is Croatia's premier adventure travel source. Even though it is based in Zagreb, Huck Finn offers an extensive slate of active Dubrovnik excursions, including sea kayaking around Koločep Island, bicycling across Šipan Island, rafting the Neretva River, and much more (Vukovarska 270, 10000 Zagreb; © 01/618-3333; www.huck-finn.hr). **Metro Tours** at Šetalište Kralja Zvonimira 40A (© 020/437-320) offers excursions to various locations each day. You can choose Mostar in Bosnia on Monday for 290kn, Cavtat on Tuesday for 125kn, and Korčula and the Pelješac wine country on Friday for 320kn. Prices include transfers, guides, bus, and boat, depending on the destination.

If you have the resources, consider booking an English-speaking private guide who not only can plan a custom itinerary for you, but also can arrange transport, transfers, and admittance to otherwise inaccessible sites. **Jelena Delić** (© 91/531-8782; damale3@ hotmail.com) is one of the best.

(*Fast Facts*) Dubrovnik

American Express **Atlas Travel**'s main office at Ćira Carića 3 (© 020/419-119; fax 020/442-645; www.atlas-croatia.com) is the American Express agent in Dubrovnik. Atlas-Amex also has an office at Brsalje 17 (© 020/442-574), open from 8am to 7pm Monday through Saturday.

ATMs Croatia's major banks operate Bankomats (aka ATMs) in Old Town and Dubrovnik proper. These are centrally located at the Stradun, Lapad, outside the Pile Gate, in Gruž, and now in hotel lobbies, restaurants, and elsewhere.

Banks Most banks are open from 7:30am to 7pm Monday through Friday and from 7:30 to 11:30am Saturday. Some banks close for lunch.

Business Hours Grocery and department stores are open from 7:30am to 8pm. Nongovernment offices generally work 8:30am to 5pm Monday through Friday.

Credit Cards Credit cards are generally accepted at hotels and larger restaurants, but be sure to ask before you order.

Emergencies Dial © 92 for the police; © 94 for an ambulance; © 93 to report a fire; and © 9155 to reach the Coast Guard.

Hospital Go to the **Dubrovnik General Hospital** (© **020/431-777;** www.
bolnica-du.hr).

Holidays See "When to Go," p. 23.

Information You can reach the **Dubrovnik Tourist Board** at © **020/323-887;**
the **Dubrovnik Neretva County Tourist Board** can be reached at © **020/413-
301.** Also see "Visitor Information," p. 60.

Internet Access There are numerous Internet centers in Dubrovnik. Try the cozy
Netcafe Internet Bar (no. 21 in the middle of Prijeko St.'s restaurant block). Connections are fast, the coffee is excellent, and the place is air-conditioned. Open
9am to 11pm daily.

Pharmacies Pharmacies in Dubrovnik have varied working hours: They're open
mornings and afternoons Monday through Friday, but only in the morning Saturday. Almost all accept credit cards.

Telephone Public telephone boxes accept phone cards available from newspaper
stands and post offices only. No cash.

Time Zone Dubrovnik is on Central European Time (GMT plus 1 hr.). Daylight
saving time starts at the end of March and ends on the last day of September.

Tipping Tipping is generally not expected, though it is appreciated. High-end
restaurants are the exception. Waiters there expect a tip.

Weather The climate in Dubrovnik is typical Mediterranean, with mild, rainy
winters and hot, dry summers. Daily forecasts are available at www.dubrovnik-
online.com/english/weather.php.

DUBROVNIK NEIGHBORHOODS

OLD TOWN The area within Dubrovnik's walls is known as Old Town, and most of
the city's main attractions are there. Besides historic buildings, Old Town is home to
restaurants, cafes, shops, and services that line the Stradun—a long (just under .5km/¼
mile) and wide street that runs from the Western Gate (Pile) to the Eastern Gate
(Ploče)—and its backstreets.

PLOČE Ploče is the neighborhood just outside Old Town's Eastern Gate. Some of the
city's classiest hotels are located on beachfront property in this area, as is the city's main
public beach, Banje.

LAPAD There are no big-time historic sites in Lapad, whose main attraction is a wide,
leafy pedestrians-only street lined with hotels and restaurants and backed by a residential
area on this peninsula west of Old Town. Lapad abuts Lapad Bay, so it has some beachfront, but the neighborhood's draw is several moderately priced hotels—moderate compared to the luxury hotels in Ploče and Old Town. Almost every bus that stops in Lapad
(nos. 4, 5, 6, 7, and 11) connects with Old Town at the Pile Gate; the ride takes 15
minutes and costs 10kn if you buy on board, 8kn from a news kiosk.

BABIN KUK On the Lapad Peninsula, at some indeterminable point less than 6.4km
(4 miles) from Dubrovnik's center and bordered on three sides by the sea and pebble
beaches, the Babin Kuk neighborhood begins. Babin Kuk is home to several hotels in
various price ranges. It also is an access point to rocky coves with what optimists call

beaches (read: major pebbles/rocks, no sand), as well as to scores of restaurants, shops, and services. Babin Kuk is connected to Dubrovnik by the city's bus system. Camp Solitudo, Dubrovnik's only close-in campground, is here.

Getting Around

There are no trains or trams in Dubrovnik, but the Libertas city bus system is fairly efficient (www.libertasdubrovnik.hr). If you are staying within comfortable walking distance of Old Town, everything important is accessible on foot.

BY BUS   Buy one-way tickets from a news kiosk or at your hotel for 8kn and save 2kn over the on-board price; an unlimited full day ticket is 25kn. All buses stop at the Pile Gate and continue on to outlying hotels, the ferry port, and beyond. Schedules and route maps are available at the Tourist Information Center in Old Town across from the Franciscan Monastery.

BY TAXI   Taxi stands are at the airport, bus station, and at the Pile Gate. Taxis can be called locally ⓒ **020/424-343** (Pile Gate), ⓒ **020/423-164** (Ploče), ⓒ **020/418-112** (ferry port), ⓒ **020/357-044** (bus station), and ⓒ **020/435-715** (Lapad). Rides start with 25kn on the meter and go up 8kn per kilometer. If you agree to a meterless ride, negotiate a price beforehand to avoid rip-offs and unwanted excursions.

ON FOOT   Negotiating the busy streets outside the walls can be confusing (and dangerous), especially at night. But once you are in the Old Town, you can devise your own walking tour using the suggestions in this book. You also can employ a private guide to accompany you on a walk, or you can book a guided Old Town walking tour through the tourist office or through a private tourist agency.

BY CAR   Congestion and parking make driving in Dubrovnik stressful, and Old Town is pedestrian-only, but if you rent a car for excursions to nearby Pelješac or Ston, car rental companies at the airport include: **Hertz** (ⓒ **01/484-6777;** www.hertz.hr), **Budget** (ⓒ **020/773-290;** www.budget.hr), **Thrifty** (ⓒ **020/773-3588;** www.thrifty.com), and

DUBROVNIK

5

ORIENTATION

Ⓕⁱⁿᵈˢ   **Nature's Waiting Room**

Make good use of flight delays at Dubrovnik Airport and go caving while you wait. You can wander with wonder around showy stalactites and stalagmites that still are growing in **Đurovic Cave** ★★ 25m (82 ft.) under one of the airport's runways. In less than half an hour you'll get a guided tour in English, Russian, or Croatian for a mere 50kn per person (35kn each for groups of 12 or more). Even if you aren't catching a flight, the cave is a nice respite from Dubrovnik's heat, with constant temperatures of 60°F (16°C). The cave opened in July 2009 after 7 years of excavation and a 2.2-million-kuna investment. Bronze and Iron Age artifacts found there confirm that prehistoric civilizations settled in the area and used the cave. During the 1991 Homeland War, Dubrovnik's citizens used the cave's entrance as a shelter. Plans are in the works for a visitor center and multimedia room. Call ⓒ **020/773-331** for reservations or e-mail the Konavle Museum at skycellar@dubrovnikpr.com for more information.

MACK, a local company that proved to be economical and reliable (Frana Supila 3; ℂ **020/423-747**). Ask for Mr. Zec. Wherever you rent, be sure to reserve a car in advance.

BY BICYCLE   No companies currently rent bikes in Dubrovnik.

WHAT TO SEE & DO

Dubrovnik sprawls well beyond the city walls, to Ploče in the east and the Lapad and Babin Kuk peninsulas in the west, but just about everything worth seeing is within the walled Old Town.

City Wall ★★★   The wall is Dubrovnik's marquee attraction, and no visit to the area is complete without at least a partial walk around the top of the medieval fortification. The wall and its fortresses and towers are works of art; they undulate around Old Town in a protective embrace, creating an architectural frame for the historic city like none other. As you make the 2km (1¼-mile) circuit atop the wall, which is 25m (82 ft.) high and 6m (18 ft.) thick at some points, greater Dubrovnik and its landmark rooftops are visible from every conceivable angle with tourists and residents below going about their lives, jumping into the Adriatic off the wall's rocky base, or dining at restaurants set on outcroppings. It takes about an hour to complete the walk around the wall, depending on how often you feel compelled to snap photos.

You can access the wall at three points: just inside the Pile Gate, near the Maritime Museum/St. John's Fortress, and near the Dominican Monastery at the Ploče Gate. From this point, you can choose a route around the wall's entire perimeter or half that distance. If you start at the **Pile Gate** entrance, take an immediate left as you enter Old Town and walk up a steep flight of stairs through an arch topped by a statue of St. Blaise. If you want to do the entire 360-degree stroll, continue straight up toward the **Minčeta Tower,** which is recognizable by its distinctive "crown." If you decide on the partial walk, halfway up the stairs you'll have to do a 180 from the stairs via a small landing to reach the wall, and you'll end your walk near **St. John's Fortress** on the south side. The 16th century **Revelin Fort** is on the eastern side of the wall above the Ploče Gate; and the 15th-century **Bokar Fortress,** which guarded against sea incursions, is at the southwestern corner across from the **Lovrijenac Fortress.**

Old Town. Daily 8am–7:30pm July–Aug. Hours vary other times. 50kn adults; 20kn children 13 and under; audio rental 40kn.

Dominican Monastery and Museum ★★★   Dubrovnik's Dominican Monastery may be one of the city's first multi-purpose construction projects. Besides its function as a home for a 14th-century Dominican congregation, it was positioned against the city wall to strengthen the ramparts' northeastern flank. The monastery is off a narrow passageway behind the Sponza Palace. An impressive stairway leads to the church doorway, which is decorated with a statue of St. Dominic; the door opens to the 15th-century Gothic cloister designed by Maso di Bartolomeo. The monastery's rooms circle the cloister, whose graceful triple arches frame a garden heady with Mediterranean plantings; and an ancient well lies in the center. But architecture aside, the real reason to visit is the museum, which holds religious art from Dubrovnik and elsewhere. Paintings, triptychs, church vessels, and a reliquary purportedly containing the skull of King Stephen I of Hungary are part of the museum's rich collection.

Sv. Dominika 4. Museum admission 10kn. Daily 9am–6pm.

ATTRACTIONS ●
Aquarium/Maritime Museum **12**
Bokar Fortress **20**
Dominican Monastery & Museum **3**
Dubrovnik Cathedral **11**
Franciscan Monastery/ Apothecary **16**
Gundulićeva Poljana **10**
Jewish Synagogue **5**
Luža Square & Orlando's Column **6**
Minčeta Tower **15**
National Theater **8**
Onofrio's Large Fountain **18**
Onofrio's Small Fountain **7**
Pile Gate **19**
Ploče Gate **2**
Rector's Palace **11**
Revelin Fort **1**
Sponza Palace **4**
St. Blaise Church **9**
St. Ignatius of Loyola Church **13**
St. Saviour Church **17**
Stradun/Placa **14**

Old Harbor

ADRIATIC SEA

500 ft
100 m

⏺ **Tips** | **The Heat**

When Dubrovnik's temperature is above 80°F (27°C)—the average temperature there May through September—tackle the wall when it opens at 9am or wait until after 5pm. Besides being atop a high roof, you'll be standing on an unshaded stone path that absorbs the sun's heat from dawn to dusk, and you'll be "cooked" from above and below. At the very least, wear a hat and take a large bottle of water.

Dubrovnik Aquarium and Maritime Museum ★★ (Kids) For a change of pace, follow the street opposite the Dubrovnik Cathedral's main door past several down-in-the-mouth side streets to St. John's Fortress and the aquarium and maritime museum. Instead of jumping into the sea, you can step back and take an intimate look at it. Located in Tvrđava Sv. Ivana (St. John's Fortress) next to the old port, the Dubrovnik Aquarium has a large array of indigenous fish and ocean dwellers on display in its 27 tanks, which are fed by a constant stream of fresh sea water. The museum has charts, documents, boat models, and artifacts from Ragusa's sea industry.

Damjana Jude 2, St. John's Fortress. ✆ **021/427-937.** Admission to both museum and aquarium 20kn adults, 10kn children. Aquarium summer daily 9am–9pm; winter Mon–Sat 9am–1pm. Maritime Museum summer daily 9am–6pm; winter Tues–Sun 9am–6pm.

Dubrovnik Cathedral (Church of the Assumption) ★★★ A gold-plated skull, arm, and leg that once were part of St. Blaise are reason enough to visit this restored cathedral built on the remains of two earlier churches. According to legend, the first church on the spot was financed by King Richard the Lion-Hearted, who was shipwrecked and rescued in Dubrovnik. He donated the funds to build a church on the ruins of a 7th-century basilica as a thank-you for his rescue. The legend probably isn't true, but historians say the original cathedral was an elaborate Romanesque affair so severely damaged in the 1667 earthquake that it had to be rebuilt. The cathedral was restored following the quake in the au courant Baroque style, and it thus became the third church to be constructed on that site. In fact, remnants of both earlier churches still are visible. *Tip:* Don't miss Titian's polyptych *The Assumption of the Virgin* (1552) in the church's apse.

Poljana Marina Držica. Treasury 10kn. Mon–Sat 9am–5:30pm; Sun 11am–5:30pm.

Franciscan Monastery ★★ Walgreens watch out. This small **apothecary** inside the 14th-century monastery complex has been in business in 1317 and claims to be the oldest working pharmacy in Europe (it still sells herbal lotions and tonic made according to ancient recipes). It has a fascinating display of ancient lab equipment, mortars, measuring implements, and decorative containers used over the centuries. The monastery is accessed via a narrow passage from **St. Saviour Church;** the complex's **Romanesque cloister** is the monastery's most compelling feature (the postquake Renaissance cloister is open to Franciscans only). The lower cloister's open wall of double columns (topped with human, animal, and plant carvings) frame a tranquil open garden area where you can imagine monks enjoying the contemplative life. The complex also is home to a **15th-century well,** the single-nave **St. Francis Church,** a **bell tower,** and the **monastery museum,** whose library contains ancient writings, music manuscripts, gold and silver objets d'art, and other items that illuminate Dubrovnik's history. Monastery museum 20kn adults; 10kn kids. Summer 9am to 6pm; erratic hours other times of the year.

Gundulićeva Poljana ★ Mountains of colorful produce, fish, plastic bottles filled with homemade wine and *rakija* (fruit brandy) and handmade table cloths greet early morning browsers to this raucous market west of St. John's Fortress behind the Rector's Palace. In the afternoon, it is a place to have coffee and in the evening, it is a venue for concerts.

Jesuit Church of St. Ignatius of Loyola ★★★ If you make a right turn from Gundulićeva Poljana, you'll run into a long set of Baroque stairs designed by Pietro Passalacqua and reminiscent of Rome's Spanish Steps. The stairs lead up from Uz Jezuite to the Jesuit Church of St. Ignatius of Loyola, Dubrovnik's largest house of worship. The stairs were severely damaged in the 1991–92 siege of the city, but they have been restored. They end at the 1658 Jesuit College (Collegium Ragusinum), the school where many of Ragusa's greatest scholars were educated. The college is next door to the Baroque church, which was modeled after Rome's Chiesa del Gesu, the mother church of the Jesuit order. The single nave church was completed in 1725 and decorated by Spanish artist Gaetano Garcia according to architect Andrea Pozzo's plan, which included frescoes depicting scenes from the life of St. Ignatius along the semicircular divided apse. The church's bell is said to be the oldest in Dubrovnik.
Poljana R. Boškovića. Daily 9am–noon and 3–7pm.

Jewish Synagogue ★★ Europe's second oldest Judaic house of worship is off the Stradun and north up a steep street and staircase on Žudioska Ulica (Jews' St.). The synagogue is on the second floor of a town house given by the city government to the Jewish community: first, those who fled persecution in Spain during the late 15th century; and later, in the early 16th century, Jews from Italy. A small museum chronicles the Jewish community in Dubrovnik and holds an ancient Torah brought to Dubrovnik by the city's first Jewish residents.

Tip: Dubrovnik Walking Tours offers a guided walk through the Old Jewish Quarter every Wednesday, Friday, and Saturday at 11:30am. Meet 10 minutes before the start of the tour at the large Onofrio's Fountain. The tour focuses on the history of Jews in Dubrovnik, and the cost is 90kn per person. It lasts about an hour.
Žudioska Ulica 5. Summer daily 10am–8pm; winter Mon–Fri 10am–1pm.

Luža Square ★★★ Luža looks like the equivalent of Times Square any time of the day or night. It's a meeting place and a crossroads where tourists stop to cool off with

---

(Kids) Getting Stoned

When you leave St. Saviour Church for the Franciscan monastery next door, keep your eyes downcast and you'll see a **12×12-inch stone** ★★ with a carved face and flat, smooth top protruding about 6 inches above the street. You'll also see a crowd watching people attempting to stand on the stone for a few seconds. Legend says that guys who can stay on the stone known as "The Mask" long enough to remove their shirts will have good luck. (Girls also try this but are entitled to the luck without removing their tops.)

water from **Onofrio's Little Fountain,** explore exhibits in **Sponza Palace,** meet friends at the **city bell tower,** take a *bijela kava* break at the **Gradska Kavana,** or take a breather on the steps of **St. Blaise Church.** Luža is also where Dubrovnik's Summer Festival kicks off and where the annual February 3 St. Blaise procession ends.

Onofrio's Fountains ★★★   When you enter Old Town through either the Pile or Ploče Gate at either end of the Stradun, the first thing you will see is one of two Onofrio fountains. Construction on both started in 1438, and they were intended to provide a place for visitors to wash away any plague lurking on their skin before they entered the city. The fountains were designed by Italian hydroengineer Onofrio della Cava and architect Pietro di Martino and they provide clean, cold water via an aqueduct from the Dubrovnik River (Rijeka Dubrovačka), 11km (7 miles) away. But the fountains' efficacy as plague prophylactics is questionable. The larger fountain at the Pile Gate looks like a giant, domed, sectioned vat; it delivers cold water from 16 carved stone heads that ring the structure's lower third. The heads are all that is left of the fountain's ornamentation after the 1667 quake and the 1991–92 sieges. Water from the Luža Square fountain flows through a more ornate device with detailed sculpture work. Many people fill their water bottles and soak their bandannas in the fountains' cold water, especially in summer when Dubrovnik is steamy.

Orlando's Column ★★   According to legend, Orlando helped the people of Ragusa fight off a Saracen attack in the 9th century. Since the Orlando of poetic lore died in battle in 778, the legend defies plausibility. Other free cities also erected statues of Orlando, with the knight's image representing a city's status as a free-trade city-state. It is likely Dubrovnik's Orlando statue had a similar purpose. This particular sculpture is chiseled into a stone column in the center of Luža Square. It was erected in 1419 and once served as the city's forum for public proclamations, notices, rallies, and punishments. In 1990 a flag with the Libertas motto was flown above the column, and it became a rallying point for Dubrovnik's freedom fighters. Today the Libertas banner is flown above the column to herald Dubrovnik's annual summer festival.

Pile Gate ★★★   In Renaissance times, a wooden drawbridge leading to this gate on the western end of the Old City was pulled up at night in an elaborate ceremony. Now, the drawbridge is a memory and the moat a green space. Instead of armor-clad sentries, kids in period costume working summer jobs stand guard as tourists shuffle in for a day of sightseeing. A stone bridge leads to the outer gate, which is embellished with a statue of St. Blaise, the city's patron saint. The outer Pile Gate was guarded from 1537 on to monitor trade in and out of the city. The interior gate was built in the 15th century and it, too, has a statue of the ubiquitous St. Blaise—this one by 20th-century Croatian sculptor Ivan Meštrović. This is Old Town's busiest port of entry, largely because buses from the city and ferry terminals deposit their passengers there.

Ploče Gate ★★★   The Ploče Gate at the eastern entrance to the Old City is becoming the portal of choice for the trendy, moneyed crowd because Dubrovnik's most exclusive hotels and most expensive restaurants are just outside the 15th century structure. It has inner and outer sections and the approach is via a stone bridge. The Revelin Fortress is built into Ploče's outer section as a lookout point. Like the Pile Gate, a statue of St. Blaise stands watch. The words, "Keep away, men of violence. For centuries, war has not affrighted this fortress, cherished by the spirit of the aged Saint" are inscribed here.

Rector's Palace ★★   The first Rector's Palace once was more a forbidding stone heap than the graceful mansion it is today, but the original 13th-century building was

Who Is St. Blaise?

According to legend, St. Blaise once saved a child from choking on a fish bone. For this reason, Roman Catholics everywhere know the Armenian physician and martyr as the patron of people with throat problems. However, the people of Dubrovnik revere St. Blaise (Sv. Vlaho) as the hero who saved their city from a sneak attack by Venetian galleys in the 10th century. When the Venetians dropped anchor off Lokrum, supposedly to pick up fresh water, the fleet actually was surveying the city in preparation for an attack. However, St. Blaise (later put to death by the Roman emperor Diocletian in 316 B.C.) appeared to the city cathedral's priest in a dream wearing a long beard with a miter and staff. He told the priest about the nefarious plot, thus thwarting the attack. Ever since, St. Blaise has been immortalized in sculpture, art, and other media as the city's protector and its biggest hero. To show their appreciation, the citizens of Dubrovnik go all out to honor St. Blaise on his feast day, which the city celebrates with food and festivities every February 3. Reliquaries purportedly containing several of the saint's body parts are carried through the streets in a parade; and people line up to have their throats blessed by local priests.

destroyed in 1435 when gunpowder stored inside exploded. The palace was rebuilt in a Venetian-Gothic style based on a design by architect Onofrio della Cava (p. 68), only to explode again just 28 years later. The current Rector's Palace is on the same site just south of Luža Square, but it is a rehab rather than a redo; its Florentine designer Michelozzo Michelozzi grafted his work onto what was left of della Cava's. Functionally, the Rector's Palace was Ragusa's governmental nerve center and housed state offices as well as a dungeon and quarters for the rector, who was required to live in the palace for the duration of his term. Today, the palace's upstairs rooms house the City Museum (Gradski Muzej), filled with exhibits depicting how people lived in Ragusa. Classical music concerts are held in the courtyard during Summer Festival.

Pred Dvorom 3. ✆ **020/321-497.** Admission 15kn. Summer daily 9am–7pm; winter Mon–Sat 9am–2pm.

St. Blaise Church ★★★ If it seems as though the original city fathers had St. Blaise's image engraved on every public building, wall, and fortress in Old Town you'd be close to correct. But nowhere is their devotion to the city's patron saint more evident than at St. Blaise Church. The present Baroque church was built between 1706 and 1714 on the site of a 14th-century Romanesque church that was damaged in the 1667 earthquake, but after the quake, the church still was usable until a 1706 fire put an end to that. Today's domed St. Blaise Church footprint is that of a Greek cross. It has a wide staircase and terrace that attracts weary tourists from Luža Square, many of whom sit on its steps for a break, much the same as flocks of pigeons settle on the square itself. Inside many works of art that were saved from the old church are on display; the most notable is a silver-plated statue of the saint holding a 15th-century model of the city as it was before the big quake.

Luža Trg (Sq.). Daily 8am–7pm.

St. Saviour Church ★ St. Saviour is one of a very few Dubrovnik structures that survived the 1667 earthquake. It was built in the early 16th century by Petar Andrijić of Korčula and its Renaissance-Gothic facade faces the larger Onofrio fountain inside the Pile Gate. Some say its design was influenced by Šibenik's UNESCO World Heritage cathedral (p. 186). It is certain, however, that St. Saviour influenced several Dalmatian churches, most notably the cathedral of Hvar. St. Saviour is no longer used for Mass. The church's interior has been recently restored.

Btw. the Pile Gate and the Franciscan Monastery at Stradun 2. Daily 9am–7pm.

Sponza Palace ★★ As you approach Luža Square from the Stradun, you'll see the arches of the 15th-century Sponza Palace on your left. Today the palace courtyard is a bright venue for art exhibits and concerts. There are several rooms off the courtyard. Two of the rooms hold artifacts significant to Dubrovnik. One contains copies of documents that chronicle Dubrovnik's history. The other is called the Memorial Room of the Defenders of Dubrovnik; it contains photos and biographies of the Croatian patriots who died during the 1991–92 siege of Dubrovnik plus a small souvenir shop. A 30m (100-ft.) bell tower to the left of the palace tolls the hour.

Luža. ✆ 020/321-032. Free admission, except for some exhibitions. Daily 9am–2pm, though times vary during exhibitions.

Stradun ★★★ Every night, Dubrovnik's maintenance crew uses fire hoses to wash down the smooth limestone pavement that is the Stradun (aka Placa), Dubrovnik's main thoroughfare. The historic street runs from the Pile Gate through the city directly to the Ploče Gate and once was a marshy dividing line between Ragusa and Dubrava on the mainland. Today the ribbon of stone is lined with neat, uniform buildings housing shops, restaurants, and entryways radiating to the alley-size side streets. Historic pictures show that buildings along the Stradun originally were far more ornate and acquired their present subtle style after the 1667 earthquake and renovation. *Tip:* To aid tourists, the city of Dubrovnik has hung banners at the entrance to each of the narrow streets off the Stradun to let people know what they'll find if they veer off the main drag.

<table>
<tr><td colspan="2">**WALKING TOUR**   **DUBROVNIK'S STRADUN**</td></tr>
<tr><td>START:</td><td>Brsalje Square outside the Pile Gate, the west entrance to Old Town.</td></tr>
<tr><td>FINISH:</td><td>St. Blaise Church/Luža Square.</td></tr>
<tr><td>TIME:</td><td>Anywhere from 30 minutes to 3 hours, depending on how much time you spend exploring side streets, in churches and museums, shopping, or dining.</td></tr>
<tr><td>BEST TIMES:</td><td>Mornings from 8am to noon before the sun is overhead; evenings after 6pm and until the last bar closes. This is when the promenade starts and segues into a fashion show for the young and beautiful.</td></tr>
<tr><td>WORST TIMES:</td><td>Noon to sundown or whenever the temperature rises above 86°F (30°C).</td></tr>
</table>

A walk up and down both sides of the Stradun is an ideal way to become acquainted with the city's charms. Old Town's smooth limestone path originally was a canal separating Old Ragusa from the mainland, and walking its length is a good way to get your bearings and become familiar with the attractions between the Pile and the Ploče Gates. There is a high concentration of important sites on and just off the Stradun, and lots of narrow side streets radiate up and out from it to intersect with cobbled streets that are packed with religious sites, historic architectural spots, shops, restaurants, a few courtyards, and even some residences.

Start your tour outside the Pile Gate in Brsalje Square next door to the Atlas Travel Agency and between the Nautika restaurant and Dubravka Kavana cafe.

❶ Brsalje Square

Rendezvous in this leafy park, but before you enter Old Town, walk away from the street to the low balustrade. You'll have an unobstructed view of the sea and **Fort Lovrijenac** to the right and the 16th-century **Bokar Fortress** to the left. Lovrijenac is built on a high, rocky peninsula that juts into the sea, and it is Dubrovnik's oldest defensive structure. These days it is used as a theater for Shakespearean productions and for performances during **Dubrovnik's Summer Festival.** Croatian native and TV star Goran Višjić of *ER* fame is a frequent performer there. Bokar was used as a prison in the 19th century.

Return to the street, turn right, approach the:

❷ Pile Gate

This is the busiest portal to Old Town, and it is really two gates you approach across a wooden drawbridge that once was pulled up each night to protect the city. Note the statue of St. Blaise carved into a niche above the opening of the 16th-century outer gate and another statue of the city's patron (by **Ivan Meštrović**) inside the even older (15th-c.) inner gate. Occasionally musicians and vendors hang out in the courtyard between the gates to catch people on their way out.

Step through the inner gate and stop a moment to orient. Walk through and note:

❸ Onofrio's Large Fountain & the Wall Walk Entrance

Walk inside the Pile Gate and immediately to the left you'll see a steep stairway that leads up to the **Minčeta Tower** at the top of the wall (see p. 64 for details). This is one of three access points to the top of the ramparts. To the right is **Onofrio's Large Fountain,** a tall concrete dome that during the Middle Ages was a collection point for water flowing into the city via an aqueduct from the **Dubrovnik River** 12km

(7½ miles) away. The fountain was more ornate when it was completed in 1444, but the iron embellishments were destroyed in the 1667 earthquake. The fountain also supplied Dubrovnik with fresh water when it was on lockdown during the 1991–92 sieges.

Stay left. The first building on your left is:

❹ Church of Our Saviour

This tiny church was built as a memorial to the victims of a 1520 earthquake, but it became a symbol of strength when it became one of the few buildings to survive the 1667 quake that destroyed most of the city. Today it is used for concerts and exhibits.

Walk on a few steps to:

❺ The Franciscan Monastery/ Museum

Before you explore this building with its columned cloister and ancient pharmacy, note the small stone protruding from the bottom left of the church's front (p. 67) and the people who keep jumping on it. This building, with its garden, architectural features, pharmacy, and museum exhibits, is worth a visit (p. 66).

Exit the monastery and begin your Stradun stroll in earnest to investigate the:

❻ Stradun Side Streets

The Stradun (aka Placa) runs to the clock tower and the **Ploče Gate.** All the buildings along the way are almost identical in style, a result of post quake construction in the 17th century. Note the arches that frame a combo door and window. The sill was used as a counter over which business was conducted. If you are up for a detour, head up **Žudioska Street** to visit the second-oldest synagogue in Europe and its original 17th-century furnishings (p. 67).

Continue along the Stradun past Zlatarska Street to the:

❼ Sponza Palace

As you approach Luža Square, look left and note the graceful Renaissance arches of the **Sponza Palace** (p. 70), which used to be Dubrovnik's Customs House. Today it houses the **Memorial Room of the Dubrovnik Defenders,** a visual tribute to the more than 300 people who were killed from October 1, 1991, to October, 26, 1992, while defending Dubrovnik against Serb attacks. Multimedia images of the destruction and photos of the young people who died in the conflict are moving reminders of the devastation that swept Croatia at that time.

Exit the palace and walk to Orlando's Column in the center of Luža Square. Pause at:

❽ Orlando's Column and Onofrio's Small Fountain

Orlando's Column (p. 68) will be in front of you as you exit the Palace, and the **Clock Tower** will be to your left. Note the statue's forearm, which was Old Ragusa's standard of measurement (512mm/20 in.). The **Clock Tower** features a pair of bronze men who move up to strike the bell on the hour. The **Town Hall** is to the right of the Clock Tower and **Onofrio's Small Fountain** is in front of that.

Turn left from the front of Orlando's Column and walk through the passageway between the Sponza Palace and the Town Hall. Turn left and head to the Dominican Monastery:

❾ Dominican Monastery, the Old Port, and the Ploče Gate

The Dominican Monastery is a complex that includes a large church, cloisters, and a museum. The original 14th-century church was destroyed in the 1667 quake, and this one was rebuilt in the 17th century. There are some interesting paintings inside, and the church doubles as a concert venue during the Summer Festival. The cloisters are a must-see with courtyard gardens and interesting stonework (p. 64).

Exit the monastery and go left onto Svetoga Dominika. Continue on to explore the Old Harbor,

Ploče Gate, and Revelin Fortress, and/or retrace your steps and return to Luža Square:

❿ Gradska Kavana & the Rector's Palace

As you return from the Dominican Monastery, the Town Hall and **Gradska Kavana** (Town Café) will be on your left. You can break for a cold drink or coffee and sit at tables facing the square or go inside to the Gradska Taverna and grab a spot on the terrace overlooking the Old Harbor. The **Town Theater** is also in this building. The Venetian-Gothic **Rector's Palace** (p. 68) is adjacent to the Gradska Kavana complex fronted by pillars made of marble from Korčula and topped with interesting carvings. The interior is used for summer concerts.

Exit the Rector's Palace and turn left:

⓫ Dubrovnik Cathedral

Note the minimalist gray marble altar that was installed when Roman Catholicism ruled that the priest should face the people during Mass—its block style is incongruent to the church's Baroque design. Don't miss the **treasury,** which is loaded with priceless relics, including the skull of St. Blaise and a piece of the True Cross (p. 66).

Exit the cathedral and walk around to the rear and walk up Androvićeva to the Jesuit Steps and Church of St. Ignatius Loyola (p. 67) or turn left and walk past the Rector's Palace to return to Luža Square.

⓬ St. Blaise Church

This 18th-century Baroque church (p. 69) is a tribute to Dubrovnik's patron saint. Inside, the altar is the main draw with its statue of the saint holding a model of the city of Dubrovnik as it was before the 1667 quake. Outside, the church's wide steps are a popular resting/meeting place for tourists.

From St. Blaise you can return to the Pile Gate and inspect the shops along the south side of the Stradun, explore what you've just seen in greater depth, or venture up the steep side streets to discover more sights.

(Finds) Jungle by the Sea

Get out of the blazing sun and take shelter in the lush oasis that is Trsteno, a 28-hectare (70-acre), 15th-century villa and garden estate overlooking the sea. Trsteno's botanic collection was acquired over the course of 5 centuries. Situated 13km (7 miles) northwest of Dubrovnik, Trsteno once was a center of gentility and culture in Dubrovnik. Today it is much more. Besides being a showcase for its Renaissance structures, fountains, and aqueduct, Trsteno serves as a shelter for a wide array of exotic plants, many brought to Ragusa centuries ago by traders from faraway ports. The villa and its land were confiscated by the Communists after World War II, and the property was sadly neglected under Communist stewardship. In 1991, the Arobretum was severely damaged by fires set by the Serbian Army, and in 2000 by a forest fire during a drought, but it has been restored and is now a national historic site protected and maintained by the government. Don't miss the statue of Neptune, which overlooks a goldfish pond and fountain deep in the gardens (② **020/751-019;** fax 020/751-268). Open daily 7am to 7pm May to October and 8am to 3pm November to April. There is a 25kn per-person entry fee, 15kn for children under 14.

Escorted Walking Tours

Mediterranean Experience Ltd. ★★, Ćira Carića 3 (② **020/442-201**), offers daily 1-hour "Discover Dubrovnik" walks from the Large Onofrio Fountain at 10am and 7pm. The itinerary introduces Dubrovnik's sights for 90kn per person.

Dubrovnik Walking Tours ★★ offers the same services as Mediterranean for the same price. Just show up at the Big Onofrio's Fountain 10 minutes before the "Discover Dubrovnik" walk (daily at 10am and 6:30pm), for the "Story About the War" walk (Mon, Tues, Thurs, Sat at 11:30am and daily at 8pm), or for the "Old Jewish Quarter" walk (Wed, Fri, Sun at 11:30am).

BEACHES

Croatians loosely define beaches as any place the sea meets the land. While some beaches may have names, most are little more than rocks used as platforms for jumping into the water. One such place is a must-see, if not a must-swim area in Dubrovnik. Just around the corner from the old port you'll find a **rocky indentation** ★★★ where those who are confident in their swimming skills routinely take a dip.

There is no such thing as a privately owned beach in Croatia. Nonetheless, several of the hotels east of the port have staked out access routes to sections of the beach for their guests, making it hard for others to get there. Dubrovnik's main public beach, **Banje,** exists as a beach club (below).

Bobin Kuk's **Copacabana Beach** ★★ is another choice. Copacabana is a pebble-and-concrete beach with a view of the graceful Dubrovnik bridge and the Elafiti Islands. It is one of the few beaches in Dubrovnik with facilities for kids, sports enthusiasts, and swimmers with disabilities. Here you can ride a jet ski, get whipped around on a banana-boat ride, or go parasailing. There also are sea slides for kids. A lift on the concrete part of the beach gives seniors and people with disabilities easy access to the water. Nonswimmers can relax in a beach bar or a beach restaurant. At night, the beach bar becomes a cocktail bar and disco.

Day or night, the **Eastwest Beach Club** ★★★ is Dubrovnik's answer for people who want to experience the luxury of a beach hotel without paying beach-hotel prices. Situated on Banje, about 46m (150 ft.) from the entrance to the Ploče (Eastern) Gate, Eastwest is also in the shadow of the upscale Excelsior and Villa Argentina hotels. The club has a restaurant with a view and a sophisticated Dalmatian menu, a cocktail bar with space for dancing, watersports galore, a beach with crystal-clear water, beach attendants, and the unique baldachin. This "bed" on the beach looks like a raised four-poster hung with gauzy curtains that blow in the breeze. You can rent the baldachin for 200kn per day and enjoy semiprivacy on the beach.

Frana Supila bb. (✆ **020/412-220.** www.ew-dubrovnik.com.

DIVING

Sometimes the temptation to jump into the deep blue sea around Dubrovnik is just too strong to resist. Get the most out of your plunge with a professional diving school like **Blue Planet** ★★. Rent equipment or use your own for SCUBA or open water dives that last from 2 hours to 6 days. No experience? Blue Planet is a certified instruction center and can teach you what you need to know.

In the Dubrovnik Palace Hotel. Masarykov Put 20 (✆ **091/899-09-73.** www.blueplanet-diving.com. 2-hr. group dive 60€. 2- to 3-day dive 264€. Prices include equipment. MC, V. Daily 9am–7pm May–Oct. By appointment the rest of the year.

WHERE TO STAY

Dubrovnik is the most expensive city in Croatia, especially in summer when prices for everything from gelato to taxis can triple over the prices charged other times. Add to that a conspicuous lack of budget accommodations and the hunt for value becomes a crusade. Even moderately priced rooms are difficult to find unless you opt for private rooms in Lapad or Gruž. Try the tourist offices or look for signs in windows that say SOBE (room available). If you arrive at the ferry or bus terminal, you'll be greeted (or accosted) by men and women waving photos of lodging options—mainly rooms in private homes. In general, the cheapest are from the seated old ladies asking you if you need a place to sleep. If you choose this option, be sure to inspect the room before you hand over any money. You never know what you'll get—perhaps a dirt-cheap find in the center, or a tiny bed (sharing a bathroom with the owner) on the outskirts of town. All of these options take cash only. If you want to be sure of what you're getting, go to a tourist office, which has screened rentals and provides photos and amenity lists.

Very Expensive

Grand Hotel Park Dubrovnik ★★ (Value) Balconies overlooking the sea or a lush garden are standard for all guest rooms in this Lapad landmark, thanks to a 2008 renovation that has transformed the formerly blah block hotel into a pretty snazzy bargain location. Decor is fresh and bright in rooms on all seven floors, and the 28 rooms in the two glass-fronted towers are unusually spacious and sport Jacuzzi tubs. The outdoor pool and sunning area are gateways to the beach beyond. The Grand Park is surrounded by green space, which acts like a privacy fence. *Tip:* The property includes two stone houses it rents as villas, one with a honeymoon suite and wraparound windows.

ACCOMMODATIONS ■
Autocamp Solitudo **1**
Grand Hotel Park Dubrovnik **5**
Hotel Dubrovnik Palace **7**
Hotel Excelsior **10**
Hotel More **3**
Hotel Rixos Libertas **8**
Hotel Zagreb **6**
Hotel Grand Villa Argentina **13**
Importanne Resort **2**
Villa Agave **11**
Villa Orsula **12**
Youth Hotel Dubrovnik **9**

DINING ◆
Restaurant Konakova **4**
Restaurant More **3**
Restaurant Satu **10**

Dubrovnik•

▲ *Mt. Srd*

NUNCIJATA

GRUŽ

Gruž Harbor

Gruška obala

Radnička

Jadranska cesta

Obala S. Radića

ŠIPČINE

Od Gaja

Gornji Kono

GORNJI
KONO

Put Republike

Branitelja Dubr.

Vladimira Nazora

A. Boškovic

BONINOVO

Splitski

Ante Starčevića

Knežije Hedranga

MONTOVJERNA

GOSPINO
POLJE

HLADNICA

Dr. A. Šercera

Liechtensteinov put

GORICA

Iva Vojnovića

K. Tomislava

BATALA

Od Batale

Papadka obala

LAPAD

SUMRATIN

Ispod Petke

VELIKA
PETKA

BABIN
KUK

Iva Dulčića

LAZARET

Ivana Žajca

Vatroslava Lisinskog

Kardinala Stepinca

Mašan Kovača put

Lapad Bay

A D R I A T I C   S E A

PILE

STARI GRAD
(OLD TOWN)

see Old Town maps

Branka Šekovica

Zagrebačka

Petra Bakića

Iza Grada

od Bosanke

Jadranska cesta

PLOČE

Kralja Petra Krešimira

Frana Supila

10 11 12   13

BOSANKA

Brune Bušića

Lokrum

■ Bus station
- - Ferry route

0 ———— 1/2 mi
0 ———— 1/2 km

Fun Facts **BLU Meets Green**

The Radisson BLU is built in the Dubrovnik Sun Garden, formerly a setting for a '70s ocean front resort popular in Socialist times. In an unusual but expensive move, BLU developers decided to move the Sun Garden's exotic, mature vegetation into "storage," during construction instead of digging it up and throwing it away. They put it in greenhouses and nurtured it during construction, then replanted it as the new BLU's landscaping. The result is a lush landscape that gives the resort a mature look. The BLU also has installed green roofs on all buildings, and it uses environment friendly heating and air-conditioning powered by heat exchange units located offshore in the ocean.

Šetalište Kralja Zvonimira 39, Lapad. ☎ 020/434-444. www.grandhotel-park.hr. 242 units, 2 villas. July 1–Sept 30 seaside double; from 320€ villa. Other times from 90€ seaside double; from 220€ villa. AE, MC, V. Rates include breakfast. Free parking. **Amenities:** Restaurant; bar; indoor and outdoor pools; sauna; free Wi-Fi. *In room:* A/C, TV, minibar.

Hilton Imperial ★★★ When we've had enough of "quaint" and "rustic," in Dalmatia, we head for the Hilton Imperial, the international chain's first hotel in Croatia. It isn't within the walls of Old Town, but it is just steps outside the Pile Gate. The 1897 Imperial (and its guesthouse across the street), sheltered refugees from Croatia's civil war and took a direct mortar hit on the upper floors. Today its new red brick-and-white stone facade and Hapsburg-flag yellow filigree balcony railings are the hotel's face to the world, but Hilton personnel are its link to guests. We like it because Hilton staff members are a class act and extend the same courtesies to Brioni-suited businesspeople and backpackers alike, an anomaly in Croatia. While Hilton was changing worker attitudes, it kept whatever it could of the old Imperial—its stone staircases, the lobby footprint—but everything else is brand-new. Rooms are spacious and done in the similar earth/sun color schemes. All are loaded with amenities whether you stay in a single room or a suite. It's easy to get comfy with room service from the hotel's **Porat Restaurant** ★★ or in the huge lobby bar where you can read a newspaper or get a snack with your coffee frappe.

Marijana Blažića 2, at the Pile Gate. ☎ 020/320-320. Fax 020/320-220. www.hilton.com. 147 units, including 8 junior suites. From 2,653kn double; from 4,523kn suite. AE, MC, V. Rates include buffet breakfast and taxes. **Amenities:** Restaurant; piano bar; pool; sauna; smoke-free rooms; steam bath; room for those w/limited mobility. *In room:* A/C, TV, hair dryer, minibar, Wi-Fi.

Hotel Dubrovnik Palace ★ As a luxury tourist destination, the Palace deserves no more than a mixed review even though it has reigned over Dubrovnik's hotel scene for years. After a 45-million-euro renovation in 2005, the hotel in the woods at the southern end of the Lapad Peninsula positioned itself as an elite facility catering to business travelers with expense accounts and others with deep pockets, but the money wasn't used with an even hand. Public areas and facilities are gorgeous and views are knockouts. All rooms have sea views, private balconies, and flatscreen TVs, but they are a bit cramped and chintzy for the price (especially bathrooms). Perhaps the most egregious failing is that service and staff friendliness leave lots of room for improvement.

Masarykov Put 20. ☎ 020/430-000. Fax 020/430-100. www.dubrovnikpalace.hr. 308 units. Doubles from 348€; suites from 495€. AE, DC, MC, V. Rates include buffet breakfast. **Amenities:** 3 restaurants; 4 bars;

nightclub; children's program; 3 outdoor and 1 indoor pool; room service; spa; tennis courts; diving center; Wi-Fi access; 1 room for those w/limited mobility; VIP wing w/private entrance. *In room:* AC, TV, hair dryer, minibar, Wi-Fi.

Hotel Excelsior ★★★

If you love the elegance and Art Deco opulence of the '20s and '30s, the Excelsior can take you back in time. The Excelsior was built in 1913, expanded in the 1960s, completely renovated in 1998, updated in 2006, and reconstructed from the wall studs in 2008. The result is a classy, comfortable accommodation that's fit for a king but affordable for commoners. Guest rooms, whether in the old or new parts of the hotel, drip with class and include windows with views of the sea and St. John's Port. Bathrooms have wraparound windows that bring the sun and sea indoors where the scent of L'Occitaine toiletries fills the air. Rooms in the older section of the hotel have gentle touches of yesteryear seamlessly melded with modern technology. Add a staff that is gracious and well trained, gorgeous drinking and dining facilities (note the sushi bar **Satu** [p. 84], adjacent to the swank piano bar, **Abakus**), the Palm Garden terrace for al fresco lounging, and you have a hotel that's hard to beat.

Frana supila 12, Ploče. ✆ **020/353-300.** Fax 020/414-214. www.hotel-excelsior.hr. 179 units, including 1 villa. From 420€ double with sea view and balcony July 1–Sept 30; from 250€ other times. Suites from 735€ July 1–Sept 30; from 359€ other times. Agave Villa (see box below) 7,000€ per day. Rates include breakfast. Half-board available. AE, MC, V. **Amenities:** 4 restaurants; sushi bar; piano bar; airport shuttle; babysitting; indoor pool; room service; sauna; rooms for those w/disabilities. *In room:* A/C, TV, fax, hair dryer, minibar, Wi-Fi.

Hotel Grand Villa Argentina ★★

Grand Villa Argentina is really a complex of five buildings—one hotel and four smaller (but just as elegant) villas, all with an aura of refined luxury. Personalized service is the Argentina's mission, and it shows. Argentina is within walking distance of Old Town and while its sea views are spectacular, its guest rooms are not as large as those in Villa Orsula (below).

Frana Supila 14, Ploče). ✆ **020/440-555.** Fax 020/432-524. www.hoteli-argentina.hr. 151 units. July 1–Sept 30 from 320€ double with sea view and balcony; from 500€ suite. Other times from 250€ double with sea view and balcony; from 420€ suite. Rates include breakfast. AE, MC, V. **Amenities:** 3 restaurants; bar; indoor and outdoor pools; sauna; spa; Internet access; casino. *In room:* A/C, TV, hair dryer, minibar.

Hotel More ★★★ (Finds)

You'll have to climb a steep hill to get to this intimate boutique hotel carved into a cliff near the tip of Lapad, but you won't regret the effort. Perhaps it's because the More is classy without being stuffy, or perhaps it's because of the staff's welcoming attitude. Either way, the More is one of Dubrovnik's hidden treasures, an all-new hotel built on the footprint of a former Socialist getaway in pine-scented surroundings that open to the Adriatic. Hotel More opened in 2008 loaded with high-style, modern conveniences, and a world-class restaurant (More, reviewed on p. 84). Most rooms have balconies with sea views on three sides; all are loaded with creature comforts,

(Kids) Down-to-Earth Dubrovnik

See the walled city from a new perspective. Panoramic Flight operates 30- to 100-minute air tours (140€–345€) of the region in open-design, single-engine planes. Destinations and itineraries are flexible. Three-persons max for each flight. For more information call ✆ **098/427-856** (www.aer-marina.com).

and all are capsules of privacy. There is a small pool on the fifth-floor terrace balcony, but it is the numerous stone staircases leading to the beach rocks and sea below that are most enchanting.

Tip: Igor of customer relations told us the builders discovered a natural cave 23m (75 ft.) beneath the hotel's foundation, and it currently is being transformed into a private room for dinners and wine tastings.

Kardinala Stepinca 33. (© **020/494-200.** Fax 020/494-210. www.hotel-more.hr. 39 units and 1 presidential apt. Sea view double with balcony from 290€ double July–Sept; other times from 180€. Suites from 500€ July–Aug; from 370€ other times. Call Igor in customer relations for special offers. Rates include breakfast. AE, MC, V. Free garage and outside parking. Closed Nov–Mar. **Amenities:** Restaurant; bar; pool; wellness center. *In room:* A/C, flatscreen TV, free broadband access, minibar.

Importanne Resort ★   Use of a luxury car, a speedboat, and valet service comes with a booking in Villa Elita, which opened in 2007 as part of the Importanne Resort. Neptun/Importanne Suites and the Ariston are the resort's other properties on the Lapad Peninsula 10 minutes from Dubrovnik's Old Town. Together, the three offer accommodations to suit a wide clientele that includes both families and tycoons.

Kardinala Alojzija Stepinca 31. (© **020/440-100.** Fax 020/440-200. www.hotel-neptun.hr. 158 units (Neptun/Importanne Suites), 116 units (Ariston), 6 units (Villa Elita). Doubles from 95€ for standard room in the Neptun to 12,000€ for Villa Elita. AE, DC, MC, V. **Amenities:** 3 restaurants; beach bar; 2 seawater pools; room service; spa. *In room:* A/C, TV, hair dryer, Internet access, minibar.

Pucić Palace ★★   Sleep where Old Ragusa's ruling class slept. Formerly the home of a nobleman, the Pucić Palace is a legend and *the* favorite Dubrovnik haven for the well-heeled. However, though the hotel combines the cachet of a Renaissance palace with contemporary creature comforts, it doesn't offer all the amenities you'd expect for the prices. Furnishings are first-rate and bathrooms are loaded with toiletries and lined with nonskid tiles and tasteful mosaics, but we're talking showers only here. The hotel maintains a yacht in the harbor for guest use; the terrace has a great view of the city; and you *are* staying in a historic monument. Service is impeccable; but you'll have to decide for yourself if those things justify the sky-high tariffs.

Ulica Od Puča 1, Old Town. (© **020/326-222.** Fax 020/326-223. www.thepucicpalace.com. 19 units. June–Sept from 515€ deluxe double; from 775€ junior suite and from 1,045€ executive suite. Other times of year from 295€ double; from 550€ junior suite, and from 825€ executive suite. Rates include breakfast but not taxes. AE, DC, MC, V. **Amenities:** Restaurant; bar; concierge; room service. *In room:* A/C, TV, minibar.

Radisson BLU ★★★   Just weeks after this sprawling resort opened in July 2009 in the village of Orašac, it still was experiencing birthing pains. Despite some minor service missteps, it was clear that the BLU is in the process of evolving into what could be Dubrovnik's showcase resort destination even though it's 12km (7 miles) north of Old Town. The hotel feels like a mini city complete with a strip of shops and restaurants on one side of the shaded promenade and pools, cabanas, park space, and fountains on the other. Beyond that is the Adriatic. The hotel is ultramodern in concept, but the renovated '80s villas built on four terraced levels have a southwestern feel and all the conveniences of home. This is a big-time, they-thought-of-everything resort in a rural setting, a sophisticated getaway surrounded by casual country simplicity. The effect is decadent without being arrogant, big without being impersonal, modern without being sterile.

ACCOMMODATIONS ■
Hilton Imperial **2**
Hotel Stari Grad **8**
Pucić Palace **15**
Sesame Inn **1**

DINING ◆
Arsenal Taverna at
  Gradska Kavana **20**
Atlas Club Nautika **5**
Bistro Teatar **16**
Café Festival **10**
The Gaffe Pub **13**
Gil's **18**
Kavana Dubravka **4**
Konoba-Café Bar
  Sigurata **9**
Konoba Lokanda
  Peskarija **21**
Pizzeria/Spaghetteria
  Baracuda **12**
Poklisar **19**
Proto **11**
Restaurant Arka **14**
Restaurant Jadran **6**
Restaurant Mimoza **5**
Rosarij **17**
Sesame Taverna **1**
Steak House Domino **7**

Dubrovnik

Old Harbor

Ploče
Gate

Dominican
Monastery

Zagrebačka

Iza Grada

Maria Petrića

Put iza Grada

Uz Posat

Đura Pulića

Dr. Ante Starčevića

Miletićeva

Plata Androvića

*ADRIATIC
SEA*

Pile
Gate

Onofrio
Fountain

Zlatarska

Kovačka

Žudioska

Boškovićeva

Prijeko

Zamanjina

Kuničeva

Antuninska

Palmotićeva

Od sigurate

Celestina Medovića

Od Puča

Nalješkovićeva

Plača (Stradun)

Izmedju Polača

Cvijete Zuzorić

Miha Pracata

Luža

Pred dvorom

Zeljarica

Marojice Kaboge

Dinka Ranjine

Gundulićeva
poljana

Poljana
M. Držića

Uz Jezuite

Bunićeva
poljana

Od Puča

Od Domina

Za Rokom

Zlatarićeva

Lučarica

Ribarnica

Siroka

Đorđićeva

Sv. Josipa

Nikole Božidarevića

Strossmajerova

Buniceva
poljana

Poljana R.
Boškovića

Od Kaštela

Crijevićeva

Zvjezdićeva

Od Rupa

Od Sorte

Na Andriji

Sv. Marije

Braće Andrijića

Đura Beljavi

Restićeva

Od Pustijerne

Stajeva

Kneza Damjana Jude

Ilije Sarake

Stulina

Pobjana

500 ft

100 m

ADRIATIC SEA

DUBROVNIK

5

ORIENTATION

Tip: Even though the BLU is outside Dubrovnik's city limits, you can go back and forth easily via the hotel's shuttle van or boat.

Na Moru 1. 20234 Orašac. ℂ **020/361-500.** Fax 020/661-501. www.radissonblu.com/resort-dubrovnik. 225 units, 207 villas. From 220€ double; from 290€ suite. From 260€ villa. Hotel rates include breakfast; villa rates do not. AE, MC, V. Free parking. **Amenities:** 7 restaurants; pastry cafe; wine bar; children's program; 3 pools; 3 beaches; room service; spa, smoke-free rooms; rooms for those w/limited mobility; sports center, bicycle rental. In room: A/C, TV, hair dryer, full kitchen (in villas), minibar, free Wi-Fi.

Rixos Libertas ★ (Overrated) Rixos's opening of the renovated landmark Libertas Hotel was delayed several times since the project started construction in 2004. Nearly 4 years and 70 million euros later, the Pygmalion project revealed a 12-story ultramodern temple of glass, steel, and stone. Unfortunately, the former refugee shelter still has some huge wrinkles despite its fancy new veneer: We noticed missing rail screws in the elevator, patches of crumbling grout in the granite floor, and the absence of a lot of "little things" guests take for granted in this price category, like pens, stationery, and tissue. One of the biggest shortcomings is the lack of a shuttle to get guests to Old Town or even to public transportation. Instead, Rixos guests must walk 2,952m (900 ft.) uphill to access city buses. The Libertas's tumbling terraces, pool, and beach area are beautiful, but sadly they do not overcome the hotel's "no frills" approach to service and amenities. *Tip:* Internet connectivity in guest rooms is broadband and guests are supposed to be given a cable for free access on registration. We weren't, so ask for one.

Liechtensteinov Put 3. ℂ **020/333-720.** Fax 020/333-723. www.rixos.com. 315 units. Doubles from 2,198kn June 15–Sept 30; from 940kn other times; suites from 5,550kn year-round. AE, DC, MC, V. Rates include breakfast; half board available. AE, MC, V. Free parking. Closed Nov–Mar unless bookings warrant opening. **Amenities:** 2 restaurants; 2 cafes; 2 bars; cigar room, casino; indoor and outdoor pools; room service; rooms for those w/limited mobility; smoke-free rooms; spa. *In room:* A/C, TV, hair dryer, minibar, broadband Internet access.

Villa Orsula ★★★ One of the best addresses in Dubrovnik, Villa Orsula is everything you would expect of an opulent 1930s Mediterranean villa. In fact, Villa Orsula was built as a private residence in that era and was converted into a hotel in 1989. Orsula is adjacent to the Grand Villa Argentina (above); the two buildings share a pool and other facilities as well as a garden leading to the sea. Villa Orsula is augmented with areas like the gorgeous **Victoria Terrace Restaurant,** which is tucked into beds of fragrant flowers

Viva Villa Agave ★★★

When the Excelsior Hotel decided to renovate an adjacent Dalmatian stone house as a private villa, it spared no expense. Villa Agave's first guests arrived in spring 2009, and there has been a steady interest in the luxury property since. For 7,000€ per day (the villa sleeps three couples, so the expense can be shared), guests have access to a private chef, a BMW sedan and driver, yacht and boat charter, and a private hot tub set on one of Agave's five stone terraces with views of Old Town. It is large enough to double as a lap pool. This is a house that is both modern and historical with living room, fireplace, dining room, bathrooms to die for, private beach, massage and beauty services, private butler, Wi-Fi, and much more. Call ℂ **020/353-291;** fax 020353-295; www.alh.hr for reservations.

and lush vegetation. The restaurant and most of the guest rooms both have sweeping views of Old Town and the sea.

Frana Supila 14, Ploče. © **020/440-555.** Fax 020/432-524. www.gva.hr. 15 units. July 1–Sept 30 from 340€ double with sea view and balcony; from 520€ suite. Other months from 254€ double with sea view and balcony; from 420€ suite. Rates include breakfast. AE, MC, V. Apr–Nov only. **Amenities:** Restaurant; bar; Internet access; indoor and outdoor pools; sauna; spa. In room: A/C, TV, hair dryer, minibar.

Expensive

Hotel Stari Grad ★   The aristocratic home that has been the tiny Stari Grad since 2002 is also a cultural monument and just one of two hotels within Dubrovnik's walls. Each room is elegantly furnished, comfortable, cozy, and augmented by bathrooms equipped with hydro massage showers. The view of Lokrum and Cavtat from the fifth-floor terrace is dynamite.

Od Sigurate br. 4, Old Town. © **020/322-244.** Fax 020/321-256. www.hotelstarigrad.com. 8 units. From 994kn double. Rates stay the same all year and include breakfast. AE, MC, V. **Amenities:** Restaurant; babysitting. In room: A/C, TV, hair dryer, minibar.

Moderate

Hotel Zagreb ★★ (Finds)   A careful restoration has turned this salmon-colored 19th-century mansion into a showplace hotel on the Lapad promenade. Each guest room is unique, and staying here is like staying in a grand Hapsburg home complete with shaded garden and sprawling lawn. Some of the staff speaks English; all are very helpful.

Šetalište Kralja Zvonimira 27, Lapad. © **020/436-146.** Fax 020/436-006. 24 units. From 1,060kn double July 1 to mid-Sept; from 700kn double at other times. AE, MC, V. **Amenities:** Restaurant; bar. In room: TV, hair dryer.

Sesame Inn ★★   We loved the Sesame Inn for its location and the personal atmosphere that made it feel like home. It really is just a few boutique rooms attached to a restaurant, but the juxtaposition blends convenience, history, and gourmet dining for anyone who is lucky enough to snag one of Sesame's four modern rooms. The 200-year-old Dalmatian stone house where they are situated has been updated with handsome white bathrooms, stylish furniture, and windows that overlook a fragrant garden and sunny terrace. Add to that reasonable (for Dubrovnik) rates, the hosts' (Ercegović family) cordiality, the **Sesame Taverna** ★★ (reviewed below), and the inn's position 158m (525 ft.) west of the Pile Gate (past and across the street from the Hilton and post office), and you have a perfect base from which to explore Old Town Dubrovnik.

(Finds) Down-Home Dubrovnik

Tiny Zaton Mali is just 15 minutes north of Dubrovnik, but the serene water-front village is galaxies away in temperament. It also is home to an exceptional inn run by a family that really knows how to put out the welcome mat.

The three Kukuljicas (Antun, Nena, and their son, Ivo) preside over an inn as deftly run as any luxury hotel. Guest rooms are spic and span, homey, and affordable. Meals are prepared using produce from the family's organic garden; wine is home produced from the family vineyards; and seafood comes from the front yard.

Little touches give Villa Kukuljica guests added value: Airport transportation to and from is free; excursions to nearby islands, Međugorje, and Mostar are handled by Ivo's brother; guests are greeted with a meal no matter how late they arrive.

For the Kukuljicas, the Villa isn't just a business; it is also home to Antun and Nena, whose strong suit is hospitality.

Rooms in Villa K vary in size and amenities—most have private bathrooms and others are multiple bedrooms with a detached bathtub on one floor suitable for a family; all are comfortable. Our favorite is either of the two balcony rooms. All rooms have air-conditioners and TV, and we even were able to pick up a free wireless network in ours.

Most people who come to Villa K stay for a week or two, but you can rent for a single night if there is availability. For more information call Ivo Kukuljica at ☎ **020/891-622** (www.dubrovnikrooms.com). Flat charge is 20€ per person with breakfast; 30€ per person half board. Open all year; credit cards are not accepted.

Don Frane Bulića 4. ☎ **020/412-910.** www.sesame.hr. 4 units. July–Aug doubles from 440kn. Other times doubles from 320kn. No credit cards. Breakfast is 25kn per person and there is a 20% surcharge for stays of less than 3 days. AE, MC, V. **Amenities:** Restaurant; terrace.

Inexpensive

Autocamp Solitudo ★ The bathrooms at this campground outside Dubrovnik (the only campground in the area) are like new, and there's a laundry area and a cafe. Shops, tennis courts, and a pool at the Valamar Club Dubrovnik are all nearby. Pets are allowed in designated zones within the camp.

Vatroslava Lisinskog 17, Babin Kuk. ☎ **020/448-686.** Fax 020/448-688. 166 campsites. Site with electricity for 2 persons 16€. AE, MC, V. Open Apr 1–Oct 15. **Amenities:** Restaurant; market; pool; excursions.

Youth Hostel Dubrovnik (Value) Unlike some of Dubrovnik's hotels and inns, this hostel stays open all year long. It is just a 10-minute walk from the Dubrovnik bus station and a 15-minute walk to Old Town. Dubrovnik's hostel has a fine reputation and some say it is the best in Croatia. You must be a member of a hosteling association to stay in these dorm-style accommodations (four- to six-person rooms), which are in high demand. Guests can use the communal kitchen and dining room, too. *Note:* Though the hostel is conveniently located near Dubrovnik's hottest nightlife areas, the hostel imposes a 2am curfew.

Vinka Sagrestana 3, near Old Town. ✆ **020/423-241.** Fax 020/412-592. www.hfhs.hr. 19 units with 82
beds. Bed only: 120kn per person July–Aug. Other times, bed-and-breakfast from 80kn per person. Extra
charge for breakfast. AE, MC, V. **Amenities:** Restaurant; TV room; membership kitchen.

WHERE TO DINE

You won't have to search for a restaurant no matter where you are in the Dubrovnik region.
Places like Prijeko Street in Old Town jam restaurants so close together you can't tell where
one ends and another begins. It's also hard to tell one from the other by the offerings
because many serve identical fare, much of it high priced and mediocre or high priced and
exotic. Our advice is to do some comparison shopping by reading menus, which usually are
posted outside. We've listed our take on the Dubrovnik restaurant scene below.

Very Expensive

Atlas Club Nautika ★ (Overrated MODERN DALMATIAN   Nautika has the best
location of any restaurant in Dubrovnik: It boasts an unobstructed view of the sea and
the Bokar and Lovrijenac fortresses. Less impressive is the light lunch menu offered from
noon to 4pm at 60kn to 120kn for one of six uninspired choices. You can skip lunch and
get the view for free in the space along the rail next to the restaurant. Dinner is a different
story: Diners can choose elegant cuisine from an extravagant dinner/tasting menu with
choices such as sea bass with cuttlefish-ink sauce, stuffed snails Pelješac style, and excellent
vintages from an impressive wine list, including international choices from nearby Bosnia
to far-flung California. *Tip:* The restaurant accepts credit cards for dinner but not lunch.

Brsalje 3, Old Town. ✆ 020/442-526. www.esculap-teo.hr. Dinner entrees 148kn–380kn; 7-course
degustation menu 730kn per person without wine. AE, DC, MC, V at dinner only. Daily noon–midnight
(light lunch served noon–4pm).

Gil's ★ FRENCH   Follow the leggy girls in micro minis and sky-high Manolos to a
hole in the wall (literally) just past the Ploče Gate entrance. On the left, a tiny sign her-
alds the entrance to Gil's, Dubrovnik's newest "in" dining and drinking establishment.
Watch Gil's French chef at work in the open kitchen from a terrace table or sit in a gun
cubby deep in St. Luke's bastion. Either way, bring your 401k to pay for the experience.
There is a huge wine list with even bigger prices to match. Gil's cuisine is the most complicated in Dubrovnik. Views of the port from strategically placed tables are superbly
romantic. This is a flashy see-and-be-seen place, but it's also a place for serious foodies.
Tip: For a mini Gil's experience, graze on tapas in the Pop Lounge on the upper level and
take your main meal at someplace less haute.

Sv. Dominika 2. ✆ **020/322-222.** www.gilsdubrovnik.com. Reservations required. Dinner entrees
250kn–400kn. AE, DC, MC, V. Dining rooms daily noon–2pm and 7–10pm; Pop Lounge bar noon–11pm.

Expensive

Ginja ★★ (Value INDIAN   In many ways, Ginja is a supper club, but it is much more.
Sink into cushioned chairs on the elevated terrace at sunset to dine on expertly prepared
tandoori chicken or satay, then stay until dawn to dance to live music and the tempo of
the waves under the moon. Or sip an exotic martini with the beautiful people inside in
the white and wood lounge/nightclub while you watch the chefs perform their magic in
the open kitchen. You even can take a turn at the hookah bar. Ginja is hard to define but
easy to describe: It's a fascinating place to feed all the senses.

In the Radisson BLU, Na Moru 1, 20234 Orašac. ✆ **020/361-500.** Fax 020/661-501. www.radissonblu.
com/resort-dubrovnik. Entrees 65kn–170kn. AE, DC, MC, V. Daily 5pm–late in summer; 7pm–2am other
times.

Dalmatia Dish Decoder

Brujet/brudet/brodetto: Casserole made with a variety of fish pieces, onions, tomatoes, olive oil, and tomatoes.

Crni Rižot: Black risotto made with cuttlefish ink

Dalmatian pršut: Dalmatian smoked ham. The ham is salted, smoked, and left to dry in the open air.

Janjetina s ražnja: Lamb barbecued on a spit over an open-wood fire.

Pašta-fažol na brujet: Bean stew with pasta. A local specialty on the island of Vis.

Pašticada: Sauce made from meat that has been marinated in vinegar and red wine, then cooked with vegetables. Usually served with gnocchi.

Rožata: Dalmatian flan.

More ★★★ MODERN DALMATIAN   More's location in the Hotel More, off the beaten pedestrian track in the Lapad district, has its ups and downs. On the plus side, it's as intoxicating by sunlight as it is by candlelight, thanks to embracing pines and an open view of the Adriatic. On the minus side, it's a little difficult to get to—but well worth the effort. Book a table on the terrace, though the dining room view of the chef at work in the open kitchen isn't bad either. Feast on mostly Dalmatian dishes prepared with a twist or try the flambé for two (steak or scampi) for the ultimate in atmospheric dining. There are vegetarian choices, a four-course chef's choice menu, and a light lunch with smaller portions and prices.

In the Hotel More, Kardinala Stepinca 33. ✆ **020/494-200.** Fax 020 494-240. www.hotel-more.hr. Entrees 90kn–650kn (lobster). Daily 11am–midnight. DC, MC, V. Closed when the hotel is (see above).

Porat ★★ MODERN DALMATIAN   Unexpected flavors and sauces are Porat's signature element. The elegant second-floor dining room offers a menu laden with local foods, but with unexpected twists. Try crispy skinned sea bass filet with sea salt and candied lemon from the lava-stone grill, or beef tenderloin with tomato-shallot marmalade. You also will find sushi and duck breast served with apricot/pancetta rolls and veggies on the menu, which is unusual in Dalmatia.

In the Hilton Imperial, Marijana Blažića 2. ✆ **020/320-320.** Fax 020/320-220. www.hilton.com. Reservations required for dinner. Dinner entrees 140kn–190kn; lunch and breakfast entrees 70kn–120kn. AE, DC, MC, V. Daily 7–10:30am, 12:30–2:30pm, and 7–11pm.

Satu ★★ SUSHI   A jaw-dropping view of the Mediterranean and Old Town are the uni on your sashimi (sea urchin roe on your seasoned raw fish) at this serene restaurant tucked into a room just off the **Hotel Excelsior's Abakus Piano Bar** in the lobby. The sushi is a work of art, the tempura light as air, and the atmosphere dreamy, especially after dark. Try the Samurai Plate, which is a combination of sashimi, nigiri, and maki. Accompany your meal with a bottle of Sapporo or even a Croatian beer.

In the Hotel Excelsior, Frana Supila 12. ✆ **020/353-440.** Fax 020/353-200. www.hotel-excelsior.hr. Entrees 15€–35€. AE, DC, MC, V. Daily 6pm–midnight.

Arsenal Taverna at Gradska Kavana ★★ CROATIAN   This upscale terrace became a popular addition to Dubrovnik's restaurant scene when it opened in 2005 on the Old Harbor near the Ploče Gate. The menu is typical of Dubrovnik with lots of fish dishes, but it also has a better-than-average selection of grilled meats and an extensive but pricey selection of Croatian wines. Appetizers include Paški sir, a specialty sheep's milk cheese from the island of Pag, and kulen, a spicy sausage from Slavonia in eastern Croatia. Service can be slow, but who wants to hurry through a meal when an illuminated Dubrovnik is the backdrop?

Pred Dvorom 1. Old Town. ✆ **020/321-065.** Entrees 70kn–140kn. AE, DC, MC, V. Daily 9am–2am. Kitchen closes 11:30pm.

Bistro Teatar ★ DALMATIAN   This strictly sidewalk restaurant across from the National Theater expands and contracts with the crowds: Tables are added to or subtracted from the space depending on the number of diners. Either way, you won't be disappointed by the food. Seafood, steaks, and pasta are touted here, but you can't go wrong with the grilled fish dishes, which are prepared in traditional Dalmatian style.

C. Zuzorić 1, Old Town. ✆ **020/323-977.** Entrees 40kn–150kn. DC, MC, V. Daily 10am–2am.

Konoba-Café Bar Sigurata ★ DALMATIAN   Order any fish dish at this secluded side-street spot and you'll be happy. If you're not in the mood for that, Sigurata offers a vegetarian platter, spaghetti, and fried calamari. Tables are covered with awnings to keep things cool on hot afternoons.

Sigurata 2, Old Town next to the Stari Grad Hotel. ✆ **098/358-818.** Entrees 40kn–90kn. AE, DC, MC, V. Daily 11am–1am.

Orsan ★ (Finds) SEAFOOD   Every terrace table is at water's edge in this little stone house in Veliki Zaton about 8km (5 miles) north of Old Town. Every table was full when we dined there, with people enjoying Orsan's reasonably priced fish and pasta dishes. We tried the gnocchi with seafood and the three portions we ordered came family style on a single platter. It was enough for four or more. We sipped the house white, which was perfect with our food. Orsan is a romantic setting with the water reflecting moonbeams and the lights around the bay. You can have a fine, special-occasion meal here without breaking the bank.

Stikovica 43, Zaton Mali. ✆ **021/891-267.** Entrees 80kn–180kn. MC, V. Daily noon–midnight Easter to mid-October.

Poklisar ★★ SEAFOOD   Poklisar has been unabashedly catering to tourists for 10 years, and its extensive menu, friendly waitstaff, and crowded tables on a street that meets the sea are testament to that. The cuisine ranges from pizza to lobster and everything is well-prepared and attractively presented. Try the house specialty, skewers of grilled shrimp resting atop blue cheese risotto, or savor one of the superthin-crust pizzas while you breathe in the scent of the sea.

Ribarnica 1, Old Town. ✆ **020/322-176.** www.poklisar.com. Entrees 41kn pizza; 590kn kilo (2.2 lb.) lobster. AE, DC, MC, V. Daily 9am–midnight.

Proto ★★ SEAFOOD   There is some sidewalk seating here, but opt for the breezy upstairs terrace or the sublime winter garden, which features lots of glass, stone walls, and dark wood. According to the menu, food is prepared "according to our grandparents' recipes" using local ingredients. Try any of the grilled meats—or even the Dalmatian ham appetizer—to see if either conjures up childhood memories. The wine list is full of reds from Pelješac and whites from Korčula.

Široka 1, Old Town. ☎ 020/323-234. www.esculap-teo.hr. Reservations recommended. Entrees 74kn–110kn. AE, DC, MC, V. Daily 11am–11pm.

Restaurant Arka ★ Value DALMATIAN   Lasagna any way you like it is the specialty of this busy dining spot in the shadow of St. Ignatius of Loyola Church. The seafood platter is piled high with various types of crustaceans, while the Plata Arka overflows with vegetables and fish. There are several vegetarian choices, too. You really get your money's worth here.

Uz Jezuite bb, Old Town. No phone. Entrees 45kn–150kn. No credit cards. Daily 11am–midnight.

Restaurant Konakova ★★ Value DALMATIAN   You'll probably have to stand in line to get a table at this second-floor Lapad terrace restaurant, which packs them in every night. Like most Dubrovnik dining spots, specialties are seafood, grilled meat, pizza, and pasta, but equal care is given to all dishes. Little touches like complimentary fish pâtés served with bread make this bargain choice even better.

Šetalište Kralja Zvonimira 38, Lapad. ☎ 020/435-105. Entrees 45kn–120kn. AE, DC, MC, V. Daily noon–midnight.

Rozarij ★★ Finds SEAFOOD   Rattan tables outside this tiny dining room are arranged on steps around Rozarij's entrance, set on a hard-to-find corner of Prijeko (corner of Prijeko and Zlatarska in Old Town). But Rozarij and its succulent seafood are worth searching out. Try the shrimp with white risotto or the mixed *buzzara,* a combination of mussels and scampi cooked in a fragrant court bouillon.

Prijeko 2, Old Town. ☎ 020/321-257. Entrees 50kn–120kn. No credit cards. Daily 11am–midnight.

Sesame Taverna ★★ REGIONAL CROATIAN   This dining room doesn't have a seaside location, but it does have a vine-covered pergola over the second-floor terrace, stone walls bathed in flickering candlelight, and a menu of beautifully presented dishes. Sesame Taverna is as romantic as it gets, especially on the terrace. Try the chicken Elafiti with rosemary and olives or any of the dishes with truffles accompanied by a bottle from the reasonably priced wine list, which features the best of Croatia's vineyards.

Din Frane Bulića 7, west of the Pile Gate. ☎ 020/412-910. www.sesame.hr. Entrees 75kn–180kn, more for seafood sold by the kilo. AE, MC, V. Daily 8am–11pm.

Steak House Domino ★ STEAK   Meat, meat, and more meat dominates at Domino, a restaurant up a narrow street off the Stradun. In summer, waiters in white shirts tend to diners seated under a canvas canopy at bench-style tables on the restaurant's charming terrace. In winter the action moves inside to the white tablecloth dining room. Portions are generous and grilling seems to be the preferred method of cooking—a good

---

Tips   **Seafood Etiquette**

In Dalmatia, scampi are almost always served whole in their shells. You'll be spotted as a tourist if you eat them with utensils, but you'll pass as a local if you pick them up with your fingers and suck on their heads.

thing since steak is a specialty of the house. Try that, or the grilled calamari with blitva (Swiss chard and potatoes). Service can be slow when all the tables are full, and they often are as Domino is a favorite stop for tour groups.

Od Domina 6. © **020/323-103.** Fax 020/323-101. Entrees 80kn–160kn. AE, DC, MC, V. Daily 10am–midnight. Closed Dec 1–Jan 20.

Inexpensive

Café Festival ★ LIGHT FARE It can get uncomfortably warm in the afternoon sun at tables under the nautical blue awning outside this smart cafe near the Pile Gate. Go inside to try the salads, pastas, fancy drinks, and homemade pastries. Café Festival is the ideal place for a light lunch or a cool drink.

Stradun bb, Old Town. © **020/420-888.** www.cafefestival.com. Entrees 15kn–45kn. AE, DC, MC, V. Daily 8am–11pm.

The Gaffe Pub (Value) LIGHT FARE If you hanker for a taste of home, try a burger at the Gaffe. Known locally as "The English Pub," the Gaffe serves a mixture of burgers, salads, and omelets on its covered terrace. Inside, patrons can watch horse racing or live sports on TV while they lift a few pints.

Miha Pracata 4 (5th street on the left from St. Blaise Church), Old Town. © **020/324-841.** Entrees 30kn–40kn. No credit cards. Daily 10am–3am during Dubrovnik's festival; till 11pm other times.

Kavana Dubravka ★★ CROATIAN The view of the fortresses and the sea is the same from Dubravka as it is from the pricey Nautika next door, but at a fraction of the cost. The food isn't bad, either. Order a prsut-and-cheese sandwich or a pastry, sit back, and congratulate yourself on finding a bargain. Dubravka is now offering dinner service on its terrace overlooking the sea, and it has added a surprisingly classy souvenir shop.

Brsalje. © **020/426-319.** Sandwiches from 15kn–25kn. Dinner entrees 35kn–70kn. No credit cards. Summer 10am–midnight daily and 10am–8:30pm daily in winter.

Konoba Lokanda Peskarija ★★ (Value) DALMATIAN Entertainment is all around you at Lokanda: Watch walkers atop the wall, see boats dock, and observe chefs working in an open kitchen that looks like a beach bar. Prices are low, main courses are limited to a few fish dishes and risottos, but portions are huge. The octopus salad and black risotto are standouts.

Gorica Svetog Vlaha 77. Old Town. © **020/324-750.** Entrees 40kn–65kn. No credit cards. Bar and snacks daily 8am–2am; kitchen noon–midnight.

Pizzeria/Spaghetteria Baracuda ★ PIZZA Baracuda may look like an everyday pizza place on a narrow side street, but its superthin pizza crust sets it apart. Outdoor tables are picnic-style with umbrellas. Space is so tight that there's barely room for a waiter carrying a large pizza to wind through the serving aisle. But the pizza is worth the squeeze: Each has a crispy upturned rim that is a perfect counterpoint to the bubbling ingredients on top.

Božidarevićeva 10, Old Town. © **020/323-160.** Pizza 25kn–50kn. No credit cards. Daily 10:30am–12:30am.

Restaurant Jadran ★ DALMATIAN Jadran is a touristy but solid restaurant with both a garden setting and an indoor dining room. The restaurant is in the former Convent of the Poor Clares and it doesn't fool with tradition. This is one of those places with all the usual Dalmatian entrees—squid, risotto, mixed grill, and the occasional omelet and salad—on the menu. But the food is competently prepared, making the Jadran a good place for a quick bite before or after tackling the city wall.

Paska Miličevića 1, Old Town. ℂ **020/323-403.** Fax 020/323-403. Entrees 19kn–49kn. AE, DC, MC, V. Daily 10am–midnight.

BARS & NIGHTLIFE

Once the sun goes down, Dubrovnik is a hive of humanity, with crowds walking in waves to one restaurant or another and then moving to the Stradun or the Lapad promenade. From about 8 to 11pm, the crowd is a diverse mix of families and couples strolling with ice-cream cones. But at 11pm, there's a changing of the crowd as the early birds file out and 18-to-20-somethings flow in dressed in outfits that rival the costumes in *Sex and the City.* Follow the throbbing music blaring from jampacked side streets where nightly block parties convene after the restaurants close and you'll experience Dubrovnik cafe society's second shift.

Buža I ★★★ People sitting at tables stuck in a rocky indentation and jumping from there into the sea are visible to anyone walking the wall, and the inevitable question is, "How do I get there?" Wonder no more. This alfresco bar is accessible from the ground via a doorway marked "8-20" opposite the terrace of the Ekvinocijo restaurant on Ilije Sarake. Open daily in summer 8am to 2am or closing. Buža II is open from 10am to 2am or closing. Ilije Sarake access. No phone.

Capitano ★ Deejay dance music is the norm at this bar near the Pile Gate, but occasionally a live band comes to jam. Capitano seems to lure a mostly young and restless crowd, as everyone in the place seems to be on the prowl. It's open daily 6pm to 4am Wednesday through Saturday. Izmedju vrta 2. No phone.

Casablanca ★ The decor and size of this popular bar almost make it seem sedate, but Casablanca can rock. There is a big TV screen playing soccer reruns and music videos; drinks range from straight up to complicated, and DJs spin a good mix of music. It's open daily 5:30pm to 1am. Zamanjina 7. No phone.

D'vino ★★ D'vino wine bar is located just off the Stradun in the heart of Dubrovnik's Old Town. With over 100 wines by the glass, it's the perfect place for a relaxing interlude after a day of sightseeing. D'Vino stocks vintages from all over the world and also offers wine flights for tasting. Open daily noon to midnight. Palmotićeva 4a. ℂ **020/321-223.** www.columis.net/dvino.

East-West ★★★ East-West has a dual personality as a restaurant for families and bikini-clad sun worshipers when the sun is up and a bar full of fashionistas when the sun goes down. However, East-West's location on the city's public beach (Banje) ensures that it's crowded 24/7. There is music, but it takes a back seat to East-West's spectacular location and clientele. Open daily in summer only from 5pm to 3am. Banje Beach, Frana Supila. ℂ **020/412-220.** www.ewdubrovnik.com.

Latino Club Fuego ★ For a disco experience, try **Latino Club Fuego** outside the Pile Gate. Don't expect nonstop salsa here despite the name: There is nothing vaguely Latino about this club. Open in summer 10pm to 4am daily; open in winter 10pm to 4am Thursday to Sunday only. Pile Brsalje 11. ℂ **020/312-871.** Cover charge is nominal and includes a drink.

Night Club Revelin ★★★ This club in the Revelin Fortress at the wall attracts a younger crowd and it's always packed. Revelin's location in the 16th century fortress affords views of the old harbor and even the sunrise if you stay that long. There is a terrace where you can catch a breather from the always-jammed dance floor. Open 9pm to 2am Wednesday through Thursday and 9am to 3am Friday through Saturday. Sveti Dominika. ✆ **020/322-164. www.revelinclub.com.**

Sunset Lounge ★★   Everything is chic in this high-end lounge with a killer view of the sea. From the hip piano player to designer drinks to the panoramic views out the floor-to-ceiling glass walls, Sunset reeks of money and style. Even if cocktails aren't your thing, check out the views. Open daily noon to 1am. In the Hotel Dubrovnik Palace, Masarykov Put 20. ✆ **020/430-000. www.dubrlace.hr.**

Troubadour ★★★   Jam to the music inside or sit back on comfy chairs outside and let the music wash over you at this venerated jazz club. Performing groups change almost nightly. Inside is cramped and tiny, but you can sit at one of the T-mobile umbrella tables on the terrace and tap away at your laptop in the Hotspot zone with a drink and sandwich. Open daily 9am to 3am in summer and 5 to 11pm in winter. Bunićeva Poljana 2. ✆ **020/323-476.**

2 DUBROVNIK DAY TRIPS

ELAFITI ISLANDS

Slow the pace and get away from Dubrovnik's glam for a day with a fish picnic excursion to the Elafiti, 14 islands and islets between Dubrovnik and the Pelješac Peninsula. These land masses are the basis for one of the most popular excursions from Dubrovnik. Only the largest of the "deer islands" (from the Greek *elfos*)—Koločep, Lopud, and Šipan—are populated. They have been inhabited since prehistoric times. During the 10th century, the islands became Dubrovnik territories and were liberally strewn with chapels, churches, and villas designed in a riot of pre-Romanesque, Gothic, and Renaissance styles. Today, the islands' few residents are indifferent to tourists, who mostly are left alone to poke around in the pine forests and crumbling ruins that cover much of the terrain. If you have the time, visit the islands one at a time instead of with the popular "overview" excursion that hits all three (it is a whirlwind, and you don't get to embrace any island fully). However, if time is short, **Vivado Travel Agency** (✆ **020/486-471; www.dubrovnik-online.com/vivado**) and many other tour operators have ticket kiosks at the Old Harbor near the Ploče Gate. They sell daily fish picnic excursions for about 250kn per person. *Tip:* "Fish picnic" means you get lunch that usually includes grilled fish, bread, potatoes, and beverages.

What to See & Do: Islands

KOLOČEP ★   Koločep is the island in this group closest to Dubrovnik; at less than a square mile, it is also the smallest. Less than 3.2km (2 miles) from Dubrovnik, Koločep is scattered with a number of sacral buildings worth visiting. Its fewer than 200 residents live in tiny villages of stone houses like Donje Čelo on the northwest side and Gornje Čelo on the island's southwest side. You can cover the distance between the two villages in less than an hour on foot unless you are lured off the path between them to explore Koločep's olive groves and church ruins.

LOPUD ★★   Lopud is the most tourism oriented of the islands. It is the midsize island and covers just under twice the territory that Koločep does. It attracts more visitors than its sister islands and has the most attractions: the shell of a Franciscan monastery, a small ethnographic museum, the ruins of a small fortress, ancient churches in various stages of decay, and a sandy beach with a restaurant and bar. Fewer than 100 families live on Lopud and they are mostly involved in farming or in providing food and services to visitors.

ŠIPAN Šipan is the largest of the Elafitis, but it is also the least developed. Ferries deposit passengers at Šipanska Luka (Šipan Harbor) every hour and a half or so. You are then free to explore what's left of the island's 15th-century manor homes and to relax on the island's tiny sand beach. There is a pleasant valley (Šipansko Polje) between Šipanska Luka and Sudurad, another village at the opposite end of the island, as well as assorted towers, houses, and a little church.

LOKRUM

Lokrum is the island closest to Dubrovnik and water taxis leave from the old harbor every 30 minutes daily in summer from 9am to 6pm. The journey takes about 15 minutes and costs 35kn round-trip. Once there, you have your choice of relaxing on the beach or exploring the woods and the vestiges of an 11th-century Benedictine monastery purchased in 1859 by Hapsburg Archduke Maximillian Ferdinand and his wife, Charlotte, as a vacation home. Maximillian didn't have much chance to enjoy his Lokrum digs: He was dispatched to Mexico to be its emperor 3 years after acquiring the property and never returned to Lokrum—he was assassinated in Mexico in 1867. But before Maximillian left, he put in a botanic garden at the monastery. The garden still is open to the public, but it is a mess. However, you can follow Maximillian's walking path to Fort Royal, a French fortification built on Lokrum's highest hill in 1806.

MLJET

Mljet's background is laced with legends, but its present condition is a real-life experience of nature and history. There is proof that ancient Greeks were familiar with Mljet, an island they called Melita, or "honey," for the swarms of bees they found there. But except for amphorae in the sea off Mljet, there is no tangible evidence that the Greeks ever settled there. However, later settlers—Romans, Byzantines, Avars, Slavs—did leave traces of their time on Mljet; the area around Polače boasts several sites with ruins from the 1st through the 6th centuries, including a 5th-century Roman palace and some fortifications.

Today the western side of Mljet is a national park known as a "green island" because Mljet is heavily wooded (more than 70% of the island is covered with forests). Its centerpieces are the two saltwater lakes. Water in these lakes is warm: 77°F (25°C) for Malo Jezero and 82° to 86°F (28°–30°C) for Veliko Jezero. The lakes' high saline concentration is said to have healing properties, especially for skin diseases and rheumatism. The smaller lake actually was a swamp until the 12th century, when Benedictine monks who built a monastery on **St. Mary's Islet on Veliko Jezero** dug a channel between **Malo Jezero** and the larger lake, which is connected to the sea by a canal.

The 12th-century monastery and its **Church of St. Mary** ★ have gone through several incarnations since they were built, including a stint as a hotel during Tito's administration. The 1991 war ended that phase, leaving the monastery and church vacant and neglected. However, there are signs that the church and monastery are being renovated; according to a Mljet tour guide, the Benedictines plan to reopen the monastery and church as soon as they can get them in shape.

The monastery is closed to visitors, but the tiny **Church of St. Mary** ★ is open, though there isn't much to see there: It is a single nave and mostly empty. Small engraved stones in the foyer floor mark graves where the monks were buried vertically.

Mljet and **Mljet National Park** ★★ are easily reached from Dubrovnik and other nearby islands and points on the mainland. Excursion and car ferries run here from Trstenik on the Pelješac Peninsula. Atlas runs excursions (8am–6pm) from Orebić that depart via water taxi from the dock across from the tourist office on Trg Mimballa; the boat also picks up people at the Orsan hotel farther up the beach. The daylong excursion costs 270kn per person. The fee includes admission to the park.

The water taxi takes you to Korčula, where you pick up the boat to Mljet. The ride to Mljet from Korčula takes an hour and 40 minutes, so you spend half a day just getting there and back. The excursion boat, which is like a crowded bus on water, disgorges passengers at Pomena, Mljet's center of tourism. Mljet is a very low-key island with just one hotel and apartments for rent. It only seems crowded when you dock at Pomena because everyone congregates around the Odisej hotel on the marina.

(Moments) Konavle Kool

The Konavle is low-key, stress-busting alternative to Dubrovnik's high-powered pace. It's a strip of fertile land flanked by mountains and the sea that stretches southeast of Cavtat and ends at the Montenegro border. A Sunday afternoon drive to watch the weekly folklore show in Čilipi and a stop for lunch in Gruda comprise the ideal itinerary for a visit to Konavle. In fact, sitting next to the River Ljuta under an umbrella of pine and laurel at the 40-year-old **Konavoski Dvori** ★★★ restaurant, we lost track of time. Waitresses in traditional regional dress served pick-your-own trout pulled from pens on site. Pag cheese, Slavonian kulen, and an appetizer of snails ragout on polenta also tempted us before the waitress brought out some of the best charcoal roast lamb in Croatia. Afterward, we walked around the restaurant grounds and its waterfalls, ancient mill wheels, and riverscapes, which are lighted at night. The air temperature that day was 100°F (38°C), but at Konavoski Dvori, it was cool and comfortable thanks to the trees and river. Entrees run 60kn to 155kn, and AE, DC, MC, and V credit cards are accepted. It's open daily noon to midnight, closed the month of December. Konavoski Dvori is 45km (72 miles) south of Dubrovnik near Gruda (20217 Ljuta; ✆ **020/791-039;** fax 020/791-435; www.esculap-teo.hr).

You can pick up a cold drink at the **Odisej Hotel** ★, and then walk just short of a mile to boats that will take you to St. Mary's Island on Veliko Jezero, where you can poke around in the 12th-century Benedictine monastery or swim in the warm, saltwater lakes. Malo Jezero, the smaller of the two lakes, has a beach, but access to Veliko Jezero is off a rock ledge. Boats between St. Mary's and Pomena leave every hour.

CAVTAT

Cavtat (pronounced Sahvtaht) is a sleepy fishing town loved by tourists for its beaches and its beautiful horseshoe-shaped harbor as well as several sights worth investigating. The town's proximity to Dubrovnik makes it an acceptable alternative place to stay when Dubrovnik is full. Just 19km (12 miles) southeast of Dubrovnik, Cavtat originally was founded by Greeks from Vis as a settlement called Epidaurum. In the 1st century B.C., the Romans under the Emperor Augustus took over, and eventually the town became known as Cavtat. Existing archaeological finds from those times include underwater ruins in the bay, foundation remains, tombs, and vestiges of a Roman road above the present town. The ancient town was destroyed at the beginning of the 7th century, during the invasions of the Avars and the Slavs, and it was then that the founders of Dubrovnik fled to the north and established their new city. Cavtat shared Dubrovnik's destiny in the years that followed.

Cavtat is an easy half-hour day trip from Dubrovnik and reachable by bus, water taxi, or organized excursion. Go there for lunch at **Restoran Leut** at Trumbićev Put 11 (✆ **020/479-050**), then browse the art at the **Pinakoteka-Galerija** (10am–1pm Mon–Sat in summer). Stop at the parish church of **St. Nicholas** ★, but don't miss the spectacular sculpture work inside **Ivan Mestrovic's Račić Mausoleum** ★★ (daily 10am–noon and 4–8pm in summer; 10kn) in the town cemetery.

VISITOR INFORMATION   The **Cavtat Tourist Office,** Tiha 3 (𝒞 **020/479-025;** www.tzcavtat-konavle.hr), can supply you with maps and information on the town's attractions. During July and August, it's open from 8am to 9pm daily. September through June, it's open from 8am to 3pm Monday through Friday, and 9am to noon Saturday and Sunday.

GETTING THERE   Cavtat is a short drive from Dubrovnik, but if you don't have your own transport, a bus (no. 10) runs from Dubrovnik's main station hourly and takes less than an hour. You also can hop a water taxi from Lokrum harbor three times a day.

GETTING AROUND   As with most towns in Croatia, walking is the best way to see the area's attractions.

What to See & Do

Franciscan Monastery and Our Lady of the Snows Church ★   The monastery recently was converted to an eight-room bed-and-breakfast, and guests can explore the adjoining church at their leisure. Look for the church's medieval altarpieces and the remains of what may be an ancient Roman amphitheater nearby. Inside, you'll find a 16th-century triptych by artist Vicko Lovrin. The most popular event on Cavtat is the festival of Our Lady of the Snows on August 5, and the church plays a pivotal role in that. The church and monastery are at the north end of Cavtat harbor at the bottom of the hill on which Ivan Mestrovic's Račić Mausoleum (above) stands.

Put Od Rata 2. 20210 Cavtat. No phone. 8 units. Apr 1–Oct 15. Doubles from 52€. **Amenities:** Breakfast served in the restaurant next door. In room: TV.

Rector's Palace and St. Nicholas Church ★   This Renaissance mansion is located near the bus station and was renovated in 1958 to make it a suitable home for the Baltazar Bogišic Collection, documents, and volumes that belonged to one of Cavtat's native sons, who was a 19th-century lawyer. The Baroque building next door houses St. Nicholas Church and its unusual wooden altars.

Obala Ante Starčevića 18. 𝒞 **020/478-556.** Rector's Palace 10kn adults, 5kn children. Mon–Fri 9am–1pm. St. Nicholas Church 5kn. Daily 10am–1pm.

Town Cemetery ★★   A long set of stairs leads from the monastery up to this cemetery, which contains the beautiful white stone mausoleum made by Croatia's preeminent sculptor, Ivan Meštrović, for the Račić family in the 1920s.

Admission to the Račić Mausoleum 10kn. Daily 10am–noon and 4–8pm.

Where to Stay

If you stay in Cavtat, there are plenty of private rooms. You can get leads on available accommodations at the tourist office (above). Cavtat also has several hotels. The Croatia is one of the country's largest, with nearly 500 rooms.

Hotel Croatia ★★   You'll find comfort and convenience at this huge package hotel, which has its own beach. Guest rooms are well appointed and spacious; suites are especially fancy.

20210 Cavtat. 𝒞 **020/475-555.** Fax 020/478-213. www.hoteli-croatia.hr. 487 units. Mid-July to Aug from 220€ double with sea view; from 460€ suite. Other times from 144€ double with sea view; from 252€ suite. Rates include buffet breakfast. **Amenities:** 2 restaurants; tavern; coffee bar; 3 bars; children's programs; 2 pools; sports programs; tennis courts; art gallery; terrace. In room: A/C, TV, hair dryer.

Hotel Supetar ★ Much smaller and older than Hotel Croatia, this value-priced hotel on the harbor is managed by the same company. Guest rooms are tiny and more modestly furnished than the Croatia's, but they are comfortable and near the beach.

Obala Anton Starčevića 27. (℡ **020/479-833.** Fax 020/479-858. www.hoteli-croatia.hr/supetar. 28 units. Mid-July to Aug from 96€ double; other times, from 56€ double. **Amenities:** Restaurant; limited access to Hotel Croatia facilities. *In room:* TV.

Where to Dine

Food is plentiful and easy to find in Cavtat. Menu choices are usually Dalmatian and the only differences are restaurant location and view. Let your nose lead the way.

PELJEŠAC PENINSULA ★★★

You'll never feel crowded in Pelješac, which is overlooked by most visitors to southern Dalmatia. Most tourists make a beeline for glitzier Dubrovnik instead. Their loss is your gain. Pelješac is low key in every respect, but that doesn't mean it lacks worthwhile attractions: Pelješac is dotted with vineyards, beaches, out-of-the-way konobas, and glorious scenery. Make a stop at **Podobuče,** a little fishing village that also has a small beach and a thriving winemaking enterprise. Stop at **Konoba Molovran,** Podobuče (℡ **020/713-569;** www.molovran.com), for a lunch of fresh-caught fish with homegrown veggies, olive oil, and wine. If you like the place, you can stay in one of Molovran's rooms for 25€ per person and enjoy a breakfast fit for a king. Call ahead for reservations for either the restaurant or accommodations. Molovran is open June to October.

Orebić ★★

This town in the southwestern part of the Pelješac Peninsula boasts that it has one of the sunniest climates in Croatia thanks to the town's position at the foot of the 961m (3,153-ft.) Mount St. Ilija. Beachgoers take advantage of this in droves, and it isn't unusual to see moms carting picnic baskets to water's edge for breakfast, lunch, and dinner. Orebić's atmosphere is definitely family focused. This is where you will find some of Croatia's best beaches and one of the most interesting and congenial promenades anywhere. Orebić is a place where you can settle in and let your mood take you to the beach, on a day trip to Korčula, or out to sea on a sailing excursion. Orebić owes much of its cachet to its history as a town of sea captains, who in the 18th and 19th centuries built many fine houses inland. Some of these structures still are standing and in use as inns and private residences.

Essentials

VISITOR INFORMATION The **Orebić Tourist Information Office** is on the beach at Trg Mimbeli (℡ **020/713-718;** www.tz-orebic.com). The staff doubles as Atlas agents and books excursions from Orebić to Dubrovnik, Mljet, and other southern islands. **Orebić Tours** at Bana Josipa Jelačića 84a (℡ **020/714-054;** fax 020/713-616; www.orebic-tours.hr) does an excellent job of booking private accommodations and arranging excursions, too.

GETTING THERE Orebić is on the farthest tip of the Pelješac Peninsula, which is a strip of hilly, fertile land noted for its vineyards. The town is about an hour by car from the peninsula's eastern border and makes a nice base for day trips to Korčula or to explore the peninsula. The Libertas no. 21 buses make two trips daily both ways between Dubrovnik and Orebić.

GETTING AROUND Everybody walks everywhere in Orebić, especially in the evening. The Riva, of course, is pedestrians-only.

(Finds) Fishing for Compliments

Tucked into a corner next door to Our Lady of the Snows Church and the start of the steps leading to the Račić Mausoleum you'll find the **Taverna Galija** ★★★, one of the most enjoyable fish restaurants we tried anywhere in Croatia. Besides its tasting menu, which pairs Croatian vintages with the chef's creative interpretations of bounty from the sea (entrees 70kn–160kn), the Galija offers cooking courses and 1-day fishing excursions (3,600kn) with the chef on his boat. When you return with your catch, you either can cook it, have the chef prepare it, or order from the menu if you come up empty at sea. This is a place that makes you feel at home. For information and reservations, contact Taverna Galija at Vuličevićeva 1, 20210 Cavtat (© **020/478-566;** www.galija.hr).

What to See & Do

Franciscan Monastery ★★   This stately 15th-century structure sits on a plateau above the beach and water with a grove of pine trees as its backdrop. It once was used as a lookout point for invasions from the sea. Inside, the walls are hung with a series of paintings done on wood, mostly donated by seafaring men. Each commemorates its donor's escape from death during a storm.

Admission 10kn. Daily 8am–noon and 5–7pm.

Maritime Museum   You have to be into boating to appreciate this shrine to things nautical. The place is filled with models of boats, paintings of boats, pieces of boats, and boating equipment. Captions have English translations.

Obala Pomoraca. © **020/713-009.** Admission 10kn. Mon–Fri 10am–noon and 6–9pm; Sat 6–9pm.

Orebić is the quintessential family resort town. The beach and the sea are its primary attractions, and all watersports are very popular there. The surrounding area is excellent for hiking, too. Don't miss the seaside promenade, which is so close to the water you can wade as you walk.

Where to Stay

To rent an apartment, try **Orebić Tours ★★**, Bana Josipa Jelačića 84a (© **020/714-054;** fax 020/713-606; www.orebic-tours.hr). The company also arranges excursions and hotel accommodations. Or walk up and down the beachfront and the main drag and look for APARTMAN, SOBE, OR ZIMMER FREI signs. We found a two-bedroom apartment that sleeps four with living room, kitchen, TV, and a washing machine for 70€ per night.

Hotel Indijan ★★   Everything about the Indijan is designed for guest comfort, even the little spa and its retractable roof over the indoor pool. The Indijan is a boutique hotel that opened in 2007 on Orebić's waterfront to target a well-heeled market. It is at the west end of the beachfront, set apart from most of Orebić's accommodations. The Indijan's 19 units all have balconies that look out to sea and beyond to Korčula and all are done in natural teak and olive tones. The Coffee Bar Kolona on an outdoor terrace, graced with palm trees and columns made of white Korčula stone, is especially nice. There's no better place to watch the sun set over the Adriatic than at the Indijan, the classiest hotel in Orebić.

Škvar 2. ℂ **020 714-555.** Fax 020 714-567. www.hotelindijan.hr. 19 units. Doubles with sea view and balcony from 1,375kn July–Aug; from 712kn other times. Suites from 1,663kn July–Aug; from 943kn other times. Free parking. May 1–Nov 1 or according to advanced bookings. **Amenities:** Restaurant; coffee bar; indoor pool; spa. *In room:* A/C, TV, Internet, minibar.

Hotel Orsan ★   Located on a sandy bay steps from the sea and backed by thick forest, the Orsan is a lovely way to spend a few days enjoying the shimmering waters of Orebić. Each room's balcony offers sea or park views.

Obala Pomoraca 36. ℂ **020/713-026.** Fax 020/713-267. www.tz-orebic.com. 94 units. Apr–Nov from 100€, half-board double. Subtract 7€ per person for rooms with breakfast only. Closed Dec–Mar. AE, MC, V. **Amenities:** Restaurant; bar; pool. *In room:* TV, minibar.

Where to Dine

The most difficult task in finding a good restaurant in Orebić is deciding which tempting aromas to follow: There are many places along the beachfront in full cooking mode simultaneously, a situation that can set off olfactory overload and salivation. Menus are posted outside most places, and the greatest danger is finding a restaurant you can't resist trying *after* your postdinner promenade along the shore.

Café/Bar Jadran ★ (**Value** DALMATIAN   This restaurant on a raised terrace above the beach uses the sea as a backdrop for its predictable Dalmatian offerings. Think beach fast food prepared with pizzazz. You have to put your faith in the chef when you order an item simply listed as "fish," but what arrives at the table is the real deal, perfectly grilled and served with just a sprinkling of herbs. Jadran has decent pizza and grilled meat, too. It's the kind of place where you can wear your grubbies and still feel like you're out on the town.

Trg Mimbeli 11. ℂ **020/713-243.** Entrees 38kn–180kn. No credit cards. Daily 9am–1am. Closed Oct–May.

Konoba Marco Polo ★★ DALMATIAN   Marco Polo is the quintessential porch restaurant set on a veranda about 1.2m (4 ft.) above the main promenade. If you snag a table near the railing, it's a great spot for people-watching and for catching the evening sea breeze. The menu has the usual Dalmatian offerings of grilled fish and seafood plus several Croatian meat dishes in case you're all fished out. Order the french fries. They aren't McDonald's, but they arrive hot and crisp.

Šetalište Kneza Domagoja 28. ℂ **020/714-214.** Entrees 65kn–97kn. No credit cards. Daily 2–11pm June 1–Sept 1.

Korta ★★ DALMATIAN   Korta's dining room is surrounded by windows on three sides, but you also have the option of dining on its terrace, which is set on the beach. The menu has the usual Dalmatian favorites—grilled fish, squid any way you want it, steak— but Korta also offers a few unique choices like wild boar or fish stew (these must be ordered ahead and for two people). Try the Pag cheese for an appetizer and the banana split for dessert.

Škvar 2. ℂ **020/714-555.** Fax: 020/714-567. www.hotelindijan.hr. Entrees 70kn–120kn, more for fish sold by the kilo. DC, MC, V. Daily 6am–midnight when the hotel is open.

Oaza Slastičarnica ★★★ (**Finds** GELATO   No meal in a Croatian resort town is complete without an ice-cream cone. There are many places to get the frozen treat in Orebić, but Oaza is the locals' choice. Oaza's gelato is homemade and the flavors are natural and truly sublime. You'll be able to spot Oaza along the promenade (Obala Pomoraca), by the line of people spilling out the door.

Obala Pomoraca 10. No phone. 5kn per scoop. No credit cards. Daily 9am–midnight.

Finds **Wine Road Detour**

East of Orebić, about 32km (20 miles) along the main road to Ston, you'll see a turnoff for Trstenik that leads to **Grgić Vina,** the ancestral home of the founders of Grgich Hills, one of America's greatest wineries. Grgić is very modest compared to its American counterpart, but it produces some of Croatia's most sought-after wines. The winery is open from 10am to 5pm daily and takes credit cards. You can contact Grgić at Grgić Vina d.o.o., 20245 Trstenik, Poluotok Pelješac (© **020/748-090;** grgic-vina@du.htnet.hr).

Note: From June 15 to September 15, you can hop a daily **Semmarina ferry** (© **021/352-533;** www.sem-marina.hr) at Trstenik and head to Polače on the island of Mjlet.

A few miles past Grgić on the way to Orebić, you'll encounter many signs advertising homemade wine and rakija. Stop if you are curious, but be sure to spend time in the **Dingać wine district ★★★** about 16km (10 miles) past Grgić. There are many big names here—Dingać, Miloś, and Vukas. As you approach you'll see a sign for Dingać and a "tunel" [sic] sign on the right. Turn left and on your left you'll find the enigmatic **Indijan Winery ★**. Its wines are usually for sale on the honor system at the giant barrel outside. Take what you want and leave your money or pound on the door and someone usually answers. Just past Indijan you'll hit the "tunel," a passage through the mountain that was carved out so vineyard workers wouldn't have to haul grapes up and down the steep hills. Make a left at the end (slow down before you get there because the tunnel leads straight to a cliff and into the sea) for a trip down a character-building road that affords some of the most beautiful coastal vistas we've seen in Croatia. There are many tasting opportunities and apartments for rent the closer you get to the water.

Ston & Mali Ston ★★★

Ston and Mali Ston are adjacent "blink-and-you'll-miss-them" towns at the isthmus where Pelješac meets the Croatian mainland less than an hour northwest of Dubrovnik (58km/36 miles). However, both bedroom community Mali Ston and its working-class sister Ston were important strategic locations for the Republic of Dubrovnik, which acquired them in the 14th century. The city-state's officials then built an amazing system of fortified walls and fortresses that still run up the southern slope of Sveti Mihaljo (St. Michael) Hill behind the town and once served to limit enemy access to the rest of the Pelješac Peninsula in medieval times.

You can climb to a lookout point on the wall via brick stairs. Some sets of stairs are overgrown and appear to lead up from various streets in town to the top of the wall. These are dead ends, so approach from the right.

The town of Ston is a small area scored with a number of very narrow streets designed to flummox would-be intruders. In addition to the walls, the towns prize their salt pans and oyster beds, which still are active today. Stay for dinner at one of the area's good restaurants to feast on oysters taken directly from nearby oyster beds and to drink Pelješac's fine wines.

VISITOR INFORMATION Ston's **tourist office** is at Pelješka cesta bb (© 020/754-453 or 098/296-192; www.tzo-ston.hr). It is on the road leading into and out of town across the street from the daily market. Maps, brochures, and information about the town and its treasures are freely dispensed here.

GETTING THERE The bus stops on the road outside Ston, but local public transportation for Ston and the whole Pelješac Peninsula is not regular or very efficient. If you want to see the exceptional but hidden gems in the hills and valleys of this rarely visited part of Croatia, you'll need a car.

GETTING AROUND The roads through Pelješac are generally narrow and winding, especially the coastal roads as you approach Mali Ston and Ston. The pavement varies from flats through the valleys to heart-stopping hairpin turns in steeper areas. Walking is the best way to explore Mali Ston and Ston, however. There is a free parking lot outside Ston near the market.

What to See & Do

Mali Ston and Ston are sentries at the entrance to the long and rugged Pelješac Peninsula, which is home to some of the most awe-inspiring landscapes in the country. Even if your objective is to follow Pelješac's wine road to sample its well-respected wines or to head to one of the peninsula's quiet beaches, Mali Ston and Ston should be one of your stops. The monumental Ston Wall and its fortifications are the obvious draw, but if you linger awhile, you'll be able to explore the towns' charming historic buildings and their still-working ancient salt pans, then stop for a sublime meal of oysters or mussels fresh from nearby Malostonski Bay.

Ston Wall and Fortifications ★★★ From afar, the 5.6km (3½ miles) of walls and their positioning resemble the Great Wall of China running straight up, down, and across Sv. Mihaljo behind the town. St. Michael's Church is just up the hill via steps leading from the center of town. The steps do not lead up to the fortress; both the wall and the city of Ston were devastated by a 1996 earthquake, and the path leading up to the fortress at the top sustained damage that has not been completely repaired. However, restoration is in progress. The climb to the top of the wall is a steep one, so be sure to ascend on the right side of the fortress as you face it because there is a metal handrail there. The view of the town and peninsula is magnificent from the top. There is no fee to climb the walls and they are open 24/7, according to the town's tourism office, but climbing the stairs to the top is not recommended after dark.

Where to Stay

The Ston region is an ideal place to stay if you want to explore the Pelješac Peninsula or if you simply want to tour the peninsula's wineries.

Ostrea Hotel ★★★ Ostrea is the Latin word for oyster, and this tiny hotel in Mali Ston is a wonderful place to stay. Oysters are a backbone of the Mali Ston economy. The hotel, which opened in 1998, is managed by the Kralj family, whose ancestors have lived in the vicinity of Ston since the 16th century. The stone house was renovated to accommodate guests comfortably in rooms that are individualized and modern, with slick bathrooms and Internet access. Staying here is like staying with a sophisticated friend in the country.

Mali Ston bb, Mali Ston © 020/754-555. Fax 020/754-575. www.ostrea.hr. 10 units. From 140€ double; 165€ suite. AE, DC, MC, V. Parking available. **Amenities:** Restaurant; bar. *In room:* TV, Internet, minibar.

Bakus ★★ MEDITERRANEAN Located in the heart of Ston, Bakus offers casual dining with a seafood emphasis. It is a good place to stop after a climb on the wall or a visit to Ston's salt pans.

Radovani 5. ☎ **020/754-270.** www.konobabaku.hr. Entrees 55kn–90kn. MC, V. Daily 8am–midnight.

Kapetenova Kuća ★★★ SEAFOOD You don't have to be a seafood lover to enjoy this excellent restaurant on the small square in front of the harbor in Mali Ston. Like the Ostrea Hotel, Kapetenova Kuća is owned by the Kralj family. It specializes in products from the twin towns, which translates to oysters and mussels. Other treats from the sea appear on the menu, too, like octopus burgers with tartar sauce and scampi flambé. Try a bottle or two of fine Pelješac wine with your meal, and the Ston *makarula* cake for dessert.

Mali Ston bb. ☎ **020/754-264.** Fax 020/754-4369. www.ostrea.hr. Reservations required. Entrees 65kn–220kn, more for lobster. AE, DC, MC, V. Daily 9am–midnight.

Konoba Kod Bače ★★ DALMATIAN As soon as you park your car in Ston, look for the veranda with an enormous mulberry tree in the midst of the umbrella tables. This is Kod Boče, a former pizzeria turned fine dining establishment thanks to its owner, Antun Tranković, who worked as a waiter at Kapetenova Kuća for 10 years before opening his own place in 2007. His talent as a restaurateur, combined with Ston's access to fabulous shellfish and seafood, make this a haute cuisine experience at a reasonable price.

20 230 Ston. ☎ **020/754-876.** Mario.delo@du.t-com.hr. Entrees 55kn–115kn. DC, MC, V. Daily 6am–10pm.

Taverna Bota ★★ DALMATIAN Taverna Bota has become a haven for foodies from Dubrovnik and others into munching Dalmatian delights taken to the next level. Try the black risotto or one of the fish soups. Everything goes with the restaurant's sublime homemade bread. Be sure to check out the wine list, which is full of local labels like Dingac and Grgić. Bota can get very crowded, especially on weekends when people are traveling to and from nearby Dubrovnik.

Mali Ston bb. ☎ **020/437-099.** Reservations recommended. Entrees 70kn–200kn. AE, DC, MC, V. Daily 8am–3am.

MEĐUGORJE (BOSNIA-HERZEGOVINA) ★★★

Note: You'll need your passport for this excursion. Međugorje isn't in Croatia, but it might as well be because almost everyone who visits this Catholic pilgrimage site passes through and spends time in Croatia on the way. Roman Catholics in the United States and elsewhere know that Međugorje is the site of purported appearances of the Blessed Virgin Mary, but many people are unclear about where Međugorje is or how this tiny village in the middle of Herzegovina came to be the second-largest Roman Catholic pilgrimage site in the world. It is a popular day trip from Dubrovnik for independent travelers, and it is also a pilgrimage package tour organized by hundreds of Catholic parishes across the United States and other parts of the world.

Essentials

VISITOR INFORMATION You find excellent private accommodations in Međugorje and the surrounding area at any house with a SOBE (rooms available) sign out front; or contact G-tour Međugorje (☎ **036/650-126;** fax 036/650-156; www.globtour-medjugorje.com) for help. G-tour also books guides who speak a variety of languages.

What Happened at Međugorje?

Međugorje is considered a holy place thanks to the testimony of six children who say the Virgin appeared to them for the first time on June 24, 1981, in Podbrdo, a hamlet of the village of Bijakovići.

Today, the children, most of whom are now in their 40s, say the Virgin continues to appear daily, inviting all people to embrace peace and conversion. During the apparitions, Mary conveys the message that "Peace, peace, peace—and only peace must reign between man and God and between men." This statement is particularly resonant for the people of this war-torn area. The Catholic Church has not formally recognized Međugorje as a pilgrimage site, but more than 20 million people have journeyed to the shrine since the first vision, many claiming they experienced miracles thanks to their visits.

GETTING THERE   Once you head north toward Hercegovina from the E65 highway, you can literally follow any bus on the road to Međugorje (although some continue past the turnoff toward Mostar). Most carry people on organized tours, but there are public buses to Međugorje, too. Makarska and Zagreb also run regular buses to the Bosnia-Hercegovina pilgrimage site.

GETTING AROUND   Everyone walks in Međugorje. In fact, many buses leave and pick up their passengers 1km (½ mile) outside of town, though St. James Church in the center has a huge, free paved lot where cars and some buses park.

What to See & Do

Since Međugorje is a Marian pilgrimage site, what people do there might seem obvious. Certainly prayer and contemplation are the focus of Međugorje, but there are many ways to show devotion at this popular holy spot. St. James Church holds regular **prayer services and masses** ★ in many languages from early morning to late at night. **Krizevac, or Cross Hill** ★★★, is a must for most Međugorje pilgrims. The base of the steep, rocky path leading to the 11m-tall (36-ft.) cross at the top of a hill at one end of town is about 1km (½ mile) from St. James Church. The climb is about 300m (984 ft.) to the peak on an uneven, inclined path strewn with rocks of various shapes and sizes. Visitors of all ages and abilities climb this path. Some do it barefoot, and some climb on their knees to show their devotion. It is not unusual to see people carrying invalids to the top or pausing to pray at the 14 stations of the cross placed along the path. **Apparition Hill** ★★★ is the site of the original appearance of the Virgin on Wednesday, June 24, 1981. As with Krizevac, the ways to the **Statue of Mary** ★★ on Apparition Hill are rocky and steep, but that's not a deterrent for pilgrims who want to reach the site.

Lower Dalmatia

The Dalmatian coastal region from Split to Dubrovnik is the inspiration for Croatia tourism's "The Mediterranean as It Once Was" slogan, and with good reason. The skinny strip of land stretching north to south between Bosnia-Herzegovina and the sea presents one breathtaking moment after another.

It's almost impossible to zip through lower Dalmatia on a scattershot tour, even though driving from Zagreb to just outside Ploče (21km/13 miles south of Split) is now a high-speed breeze on the country's new toll road. However, once you run out of divided highway, traffic—and life—slows to a languid tempo. Visitors to this Mediterranean rat-race-free zone are forced to go with the flow. There's so much to see in 436km (260 miles) of old road between Zagreb and Dubrovnik that at least one pit stop to smell the lavender

is necessary to understand the Dalmatian way of life. Split is Croatia's second-largest city and home to some of the best-preserved Roman ruins in the world. Hvar surrounds visitors in a cloud of glamour and herbal fragrance while Brač puts wind in the sails of board bums off its Golden Cape. Korčula draws people through Marco Polo lore, its endless vineyards, and the white stone of its medieval walls. Farther out on the Adriatic, Vis and Biševo islet beckon travelers to bask in the blue glow of an underwater cave and to explore what was Tito's war room. In between, multiple towns, islands, and beaches; historic sites, architectural gems, natural wonders, and age-old traditions are the keys that unlock the doors to treasures waiting for anyone savvy enough to seek out this stretch of the Dalmatian coast.

1 ORIENTATION

ARRIVING

How you get to Dalmatia's coastal playgrounds depends on your wallet, time, and whether you want to settle in at a single destination or move around to see as much as possible. Split is the logical northern starting point for any trip along the southern coast unless you are traveling by boat and can pick your ports of call without worrying about traffic, bus schedules, or flight plans. You'll have the most flexibility if you have your own wheels, but you also can travel by bus or ferry or a combination of the two.

2 SPLIT

Split celebrated its 1,700th birthday in 2005, an anniversary that marked the dual event of the city's founding and the completion of Diocletian's grandiose palace in A.D. 305. Diocletian deliberately chose a tract of land near ancient Salona, thereby securing a location that could provide the best of both country and city pleasures for his retirement years. As emperor emeritus in Split, Diocletian might not have had the power of a sitting Roman ruler, but he still had some clout. (It didn't hurt that he claimed to be a descendant of the god Jupiter and that he had a worshipful following.)

When in Split, Diocletian was just 6km (4 miles) from Salona, close enough for drop-in visits to Dalmatia's provincial center of power. Off duty, Diocletian retreated to the Split palace, where he maintained the illusion of imperial position by receiving heads of state and others, all of whom paid lavish homage to the former emperor.

Today greater Split is a mostly working-class city of 250,000 and one of Croatia's busiest ports. It has a population of rabid sports fans; it functions as a transportation hub; and it is home to some of the most spectacular Roman ruins in the world.

ESSENTIALS

Split is a transportation hub for the Dalmatian coast, which makes it a busy crossroads. Despite the city's spectacular Old Town, whose borders are defined by the walls of Diocletian's 3rd-century palace, Split never has had the exotic cachet of other Dalmatian destinations, though most travelers who head for Dubrovnik or Croatia's islands pass through Split or make connections there. Today, Split is the source of an extensive transportation network and it is one of the most accessible cities in Croatia.

VISITOR INFORMATION   Finding the official **Tourist Information Center** in Split can be confusing. When we visited in summer 2009, the main bureau was in temporary quarters next to the Luxor cafe in the Peristil (© **021/342-666;** www.visitsplit.com). Ask any shopkeeper in the Peristil to direct you. There also is a private **tourist agency** at Obala Hrvatskog Narodnog Preporoda 7 (Riva; © **021/348-600;** fax 021/348-604), across the street toward the ferry port. Locate private accommodations there.

GETTING THERE

BY CAR   Before May 2005, it took 5 hours or more to drive from Zagreb to Split. That changed when Croatian officials cut the ribbon to open the new Zagreb-Split autocesta that flows through mountains and bypasses country roads. The new route isn't quite as scenic as the old, but this toll way has cut about an hour from the trip. Except for weekends in July and August, the 364km (226-mile) drive from Zagreb to Split now takes less time than the 217km (135-mile), south-to-north drive from Dubrovnik to Split on the Adriatic Coastal Highway. In 2007, another 27km (16 miles) of highway opened between Split and Omiš. In summer 2009, the autocesta was at Ravča (almost to Ploče) and less than 100km (60 miles) from Dubrovnik.

BY PLANE   Split's **airport** (© **021/203-171;** www.split-airport.tel.hr) is 26km (16 miles) northwest of the city center between Kaštela and Trogir. Flights from all over Croatia as well as from many European cities fly in and out on regular routes. Service is more frequent in the summer months than in the winter, and an airport bus shuttles passengers between the airport and Split's main bus station for 30kn each way. Contact the **main bus station,** next to the Split train station at Obala Kneza Domogoja 12 (© **021/203-305**), for schedule information.

BY BOAT   Except for its historic core, Split's ferry port directly across the street from the Riva and palace is the busiest part of town. International, local, and island ferries move in and out of the area Brač, Hvar, Vis, Korčula, Lastovo, and Šolta. The port also accommodates daily fast catamarans to those destinations as well as car/passenger ferries that make overnight runs to Ancona, Italy. Contact the local Jadrolinija office

(✆ **021/338-333**), Semmarina (✆ **021/338-292**), or Adriatica (✆ **021/338-335**) for schedule and price information. From June to September, a high-speed catamaran runs between Split and Ancona, Italy daily. **SNAV,** an Italy-based company, can be reached locally at ✆ **021/322-252.** SNAV also runs high-speed ferries (4 hr. or less) to Ancona from June to mid-September.

BY BUS   Split is well served by local, national, and international buses and the station is conveniently located next to the ferry port. Local bus lines run through Split and its suburbs, including Salona, Klis, Omiš, and Trogir, while others travel many times a day to Zagreb, Zadar, Rijeka, Dubrovnik, and destinations beyond. International buses provide daily service to Slovenia, Germany, and Italy, and weekly service to Austria and England. Get schedule and fare information at ✆ **021/338-483.**

BY TRAIN   Split's main train station is next to the main bus station at Obala Kneza Domogoja 10 near the town center. It runs between Split and Zagreb, Knin, and Šibenik. There is also an overnight train between Split and Zagreb. Call the **Split train station** (✆ **021/338-535**) or the **national train office** (✆ **060/333-444;** www.hznet.hr) for schedule and fare information.

GETTING AROUND Most of Split's best sights are within the walls of Diocletian's Palace or nearby. The walled city is limited to pedestrians; even the street skirting the Riva immediately outside the palace walls is closed to motorized vehicles. There are a few sights worth taking in outside the historic core—the **Meštrović Gallery** ★★★ in Marjan, the public beach at **Bačvice** ★—and you can reach those via bus or taxi. The main taxi stands are at each end of the Riva (in front of the town market and in front of the Bellevue Hotel). If you don't see a cab, call ✆ **970.**

Tip: Be sure to negotiate your taxi fare before getting in the vehicle. Prices for the same ride can vary wildly and cabbies will compete for your business if more than one is available.

CITY LAYOUT

Split's historic core is bounded by Obala Hrvatskog Preporoda (Riva) in the south, Marmontova Street in the west, Kralja Tomislava in the north, and Hrvojeva in the east; Old Town's main square, Narodni Trg, is almost in the center of the rectangle.

(*Fast Facts*   Split

Ambulance Call ✆ **94.**

American Express/Atlas Travel Atlas is the official American Express agent in Croatia. You can buy maps, arrange accommodations, and book excursions at this office at Nepotova 4 (✆ **021/343-055**). To get to Atlas from the Silver Gate, head west on Poljana Kraljice Jelene; then north on Nepotova.

ATMs Available all over Split, with several on the Riva.

Banks Many of Croatia's banks have branches in Split. Zagrebačka Bank has an office on the Riva at Obala Hrvatskog Narodnog Preporoda 10. It is open from 7:30am to 12:30pm and 2:30 to 7pm Monday through Friday.

Fire Call ✆ **93.**

Holidays Split Summer Festival is from mid-July through mid-August. The Split Melodies of the Adriatic Festival is in August.

Hospitals Firule hospital is located at Spinciceva 1 (✆ **021/556-111**); it is open 24/7.

Pharmacy There is a pharmacy at Guduliceva 52 (✆ **021/341-190**), and one at Pupačićeva 4 (✆ **021/533-188**).

Police Split's main police station is at Trg Hrvatske Bratske Zajednice 9 (✆ **021/307-281**).

Post Office Split's main post office is at Kralja Tomislava 9. Hours are 7am to 8pm Monday through Friday, 7am to 3pm Saturday.

WHAT TO SEE & DO

Be sure to stroll down Split's spiffed up **Riva** ★★, one of Croatia's busiest promenades. In the morning, people linger over coffee at the Riva's sidewalk tables before work, after the market, or before a day of sightseeing. From then on the tables aren't empty until closing time. Never deserted, the Riva is at its busiest in the evening when people dine, stroll the concrete length, or arrive and depart on the late ferries.

LOWER DALMATIA 6 SPLIT

ATTRACTIONS ●
Cathedral of St. Dominus 17
Ethnographic Museum 12
Papalić Palace & the City Museum 19
Split Archaeological Museum 22
Temple of Jupiter 14

ACCOMMODATIONS ■
Hotel Adriana 6
Hotel Bellevue 4
Hotel Caštel 10
Hotel Globo 5
Hotel Peristil 18
Hotel President 3
Hotel Vestibul Palace 13
Pansion Jupiter 11

DINING ◆
Bistro Black Cat 21
Bistro XVIII Stoljeća 16
Cafe Luxor 15
Caffe/Bar Gaga 8
Gradska Kavana 9
Kalumela 6
Konoba Varoš 2
Restaurant Nostromo-Bellevue 3
Restoran Boban 21
Restoran Kod Jože 20
Restoran Sarajevo 7
Restoran Šumica 21
Skipper Club 1

Another must is **Marmontova Street** ★, a broad, brick-paved pedestrian street that forms Old Town's western border. You won't find too many quaint shops here, but you will find some international retail outlets (Tommy Hilfiger, Benetton) and a set of McDonald's golden arches. There are smaller shops, too, and some stalls selling Croatian crafts and handiwork at the north end of the street. Just south of the walls at Marmontova, you'll run into the Bellevue Hotel and the **Prokurative,** a horseshoe-shaped set of neoclassical government buildings on **Trg Republike.**

Braće Radić Trg (Voćni Trg or Fruit Sq.) ★   Smaller than Narodni Trg, this medieval square is dominated by Ivan Meštrović's sculpture of Croatian author **Marko Marulić,** who wrote "Judita," the first narrative poem in Croatian. Marulić (1450–1524) is revered as the father of Croatian literature and his statue shows him with—what else?—a book.

Cathedral of St. Domnius ★★★   In its former life, the Cathedral of St. Domnius was Diocletian's mausoleum, an elaborate domed structure that local Christians converted to a church in the 7th century. The original structure was built from massive stone blocks and framed by 28 granite and marble columns that Diocletian supposedly brought to the palace after looting them from Greek and Egyptian temples during one of his campaigns. Because of its proximity to the Silver Gate, which leads to Hrvojeva Street and access to the Riva, the cathedral is a popular meeting place and its courtyard hosts performances during the **Split's Summer Festival** ★★★ in July and August.

Diocletian, who is known for his brutal persecution of Christians, was buried in the mausoleum in A.D. 316, following a focused campaign to eradicate Christianity. His body was removed from the mausoleum in the 7th century while the building was being converted into a church. The emperor's mortal coil was replaced with a shrine to St. Domnius (Sv. Duje). There is no record of who took Diocletian's body or where his remains are today. Ironically, part of the cathedral/mausoleum is now used as a reliquary for the bones of the same Christian martyrs slaughtered by Diocletian.

The **cathedral treasury** ★★ above the sacristy contains valuable church documents and artifacts. Enter through the cathedral's carved wooden doors leading to the interior, which has been purged of its pagan decoration but still sports reliefs of Diocletian and his wife Priscia around the dome. The doors are protected by glass, but you can see its carvings depicting scenes from the life of Christ done by Croatian sculptor Andrija Buvina in the early 13th century. Note the 15th-century altar of St. Anastasius on the left as you enter. It was created by Croatian architect Juraj Dalmatinac, who also designed the UNESCO protected Šibenik Cathedral

After viewing the church's cache of gold and silver in the treasury, you can climb the bell tower for 10kn from 8am to 8pm in summer and whenever it is open in winter. You also can explore the cathedral crypt, though it has no posted hours and was closed whenever we tried to visit during the height of the 2009 summer season.

Kraj Sv. Duje 5. ℂ **021/342-589.** Admission 5kn. July–Aug daily 8am–8pm; other times daily 7am–noon and 5–7pm. You can see the cathedral treasure for an extra 5kn: saints' heads done in silver, body-part reliquaries, plus body relics displayed behind glass. When you're finished in the treasury, you can climb the adjacent campanile for another 5kn 8am–noon and 4–7pm daily. Note that the church is open for masses that are said from 7am to 7pm daily.

Croatian National Theater ★★   The theater is outside the walls directly north of the intersection of **Marmontova and Kralja Tomislava.** Once a nondescript mousy brown, the exterior of this graceful 19th-century building has been restored to Hapsburg yellow splendor. The cool, dark interior is no less impressive than the exterior. The theater is the setting for assorted performances during Split's summer festival and periodically during the rest of the year.

Trg Gaje Bulata 1. 🕾 **021/585-999.**

Diocletian's Palace ★★★ Whatever Diocletian's intention in building a mega-estate with seaside frontage, this project was no prefab getaway cottage on the beach. It was a heavily protected enclave that included a military installation with a footprint covering nearly 3 hectares (10 acres). It included the emperor's apartments, several temples, and housing for soldiers and servants. Some say Diocletian (A.D. 245–316) began building his imperial retirement home while he was still in power so he could live out his golden years near Salona, his birth place. Some say he just wanted to stay near the region's seat of power. Either way, after 21 years as emperor, Diocletian lived in the palace built of local limestone (mostly from Brač) after abdicating his throne in A.D. 305. According to historians, he commissioned construction of the palace in A.D. 293 from the architects Filotas and Zotikos, whose names are engraved on palace foundation stones found during recent excavations.

In the years immediately following Diocletian's death, the palace was converted to government office space, but it inadvertently became a shelter for refugees in the early 7th century when the Avars and Slavs attacked and destroyed Salona. Salona's residents first fled to nearby islands and later sought the security of the palace walls, which were 2m (6 ft.) thick and nearly 30m (100 ft.) high at points.

The huge influx of refugees overcrowded the palace compound, and the new settlement spread outside its walls. Successive rulers, including the Byzantine emperors, the Croatian kings, the Hungarian-Croatian kings, and the Venetians, later built structures within and outside the complex, changing it so much that its Roman character all but disappeared.

After the fall of Venice in 1797, the Austrians took over, ceded control of the city to France for a short time in the early 19th century, and then took over again until World War I, when control reverted to the Yugoslav government and ultimately Croatia.

Because of its size and because it has undergone so much change, imagining what Split's UNESCO World Cultural Heritage gem must have looked like in its prime is difficult. You can, however, get a feel for the original floor plan by exploring the palace's lower level (podrum), whose layout is a mirror image of the upper floors'.

Ethnographic Museum ★ This small museum founded in 1910 has limited collections of Dalmatian folk costumes, jewelry, and arms, but its setting in Diocletian's former apartment in the south part of the palace adds an extra dimension to the displays. The museum also houses the church of St. Andrew de Fenestris and the former convent of St. Clare. Of special note are the collection of chests that were used for storing valuables and the collection of 20th century art, from mostly Split artists.

Severova 1. 🕾 **021/343-108.** Admission 10kn adults, 5kn children. Mon–Fri 9am–9pm; Sat 9am–1pm. Closed Sun and holidays.

Meštrović Gallery (Marjan) ★★★ The Meštrović Gallery was envisioned as a home/atelier for Croatian sculptor Ivan Meštrović and his family, but they lived there for just 2 years before emigrating from Croatia. The house and garden hold some of the artist's best work, including a pair of huge walnut Adam and Eve figures and the powerful bronze Cyclops. Meštrović's religious art comprises much of the gallery's permanent

Exploring the Palace

There are several access points for entering Split's historic core, but the best place to start your exploration is the **Bronze Gate** where the sea once lapped at the palace's back walls. Today the Bronze Gate opens outward from the palace's southern flank to Split's Riva and the ferry port beyond. Inside, it leads to the *podrum,* or basement, that meanders under the structure. The podrum was the palace's "plant" where support staff cooked meals for Diocletian and his guests, fixed palace equipment, and took care of day-to-day maintenance. The underground space was sadly neglected until the mid-1950s, and parts of it have yet to be restored and cleared of centuries of debris. The *cryptoporticus* (gallery) that runs east-west from the Bronze Gate was an open promenade and probably the site where Diocletian went to catch a sea breeze. Today the outdoor promenade can only be imagined from the form of the long corridor beneath it. The part of the podrum that extends from the Bronze Gate toward the steps to the Peristil above is a brick-lined minimall filled with merchants and craftspeople selling jewelry, maps, and other souvenirs of Split.

At the far end of the aisle that runs through this section of the podrum, you'll find a staircase that leads up to the *Peristil,* which was the palace's main courtyard and the place where Diocletian received important visitors. Today, the Peristil is one of the busiest spots in the historic city and home to cafes, **boutique hotels,** the cathedral, and passages leading to the heart of Old Town. It also functions as a stage during the Split Summer Festival, and on May 7 when the city celebrates the feast of St. Domnius.

Note the **black granite sphinx** standing guard outside the cathedral. It was one of 11 acquired by Diocletian during battle in Egypt and it is the only one left.

If you are approaching the palace from the **Silver Gate** on the eastern wall, you first must walk through the jumble of stalls that is the **city fruit and**

exhibits, but traveling exhibitions from Croatia and other locations periodically are on display. The stately mansion was under construction from 1937–39. Walk up the road to Šetalište Ivana Meštrovića 39 to visit the 16th-century **Kaštelet** ★★, a Renaissance-style summer house on the gallery property purchased and remodeled by Meštrović in 1939 as a showcase for his "Life of Christ Cycle" reliefs. The room-size wood carvings were completed over the course of Meštrović's lifetime between 1916 and 1950, and they line Kaštelet's Holy Cross Chapel. There is no extra charge to enter Kaštelet if you have a ticket to the main gallery.

Šetalište Ivana Meštrovića 46. ✆ **021/358-450.** Admission 30kn adults, 15kn children, 50kn family. Summer Tues–Sun 9am–7pm; closed Mon, winter Tues–Sat 9am–4pm; Sun 10am–3pm. Closed Mon and holidays.

Museum of Croatian Archaeological Monuments (Marjan) ★★

Take a bus (no. 12) or a taxi to this block-style building with a view of the sea at Marjan just west of the center. Like many museums in Croatia that display artifacts from ancient cities, exhibits are both inside galleries and outside on the museum grounds. Early Croatian

vegetable market (Pazar). Making this walk is fine during the day, but it can be dicey at night, even though the market often stays open until 10pm or later during the summer. The Silver Gate leads directly to **Decumanus,** the original east-west street that intersects with **Cardo,** the original north-south artery, at the Peristil. These former thoroughfares sectioned the palace into quadrants, which in turn became districts. The medieval **Church of St. Dominic** outside the Silver Gate was completely rebuilt in the 17th century and is home to good sacral art.

The **Golden Gate** at the north end of the wall was the portal to Salona and was the most ornate gate into the palace. It has a guardhouse that contains the 9th-century **Church of St. Martin.** Ivan Meštrović's largest **statue of Bishop Grgur (Gregorius of Nin) Ninski,** a 9th-century bishop who defended church use of the Glagolitic script and Slav language, towers over visitors approaching the gate. The sculpture is entirely black except for one toe, which is bronze because visitors inevitably touch it for good luck as they pass. To the west, the **Iron Gate**'s guardhouse is the site of the oldest Romanesque belfry in Croatia and the 10th-century **Church of Our Lady of Belfry.**

The **Cathedral of St. Domnius** (below) is on the eastern side of the Peristil. The **Temple of Jupiter** (now the cathedral's baptistery) and what's left of the small, round **temples of Venus and Cybele** are on the Peristil's western side. *Tip:* To gain perspective on the palace's footprint, take a walk through the subterranean halls that run beneath it. The vaulted halls were built to support Diocletian's living quarters, but they mirror the original palace layout before development infringed. For 30kn you get a helpful guidebook with map. The halls are open from 9am to 9pm Monday to Saturday and from 9am to 6pm Sunday from June to September.

sacral art from the 7th to the 12th centuries and other medieval pieces are the focus here, but the most interesting pieces are those reminiscent of Celtic art.

Stjepana Gunjace bb. ✆ **021/343-983.** Fax 021/345-255. http://mdc.hr/hrv-arh-split/en/1-opci.html. Admission 20kn. 9am–1pm and 5–8pm Mon–Fri; 9am–2pm Sat; closed Sun July–Sept. Other times 9am–4pm Mon–Fri; 9am–1pm Sat, closed Sun.

Narodni Trg (People's Sq.) ★★ If you walk west along Krešimirova (formerly the Decumanus) through the Silver Gate, you will come out on Narodni Trg, Old Town's current main square. West of Narodni Trg you'll find the indoor fish market **(Ribarnica)** at Kraj Sv. Marije. It is open from 7am to 1pm Monday through Saturday, and from 7 to 11am Sunday. You'll smell it before you see it.

In the center of town.

Papalić Palace & the City Museum ★ Croatian designer Juraj Dalmatinac designed the 15th-century Gothic town house that is the Papalić Palace on Papalićeva Street north of the Peristil. Note the star-and-feather coat of arms over the portal leading to the building's charming courtyard: It represents the Papalić family's symbol. **Split's**

Split Walking Tours

Even if your time in Split is limited to a layover between ferries, you can hit the city's highlights via an organized walking tour that starts a few hundred yards from the ferry port at the tourist office outside the Peristil, just inside the Silver Gate. You'll see the Riva, the palace basement halls, all four palace gates, Narodni Trg (Peoples Sq.), Voćni Trg (Fruit Sq.), the iconic statue of Gregory of Nin, and Marmontova Street. Tours last 60 to 90 minutes and leave 3 times daily at 10 and 11:45am, and 7pm and cost between 70kn and 90kn per person, depending on the agency. *Tip:* **Split Walks,** which meets under a red umbrella at the Peristil, conducts all tours in English from June 15 to October 31. For more information call (℃) **091/537-9538** or go to www.mediterranean-experience.hr.

City Museum ★ is on the town house's first floor; it contains a hodgepodge of artifacts from the city's past. Sculptures, documents, medieval weaponry, and coins stamped with Diocletian's image form the crux of the exhibit.

Papalićeva 1. (℃) 021/344-917. www.mgst.net/eng/indexEFrameset.htm. Admission 10kn adults, 5kn children. Summer Tues–Fri 9am–9pm; Sat–Sun 9am–1pm. Winter Tues–Fri 10am–5pm; Sat 10am–noon; closed Sun–Mon.

Split Archaeological Museum ★★ This is Croatia's oldest museum. Founded in 1820, it is a repository for artifacts—jewelry, coins, and pottery—mostly unearthed at Salona in the hills above Split. The collection includes many religious objects used by the people who fled to the palace from Salona during the Avar-Slav invasion in the 7th century. It also displays heavier stone objects such as sarcophagi outdoors. It is a 10-minute walk north of the historic core.

Zrinjsko-Frankopanska 25. (℃) 021/318-714. www.st.carnet.hr./split/arheol.html. Admission 20kn. 9am–2pm and 4–8pm Mon–Sat. Closed Sun.

Split Summer Festival ★★★ Split salutes the arts from mid-July to mid-August. During this time, culture takes center stage, usually in the Croatian National Theater, in the Peristil, in Old Town squares, and at other venues around town. Theatrical performances, classical musical concerts, operas, puppet shows, dance performances, and other arts performances attract thousands of visitors to the city, so if you go, be sure you have hotel reservations and tickets to the events you want to see. Contact the Croatian National Theater for information and tickets to various performances.

Gaje Bulata 1. (℃) 021/585-999. www.hnk-split.hr.

Temple of Jupiter (Baptistery) ★★ This small structure directly facing the mausoleum probably was a temple dedicated to Jupiter in Diocletian's time. During the Middle Ages, the building was converted into a baptistery, but only the enclosed part of the temple and its richly decorated portal remain. The baptistery also contains a **Meštrović statue of John the Baptist** ★ and the 7th-century sarcophagus of Ivan Ravenjanin, the first archbishop of Split who had the martyrs' relics taken to the cathedral. In the 19th century, the baptismal font was decorated with stone carvings that portray a Croatian ruler (possibly the Croatian King Zvonimir) on his throne.

Hotel rooms in Split are scarce in general, and reasonably priced hotel rooms are almost nonexistent, though private accommodations are fairly easy to secure. Split never has been known as a vacation destination in Croatia. Rather, its reputation has been that of a gateway to the Dalmatian coast, and as the birthplace of such sports stars as Tony Kukoc (Chicago Bulls) and Goran Ivanisevic (tennis). Until recently not much attention was paid to tourist lodging in Split, but that attitude is changing. Existing hotels are renovating, small boutique hotels are entering the market, and one large luxury chain has opened a resort complex on the site of a historic landmark hotel. The socialist-drab Marjan Hotel failed to meet its renovation schedule and 2009 reopening as a Hilton, and is now hoping for late 2010.

Very Expensive

Art Hotel ★   The guest rooms in this converted Bobiš Bakery building are comfortable and better equipped than rooms in most of Split's hotels, but the Art Hotel's location in a nondescript neighborhood a good 15-minute walk from the Old Town will deter some visitors. The bland rectangular structure got its name because the designer's vision was that of a hotel *cum* showcase for local artists, but that didn't materialize. You might think the designer then used the hotel as a canvas for kindergarten kids because the exterior walls and interior public spaces are liberally doused with ribbons of red, yellow, and blue paint, a decorating scheme that makes the Art Hotel feel like a graffiti showcase. Guest rooms are more sedate with decent-size bathrooms with white enamel and stainless fixtures, including cigar-shaped shower heads from Italy. A big plus—the whole hotel is wired for Internet use and both Wi-Fi and broadband are free to guests.

Ulica Slobode 41. ✆ 021/302-302. Fax 021/302-300. www.arthotel.hr. 36 units. Doubles from 1,330kn. Rates include breakfast and taxes. Parking 50kn per day. AE, DC, MC, V. **Amenities:** Restaurant; bar; fitness center. *In room:* A/C, TV, hair dryer, free broadband Internet access, minibar.

Atrium Hotel ★★   Guest rooms are light and airy, oversize, and lavishly outfitted with ultramodern bathrooms, desks, and high-speed Internet access. The hotel also had the foresight to put in an underground garage that comes in handy in parking-challenged Split. Add to that pieces of Diocletian's aqueduct out back, a spa pool with a panoramic view of the city, and a stand-alone dining destination, **Restaurant Cardo,** and you have the makings of a fine hotel. However, the Atrium's setting in the shadow of a cluster of brand-new, garishly painted apartment high-rises in Brodarica, 15 minutes from the Old Town, will be a turnoff for some.

Domovinskog Rata 49a. ✆ **021/200-000.** Fax 021/200-100. www.hotel-atrium.hr. 101 units. Doubles from 1,425kn; suites from 1,800kn. Rates include breakfast and VAT. AE, DC, MC, V. **Amenities:** Restaurant; bar; indoor pool; spa. *In room:* A/C, TV, hair dryer, high-speed Internet, minibar.

Hotel Marmont ★   The Marmont is a clever blend of ultramodern and old-world style, and it is just a minute away from Diocletian's Palace, but its amenities don't justify the high room rates, especially in summer. Marmont is the third and newest small luxury to open in the vicinity of the Diocletian's Palace area since 2005. It opened in July 2008 with rooms done in minimalist browns and creams and a wall in the breakfast room that was rebuilt from bricks that were salvaged from the wall of a 15th-century fortress. There are no balconies, pool, or fitness center, and there is no on-site restaurant even though the owners also own the Luxor Café in the Peristil. Parking is outside the palace walls, and guests have to schlep their luggage through town. Stay here only if you yearn to be in the heart of Old Town and can't get into or can't afford the Vestibul Palace (below). The Marmont is gay friendly.

Zadarska 13. (C) **021/308-060.** Fax 021/308-070. www.marmonthotel.com. Doubles from 250€ in summer; from 119€ other times. Rates include breakfast, but not VAT. All rooms are furnished with king beds only. AE, DC, MC, V. No pets. **Amenities:** Bar; smoke-free rooms. *In room:* A/C, TV, minibar, free Wi-Fi.

Hotel Vestibul Palace ★★★　Brilliant 21st-century architects carved this intimate boutique hotel into the space next to what was Diocletian's boudoir. The hotel opened in 2006, and the interior uses high design to meld glass with the ancient stone palace walls. The result is spectacular. Most of the bathrooms have tubs, but those without have high-tech showers and black marble fixtures. Each room is different but each incorporates some detail of the palace with modern comforts like flatscreen TVs. The **Caffe Restaurant Vestibul** (p. 115) serves Dalmatian food and is open for breakfast and dinner only.

Vestibula 4. (C) **021/329-329.** www.vestibulpalace.com. 7 units. Doubles July–Aug from 240€; suites from 300€. Other times doubles from 210€; suites from 285€. Rates include breakfast and VAT. AE, MC, V. **Amenities:** Restaurant. *In room:* A/C, TV, hair dryer, minibar, Wi-Fi.

Le Meridien ★★　Le Meridien Lav was unveiled in fall 2006, and the facility's metamorphosis from package hotel to exclusive resort is a mixed success. The 381-unit hotel has been positioned as a seafront destination, and it certainly has the appropriate real estate, plus a more posh, colorful interior (lots of candy-red accents in the rooms); a Diocletian spa area with an indoor pool; and even an elegant modern library area. However, a few vestiges of the former Hotel Lav's Socialist roots detract from the ambience. The **Restaurant Spalatum ★** has an ambitious menu executed by a talented chef, but the room is a brightly lit cavern more suited to a cafeteria than an elegant dining experience. (The Art Café across from the reception is a more welcoming, art-filled space.) Also, the Meridien's staff is courteous and helpful, but we did encounter some serious service lapses that should not occur at this pricing level.

Grljevač 2a, 21312 Podstrana, 6km (4 miles) from Split's Old Town (20 min.) and 40 min. from Split-Kastela International Airport.. (C) **021/500-500.** Fax 021/500-705. www.lemeridien.com/split. 381 units. Doubles from 275€; suites from 462€. Rates include VAT but not breakfast, which is 30€ per person. AE, MC, V. Valet parking. **Amenities:** 2 restaurants; cafe; pub; 2 bars; children's program; private beach; marina; indoor and outdoor pools; smoke-free rooms and rooms for those w/limited mobility; spa; tennis courts; casino; nightclub. *In room:* A/C, TV, broadband Internet access (45kn per hour/145kn per day), minibar.

Expensive

Hotel Peristil ★★ (Finds)　The Peristil opened in 2005, giving guests a place to sleep in the middle of Diocletian's former living room and next door to the Cathedral of St. Domnius. It has made several cosmetic improvements since, but it hasn't changed its prices. The Peristil is just inside the Silver Gate and shares walls with the palace, which puts guests in literal touch with history. The Peristil's owners worked with conservators for 6 years to come up with a design that respects the surrounding ancient architecture before they built their hotel, and they have done an excellent job. Guests can eat breakfast on the limestone terrace surrounded by the hotel and palace walls; inside, they can listen to the annual Split Summer Festival performance of *Aida* and other musical masterpieces from any of the rooms when the windows are open. All guest rooms are comfortably sized and have original artwork on the walls. Most have showers rather than tubs. The rooms are equipped with dial-up Internet access via the phones, though this service can be pricey. Restoran Tifani (reviewed below) downstairs is a delight.

Poljana Kraljice Jelene 5. ℭ **021/329/070.** Fax 021/329-088. www.hotelperistil.com. 12 units. July–Aug from 1,200kn double; other times doubles from 900kn. AE, MC, V. Rates include breakfast. **Amenities:** Restaurant; bar. *In room:* A/C, TV, hair dryer, dial-up Internet access.

Moderate

Hotel Adriana ★★   The Adriana's accommodations are really rooms over its popular **Adriana Restaurant** (p. 115), right on the Riva. If you can snag one of these rooms, you will be in an ideal location for sightseeing and close to the sea. Guest rooms are plain but comfortable, especially those with a sea view.

Preporoda 8. ℭ **021/340-000.** www.hotel-adriana.hr. 5 units, 2 apts. Mid-Apr to mid-Oct from 850kn double; 1,200kn apt. Mid-Oct to mid-Apr from 750kn double; from 1,000kn apt. AE, DC, MC, V. **Amenities:** Restaurant. *In room:* A/C, TV, minibar.

Hotel Consul ★   The Consul is a bit of a hike northeast of the center of town, but with Split's dearth of hotel rooms, it's an option worth considering if you can't book anywhere else. The Consul has the aura of a business hotel with large, bright guest rooms, traditional furnishings, and bathrooms with Jacuzzis. The hotel's Consul Restaurant is quite good, and its partially covered terrace restaurant is surprisingly stylish, with a menu to match.

Tršćanska 34. ℭ **021/340-130.** Fax 021/340-133. www.hotel-consul.net. 19 units. From 820kn double; from 1,100kn suite. Rates include breakfast. Half- and full board available. Limited free parking. AE, DC, MC, V. **Amenities:** Restaurant; bar. *In room:* A/C, TV, fax, hair dryer, Internet, minibar.

Hotel Globo   This is a good choice if all you need is a room. The Globo was constructed in 2001 in a residential area 10 minutes southeast of the city center, an area that has nothing to recommend it. Guest rooms are pleasant and comfortable, but besides the breakfast buffet, the hotel has no real amenities.

Lovretska 18. ℭ **021/481-111.** Fax 021/481-118. www.hotelglobo.com. 25 units. From 1,100kn–1,350kn double. AE, DC, MC, V. Limited free parking. **Amenities:** Breakfast room. *In room:* A/C, TV, Internet, minibar.

Hotel Park (Bačvice) ★★   Even though this elegant hotel was modernized in 2004, Hotel Park's hallmark is its old-world formality, as it was quite exclusive during its heyday in the 1920s and '30s. Guest rooms are a departure from the grand atmosphere of the public areas, however, as they have been outfitted with modern furniture and bathrooms. The rooms can be noisy, especially those in the front of the house, so book accordingly. At this time, the Park is one of the nicer hotels in Split, partially because of its excellent **Restaurant Bruna** and partially because of its proximity to Bačvice beach and park. But be warned that the short walk from the hotel to the city center is rather convoluted and takes longer than you'd expect.

Hatzeov Perivoj 3. ℭ **021/406-400.** Fax 021/406-400. www.hotelpark-split.hr. 54 units, 3 apts. From 465kn double; from 700kn apt. AE, DC, MC, V. **Amenities:** Restaurant; bar; money exchange; room service; sauna; solarium. *In room:* A/C, TV, Internet, minibar.

Hotel President ★★   The President is one of the most conveniently located hotels in Split and very close to the Croatian National Theater at Trg Gaje Bulata just north of the walled center. The President isn't a lavish hotel, but guest rooms are tastefully done in soothing earth tones with good quality furnishings. Regular doubles are smallish, but the next grade up is more than adequate.

Starčevićeva 1. ℭ **021/305-222.** Fax 021/305-222. www.hotelpresident.hr. 44 units. From 975kn standard double; from 1,125kn superior double; from 1,575kn suite. AE, DC, MC, V. Rates include breakfast. Garage 75kn per night. **Amenities:** Restaurant; bar; smoke-free rooms. *In room:* A/C, TV, minibar, hydro massage bath (some rooms).

Hotel Bellevue The Bellevue is a Sleeping Beauty waiting for a wealthy prince to kiss it with a renovation. The 115-year-old hotel saw its last upgrade in 1979, and it shows. Situated on lovely but nearly deserted Prokurative Square outside Old Town's western wall, the hotel is spitting distance from Old Town and its attractions and the water. It is also one of the few lodging options close to Split's Old Town. *Tip:* The Bellevue overlooks one of the Summer Fest sites that host televised performances so beware the noise and klieg lights when the show is on. The **Restaurant Noštromo-Bellevue** (p. 115) serves up fresh fish on the first floor.

Bana Josipa Jelačića 2. ☎ **021/345-644** or 021/347-499. Fax 021/362-382. www.hotel-bellevue-split.hr. 50 units. From 682kn double; from 986kn suite. Rates include breakfast. Limited free parking. AE, DC, MC, V. **Amenities:** Restaurant/bar; concierge; money exchange; room service. *In room:* TV, hair dryer, minibar (suites only).

Hotel Jupiter ★ ⓥ**alue** When you find clean, attractive rooms at bargain prices in Split, you have found a treasure. The Jupiter is located next to the 1,700-year-old Temple of Jupiter near Narodni Trg and in the midst of Split's nightlife action. The hotel is really a guesthouse that rents rooms with shared bathrooms, but it is an excellent place to bunk if you don't mind not having a private bathroom. Jupiter had an overhaul for the 2005 season, and the Spartan rooms and bathrooms are clean and well kept, though they are light on luxuries.

Grabovčeva Širina 1. ☎ **021/344-801.** www.hotel-jupiter.info. 25 units. 250kn per person. No credit cards. **Amenities:** Cafe/bar; TV room. *In room:* A/C double and triple rooms, fans in singles. Towels supplied but bring soap.

Hotel Kaštel ★★ ⓥ**alue** The Kaštel is really a well-placed pension and the least expensive of the three hotels built into the palace walls. Rooms are clean but modest and the place is a family enterprise. Unless you need absolute quiet, choose a room overlooking the Riva. Rooms have sound-reducing windows, but they aren't perfect.

Mihovilova Širina 5. ☎ **098/973-8601.** www.kastelsplit.com. 12 units. Doubles from 80€ June–Sept; doubles from 50€ other times. *In room:* A/C, TV.

WHERE TO DINE

Pizzerias and konobas dominate Split's restaurant scene, but the influx of tourists and new hotels is spurring more sophisticated restaurant choices.

Very Expensive

Restoran Boban ★★★ DALMATIAN Boban is one of Split's finest restaurants, with a reputation that dates from its founding in 1973. Both the indoor dining room and outdoor terrace are beautiful settings for the consistently excellent food that comes out of Boban's kitchens. From seafood to grilled meat to traditional Croatian fare, this place does it all. Boban also makes good use of Istrian truffles in pasta and meat dishes, paired nicely with wines from Grgić, Zlatanotok, or Dingač.

Hektorovićeva 49. ☎ **098/205-575** or 021/543-300. www.restaurant-boban.com. Entrees 70kn–330kn. AE, DC, MC, V. Mon–Sat 10am–midnight; Sun noon–midnight.

Spalatum ★ MODERN DALMATIAN (Le Meridien Lav) Its name is Latin for "Split" and its cuisine is creatively prepared to showcase local products. Spalatum tries to be both a glitzy hotel restaurant and family friendly buffet, and the result is that neither effort is as good as it could be or should be. There is potential: One wall of the restaurant showcases the city of Split and an outdoor terrace through floor-to-ceiling glass, and the chef has talent. However, the overall ambience of the place is too institutional, even for a hotel as large as the **Lav** ★★. Don't let that deter you from trying dishes such as the trio of Dalmatian lamb or olive oil poached tuna. Bigger appetites can choose the "all-you-can-eat" option from the mind-boggling choices offered at the nightly buffet for 220kn. Service for the a la carte menu is top-notch, and the breakfast buffet has lots of options.

Grljevačka 2a. 21312 Podstrana. ℂ **021/500-500.** Fax 021/500-705. www.lemeridien.com/split. Entrees 85kn–350kn. AE, DC, MC, V. Daily 6:30–10:30am, 12:30–3:30pm, and 6:30–10:30pm.

Expensive

Caffe Restaurant Vestibul ★★ DALMATIAN Vestibul is open for breakfast and dinner only, but this restaurant in the Hotel Vestibul Palace (reviewed above) is worth putting on your schedule if only to dine surrounded by history. Vestibul's food is Dalmatian in character and full of elegance to match the hotel's mood. Try grilled fish at dinner.

In the Hotel Vestibul Palace, Iza Vestibula 4. ℂ **021/320-329.** Fax 021/329-333. www.vestibulpalace.com. Breakfast 40kn–110kn; dinner entrees 80kn–150kn. AE, DC, MC, V. Daily 7–10am and 7–10pm.

Restaurant Noštromo-Bellevue ★★ SEAFOOD Noštromo has a respectable menu, but it is disadvantaged by being on the first floor of the Hotel Bellevue (see above), which has seen better days. Noštromo's outdoor tables are set on what looks like a miniature St. Mark's Square (minus St. Mark's) under the Venetian balustrades of the Bellevue. The menu lists lots of fresh fish entrees, and the tux-clad waiters lend a formal air, but you may be the only patron in the place unless it's Summer Fest time.

In the Hotel Bellevue, Kraj Sv. Marije 10. ℂ **091/405-666.** Entrees 45kn–200kn. MC, V. Daily noon–11pm.

Restoran Šumica ★★★ SEAFOOD Šumica is an upscale restaurant with one of the most romantic atmospheres in Split, and it serves some of the most pristinely fresh seafood in town. Choose the house specialty of tagliatelle with scampi and salmon, and pair it with a bottle from Šumica's excellent cellar. You can dine under pines on the outdoor terrace or in the slightly formal but airy dining room. Either way, Šumica is a good but pricey choice if you want something special.

Put Firula 6. ℂ **021/389-897.** Fax 021/389-894. Entrees 80kn–300kn, more for seafood sold by the kilo. AE, DC, MC, V. Daily 10am–midnight.

Moderate

Adriana ★★ DALMATIAN This sprawling restaurant on the Riva near Old Town is always crowded. Perhaps that's because the excellent food is fairly priced or perhaps it's because of the Adriana's prime location for people-watching. Try the seafood risotto or any grilled meat or fish dish. There is live music on weekends and sometimes on

360 Degrees of Beauty

The island of Šolta, 35 minutes across the water from Split, will be the site of Europe's first rotating hotel. According to *World Architecture News,* the hotel will be constructed on an axis that will make 1¹/₂ complete circles daily to give all guests a sea view for at least part of their stay. The island resort development site is a hillside olive grove that allows views across the bay. No estimated date of completion was available at press time.

weekdays during the summer, which is great for patrons but which can be annoying if you're staying in one of the Adriana's rooms upstairs. Service can be slow when the restaurant is crowded.

Obala Hrvatskog Preporoda. ℂ **021/344-079.** www.dalmatianet.com/adriana/indexhrv.htm. Entrees 45kn–160kn. AE, DC, MC, V. Daily 8am–11pm.

Gradska Kavana ★ DALMATIAN   This staid cafe and restaurant across from Narodni Trg is obviously geared toward tourists. Most of GK's fare is traditional Dalmatian and a bit overpriced, but there are a few surprises. If you're feeling adventuresome, try the special lasagna, which includes prawns, Dalmatian smoked ham, vegetables, cheese, tomato sauce, eggs, and cream.

Narodni Trg 1. ℂ **021/317-835.** Entrees 40kn–90kn. Lobster (per kilo) up to 650kn. AE, DC, MC, V in the restaurant; cash only in the cafe. Daily 7am–midnight.

Restoran Sarajevo ★★ TRADITIONAL CROATIAN   Grilled meat dominates the menu at this old-style dining room housed in a space supported by vaulted arches constructed at the beginning of the last millennium. Try the *ražnjići,* chunks of grilled meat skewered on tiny swords. The mixed-grill plate is excellent, too, but be warned that one of the meats is liver. There's a nice wine list, but service can be slow, even frosty.

Domaldova 6. ℂ **021/347-454.** Entrees 62kn–150kn. AE, DC, MC, V. Daily 9am–midnight.

Restoran Tifani ★★ (Finds MODERN DALMATIAN   Tifani (in Hotel Peristil) is a welcome departure from the same old, same old that characterizes most of the Split's restaurants. Grilled meats and fish are menu staples, but Tifani's young chef also tries to spread his culinary wings. House-made noodles with mussels, mortadella, and peppers come together in a creamy sauce laced with cheese. Sautéed stroganoff is a happy mix of beef, Madeira sauce, mushrooms, gherkins, and cream. Tifani has a nice wine list and even nicer prices and servers.

In Hotel Peristil, Poljana Kraljice Jelene 5. ℂ **021/329/070.** Fax 021/329-088. www.hotelperistil.com. Entrees 45kn–160kn. AE, DC, MC, V. Daily 7am–midnight.

Inexpensive

Bistro Black Cat ★ LIGHT FARE   This addition to Split's dining scene is a 5-minute walk from the Riva and easy on the pocketbook. Black Cat also offers food that departs from the usual Croatian grills and pizzas. Croissant sandwiches, wraps, curry concoctions, and wonderful home-style desserts star here. Full English breakfasts are available as are main courses with Thai, Indonesian, and vegetarian flavors.

Segvičeva 1. ℂ **021/490-284.** Entrees 45kn–65kn. AE, DC, MC, V. Mon–Sat 8am–11pm; closed Sun.

Konoba Varoš ★★ DALMATIAN   A little off the beaten path, Varos is not too far from the town center and it charges decent prices for a good meal in a creatively designed atmosphere full of fishnets and nautical kitsch. You'll see lots of locals here, which is usually a sign of a good restaurant in Croatia. Dig in to a big plate of lamb or veal hot from the *peka* (grill); or try the bluefish or octopus. Varos has an unusually long and varied wine list for a simple *konoba,* which translates to fair bottle prices.

Ban Mladenova 7. ℂ **021/396-138.** Entrees 60kn–80kn. AE, DC, MC, V. Daily 11am–midnight.

Luxor ★★ LIGHT FARE   You can't get much closer to the palace walls than this cafe in the Peristil, across from the cathedral. In fact, Luxor shares a wall with the ancient structure, and the waitstaff will bring your *biela kava* to you while you take in the sights

---

> ## (Tips) Split Card
>
> Consider picking up a Split Card, which entitles you to discounts at more than 40 hotels, restaurants, museums, and merchants. The card is free and available from hotel reception desks and at the Tourist Info Center at the Peristil if you are staying in Split for at least 3 days. If you are staying fewer than 3 days, you still can save by purchasing a card for 5€.

---

sitting on cushions on the steps outside. If you do that, be sure to poke your head inside to see the dining room, which recently has been restored. The Luxor also offers value-added services like free Wi-Fi, international newspapers, and cocktails.

Kraj Sv. Ivana 11. ✆ **021/341-082.** www.kavanaluxor.com. Sandwiches 35kn–65kn. AE, DC, MC, V. Sun–Thurs 8am–1am; Fri–Sat 8am–2am.

Pizzeria Galija ★ (Value PIZZA   Galija is tiny, but it serves some of the best pizza in Split at a fair price. Galija is a little off the tourist track on the western edge of town, but it is a worthwhile detour if you just want a relaxing beer and pizza. *Note:* You have to buy pizza whole at Galija, so take a friend.

Kamila Tončića 12. ✆ **021/347-932.** Pizza 26kn–100kn. AE, DC, MC, V. Daily 10am–11pm.

Skipper Club Grill ★ PIZZA   The view from this informal dining spot above the ACI Marina is nothing short of spectacular. Whether you are at an umbrella table on the deck or at a table next to the windows in the air-conditioned dining room, you can see all the activity in the harbor below, the Split skyline, and everything in between. Skipper specializes in pizza (there are 34 kinds sold whole or by the slice), but the huge, freshly made salads and pasta dishes are satisfying, too. Be sure to ask for bread. Skipper's variety is a cross between pita and nan, and it comes to the table hot and freshly baked.

Uvala Baluni bb. ✆ **021/398-222.** Entrees 35kn–60kn. AE, DC, V. Daily 7am–midnight.

NIGHTLIFE

Finding something to do in Split after 11pm isn't too difficult if you know where to look. Or you can just follow the music and the dressed-to-party pedestrians. After dark, the beach and the warren of streets inside the palace walls become singles bar central. Many places get going around 10pm and stay open until the last patron goes home. Bars within the palace boundaries must close at 1am.

Gaga ★   This coffeehouse/bar is lively all the time, but especially after 11pm when everything else closes down. Crammed into a narrow street junction, Gaga by day is a crowded coffee stop, and by night is a collection of tables on the street where wall-to-wall people try to hold conversations over throbbing disco music. Daily 7am to whenever (officially 1am). Iza Loža 5. ✆ 021/342-257.

Ghetto ★★   Art and drinking combine in this multilevel gallery-cum-bar near Trg Brać Radića (Fruit Sq.) just off the Riva. When both are busy, the place rocks. Academia is one of a triad of hot spots in the area (Fluid, Puls) perfect for bar-hopping within the palace confines. Daily 10am to 1am. Dosud 10. ✆ 021/346-879.

Quasimodo ★★   Don't let Quasimodo's facade put you off. Inside the plain gray brick building is one of Split's best venues for jazz, blues, and alternative rock. The groups that play here are a mix of locals and acts from the western Balkans and Croatia. Open Friday 7am to 3am and Saturday 7am to 4am. Closed Sunday. Gundulićeva 26. ✆ **091/934-273.**

Vanilla ★   Vanilla overlooks the pool in the sports complex on the beach near the Poljud soccer stadium. It is more upscale than most Split bars; it attracts an affluent clientele and serves complicated mixed drinks. Open Friday and Saturday midnight to 4am. Baženi Poljud Put bb, Poljudsko Šetalište. ✆ **021/381-283.**

---

3 SALONA

Anyone wandering the remains of deserted, windswept **Salona ★★** in the hills above Split inevitably will wonder what it was like to live in the provincial Roman settlement during its prime. The archaeological leavings are so spread out and so vast that the city's former status in the empire is unmistakable. There is just enough left of the original ancient structures to paint a good picture of what the city of 60,000 must have looked like, but a depressed economy has left Salona neglected and overgrown.

When you buy your ticket, you will be given a map, but the gravel paths meander— and sometimes disappear—without many signs defining the tract, which seems to blend into patches of working farmland. Oddly, none of these "flaws" detract from Salona's mantle of history, and even if you get lost, it is clear that Salona is an integral cog in Split's, and Croatia's, heritage.

Salona originally was a sheltered town on the Jadro River that was settled primarily by Illyrians and Greeks from Vis (Issa) who were trading partners. In the 2nd century B.C., the Romans began to infiltrate, and eventually Salona was named Colonia Martia Julia Salona and transformed into Rome's administrative center for the province of Dalmatia. It subsequently became the largest city on the eastern Adriatic coast.

During Diocletian's reign, Salona prospered and the Romans undertook extensive building projects there, most notably a huge gate on the eastern boundary (Porta Caesarea); a theater; a forum with a temple consecrated to Jupiter, Juno, and Minerva; and a three-story amphitheater that could seat more than 15,000 spectators and that served as the city's primary sports and entertainment venue.

At the same time, Salona became a magnet for adherents of various spiritual movements of the times. According to scholars examining the ancient city's archaeological leavings, these immigrants brought their customs and beliefs with them from such far-flung places as Egypt, Asia Minor, and Persia.

The new Christian faith was also in the mix of emergent religions sprouting in Salona, a situation that particularly vexed Diocletian, who was devoted to his pagan gods and claimed to be a descendant of Jupiter. In A.D. 303, toward the end of his reign, Diocletian solidified his reputation as one of Christianity's most zealous persecutors. He attempted to purge his corner of the empire of the new religion by ordering the churches to be razed to the ground and the Scriptures be burned. He warned that high-ranking Romans would lose their places and domestic staff if they continued to profess Christianity, and they would be deprived of their liberty. Other decrees arrived in rapid succession, ordering that "the presidents of the churches in every place should all be first committed to prison and then coerced by every possible means into offering sacrifice."

Bishops Domnius and Anastasius of Aquileia were among the Christian proselytizers of the times and both probably were among those martyred in Salona's amphitheater for their beliefs. Ironically, the bodies of both these martyrs replaced Diocletian's in the Cathedral of St. Domnius in Old Town Split after Christianity was legalized and after it became the religion of the majority in the realm.

At the beginning of the 7th century, the Avars and Slavs invaded Salona, driving the city's residents to nearby islands from which they later fled to Diocletian's palace.

Today Salona is a ghost city of ruins, and little of its former glory remains, though it still affords a panoramic view of Split and the surrounding area. The amphitheater's foundation is breathtaking in its scope and size, and historians say the arena still was standing in the 17th century when it was deliberately destroyed by Venetian generals who decided it was better to level the structure than leave it for encroaching Turks. After that Salona was ignored until a Split priest and well-regarded archaeologist, the Rev. Frane Bulić, began an excavation in the late 19th century. He sent most of his significant finds to Split's archaeological museum, where they are on display.

ESSENTIALS

Salona is suitable for a day trip rather than a place for an extended stay, so you will likely approach from Split or Trogir and move on the same day. If you brush up on Salona's history and know what you are looking at when you get there, your visit will be more meaningful.

VISITOR INFORMATION Before going to Salona, check with the tourist office of the Town of Solin at Ulica Kralja Zvonimira 69 (② **021/210-048;** fax 021/269-900; www. solin.info.com) for directions and information. When you arrive at Salona, you will encounter an information/ticket booth at Tusculum, portal to the ancient city. Tickets are 10kn; maps and other printed material related to the site are also available. Salona is open from 7am to 7pm Monday through Friday, from 10am to 7pm Saturday, and from 4 to 7pm Sunday.

GETTING THERE & GETTING AROUND Salona occupies 156 hectares (385 acres) about 6km (4 miles) from Split. If you are driving, take the Trogir-Split road (D8) directly to the parking lot. If you are using public transportation, buses to Salona leave Split every 20 minutes from 7am to 10pm from the stop across the street from the Croatian National Theater, and the trip takes about half an hour.

WHAT TO SEE & DO

Salona is navigable on foot only. You should wear sturdy shoes to tramp around the overgrown fields and gravel paths, and if you are visiting during the heat of the day, be sure to take ample water and wear a hat and sunscreen. Except for the arbor near the entrance, there is no shade.

Caesarea Gate ★★ The Caesarea Gate is a good example of imperial Roman architecture. It lies just past Tusculum in an area where the foundations of two basilicas have been unearthed. The gate's arches are no longer discernible, but you can still make out the octagonal shape of the two towers that flanked it.

Near Tusculum.

Manastirine Necropolis ★ From the 4th century on, Christians from Salona and Split buried their martyrs outside the walls of this site south of Tusculum. The sarcophagus of Salona Bishop (and later Saint) Domnius was buried here, as were countless other Christian martyrs. As with many Christian burial sites of the times, the Manastirine evolved into a place of worship where Christians gathered to pray for and to their dead, and in the 5th century, a basilica was built over the graves. Rev. Bulić is buried near the Manastirine. He died in 1934.

South of Tusculum.

Salona Amphitheater ★★★   The amphitheater is a good 20-minute walk from the Tusculum entrance at the easternmost part of the ancient city, but it is a walk worth taking. The 2nd-century ruins are very impressive as a huge circular footprint above chambers that are still hidden underneath. The site has not yet been excavated completely, and archaeologists say there is much more to discover there.

Tusculum ★★★   This structure just outside the entrance was built in 1898 by Rev. Frane Bulić at Manastirine next to the ruins of an early Christian basilica. Rev. Bulić is responsible for saving Salona from disappearing into the earth: He started excavating the site in the late 1800s after decades of neglect had left it a mess. His purpose in building a house at Tusculum was to provide the archaeologists who were excavating Salona with an on-site place to stay. Today the house is a memorial museum for Rev. Bulić and a regional branch of the Split Archaeological Museum. A display of furniture from Rev. Bulić's time, his personal belongings, and photographs documenting his work are on display on the first floor. The building's exterior is decorated with capitals, inscriptions, and statues. Note the garden and walkway framed by a variety of columns from old Salona.

Put Starina bb, Manastirine. ✆ **021/212-900.** Mon–Fri 7am–7pm; Sat 10am–7pm; Sun 4–7pm.

4 TROGIR

Trogir ★★★ is the stuff of fairy tales and one of the most enchanting towns on the Adriatic coast. It was founded in the 3rd century B.C. by the Greeks of Issa (Vis), occupied by the Romans, and it escaped destruction by invading Slavs in the 7th century. Trogir prospered and eventually became part of Venice's portfolio, where it remained until Austria took over in 1797. Today's Trogir is a jewel in Croatia's crown with its postcard-perfect profile, its well-preserved stonework, and its excellent tourism infrastructure. In fact, these things and the medieval character of Old Town prompted UNESCO to add the entire town to its World Heritage List in 1997.

Trogir's **historic center ★★★** is actually on an islet on part of Kaštela Bay that flows between the mainland and the island of **Čiovo ★**. Čiovo was a settlement in prehistoric times, a place of political exile in Roman times, a pariah in the Middle Ages when it served as a leper colony, and now home to a cluster of communities best described as suburbs. Čiovo is connected to Trogir by a bridge and resembles a series of bedroom communities in the middle of a housing boom with closely packed pensions, summer homes, and permanent residences in various stages of construction scattered along the shoreline and in the hills.

Trogir is just 16km (10miles) from Split and the region's airport actually is closer to Trogir than it is to Split. But it is **Old Town Trogir ★★★** that is the biggest draw and the source of the area's greatest treasures. Almost all houses and structures in the Old Town are emblazoned with stonework that hints at the past by depicting a coat of arms or some other family symbol over doorways or windows on most buildings, some of which are more than 700 years old. Ambling through the town's narrow streets or promenading along the waterfront is almost like walking back in time. And at night, the **Riva** ★★ comes alive with vendors selling everything from candy by the kilo to lavender oil by the liter. There is also street entertainment in the forms of fire-baton twirlers, mimes, and impromptu singing groups. On the mainland, the city market stays open until midnight to give you one more chance to buy something before you leave.

ESSENTIALS

VISITOR INFORMATION Trogir's **tourist office** on the main square at Trg Ivana Pavla II/I (✆ 021/885-628; fax 021/881-412; www.dalmacija.net/trogir.htm; 8am–9pm June–Sept and 8am–2pm other times) is a gold mine of information. The office can provide you with maps, brochures, and even restaurant recommendations. The staff will give you a short course on the city if they aren't too busy. **Vila Sikaa Travel Agency,** across the strait on Čiovo at Obala Kralja Zvonimira 13 (✆ 021/881-223; fax 021/885-149; www.sikaa-travel.com), is a full-service agency on the first floor of the Vila Sikaa Hotel. This agency does it all—excursions, private accommodations, boats, cars, and scooters—and even serves breakfast. **Atlas Travel Agency** at Obala Kralja Zvonimira 10 (✆ 021/881-374; fax 021/884-744) is headquarters for rafting trips, fish picnics, and trips to Brač and Hvar and beyond.

GETTING THERE The bus station is just outside the city gate next to the outdoor market and across the street from the local Konzum supermarket. Buses between Split and Trogir run about every half-hour; others that travel between Split and Šibenik stop there as well. In addition, at 4km (2½ miles) from Trogir, Split's airport is closer to the island city than it is to Split. See "Getting There" and the section on Split (p. 101).

GETTING AROUND Trogir's core is a pedestrian zone, so walking is the only option. If you stay outside town, there is a local bus system and a few taxis.

WHAT TO SEE & DO

Trogir can best be characterized as a happy city. Walking along the water, you'll feel positive energy flowing through this delightful town, which has just about everything—beaches, harbor, historic town, nice restaurants, comfortable accommodations—that any visitor could want.

Cathedral of St. Lawrence ★★★ Like many churches in Dalmatia, the Cathedral of St. Lawrence is built on the site of an earlier church that was destroyed by medieval invaders. Construction on the current church building began in the late 12th century, but it wasn't completed for decades and it is done in a variety of styles (Romanesque, Gothic, and Mannerist) that reflect the ages. The triple-nave St. Lawrence is one of Trogir's singular buildings and one of its best examples of medieval architecture. Inside, the Chapel of St. John is the cathedral's principal feature; numerous statues in a tableau-like scene include the coffin of St. John of Trogir. The chapel was built by Nikola Fiorentinac, the architect who continued the work on Šibenik's Cathedral of St. James after the death of its principal designer and his patron, Juraj Dalmatinac.

Trg Ivana Pavla II. ✆ 021/881-426. Daily 8am–noon and 4:30–7pm.

Čipiko Palace ★ During the 15th century, Čipiko Palace was home to Trogir's most prominent family. Today its architecture and furnishings are what draw visitors, who also marvel at an intricately carved Venetian-Gothic triple window.

Trg Ivana Pavla II.

Church of St. Dominic ★   Nikola Fiorentinac was a busy man in Trogir. Besides working on the Cathedral of St. Lawrence, he updated the single-nave 14th-century Romanesque-Gothic St. Dominic and its monastery in Renaissance style.

Obala Bana Berislavića. Summer only; daily 8am–noon and 4–7pm.

Clock Tower & Loggia ★★   The 15th-century Loggia on Trg Ivana Pavla II probably was used as a courtroom where town trials were held in Renaissance times. The walls behind the judge's table are decorated with a 1471 relief portraying Justice, done by Nikola Fiorentinac; another has a 1950s relief by Ivan Meštrović. The clock tower once was part of the Church of St. Sebastian.

Trg Ivana Pavla II.

Delicium Nostrum ★   Take the aromas and flavors of Dalmatia home with items from this elegant shop that stocks local foodstuffs, wines, soaps, and other sensory reminders of southern Croatia. You can sample many of the wares on site.

Obrov 2. ℭ 021/884-572. Daily 10am–11pm May1–Oct. 1. AE, DC, MC, V.

Kamerlengo Castle & St. Mark's Tower ★★★   The Kula fortress of Kamerlengo (Fortress Sv. Marko) was built in the mid–15th century by Marin Radoj as part of an expansion of the Veriga Tower, built on the site in the late 14th century. As part of the defense system, the fortress was surrounded by a ditch filled with sand; inside the walls were a well and other structures for withstanding long sieges. St. Mark's Tower on the north end of the fortress was built shortly after the castle in typical Renaissance style and its roof once was ringed with guns at the ready to repel invaders. Kamerlengo began to deteriorate at the end of the 19th century and was renovated after World War II. Today the castle's interior courtyard is used as a summer stage and open-air cinema. Tourists can climb to the top of the tower and enjoy the view during the day and also at night when no movie is showing.

Kaštel Kamerlengo. Admission 10kn. Daily 9am–10pm.

Land Gate ★★   This city gate is emblazoned with St. Mark's lion and a statue of the town's patron saint, John of Trogir. The Renaissance-style portal was built after the city walls (15th c.) and renovated in the 17th century.

Southwest corner of the islet on the Riva.

WHERE TO STAY

There is no shortage of accommodations in the Trogir "metro" area, though there are few rooms on the island itself. You may need to cross the bridge to Čiovo to find a place to stay.

Hotel Concordia ★★   The facade of this hotel in Trogir's core on the Riva is 300 years old and fits right in with the neighboring Kamerlengo fortress a couple of doors down. The terraced hotel opened in 1995, however, and guest rooms, though simple, are much more contemporary than the outer walls. Most have a sea view and fit the needs of today's tourists better than the rooms of other hotels in Trogir. Because of its great location and modern facilities, the Concordia's guest rooms are in high demand, so reserve early. *Note:* Some rooms are much smaller than others. Ask for nos. 3 or 5 and skip nos. 1 and 4.

Obala Bana Berislavića 22. ℭ 021/885-400. Fax 021/885-401. www.concordia-hotel.htnet.hr. 14 units. From 600kn double. Rate includes breakfast. AE, MC, V. Free parking. **Amenities:** Restaurant. *In room:* A/C, TV, free Wi-Fi (some units).

Trogir Walking Tour

Take a leisurely walk around Old Town with a guide who can tell you about the treasures that make Trogir a UNESCO World Heritage Site. You'll learn about Trogir's 2,000-year history and hear stories and legends that make Trogir a living museum. Tours start in front of the **Portal Travel Agency** at Obala Bana Berislavića 3 (℃ **021/885-016;** www.portal-trogir.com). Tours are available in several languages and run 11am and 7pm daily from May to October and last 90 minutes. Admission is 90kn per person.

Hotel Fontana ★   This waterfront hotel on Trogir Channel was renovated in 1999 to house a classy pension that has 13 rooms and one apartment. Three rooms and the apartment have Jacuzzis, and the rest have showers, so ask for the former for a real treat. Some of the guest rooms are a little tight, but each is different because of the building's historic status. The Fontana's location on the Riva is unbeatable.

Obrov 1. ℃ **021/885-744.** Fax 021/885-755. www.fontana-commerce.htnet.hr. 14 units. From 700kn double; from 1,000kn suite. Rates include breakfast. AE, MC, V. **Amenities:** Restaurant; bar; excursions. *In room:* A/C, TV, minibar, Jacuzzi; suite has living room and kitchenette.

Hotel Pašike ★★   Old World meets new in this boutique hotel a few steps inland from the Riva. Pašike is close enough to the action to be convenient and far enough away so you won't have to listen to merrymaking until the wee hours. The hotel is divided into old (2004) and new (2009) sections and both offer value. The seven-room "older "section offers six rooms and one suite full of Victorian-looking furniture complemented by modern touches like flatscreen TVs and Wi-Fi. The new six-room section is similar, but the rooms are much larger and airier. Opt for a room in the new section if possible. Note the Oriental rugs and overstuffed cobalt-blue furniture in the lobby, especially the antimacassars on all the seats. Restaurant **Pašike** (p. 125) serves up Trogir home-cooking.

Sinjska bb. ℃ **021/881-629.** Fax 021/797-720. www.hotelpasike.com. 13 units. Doubles from 800kn July–Aug, from 700kn other times; suite 1,200kn July–Aug, 1,100kn other times. 10% discount for stays longer than 3 days; 10% discount for cash payment. Rates include breakfast. **Amenities:** Restaurant; bar. *In room:* A/C, TV, hair dryer, Wi-Fi.

Tragos ★★   Tragos was a palace in the 18th century, and there has been a **Tragos restaurant** at this location about 18m (60 ft.) off Trogir's main square since 1972. In 2004, the nobleman's residence above it morphed into a cute hotel with an entrance on a narrow cobblestone street. Inside the hotel is cheery and bright with interior stone walls, lots of pine furniture, and brightly colored fabrics throughout. Each of Tragos's rooms is named after a Dalmatian town, and the staff of the family run hotel couldn't be friendlier. *Tip:* Tragos gets a lot of repeat business and rooms are often booked a year in advance, so plan accordingly.

Budislavićeva 3. ℃ **021/884-729.** www.tragos.hr. 12 units. Doubles from 110€. Rates include breakfast. AE, DC, MC, V. Pets allowed. **Amenities:** Restaurant; room service; excursions. *In room:* A/C, hair dryer, Internet access, minibar.

Vila Liza ★ (Value)   This budget entry into the Trogir hotel market has four rooms, a tiny terraced dining area, and a veranda. It's in the same building as the Vila Sikaa, sandwiched between the Sikaa and its travel agency. Rooms are surprisingly large, though furnishings are plain. Bathrooms have showers only, but they are adequate.

Kralja Zvonimira 1. (②) **021/884-690.** www.vila-liza.hr. 4 units. From 550kn double. Rates include breakfast. AE, DC, MC, V. *In room:* A/C, TV, Internet access.

Vila Sikaa ★★ This tiny hotel in a renovated medieval house has a view of Trogir across the channel. It's only a short walk across the bridge to the UNESCO-protected city. The Sikaa is above the Vila Sikaa travel agency, which also rents scooters, so it can be noisy, but another tiny hotel is on the floor between them. Ask for a room with a view of the Old Town.

Obala Kralja Zvonimira 13, Čiovo. (②) **021/881-223.** Fax 021/885-149. www.vila-sikaa-r.com. 7 units. June 1–Sept 1 from 81€ double, from 108€ suite; rest of year from 68€ double, from 95€ suite. AE, DC, MC, V. **Amenities:** Restaurant; bar; room service; valet service; excursions. *In room:* A/C, TV, Internet access.

Villa Meri ★★ (Finds) Statues and pictures of St. Anthony abound in this tiny inn in Trogir's center because its owner, who also runs the **Don Dino restaurant** across the street (reviewed below), reveres the saint. Meri even opened on the saint's feast day (June 15) in 2006 for good luck. So far, the strategy is working. The inn is a family operation run by the owner's daughter and her husband. The couple has effected a transformation on the seven-room structure—from an elderly woman's home into a charming B&B. Staying at Villa Meri is like being an honored guest in a friend's home.

Splitska 1. (②) **021/882-555.** Fax 021/882-533. www.villa-meri.com. 7 units. Doubles from 120€. Rates include breakfast. AE, DC, MC, V. Closed Jan. **Amenities:** Restaurant. *In room:* A/C, TV, hair dryer, dial-up Internet, minibar.

Villa Sv. Petar ★★ This tiny inn opened in 2005 in a 14th-century town house that was restored using stone, wood, and hand-carved beds mingled with modern electronics like air-conditioning and flatscreen TVs. Instead of numbers, rooms are named for local fruits, such as olives, figs, and cherries, and all are decorated with original art from Croatian artists. This is an intimate hotel in a historic setting, and you can't get any closer to the action in Trogir than this.

Ivana Duknovića 14. (②) **021/884-359.** Fax 021/884-350. www.villa-svpetar.com. 6 units. Doubles 715kn July 1–Sept 30, from 550kn other times; suites from 1,090kn July 1–Sept 30; from 902kn other times. Rates for doubles include breakfast; suite rates do not. *In room:* A/C, TV, hair dryer.

WHERE TO DINE

Restaurants are plentiful in the Trogir area, though during the July-August tourist season, they can be crowded. Occasionally, Trogir restaurants that usually take credit cards refuse to take them in July and August, according to one waiter. Nonetheless, you won't go hungry. *Tip:* For a sweet treat, head to the area around Gradska 16 in the center of town. It features a large block of tables surrounded by ice-cream shops.

Alka ★★ SEAFOOD Alka has been a fixture deep in the heart of Trogir for more than 40 years. Diners feast on classic preparations of seafood, pasta, and even sautéed veal liver at white-cloth-covered tables surrounded by potted hedges while tuxedo-clad waiters rush around deboning fish and mixing up steak tartare. Beware the dipping oil that comes with the bread: It is 100-proof garlic juice.

Bl. Augustina Kažotića 15. (②) **021/881-856.** Fax 021/882-730. www.restaurant-alka.hr. Entrees 70kn–140kn. V. Daily 9am–midnight May 1–Aug 30.

Don Dino ★★ DALMATIAN Dalmatian specialties are the emphasis at this beautiful little restaurant in Trogir's center. The terrace is an especially nice setting for feasting on excellent grilled specialties and deftly prepared Italian choices such as seafood risotto and spaghetti carbonara. For a special treat, try Don Dino for breakfast, and order the ham omelet made with local pršut. Yummy. *Tip:* Try to book a room at the **Villa Meri** (p. 124) across the street. It's run by the restaurant owner's daughter and son-in-law.

Augustina Kažotica 8. ☎ **021/882-656.** www.dondino.hr. Entrees 60kn–170kn. AE, DC, MC, V. Daily 9am–1am.

Fontana ★★ SEAFOOD   The Fontana Hotel's restaurant in the shadow of St. Dominik Church is a classy, mostly alfresco watering hole on the Riva that offers rather pricey but excellent grilled fish, some pizzas, and a bit of attitude toward tourists. Outdoor tables are scattered among three terraces separated by potted palms and rosemary hedges; you can watch the Riva action while you dine. Black-suited waiters provide competent, slightly formal service but tell obvious foreigners (us) they must pay in cash during the season.

In the Fontana Hotel, Trogir Obrov 1. ☎ **021/885-744.** Fax 021/885-755. www.htnet.hr/fontana-commerce. Entrees 30kn–240kn. No credit cards in summer. Daily 7am–midnight.

Jambo Bistro Pizzeria ★ (Value) PIZZA   At first glance there doesn't seem to be much difference between Jambo and its courtyard neighbors—until you look at the menu and see the prices. Risotto con funghi and pizza picante are among its offerings. Jambo's fare is similar to that of the restaurants that flank it, but it is a better bargain— one of the best in Trogir, in fact.

Obrov 6, 21220 Trogir. ☎ **021/885-630** or 091/510-4924. Entrees 33kn–60kn. No credit cards. Daily 4pm–midnight.

Pašike ★ DALMATIAN   Pašike is an odd mixture of styles. Blue upholstered chairs, silver candelabra, and lots of crystal adorn tables on the Hotel Pašike's terrace under a white tent, but the cuisine is pure Trogir home cooking. Savor local dishes including Kaštela macaroni, pasticada with gnocchi (meat and cheese stuffed noodles), and brodetto with polenta (fish stew). Prices are higher than in similar restaurants nearby, but the menu's homage to family recipes is worth it.

In the Hotel Pašike, Sinjska bb. ☎ **021/797-728.** Fax 021/797-729. www.hotelpasike.com. Entrees 50kn–150kn. MC, V. Daily noon–5pm and 6–11pm.

Restaurant Kamerlengo ★★★ CROATIAN   Like a lot of Trogir's restaurants, Kamerlengo does most of its tourist business from an open-air site wedged between the walls of the city's ancient stone buildings. Kamerlengo has a nice inside dining room, too, and it is dominated by a huge wood-burning oven in the center of the room. Order grilled fish or meat and you can't go wrong.

Vukovarska 2. ☎ **021/884-772.** www.trogir.com. Entrees 30kn–150kn. AE, DC, MC, V. Daily 10am–midnight; 10am–1am early July to end of Aug.

Sv. Dominik ★★ DALMATIAN   Sv. Dominik is a summer restaurant in that it sets up on the plaza between St. Dominic church and the harbor in the summer and disappears in the winter. But as long as the weather is warm, this is the ideal setting for an evening meal with friends who enjoy pizza, salad, or fish accompanied by a fancy cocktail or local beer.

A. Kažotića 1. ☎ **091/530-1620.** www.svdomink.com. Entrees 48kn–138kn. No credit cards. Daily 8am–midnight Apr 15–Nov 1.

Top Baloon Grill and Pizzeria ★ PIZZA It's just another courtyard pizza joint, but this restaurant and its neighbor (below) really pack them in. Pizza, pasta, meat, fish, and salads offer diners a hefty list of choices. Try the Top Baloon pizza made with tomatoes, ham, mushrooms, bacon, pepperoni, and cream.

Obrov 7. ℮ 021/884-869. Entrees 38kn–100kn. No credit cards. Daily 10am–midnight.

---

5 MAKARSKA RIVIERA

This stretch of waterfront property from Omiš south to Gradac is dedicated to sea and surf aficionados. Pebbles cover every semi-gentle slope that leads into the sea; and in July and August, well-oiled bodies cover the pebbles from sunup to sundown almost the entire length of the 58km (36-mile) strip of coastline. There are six recognized resort towns along the Riviera and the Cetina Gorge; **Brela** ★★ and **Makarska** ★ are the most notable, but the two towns couldn't be more different.

Brela is a low-key resort composed of boutique hotels and family-run restaurants, while Makarska caters to families with large, package-oriented resort hotels.

Brela, at the top of the chain of pebble beaches that punctuate the coast south to Gradac, is a two-level town. Most of the town's motor traffic, commercial enterprises, and private accommodations are on the road that continues down the coast. The major hotels and the town's nearly 6km (4 miles) of beach are at the bottom of a terraced, pine-forested slope. Near the bottom, a lovely walkway wends its way along the coast.

ESSENTIALS

VISITOR INFORMATION The **Brela city tourist office** at Trg Alojzija Stepinca bb (℮ 021/618-455; fax 021/618337; www.brela.hr) and the private agencies in town are very helpful and courteous. Through them you can secure accommodations and pick up maps and brochures. **Berulia Travel** (℮ 021/618-519), one of the most helpful private agencies in the area, has a huge inventory of private accommodations. **Bonavia Travel Agency** at Obala Kneza Domagoja 18 (℮ 021/619-019; www.bonavia-agency.hr) also finds private rooms and books excursions. The **Makarska city tourist office** at Obala Kralja Tomislava 16 (℮ 021/612-002; www.makarska.com) is open daily June through September, 7am to 9pm; and Monday through Friday, October through May, 7am to 2pm.

GETTING THERE The bus line that runs up and down the coast and through the Makarska Riviera stops at Brela behind the **Hotel Soline** and goes on to Makarska, where it stops at Ante Starčevića 30. Makarska also has a Jadronlinija office on Obala Kralja Tomislava (℮ 021/338-333). It's a 2-hour or longer drive to Brela from Split along the Adriatic Coastal Highway, but that time could be cut in half if you didn't have to drive through Omiš, an overcrowded resort town north of Brela that is clogged with pedestrian and auto traffic all summer.

GETTING AROUND With most traffic relegated to the part of town above the beach, Brela is a wonderful walking town (though some of the paths are vertical). In fact, it is possible to navigate the 14km (8½-mile) path along the water all the way to Makarska, though you will pass through the town of Baška Voda 5km (3 miles) into it. Makarska's waterfront has the usual pedestrian promenade, but the town can turn into a massive traffic jam on any weekend day or night during July and August.

Biokovo Nature Park

The majestic peaks of the Biokovo Mountain Range rise about 3km (2 miles) northeast of Makarska and beckon those who want to supplement beach time with aerobic activity. The range is home to the **Biokovo Nature Park ★★★**, which is honeycombed with caves and landscapes, botanical gardens (at Koto-sina), and some challenging hiking and climbing trails. More experienced mountaineers can tackle the peaks of Sveti Jure, Vošac, or any of 10 other peaks. The rewards are breathtaking views and a sense of accomplishment. You can also drive the 7km (4¹/₂ miles) to the summit in the summer, but that can be scarier than climbing thanks to lots of hairpin turns. As with any climbing adventure, you should pack emergency gear, check the weather, carry an accurate map and water, and wear good climbing boots.

WHAT TO SEE & DO

The centerpieces of each of these towns are the beach and the sea, with a lot of watersports and spectacular scenery; but several historic churches and a monastery are sprinkled here and there, too. Brela is also home to several sports centers.

Aquanaut Diving at Bartola Kašića 50 (*©* **021/618-664** or 098/371-651; ines. medic@st.htnet.hr) outfits novice and experienced divers and conducts excursions off Brela. **Mountaineering Club Pozjata,** Sv. Juja 1 (*©* **021/618-337**), conducts hikes and climbs in the area.

WHERE TO STAY

There are lots of big, impersonal package hotels up and down the Makarska Riviera, but there are also many charming private accommodations and a few small hotels, too. During July and August it is difficult to find a parking place at Makarska or Brela, much less a room. If you do choose to visit then, you will have to book for at least 7 days in most places.

Biokovo ★★　This medium-size hotel is on the city promenade and close to the city center—a superb location, especially if you decide to leave the beach for lunch. Rooms are large and bright. The **Biokovo Dining Room** is quite elegant. There is a pretty outdoor terrace cafe.

Obala Kralja Tomislava bb, Makarska. *©* **021/615-244.** Fax 021/615-081. www.hotelbiokovo.hr. 60 units. July–Aug from 122€ double; from 136€ suite. Rest of year from 86€ double; from 122€ suite. 20% surcharge for stays fewer than 4 days. AE, DC, MC, V. Rates include breakfast. Half- and full board available. **Amenities:** Restaurant; cafe; pizzeria; Internet access, room service. *In room:* A/C, TV, minibar.

Hotel Berulia ★★　Pine trees provide scent and privacy for this large white structure set back from Brela's pebble beach. Though the Berulia is a fairly large and well-equipped facility, its layout and landscaping create an illusion of intimacy. Rooms are average but with decent appointments; most have balconies that overlook the sea, the park, or the mountains. Bathrooms are immaculate but nothing special, and almost all have showers only.

Trg Gospe od Karmela 1, Brela. © **021/603-599.** Fax 021/619-005. www.brelahotels.com or www.brela.
hr. 199 units. July–Aug from 916kn double with sea view; rest of year from 400kn double with sea view.
Rates include breakfast. Limited free parking. Closed Nov–Mar. AE, DC, MC, V. **Amenities:** Restaurant;
terrace cafe; beach restaurant; bar; minigolf; pool; sauna; solarium; tennis courts, bocce. *In room:* A/C, TV,
hair dryer, minibar.

Hotel Meteor ★★   The Meteor is the largest and the best of the three major hotels
at Makarska. It also has the most amenities and is the only one that is open year-round.
There are seven tiers of rates through four seasons here. The best accommodations are
the terrace rooms that face the pool, though the decor tends to be bland at every level.

Kralja P. Krešimira IV bb, Makarska. © **021/615-344.** Fax 021/611-419. www.hoteli-makarska.hr. 275
units. July–Aug from 130€ double, from 140€ suite; rest of year from 84€ double, from 110€ suite. AE, DC,
MC, V. Rates include breakfast. Half- and full board extra. **Amenities:** Restaurant; tavern; disco; snack bar;
2 pools; sauna; whirlpool. *In room:* A/C, TV, minibar.

WHERE TO DINE

Makarska is a resort area that lives or dies on tourism. Almost all its restaurants serve
decent food, but few venture into gourmet territory with menu choices or preparations.
Brela's eateries are even more casual and predictable, perhaps because of board arrangements at the hotels and because many people prepare meals in their private accommodations. Several restaurants in both towns do try a little harder than the rest and they're
noted below.

Jež ★★ DALMATIAN/SEAFOOD   Another perennial on the "100 best restaurants
in Croatia" list, Jež richly deserves the honor and is a great choice for a special occasion.
Located near the beach, Jež specializes in fresh seafood in a variety of preparations, has
an excellent list of Croatian wines, and offers terrace dining. Be sure to try the pineapple
torte for dessert.

Petra Krešimira IV 90, Makarska. © **021/611-741.** Reservations recommended. Entrees 60kn–130kn. MC.
Daily 11am–midnight.

Konoba Decima ★★ DALMATIAN   It's in the city center rather than on the beach,
but the energy at this family konoba makes up for its location. The food is well prepared
though the choices are run-of-the-mill Dalmatian with lots of grilled fish and meat. But
the grapevine-arbor covered terrace and the live traditional Dalmatian music performed
by *Klapa* musicians make dining here memorable.

Trg Tina Ujevića, Makarska. © **021/611-374.** Entrees 50kn–110kn. No credit cards. Daily 8am–1am.

Riva ★ DALMATIAN   This restaurant near the harbor routinely shows up on "best
restaurant" lists in Croatia. Enjoy fish and meat specialties and a great wine list in a
white-tablecloth dining room or on the terrace under palm and pine trees. Specialties
include grilled seafood and filet mignon.

Obala Kralja Tomislava 6, Makarska. © **021/616-829.** Fax 021/615-422. restoran.riva@htnet.hr. Entrees
75kn–180kn. AE, DC, MC, V. Daily 11am–midnight.

Stari Mlin ★★ FUSION DALMATIAN–THAI   Dalmatia meets Thailand on the
interesting menu in this restaurant set in an old stone mill. The patio is an oasis of
green—the perfect setting for savoring steamed mussels, shrimp curry, or grilled fish with
Thai sweet-hot sauce. Mlin also has a solid wine list and a children's menu.

Ulica Prvosvibanjska 43, Makarska. © **021/611-509.** Entrees 68kn–150kn. AE, DC, MC. Mon–Sat 10am–
3pm and 6pm–1am; closed Sun.

6 BRAČ

Brač ★★★ is both a windsurfer's paradise and one of Croatia's least-developed populated islands. This rugged land mass is about an hour's ferry ride from Split, and it also
is famous as the source of the stone that built Diocletian's palace on the mainland, the
White House in Washington, D.C., and the Reichstag in Berlin. Brač also has a reputation as the source of Bolski Plavac and other highly regarded, locally produced wines. It
is the third-largest island off Croatia (Krk is the largest, followed by Cres), and it is home
to **Zlatni Rat (Golden Cape)** ★★, Croatia's most famous beach.

Despite its size, Brač is really just a two-town island. That's because only **Supetar** ★
on Brač's northern shore and **Bol** ★★★ on its southern shore are frequently visited by
those who love the island's Mediterranean climate and unspoiled countryside. Tourism
currently supplies most of Brač's revenue.

ESSENTIALS

VISITOR INFORMATION **Turistička Zajednica Grada Supetar** is at Porat 1 (② **021/
630-551;** www.supetar.hr). Hours are 8am to 10pm daily from June to the end of September. At other times, it's open 8am to 4pm Monday through Friday. Bol's tourist office is at
Porat Bolskih Pomoraca bb (② **021/635-638;** www.bol.hr). Both offices can help you
locate private accommodations, provide you with maps, and even suggest excursions and
walking routes.

GETTING THERE In the summer, more than a dozen car ferries make the daily hour-
long journey from Split to Supetar on Brač's northern shore; and high-speed catamarans
travel to Bol on the southern shore. Car ferries from Makarska run to Sumartin on Brač's
eastern shore. Several independent ferry services run between Brač and Hvar.

GETTING AROUND Buses run from Supetar to Bol six times a day and to several
other towns and villages on Brač three times daily, but making connections can be limit-
ing. The best way to explore more than one town per visit is to rent a car, a motor scooter,
or even a bike (in Supetar) and explore the island independently. If you plan to stay in
one place on Brač, walking is the preferred mode of travel. There are a limited number
of bikes and mopeds for rent in Supetar, but there are no cars for rent unless you arrange
to have one available before you arrive.

WHAT TO SEE & DO

Supetar and Bol are the locations most frequented by visitors to Brač. Supetar is by far
the closer landing point from Split, but its **horseshoe-shaped beach** ★ is quite ordinary
and not as interesting or as attractive as the famous **Zlati Rat (Golden Cape)** ★★ at
Bol. Supetar does have a resort hotel complex and a decent-size pebble beach, but it
doesn't have the cachet of its glamorous counterpart on the other side of the island.
However, both towns are ideal locations for diving and other watersports thanks to their
clear water and prevailing winds.

Supetar ★

With 3,500 inhabitants, Supetar is the largest town on Brač. The ferries landing at Supetar deposit passengers on a dock that sits just outside the town's quaint center at the
business end of the beach. The beach starts south of the dock and curves away from the

town toward the west up to the island's main hotel complex, which is home to three large package hotels and several smaller establishments.

Supetar's tourism revolves around its beach, which arcs away from the ferry port and is the center of almost all activity. The town does have a few other sites that can keep anyone busy for an afternoon. The best of these is the Baroque **Church of the Annunciation** ★, which is a short uphill walk from the port toward the city center. Next to the church on the left, you'll find remnants of a **mosaic floor** ★★ that was part of an early (6th c.) church dedicated to St. Peter and built on this site. The present church was built on top of its predecessor. What's left of the original church's floor is in sections *in situ* on the ground, open to the elements and foot traffic. The courtyard entrance is graced by a very modern bust depicting **Mother Teresa** ★.

As you explore the church grounds, you should note the church's bronze doors and the Stations of the Cross chiseled in stone and hung on the rock wall that leads to a bell tower to the right of the church.

Supetar's **cemetery** and its ornate **Petrinović Mausoleum** ★ are other attractions worthy of a stop. The cemetery is at the far end of the beach on a small, eerie-looking peninsula draped with cypress trees. Supetar native Ivan Rendić (1839–1932) is responsible for creating many of the unique grave markers there and for the huge Petrinović tomb built for shipping tycoon Francisco Petrinović, who was born in Croatia. The cemetery is also home to two stone Christian sarcophagi and the ruins of a Roman *villa rustica*. Sculpture in the cemetery ranges from classical to Byzantine, and if you enjoy necropolis art, you'll love poking around this collection.

After you've investigated the cemetery, you'll find that the allure of Supetar's attractions falls off sharply. However, you can take quick bus trips from Supetar to **Škrip**, the oldest settlement on Brač; or to **Milna**, birthplace of tennis ace Goran Ivanisevic. Or you can take the ferry back to Split or hop a bus to Bol.

Bol ★★★

Bol is home to what may be Croatia's most publicized beach. Almost every photo touting the country's unspoiled landscapes uses an aerial shot of **Zlatni Rat (Golden Cape)** ★★ beach in its promotions. From the air, Zlatni Rat does look like a long, inviting tendril of white sand lazily stretching into the sparkling azure sea. Add a gorgeous sunbather lounging here and there and the shape-shifting strip of land appears to be the perfect place for an idyllic sojourn. In reality, Zlatni Rat is a sun-washed finger of land that juts into the sea west of town. The Golden Cape is anything but a good choice for a dreamy vacation; and it isn't made of sand. Rather, Zlatni Rat is a mini-peninsula topped with chicken-egg-size pebbles and packed with people during the summer months. You can rent a beach chair and umbrella for 60kn a day if baking on hot rocks under a relentless sun doesn't appeal to you. If you don't enjoy sharing a beach and bathing area with a cast of thousands, you may wonder what all the Zlatni Rat fuss is about. On the bright side, the water off Zlatni Rat deepens gradually from the shore, and it is interesting to hear the cacophony of languages and pickup lines tossed about on the beach and to see the various sunbathing "styles" present there. If you just want to see the place but don't want to invest in the 20-minute walk each way to get from town to the beach, a water taxi shuttles passengers between the dock at the west end of town and the beach for 5kn.

To be sure, Zlatni Rat is more upscale and tourist-savvy than the beach at Supetar, its sister to the north, and there is a certain satisfaction in setting foot on this super-hyped playground. But if sun worship isn't for you, stay in town and duck into

Branislav-Dešković Modern Art Gallery at Porat Bolskih Pomoraca bb near the tourist office in Bol. It is open in July and August only (daily 6pm–midnight) and has a fine collection of Brač landscapes from such renowned Croatian artists as Ivan Rendić, the man who created much of the sepulchral art in Supetar's cemetery.

Watersports ★★★

Bol has a worldwide reputation as a windsurfer's paradise. It's not unusual to see "schools" of boarders riding the waves around the island, especially near Potočine beach west of Bol.

Big Blue Big Blue is the big kahuna of watersports in Bol, a thriving operation that caters to all levels of athletes. You can rent a board for an hour for 15€ or for a week for 150€. Big Blue also rents equipment for mountain biking, diving, and sea kayaking. You also can take a 6-day (2 hr. per day) scuba certification course for 139€, certification fee not included.

Podan Glavice 2 (near the Hotel Borak btw. Zlani Rat and town). ℂ 021/635-614. www.big-blue-sport.hr.

WHERE TO STAY

In Supetar, most accommodations consist of package hotels at the west end of town, though you can secure private accommodations at the tourist office near the dock (p. 129). You also can inquire wherever you see a SOBE sign. Bol has rooms in well-equipped resort hotels, too, but it also has some charming private accommodations.

In Bol, you can book private accommodations at Boltours at Vladimira Nazora 18 (ℂ 021/635-693; fax 021/635-695; www.boltours.com).

Dominikanski Samostan Campground (Dominican Monastery) ★★★ (Finds) This campground east of town near the Dominican Monastery has limited space (70 sites) and is run by monks. Exceptionally popular because of its location near the sea and its well-kept facilities, it is always full. However, if you are inclined to walk around in a state of skimpy dishabille, this is not the place for you. The site is posted with dress-code signs.

Šetalište Andeleka Rabadana. ℂ 021/635-132. 70 campsites. May–Oct: 105kn 2 adults. No credit cards.

Hotel Kaktus ★★ This Supetar hotel is one of several managed by the same company (Waterman Resorts) in a gated compound on the west side of the city and beach. Kaktus is the epitome of a resort hotel, a white multilevel building with services galore. Guest rooms are smallish but immaculate, and most have balconies that overlook the pool or the sea. In reality, the facilities here outshine the town's offerings, but be warned that if you make a reservation for a single night (if you can get one), you'll pay considerably more than the going rate for multiday stays, a practice that is all too common in Croatia.

Put Vela Luke 4, Supetar. ℂ 021/640-155. Fax 021/631-344. www.watermanresorts.com. 120 units. Mid-July to mid-Aug from 100€ double with half-board. Rest of year from 46€ double with half-board. **Amenities:** 3 restaurants; bar; 2 pools; sauna; spa; tennis courts; diving school. In room: A/C, TV, Internet access, minibar.

Hotel Kaštil ★★★ Hotel Kaštil is loaded with personality thanks to its location in an old Baroque fortress on the water near the town center. It is the most interesting place to stay in Bol. Each of the Kaštil's 32 guest rooms is unique, modern, and cheery, in keeping with the welcoming atmosphere of the hotel's public spaces. The partially covered pizzeria on a terrace overlooking the water is an especially nice place to dine.

Frane Radića 1, Bol. ℂ 021/635-995. Fax 021/635-997. www.kastil.hr. 32 units. July–Aug from 140€ double. Rest of year from 64€ double. Rates include breakfast. MC, V. **Amenities:** 2 restaurants; pizzeria; bar. In room: A/C, TV.

Hotel Pastura ★★ (Finds) This blue and white hotel is right on the water in Postira, 10km (6 miles) from the Supetar ferry port, making the hotel close enough for convenience and remote enough for a vacation that makes rat-race stress disappear. The architecture and interior design are reminiscent of an Art Deco ocean liner, and guest rooms in the hotel are furnished accordingly. All have barrier-free views of the sea, too. There is a gorgeous, oval, fresh water pool, a pretty restaurant whose glass walls showcase the scenery, and bike rentals if you decide you want to commune with nature at close range.

21410 Postira. ✆ **021/740-000** or 021/632 100. Fax 021/632-109. www.hotelpastura.hr. 50 units, including 4 apts. Early Apr to mid-Oct. Doubles from 110€. **Amenities:** Restaurant; bar; fitness center; pool; sauna. *In room:* A/C, TV, minibar.

Hotel Riu Borak ★★ This all-inclusive Blue Sun hotel, just a 10-minute walk from either Zlatni Rat or town, is set back in the trees so you are away from the constant stream of people heading to the beach. Guest rooms in the renovated hotel are spacious and equipped with all the comforts of home. In addition, most rooms have balconies that overlook the pool or the beach.

Bračka Cesta 13. 21420 t, Bol. ✆ **021/306-202** or 021/635-210. Fax 021/306-215. www.riu.com. 234 units. July–Aug from 185€ double; from 210€ suite. Rest of year from 145€ double; suite 117€. Rates include breakfast and dinner. AE, MC, V. **Amenities:** Restaurant; 2 bars; children's program; Internet; pool; solarium; tennis center; live music. *In room:* A/C, TV, hair dryer, minibar.

Hotel Villa Adriatica ★ This small hotel is more intimate than the neighboring resort hotels. If you are looking for a more personal experience, this is the place. Guest rooms are spare, but each is decorated with quality furniture and lively colors, and each has a balcony. The tiled bathrooms are adequate; most have showers. The individual attention you'll get from the staff makes up for any shortcomings. *Tip:* Proprietors Zlatan and Nevenka Jelovac are walking encyclopedias when it comes to Brač's history and little-known treasures. Ask them for suggestions about hiking trails, secluded coves, and other "discoveries."

Put Vele Luke 31, Supetar. ✆ **021/343-806.** Fax 021/755-015. www.villaadriatica.com. 22 units. Late July to late Aug from 108€ double. Rest of year from 66€ double. Closed Nov–Mar. Rates include buffet breakfast. MC, V. **Amenities:** Restaurant; cafe; bar; bike rental; minigolf; pool; tennis courts; volleyball; watersports; excursions. *In room:* A/C, TV.

Palača Dešković ★★★ Rooms in this 15th-century former mansion are filled with art, antiques, and other beautiful accoutrements; Countess Ružica Dešković is the hotel's charming hostess. Palača Dešković is on Brač's north coast, 21km (12 miles) east of Supetar, and out of the center of the island's tourism flow, but that's part of its allure. You can pretend that you are as royal as the countess herself in the hotel's elegant restaurant, on a yacht in its private harbor, or even in your room surrounded by period furniture and the countess's artwork. Modern touches like heated bathroom floors, Jacuzzis, and Internet connectivity add to, rather than detract from, the hotel's Renaissance ambience.

21412 Pučišč, Brač. ✆ **021/778-240.** Fax 021/778-247. www.palaca-deskovic.com. 15 units. Doubles from 206€; suites from 248€ July–Aug. Other times doubles from 124€; suites from 148€. Closed Jan to mid-Feb. DC, MC, V. **Amenities:** Restaurant; bar; marina. *In room:* A/C, TV, Internet, Jacuzzi, minibar.

WHERE TO DINE

Restaurants in both Bol and Supetar are pretty predictable, though Bol has a better selection. Most of the people who book rooms on Brač stay in the resort complexes and take few and far between except for cafes and pizzerias.

Bistro Palute ★ (Value DALMATIAN   You can watch locals demolish huge plates of fish at this local hangout with tables inside and out. *Janjetina* (roasted or grilled lamb) is one of the specialties. Palute also operates a bed-and-breakfast.

Put Pašike 16, Supetar. ✆ **021/631-730.** palute@st.htnet.hr. Entrees 35kn–49kn. AE, MC, V. Daily 8am–3am.

Bistro Pumparela ★ DALMATIAN   This little place on the harbor serves breakfast, lunch, and dinner. You can eat indoors or outdoors in little wooden booths. Well-prepared fish and pasta are the menu mainstays for dinner.

Porat Bolskih Pomoraca bb, Bol. ✆ **021/635-886.** Entrees 50kn–140kn. No credit cards. Daily 6am–2am.

Konoba Gušt ★★ DALMATIAN   A limited menu is listed on a chalkboard at this taverna near the Hotel Kaštil and just behind the Riva, but it offers the fish and pasta dishes you would expect at any good island restaurant in Dalmatia. Gušt also has a few traditional beef preparations and a dynamite lobster salad. The dining room is air-conditioned and decorated with agri-art (farming implements). The terrace has just six tables and a great breeze. Regardless of where you sit, start your meal with a bottle of local wine and end with herb-infused *rakija* (a strong brandy), if you dare.

Frane Radića 14, Bol. ✆ **021/635-911.** www.bol.hr/index.php?ukljuci=taverna%20gust. Entrees 122kn–175kn. No credit cards. Daily noon–2am.

Restaurant Dolac ★★ DALMATIAN   You can't really call Dolac a fancy restaurant, but it is a little more upscale than most of the places in Supetar. Dolac sits behind a stone wall and has lots of courtyard tables shaded by trees and a tiled canopy. The menu lists the usual assortment of grilled fish and pasta, but there are some very nice steaks offered here, too.

Ulica Petra Jakšića 6, Supetar. ✆ **021/630-446** or 021/630-445. Entrees 40kn–80kn. AE, DC, MC, V. Daily 3pm–midnight.

Taverna Riva ★★★ DALMATIAN   Riva is next door to the Hotel Kaštil. It is also at the edge of the sea, which makes dining at the outdoor terrace tables an invigorating and romantic experience. Try a creative fish dish like squid Pandora (cylinders of tender calamari stuffed with Dalmatian ham and cheese) or one of the steaks. If you make reservations 48 hours ahead and can muster a party of four, Riva will prepare lamb or veal on the *peka.* One server unabashedly said that Riva is the best restaurant in Bol, bar none; he recommended the Vrhunsko vino Bol, the area's best wine. Riva is much pricier than any other restaurant in town, but it is also Bol's finest dining experience.

Frane Radica 5, Bol. ✆ **021/635-236.** www.bolnabracu.com/eng/taverna.htm. Reservations required. Entrees 58kn–200kn. AE, DC, MC, V. Daily noon–2pm and 6pm–midnight.

LOWER DALMATIA

6

BRAČ

Ordering a "Peka" Dish

Food cooked under a *peka,* or cooking bell, is usually ordered 24 hours ahead of time. The peka is covered with hot ashes while underneath it the meat (lamb) bakes with potatoes and vegetables. Complete cooking usually takes 2 hours.

7 HVAR

St. Tropez, Majorca, Aspen, and other glamour destinations don't have anything on Hvar, the glitzy Croatian playground patronized by celebrities, the idle rich, and the average Joe tourist who wants to be part of the Hvar hoopla.

Hvar is indeed a lush, sunny Shangri-La with more hours of sunshine (2,724) than any other place in Croatia, according to the literature. But when you're talking just 24 more hours of rays than Brač (2,700) and only 124 hours (4 days) more than most of Croatia's other islands, you're splitting hairs. Ultraviolet rays aside, Hvar is a hilly piece of real estate with vineyards, lavender fields, a few interesting sites, a lot of good restaurants, and some überexpensive places to stay.

Hvar's principal towns are Hvar Town, Stari Grad, Vrboska, Jelsa, and Sucuraj, though Hvar Town seems to be the center of current interest in the island.

ESSENTIALS

VISITOR INFORMATION   Hvar Town's principal **tourist office** is at Trg Sv. Stjepana bb, Hvar's main square (✆ **021/741-059;** fax 021/742-977; www.tzhvar.hr; 8am–2:30pm and 3:30–10pm daily June–Oct, 8am–2pm Mon–Sat Nov–May). Stari Grad's is at Nova Riva 2 (✆ **021/765-763;** www.hvar.hr; summer 8am–10pm Mon–Sat, 9am–1pm and 5–8pm Sun; winter 8am–2pm Mon–Sat). Jelsa's tourist office is at Mala Banda (✆ **021/761-017;** summer 8am–11pm Mon–Sat, 10:30am–12:30pm and 7:30–9:30pm Sun; winter 8am–1pm Mon–Fri). Each can provide literature and maps, but if you want accommodations in Hvar Town, go to **Pelegrini Travel,** steps from the boat landing (✆ **021/742-743;** pelegrini@inet.hr), open 8am to 10pm Monday through Saturday and 6 to 8pm on Sunday. Pelegrini handles most of the private accommodations in Hvar Town and books rooms through travel agencies in Split and other towns. **Atlas Travel,** on the west side of the harbor (✆ **021/741-670**), is an excellent place to book excursions. During July and August, there is the potential for a reservation snafu, so be sure you have confirmed—and preferably paid for—accommodations before arrival.

GETTING THERE   Jadrolinija operates car ferry service between Split and Stari Grad (38kn per person and 250kn per car each way), and some runs also stop at Korčula and Dubrovnik. Car ferries from Dnvenik, just south of Makarska, dock at Sucuraj at the extreme southern tip of the island (13kn per person and 95kn per car each way). From May through September pedestrian-only ferries and catamarans dock at Hvar Town at the extreme northern end (30kn per person each way). Stari Grad and Hvar Town are 77km (46 miles) and a narrow, hilly, serpentine road with spectacular views of the sea apart. Buses connect from the ferry port in Stari Grad and go across the island to Hvar Town and Jelsa seven times a day (20kn per person each way). Jadrolinija has an office on the Riva in Stari Grad (✆ **021/741-132**) and can provide prices and schedules. In summer, there usually are half a dozen or so buses that ply the route between Stari Grad and Hvar Town, but Sundays, holidays, and other times, service is spotty. Catamarans that carry only foot passengers also serve the island, and they are faster than the car ferries. Most pick up and drop off passengers at the Hvar Town marina. It is possible to spend the morning in Korčula and go on to Hvar in the afternoon. However, you'll have to overnight on Hvar because the last boat arrives there about 6:15pm, and nothing leaves late at night. In addition, it is very difficult to see much on Hvar if you only have a day.

ACCOMMODATIONS ■
Hotel Adriana 2
Hotel Amfora 1
Hotel Croatia 1
Hotel Palace 3
Hotel Podstine 1
Hotel Riva 12

DINING ◆
BB Club 12
Buffet Đorđe Pošteni 10
Đordota Votal 13
Hanibal 9
Lucullus 4
Macondo 8

Palača Paladini 5
Restaurant Kod
    Matkovića 11
Restaurant Luna 7
Sora 2 12
Val Marina 2
Zlatna Školjka
    (Golden Shell) 6

GETTING AROUND   Hvar Town is closed to motorized traffic from the bus station to the Riva, which is also the busiest thoroughfare until after nightfall, when the long, rectangular main square, Trg Sveti Stjepana, becomes a circus. If you want to see anything besides Hvar Town and Stari Grad, a car is a time saver, but Hvar Town is best covered on foot.

WHAT TO SEE & DO

Hvar Town is St. Moritz with surf instead of snow. It's Hollywood meets Nice, Milan sophistication melded with Mediterranean relaxation, and the Las Vegas Strip transported to Tuscany. Hvar Town is a magnet for rock stars, tycoons, and the hip beautiful people drawn to their blazing orbits.

The uniqueness of the place is that everyone looks rich and famous. It's difficult to recognize even a well-known face because in Hvar Town a pair of Maui Jim's sunglasses, designer jeans, and a look of ennui are enough for anyone to blend into the sculpted, perfumed crowd.

Make no mistake, Hvar Town has a nice cache of lazy, sensual countryside and 13th-century attractions. However, it's really the sun, the sea, and the 21st-century social scene that pull in visitors, who make their entrances on everything from sleek yachts to ferries packed sardine-style. But even if you're here for the beach scene, be sure to check out **St. Stephen's Square (Trg Sveti Stjepan)** ★★★. Dating from the 13th century, this square is Hvar Town's center of activity. It is book ended by St. Stephen's Cathedral at its east end and by a small harbor on the west. The square's borders are lined with restaurants, cafes, and galleries. A 16th-century well sits in the center of the paved space, which was redone in the late 18th century.

Fortress (Fortica) ★★   The large 16th-century fortress that stands above Hvar Town once was a medieval castle. The current structure, built by the Venetians, is worth the climb to see spectacular views of Hvar Town's rooftops and its harbor from the ramparts. Inside the fortress you'll find displays of amphorae found offshore; and you can visit a spooky dungeon. There is a small cafe atop the castle. The walk up to the fortress is a nice but challenging trek during the day, but at night the climb can be treacherous because the steps/path leading up to the site are not lighted.

North of Hvar Town center. ℂ **021/741-816.** Admission 10kn. Summer daily 8am–midnight; by appointment only in winter.

Franciscan Monastery ★★   Walk along the sea to the 15th-century monastery south of the center and enter through a graceful cloister, where concerts are held every 2 days during the summer. Inside there's a nice museum with a collection of sacral art. The museum opens to an idyllic garden with a view of the sea. The adjacent church, Our Lady of Mercy, also dates from the 15th century and it is home to three notable polyptychs and many other pieces of religious art.

Hvar Town. ℂ **021/741-123.** Admission 10kn. Summer daily 10am–noon and 5–7pm; winter daily 10am–noon. Performance times and prices vary.

St. Stephen's Cathedral ★   St. Stephen's is an unremarkable triple-aisled church with a nice 17th-century bell tower. The inside has quite a few late-Renaissance paintings and a nice wooden 16th-century choir area.

Trg Sv. Stjepana bb. Daily 7am–noon and 5–7pm. Hours sometimes extended during tourist season.

Venetian Loggia & Clock Tower ★★★ The Loggia and Clock Tower are part of the Hotel Palace's face to the world. The Loggia is a fine example of Renaissance architecture, but it was damaged by the Turks in 1571, repaired, and then used as a cafe from the late 19th century to as recently as the early 1970s. Today it frames elegant vintage salon in the Hotel Palace, complete with a grand piano. The clock tower was built in the 19th century on the site of the ducal palace, which was destroyed in the same assault that damaged the Loggia.

Trg Sv. Stjepana bb.

Beaches

Hvar Town has a public beach west of the center. It is a pebble beach and, like most of the patches of Croatian land that have either been turned into paved strips or covered with pebbles and proclaimed a beach, this one is usually crowded with sunbathers from the nearby package **Hotel Amfora.** However, for a mere 10kn, you can hop a taxi boat to nearby **Pakleni Otoci,** a cluster of pine-forested, uninhabited islands whose coastlines are alternately rimmed with rocks and little pebble beaches. The **Bonj Les Bains beach club** at the Hotel Amfora is a swanky addition to the Hvar beach scene. All beaches in Croatia are open to the public by law, but you have to pay to use the Amfora's cabanas and sun beds, which are on the free beach. You don't have to stay at the Amfora to use Bonj Les Bains, but you do have to pay a hefty daily fee to use the equipment on its beach—from 48€ per day for two sun beds, two towels, an umbrella, and a table to 111€ per day for the same equipment plus a stone cabana.

Watersports & Excursions

This part of Croatia is home to some of the best conditions in Europe for windsurfing, kite boarding, jet-skiing, sailing, diving, and swimming.

Dive Center Jurgavan ★★★ This large professional dive center near the Hotel Amfora runs diving trips between Hvar and the island of Vis, which recently has become the darling of extreme sports enthusiasts. The Dive Center offers a long menu of dive services and trips and supports other watersports such as water-skiing, snorkeling, kite boarding, windsurfing, and banana boating. It also rents boats, kayaks, and equipment to go with all its sports. Dives cost from 250kn for a single dive including equipment to an all-inclusive certification course for 2,360kn.

At the Hotel Amfora. ✆ **021/742-490.** www.divecenter-hvar.com.

Sunčani Hvar Hotels ★★★ The folks here will customize a tour according to guests' specifications whether you are a guest of a Sunčani Hotel or not. Choose from hiking, diving, boating, or combination experiences. Go to the front desk of any Sunčani hotel on the island (Adriatic, Riva) for details or contact concierge@suncani.com. Prices vary according to tour features and duration.

Viking Diving Center ★★ The Petrinovic family runs this establishment next to the Podstine Hotel, and it can furnish equipment, instruction, and even rooms. Many of Viking's diving excursions go to the waters off Pakleni Otoci. Viking offers a wide range of options: You can buy almost any service, from a single dive at 220kn, to a package of 5 days and 10 dives for 1,720kn, to a full-day trip with cave diving for 490kn, and everything in between. Equipment rental is extra.

Podstine bb. 21450 Hvar. ✆ **021/742-529.** www.viking-diving.com.

> **(Fun Facts** Hvar Hero
>
> Petar Hektorović (1487–1572) was a Hvar local and a poet who lived during the Croatian Renaissance. He built the Tvradlj (palace) on the south side of Stari Grad's harbor as his summer house and as a kind of safe house for the island's people in case of attack. The interior features a courtyard garden and trout pond. The pond's purpose was to provide food, should the island come under attack.

WHERE TO STAY

There are no hotel bargains in Hvar Town, and most of the accommodations in Stari Grad are huge, impersonal package resorts. Since the island became all the rage, innkeepers have been scrambling to expand and renovate, and the result is that prices are escalating faster than the hotel improvements. You still can find modestly priced private accommodations, but in the summer you probably will have to book for 4 days or more just to get a reservation.

Very Expensive

Adriana ★★★   After a 2-year renovation, the Adriana emerged in 2007 as Croatia's first member of the Leading Small Hotels of the World. Adriana deserves the recognition. Its rooftop terrace has a heated indoor/outdoor seawater pool plus bar and lounge area. Guest rooms are spacious and full of light, which makes for a relaxing ambience. Bathrooms are big and ergonomic and stocked with plenty of toiletries. Adriana's Sensori Spa is the Adriana's showpiece. Besides the usual beauty and massage services, the spa offers boutique services like a VIP suite for couples, an olive leaf and salt scrub, and a sea mud wrap.

Fabrika bb. ℂ **021/750-200.** Fax 021/750-201. www.suncanihvar.com. 59 units. Doubles from 350€; suites from 420€. Rates include breakfast. **Amenities:** Restaurant, cafe; 2 bars; pool; spa. *In room:* A/C, TV, hair dryer, minibar, free Wi-Fi.

Hotel Amfora ★★★   The Amfora opened to great fanfare in 2008 in a pine forest 10 minutes from St. Stephen's Square in Hvar Town. Everything in the newest kid on the block is luxe, including a pool with cascading waterfalls and garden islands, the **Maestral restaurant** (see below) set on a yacht, lush landscaping, and a spa. Rooms are outfitted with modern electronics and decor, and all have park or sea views. *Tip:* The Amfora's **Bonj Les Bains private beach club** ★★★ is an oasis of decadence from yesteryear. Rent a stone cabana with sun beds and table for 111€ per day for two at the refurbished 1930s facility.

Majerovic bb. ℂ **021/750-300.** Fax 021/750-301. 319 units. Doubles with sea view from 275€; studio suites from 384€; 2-bedroom suites from 590€. **Amenities:** 3 restaurants; 4 bars; pool; private beach club; spa. *In room:* A/C, TV, hair dryer, minibar, free Wi-Fi.

Riva ★★   Riva (formerly Slavija) wins the ugly-duckling-to-swan award and it's *still* all about location. Anyone who stays at this hotel about 9m (30 ft.) from the pier where catamaran passengers disembark and luxury yachts tie up has a bird's-eye view of the waterfront action and now they also have plush surroundings: Renovation and cutting-edge design turned this historic building into a hip place to stay, dine, and socialize. Rooms are small because of the building's protected status, but now they have ultramodern bathrooms, flatscreen TVs, slick designer colors, and walk-out patios. The hotel's

terrace is home to a **pizzeria** ★ and **Sora 2** ★★, a sushi house that leaves Zagreb for
Hvar in summer, then goes back to the big city when the tourists do.

Riva bb, Hvar Town. ☎ **021/741-820.** Fax 021/741-147. www.suncanihvar.com/riva. 54 units. July 4 to
late Aug sea-view/balcony doubles from 319€; sea-view suites from 394€; Riva suite from 515€. Rest of
year sea-view doubles from 308€; sea-view suites from 381€; Riva suite from 515€. Rates include breakfast. AE, DC, MC, V. **Amenities:** Restaurant; bar; spa access. *In room:* A/C, TV, hair dryer, free Wi-Fi.

Expensive

Hotel Croatia   From the outside, Hotel Croatia looks like an upscale mansion nestled
in a woodsy flower garden. Inside, it's evident that the hotel was built during the Tito
regime and is caught in a time warp. Rooms are tiny, dark, and cooled by a table fan,
while the bathrooms are closet-size and dimly lit. While the hotel's location a few yards
from the sea is a plus, its value-for-dollar is very low.

Majerovica bb, Hvar Town. ☎ **021/741-707.** Fax 021/742-400. www.hotelcroatia.net. 28 units, including
6 family units joined by a bathroom. Mid-July to Aug seaside doubles from 140€; family units (4 persons)
from 252€. Other times seaside doubles from 58€; family units (4 persons) from 154€. Rates include
breakfast. **Amenities:** Restaurant; bar; Internet. *In room:* TV, fan, hair dryer.

Hotel Palace ★ (**Overrated**   This grande dame is behind the 16th-century loggia that
once graced the town's ducal palace. The Palace was built in the early 20th century and
has many elegant features that haven't changed much over the years. Despite its soaring
ceilings and architectural appointments, the Palace's guest rooms are small, dated, and
without air-conditioning. Oddly, the color scheme on the guest floors is peach and
Miami aqua, which only ages this lady more. If you open a window in your room, you'll
hear the noise on the square or beyond, and that can last until sunrise.

Trg Sveti Stjepana bb. ☎ **021/741-966.** Fax 021/742-240. www.suncanihvar.hr. 73 units. Mid-July to Aug
from 916kn. double. Rest of year from 420kn double. AE, DC, MC, V. Rates include breakfast. **Amenities:**
Restaurant; bar; pool. *In room:* TV.

Hotel Podstine ★★★   The Podstine is surrounded by palm and citrus trees and is
next to its own beach, which is actually a concrete strip with a view of the Pakleni Islands.
The hotel is a good 20-minute walk from the hotel to the center of town but it has its
own shuttle, which will take you to the ferry landing or pick you up when you arrive.

(Fun Facts   Lavender Blues

Hvar is sometimes known as "Lavender Island" because the graceful plant with
silver-green foliage and a hypnotic, soothing fragrance grows all over the place.
Lavendula, as the plant is known in botanical circles, is a native of the dry Mediterranean climate and is the subject of many legends and superstitions. It is also
thought to have medicinal properties.

   On Hvar, lavender is an industry and you'll pick up the lavender scent as soon
as you disembark from the boat that brought you there, because it is sold in
kiosks up and down the dock at Hvar Town and at the ferry port at Sucuraj. It is
said that the whole island is enveloped in a cloud of lavender scent in the spring,
and that may be so. But even after hiking in the Hvar hills, the only lavender we
saw or smelled originated at the kiosks at the dock.

Guest rooms are clean and those on the upper floors have nice views. The shaded dining terrace is a wonderful place to kick back with a glass of wine.

Pod Stine. ℂ 021/740-400. Fax 021/740-499. www.podstine.com. 40 units. Mid-July to late Aug from 1,860kn seaside double. Rest of year from 1,085kn seaside double. AE, DC, MC, V. Guarded parking. **Amenities:** Restaurant; bar; diving center; excursions; bike, scooter, and car rental; room service. *In room:* A/C, TV, minibar.

WHERE TO DINE

Most of the restaurants up and down the Hvar Town harbor serve similar fare—pizza, pasta, and grilled fish. However, restaurants in richly renovated hotels and in the narrow, unnamed streets off squarest. Stephen's Square and the Riva offer distinctive dining experiences.

Very Expensive

Luna ★★★ DALMATIAN   Few experiences are more romantic than dining alfresco on a flower-filled rooftop terrace under a sky ablaze with stars, especially when the food is superb and the service impeccable. Don't let the arrival of the bill spoil the mood—the experience is worth every penny, especially if you've splurged on the Lobster Lunatic, a dish using the pricey crustacean, white wine, tomatoes, and brandy (490kn). A gratis pâté helps ease the pain of sticker shock.

Petra Hektorovića, Groda. ℂ 021/741 400. Entrees 80kn–490kn. AE, DC, V. May–Sept daily noon–midnight; Oct–Apr daily noon–3pm and 6pm–midnight.

Maestral ★★★ SEAFOOD   There's something seductive about dining on a yacht even if the yacht is moored in a harbor at the Hotel Amfora. Besides the rush of being on the water instead of next to it, the exclusivity of sitting at a table on a polished teak deck under a floaty white tent gazing at a horizon that melts into the water adds a unique dimension to every bite. Not that the Maestral's creations need help. Any grilled Adriatic fish dish is a winner. Did we mention the *Klapa* singers whose a cappella strains float through the night air during dinner?

At the Hotel Amfora, Amfora Bay. ℂ 021/750-300. www.suncanihvar.hr. Entrees 70kn–250kn. AE, DC, MC, V. Daily 11am–midnight June–Sept.

Val Marina ★★★ SEAFOOD   The lobby of the ultrachic Hotel Adriana is the setting for this inventive, classy restaurant, whose menu is based on local produce and seafood, Hvar wines, and the chef's talent and imagination. For an unforgettable dining experience, book a table with a view of the harbor and try the divine but pricey five-course Dalmatian Blue, which features Dalmatian lobster.

In the Hotel Adriana, Fabrika. ℂ 021/750-750. www.suncanihvar.com. Reservations recommended. Entrees 75kn–180kn; 400kn for the Dalmatian Blue experience. AE, DC, MC, V. Daily 11am–midnight.

Expensive

Đorđota Vartal ★★ DALMATIAN   This terrace restaurant on an elevated stone porch is a world all its own, with a vine-covered canopy and potted lavender plants. The menu is typical Dalmatian with pasta and grilled meat and fish. There is also a great *brujet* (spicy fish stew) and, of course, lobster.

Križna Luka 8. ℂ 021/743-077. djordje.tudor@st.t-com.hr. Reservations recommended. Entrees 45kn–160kn, more for lobster and fish by the kilo. AE, MC, V. Daily noon–midnight. Closed Oct 15–Apr 1.

Gostiona Kod Matkovića ★ Ⓥⓐⓛⓤⓔ SEAFOOD   This courtyard restaurant off the Riva isn't anything unusual in fish-crazy Dalmatia, but besides its well-rounded

The Rest of Hvar

Hvar Town has become synonymous with the island itself, but Hvar is blessed with beautiful real estate away from the glitzy enclave that is perfect for nature and history lovers.

If you hit Hvar at Stari Grad, resist the impulse to cover the 77km (46 miles) between there and Hvar Town as fast as possible and take time to see the land between the two. History is on display at **Stari Grad** ★, the island's main ferry port. Head for **Tvrdalj** ★★, 16th-century poet Petar Hektorović's castle, which has a fine garden and a trout pond inside (✆ **021/766-324;** admission 15kn). Then take a peek at the **Dominican Monastery** ★ off the harbor; admission 10kn. Both are open 10am to noon and 6 to 8pm daily in summer only.

As you leave Stari Grad, look for signs directing you to **Vrboska,** 6km (4 miles) east. Stop at the **Church of St. Mary,** which is only open for Mass. If you can't get in, go to the nearby **Church of St. Lawrence,** which houses some of the Venetian art that once adorned St. Mary's. Open daily 10am to noon and 5 to 7pm.

Go back to the main road, which is narrow, twisting, hilly, and a vantage point for gorgeous views of the sea. Eventually, you'll come to **Jelsa** ★, Hvar's family resort town. Stroll around **Old Town** on the harbor; visit the **Church of St. Ivan** (irregular hours), and stop for gelato at any of the cafes that line the harbor. From Jelsa, you can detour to any of the villages that dot the hilly Hvar interior for a look at lavender fields, olive groves, grazing sheep and goats, and abandoned stone dwellings. You'll arrive at Hvar Town rested and ready to party.

seafood/shellfish offerings, Matkovića also has a nice selection of meats, including spit-roasted lamb. Wine selections are limited to the house white or red. Service can be very slow when all the tables are taken.

55 Godina Tradicije. Hvar Town. ✆ **021/741-854.** Entrees 35kn–150kn, more for fish sold by the kilo. AE, DC, MC, V. Daily noon–2pm and 6pm–midnight.

Hanibal ★★ DALMATIAN Hanibal has been a fixture in Hvar Town since 1997 and it's a good choice. The tables outside are usually crammed until midnight, so you might have to settle for a spot in the polished wood interior where model ships are mounted on Plexiglas. Try the stuffed squid, the scampi risotto, or the grilled lamb, and you can be sure it will be prepared to your liking. Service is cordial and attentive.

Trg Sv. Stjepana 12. ✆ **021/742-760.** Reservations recommended. Entrees 70kn–140kn. AE, DC, MC, V. Daily 10am–midnight.

Lucullus ★★ DALMATIAN Light-slow food is how the chef describes his menu. That translates to a leisurely meal of well-prepared seafood and Dalmatian specialties served in a convivial atmosphere. Wood-grilled pizza is on the menu, but try the island lobster *brodeto* in Lucullus's cozy dining room or at home—the chef shares his recipe for *brodeto* and for lobster stew with tomatoes and onions *(gregada)* on restaurant flyers. Peka-grilled meat is available if ordered 3 hours in advance.

Off the main square. ✆ **021/742-498.** Reservations recommended. Entrees 60kn–175kn. AE, DC, V. Daily noon–1am. Closed Nov–Apr.

Macondo ★★ SEAFOOD   Macondo is a seafood restaurant off St. Stephen's Square that spills into a nameless alley. Portions are huge, prices are moderate, and the waitstaff is young and friendly. Try the *gregada,* a garlicky seafood stew.

Groda bb. ✆ **021/742-850.** Entrees 45kn–110kn. AE, DC, MC, V. Daily 11am–midnight.

Palača Paladini ★★★ SEAFOOD   A beautiful garden setting with stone walls and orange trees is the setting for this attractive bi-level restaurant specializing in slow food. Try anything grilled from the huge seafood menu, or go vegetarian with an amazing creation called "vegetarian pleasure."

Petra Hektorovića 4. ✆ **021/742-104.** www.tihi-hvar.com. Reservations recommended. Entrees 70kn–160kn. AE, DC, MC, V. Daily noon–3pm and 6pm–midnight. Closed Jan 15–May 15.

Zlatna Školjka ★★ MODERN DALMATIAN   The affable owner says that slow food is the opposite of fast food, which doesn't begin to explain this Croatian style of dining. It's really a leisurely presentation of courses, leaving time for diners to savor their meals. Start with Dalmatian ham and goat cheese in olive oil, and follow that with steak stuffed with goat cheese and capers, the excellent lamb stew, or grilled fish. This is a place where food is an art form.

Petra Hektorovica 8. ✆ **098/168-797.** Entrees 75kn–175kn. No credit cards. Daily noon–3pm and 7pm–midnight. May–Oct only.

Inexpensive

BB Club ★ PIZZA   Hotel Riva's high-priced, gourmet restaurant Roots is gone, and in its place is the BB Club, a shabby-chic pizzeria that caters to sightseers on the run. Besides pastas, a dozen varieties of pizza, and meal-size salads, you can get a pretty decent burger and fries at BB. *Tip:* BB closes when the Riva Hotel closes for winter renovations, but the Val Marina at the Adriana Hotel a few blocks away picks up the slack.

In the Hotel Riva on the harbor. ✆ **021/750-750.** www.suncanihvar.com. Pizzas 45kn–65kn. Entrees 6kn–80kn. Breakfast 95kn. AE, DC, MC, V. Daily 7am–midnight; bar till 1am.

HVAR AFTER DARK

Celebrities, royalty, and business tycoons firmly established Hvar as the beautiful-people capital of Croatia a decade ago when they started parking their yachts in the island's secluded harbors. While they usually rent exclusive properties surrounded by security or use their floating palaces as portable beachheads, the well-heeled guests are often seen drinking and discoing at the iconic **Carpe Diem** ★★★ on the Riva next door to Hotel Riva (✆ **021/742-369;** 9am–3am daily in summer and 9am–midnight daily other times). The **Hula Hula Beach Bar** ★★ near the Hotel Amfora on a tiny peninsula called Majerovića is the place to go for après beach cocktails, at Majerovića (no phone; 9am–9pm daily mid-May to late Sept). Champagne cocktails and late-night grazing are specialties the **Colonnade Beach Bar** ★★★ on Amfora Bay at the **Bonj les Bains beach club** at the Hotel Amfora (✆ **021/750-750;** 11am–2am daily summer only). **Zimmer Frei** ★ near the Zlatna Školjka restaurant seats patrons on chairs with white cushions spread along the narrow street in front, at Petra Hektorovića, Groda (✆ **098/559-6182;** 8pm–3am daily in summer). For the ultimate decadent Hvar cocktail experience, go to the **Top Sky Bar & Terrace** ★★★ atop the Hotel Adriana (✆ **021/750-200;** 11am–2am daily). There's a 360-degree view of the Hvar Town Harbor, call-brand cocktails, and even massages.

8 KORČULA

There is more to the island of **Korčula** ★★★ than the walled city of Korčula Town. In the less than 50km (30 miles) between the picturesque walled city at the eastern end of the island and the Vela Luka at the other end, you'll find vineyards and wineries, hills and hiking trails, and quiet towns like **Lumbarda, Smokvica,** and **Blato** with out-of-the way beaches along the coastal areas between.

KORČULA TOWN ★★★

No matter what time you arrive at Korčula Town on this close-in Adriatic island, you'll encounter crowds of people mobbing the tourist agencies on the dock looking for accommodations, maps, directions, and other information about the island before they disappear through the Land Gate and into Korčula Town's historic walled core. The island is a popular day trip from Split, Dubrovnik, and Orebič on the Pelješac Peninsula, and Korčula Town is the focus of most tourist activity on the island as well as its main transportation hub. KT's ferry landing is full of shops, kiosks, cafes, and tourism-related offices that make a disconcerting Grand Central Station impression to visitors and your first instinct might be to get back on the boat and go someplace else, but don't. Once you climb the 19th-century Grand Staircase with its 15th-century Revelin tower and walk through the 14th-century Land Gate, Korčula Town becomes a medieval cocoon that wraps you in a sense of how life was lived there centuries ago.

Behind the wall, Old Town is crisscrossed with picturesque structures built with materials cut from local islands' stone quarries. These house restaurants, museums, families, and offices. Hilly, dark, narrow streets branch off from the enclave's major north-south thoroughfare (Korčulaskog Statuta) in a pattern that resembles a trout skeleton. The street grid creates the illusion of a central boulevard with a lot of short side streets radiating from it. You can spend hours walking up and down these narrow offshoots and never know exactly where you are in relation to the walled town's exit. *Tip:* The approach to Korčula Town on the morning ferry from Orebič makes one of the best vacation pictures ever.

The island of Korčula, which is just a little over a mile from the mainland across the Pelješac Channel, once was covered with so many pine trees that the sight led the Greeks who settled there around 400 B.C. to dub the island Kerkyra Malaina (Black Corfu). As with many of the islands in the southern Adriatic, there is evidence that Korčula was the site of Neolithic settlements. Records show that it also experienced much the same historic string of takeovers and changes of fortune as the rest of Dalmatia's coastal settlements, including long stretches of Venetian rule.

Today, tourists are drawn by Korčula Town's well-preserved walled city and its medieval attractions, plus the city's claim that it is the birthplace of legendary explorer Marco Polo. Tourists also travel to Korčula to see the traditional **Moreška Sword Dance** ★★, an annual spectacle that recalls a battle between Christians and "infidels" that was fought over a woman. And finally, the island is the source of excellent olive oil and wine, most notably white wines (Pošip, Grk) produced from grapes grown in the island's interior.

ESSENTIALS

VISITOR INFORMATION The folks in Korčula Town's tourist office are courteous and helpful. With a little notice, they will gladly help bewildered tourists and will sometimes even arrange for guides. Their office is next door to the Hotel Korčula at Obala Dr. Franje Tuđmana bb (© **020/715-701;** www.korcula.net). You can rent a motorbike or

> **(Fun Facts) The Legend of Marco Polo**
>
> Legend, but not documentation, says that explorer Marco Polo was born in 1254 in Korčula Town in a modest stone house to the right of the cathedral's bell tower. Korčula Town's city fathers have not hesitated to capitalize on the city's supposed link to greatness; there is at least one restaurant, hotel, boat, and sandwich in this town named after the legendary navigator. However, according to a tour guide, there is no concrete evidence that Marco Polo ever set foot in Korčula Town even though as a captain of the Venetian navy he was involved in a sea battle with the Genoese navy off Korčula in 1298. Marco Polo was taken prisoner, and sent to a jail in Genoa, not Korčula. The alleged **birth house** at Put Sv. Nikol bb (admission 10kn; daily 9am–1pm and 5–7pm in summer, closed in winter) postdates Marco Polo's death by a couple of centuries and the claim that Marco Polo was born there actually grew from the fact that someone with the surname "DePolo" once lived in the house.

jet-ski at **Rent-a-Scooter** (℗ 091/787-754), open daily from 8am to 8pm. **Kantun Tours** (℗ 020/715-622; www.kantun-tours.com) offers Internet access and luggage storage and arranges tours. **Atlas Travel** (see "Fast Facts: Split," earlier in this chapter) also rents cars, but reserve ahead. In Vela Luka, try the **Mediterano Tourist Agency** at Obala 3 bb (℗ 020/813-832; www.mediterano.hr). Mediterano is a full-service agency specializing in private accommodations.

GETTING THERE   Korčula is linked to Split by speedy catamarans and ferries, each of which makes the round-trip at least once per day. A few ferries serve Korčula from nearby Orebić, with pedestrians landing at Korčula Town and car ferries landing at Dominiče, 3km (1¾ miles) southeast of there. There is also daily bus service from Dubrovnik via the car ferry. For ferry information, contact the Jadrolinija office in Korčula Town (℗ 020/715-410; 8am–8pm Tues–Thurs, 8am–9pm Monday, 8am–1pm Sat, 6am–2pm Sun). Ferry service runs from Orebić through **Jadrolinija** (℗ 020/711-156). Bus schedules and fare information can be obtained at the Korčula Town bus station (℗ 020/711-216).

GETTING AROUND   Local buses make five runs daily from one end of the island to the other. You can also rent a bike and easily pedal the 6km (4 miles) between Korčula Town and Lumbarda (where the best beaches are). At its widest point, Korčula is about 8km (5 miles) wide and it is less than 32km (20 miles) long.

WHAT TO SEE & DO

Korčula's main attraction is the medieval Korčula Town and its walls, where you will find several historic churches, museums and other points of interest. Korčula Town likes to promote a once-nondescript stone edifice as the birthplace of Marco Polo, but there is no credible documentation that the great explorer ever set foot on the island.

Cathedral of St. Mark (Katedrala Sv. Marka) ★★   One of the main points of interest on the facade of this Gothic Renaissance building is the curious collection of sculpture at the entrance. You'll see statues of Adam and Eve carved from Korčula limestone at the main door, and above it a statue of St. Mark. Add to that sculptures of a mermaid and an elephant, and the result is a weird mix of imagery. Inside, the sculpture is more modern and more classic, too. Note the Pieta by renowned Croatian sculptor Ivan Meštrović in the

baptistery. There is also a Meštrović sculpture of St. Blaise near the altar, and an altar paint- **145**
ing allegedly done by Tintoretto.

Strossmayer Trg. Summer daily 7am–9pm; winter daily 7am–7pm.

Land Gate ★★★   This 14th-century portal and its 15th-century Revelin tower
frame the only land access to the walled Old Town. The gate (Kopnena Vrata) is embellished on the inside with a sculpture of St. Mark's lion over its arch. It leads to the core's
main square, Trg Bracé Radića, which is home to a 16th-century column, the town hall,
and the 17th-century Church of St. Michael.

At Trg Bracé Radića.

St. Peter's Church ★   You'll notice this modest 14th-century church because of the
rope gate and ticket takers outside. In the summer of 2009, an 18th-century statue of St.
Peter made by an anonymous Venetian artist was sharing the formerly hallowed space
with a bizarre Marco Polo exhibition. Displays of model ships and statues make for a
garage-sale atmosphere for exhibits that include tacky cardboard standup figures dressed
in period garb representing Korčula's favorite son and his contemporaries. The exhibit's
centerpiece is a board that lights up as it traces Marco Polo's trips on a poster-size map.

Admission 15kn. Summer daily 10am–2pm and 6–10pm.

Town Museum ★★   This three-story museum in the 16th-century Gabriellis Palace
(across from the treasury) is a repository of Korčula culture and history. Here you will see
amphorae and stone remnants. The second-floor displays concentrate on furniture, textiles, and glassware. An exhibit features wall remnants still decorated with old frescoes.
Most captions have English translations.

Trg Sv. Marka Statuta. ✆ 020/711-420. Admission 10kn. Daily June–Aug 9am–1:30pm.

Town Treasury/Abbey Treasury ★★   The collection of paintings, religious art,
jewelry, furniture, and ancient documents from Korčula's past may not have great monetary
value, but they are precious vestiges that help put today's the island in historical perspective.

Trg Sv. Marka Statuta. Admission 15kn. Daily May 1–Oct 31 9am–8pm.

WHERE TO STAY

With one, sparkling. upscale exception, hotels on Korčula tend to be large out-of-date
package-type places that haven't been improved much since they were built, but most
have raised their prices as if they were refurbished early and often. These hotels also
charge a premium if your stay is less than 4 days, so unless you intend to make Korčula
your base, you are better off looking for private accommodations.

Hotel Korčula ★★   Situated on the west side of Korčula Town, the Hotel Korčula
has a lovely veranda and an expansive terrace that lets you linger over breakfast with a
view of the Riva. Built in 1912, the Korčula has the most personality of all the hotels on
the island. Most of the rooms are small but nicely decorated; none have air-conditioning.
Even though each room has a fan, try to book one of the rooms facing the sea.

Šetalište Frana Kršinića. ✆ 020/711-078, or 020/726-336 reservations. Fax 020/711-746. www.korcula-
hotels.com. 24 units. From 160€ double. Rates include breakfast but not taxes. AE, DC, MC, V. Closed
Jan–Mar. **Amenities:** Restaurant. *In room:* Fan, TV.

Hotel Marko Polo   The Marko Polo was built in 1972 and was completely renovated
for the 2007 season. Both guest rooms and public areas have been spiffed up for looks
and comfort, and prices have been hiked accordingly.

Šetallište Frana Kršinića. ☎ **020/726-306.** www.korcula-hotels.com. 94 units. July–Aug from 220€ for a superior double with a sea view. Other times sea view doubles from 143€. Rates include breakfast but not taxes. AE, DC, MC, V. Closed Nov–Mar. **Amenities:** Restaurant; 2 bars; indoor/outdoor pools; money exchange. *In room:* A/C, TV, hair dryer, minibar.

Lešič Dimitri Palace Korčula ★★★ (Finds) It took 6 million euros and 6 years to turn this 18th-century bishop's palace into a luxurious boutique hotel. Each of the hotel's six residences is themed after a different country (Arabia, Ceylon, India, China, Venice, Korčula) and each has distinctive furnishings and a unique layout with from one to four bedrooms. Take sleek kitchens, decadent bathrooms, and personalized service, and add a location steps from the sea and you have vacation digs fit for royalty. Amenities vary with unit; all have espresso machines. Some units have hot tubs, and management treats guests to various "surprise" extras during their stay.

Tip: The former palace's original kitchen is in the Korčula suite.

Ulica don Pavla Poše 1-6. ☎ **014/817-596.** www.lesic-dimitri.com. 6 units. Doubles from 395€ July–Sept; from 180€ other times, more for units that sleep more than 2. Year-round. **Amenities:** Cafe; bar. *In room:* A/C, TV, kitchen, minibar.

Campsite

Autocamp Kalac ★ Kalac is near the Bon Repos on the Bay of Shells and has room for 600 guests. There are bathroom facilities, refrigerators, hookups, a snack bar, and a small market, but compared to most campgrounds in Croatia, Kalac is light on services. Right next to the water, it offers some shade.

Šetalište Frana Kršinića. ☎ **020/711-078.** 162kn for site, car, and 2 people. Hookup and fridge extra. No credit cards. Closed June–Sept.

WHERE TO DINE

Dining tends to be a pretty informal affair in Korčula, and because most of the people who stay here take board at their hotels. However, without much competition, the menus at most places are all about the same.

Very Expensive

Gradski Podrum ★ (Value) DALMATIAN A 40kn daily plate is one of the draws at this Korčula institution. Any of the fish dishes done "Korčula-style"—with boiled potatoes and tomato sauce—are yummy. Try mixed meat and veggies (roasted in a closed pot covered with burning embers and ash); or savor the *pasticada* (marinated beef cooked with dumplings and gravy).

Put Sveti Antuna bb. ☎ **020/711-222.** Entrees 40kn–280kn. The latter price is per kilo. AE, DC, MC, V. Daily 11am–2pm and 6–10:30pm. Closed mid-Oct to mid-Apr.

Konoba Mareta ★ DALMATIAN This spot is a little pricier than most in its class, but its limited menu is a little better executed than some. Nice wooden bench tables are set up outside, where you can soak up the town's atmosphere while you dine. Try the salted fish appetizer; it's a Dalmatian specialty.

Plokata bb. No phone. Entrees 50kn–270kn. No credit cards. Daily 10am–2pm and 6–11:30pm.

Expensive

Konoba/bar Adio Mare ★★ DALMATIAN Local specialties and fish are the highlights of this atmospheric dining spot, whose rustic stone walls on the first floor of an old house make it resemble a fancy bunker. You'll be seated at long wooden tables with

Moreška Sword Dance

The **Moreška Sword Dance** ★★ is a 15th-century narrative in motion that tells the story of two kings who compete for the love of a princess. As the story goes, the Black King kidnaps the young woman after she declares her love for the White King, who retaliates by initiating a battle. The kings and their armies then engage in an intricate "ballet" with swords drawn as they "fight" to musical accompaniment. The Moreška Sword Dance is thought to commemorate a real clash between Christians and Moors, precipitated by the Moors' abduction of a young girl. The traditional dance is performed by townspeople, usually outside the town walls, every Monday and Thursday at 9pm in July and August; several times on July 29, the town's festival day; on Thursdays in June and September; and other times when tourist traffic is heavy.

other patrons a la Japanese teppanyaki style. Try some of the meat grilled right before your eyes while you and your tablemates make small talk with the restaurant's jovial chef. Adio Mare has a very nice selection of wines—including several versions of Korčula's famous whites—to accompany your food.

Sv. Roka 2. ✆ **020/711-253.** Reservations recommended. Entrees 40kn–130kn. AE, DC, MC, V. Mon–Sat 5:30pm–midnight; Sun 6pm–midnight. Closed mid-Oct to mid-Apr.

Moderate

Konoba Adriana ★ DALMATIAN   Fish and Dalmatian specialties crowd the menu here. Try the fish stew Adriana, something like bouillabaisse but not as spicy. There is a very nice terrace for dining, but even with umbrellas, it can get extremely hot on a sunny day.

Near the Hotel Park. ✆ **020/715-661.** Entrees 35kn–100kn. AE, DC, MC, V. Daily 11am–11pm.

Konoba Gajeta ★★ (Finds) DALMATIAN   This 5-year-old (2005) spot under the trees along the Riva serves some of the best food in Korčula Town. Specialties are pancakes with cheese and scampi, as well as Žrnovski macaroni, handmade pasta lovingly produced by a local woman especially for the restaurant.

Setaliste Petra Kanavelića bb. ✆ **020/716-359** or 091/503-2829. Entrees 50kn–90kn. No credit cards. Daily 11am–11pm. Closed Nov–Apr.

Konoba Marco Polo ★ DALMATIAN   One of the nice things about konobas is that each has its interpretation of traditional dishes. Marco Polo is no different. Tables here are set on tiered wide steps that descend onto the street. The menu is mostly grilled fish and meat. You can't go wrong with grilled octopus.

ACI Marina. ✆ **020/715-662.** Entrees 50kn–95kn more for fish by the kilo. AE, DC, MC, V. Year-round daily 11am–midnight.

Inexpensive

Konoba Briskule ★★★ (Finds) DALMATIAN   The food here isn't just good, it's *very* good, according to the restaurant's jovial owner Damir Plaziblat. Briskule is a fairly new entry in the Korčula dining scene, but since its opening in 2003, it has gained quite a

The Rest of Korčula

Don't ignore the Korčula beyond Old Town. **Lumbarda** ★, 7km (4 miles) south-east of Korčula Town was planted with vineyards by the Greeks, cultivated by the Romans, and used as a summer playground by the island's wealthy citizens. Today, it is a major producer of Grk, the island's signature white wine.

Pupnat Harbor and a lazy pebble beach lie about 9km (5¹/₂ miles) west of Korčula Town and beyond that, there's **Smokvica** ★★, a village set high above a valley planted with grapes used by **Vinarija Toreta** ★, a family winery open 8am to 8pm daily June through September that is a popular stop for tourists following Korčula's wine road. Early one Sunday morning we ran into a group of Americans sampling Toreta's varietals. They were heading across Korčula as part of a food and wine cycling tour.

You'll run into **Blato** ★★ about 10km (6 miles) west of Smokvica. The approach is on a wide road shaded by a canopy of arching trees. Don't miss Blato's pilgrimage site dedicated to **Marija Petkovi,** a daughter of Korčula who became a nun and devoted her life to helping others. The Roman Catholic Church beatified Petković in 2002 and she is in the Church's pipeline to become a saint.

Vela Luka ★ is the last stop in the trek across the island (or the first if you arrive there). It is 7km (4 miles) past Blato and it's full of harbor-side cafes and pizzerias. If you're lucky, you might hear a **Klapa** performance while you break for a snack as Vela Luka is a center of the Croatian a cappella–style performance art.

following. This is because of its low prices, high quality, and, as Plaziblat says, because the cooking is "from the heart." The menu is flexible because he or chef Ðuro Petrović buys whatever looks good that day at the fish market. The mussels, at 50kn for a huge portion, are a steal.

Setaliste Frana Kršinića bb. ✆ **091/242-245.** Entrees 35kn–65kn. No credit cards. Daily 10am–midnight. Closed Nov 1–May 1.

Nautica ★★ LIGHT FARE Big polished wood picnic tables are scattered on the veranda at this harbor-side spot in Vela Luka. The menu is loaded with variety that includes burgers and fries, spaghetti and risotto, 14 kinds of pizza, vegetarian burritos, and even a couple of curry dishes. It's a pleasant place to stop for lunch.

Obala Vela Luka. ✆ **080/796-838,** -823, or -807. Entrees 50kn–100kn. MC, V. Daily 8am–11pm.

9 VIS ★★★

Vis is the inhabited island farthest from Croatia's mainland, and it has only recently become a hot destination. Vis was closed to visitors until 1989 because of its status as a military base. Almost as soon as the island opened its shores to the world, the 1991 Homeland War threw a wet blanket over tourism in Croatia and Vis's debut as a vacation spot was delayed.

Today's Vis is a perfect poster child for the country's "Croatia: The Mediterranean as It Once Was" promotion. It is developing into the country's next exclusive tourist draw precisely because previous booms bypassed its shores, leaving it undeveloped.

The downside is that Vis is short on hotel accommodations and tourism infrastructure, but it is beginning to catch up. The island's two main towns, **Vis Town** and **Komiža,** are seeing increased tourist days thanks to an unspoiled interior, deserted beaches and clear-as-glass water, and fine, authentic restaurants. Travel routes between the island and the mainland have increased with the introduction of new fast-boat routes blessed by Croatia's government, though most of the added routes are active July and August only.

Vis's recorded history dates from the 4th century B.C., when Dionysius of Syracuse founded Issa (Vis), presumably as a strategic base for Greek enterprises in the Adriatic. Issa became a city-state and eventually was taken over by the Romans, the Byzantines, and the Venetians, in that order. Vis attained its greatest notoriety during World War II, when Marshal Tito used a cave on the island as his base for masterminding Partisan strategies. Called **Tito's Cave ★**, the chamber on the south side of Mount Hum is interesting even though you have to climb 245 overgrown stone steps to reach it.

There are many secluded bays on Vis **(Rukavac, Stiniva, Milna, Srebrna),** particularly on the island's southern side, where most of the time you'll have the rocks and sea to yourself.

ESSENTIALS

VISITOR INFORMATION The **tourist office** in Vis Town is the best place to get information and maps. It is at Šetalište Stare Isse 5 (✆ **021/717-017;** fax 021/717-018; www.tz-vis.hr), across the street from the ferry port and adjacent to the Jadrolinija ticket office. Žarko is in charge and he knows all the places off the beaten track. You can book private accommodations through the **Ionios Agency** at Obala Svetog Jurja 36 (✆ **021/ 711-352;** fax 021/711-356). Ionios also rents scooters and bikes and arranges excursions. Navigator is another reliable tourist service that books accommodations. Komiža's tourist office, at Riva bb (✆ **021/713-455**), provides the usual services. Jadrolinija's local office is in Vis Town at Šetališe Stare Isse, in the same building as the tourist center (✆ **021/711-032**).

Tip: None of the private accommodations we found accept credit cards. Cash is king on Vis.

GETTING THERE Besides private excursions offered by Atlas and other tourist agencies in various cities on mainland Croatia, travel to Vis is possible on "public" transportation thanks to regular ferry and catamaran from the mainland. Both Jadrolinija and Semmarina operate routes from Split (see p. 101 for details).

There are numerous sites worth investigating in the rural areas between Vis Town and Komiž. Wineries, countless coves with spectacular scenery that can be approached only from the sea, beachfront restaurants, caves, and abandoned military installations lead the list. If you have access to a boat or if you can book a tour, your choices expand to eerily illuminated underwater caves, lighthouses on tiny windswept islands, and vestiges of military operations carved into the rocky hills. You can even go to the mysterious **Jabuka Island,** an uninhabited volcanic land mass where compasses spin out of control thanks to a high concentration of iron in the soil.

GETTING AROUND Vis Town is the island's main port. Buses shuttle passengers between the ferry port and Komiža, currently the island's most visited population center. However, if you want to see the inland villages, enjoy the more secluded beaches, or travel the Vis wine road, you'll need your own transport.

Vis Town ★★★ has a permanent population of 1,700 and is the island's largest town and its major center of commerce. It is a combination of two separate settlements: Kut is on the east side of town and Luka is on the west end. Kut is a prosperous-looking residential neighborhood and home to numerous art galleries and the town's best restaurants. A seaside promenade connects the two neighborhoods and most of the town's beaches (concrete slabs) are along this path. One of the most interesting sites on the island is located near the Kut neighborhood: Just west of Kut, there is a **British naval cemetery** that is walled and locked. It dates to the War of 1812 and is the resting place of fallen British soldiers who fought in battles from the Napoleonic Wars through World War II. There is another (unlocked) British burial site along the old road between Vis Town and Komiža. Luka is where you will find the ferry port, the tourist office, and a **Franciscan Monastery.** Vis Town has a pleasant beach in front of the Hotel Issa north of the promenade on Vis Bay, about .5km (¼ mile) from the center. It has "snack" huts where you can get lunch or a cool drink.

A wharf, a castle built by the Venetians, a 17th-century church, and several beaches are the main attractions in **Komiža.** One of the beaches is in front of the **Hotel Biševo,** but the water there is not as clear as it is at other parts of the island. Another beach a short distance northwest of Komiža at Uvala Srebrna has clearer water, but less hospitable rocks to lie on.

Biševo Island ★★★ is a tiny piece of land 5km (3 miles) southwest of Vis. This is the site of the eerie **Blue Cave (Modra Špilja)** ★★, a sea cave that "lights up" in shades of blue and silver for an hour each day between 11am and noon. Boats leave Komiža at 9am to make it to the cave in time for the light show. The Blue Cave is one of 26 underwater caves on Biševo and the most showy. For centuries, the only way to enter the Blue Cave was by diving into the sea and swimming in, but more than 100 years ago the cave was altered so visitors could enter by boat, a setup similar to the one at the Blue Grotto near Capri off southern Italy. If you visit the Cave earlier or later than the optimal hour, you'll be disappointed because the blue color will not be visible. To get there, you can either book an excursion or take your own boat to the Cave. Almost every agency in Komiža offers Blue Cave "picnic" tours for about 140kn per person. Some also offer extended tours that also visit the **Green Cave (Zelena Špilja)** ★★★, where you can swim in the water inside, and other remote sites for 220kn per person. *Note:* Crowds and the unpredictable *Jugo* (south wind) can be deterrents to investigating the Blue Cave and visiting neighboring islands. To fit through the entrance to the Blue Cave, we had to lie flat in the small boat that took us there because the water was so high.

Low-Velocity Vis

Leave your car on the mainland when you visit Vis and rent a scooter or bicycle on the dock from the Ionios tourist agency. It's more environmentally responsible, better for getting exercise, and cheaper by the day than the fee for transporting your auto on the ferry (200kn per day for a scooter; 100kn per day for a bicycle). Ionios is at Obala Sv. Jurja 37 (© **021/711-532**).

Diving

Vis has become a hot spot for the yacht set and for diving enthusiasts. Try the **Issa Diving Center** ★★ at the Hotel Biševo in Komiža (✆ **091/201-2731;** www.scuba diving.hr) or the **Dodoro Diving Center** ★★ at Trg Klapavica 1 in Vis Town. Call ✆ **021/711-913,** or log on to www.dodor-diving.com for lessons or excursions.

Stiniva Beach ★★★ No beach on Vis (or just about anywhere else) has the powerful, serene beauty of Stiniva, a tiny cove tucked behind two towering rock curtains that separate it from the open sea save for a slit of an opening. Stiniva, which is the subject of many of Vis's tourism posters, is about 4km (2½ miles) southwest of Vis Town, though it will take about half an hour to get there by land, longer if you approach by sea. There are just two ways to access Stiniva. Lacking our own yacht, we chose the land route. We took the main road south from Vis Town, then followed the signs about 1.6km (1 mile) to Stiniva. Parking is at the top of the road for 20kn, which is paid to the lady sitting behind a folding table at the trail's head. She directs visitors to the long, rocky path to the beach. There is a small restaurant at the bottom, but you should take ample water with you on the climb. Even if you don't swim, a trip halfway down the path will yield breathtaking photos. *Tip:* Don't attempt the path wearing flip-flops. Besides being almost vertical in places, it is full of loose rocks and slippery, jagged boulders, and you'll eventually have to walk back up besides.

Vis Archaeological Museum ★★★ Lemon trees, a grassy moat, and the remains of a fortification built by the Austrian monarchy in the 19th century are the frame for this multifaceted museum that houses both ancient artifacts and ethnographic treasures. The second floor has a large collection of treasures from Vis's Greek past, including a mesmerizing 4th-century bronze head of the goddess Aphrodite. This place looks dull at first, but keep going. The more you look, the more fascinating it becomes.

Šetalište Viš Boj 12. ✆ **021/711-729.** Admission 20kn adults/10kn children. No credit cards. 10am–1pm and 5–9pm Tues–Sun June–Aug and 9am–1pm Tues–Sun Sept–May. Closed Mon. Closed in winter, but visits can be arranged.

WHERE TO STAY

Vis is short on hotel rooms and campgrounds, but private accommodations are plentiful. People with rooms to rent whip out their APARTMAN FREI signs when the ferry pulls in, and their private digs are generally good. Check with Navigator or Ionios Agency (see above) for bookings. Several nice places include **Apartments Marinković** ★★ at Mihovila Pavlinovica 9 in Komiža (✆ **021/713-821**). For 35€ per night for two, you get a room on the top floor with a balcony and a great view of the harbor. The units in **Apartmani Bellevue** ★★★ at Zagrabačka bb in the hills above Vis Town are a little more luxe. Bellevue is a cluster of three two-apartment structures with expansive balconies overlooking the town and harbor (amenities include A/C, TV, dishwasher, washing machine, and a complete kitchen). A one-bedroom rents for 657kn per day. Contact Darka Rakić at ✆ **021/388-750,** www.apartment-bellevue.com, for availability. A car is handy for staying at the Bellevue, but there is a footpath to town just below the road that passes in front.

Hotel Biševo ★   Komiža's only hotel has a decent beach and a nice view of the water. Guest rooms are smallish and a few of them have been renovated; some have air-conditioning, so ask for one that has been redone.

Ribarska 72, Komiža. ☏ **021/713-008.** 135 units. From 610kn double. Rate includes breakfast. AE, DC, V. Parking. **Amenities:** Restaurant. *In room:* TV, minibar.

Hotel San Giorgio ★★   You'll feel welcome at this 10-room inn (formerly Hotel Paula) in a vintage stone building in the Kut district of Vis Town just 90m (300 ft.) from the beach. Each room in the family run establishment is unique in design and updated with modern conveniences. You will love having breakfast in the terrace restaurant, which is surrounded by a stone wall and dripping with flowers. The owner also runs a small wine bar across the street where you can sample the island's best vintages.

Petra Hektorovića 2. ☏ **021/711-362.** Doubles from 100€. AE, DC, MC, V. **Amenities:** Restaurant. *In room:* A/C, TV, hair dryer, minibar, free Wi-Fi.

Hotel Tamaris ★   Tamaris is steps from the Vis Town waterfront promenade and walking distance to the ferry port. The 19th-century building itself is a squarish red structure adorned with brick gingerbread. It is in the center of town and convenient.

Svetog Jurja 30, Vis Town. ☏ **021/711-350.** 26 units. From 650kn double. AE, DC, MC, V. **Amenities:** Restaurant; bar. *In room:* A/C, TV.

Villa Nonna and Casa Nonno ★★   Wood floors, stone accents, and lots of light were incorporated into the 2003 renovation plan for Villa Nonna, a 400-year-old Komiža town house that once was a tavern. The result is seven studios with personality and plenty of elbow room. If self-catering doesn't appeal and you don't need that much space, book a room at Casa Nonno, a four-room sister facility on the parallel street behind and up from Villa Nonna. Casa Nonno was restored in 2005 and it has a central kitchen for guests' use. Restaurants are steps away from both for those who don't want to be bothered with cooking. Both facilities require week-long bookings from Saturday through Saturday (except in the off season, which is Jan 1–Apr 28).

Ribarska 50, 21485 Komiža. ☏ **098/380-046.** Fax 021/713-500. www.villa-nonna.com. Villa Nonna: 7 units. From 476€ per week. Casa Nonno: 4 units. Doubles from 310€ per week. No credit cards. **Amenities:** Garden; excursions; use of private yacht. *In room:* A/C, full kitchen in Villa Nonna units.

WHERE TO DINE

The restaurants on Vis are always good, but some are outstanding. Their proximity to the source of the catch makes any fish dish you order a sublime dining experience.

Kantun ★★ REGIONAL DALMATIAN   A recent renovation has made Kantun a destination restaurant that is at once urban and homey in feel: The place looks like a laid-back konoba, but the food is laced with subtle sophistication. Try the smoked tuna carpaccio appetizer or the succulent fish soup. There is a great selection of local wines.

Biskupa Mihe Pusića 17, Vis Town. ☏ **021/711-306.** Entrees 60kn–160kn. No credit cards. Daily 6pm–midnight.

Konoba Stončica ★★ GRILL   You can get to this homey beachfront grill by land, but that way it is a 5-minute hike down a hill from the road that runs to the northeast part of the island and Stončica Beach. It's more fun to arrive by boat and to tie up in the quiet, protected bay out front the way Princess Caroline of Monaco and the president of Croatia do. You can dine on peka roasted lamb or fish grilled over charcoal while you sit

---

> ### (Moments)   Heard It on the Grapevine
>
> Visiting Vis's vineyards and wineries is one of the island's delights. During the day, vineyards are deserted, but when the sun goes down, the owners come out to tend their vines and talk about the harvest. While meandering along Vis's *vinska put* (wine road), we saw huge mounds of rocks scattered about in what looked like patterns to us and asked a vineyard worker what they were. He said the rocks were piled around by people clearing the land and the result of hundreds of years of work. We also stopped at the **Vinarija Lipanović ★★★**, which is housed in a cave that once was a Yugoslavian Army installation. Antonio Lipanović rents the space from the Croatian government and the cave keeps his wine at a perfect temperature. But, he said, there still are "ghosts" of war the military left behind. He showed us an old army phone and steel doors at the end of each of two side tunnels. The doors are sealed shut and Lipanović says that's the way they were when he set up shop a decade ago. He has no idea what's behind them. Trg Karolina, Vis Town. Call ✆ **021/711-386** to arrange a tour.

at tables shielded by bamboo plants. After dinner, take a walk through the vineyards out back and pick up a bottle of vugava from the vineyard store.

P.U.R.O. Dobra Luka. ✆ **021/711-952**. Entrees 20kn–80kn, more for fish by the kilo or lamb from the peka. AE, DC, MC, V. Daily noon–2am.

Limoncello ★★ DALMATIAN   Limoncello is a true garden restaurant—there is no indoor dining room—and its polished pine tables are "terraced" on multilevel decks that look down on lemon trees, flowers, herbs, and other greenery. Our waiter told us the property once belonged to sculptor Ivan Meštrovic's daughter Ivana as he explained how two original Meštrovic works of art came to rest in the middle of the 2-year-old (2008) restaurant's courtyard. Like most Vis restaurants, Limoncello's menu is heavy on fish, but supplemented by a few unusual (for Croatia) entrees like paella. Unlike most, ambience includes music provided by top 20 hits from the 1960s.

M. Gupca 10. Luka, Vis Town. ✆ **091/1100-312** or 021/711-823. www.horizon-issa.hr. Entrees 85kn–260kn (paella for 2). No credit cards. Daily 6pm–midnight May 1–Oct 20 or whenever the last regatta ends.

Pojoda ★★★ (Value) SEAFOOD   Pojoda is famous for its creative cuisine and its starters, and once you see the menu you might not get to the main course. Try the tuna in caper sauce or the pasta and beans. If you do have room for an entree, any of the barbecued fish dishes are luscious, as is the fish cooked in wine. The garden is fringed with orange and lemon trees. Reserve a table on the upper floor for the view.

Don Cvjetka Marasović 8, Kut, Vis Town ✆ **021/711-575**. Fax 021/718-031. Entrees 40kn–125kn. AE, DC, MC, V. Daily in summer noon–3pm and 5pm–1am; in winter 5pm–midnight.

Val ★★ REGIONAL DALMATIAN   Val's outdoor tables are surrounded by palm trees while indoors the atmosphere is nautical and done in cheery blue and white. Whichever you choose, call ahead, because Val is always crowded thanks to its devotion to well-prepared local specialties like *pašta fažol na Brudetto*, a Croatia-meets-Italy bouillabaisse of fish, beans, pasta, tomatoes, and onions.

Kut, Vis Town. ✆ **091/508-2015**. val_restaurant@yahoo.com. Entrees 50kn–100kn. No credit cards. Daily noon–3pm and 5pm–1am Apr–Oct.

Villa Kaliopa ★ ⟨Overrated⟩ SEAFOOD   Situated in the garden of the 16th-century Garibaldi Palace on the outskirts of Kut, this stylish place set among palm trees and sculptures is a favorite of the yacht set that ties up in the harbor. Besides serving fresh local catch, Kaliopa serves Vis wine, which has been made on the island since the time the Greeks called Vis "Issa." This restaurant is a romantic (and expensive) choice.

Tip: We ordered Kaliopa's "special" appetizer of various fish, cheese, and olive canapés. However, we later felt duped when we spotted identical prepackaged fish tidbits in the dairy case of several Croatian grocery stores on the mainland.

Vladimira Nazora 32, Kut, Vis Town. ⟨© **021/711-755** or 099/529-667. Entrees 250kn–600kn. No credit cards. Daily in summer 5:30pm–12:30am.

VIS AFTER DARK

Komiža is party central for singles on Vis, while Vis Town's action is more family oriented. **Aquarius Bar** ★ on Kamenica beach in Komiža is the island's summer headquarters for mingling under the moon. It is really the only place dedicated to serious partying, and it is open 24/7 July and August only (© **095/902-7701**). **Zadruga** is another Komiža hot spot, but tamer than Aquarius. It has a fine location next to the town wine press where locals deposit their grapes at harvest time, and it's decorated with antique winemaking equipment. Zadruga is the most sophisticated and expensive watering hole on the island (© **021/713-023;** daily 8am–2pm). Vis Town's bars are mostly alfresco and concentrated along the waterfront promenade. **Caffe Bar Biliba** ★ in the Luka section of Vis Town attracts a large crowd, perhaps because it also has Internet services and big-screen TV (© **021/717-475;** daily 7am–11pm). No credit cards are accepted.

Upper Dalmatia

The region known as Upper Dalmatia (Senj to Zadar) is a collection of contradictions: The cities and sites are among some of Croatia's most accessible and enchanting; but the region also is home to what is arguably some of the most forbidding and barren terrain in the world. Still, there is something for everyone in this gateway to Croatia's coastal playground, whether your interests tend toward poking around ancient ruins, getting an adrenaline rush rock climbing the challenging Velebit range, or feeding your cultural appetite with classical music at the Church of St. Donat in Zadar.

All roads to and from Upper Dalmatia seem to go through Zadar, the largest city on the region's coastal highway. In many ways, Zadar's mix of monuments and commerce, of ancient history and proactive civic vision, make it one of Croatia's most cosmopolitan centers. Senj, the Velebit, and Pag Island make up the Velebit Coastal Area in the northern part of Upper Dalmatia, while Paklenica National Park, Nin, and Zadar and the Kornati Archipelago offshore to the west are its center. Krka National Park, Primošten, Šibenik, and other smaller resort towns extend to the south just above Split, which is the trail head for Lower Dalmatia.

1 ORIENTATION

EXPLORING THE REGION

Transportation vagaries in Upper Dalmatia make logistics difficult for people who want to see a lot in a short time. But covering the maximum amount of territory during a trip to the coast north of Split can be accomplished with careful planning.

For example, most visitors to Pag spend a weekend or more on the beach or on the water, while visitors to Zadar might make that city a base for a week or more for excursions to nearby Paklenica National Park and Nin. Others might spend their whole stay in Zadar, investigating its imposing churches and monuments, and then venture out of the city for half- or full-day trips with local cruise lines to see some of the area's numerous offshore islands. The latter is a strategy that makes good sense for those who don't like roughing it, but do want to see Dugi Otok and Pašman in the Zadar Archipelago. Those two island destinations and several others have few accommodations options and taking day trips is the pragmatic way to see them.

Senj, Nin, and Primošten each can be thoroughly explored in a few hours, but you'll need at least a day each to discover Zadar or Šibenik, a day to see each of the national parks (more if you want to do some hiking or camping); and a day or more for each of the islands you choose to visit (mostly because of ferry timetables).

It's fairly simple to access all the major coastal sites in Upper Dalmatia by driving from Senj down, but it's much trickier to coordinate ferry connections from the mainland to the islands or to travel between islands.

VISITOR INFORMATION   Coastal Dalmatia is Croatia's most celebrated region, so it is not surprising that tourism services are well organized and developed. For tourist office contact information in Upper Dalmatia, see "Visitor Information" for individual cities; or contact the Croatia National Tourist Office (p. 335).

GETTING THERE   **Bus** travel is the most popular mode of public transportation in Croatia and many other European countries because it is the most efficient and economical. Croatian buses are air-conditioned and not only can get you from one mainland destination to another, but they also can get you to islands served by larger ferries. See contact details for the Jadrolinija ferries (p. 168).

GETTING AROUND   Private **auto** is the most efficient and comfortable way to visit the Upper (or Lower) Dalmatian coast because you'll be able to set your own schedule, linger where you find something you like, and move on when you don't without worrying about bus or ferry schedules. For those who don't have their own transportation, **buses** are the next best way to get around because they are frequent and serve almost all coastal towns. **Ferries** link coastal towns with major Croatian islands and with each other or, if you have the means, you can rent a **yacht** and map out a sea tour of your own. Split and Dubrovnik have major airports, and Zadar has a small one. All are connected by **air** with Rijeka and Zagreb. **Rail** travel is the least desirable way to travel up and down the coast because not all towns have train service and connections are often difficult.

2 SENJ & THE VELEBIT

Senj, dubbed "the fortress city," has two dubious distinctions: First, it has a reputation as the coldest, windiest town in Croatia; and second, it is the site of an infamous 16th-century pirates' den that was home to the flamboyant Uskoks, who lived in Senj in the 16th century and preyed on passing merchant ships.

In 1535, the Uskoks were a community of controversial anti-Turk fighters who helped fend off Ottoman assaults on the city and later channeled their aggression toward more lucrative pursuits until they were driven out in the early 17th century.

Today's Senj is worth a stop to see **Nehaj Fortress ★★**, which was built by the Uskoks and which makes a great photo op from the sea or highway and a great perch For photos of the sea and skyline. The **Senj Town Museum ★★** is also worth a quick look to get a sense of Senj's history, but neither is worth a lot of time.

South of Senj, you can catch the ferry to Pag Island at Prizna or a ferry to Rab from Jablanac, but on land there aren't many settlements of note between Senj and Zadar—and the ones that are there don't have much to recommend them. In fact, Zadar is the next major population center on the coast south of Senj.

Those who prefer uninhabited, unspoiled, rugged terrain to city development can veer off the coastal highway to the Velebit Range, which includes Paklenica National Park south of Senj. It extends almost the entire length of the coast from Senj to Zadar.

ESSENTIALS

VISITOR INFORMATION   The **Senj tourist office** is at Stara Cesta 2 on the waterfront (℃ **053/881-068;** fax 053/881-219; www.senj.hr). The staff can provide a city map and information about the town. It is open from 7am to 8pm daily in July and August and from 7am to 2pm Monday through Friday the rest of the year.

GETTING THERE   Senj, just 69km (43 miles) from Rijeka and a little over 161km (100 miles) from Zagreb, is easily reached from the Rijeka-Split highway. In addition, most buses routed through coastal cities stop at Senj on their way to somewhere else. See "Getting There" under "Essentials" in "Orientation," above, for transport contact information.

GETTING AROUND   Senj is a very walkable city, and you don't have to walk too far because except for the fortress on the harbor and the town's quaint center, there isn't that much to see.

WHAT TO SEE & DO

Nehaj Fortress (Kids) ★★   Senj's biggest (and some say only) attraction is the Nehaj Fortress, which was built in the mid–16th century by Uskok Captain Ivan Lenković. Ivan tore down unprotected buildings outside the fortifications to get construction materials because he reasoned the structures would be sitting targets anyway. The exhibits inside the three-story fortress trace the history of the Uskoks and display weapons, clothing, and other artifacts related to the times. Captions are in Croatian and English. The fortress was rehabbed in 1977 and now serves as the city's symbol. You can climb to the top for unparalleled views of the sea and Senj.

Above the harbor. Admission 15kn. Daily July–Aug 10am–9pm; May–June Sept 10am–6pm. Closed Oct–Apr.

Senj Town Museum ★   The 15th-century Gothic-Renaissance Vukasović Palace in the town center is the site of the town's museum, which has a good collection of local architecture and botanical specimens. There is also a collection of modern artifacts (1914–45) and another showing the development of Glagolitic writing and printing.

Ogrizovićeva 7. ☎ **053/881-141.** Admission 15kn adults, 10kn children. July 15–Sept 1 Mon–Fri 7am–3pm and 6–8pm; Sat 10am–noon and 6–8pm; Sun 10am–noon. Rest of year Mon–Fri 7am–3pm; closed Sat–Sun.

WHERE TO STAY

Private accommodations are the way to go if you intend to spend any time in Senj. Inquire at the tourist office (above).

WHERE TO DINE

Dining is casual in Senj. Most places have the same menu—grilled fish, meat, and pastas/pizza—and all are quite good.

Konoba Stari Grad ★ CROATIAN   A stone interior and shaded tables outside make this small dining spot a good place to get a break from the heat. The fare is simple and the prices low, with soups, pastas, and risottos taking center stage. Try the risotto with truffles for 55kn or the tagliatelle Montarana (pasta with smoked ham, cream, and mushrooms) for 50kn. They're a steal.

Uskočka 12. ☎ **053/885-242.** Entrees 40kn–100kn. No credit cards. Daily 7am–1am.

Lavlji Dvor ★ CROATIAN   This cute *konoba* in a former 16th-century farmhouse has a shaded terrace with an old well as centerpiece and a dining room loaded with Croatian antiques. The predictable menu offers pizza and grilled meat and fish, but the atmosphere provides a nice respite from sightseeing.

P. Preradovića 2. ☎ **053/881-738.** www.lickosenjska.com/turizam/52.htm. Entrees 35kn–180kn. No credit cards. Daily 10am–11pm.

3 PAG ISLAND ★★★

60km (36 miles) N of Zadar; 240km (150 miles) W of Zagreb

When you approach **Pag Island** on the ferry from mainland Prizna south of Senj, you'd never guess that it is home to one of the biggest party beaches in Europe. At first glance it looks as if you're headed for a landing on Mars rather than a sojourn on an island awash with nouveau riche villas, condominiums, and a pedigree that goes back to the Roman Empire.

It's difficult to imagine that anything could survive for long on Pag's barren terrain, which appears to be either entirely karst (limestone) or dry dust, but the island once was covered with lush forests. Agriculture thrived on Pag when the Romans settled here in the 1st century, and during the next 1,300 years or so, not much disturbed Pag's flora, not even the Slav invasion in the 7th century or Pag's fights over its prized salt fields.

In the 15th century, however, the rulers of Venice and Zadar were in competition for the island and its natural resources. Venice won when it took control of most of Dalmatia in 1409. That included Pag and Zadar. Some might say that Pag lost because once the Venetians had control, they used the island's vast tracts of timber as their private lumber yard and stripped the island of its trees to build ships. The hat trick of Venetian deforestation, grazing sheep, and fierce northwestern wind *(bura)* that frequently hammers the Kvarner and northern Dalmatian coast so traumatized the environment that it has never recovered.

Even though the Venetians showed little concern for ecology, they were engrossed in building and by the mid–15th century, salt trade on Pag had grown so much that the island's Old Town could no longer handle the population or the business. Consequently, the Venetian administrators hired Juraj Dalmatinac to design a new city, which became Pag Town.

Sheep breeding and salt production always have been and still are mainstays of Pag's economy, but it is tourism that now contributes the biggest chunk of revenue to the island. Thanks to that trend, Pag recently has been the site of a building boom that is driving development of other commerce on the island. While tourism is increasing on Pag, it is mostly undiscovered and underrated, leaving it a good vacation opportunity for the knowledgeable traveler.

Pag Island is 60km (36 miles) long and 10km (6 miles) wide at its broadest point. Most of the island's eastern side is barren or covered with a freehand grid of rock walls that delineate property lines and keep sheep from wandering from one patch of scrub grass to another. However, on the northwest end of the island, from Šimuni to Lun, olive trees and other vegetation have taken root in large fertile sections.

Several small islands surround Pag. Some are inhabited only by sheep (Škrda) and others aren't inhabited at all, but they offer secluded pebble beaches for anyone who arrives from the sea. Most of Pag's irregular coastline is indented with countless coves sparkling with water so clear you can see the sandy bottom 6m (20 ft.) down, a siren's song for swimmers, snorkelers, and scuba divers. Pag Island is not densely populated—yet. In fact, most of the time, visitor numbers for Pag's waters and beaches are thin, and FOR RENT signs are numerous—except from July 15 to August 15, when it seems as if half of Italy descends on the island, fills its rooms and apartments, and takes over its party beaches and restaurants. Those 4 weeks often find Pag on the 10pm news throughout Europe as a video clip showing scantily clad women and men engaging in wild, nonstop partying.

But most of the year, Pag is a quiet island whose permanent residents produce and promote four products for which the island has become famous—cheese, lamb, lace, and salt. The cheese is known as **Paški sir ★★★**, and it is reminiscent of Parmesan, though a bit saltier. It is sold throughout the island by both commercial and home-based producers and usually served sliced and drizzled with olive oil. Paški sir is exported to Croatia's larger population centers, where it goes for a much higher price than it does on Pag.

The second is **Paški lamb ★★★**. Pag is home to many herds of sheep, and meat from the island's lamb is prized because of its high quality and unique flavor, a result of the lambs' diet of scrub grass and local herbs that grow wild in the rocky soil and the salt-infused air they breathe. The combination creates lamb that has a singular taste sought after by Croatian gourmets.

The third Pag product worth noting is **Paški lace.** The art of lace making is a tradition that has been preserved and nurtured on Pag. Authentic Pag lace can be very expensive even if you buy it straight from the woman who tatted it. A 6-inch round can sell for 750kn or more, but it makes a beautiful souvenir that will last indefinitely. Look for elderly ladies dressed in black sitting in Pag Town's center square or near Novalja's market for the best examples of this art. Usually these are the lace makers themselves, who will bargain with you on the price of their wares. Once you see real Pag lace, which is incredibly intricate, you'll be able to tell imitations from the genuine article.

Finally, there is the salt once fought over by would-be conquerors. Pag's salt pans are still in production, mostly in the island's central valley. Pag salt is commonplace in Croatian supermarkets, and it is exported as well. Many of the island's souvenir shops sell decorative bottles of pebble-size Pag salt as an inexpensive souvenir.

It's a shame that "the season" on Pag isn't longer than the traditional mid-July to mid-August rush because the climate is still warm in spring and fall, and the island offers lively nightlife, crystal-clear azure water for swimming, plenty of first-class accommodations, historic sites, and quaint attractions.

ESSENTIALS

VISITOR INFORMATION   The **Pag Tourist Board (Turistička Zajednica)** can provide helpful maps, brochures, ferry schedules, and information on excursions from and around Pag. The board's office is at Ulica Od Spitala 2 in Pag Town (℃ 023/622-301; fax 023/611-311; www.pag-tourism.hr). Novalja's **tourist office** can be reached at P.O. Box 20, 53291 Novalja (℃ 053/661-404; www.tz-novalja.hr). It is open from 7am to midnight mid-June to mid-September, and from 7am to noon and 6pm to midnight during most of May and October. Hours and opening days vary the rest of the year.

Various private tourism agencies on the island are helpful for finding private accommodations and for directing you to diving centers where you can arrange dives at some of the marked sites in the sea around the island. **Meridijan 15** and **Mediteran** are two of the better agencies. Both are located in Pag Town, with Meridijan 15 at Ante Starčevića 1 (℃ 023/612-162; fax 023/612-121; www.meridijan15.hr); and Mediteran at V. Nazora bb (℃ 023/600-042; fax 023/611-238; www.mediteran-pag.com). These private agencies are open from 8am to 8pm daily May through September, but their hours and open days vary the rest of the year. In Novalja, try **Sunturist** at S.S. Kranjčevića (℃ 053/611-611; www.islandpag.com) or **Novalja Kompass** at Slatinska (℃ 053/661-211; www.navalija-kompas.hr) for private accommodations.

GETTING THERE   If you are traveling to Pag Island from Zadar and points south, the island is reachable from Posedarje on the mainland via **Pag Bridge,** which takes visitors to the island's south end. Jadrolinija ferries (p. 168) make hourly runs from mainland Prizna to Žigljen on the island's north end, depositing visitors about 4.8km (3 miles) from Novalja. When demand is high during peak season, the ferries often throw out their schedules and leave port as soon as they are full. Nonetheless, waits to board can approach several hours during July and August. A one-way ferry ride for a car with two people costs about 100kn.

Tips   **Bura Winds**

Check the weather reports before you head out for a weekend on Pag. Ferry traffic, and sometimes bridge traffic, is halted when the *bura* winds are strong.

Backups at the Pag Bridge are rarely more than half an hour, except for weekends during July and August. Unless you are coming from Zadar and points south, getting to the bridge involves a few extra driving hours. During the summer, a fast boat (catamaran) runs between Novalja and Rijeka with stops at Rab Island three times a week. Eight daily buses from Rijeka stop in Pag Town and Novalja and go on to other stops along the Dalmatian coast. See "Getting There" under "Essentials" in "Orientation," above, for transportation contact information.

GETTING AROUND   Except for private taxis and intercity buses that run from the mainland and between Pag Town and Novalja, there is little public transportation on Pag. Luckily, both Pag Town and Novalja are compact enough to explore on foot, as are their waterfronts—but travel between the two towns can be time-consuming unless you have your own car. Most visitors spend just a few hours touring the town and head directly for the beach. Thus, cars are the transportation mode of choice, and you'll want a rental car or motor scooter here if you intend to explore more than one area of the island or if you want to go beach-hopping. Rental agencies, including Budget, Dollar, Hertz, and Avis, have kiosks at the Zagreb airport and in other major Croatian cities.

WHAT TO SEE & DO

Besides hauntingly beautiful landscapes, clean waters, and deserted beaches in isolated coves, Pag has a nice collection of Roman ruins, medieval walls, churches, and cultural icons. Most of the attractions worth seeing are concentrated in Pag Town and Novalja, which are separated by about 19km (12 miles) and a big socioeconomic gap. **Pag Town ★★** has a partial **15th-century wall** and an **Old Town** complete with the last of four standing **watch towers** that once rose from the town fortifications. The town center is home to two original Juraj Dalmatinac (a prominent Renaissance stonemason) buildings: the **Rector's Palace (Knežev dvor),** which is now a cafe; and the **Parish Church of St. Mary** opposite **Trg Kralja Krešimira IV,** Pag Town's center of social activity. Pag Town is nearly a mile south of the original 14th-century settlement that preceded it, and a few crumbling remnants of the ancient town are still visible and can be visited. There is also a small **lace museum ★** near the square where you can see what genuine Pag lace looks like before you consider a purchase. Pag Town is where most of the island's locals live and where its salt fields are situated, but it is not as populous as Novalja. You can also see the town's "wall" of windmills on the hills above Pag, an energy-generating project that takes advantage of *bura* wind power.

If Pag Town is the island's historic center, then Novalja is its New World colony, because **Novalja ★★** is oceans away from Pag Town in atmosphere. Novalja is about 19km (12 miles) north of Pag Town and far wealthier and trendier. Its charming square, **Trg Bazilike ★,** is on the same waterfront spot where the Romans used to hang out when Novalja was one of their ports. Now it seems as if everyone in town stops at Bazilike for morning coffee before picking up a few *buhtle* (rolls filled with cheese or jam) to take back to their plush multistory vacation homes. Novalja is also home to a huge auto campsite with its own fine beaches (**Straško ★★**), numerous konobas and cafes, and countless private rooms and rental condos. There is also **Boš-ki-nac hotel/winery/ restaurant ★★★** set in the middle of a vineyard outside Novalja, and more **secluded coves ★★★** (that double as Adriatic swimming holes) than there are tourists to splash around in them.

Zrće Beach ★★★ is a nice pebble beach a little over a mile south of Novalja and the epicenter of Pag's swinging nightlife. Almost every bar in town (and some from Zagreb

---

(Fun Facts) Pag Patterns

Pag is best known for its forbidding naked terrain, its salty sheep's-milk cheese (Paški *sir*), its herb-infused lamb, and its wild party beaches. But Pag also has a reputation as the source of the intricately patterned lace produced by local women who can spend days creating a single 6-inch round. Pag lace is quite expensive and used as trim on clothing and tablecloths, as home decorating accents, and sometimes as framed art. Older women dressed in black from head to toe hawk large and small pieces of lace in other cities besides Pag, but once you've seen genuine Pag lace, you won't have trouble recognizing inferior imitations. Each piece of Pag lace is as complex and unique as a snowflake and a wonderful souvenir from this diverse island.

---

like Papaya and Aquarius) has set up shop on this stretch of real estate, which in summer vibrates with nonstop rock music and gyrating bodies during the day but doesn't *really* get going until 10pm. Zrće draws hordes of the 18- to 29-year-old demographic and has become Croatia's answer to "Where the Boys Are" in the Balkans. In a nod to Croatia's strict drinking/driving laws, minivans run partygoers from Zrće to Novalja's harbor through the night, but action on the beach usually continues until dawn.

Church of St. Mary ★ This Gothic-looking church was built by Pag Town's civil architect Juraj Dalmatinac, and today it is an amalgam of styles that reflect its history. The church was begun in the 15th century, completed in the 16th, and renovated in the 18th. Inside, you'll find sculptures and sacral art from other eras, including a Gothic wooden crucifix from the 12th century.

Trg Kralja Krešimira IV. *(C)* **023/611-576.** May–Sept 9am–noon and 5–7pm. Other times for Mass only.

Pag Carnival ★★ This joyous celebration is held mostly in Pag Town's main square on July 31 at the height of the tourist season. Activities include Slavic dancing *(kolo)* by performers wearing traditional Pag costumes, as well as the folk play *Paška Roninja (The Slave Girl of Pag).*

Pag Lace Museum ★ Information on the history of lace making and examples of this intricate craft are the focus here. The museum also houses a school that ensures there will be new lace makers trained to carry on this delicate tradition.

Kralja Zvonimira. Free admission. Mid-June to mid-Sept daily 8am–11pm.

Pag Watersports ★★★

Pag is a favorite of snorkelers and scuba enthusiasts because of its crystal-clear water and the underwater cliffs, caves, and wrecks where remnants of Rome and other eras rest. Stara Novalja across the Novalja inlet is a haven for diving schools and suppliers.

Connex Diving ★★ Besides excursions for accomplished divers, Connex offers a "Discovery" program that combines 30 minutes of instruction with a 30-minute dive in fairly shallow 6m (20-ft.) water. The package includes all necessary equipment. Connex also rents Zodiac craft.

Kunera bb, Stara Novalja. *(C)* **091/721-3234.** www.connex.diving.cz. Discovery Program 30€. May–Oct.

Pag has become a popular weekend getaway for people who live in north-central Croatia or within a 4-hour drive of the island. Rather than build single-family dwellings as second homes, most construction consists of multiunit buildings or even multibuilding complexes to accommodate extended family and renters during the high season. Consequently, in addition to a few hotels, there is an abundance of reasonably priced, modern, private accommodations on Pag.

Hotel Biser ★★   This sun-washed hotel at water's edge is an excellent place to chill or to use as a base while exploring Pag's charms. Most guest rooms have balconies and sweeping views of the bay plus plain but pleasing furnishings. Hotel Biser also has a sister location, Vila Bisera, next door with similar accommodations in six more rooms and six apartments.

A. G. Matosa 46, Pag Town. ⓒ **023/611-333.** Fax 023/611-444. www.hotel-biser.com. 20 units. From 54€. DC, MC, V. **Amenities:** Restaurant; tennis courts. *In room:* A/C, TV.

Hotel Boškinac ★★★   Boškinac is one of the finest hotels on the northern Adriatic coast, and its surrounding pine forest and vineyard in a secluded location near Stara Novalja 3.2km (2 miles) north of Novalja add to the hotel's exclusivity. Guest rooms and suites in this family-owned establishment, which opened in 2003, are named after local plants and decorated in chic Mediterranean style and colors that reflect the seasons. Every unit includes a sitting area and a bathroom luxuriously appointed with every convenience imaginable, including a Jacuzzi tub, making the whole effect one of warmth and tranquillity. Add to this the exquisite meals in the hotel's **Restoran Boškinac ★★★**, excursions such as grape or olive picking, horseback riding, gourmet cooking classes, a terrace, and a wine study, and you have the makings of a memorable getaway.

Novaljsko Polje, 53291 Novalja. ⓒ **053/663-500.** Fax 053/663-501. www.boskinac.com. 11 units, including 3 apts. Deluxe doubles from 227€ July 1–Aug 22; other times from 130€. Suites from 248€ July 1–Aug 22; other times from 151€. AE, DC, MC, V. Rates include breakfast but not taxes. A 5% discount is given for cash payment, bookings of more than 2 days, and for advance payment. **Amenities:** Restaurant; konoba/wine cellar; bikes; horseback riding; cooking classes. *In room:* A/C, TV, Internet access.

Hotel Luna ★★   The Luna is a modern three-story hotel north of Novalija. It incorporates comfort and a fabulous seaside location and eliminates the crowds that flock to Pag in summer. Guest rooms are spacious and 70% of them have seaside views. Hotel Luna is in Jakišnica, 14km (8½ miles) north of Novalija, a bit of a hike from the island's larger population centers, but if you want to get away from it all, this is the place.

Jakišnica bb. ⓒ **053/654-700.** Fax 053/654-754. www.luna-hotel.hr. 93 units. Doubles with a sea view from 136€ in high season. **Amenities:** 2 restaurants; 2 bars; Internet access; indoor and outdoor pools; tennis, basketball, handball, and soccer courts. *In room:* A/C, TV, hair dryer, minibar.

UPPER DALMATIA

7

PAG ISLAND

Fun Facts   Honey Buns

Paški *sir* may be synonymous with Pag, but *baškotini,* a hard roll made only in the kitchens of the island's Benedictine convent of St. Margarita from a secret recipe, is one of Pag's trademarks. These crunchy biscuits usually are eaten plain or dipped in *bijela kava* (literally, white coffee), but they also are good drizzled with the honey produced at the convent. *Tip:* The sweet golden nectar is rumored to have healing properties.

Hotel Tony ★★   Large rooms, a long list of services, and proximity to the beach more than make up for the hotel's location 1.2km (¾ mile) from Pag Town's center. Hotel Tony has its own cinema with movies in English.

Dubrovačka 39, Pag Town. ℂ **023/611-370.** www.hotel-tony.com. 12 units, 1 apt. From 300kn double. AE, DC, MC, V. Rates include breakfast. Half- and full board available. **Amenities:** Restaurant; bar; disco; free airport transfers; boat rental; diving center; tennis courts; rooms for those w/limited mobility. *In room:* TV, Internet access.

Straško & FKK Campsites ★★   As campsites go, Straško is big enough for 4,000 campers and loaded with amenities. It's also less than a mile from the center of Novalja on the 2.4km (1½ miles) beach of the same name. Besides being able to pitch your tent or park your camper in the shade of pine and olive groves on a site near the water, you can take advantage of Straško's restaurants, markets, bars, an Internet cafe, sports facilities, a gas station, and a boat launch, all there for the use of its guests. For those who like more permanence, Straško also has well-equipped, air-conditioned bungalows for rent on the premises. As is customary in much of Croatia, about one-third of the camp is reserved for nudists, but that part of the camp is well marked and partitioned, and has separate dining and recreation facilities.

Pag Island. ℂ **053/661-226.** Fax 053/661-225. www.turno.hr. Accommodates 4,000 people. From 29€ site plus 2 adults; from 85€ bungalow. AE, DC, MC, V. Closed May–Sept. **Amenities:** 3 restaurants; 2 bars; children's programs; fitness classes; golf; market; tennis; rock climbing; hiking; biking; bowling; scuba diving; excursions.

WHERE TO DINE

There are plenty of family-style konobas and pizzerias on Pag, as well as a few places where cuisine is an art form.

Konoba Kormil ★★ CROATIAN   Kormil isn't much more than a few bench-seat tables tucked into an alley-size side street off Novalja's main square, but the local hangout is definitely worth seeking out for its atmosphere and its food. The menu is limited to a few dishes served family style, and each is enough for a very large family. Don't miss the fried calamari, which is among the best prepared in Dalmatia. Not far behind are the pan-fried sardellen and local pršut, each of which can be ordered separately or as part of a variety platter that lets you taste everything.

Zrinsko-Frankopanska bb, Novalja. ℂ **053/662-332.** Entrees 23kn–45kn. No credit cards. Daily 8am–11pm.

Restoran Boškinac ★★★ (Finds) MODERN CROATIAN   You can dine in Boškinac's richly appointed second-floor dining room agleam with crystal and silver, or move outside to a table on the adjacent balcony overlooking the Boškinac vineyard. Either way, superbly prepared Mediterranean cuisine will be yours. Boškinac prides itself on its creative use of fresh, local ingredients, and you won't be disappointed in any of the dishes served here or in its more informal taverna/wine cellar. Try the Pag lamb roasted with domestic herbs, any of the fresh Adriatic fish dishes and, of course, wine produced on the premises. The Boškinac Taverna on the lower level serves more casual fare but with the same attention to quality.

Novaljsko Polje, 53291 Novalja. ℂ **053/663-500.** Fax 053/663-501. www.boskinac.com. Reservations required. Entrees 70kn–220kn. AE, DC, MC, V. Tues–Sun 10am–1am. Closed for vacation and Jan 3–Feb 10.

4 ZADAR ★★★

Zadar has had its ups and downs through the ages, and over time this beautiful city by the sea suffered grave wounds at the hands of the same factions that aspired to control it. However, today's Zadar seems to have shaken off most of its injuries, though the healing process is ongoing.

Despite frequent reconstruction, Zadar remains a city brimming with more than 3,000 years of history and culture. Like most cities on the Dalmatian coast, Zadar evolved from a prehistoric settlement to an Illyrian village to a Roman municipality, and survived other incarnations involving administrative changes and foreign assaults that finally ended with the city's liberation and reunion with Croatia in 1993.

Zadar is first mentioned in 9th-century writings as the residence of Bishop Donat, the cleric who built the **Church of the Holy Trinity** in the former **Roman Forum,** remains of which lie next to the cathedral. Today that 9th-century church is known as St. Donatus to honor Bishop Donat, and it has become the city's symbol. After the construction of **St. Donatus,** many other churches were built in Zadar, making it a center of Roman Catholicism.

When Venice tried to capture every city on the Dalmatian coast starting in the late 10th century (it finally succeeded in the 15th c.), Zadar fought back harder than any other municipality. From 1096 to 1346, Zadar was conquered and liberated an incredible seven times and taken over six more times until it was sold in 1409 to Venice by King Ladislav of Naples, who was Zadar's ruler du jour. Following the sale, Venice had authority over Zadar for almost 4 centuries until 1797. During that time, the Venetians developed the city and its economy, but only to the extent that those efforts benefited Venice.

Eventually, the Venetians were driven out, and for 120 years or so after that Zadar was governed by Austria (with a short stint of French rule), a regime that ended with World War I but did not end Zadar's occupation. From 1920 to 1944 Zadar was governed by Italy and forced to accept Italian acculturation, though many citizens left rather than become "Italianized."

During World War II, Zadar was almost destroyed by Allied forces, though it was mostly rebuilt during the postwar Yugoslavia era. Then, during the 1991 war, the city took another devastating hit when Serb forces cut the city off from Zagreb and reduced it to rubble once again. The Croatian army at last liberated Zadar in 1993 and the outlying areas in 1995.

UPPER DALMATIA

7

ZADAR

| ⓘ **Fun Facts** **Cherries in a Glass** |

Before you leave Zadar, try the local drink that has become one of the city's specialties. Maraschino is a drink made from a unique variety of maraska cherry grown in the region, and it can be had in alcoholic or nonalcoholic forms. According to legend, alcoholic Maraschino, usually a treacly sweet cherry liqueur, was first made by monks in the 16th century and was thought to improve the disposition. Today the liqueur is made in Zadar in a factory near the footbridge.

Today's Zadar is an exceptional mix of new and old architecture and a diverse mix of cultures. It is also fiercely nationalistic, a characteristic that took hold while the city was isolated from the rest of Croatia by the Serbs.

ESSENTIALS

VISITOR INFORMATION   Zadar is a tourist-friendly town with well-marked streets and addresses and large, illustrated explanatory posters installed in front of almost every notable building. For more detailed information, maps, and brochures, you can check with the local **Tourist Information Center** at Narodni Trg 5 (✆ **023/316-166**). Or try the **Zadar Tourism Board** at Ilije Smiljanića 5 (✆ **023/212-222**; www.tzzadar.hr; 8am–4pm Mon–Sat). For information on Zadar and the surrounding region, contact the **Zadar County Tourist Board** at Sv. Leopolda B. Mandića 1 (✆ **023/315-107**; www.zadar.hr).

Most accommodations near the city center are private and can be secured through **Aquarius Travel Agency** at Nova Vrata bb (✆ **023/212-919**), which can get you a room or book an excursion to regional sites, too. **Atlas Agency** at Branimirova 12 near the footbridge (✆ **023/235-850**), one of Croatia's largest, offers lodging and excursion bookings plus access to some transportation services.

GETTING THERE   Almost every mode of transportation flows through Zadar, but some methods of getting there are better than others.

By Car   Driving is one of the easiest ways to reach Zadar thanks to the A1 superhighway along the coast. The drive time between Zagreb and Zadaris about 3 hours.

By Bus   Bus service to Zadar from Zagreb is convenient and inexpensive at about 100kn each way. The Zadar bus station, just northeast of Old Town, is as busy and bright as any suburban shopping mall, perhaps because it has so much traffic. There is a place to leave your luggage for 1.20kn per hour; it's open from 6am to 10pm. You'll also find cafes, bakeries, and a market open the same hours. There are two ATMs and a couple of travel agencies for those who need local money, plus public phones for those who want to call home. For schedule and ticket information, contact the **Zadar Coach Station** at Ante Starčevića 2 (✆ **023/211-555**; www.liburnija-zadar.hr).

By Boat   Ferry travel is common up and down the Dalmatian coast, whether the route originates in Rijeka or Italy, and Zadar is a major stop for most lines during the summer months. Jadrolinija runs ferries between Ancona and Bari (Italy) and Zadar, and between Zadar and just about all Croatian coastal cities. See "Getting There" under "Essentials" in the "Orientation" section, above, for Jadrolinija contact information.

By Plane   Zadar Airport, about 8km (5 miles) south of the city, handles an average of four domestic and international scheduled flights per day (more on weekends)—from

---

ⓘ Tips   Weekend Traffic

Avoid driving to Zadar or anywhere on the coast Friday morning through Sunday afternoon during July and August. The sheer volume of traffic that descends on Croatia from outside its borders combined with local traffic heading to the same destinations can create backups 32km (20 miles) or longer, especially at border crossings and at tunnels.

Croatia Airlines shuttles to flights on private planes, international carriers, and commercial airlines. Contact the airport at P.O. 367, 23000 Zadar (*C* **023/313-311,** or 023/205-800 flight information; fax 023/205-805; www.zadar-airport.hr).

Croatia Airlines in Zadar, Poljana Natka Nodila 7 (*C* **023/250-094;** fax 023/250-109; zadto@croatiaairlines.hr), is open 8am to 4pm Monday to Friday, 9am to noon Saturday, closed Sunday.

By Train Train travel in Croatia is improving, including travel to Zadar. That said, it should be noted that it still takes 7 hours to get to Zadar from Zagreb via train because rail travelers must change trains at Knin on that route. Thus it takes roughly twice as long to get to Zadar from Zagreb by train than it does by car. The Zadar train station (Ante Starčevića 4; *C* **060/333-444;** www.htnet.hr) is adjacent to the bus station.

GETTING AROUND Croatia Airlines provides shuttle service between the airport and Zadar's center every hour for 15kn. Zadar's Old Town is closed to vehicular traffic. However, most of the hotels are outside the center and reachable by city bus or car.

(*Fast Facts* Zadar

Airport **Airport Zadar** (© **023/313-311;** www.zadar-airport.hr).

ATMs **Privredna Banka,** Stjepana Radića 3; **Raiffeisen Bank,** Široka Ulica bb; **Zagrebačka Banka,** Brne Krnarutića 13.

Banks **Hypo Alpe-Adria Bank,** Jurja Barakovića 4 (© **023/200-999;** www. hypo-alpe-adria.hr). Hours 8am to 8pm Monday to Friday; 8am to noon Saturday; closed Sunday.

Bus Station **Zadar Bus Station,** Ante Starčevića 1 (© **023/211-555;** www. liburnija-zadar.hr). Ticket office open 6am to 10pm.

City Buses **Liburnija,** N. Jurišiśa (© **023/343-730**).

Currency Exchange **Aquarius,** Nova Vrata bb (© **023/212-919**). Hours 7am to 11pm daily. **Croatia Express,** Široka Ulica 12 (© **023/250-502**). Hours 7:30am to 8pm Monday to Friday; 8:30am to 1pm Saturday; closed Sunday.

Emergency **Emergency 94,** Ivana Mažuranića 28 (© **023/239-800**). Open 24 hours.

Express Mail **DHL,** Franje Tudmana 2 (© **023/224-444**). Hours 8am to 4pm Monday to Friday; closed Saturday and Sunday.

Ferry Office **Jadrolinija,** Liburnska Obala 7 (© **023/254-800;** www.jadrolinija. hr). Hours 6am to 4pm and 6 to 10pm Monday to Saturday; 7am to 1:30pm and 3 to 10pm Sunday. **Jadroagent,** Poljana Natka Nodila 4 (© **023/251-447**).

Hospital **Hospital Zadar,** Bože Peričića 5 near the Hotel Kolavare (© **023/315-677**). Open 24 hours.

Internet **Arsenal,** Trg Tri Bunara 1 (© **023/253-833;** www.arsenalzadar.com). Open 7am to 3am daily.

Laundry **Lotos,** Miroslava Krieže 19a (© **023/335-140**). Open Monday to Saturday 6am to 10pm, and Sunday 6am to 2pm.

Pharmacy **Ljekarna Centar,** Jurja Barakovićca 2 (© **023/302-931**). Hours 7am to 8:30pm Monday to Friday; 8am to 1:30pm Saturday; closed Sunday. **Ljekarna Donat,** Braće Vranjanin bb (© **023/251-342**). Hours 7am to 8:30pm Monday to Friday; 7am to 1:30pm Saturday; closed Sunday.

Photocopying **Pharos,** Široka Ulica 6 (© **023/317-054**). Hours 8am to 1pm and 6 to 8:30pm Monday to Friday; 9am to 1pm Saturday; closed Sunday.

Police Police Station, Zore Dalmatinske 1 (© **023/345-141;** www.mup.hr).

Post Office Central Post Office, Kralja S. Držislava 1 (© **023/316-552**). Hours 7am to 9pm Monday to Saturday; closed Sunday.

Taxi Call © **023/251-400.**

WHAT TO SEE & DO

Zadar is a city of dichotomies that juxtapose modern construction with ancient architecture, live-and-let-live attitudes with fiercely patriotic conviction, and bustling entrepreneurship with laid-back Mediterranean style. You can visit the city's historic sites and countless churches, stop for gelato in Old Town, then go on to browse in the glitzy shops that line the narrow streets, but it's much more interesting to seek out Zadar's less obvious charms.

For example, one of Zadar's best features is its sights and sounds, which emanate from the city's busy ferry port and other points on its open-air stage. At one end of the Riva you can watch one of the world's most beautiful sunsets accompanied by a fanfare of ferry horns. At the other end, you can sit on steps that disappear into the sea side by side with scores of people who fall silent to listen to the eerie melody created by the waves and the city's ingenious **sea organ** (see below). At night, the organ's ingenious sister installation called **"Greeting to the Sun"** (see below) keeps time by releasing beams of light stored during the day. Whatever your interests, you'll find something to pique them in Zadar.

Archaeological Museum ★ This museum on Forum Square holds many artifacts that chronicle Zadar's development and history as well as items that represent the evolution of northern Dalmatia. The museum houses a well-designed, well-captioned collection of exhibits, but watching kids skateboard or couples picnic among the Roman ruins out in front is much more interesting.

Trg Opatice Čike 1. (✆) **023/250-542** or 023/250-516. arheoloski-muzej-zadar@zd.htnet.hr. Admission 10kn adults, 5kn children. Mon–Fri 9am–1pm and 6–9pm; Sat 9am–1pm; closed Sun.

Church of St. Mary ★★ The Romanesque Church of St. Mary dates from the early 11th century, but its present look is a result of a 16th-century renovation. The bell tower, sometimes called Koloman's Tower in honor of the 12th-century Hungarian king of Croatia, was built around 1110. St. Mary's and its bell tower were severely damaged during World War II and it took almost 30 years to rebuild them. The church is open for Mass only, but glass doors in the vestibule allow you to peek inside when the church is closed.

Masses daily 7:30 and 8:30am.

Church of St. Simeon ★★ Visit this 17th-century church to see what's inside—an ornate 14th-century silver casket containing the remains of St. Simeon, one of Zadar's patron saints. The casket sits on the church's altar supported by four bronze angels, and its intricate detail shows scenes from the saint's life. Created by Zadar silversmiths in 1381 at the request of the wife of King Ludwig I of Anjou, one of Croatia's Hungarian rulers, it is hailed as one of the finest examples of silverwork ever produced in Zadar. If you happen to be in Zadar on October 8, the saint's feast day, you will be able to view his mummified body *in situ* during the annual opening of the casket.

Trg Šime Budinića. Open during Mass only.

City Walls and Gates ★★★ At one time, Zadar was the largest fortified city in Venice's portfolio. Today the walls and military facilities once devoted to defense are used as parks and backdrops for walking paths. Some sections of the walls were built by the Romans, and some were built by the Venetians much later as fortification against the Turks, who mounted relentless attacks on the city during the Middle Ages. Today only portions of the walls and four gates remain. The most impressive of these is the **Land Gate** on Foša Harbor, built by the Venetians in 1543 and decorated with sculptures that include the winged lion of St. Mark and the city's coat of arms. The **Sea Gate** is behind the Church of St. Chrysogonus between the ferry port and the market. It contains part of a Roman arch, but it was redone by the Venetians in 1573 to celebrate a Christian victory over the Turks. The gate is adorned with a relief of St. Mark's lion on the side facing the sea and is dedicated to Pope Alexander III, who visited Zadar in 1171. It also has a plaque noting the visit on the gate's land-facing side, and the street leading up to it is named Alexander. The **Bridge Gate** is the newest opening in the wall, cut through to Narodni Trg by the Italians in the 1930s. The last and smallest gate is **St. Rocco Gate.** It connects Three Wells Square with the harbor.

Five Wells Square (Trg 5 Bunara) ★★   Zadar survived Turkish attacks during the 16th century, in part by building a huge water tank and five ornate wells. After the Turks retreated, the city built a park over the fortifications and it includes a concrete square built around the wells. The wells no longer provide drinking water, but they do serve as "gates" for skateboarders, who like to practice their techniques on the span.

Forum ★★★   Zadar's Roman Forum was constructed between the 1st century B.C. and the 3rd century A.D. but was dedicated during the reign of the Emperor Augustus, as evidenced by one of its cornerstones. The Forum included a temple consecrated to Jupiter, Juno, and Minerva, and it had meeting rooms and other "offices" that sat above subterranean shops and workshops. The Forum's paving stones still are there, as is a stairway leading inside, some walls, and one of a pair of huge columns. The tall stone stand-alone column is known as the "Pillar of Shame," and in the Middle Ages, transgressors were tied to it so the public could humiliate them for their sins. The Forum ruins weren't discovered until the 1930s, and the site was damaged during World War II when Allied troops bombed the city.

In front of the Church of St. Donatus and the Archbishop's Palace.

The Gold and Silver of Zadar ★★★   The Benedictine Convent next to the Church of St. Mary doesn't look like much from the street, but inside you'll find one of the most impressive museums in Croatia. The church dates from the 11th century, and its collection of precious sacral art and even more precious relics is displayed on three floors and in the basement of the convent next door, where the church treasures have been guarded by Benedictine nuns since the end of World War II. The collection includes elaborate reliquaries for various saints' remains, many in the shape of an upraised arm or hand done in gold or silver. Paintings, crucifixes, vestments, and other examples of religious art from Croatia are also installed in the museum's well-designed rooms, where nuns in flowing black robes keep an eye on visitors and explain the exhibits. Before you leave the building, stop in at the ground-floor chapel of St. Nediljica behind the ticket office at the main entrance and take a peek at the tranquil convent garden that is visible only from inside the building. This is a fitting home for one of the most important cultural collections in Croatia. *Tip:* The ticket office/entrance to the museum is staffed by a nun in full-length black habit who will enforce the museum's dress code, which is similar to the dress code in many Croatian churches: You will be turned away if you are wearing revealing clothing.

Trg Opatice Čike 1. © **023/211-545.** Admission 20kn. Mon–Sat 10am–1pm and 6–8pm; Sun 10am–1pm.

The Riva ★★★   In most Croatian cities that face the sea, the Riva is usually a public "runway" where people go to see and be seen dressed in their trendiest outfits, always accessorized with an ice-cream cone. In Zadar, the Riva is a path called Petra Krešimira IV through a sort of waterfront park between Old Town and the sea, more garden walk than sidewalk. At night Zadar's beautifully landscaped Riva is a hive of activity, with a few vendors' stalls, traditional a cappella groups singing as they stroll, and folks getting exercise. By day, the Riva is a park and beach where people aren't shy about stripping down and taking a dip. The Riva also goes past Zadar's university, which overlooks the sea. Founded in 1396, it is the oldest university in the region and the oldest in Croatia.

Tip: When the sea is angry, Riva traffic moves off the stone promenade and behind the grassy park area that borders it except for those who don't mind getting soaked by crashing waves.

Midway along the Riva, you'll come across **The Sea Organ** ★★★, a one-of-a-kind pipe organ that employs air and water movement rather than an organist. It is difficult to classify the Morske *orgulje* (sea organ) as anything but an art installation with its smooth, wide, white-stone steps and ever-changing audience of passersby who come to marvel at the sea's musical talent. The exhibit is a source of constantly changing sound created by the organ's 35 pipes, which have underwater whistles. Sea motion drives air and water through the whistles' openings, producing an endless string of sounds that vary according to the force and speed of the waves and that is best described as a mellow whale-cello duet. The organ was designed by architect Nikola Bašić and built by experts from Zagreb and Murter Island. It was installed in spring 2005 and won the European Prize for Urban Space shortly thereafter.

Tip: The Sea Organ now has backup in the form of **"Greeting to the Sun"** ★★★, a solar-powered sculpture that collects energy during the day and releases it in the form of dancing light beams at night.

On the south end of the Old Town.

St. Anastasia Cathedral and Bell Tower ★★

This Romanesque cathedral built during the 12th and 13th centuries is the biggest in Dalmatia. The cathedral's facade is interesting because of its three doors, arches, and rose windows. Inside it are an understated stone main altar and a smaller side altar that contains the remains of its namesake saint. But it is the cathedral's detached 15th-century bell tower that attracts the most attention because you can climb to the top to take in a great view of the city.

Trg Sveti Stošije 1. ✆ **023/251-708.** Admission 15kn.

St. Chrysogonus Church ★★

Notable for its frescoes, high altar, and exterior stonework this 12th-century Romanesque church's facade is very plain, but the sides are adorned with elaborate columns whose shapes resemble Twizzler sticks. The exterior walls of three apses at the back of the church have several graceful blind arches. The altar was built in 1701 by grateful Zadar citizens who had escaped the plague, and it is adorned by statues of Zadar's four patron saints—Chrysogonus, Zoilus, Simeon, and Anastasia. The church is almost never open, but in July and August a few evening concerts are held there.

North of the Forum on Pape Aleksandra St.

St. Donatus ★★★

This unusual 9th-century church and the buildings around it were erected on the ruins of the city's Roman Forum. Some of the Forum's foundations lie exposed outside like an ancient sculpture garden. Kids play on them, people sit on them, and sellers display their wares on them all day and far into the night, oblivious to their history. St. Donatus originally was called the Church of the Holy Trinity, but eventually it was rechristened with its present name in honor of the bishop who founded it. The church's interior has a circular center and three apses; the narthex lies between the principal entrance and the rotunda. A circular stairway leads to the first floor. The church grew into a complex of ecclesiastical buildings over the years, and the cathedral itself is very plain inside with walls and altars devoid of statues, paintings, and other ornamentation. Mass has not been said in St. Donatus for more than 2 centuries, but the church is used for classical and sacral concerts because of its superior acoustics.

At the Forum. Admission 20kn. Daily 9am–1pm and 5–7:30pm.

> **Fun Facts   Full Moon Festival**
>
> Every year on the night of July's full moon, Zadar's electric lights are turned off for *Noć Punog Miseca* (Night of the Full Moon), and the Riva glows under the lights of the moon, torches, and candles. It is on this night that Zadar celebrates regional Croatian culture and customs with floating markets, impromptu restaurants, singing, dancing, and plenty of food. Local specialties from towns and islands in Zadar's vicinity are available up and down the waterfront from boats and kiosks, where people sample them and listen to traditional music all without benefit of electricity. On this night you can really get to know the region's culture through the sounds, tastes, and aromas of enthusiastic Mediterranean merrymaking.

Watersports

Anyplace you can touch the water on the Dalmatian coast is a potential swimming hole, but diving opportunities are fewer and require planning. If you are in Zadar, you can access diving operations on offshore islands and up and down the coast.

Zlatna Luka Diving Center ★★   Half-day excursion includes two dives, full tanks, and weights. Zlatna Luka offers weekend tours to Kornati National Park and other Adriatic locations. The center is about 7km (4½ miles) south of Zadar, at Marina Dalmacija, Bibinje-Sukošan (© **023/263-121;** www.diving-zlatnaluka.net).

WHERE TO STAY

There are no hotels in Zadar's Old Town, although one is just outside the wall. Most accommodations are more than 3.2km (2 miles) away in Borik, a suburb on the sea northwest of town. However, there is good public transportation between the central city and the surrounding resort areas.

Expensive

Hotel Bastion ★ Overrated   Stone from Zadar's 13th-century Kaštel fortress meets bordello-inspired design in this sometimes over-the-top boutique hotel adjacent to Zadar's wall. Our smaller-than-average room was outfitted with a gorgeous wood floor, heavy red brocade drapes and spread, numerous mirrors, and light fixtures made of chrome, smoked plastic, and drop crystals. While we found the Bastion reasonably comfortable and its location just outside the walls near the Tri Bunari in Old Town superconvenient, the price tag for a double with no unique amenities seemed excessive.

Bedemi Zadarski Pobuma. © **023/494-950.** Fax 023/494-951. www.hotel-bastion.com. 28 units. Doubles from 191€; suites from 307€. Rates include breakfast but not taxes. Parking 10€ per day. **Amenities:** Restaurant; bar; garden bar/sun deck; spa (7€ per day for guests). *In room:* A/C, TV, hair dryer, broadband Internet (ask for a cable at the desk), minibar.

Hotel President ★   Privacy and pampering are the President's strategy for making guests feel at home. There are no doodads like a pool or spa here, just an award-winning gourmet restaurant, **Vivaldi** (see below), quietly elegant rooms and suites, and attentive service that drips with class. Guest rooms and suites are outfitted with Biedermeier-style furniture and have balconies. The large granite bathrooms are filled with a generous array of toiletries, though a bubble bath is impossible since the bathrooms are outfitted with showers only. Each room has individual temperature controls within 3° of the default,

which can be overridden by the front desk. There is 24-hour room service from the **173**
Vivaldi.

Vladana Desnice 16, north of Borik. ✆ **023/333-696.** Fax 023/333-595. www.hotel-president.hr. 27 units. July–Aug from 222€ double; from 394€ suite. Rest of year from 178€ double; from 296€ suite. AE, DC, MC, V. Parking. **Amenities:** Restaurant. *In room:* A/C, TV, hair dryer, Internet access, minibar.

Moderate

Hotel Kolovare ★★ The Kolovare is a 15-minute walk along the Zadar Channel from the Land Gate and Old Town in the Kolovare district, walking distance to the central city. It is also one of the largest hotels in Zadar and you'll run into lots of tour groups there. However, thanks to a recent renovation, the Kolovare's guest rooms are brighter, more spacious, and more comfortable than those in most package hotels, especially guest rooms with balconies facing the pool and the sea beyond. All major car-rental agencies—Thrifty, National, Budget, and Dollar—have offices in the lobby.

Bože Peričića 14, Kolovare. ✆ **023/211-017.** Fax 023/213-079. www.hotel-kolovare-zadar.htnet.hr. 203 units. July–Aug from 1,310kn double; other times: 825kn double. Suites from 2,145kn July–Aug; from 1,825kn other times. AE, DC, MC, V. Rates include breakfast. Half- and full board available. **Amenities:** Restaurant; bar; pool. *In room:* A/C, TV, hair dryer, minibar.

Hotel Niko ★★★ ⓥ**Value** The Niko is a hike from Old Town, but it is one of the nicest hotels in the area and definitely worth the extra effort. The huge guest rooms have balconies large enough for a table and chairs, and half the rooms face the sea. Decor throughout is high quality and extends to the bathrooms, where the gleaming modern appointments reflect the fact that the all-season hotel was built in 2003. Add to that the hotel's magnificent **Niko** restaurant (reviewed below) and you have a recipe for success.

Obala Kneza Domagoja 9, Puntamika. ✆ **023/337-880.** Fax 023/337-890. www.hotel-niko.hr. 12 units. Doubles from 120€ July–Aug; from 85€ other times. AE, DC, MC, V. Rates include breakfast. **Amenities:** Restaurant; bar. *In room:* A/C, TV, hair dryer, minibar.

Mediteran ★ It's not on the beach but it is within walking distance of the water; some rooms even have sea views and balconies and it's painted peach. Only a few rooms in this delightful family-run hotel have air-conditioning and a minibar. Book these if you have a choice, especially in summer.

Matije Gupca 19, near Borik. ✆ **023/337-500.** Fax 023/337-528. www.hotelmediteran-zd.hr. 30 units. Doubles from 660kn July–Aug; from 520kn other times. Rates include breakfast. AE, DC, MC, V. **Amenities:** Restaurant; bar. *In room:* TV.

Inexpensive

Borik Youth Hostel A recent redo of the pavilion has spiffed up this budget stop near the beach. Well-kept rooms are dorm-style. You can get a bed with breakfast or half-board, but don't expect gourmet chow or many creature comforts.

Obala Kneza Trpimira 76, Borik. ✆ **023/331-145.** www.hfhs.hr. Bed with breakfast from 90kn. AE, DC, MC, V.

Camping Borik ★★ Woods and access to sand and pebble beaches are two of the amenities that make this campground tucked in the midst of houses, hotels, sports facilities, and convenient roads a desirable location. In addition, washroom facilities are clean and well equipped. The campground is a short ride from Zadar's center if you use public transportation.

Majstora Radovana 7, Borik. ✆ **023/332-074.** Fax 023/332-065. www.hoteliborik.hr. Capacity 1,800 people. Tent sites with 2 people 250kn. MC, V. **Amenities:** Restaurant; bar; market; sports facilities.

Zadar offers a wide range of dining choices. Hole-in-the-wall konobas serve everything from tasty stew to pizza to Continental cuisine. Modest establishments offer a large repertoire of Croatian and Italian fare, while classy, expensive gourmet restaurants feature inventive menus with blow-out prices.

Foša ★★★ SEAFOOD   Named after the harbor that flows next to the city's east wall, which is just outside its front door, Foša has the best location of any restaurant in Zadar. When you enter, skip the inside dining room and go straight to the terrace, which opens to the sea. By day your table is the best place to catch a cool breeze, and by night you'll have an unobstructed view of the water and the city lights. Foša is a local favorite for its well-prepared fish dishes. There are other choices, too, like the omelet with smoked ham.

Kralja Dmitra Zvonimira 2. ⓒ **023/314-421.** Reservations recommended. Entrees 40kn–80kn. AE, DC, MC, V. Daily noon–11pm.

Konoba Stipe ★ CROATIAN   Konoba Stipe isn't an ordinary pizzeria/grill restaurant, though the food is pretty predictable. This konoba also has a pretty garden setting done in dark green and white, though you have to walk through a mall passageway to get there.

Plemića Borelli 5a. ⓒ **023/213-275.** Entrees 30kn–70kn. AE, DC, MC, V. Mon–Sat 7am–midnight; Sun 11am–midnight.

Konoba Stomorica ★ (Value) DALMATIAN   It might have been the sound of locals belting out off-key renditions of Croatian songs that drew us to this place where tables are filled from morning to night. This traditional Dalmatian konoba serves huge portions of good food at reasonable prices. Seating is indoors or out. The black risotto is probably the biggest and cheapest portion around, at 30kn.

Stomorica 12. ⓒ **023/315-946.** Entrees 25kn–35kn. No credit cards. Daily 9am–midnight.

Kornat ★★★ (Finds) MODERN CROATIAN   This chic restaurant doesn't look like much when you see it from the ferry port across the street, but it is a hidden oasis of imaginative Croatian cuisine served in a refined atmosphere. Kornat is cleverly protected from street noise, fumes, and ferry horns by glass baffles that make it possible to enjoy a tranquil meal while sitting outside on the wooden deck or inside, where the dining room is all high style. After you finish the complimentary *amuse bouche,* try the octopus fish balls with potatoes and rosemary—two fish patties covered with arugula and large slices of shaved Parmesan with escalloped potatoes. Any grilled fish—sea bass with scampi sauce and tiny shrimp—is done to perfection. For meat eaters, the lamb with rosemary

---

(Fun Facts)   **Outdoor Ed**

It's a mystery how students at Zadar's University concentrate on their work: This white stone classroom building surrounded by lush vegetation on Zadar's Riva faces the sea and is a stone's throw from Old Town action. The Dominican monks who founded the institution of higher learning in 1396 must have known what they were doing, however—Zadar University is Croatia's oldest and has been attracting students for more than 600 years.

and red wine can't be beat, especially if you pair it with a selection from Kornat's excellent wine list. Top off your meal with one of the menu's light but sophisticated desserts such as melon in champagne, or go all out and choose a richer treat.

Liburnska Obala 6. ✆ **023/254-501.** Reservations recommended. Entrees 45kn–100kn, more for fish or lobster served by the kilo. AE, DC, MC, V. Daily 11am–midnight.

Niko ★★★ CROATIAN   With a history that dates from 1963, Niko qualifies as an institution in the Zadar area and it is also one of the best restaurants around, hands-down. Casual elegance, a great sea breeze on the awning-covered terrace, and a view of the harbor combined with a congenial waitstaff make this restaurant in Hotel Niko a great place for a leisurely lunch or a special night out. Any grilled fish dish is worth a try, but those with smaller appetites should try the scampi salad, a plate of little shrimp and cold potato salad. The Dalmatian plate is a generous sampling of pršut, sardellen, and Paški cheese; accompany it with a bottle of local white wine. A bonus: Real Maraska (cherry juice) is served here.

In Hotel Niko, Obala Kneza Domagoja 9, Punamika. ✆ **023/337-888.** www.hotel-niko.hr. Reservations recommended. Entrees 38kn–150kn. AE, DC, MC, V. Daily noon–midnight.

Trattoria Canzona ★★ ITALIAN   Just down the street from Konoba Stomorica, this traditional pizzeria is all Italian all the time. The menu has a huge array of pastas and pizzas and a Chicago tribute called Al Capone steak that comes topped with ham, cheese, peppers, and tomatoes. Canzona, a spinoff of a pizzeria with the same name in Zagreb, has both indoor and outdoor seating.

Stomorica 8. ✆ **023/212-081** or 023/212-080. Entrees 33kn–60kn. No credit cards. Mon–Sat 10am–11pm; Sun noon–11pm.

Vivaldi ★★ (**Overrated**) MEDITERRANEAN/CONTINENTAL   Vivaldi has a reputation for haute cuisine and even "hauter" prices. The decor of this restaurant (located in the lower level of the exclusive Hotel President in the Borik area outside of town) doesn't contradict that. The entryway is covered by a canopy and flanked by high hedges that would protect the identity of any celeb on a night out. Once inside the almost painfully formal dining room, you'll encounter lots of silver and crystal, a Continental menu, and a small but well-chosen list of high-end Croatian wines with prices to match. The menu seems a bit pretentious, with a mix of classic and contrived dishes such as duck in orange sauce, *pescano* Mexicano (mixed fish with Tabasco), fish rolled in citrus fruits and bread crumbs, and lots of big steaks as entrees. Save room for Vivaldi's version of cherries jubilee, made with local fruit.

In Hotel President, Vladana Desnice 16. ✆ **023/333-696.** www.hotel-president.hr. Reservations required. Entrees 115kn–250kn. AE, DC, MC, V. Daily 7am–1am.

Coffee, Pastries & Ice Cream

A visit to Zadar is not complete without doing a bit of cafe hopping. It's fun, it's cheap (around 5kn–10kn for a coffee, pastry, or ice cream), and you'll get a chance to relax with the locals.

Café Gallery Gina ★★ COFFEEHOUSE   If you're over 30, this is the place for you. Gina attracts a crowd that's more "mature" than most, perhaps because it also has a little art gallery and more mellow music.

Varoška 2. No phone. No credit cards. Daily 7am–1am.

(Fun Facts) **Sun Spot**

If you happen to be on Zadar's Riva at sunset, you'll be bathed in the reddest glow imaginable, a phenomenon that is the result of Zadar's setting in the middle of several islands and the Velebit range. You'll also see a large poster of Alfred Hitchcock under glass on the south end of Obala Kralja Petra Krešimira IV. It is captioned in five languages and tells the story of how "Hitch" strolled the Riva during a visit and proclaimed that "Zadar has the most beautiful sunset in the world." It's an observation that can withstand any challenge.

Corso ★ COFFEEHOUSE   If you want to try cafe-hopping, Corso is right next door to In Time (see below). However, Corso is a little more upscale with a polished modern interior and almost nonstop DJ music on weekends.

Milhovila Pavlinovića 4. ✆ **098/182-7741.** No credit cards. Daily 7am–2am.

Forum Café ★ DESSERT   This cafe's location couldn't be better. Set on a shaded terrace on the Kalelarga between St. Donatus and the Forum, the cafe is a natural stopping point for a cappuccino or a *bijela kava* for anyone exploring Old Town Zadar. However, despite the table umbrellas, the Forum can get uncomfortably warm in the afternoon.

Široka Ulica bb. ✆ **023/205-554.** No credit cards. Daily 7:30am–1am.

In Time ★ COFFEEHOUSE   In Time is one of those local hangouts where cruisin' and schmoozin' are de rigueur. It's in the path of Riva walkers, so it's also an excellent spot for people-watching.

Mihovila Pavlinovića 6. ✆ **091/536-8840.** No credit cards. Daily 7am–1am.

Kult ★ COFFEEHOUSE   This is the shadiest cafe in town, which is important during Zadar's blazing heat in July and August. Kult has the usual umbrella-protected tables, but they are double-insulated by their position under leafy trees. Kult is a popular gathering place for locals, who know how to keep cool.

Stomorica 6 at the junction of Stomorica and Svete Nediljice. ✆ **091/392-2595.** No credit cards. Daily 7:30am–1am.

Slastičarna Donat ★★★ GELATO   Even people from out of town have heard of Donat, reputed to have the best ice cream in Zadar due to its creative flavors and funny, congenial scoopers. This is no small feat in ice-cream-mad Dalmatia, where competition among *slastičarnama* is fierce and people aren't properly accessorized without a cone. There is always a long line waiting to place orders. The tables outside are full for good reason. The ice cream is superb and available in an endless array of concoctions.

Trg Sv. Stošija. ✆ **023/250-829.** No credit cards. Daily 7am–midnight.

Zadar After Dark

Much of Zadar's nighttime action is outdoors on the Riva or at other seaside locations. However, there are a few rockin' indoor spots worth a mention.

Barbara Bar ★★   The hotel Club Funimation's decor is tropical/Afro and Barbara carries out that theme, too. Barbara's wicker chairs and chaises with cool white upholstery,

lots of plants, and a languid vibe are make for a relaxing break. Open daily 8am to 1am. **177**
At Club Funimation, Majstora Radovana 7. Borik. 𝄐 **023/206-100.**

City Club Forum ★★   Togas are optional and you won't hear strains from Nero's fiddle at this trio of bars designed to conjure the fall of Rome. Music is mostly pop and rock and the ambience is all Roman excess. Open daily 11pm to 4am in summer and 11pm to 4am Thursday to Saturday in winter. Marka Marulića bb. 𝄐 **023/214-556.**

The Garden ★★★   There is nothing closer to nightclub Nirvana than the Garden, a cool, understated club on an expansive terrace high up in the city's walls. During the day, the Garden is park like with people playing outdoor chess, reading, or daydreaming on its terrace. As the sun sets, the Garden becomes a glowing red planet; then as darkness takes over, it roars to life as a sophisticated alfresco dance club. This is a don't-miss experience no matter the time of day. Open daily 10am to 1:30am May to September. Liburnska Obala 6. 𝄐 **023/364-739.** www.thegardenzadar.com.

Mango ★   As waterfront bars go, Mango is a cut above. It has an energized atmosphere, an interesting drink menu, and it is a vantage point for Zadar's unmatched sunsets. Open daily 8am to 1am. Krešimirova Obala. Diklo. **No phone. No credit cards.**

5 ZADAR ENVIRONS

Zadar is truly the center of activity for northern Dalmatia and also a point of departure for many other destinations. The medieval city of **Nin** is just a short drive north of Zadar. It is a town with funky charisma, the smallest cathedral in the world, and entrancing spirit legends. Zadar is also a ferry port for the decidedly undeveloped northern Dalmatian islands of **Silba, Ugljan, Pašman,** and **Dugi Otok.** Sometimes known as "the islands of the Zadar Archipelago," Ugljan, Pašman, and Dugi Otok are the three most visited of the offshore islands, but none are overrun by tourists. From Zadar, it's an easy drive to **Paklenica National Park,** a challenging environment for hikers, rock climbers, and spelunkers. And Zadar is also a major departure point for tours to the Kornati National Park, which is really a portion of the southern islands of the Zadar Archipelago. South of Zadar on the way to **Šibenik** ★, you'll hit **Biograd** ★★, once a medieval metropolis and now a crowded package resort. Each of these locations has its own charms, and each is a reasonable distance from Zadar—accessible either by private or public transport.

6 PAKLENICA NATIONAL PARK & NIN

ESSENTIALS

VISITOR INFORMATION   Paklenica information can be had at the Starigrad **tourism office** at Trg Tome Marašovića 1 (𝄐 **023/369-255;** www.rivijera-paklenica.hr), which is open from June 6 to September 15. Nin's **tourist office** is at Trg Braće Radića 3 (𝄐 **023/265-247;** www.nin.hr). The tourist office can provide maps, brochures, and information about Paklenica and private accommodations in the area.

GETTING THERE   Paklenica is a little less than 3 hours from Zagreb on the Zagreb-Split highway. Exit at a sign for the park before you get to Zadar and continue on the old road that skirts the sea. You'll pass lots of sobe signs before you get to Stari grad; a sign leading to the park turns into a one-lane road that appears to go through a residential area. The road leads to park reception, where you can leave your car, buy a ticket, fill your water bottle, and enter the park on foot. There is no direct public transportation to the park.

Nin is easy to get to by car or bus. Buses run between Zadar and Nin frequently; and the 16km (10-mile) ride takes less than half an hour.

GETTING AROUND   Paklenica is all about walking and climbing. No motorized vehicles are allowed inside the park boundaries, though they do stop at Starigrad, a little over a mile away. Nin is very compact and semi-pedestrianized, and walking is necessary to take in the sights.

WHAT TO SEE & DO

There is a beautiful karst landscape between **Paklenica National Park** and **Nin,** but there are some land-mine warning signs, too. Those are alarmingly near weekend homes and all along the way to Zadar, but the people staying there seem pretty blasé about them; you'll see houses and people precariously close to the signs as you drive through. Paklenica is the Velebit's best hiking territory and has many gorges, mountains, and caves to tempt adventurous explorers. Nin is a quaint medieval town with ancient churches and an excellent grill restaurant.

Paklenica National Park ★★★   Once you get to the entrance of Paklenica National Park, you'll think you know what to expect because you will have been looking at the Velebit's breathtaking rock walls and vertical landscapes for miles along the highway. However, when you stop at the reception kiosk at Starigrad, you'll be amazed at the park's softer side—the sound of locusts, the caress of the wind, the colors of wildflowers, and the scent of pine in the air.

Paklenica, which was proclaimed a national park in 1949, is a do-it-yourself experience: The only drinking water source is at reception, and you have to carry everything in yourself. There is no overnight camping at the park, but if you can't bear to get off the trail, you can book a bed at either of two communal huts on the mountain. Paklenica offers a huge choice of rock-climbing experiences, from beginner to expert, and there are more than 40km (60 miles) of hiking trails that can be charted for treks of a couple of hours or a couple of days.

Starigrad Reception Office: Admission 30kn adults, 20kn ages 7–18. Daily 6:30am–8pm. Cave 10am–1pm for 10kn surcharge. **Paklenica Park Office:** F. Tuđmana 14a, 23244 Starigrad-Paklenica. ✆ **023/369-202.** Fax 023/359-133. www.paklenica.hr. Apr–Oct Mon–Fri 8am–3pm.

NIN ★★★

Most people who explore this little town on an island don't stay overnight, but visit as part of a 1-day outing. Nin is connected to the mainland by a couple of stone pedestrian bridges (*Gornji most* and *Donji most*) and there aren't many facilities for housing tourists in town. In addition, there isn't a lot to do in Nin except explore the historic churches and a few shops, and rub the toe of yet another Meštrović statue of Grgur of Nin for luck. Nonetheless, the little town that once was an important center of Catholicism in medieval times is alluring.

Nin thrived during Roman times and became a municipality at the end of the 1st century under the Emperor Augustus. As with most Roman settlements, Nin had its own Forum, an amphitheater, and a temple that is the largest discovered in Croatia so far.

(Fun Facts) Bishop Gregorius of Nin

Gregorius of Nin was a Croatian bishop from the end of the 9th century to the beginning of the 10th. He was chancellor of the Croatian court and is known for his defense of Croatian culture, specifically the Glagolitic language. Gregorius was a scholar, a high-ranking cleric, and an adviser to the Croatian royalty who became Bishop of Nin in A.D. 867, the third priest to hold that office. Gregorius became known as a courageous fighter when he stood up against attempts to abolish the Glagolitic Mass. However, he lost that battle in a political struggle with the archbishop of Split when the Church Synods of A.D. 925 and A.D. 928 forbade priests from using Glagolitic language in their liturgies and ordered them to use Latin instead. The Synod subsequently gave control of Dalmatia to the Archbishop of Split, and Gregorius was transferred to Skradin, a city that is now the main portal to Krka National Park.

The Romans kept control of Nin until the 7th century, when the Avars and Slavs appeared on the scene, but the invaders didn't completely destroy the town and it managed to maintain its way of life to a degree. From then on, Nin developed culturally and politically and became a center of church activity and a headquarters for some of Croatia's kings and bishops. When the Venetians conquered most of the Dalmatian coast in 1409, Nin was included in the takeover. A century later, Nin became the target of Turkish attacks, and in 1570, Venice destroyed most of the city rather than let it become an enemy stronghold. Nin was rebuilt at the start of the 18th century, but it did not regain its former glory.

Bishop Grgur Ninski (Gregorius of Nin) Memorial ★★ Ivan Meštrović's sculpture of the famous cleric is sometimes mistaken for a statue of Merlin the magician from Arthurian times, and versions of it can be viewed in many locations and in many sizes in Croatia. This one in Nin is larger than all except the mammoth version in Split. It is surrounded by a small garden.

In the center of town, Nin.

Church of St. Anselmo and Treasury ★ The plaque outside identifies this parish church as the town's former cathedral with a construction/renovation history spanning the 6th to the 18th centuries. It is dedicated to St. Anselm who, according to legend, was Nin's first bishop and also one of Christ's early disciples. The church's side chapel is the only remaining part of the original church. The treasury next to the church has just over two dozen exhibits, most of which are gold. The treasury also contains a gold reliquary in the shape of a hand that is said to contain St. Anselm's shoulder bone.

Trg Sv. Marcele 1 XV Anselma, Nin. Admission 10kn adults, 5kn kids. Church rarely open. Treasury Mon–Sat 9:30–noon and 5:30–9:30pm; closed Sun and holidays.

Holy Cross Church ★★★ At first glance, the 9th-century Holy Cross Church is reminiscent of any pueblo church in America's Southwest. The church's whitewashed exterior is all shadow and angle in the direct Mediterranean sun, thanks to the cathedral's shape in the form of a cross. Holy Cross bills itself as the world's smallest cathedral, and it is a mysterious showstopper. According to Mladen Pejaković, a Dubrovnik artist, besides being a place of worship, Holy Cross is also a giant sun dial and calendar. Pejaković posits that the church is situated and constructed according to exact mathematical calculations that allow the sun's rays to fall on the floor and walls in such a way that they can be used to tell time and graph the summer and winter solstices.

In the center of town, Nin.

WHERE TO STAY

Most of the accommodations near Paklenica are private or at campsites, though there is one high-rise hotel in Starigrad and several small, family-run hotels in town. Contact the Starigrad tourist office (above) for accommodations information. You can also check out the ubiquitous SOBE signs around the park. Prices for sobe doubles start at 100kn without breakfast. For hard-core hikers, there is overnight shelter in a bare-bones mountain hut available in the park. In Nin, private rooms are the only options; the tourist office (above) can help you locate those.

Hotel Alan ★ This hotel is a regular stop for organized tours, but the guest rooms are better than adequate and they are less than a mile from the park entrance. The hotel also has a surprising array of amenities like tennis courts, an outdoor pool, and children's programs, and it is just half a football field away from the Starigrad town beach.

Franje Tuđmana 14, 23244 Starigrad Paklenica. ℭ **023/369-236.** Fax 023/369-203. www.hotel-alan.hr. 138 units, including 24 apts. From 89€ double; from 134€ apt. Rates include breakfast. Half-board available. AE, DC, MC, V. **Amenities:** Restaurant; pizzeria; bistro; bar; outdoor pool; sauna; room for those w/ limited mobility. *In room:* A/C, TV, hair dryer, minibar (fee).

Hotel Vicko/Villa Vicko ★★ The luxury you'll find at this small family-run hotel near the tourist office seems almost incongruous against the rugged wildness of Paklenica, but the Vicko is a nice place to stay whether you're seeing the park or not. Hotel guest rooms are roomy and bathrooms are up-to-date. Accommodations in the Villa Vicko annex on the beach, which opened in 2004, are even more plush.

Jose Dokoze 20, 23244 Starigrad Paklenica. ℭ **023/369-304.** Fax 023/359-191. www.hotel-vicko.hr. In hotel from 73€ double with balcony; in villa 75€. AE, DC, MC, V. Rates include breakfast. Half- and full board available with 7-day stay. **Amenities:** Restaurant; cafe/bar; room for those w/limited mobility. *In room:* A/C, TV, Internet access.

WHERE TO DINE

The Alan and Vicko hotels above both have good restaurants and there are lots of pizzerias and grill places throughout Starigrad and along the road leading to it. In addition, there are several markets and bakeries where you can stock up on sandwich makings and bottled water. In Nin, there are several cafes and grill restaurants near Donji Most and a few others on the main square, but the restaurant below is the best place in town.

Konoba Branimir ★★ GRILL This ambitious restaurant is right behind the Holy Cross Church. Branimir's architecture was cleverly designed to blend with the 9th-century church and the ruins in front, so its rustic look is an illusion. A bar and a huge *peka* are located in back of the restaurant and used for roasting lambs and suckling pigs; if you happen along when a roast is in progress, you won't be able to resist taking a table on the lovely stone terrace. Besides the usual grilled meat, the menu lists chicken breasts stuffed with bitter lettuce and bits of melon, and several special dishes like grilled lamb or *tingul*

The Zadar Archipelago

Ugljan, Pašman, Murter, and **Dugi Otok** all are part of what is sometimes called the Zadar Archipelago, a group of more than 300 islands. Three of the most popular with tourists are detailed below. Each has a distinct personality. All the inhabited islands in the archipelago are accessible by ferry only, with the exception of Murter, which is connected to the mainland by a bridge.

Ugljan is the island closest to Zadar and one of the most populous, though it is never very crowded. Ugljan has been inhabited since prehistoric times. It was once the site of Roman habitation, as indicated by the *villa rustica* still found there. Today nearly 8,000 people call it home, including some who work on the mainland. Ugljan's main industries are farming, animal husbandry, and fishing, though tourism is becoming a growing source of revenue.

Pašman, like Pag, has barren and fertile areas. Most of the sites on Pašman date from medieval times. The only occupied Benedictine monastery in Croatia (Sts. Cosmos and Damian) is behind walls and atop a hilltop near Tkon. That and the island's Franciscan monastery in Kraj are worth a stop.

Murter is south of Pašman and closer to Šibenik than it is to Zadar. However, it is mostly under Zadar's jurisdiction. Murter doesn't have much to recommend it except that it can be accessed from the mainland by a short bridge and it is also just south of the islands that make up Kornati National Park, making it a good staging area for visits to Kornati. Murter's largest and most interesting town, Murter Town, is the site of the Kornati National Park's office. Murter is also the best place to book an excursion to Kornati National Park, as its citizens own 90% of the park (p. 183).

Dugi Otok is the biggest island (117 sq. km/45 sq. miles) in the Zadar Archipelago, the farthest from the mainland. It also boasts the most irregular and "wild" coastline, which makes it particularly appealing to those who like adventure and who want to avoid the usual tourist haunts. Eleven villages are strung out along the northeastern side; on the western side, Dugi Otok's cliffs rise almost vertically from the sea. Dugi Otok also offers the remains of several medieval churches, as well as a gorgeous beach on Sakarun Bay at the island's north end.

Ferry service exists to Dugi Otok from Zadar, but there is little transportation on the island itself, so if you want to thoroughly explore it, you will need a car. The extreme southern portion of Dugi Otok is part of Kornati National Park (below). ***Tips:*** The lighthouse at Veli Rat is one of the best attractions on Dugi Otok. It is at the extreme western tip of the island and is surrounded by pines, bays, and beaches. The lighthouse is an unusual shade of yellow, said to be the result of the inclusion of 1,000 eggs in the paint.

(turkey stew with prunes and potatoes) that have to be ordered 24 hours ahead. Luckily, the restaurant will prepare the roasted specials for even just one person, so it's worth a call if you can plan that far ahead.

Viseslavov Trg 2, Nin. ☎ **023/264-866.** Entrees 50kn–300kn. MC. Daily 8am–1am.

7 BIOGRAD NA MORU ★★

Biograd na moru translates to "Biograd on the sea." Located about half an hour's drive southeast of Zadar, it's a huge resort town catering to families. In medieval times, Biograd was home to many aristocrats, but in the early 12th century (1115–25), the city was taken over and destroyed by the Venetians, rebuilt, and destroyed again by the Turks in the mid–17th century. There isn't much left that's older than 18th century except its magnificent waterfront location.

WHAT TO SEE & DO

As a seaside resort, Biograd has impeccable credentials. And Biograd's position near the **Kornati Islands ★★★**, the **Velebit ★★**, **Paklenica ★★★ and Krka National Parks ★★★**, and the historical cities of **Zadar ★★★**, **Šibenik ★**, and **Nin ★★★** makes it a good choice as a base for exploring the immediate area. Kornati excursions can be booked on the waterfront from several providers. Most excursions go from 8:30am to 5:30pm and cost 150kn per person. For those who want to stay put in Biograd, the Riva offers nightly possibilities ranging from kiosks selling souvenirs, gelato, and candy to electric go-carts to entertainment to seaside tables meant for conversation. There is a tram that takes visitors on a quick tour and to hotels along the waterfront. Cost is 10kn for adults and 5kn for children.

WHERE TO STAY & DINE

Hotel Villa Donat ★★ (Finds)   Donat, formerly the Hotel Mayica, is actually a hotel and an adjacent annex. It was renovated and landscaped in 2007 and the result is a couple of long, three-story (no elevator) buildings painted deep salmon to show off the masses of lavender and greenery planted all around them. Donat is walking distance to the beach but it is in Sv. Filip I Jakov, 4km (2½ miles) from Biograd proper, so if you stay at the Donat, you have the best of two resort towns at your disposal. Rooms are large and showers are outfitted with sleek Italian fixtures.

Liburnska 1. Sv. Filip I Jakov. ℂ **023/383-556.** Fax 023/383-008. www.ilirijabiograd.com. 72 units. Doubles in the Villa from 150€; doubles in the annex from 100€. Rates include buffet breakfast. Half-board available. Pets allowed for 10€ per day. **Amenities:** Restaurant; bar; volleyball court. *In room:* A/C, TV, hair dryer, minibar. May–Oct only.

Ilirija Hotels ★   The Donat (above) is part of a group of package hotels that includes the Adriatic, Ilirija, and Kornati, each of which has a different exterior look, but similar rooms, prices, and facilities. These hotels have been updated in the last 5 years, but their renovations can't disguise that they were built and designed for family getaways during Croatia's Socialist era. The Adriatic is open all year, while the Kornati is open from April to October, and the Ilirija from mid-March to December.

Tina Ulevića 7. ℂ **023/358-333.** Fax 023/383-008. www.ilirijabiograd.com. 364 units. Doubles with sea view from 130€. Rates include breakfast. AE, DC, MC, V. Pets allowed (20€). **Amenities:** Restaurant; bar; indoor and outdoor pool. *In room:* A/C, TV, hair dryer, minibar.

Restaurant Aquarium ★ DALMATIAN   Watch the evening promenade and boats docking in the harbor from your table at this waterfront terrace restaurant. Fish fresh from the Adriatic is the specialty of the house and it's wonderful with a side of grilled vegetables. Menus are printed in four languages in this tourist restaurant with very casual, family friendly ambience.

Krešemira IV 10. ℂ **023/383-883.** Entrees 50kn–110kn, more for fish sold by the kilo. No credit cards. Daily 8am–11pm Apr–Oct.

Restaurant Marina Kornati ★★ CROATIAN   The contemporary design and sophisticated ambience of this lovely restaurant at the Biograd marina are the perfect setting for a special meal whether you are a yacht owner or day-tripper. Dark wood floors, subdued lighting, and a menu that features Croatian cuisine with an emphasis on Dalmatian specialties are the draw.

Marina Kornati, Šetalište Kneza Branimira 1, Biograd. ℂ **023/384-505.** Entrees 60kn–140kn; more for fish sold by the kilo. AE, DC, MC, V. Daily 7am–midnight.

BIOGRAD AFTER DARK

Lavender Bed Bar ★★ COCKTAILS   This bar on the terrace of the color-coordinated Adriatic Hotel really does use beds as seats and they really are lavender. You can pretend you're in ancient Rome while sipping cocktails and listening to music among the trees at night or you can visit during the day and use the beds as a base for gazing at the sea. Daily 8am to 1am. Tina Ujevića 7. ℂ **023/290-700.**

---

8 KORNATI NATIONAL PARK ★★★

Kornati National Park is part of a group of nearly 150 mostly uninhabited islands south of Pašman and Dugi Otok. The park's 89 islands, islets, and reefs are scattered across an area of about 78 sq. km (30 sq. miles) of land and 207 sq. km (80 sq. miles) of sea. Kornati's unusual landscape of mostly barren, irregular karst terrain is a submerged mountain range; the visible parts are ancient mountaintops and valleys that now are islands and channels. Less than a quarter of the Kornati area is land, while the rest of the park is under the sea, and the park's underwater landscape is perhaps its most fascinating feature. Kornati is renowned as a diver's paradise with unusual rock formations where many species of fish and plant life thrive. Both scuba divers and snorkelers will enjoy Kornati, but scuba enthusiasts must be part of a group approved by the National Park if they want to explore any of the seven zones set aside for diving visits.

If you'd rather explore land, don't miss the Kornati "crowns," steep island cliffs that face the sea, a result of a rift caused by a continental collision millions of years ago.

Kornat is the largest of the park's islands and the site of the 6th-century **fortress of Toreta** ★, an excellent example of Byzantine architecture. The precise history of Toreta is not known, but it's probably safe to assume that the fortress was built to protect navigation on the Adriatic. Near the fortress, you also can see the remains of an early Christian three-nave church from the same period.

The islands were sold in the 19th century to the people of Murter by the Zadar aristocrats who owned them. Today the inhabitants of Murter own 90% of the land, and use it to raise sheep or to grow olives and other crops suited to its rocky soil.

There are no permanent residents on the Kornati islands, but some people do have houses that they use when tending sheep or taking care of their crops. It is possible to stay on Kornati with one of the families who have cottages there. To room with a Kornati family, make arrangements with any tourist agency in Murter. Kornati also has 16 bays with mooring areas designated for boaters who want to drop anchor overnight.

VISITOR INFORMATION For information on visiting Kornati National Park, contact the Kornati National Park office at Butina 2, Murter (© **022/434-662;** www.kornati.hr). The park office can direct you to approved dive escorts. The tourist office can direct you to private agencies approved to run individual tours and accommodations on Kornati.

GETTING THERE There is no ferry service between the Kornati Islands and the mainland, and the only way to get there is by boat. You'll have more travel flexibility if you have your own vessel, but you can't dive unless you are with an approved dive group. You can book excursions to the islands from Zadar, Šibenik, or Split. You can arrange for private boat tours and accommodations at the travel agencies on Murter.

9 ŠIBENIK ★

Šibenik fell on hard times after the 1991 war, and the former industrial port town still is suffering from the economic fallout. However, as coastal towns go, Šibenik offers a change of pace from Dalmatia's strong Italianate influences since its origins are pure Croatian rather than Roman.

Situated on a broad bay at the mouth of the Krka River, Šibenik's footprint is sometimes likened to that of an amphitheater as it hugs the slopes emanating from St. Anne's Fortress, a sprawl that began shortly after the city first was mentioned in Croatian historical writings in 1066. Today, much of Šibenik's charm comes from the warren of steep, winding streets and passages, the many sets of stone steps leading up to the center, and the ruins of city fortifications that fan out from St. Anne's to the water. Above the harbor, Šibenik's center is crowded with churches and monasteries as well as stone dwellings on narrow, covered streets that open to a series of interior town squares.

Šibenik's most prominent attraction is the Cathedral of St. James, which made the UNESCO World Heritage List in 2000. St. James is a must-see for anyone who comes to town, even the upscale tourists who berth their yachts overnight in Šibenik's harbor. Indeed, the city is a favorite port of call for yachts touring the eastern Adriatic and the Kornati National Park. It also is within easy access of Krka National Park, a region in the Dinaric Alps with karst and waterfalls similar to those of Plitvice, though Krka has the bonus of ruins from medieval fortified cities.

Immediately offshore, Šibenik has an archipelago of its own, a group of small islands with picturesque coves, blue Croatian sea, idyllic beaches, and few inhabitants. Two of them, Zlarin and Prvić, once were summer havens for Croatian writers, who retreated there to find their muses. Zlarin is known for its coral, while Kaprije and Žirje are centers for grape growers, olive growers, and fishermen. The islands are linked to Šibenik by ferries on regular runs to the Vodice resort area north of town.

ESSENTIALS

VISITOR INFORMATION Šibenik's tourist information bureau is at Fausta Vrančića 18 (© **022/212-075**). It can provide maps, brochures, and basic information about the city and neighboring sites. However, excursions to Kornati and nearby islands are booked through private agencies such as Atlas Travel on Trg Hrvatske 2 near the cathedral (© **022/330-232;** www.atlassibenik.com); or by Mag Tours at Franje Tuđmana 2a (© **022/201-150**). It's a good idea to call ahead to find out which tours are offered, and

Rest in Peace

The tiny farming village of Otavice west of Šibenik in the Dalmatian interior is the site of a stately church/mausoleum designed and built by Croatian sculptor **Ivan Meštrović** to serve as his family crypt. The road to **Otavice** from Šibenik is clearly marked, but this is land that was occupied by Serb forces during the Homeland War. If you venture here, you will pass through the town of **Drniš,** where there is a museum displaying several Meštrovic works. You also will see quiet, pastoral landscapes, some marred by crumbling homes that sustained war damage. Occasionally, you may spot a "Go no farther" land mine warning off-road. The **Meštrović family mausoleum** sits on a high hill overlooking the valley and the 1930s-era home the artist built for his mother in town. At the moment the house is in ruins and the mausoleum is neglected. During the Homeland War, Serb forces desecrated the crypt beneath the little chapel in the mausoleum and stole the bronze Meštrović reliefs of his wife and children that served as decorative panels on the mausoleum door. Today a lone care-taker keeps the mausoleum presentable—and open—for tourists.

when. For example, Atlas's Kornati tours leave just three times a week (Sun–Mon, Thurs) and if you aren't in town that day, you miss the tour. Atlas also runs bus tours to Krka National Park (Tues–Wed, Fri) and other regional sites.

GETTING THERE   There is decent bus and train service to Šibenik from larger cities in Croatia as well as from select international locations. The bus station is on the seafront at Draga bb. The train station is south of the bus station at Milete bb. They are just 5- and 10-minute walks from the Jadran Hotel, respectively.

GETTING AROUND   Driving in Šibenik is a nightmare. There is street parking on the waterfront, and the Jadran has a private lot, but the tangle of narrow streets that serve the outer town is almost always jammed with cars. In addition, the town core is pedestrian-only. You must climb a long, fairly steep staircase to get there, and the streets themselves can be difficult to navigate because of their incline.

WHAT TO SEE & DO

Šibenik isn't positioned as a vacation destination, but it can provide a nice sojourn from the rigors of a trip through Croatia. Its marquee attraction is the Cathedral of St. James and the quirky town center, but there are several beaches and two national parks within easy reach, too.

Bunari Secrets of Šibenik ★★★ (Kids)   This award-winning exhibit underwent renovation for more than a year and reopened in June 2009 better than ever. It is a mul-timedia interpretation of Croatian milestones built around four 15th-century *bunara* (water storage tanks) about 46m (150 ft.) from St. James Cathedral. Inside, two floors of sequentially arranged exhibits trace the city's history in words, photos, and even film. All exhibits are numbered so visitors can follow the displays in a specific order using a timeline that traces the city's evolution from its origins to the present day. The self-guided tour of

Krka National Park ★★★

Waterfalls, gorges, and traces of ancient settlements along the Krka River are some of the attractions at this national park less than 16km (10 miles) outside Šibenik. Krka was proclaimed a national park in 1985. You can tour as much or as little of the park as you like via boat, car, or shoe leather. All public roads marked on the park map are open to cars, except for pedestrian areas of Skradinski buk and Visovac Island and its 15th-century Franciscan monastery, which are accessible only by bus and the Krka National Park boats.

Like the falls at Plitvice, Krka's were formed from deposits of limestone sediment (travertine). But Krka's are considered more dramatic. In fact, Skradinski Buk is considered one of the best falls in Europe as it tumbles from 46m (150 ft.) over 17 distinct travertine deposits.

Krka National Park begins at the Šibenik bridge and continues to Knin. Road signs along the way are numerous and clear, marking all the park entrances. Each entry point has a parking lot (free), an information office, and a ticket office (60kn adults, 45kn children July–Aug). Like Plitvice, boats connect several parts of the park (Skradin and the Skradinski buk waterfalls, for example). Boats also take visitors to the monastery on Visovac Island.

Krka National Park Tourism Office is at Trg Ivana Pavla II, b.r. 5, p.p. 154, 22001 Šibenik (© 022/217-730; fax 022/336-836; www.npkrka.hr). Hours are 8am to 8pm all year.

Šibenik's culture, development, and famous native sons ends at a coffeehouse/wine bar/jazz club on the bottom level, where you can ruminate about what you've just seen.

Palih Omladinaca 2. © 098/341-175. Admission 30kn adults, 20kn children 7–14. Daily 10am–11pm. June–Sept, entrance through main door. Other times, entrance through cafe downstairs.

Cathedral of St. James ★★★ This Gothic-Renaissance church took more than a century to build between 1431 and 1536 because of its complex design and emphasis on craftsmanship. The Venetians initiated the project, but architect Juraj Dalmatinac (who designed Pag Town on Pag Island) is recognized as the principal designer. Dalmatinac worked on the project for more than 30 years, but died in 1473 before it was finished. In the end, one of Dalmatinac's protégés, Nikola Fiorentinac, supervised the rest of the project, including construction of the exterior's unique stone masonry, which consists of interlocking stone slabs and bricks custom-fit without mortar. Inside, the cathedral's walls and furnishings are richly embellished with intricate carvings and sculpture, as is the baptistry. The cathedral is a blend of styles and features incorporated into the design by each of the architects who worked on the project. Dalmatinac, however, is credited as the plan's visionary. Among St. James' best features is a whimsical frieze of 74 faces that festoons the outer walls. Legend says that these sculptures—which are almost caricatures set in stone—were created to take a jab at penurious citizens who refused to give their fair share toward the building of the cathedral, which is now on the UNESCO World Heritage List.

Trg Republike Hrvatske. Daily 9am–7pm.

England ★★ (Kids) (Finds) Dalmatian cultural amusement park aptly describes this
center in the village of Pskov Silo between Šibenik and Drniš in eastern Dalmatia. Experience how Dalmatians of old lived without electricity and other conveniences. You can visit by yourself, but unless you take the tour or are accompanied by a Croat who knows the region's history, you will miss the point.

Postolarsko 6. Drniš. ℂ **060/486-486** or 099/220-02-00. www.dalmati.com. 35kn adults; 18kn children 6–12; 5 and under free. Tours with lunch 299kn. No credit cards. Daily noon–6pm Easter–Oct.

St. Anne's Fortress ★ As castles go, this one is all show and little substance. St. Anne's is more impressive from afar than it is close up, but it is a great place to get a view of the city, the remains of Šibenik's walls, and the sea beyond. However, its interior has fallen to ruin, and there isn't much to see inside.

   Note: This is quite a hike, and it is really only worth it for the panoramic view of the Old Town.

Above (northeast of) the Old Town.

WHERE TO STAY

Accommodations in the Šibenik area are mostly in big resort settlements north and south of the city with a few small hotels and lots of private accommodations in between. There is just one hotel in Šibenik itself.

Hotel Jadran The marina near St. James Cathedral is its front yard; it's convenient to most of the city's attractions; and it's the only game in the town core. If you do stay in the dowdy, overpriced Jadran, ask for a room on the sea to take advantage of the breeze: The guest rooms are not air-conditioned. If you get one of the small rooms at the hotel's rear, you'll be close enough to neighboring buildings to see what's for dinner, and you won't get any air even if the window is wide open. However, if you're at the front and you *do* keep your window open, you'll be an accidental audience for the live music on the terrace and you'll be able to keep an eye on the folks in their luxury yachts moored out front.

Obala Dr. Franje Tuđmana 52, Šibenik. ℂ **022/212-644.** Fax 022/212-480. www.rivijera.hr. 57 units. July–Aug from 116€ double. Rest of year from 100€ double. Rates include breakfast. Parking (5.50€ per day). AE, DC, MC, V. Half- and full-board rates available. **Amenities:** Restaurant; terrace; bar. *In room:* TV, minibar (some rooms).

Hotel Imperial ★ The Imperial is a huge hotel complex with a pebble beach in the resort town of Vodice, less than 16km (10 miles) north of Šibenik. It is within easy reach of Krka National Park and the Kornati Islands. Only 170 rooms and 15 suites of its more than 400 units are in the main building, so if convenience is a concern, ask for one of these. The others are in annexes/villas. Only some of the rooms are air-conditioned; you should request one when booking.

Vladimira Nazora 53, Vodice. ℂ **022/454-437.** Fax 022/442-611. www.rivijera.hr. 423 units, including 12 apts. Aug from 177€ double with A/C; 20% supplement for suite. Rest of year from 84€ double; 10% supplement for suite. AE, DC, MC, V. **Amenities:** Restaurant; bar; children's program; indoor heated seawater pool; access to outdoor pool; diving school. *In room:* TV, phone.

Solaris Holiday Resort ★★ Five separate hotels comprise this huge development 4km (2½ miles) southwest of Šibenik that collectively can accommodate more than 3,000 guests at once. To be sure, the hotels are designed for families and tour groups who need value for their kunas, but they also are an ideal base for exploring Šibenik and nearby Krka National Park. The complex also has a spa where you can destress tired feet after hiking around the Krka waterfalls. Most rooms are the same compact, no-nonsense dorm style, but the Ivan and Niko were updated most recently (2005) and are the freshest.

Hotel Niko: Hotelsko naselje Solaris bb, 22000 Šibenik. ☎ **022/361-001.** Fax 022/361-801. www.solaris. hr. 218 units, 2 apt, all with shower only. Aug from 82€ double; from 88€ suite. Rest of year from 46€ double; from 37€ suite. All rooms have balconies. Rates include breakfast. Half- and full board available. Rates based on stays of 4 days or longer. AE, DC, MC, V. Free parking. **Amenities:** Restaurant; bar; seawater pool. *In room:* A/C, TV, hair dryer.

WHERE TO DINE

Like most of Dalmatia, Šibenik and the surrounding area are full of pizzerias and simple grill restaurants where you can get excellent fish and pastas. If you want a dramatic setting, walk north from the ferry terminal to the Dolac area, which has become a neighborhood food/entertainment court with numerous restaurants, cafes, and bars, many with live music.

Gradska Vijećnica ★★ DALMATIAN   Its name means "City Hall" and it has made Croatia's largest newspaper's "100 Best Restaurants" list. The "best restaurant in Šibenik" is situated in the loggia (first floor of the old town hall) on the north side of Trg Republike Hrvatska, across from St. James Cathedral. Vijećnica is the picture of elegance thanks to its loggia setting and an abundance of woodwork inside. The menu is pure Dalmatia, with lots of grilled fish and a few Italian-inspired pasta dishes. Try the peppers stuffed with cheese or the very generous portion of super-big scampi while you enjoy the pure, languid, Venetian ambience at tables that spill onto the square.

Trg Republike Hrvatska 1. ☎ **022/213-605.** Entrees 40kn–110kn. AE, DC, MC, V. Daily 9am–midnight.

Tinel ★★ SEAFOOD   This unusual multistory restaurant stresses whimsy and originality in the decor, but the ingredients—and many preparations—are unadulterated Dalmatia. Fish dominates, but options include lamb and baked dishes. Try the *brodet* (fish stew), and match it with a local wine from the restaurant's nicely balanced cellar.

Trg Pučkih Kapetana 1. ☎ **022/331-815.** Entrees 65kn–120kn. AE, DC, MC, V. Mon–Sat noon–3pm and 6:30–11pm.

8

The Kvarner Gulf

Experiencing all the charms of the Kvarner Gulf region requires a strategically orchestrated campaign. Some visitors to Opatija ensconce themselves in 19th-century villas, emerging only to luxuriate in the sun and surf by day and dine and dance by moonlight. Others hop-scotch among Kvarner's many islands, where yachts from all over Europe dock at marinas in the shadow of ancient waterfront buildings.

Ecologically savvy tourists can explore Mount Učka, which looms over the Opatija Riviera and offers hikers the opportunity to wander for hours among its wonders. Others prefer the rocky hills of Cres Island, where rugged paths monitored by grazing sheep run a dizzying course to deserted azure coves.

It's fairly simple to visit all the major mainland towns that dot the Kvarner coast by driving the coastal highway from Opatija to Senj, but it's much trickier to coordinate ferry connections to, from, and between the islands. Indeed, except for the facilities along the Opatija Riviera, the region's infrastructure is uneven at best, though tourism services on the offshore islands are improving. Visitors to the mainland can expect a broad range of accommodations and services, while island hoppers will find large package-hotels, a respectable selection of campgrounds (including many naturist colonies), and modest family-run hotels, usually in old homes or simple villas.

1 RIJEKA

142km (88 miles) SW of Zagreb; 615km (382 miles) NE of Dubrovnik

No matter which part of the Kvarner Gulf region you explore, you'll probably go through Rijeka, which is at the southern end of the Zagreb-Rijeka autocesta. There are no beaches or resorts on Rijeka's shores, so most people breeze past on their way to somewhere else without a thought to stopping. Rijeka's collection of 19th-century buildings and monuments is important. Many have been or are in the process of being restored, but most *could* use a good power-washing and a little paint. For now, you need to look beneath the grime and imagine Rijeka the way it once was.

GETTING THERE & GETTING AROUND

BY CAR   Almost all roads in Croatia eventually lead to Rijeka, but you can drive there from Zagreb in less than 2 hours on the Zagreb-Rijeka autocesta (A-6) from the north. A-6 also connects to the A-1 autocesta from Split in the south. From Ljubljana in Slovenia, take E-70 via Postojna and connect with local Route 6 at Illirska Bistrica. You will encounter a border crossing at Rupa. Occasionally there is some hassle here so be sure your documents are in order, and follow E-61 to Rijeka. Ferries from several nearby islands stop at Rijeka and dock near the Riva south of the center. A schedule and prices can be obtained from www.jadrolinija.hr; or call © **06/032-13-21** for schedule and price info.

Fun Facts   **Rijeka's Morčić (Moretto, Moro)**

A ceramic-and-gold rendering of a black woman in a turban has become a distinctive design for jewelry and a symbol of Rijeka, where the baubles are made. The colorful Morčić is mostly used in earrings, though the image of a Moorish woman is a popular mask worn by revelers during Rijeka's huge pre-Lenten carnival. There are many legends about the Morčić, including tales of a victory over the Turks thanks to a Moorish woman's prayers, but in reality, the Morčić probably is a vestige of 17th- and 18th-century European fashion, which was mad about anything Asian. As earrings, Morčić were worn by upper-class married women, sailors, fishermen, and only sons (in the right ear) to ward off evil spirits.

BY TRAIN   Except for fast-train service between Zagreb and Split, rail service in Croatia can be cumbersome, but the train stations usually are something to see. That's especially true of the terminal in Rijeka, which is straight out of the 19th century. Trains stopping in Rijeka connect with Opatija and other Croatian towns and with some European hubs, too. For a schedule, check the website, www.hznet.hr, which has routes and prices in English. Or you can call the central office (Željeznički Kolodvor; ☎ 060/333-444), though you might not be able to find anyone who speaks English. The station's ticket office is open from 9am to 4pm and from 5:30 to 8:45pm. At other times you can buy tickets on the train.

BY BUS   Buses to and from Rijeka connect with other parts of Croatia and run frequently. Fares are affordable: A one-way ticket to Zagreb costs 1.5€ to 16€, depending on the route. Buses also connect with other cities in Europe. The main bus hub is at Trg Žabica 1 and is open from 5:30am to 9pm (☎ 060/302-010 reservations and information). You can buy tickets on board the bus, but getting a seat is uncertain in summer.

BY PLANE   Rijeka is accessible by air, though the airport is actually near **Omišlj** on **Krk Island** 24km (15 miles) south of the city. After you deplane, you can get to town on the Autotrolej bus, which lets you off at the station at Jelačić Square for 2€ one-way. Or you can grab a taxi outside the airport and pay as much as 31€ for the same ride. Call the Rijeka airport (☎ 051/842-040); for flight info, call ☎ 054/842-132 or check www. rijeka-airport.hr.

GETTING AROUND

Navigating Rijeka and the surrounding area is fairly easy whether you wander around the center or go farther afield. City bus tickets can be purchased at **Tisak** kiosks (newsstands) or from the bus driver, and fares depend on how far you are going. You can go to **Lovran** for 2.5€, or to the nearby 'burb of **Trsat** for less than 1.5€. Walking is the favorite travel mode in Rijeka, and maps and other information about restaurants, shows, and monuments can be obtained at the **tourist office** at Korzo 33 (☎ 051/335-882; www. tz-rijeka.hr).

Taxis are plentiful and you can hail one off the street that will take you anywhere within the city limits, but you should always confirm the fare with your driver before getting in the car. Buses make regular runs from 5am to 11:30pm daily.

WHERE TO STAY & DINE

Despite its position as the third-largest metropolis in Croatia, Rijeka has few standout hotel and restaurant options but you won't go wrong with the selections below.

Bitoraj Hotel ★★ (Finds)   The Bitoraj opened in August 2007, shortly after the legendary **Bitoraj restaurant** (below) moved into its new quarters on the main floor of a new building—and one of the best things about this property is the pleasure and convenience of staying above a fine restaurant. Guest rooms are done with lots of wood and soft colors with big windows for natural light. Most rooms have showers, but some have tubs. The Bitoraj Hotel is about half an hour from Rijeka.

Sveti Kirž 2 in Fužine, first exit on the Rijeka/Zagreb autocesta. ℂ **051/835-019.** www.bitoraj.hr. 20 units. Doubles from 598kn July–Aug; from 450kn other times. Rates include breakfast. Free parking. AE, DC, MC, V. **Amenities:** Restaurant; bar/pub; room service; smoke-free rooms; tennis courts; rooms for those w/ limited mobility. *In room:* A/C, TV, hair dryer, minibar, free Wi-Fi.

Bitoraj Restaurant ★★★ CROATIAN   Bitoraj is a 30-minute drive from Rijeka, and the 75-year-old restaurant will transfer you to a completely different mindset about food from that of the Adriatic coast. In 2007, Bitoraj moved to a beautiful new space that includes the Bitoraj Hotel, but thankfully the owners didn't change anything about the restaurant's exceptional food. The menu offers huge selection of meals heavy on various game and forest vegetables, and you will be able to choose from exotic appetizers and main courses available few other places. From bear and deer ham, to Bitoraj's signature dish of young wild boars baked under a lid on an open fire *(peka)*, to great desserts, all dishes utilize the best ingredients the surrounding woods can offer.

In the Bitoraj Hotel, Sveti Kirž 2 in Fužine, first exit on the Rijeka/Zagreb autocesta. ✆ **051/835-019.** Fax 051/830-005. www.bitoraj.hr. Entrees 55kn–160kn, more for meat/fish by the kilo. AE, DC, MC, V. Daily 7am–11pm.

Grand Hotel Bonavia ★★   The 125-year-old building in the city's Old Town was completely redone in 2006 with big-city amenities and a covered dining terrace. The standard rooms are a bit small for the price, but some rooms have balconies; all have roomy ceramic tiled bathrooms.

Dolac 4. ✆ **052/357-100.** Fax 052/335-969. www.bonavia.hr. 121 units. Doubles from 162€; suites from 317€. Rates include breakfast. AE, DC, MC, V. Pets allowed. **Amenities:** Restaurant; bar. *In room:* A/C, TV, hair dryer, minibar.

Hamby ★ FAST FOOD   There *is* a McDonald's in Rijeka, but why settle for the predictable when you can feast on pizza slices, hot and cold sandwiches, and even pasta or salad for about the same price? This fast-food franchise at the train station even has outdoor dining.

Krešimirova 10. ✆ **051/332-535.** Sandwiches from 18kn. No credit cards. Daily 7am–9pm.

Hotel Continental ★   A 2009 mini-renovation has brought the Continental up to acceptable status, but its 19th-century exterior still is far more elegant looking than its guest rooms. Public areas are a frayed but the hotel *is* in Rijeka's center and overlooks a park near the river. There is a nice terrace and the coffeehouse serves great desserts.

Šetalište Andrije Kačiča-Miošiča. ✆ **051/372-008.** Fax 052/372-009. 69 units. Doubles from 90€. Rates include breakfast. AE, DC, MC, V. **Amenities:** Restaurant; cafe. *In room:* TV.

Hotel Jadran ★★   The Jadran is less than a mile from Rijeka's center in the Pećine neighborhood on the road to Split, but its location in a 1911 building and an extensive 2005 renovation put it in a class by itself (for Rijeka). The Jadran even has its own beach and restaurant.

Šetalište XIII Divizije 46. ✆ **052/494-000.** Fax 052/216-458. www.jadran-hoteli.hr. 69 units. Doubles from 135€; suites from 170€. Rates include breakfast. AE, DC, MC, V. **Amenities:** Restaurant; cafe; bar; beach; car rental. *In room:* A/C, TV, hair dryer, Internet connection, minibar.

Kamov ★★ INTERNATIONAL   Hotel Bonavia's ambitious restaurant has developed a menu that combines the best of Croatian produce with several inspired preparations. Begin with Nobleman's Nettle soup before you try the stuffed squid LaGuardia, brie-stuffed calamari tubes with Istrian pršut and scampi tails grilled on lava rocks. If you still have room, the truffle-infused cheese with a glass of dessert wine is a taste sensation.

Dolac 4. ✆ **051/357-100.** Fax 051/335-969. www.bonavia.hr. Reservations recommended. Entrees from 50kn. AE, DC, MC, V. Daily 11am–midnight.

Konoba Feral ★★ SEAFOOD   A nautical theme pervades this cellar restaurant where anything with shellfish is sublime. The scallops gratin with tomatoes, cheese, and white wine is especially good. The menu also lists some classic grilled Croatian choices, too.

Matije Gupca 5b. ✆ **051/212-274.** Entrees 45kn–90kn or more for fish by the kilo. AE, DC, MC, V. 9am–10pm Mon–Sat. Closed Sun.

Municipium ★★★ CROATIAN   Rijeka's most upscale restaurant is set in a restored Hapsburg building that housed the city's government in the 19th century. The atmosphere is formal but not stuffy, and the specialties of the house are mostly fish dishes. Regional foods like Pag cheese (Paški sir) and Dalmatian ham (pršut) are offered, as is steak Municipium, beef garnished with smoked ham, basil, and potatoes. *Tip:* Municipium will prepare steak tartare for two after 6pm.

Trg Riječke Rezolucije 5. $\textcircled{C}$ **051/213-000.** www.municipium.hr. Reservations recommended. Entrees 70kn–150kn, more for fish and meat by the kilo. MC. 10am–11pm Mon–Sat. Closed Sun.

Rijeka Youth Hostel ★ (**Value**)   The former Villa Kozulić was transformed into Rijeka's first hostel in 2006 and it is a better choice than a couple of Rijeka's "basic" hotels. The setup is standard dorm, but there are three doubles in the attic, a TV room, Internet, and a communal kitchen. RYH is less than a mile from the center in the Pećine neighborhood near the Jadran (above).

Šetalište XIII Divizije 23. $\textcircled{C}$ **051/406-420.** www.hfhs.hr. 60 beds, 3 doubles. 18€ per dorm bed; 42€ double. No credit cards. Year-round. **Amenities:** Communal kitchen; TV room; Internet.

Trsatika Grill and Pizzeria ★★ PIZZA GRILL   If you hit Trsat at lunchtime or if you need a break, try this restaurant-cum-terrace across the street from Our Lady of Trsat Church. The pizzas grilled in a wood-burning oven taste even better when eaten on the terrace perched above Rijeka. Inside, the front dining room is dark and cozy but there are more tables in a cavernous banquet room in the back. If you don't have a yen for pizza, try the green noodles carbonara or the roast veal knuckle, traditional Kvarner treats. Service is attentive and the view is free.

Šetalište Joakima Rakovca 33. Trsat. $\textcircled{C}$ **051/217-087.** Fax 051/217-455. Entrees 25kn–130kn. AE, DC, MC, V. Daily 11am–11pm.

Zalogajnica Grandis Placa ★★ (**Value**) CROATIAN   Order a *plat du jour* in this unpretentious restaurant and you won't be hungry for a week. This establishment at the market specializes in such slow-cooker classics as stews, goulashes, and casseroles. It's an ideal place to see how and what the locals eat without emptying your wallet.

Zagrebačka 16. $\textcircled{C}$ **051/331-981.** Entrees 23kn–60kn. No credit cards. Daily 5:30am–9pm.

EXPLORING RIJEKA

The wide pedestrian street called **Korzo** ★★ originally was constructed along the path of the town walls. It was rebuilt after the 1750 earthquake that just about leveled the city. Today the Korzo is lined with stores, cafes, restaurants, and even an enclosed shopping mall, which makes it a center of commerce and a great meeting place in the city. However, most stores on the Korzo close at 1pm on Saturday and don't reopen until Monday morning, making the area pretty dead on weekends.

Also noteworthy is **Gradski Toranj (City Tower)** ★. Baroque and bright, this yellow tower above the preserved city gate once was Rijeka's main entry point. It is one of the few structures left after a 1750 quake, but it was renovated and tinkered with for 140 years or so after the seismic event, which further altered its appearance. The clock was added in 1873 and the dome at the top in 1890. Today, fashionable retail outlets flank the tower, which is a popular meeting place.

Walk through the portal below the City Tower from the Korzo to **Trg Ivana Koblera,** where you will run into the **Stara Vrata (Roman Gate)** ★, Rijeka's oldest surviving structure. The Roman Gate once served as the portal to the Roman Praetorium, which

(Fun Facts)   **St. Vitus Church ★★**

Legend has it that when a disgruntled 13th-century gambler threw a rock at the crucifix that now resides on St. Vitus's main altar, the rendering of Christ's body on the cross began to bleed and the gambler was swallowed up by the earth except for his hand. How the church got the crucifix is a mystery, but it is known that the Jesuits built the current church in 1638 in honor of St. Vitus, Rijeka's patron saint. The church is an unusual rotunda containing touches of Baroque and Gothic and has a separate bell tower.

was Rijeka's military command center. The gate looks like a loose arrangement of cemented rocks growing out of a strange mixture of buildings, including a Hapsburg residence, a church, and a building left over from the socialist era. Once you pass through the gate, you will see more Roman excavations.

Much of Rijeka's Old Town (Stari Grad) was demolished to make way for modern infrastructure, but vestiges still remain. Remnants of the ancient city of **Tarsatica** that once stood in what is now the middle of town are visible in the vicinity of **St. Vitus Church** at Trg Grivica 11 (✆ 051/330-879). *Tip:* Take time to explore **Rijeka's city market.** It's just east of the Korzo and it meanders through several streets, alleys, and squares. It's the largest city market we found in Croatia.

TRSAT ★★★

Trsat is an attractive suburb in the hills above Rijeka with terraced gardens, villas, and tree-lined streets that skirt a cute center and a beautiful castle. Trsat is older than Rijeka proper: It was founded by the Illyrians and the Romans. Today it's a frequent tour-bus stop for pilgrims who want to visit the church where Jesus' boyhood home allegedly stood for a few years.

Our Lady of Trsat Church ★★   Legand says that when the Crusaders were relocating the home where Mary agreed to the angel Gabriel's proposal to become Jesus' mother (The Annunciation), they left it in Trsat. Franciscan monks built a church on the site where it allegedly was deposited in 1294, and today the church and adjacent 17th-century **Franciscan Monastery** are visited by thousands of pilgrims every year. Whether you believe the legend or not, the 15th-century church is notable for its stonework and artwork and for a **painting of the Virgin Mary** that is said to have been done by the apostle Luke. The small painting is on the main altar, which is in turn behind beautiful wrought-iron gates, but you can get fairly close if Mass isn't in progress. The monastery has a nice collection of sacral and other art, which you must see by appointment unless you happen to run into an agreeable friar who will take you around.
Trsat Hill. ✆ 051/217-018.

Trsat Castle ★★★   This remarkably well-preserved castle on a hill above Trsat is a second reason to visit the town. The castle dates from the Middle Ages but its last owner was a 19th-century count who purchased it as a ruin and transformed it into a neo-Gothic showplace complete with a mausoleum guarded by stone griffins. Today the castle is in *primo* condition, and the explanations on the exhibits inside are in Croatian and English. Admission is free, except for large groups. Both castle and fortress are open to visitors. Art galleries, concerts, and theater productions set up shop in the fortress during the summer. The **city tourist office** at the entrance to Trsat Castle is open from 9am to 8pm daily.

Trsat Castle. ✆ **051/217-714.** Free admission except for groups, which are charged about 15kn per head.

2 CRIKVENICA & NOVI VINODOLSKI

Croatians sometimes refer to Crikvenica as the "poor man's Opatija." Like the glitzy strip of real estate that skirts Kvarner Bay, Crikvenica is a resort town and has been since the late 19th century. Unlike Opatija, Crikvenica is a comfortable, affordable weekend getaway where folks who live in Rijeka and central Croatia are the most frequent guests. They stay in the town's post–World War II hotels and apartment complexes or at weekend homes, and take advantage of Crikvenica's long waterfront promenade, which is lined with shops, cafes, and acres of pebble beach. Nearby Novi Vinodolski has many of the same features as Crikvenica, but it is smaller and even *more* "down home."

GETTING THERE & GETTING AROUND
Crikvenica is a 2-hour drive from Zagreb and half an hour from Rijeka. Hourly buses travel the 30km (18 miles) between Rijeka and Crikvenica and deposit passengers a block from the city's tourist office at Trg Stjepan Radića 1c at the south end of the promenade (✆ **051/241-051**). It is open every day from 8am to 10pm July to August and from 8am to 2pm Monday through Friday the rest of the year. The Crikvenica Tourist agency (✆ **051/241-249**) is open 8am to 10pm daily June to September and from 8am to 3pm October to May. It books rooms and apartments from the same office. The office is stocked with maps, brochures, and books on the area and the rest of Croatia.

WHAT TO SEE & DO
Crikvenica caters to families and an older clientele seeking a beach vacation Sometimes it seems as though the entire town is arranged around that concept. However, if you're a history buff and want to take a break from the sun, the nearby town of **Novi Vinodolski** just 9km (5½ miles) south of Crikvenica will fill the bill. The Vinodol Statute recognizing the rights of local citizens and Frankopan rule was signed in Novi Vinodolski in 1288. You also can explore the remains of a 13th-century Frankopan castle in the hills above the town.

WHERE TO STAY & DINE
Hotels in Crikvenica and Novi Vinodolski are, for the most part, bland, and restaurants all have similar menus. However, there are a couple of notable exceptions.

Amor ★ SEAFOOD   Amor stands out as the best, and most expensive, restaurant in Crikvenica based on its selection of fresh seafood. Even if the interior appears to have been decorated by a Hawaiian pirate, the black and gold palms on tall stands that are stuck behind and between tables in this otherwise pleasant dining room don't detract from the food.

Frankopanska 35. ✆ **051/242-017.** Fax 051/242-017. Entrees 110kn–160kn. More for fish sold by the kilo. AE, DC, MC, V. Daily 8am–11pm.

Ethno Hotel Balatura ★★ (**Finds**) A 300-year-old collection of stone houses surrounded by karst mountains and woodlands is now an eco-friendly guesthouse near Novi Vinodolski and less than 6km (4 miles) from the sea. Gordon and Anne-Kathryn Godec and their five children moved to the Vinodal Valley from Germany in 2000. It took the Godecs 8 years to complete their environmentally conscious restoration, which also preserved historical detail. Each of the Balatura's 10 rooms is named after a flower and each is unique in size and configuration. Two of them, Violet and Lavendar, have Internet access through the rooms' TVs.

Mali Sušik 2. 51243 Tribalj. ⓒ **051/455-340.** Fax 051/455-344. www.hotel-balatura.hr. 10 units. Doubles from 130€ July–Aug; from 70€ other times. Rates include breakfast but not taxes. *In room:* TV, minibar, heated floors.

Falkensteiner Hotel/Residences Therapia ★★★ (**Finds**) When Archduke Josef, brother of Hapsburg Emperor Franz Josef, built Crikvenica's first hotel in 1895, he was so proud of the effort that he named it "Nadvojvoda Josip," after himself. The hotel became *the* place to be for the aristocracy, and during the 1930s the hotel became part of the same luxury chain as the Georg V in Paris. Fast forward through several wars and economic catastrophes to May 2006, the date that the hotel reopened as the Palace Hotel Therapia after a long and painstaking renovation. From its Hapsburg yellow facade to its gorgeous full-service spa and handsomely refurbished rooms, the Therapia is now a destination all by itself. The hotel's designers wisely incorporated features like the building's original stone stairways and ironwork into their plan while adding all the conveniences expected of a first-class hotel so guests could soak up history along with the hotel's thermal indulgences. *Tip:* The Falkensteiner group based in Austria acquired Therapia in 2009 and is making select units in the hotel available for purchase.

Braće Buchoffer 12. 51260 Crikvenica. ⓒ **051/209-700.** Fax 051/785-072. www.therapia.hr. 123 units. Doubles with balcony and sea view in July–Aug from 730kn; suites from 1,153kn. Other times doubles from 621kn; suites from 1,037kn. Rates include breakfast and use of the pool. Free parking. **Amenities:** Restaurant; bar; pool; full-service spa; tennis courts. *In room:* A/C, TV, hair dryer, broadband Internet, minibar.

Hotel Villa Ružica ★ (**Value**) Ružica was built in 1912 as a getaway hotel for Rijeka's workers. It is one of the few Crikvenica hotels with personality, even after a 2001 renovation that updated its guest rooms (on a budget). *Tip:* One-third of Ružica's 36 rooms are affordable suites, which makes it a good choice for families.

Bana Jelačića 1, PP: 22, 51260 Crikvenica. ⓒ **051/241-959.** Fax 051/784-378. www.vila-ruzica.hr. 36 units. Doubles July–Aug from 126€; suites from 144€. Other times doubles from 66€; suites from 80€. **Amenities:** Restaurant; bar; Internet cafe; excursions. *In room:* A/C, TV, hair dryer, minibar.

Novi ★★★ In 2006, Novi Vinodolski was just a quiet, small town south of Rijeka with a nice beach and modest accommodations. Since early 2009 it has been home to

---

Exceptionally Eco

The Novi resort's size doesn't keep it from being environmentally responsible. All its roofs are "green" in that they are planted with grasses and other local vegetation, and the vehicles that shuttle guests around the grounds all run on clean fuel—electricity.

Novi Spa Hotels and Resort, the largest facility of its kind in Europe and one whose attention to detail is reminiscent of the operations style of a Disney theme park. This is a huge complex with three restaurants, nine swimming pools, a kids' compound with pool and water slides, and a sports complex. Guest rooms are oversized and every room has a balcony and a view of the sea. Bathrooms are done in marble and have state-of-the-art fixtures, heated floors, a rain shower separate from the tub, and a generous supply of L'Occitaine toiletries. *Tip:* The spa has 14 saunas and a huge complement of fitness machines that are set in front of two-story floor-to-ceiling windows overlooking the sea.

Kralja Tomislava 4. ☎ **051/702-410.** Fax 051/244-540. www.novi.hr/en. 572 units, including 336 apt. Doubles from 240€, suites from 355€. Rooms booked online will be discounted during all seasons. Apt prices 240€–720€ depending on size. (200 more hotel rooms to open as we go to print.) Rates include breakfast in the hotel rooms and suites but not in the apts. Taxes are included in all rates. Year-round. Valet parking, garage. Pets allowed (15€ per day 12 lb. and under; 25€ per day over 12 lb.). **Amenities:** 8 restaurants; 6 bars; babysitting; children's program; 9 pools; sand and pebble beaches; spa. *In room:* A/C, TV, Internet access, minibar.

---

3 THE OPATIJA RIVIERA

OPATIJA

Opatija started as a tiny, nondescript fishing village with a church and a population in the low double digits. But in the mid–19th century, the mild climate and spectacular seashore caught the fancy of **Iginio Scarpa,** a wealthy Italian businessman who built the lavish **Villa Angiolina** ★★ (named after his late wife), surrounded it with a jungle of exotic flora from around the world, and invited all his aristocratic friends for a visit. Privileged Europeans were so taken with Villa Angiolina and Opatija that they erected villas of their own, each bigger and more ornate than the next, thus cementing Opatija's reputation as a winter playground for the wealthy.

It didn't hurt that in 1873 the railroad built a spur to connect Opatija to Ljubljana and beyond, and that the town was given a medical imprimatur as a healthy environment. In fact, Opatija originally was a health resort for Austrian snowbirds; its season ran from October to May. Thanks to word of mouth from the railroad and from prominent folks who visited Opatija, the city became wildly popular. Regal hotels such as the **Kvarner** ★ (Opatija's first hotel), **Imperial** (formerly Kronprinzessin Stephanie), and **Palace-Bellevue** were built to accommodate the fancy new tourists.

From the mid-1880s to the start of World War I, Opatija was the retreat of choice for such notables as dance maven **Isadora Duncan,** author **Anton Chekhov,** and a horde of Hapsburg aristocrats. World War I put a crimp on European vacations, and Opatija was not immune to the downturn, but tourists never really abandoned it, either. After two subsequent wars, modern Opatija still is popular with European tourists, who flock to the resort all year long, but especially from mid-July to mid-August.

GETTING THERE

BY CAR If you've driven to Rijeka, it's only another 20 minutes to Opatija via the coastal highway.

BY BUS The bus (no. 32) stops in front of the Rijeka train station and travels the length of the Riviera from there to Lovran every 20 minutes for 10kn one-way.

Operetta ★   To some it's just a shopping mall in a fixed-up old building, but the Operetta is really a cleverly restored and partitioned 19th-century villa at Sv. Florijana 1, next to the Bristol Hotel. It houses several upscale stores including Benetton as well as a pizza-by-the-slice fast-food emporium. If nothing else, you'll be able to marvel at the clever interior architecture. *Tip:* The mall is open for browsing until 11pm, but the stores inside set their own hours.

Šetalište Franza Josefa (aka Lungomare) ★★★   Promenading in the evening is an art form in Croatia in general and in Opatija in particular, and this 12km (7¼ miles) flagstone walkway along the shore from **Volosko** ★★ (4.8km/3 miles north of Opatija) to **Lovran** ★★ (9.6km/6 miles south of Opatija) is the granddaddy of them all. Along the way you can observe street theater, check out what people are having for dinner in the seaside restaurants that flank the path, take a dip from a rocky outcrop, or simply enjoy the stroll along the shore.

Villa Angiolina ★★   This is the villa that started it all, and thanks to careful restoration, it's easy to see why. Neoclassical design, mosaics, frescoes, and lush landscaping combine to illustrate why every rich 19th-century aristocrat wanted a place like this. The villa was built in 1844 and was renovated completely in 2000. Villa Angiolina is now a popular venue for weddings when it isn't being used for art exhibits and other cultural events. The Villa now serves as a museum for Croatian tourism. The surrounding **Park Angiolina** ★ is a monument to horticulture with colorful formal gardens as well as many tropical species that include the camellia, Opatija's official flower.

Park Angiolina 1. *©* **099/239-14-16.** Tues–Sun 10am–6pm.

Volosko ★★   This Mediterranean fishing village is a 20-minute walk north of Opatija along the promenade, but it is free of the Hapsburg bling that characterizes its sprawling neighbor. Volosko is also known for outstanding restaurants, which include **Amfora** ★★★ and **Le Mandrać** ★★★, two of the area's best. There aren't any important monuments or museums there, but Volosko's winding streets, modest vintage buildings, and decent beach are good places to explore when you are in the mood for some quiet time or a fabulous meal.

WHERE TO STAY
Very Expensive
Milenij ★★ (Overrated)   If your idea of the perfect hotel is one so loaded with features that you never have to leave the property, you can't beat the pricey Milenij/Millennium. The questions are, how much of this stuff do you really need and what are you going to use on vacation? Sure, the spa offers 10 kinds of facials, but standard guest rooms are typical hotel-chain, even the ones with tiny balconies and views of the water. The oversize bathrooms are better than average, with double marble sinks and conveniences like retractable clotheslines, and the windows have remote-control awnings, but the pillows are flat as pancakes, and the towels are skimpy. Three units have kitchenettes. The buffet breakfast in the hotel's Restaurant Argonauti is the best in Opatija; tables on the columned terrace make morning coffee an event. Guests have pool and gym privileges, and the staff will make dinner reservations or send your faxes, but except for those and a piece of chocolate on your pillow at night, most services outside the basic room tab

require an extra fee. When you add on all the charges for extras, the Milenij is Opatija's
most expensive hotel.

Maršala Tita 109, 51410 Opatija. 🕿 **051/278-007.** Fax 051/278-021. www.milenijhoteli.hr. 91 units. High season from 162€ double; from 335€suite; from 425€ kitchenette unit. Rest of year from 135€ standard double; from 300€ suite; from 375€ kitchenette unit. Rates include breakfast. AE, DC, MC, V. Parking 90kn per day May–Sept; 70kn per day other times. **Amenities:** 2 restaurants; bar; babysitting; car rental; concierge; room service; smoke-free rooms; spa; tennis courts; travel agency; excursions; currency exchange; valet services. *In room:* A/C, TV w/pay channels, hair dryer, minibar.

Miramar ★★★   The Miramar is a spa hotel in the heart of the Opatija. It started out in 1876 as the Villa Neptune; now, as the Miramar, it is vying to be the top choice of discriminating travelers. Since its transformation, the hotel's rooms sparkle. Bathrooms are outfitted with the latest fixtures and toiletries and are large enough to accommodate two. Some rooms have sea views and three have kitchenettes. Everyone has easy access to the hotel's spa, which includes a seawater pool, sauna, and salon.

Kaline 11. 🕿 **051/280-000.** www.hotel-miramar.info. 85 units. Summer from 275€ double; from 320€ suite/ kitchenette unit. Rest of year from 120€ double; from 220€ suite/kitchenette unit. Limited free parking. **Amenities:** Restaurant; cafe; bar; pool; spa. *In room:* A/C, TV w/pay channels, hair dryer, Internet, minibar.

Expensive

Agava ★★   Opatija is awash with Art Nouveau villas that are slowly being converted to exclusive inns. As of 2006, Agava comprises two of them. Rooms are stylish with wood floors, period furniture, and extras like room service and international newspapers. Agava is managed by the same folks who take care of the luxury Milenij Hotel. It is steps from the sea and Angolina Park, too.

Obala Maršala Tita 89. 🕿 **051/278-100.** www.milenijhoteli.hr. 76 units. Doubles from 1,150kn July–Aug; from 867kn other times. DC, MC, V. Garage (90kn per day July–Aug; 70kn per day other times). **Amenities:** Restaurant; bar. *In room:* A/C, TV, hair dryer, Internet, minibar.

Ambassador ★★★   Of all the hotels in Opatija that advertise "wellness" services, the Ambassador is the one with the most comprehensive program devoted to rejuvenation. Five Elements Spa is spread over two of the recently renovated (2007) Ambassador's 10 floors. Guests can float in the heated seawater pool, simmer in an eight-person whirlpool, sweat in a sauna, or indulge in one of the spa's numerous treatments. Rooms live up to the hotel's designation as Liburnia's best, but most guests probably will spend most of their time on the beach or getting pampered in the spa.

F. Persiča 1. 🕿 **051/710-444.** Fax 051/271-503. www.liburnia.hr. 180 units. Doubles from 180€ July–Aug; from 135€ other times. Rates include breakfast. **Amenities:** Restaurant; cafe; bar; children's program; spa. *In room:* A/C, TV, hair dryer, Internet access.

ⓘ **Fun Facts**   **Royal Trend Setter**

Croatia was the first country in the world to offer nudist vacations. It's common to find naked people on beaches all over the coast, not just in nudist camps. The Croatians say the British royals started the whole thing off when King Edward VIII and his mistress, Wallis Simpson, vacationed there in the 1930s to enjoy the view from the island of Rab and she took a nude swim in the Bay of Kanda.

Bristol ★★ Don't confuse this *fin de siècle* gem with the creaky Bristol in Lovran, and don't be put off by the egg-yolk-yellow color of its facade. This hotel reopened in late June 2005 nearly 2 decades of being closed to the public while it served as a shelter for Slavonian Croats who were displaced by the Homeland War. Happily, an extensive renovation turned the Bristol into a sophisticated, tastefully decorated showpiece. Guest rooms are spacious and done in soothing earth tones, and most have at least partial sea views. The Bristol is more buttoned-down than its avant-garde sister, Hotel Astoria, but its traditional atmosphere exudes comfort and confidence. The Bristol's exceptional English-speaking staff will help guests find a restaurant, book a bike tour/countryside picnic, and everything in between. Guests have access to the saltwater swimming pool at the regal **Opatija Hotel** down the block.

Maršala Tita 108, 51410 Opatija. ✆ 051/706-300. Fax 051/706-301. www.hotel-bristol.hr. 78 units. High season from 145€ double; from 215€ suite. Rest of year from 100€ double; from 200€ suite. Rates include breakfast. AE, DC, MC, V. Parking 30kn per day. **Amenities:** Restaurant; cafe; pool (at Hotel Opatija); excursions; room for those w/limited mobility. *In room:* A/C, TV w/pay channels, hair dryer, Internet access, minibar.

Design Hotel Astoria ★★ (Finds) High design is the guiding principle behind the new look of the Hotel Astoria, which opened in July 2005 after a year of renovation. When it was built in 1904 as Villa Louise, the hotel was an excellent example of stately Austrian-Mediterranean style. Today the hotel's new look is more Guggenheim Museum with touches of whimsy. Guest rooms are comfortable with sophisticated bathroom fixtures that make use of every inch of space. Lots of details such as artwork on the walls and vases filled with lucky bamboo make the spaces seem lived in, but it is big flatscreen TV that makes each room feel like home. If you can swing it, ask for a suite on the sixth floor, which was built atop the old hotel and is completely new, including balconies with louvered awnings and wood plank floors on three of the floor's six units.

Maršala Tita 174, 51410 Opatija. ✆ 051/706-350. Fax 051/706-351. www.hotel-astoria.hr. 51 units. High season from 137€ double; from 200€ suite. Rest of year from 93€ double; from 220€ suite. Rates include breakfast. Children 6 and under free in parent's room. AE, DC, MC, V. Parking 70kn per day. **Amenities:** Restaurant; pool (at Opatija Hotel); excursions. *In room:* A/C, TV w/pay channels, hair dryer, Internet access, minibar.

Mozart ★★ Spending a night in this pink confection on Opatija's "Hotel Row" is like being a guest in a regal Art Nouveau home. In fact, that's what the Mozart was when it was built in 1895. Since then, the building has undergone renovation (1995, 2006) and has added modern conveniences such as air-conditioning and a spa without changing its original character. Features include a stone-walled terrace and garden that serves as a backdrop for dining, polished wood floors strewn with Oriental rugs, guest rooms decked out in period furniture that include canopied beds, and modern bathrooms. One unit has a kitchenette. The liveried staff will jump in the gulf to make guests comfortable. Wolfgang Amadeus Mozart memorabilia is everywhere.

Maršala Tita 138, 51410 Opatia. ✆ 051/718-260. Fax 051/271-739. www.hotel-mozart.hr. 25 units. High season from 1,289kn double; from 2,062kn suite. Rest of year from 1,031kn double, from 2,580kn suite. AE, DC, MC, V. Parking 40kn per day. **Amenities:** Restaurant; cafe/piano bar; excursions. *In room:* A/C, TV w/pay stations, minibar.

Moderate

Admiral ★ This refurbished hotel (2005) is a favorite destination for tour groups. The rooms are serviceable but small for the price, and not all amenities work all the time. However, every room has a balcony that overlooks the Kvarner Gulf and the huge outdoor pool. The Admiral doesn't have much history or atmosphere, but it is well placed, with Maršala Tita at its front door and the sea and marina at its rear. If you just want a comfortable place to sleep with a pool and easy access to shopping and the water, and if you don't mind staying in a large, generic hotel that caters to tour groups, this is one of the best choices in town.

Maršala Tita 139, 51410 Opatija. (C) **051/271-533.** Fax 051/271-708. www.liburnia.hr. 180 units. High season from 1,075kn double; from 1,160kn suite. Rest of year from 800kn double; from 930kn suite. Rates include breakfast buffet. AE, DC, MC, V. **Amenities:** 2 restaurants; cafe; bar; outdoor pool; indoor pool w/ heated seawater; marina. *In room:* TV w/pay stations, Internet access, minibar.

Kvarner-Amalia ★ The oldest Croatian hotel on the Adriatic has a prime location on the sea and an exquisite terrace that abuts the Lungomare. The Kvarner's park setting and Austro-Hungarian pedigree create an old-world atmosphere that makes you feel as if you've just hit a time warp. Antique furniture, high ceilings, and lots of sparkling crystal and gleaming wood enhance the effect. Be sure to take a peek at the Crystal Ballroom, which looks poised for a formal Viennese ball. The indoor/outdoor pool that opens to the sea is another draw, as is the Villa Amalia Annex, which once was an official Hapsburg hangout. Rooms are anything but cookie-cutter, but those on the sea are head and shoulders above the rest (in price, too).

P. Tomašića 1–4, 51410 Opatija. (C) **051/271-233.** Fax 051/271-202. www.liburnia.hr. 83 units. From 550kn double; from 655kn suite. Rates include breakfast. AE, DC, MC, V. Limited free parking. **Amenities:** Restaurant; bar; 2 pools; sauna. *In room:* TV, minibar.

Villa Ariston ★ The terraced gardens behind this 19th-century villa are the setting for its renowned **Villa Ariston restaurant** (see below), which is a knockout, as are the views of the sea. But despite Viennese architect Carl Seidl's artful 1924 reconstruction of the villa, the guest rooms—especially the doubles on the top floor—are disappointingly cramped, dim, and in need of updating. The presidential suite, however, has a fabulous balcony and an unsurpassed view of the garden and water; it is even equipped with period furniture that includes a fainting couch. It is said that Coco Chanel and JFK slept there, but no one on staff knows which rooms they used.

Maršala Tita 179, 41310 Opatija. (C) **051/271-379.** Fax 051/271-494. www.villa-ariston.hr. 10 units. High season from 110€ double; from 169€ suite. Rest of year from 82€ double; from 123€ suite. Rates include breakfast. AE, DC, MC, V. Limited free parking. **Amenities:** Restaurant; wine cellar; garden. *In room:* TV, hair dryer, minibar.

Inexpensive

Hotel Imperial (Value) Walking up the long, wide staircase to the Imperial's front door makes you feel like you're approaching a monument, and once inside, the impression sticks. Staying in the 1885 hotel is like staying in a fine old opera house—crystal chandeliers, soaring ceilings, long corridors, heavy velvet curtains, etched glass doors, and a dining room fit for a royal banquet. Guest rooms are generous spaces complete with updated bathrooms and period furniture, but they are dark and tired-looking even if they have balconies. Asking for a room that opens to the sea is a catch-22 because the sea is across busy Maršala Tito: You'll get a good breeze but the noise might keep you awake. Be sure to walk to the back of the hotel on the first floor and see the black-and-white photo exhibit made from negatives shot when the hotel was new.

Maršala Tita 124/3, 51410 Opatija. (C) **051/271-577.** Fax 051/272-848. Imperial@liburnia.hr. 127 units. High season from 585kn double. Rest of year from 375kn double. AE, DC, MC, V. **Amenities:** Restaurant; cafe; bar. *In room:* TV.

Accommodations in Opatija are expensive, especially during July and August, unless you stay in private rooms (sobes) and apartments available through private agencies. One of the most helpful agencies is **Da Riva,** which has an office at Maršala Tita 162 (✆ **051/272-990,** 051/718-249, or 051/718-248; fax 051/272-482; www.da-riva.hr). The agency can find rooms from 145kn to 210kn per night without breakfast, but you may have trouble securing one unless you book for at least 3 nights, especially during the summer. Besides rooms, Da Riva also books excursions.

Camping

There are no campgrounds within Opatija, but there are a few both north and south of the city. During peak season, camps can be crowded, but they also may be your only chance for a place to sleep.

Autocamp "I" ★   Everything you need is in this resort/camp 12km (8 miles) south of Opatija. The grounds are well kept and the excellent beach is usually crowded.

A. Slatin bb, Mošcenicka Draga. ✆ **051/737-523.** Fax 051/737-460. 45kn per person including tax, plus another 45kn for car and tent site. Open May–Sept.

Ičići ★★   This camp has one of best beaches around, plus it throws a Saturday barbecue. It is 4.8km (3 miles) south of Opatija and is set into a hillside near the sea and Mount Učka.

Liburnijska 46, Ičići. ✆ **051/704-387.** Fax 051/704-046. 31kn per person per day; 105kn for 2 people, car, and tent site. Pets allowed. Open May–Sept.

Medveja ★★★   This campsite is a little farther south of Ičići and can accommodate 1,200 people with its combination of sites, rooms, and a few bungalows. Private rooms are available in the village. Like Ičići, Medveja is on the water but its beach is *the* best in the area.

Medveja bb. ✆ **051/291-191.** Fax 051/292-471. ac-medveja@liburnia.hr. From 455kn bungalow; from 235kn single room; 35kn campsite per person plus 47kn for car and tent site. Fido is welcome for an additional charge. Open May–Sept.

Preluk ★   About 4.8km (3 miles) north of Opatija near Volosko, Preluk is particularly well situated for those who love watersports.

Preluk bb. ✆ **051/622-249** or 051/621-913. Fax 051/622-381. tranzit@ri.htnet.hr. 32kn per person, 23kn per child; 45kn for car and tent site. Dogs allowed.

WHERE TO DINE

Expensive

Amfora ★★★ SEAFOOD   There is no question that Amfora has the most spectacular setting on the Opatija Riviera. Perched on a hill in the picturesque fishing village of Volosko a little more than a mile from Opatija's main drag, its ambience and menu are good enough to hold up anywhere in the world. After you order, you'll be served a complimentary taste of marinated and grilled sardella and shrimp or some other tasty *amuse bouche.* Try the savory black risotto done to creamy perfection and full of tender pieces of squid—it's an Adriatic specialty. The lobster tails are huge and attractively presented with melon, and salads are large and made with just-picked ingredients. Service is exceptional. Parking is free, though timid drivers might want to park on the road above the restaurant and walk down instead of attempting the steep turns to the parking lot.

Črnikovica 4. ✆ **051/701-222.** Fax 051/741-016. www.restaurant-amfora.com. Reservations recommended. Entrees 58kn–255kn. AE, DC, MC, V. 10% discount for paying cash. Daily 11am–midnight (until the last guest leaves).

Bevanda ★★ SEAFOOD   There are lots of seafood restaurants to choose from in Opatija, but if you want a table with a view of Rijeka's shimmering lights at night, sound effects provided by the sea lapping at the shore, and the kiss of a gentle sea breeze on your face while you nibble on mussels *buzara,* then Bevanda is for you. Bevanda hugs Opatija's famous promenade, so strollers might pass within a few feet of your table in the middle of dinner, but it's all part of the atmosphere. The restaurant also has indoor seating in a handsome candlelit room with a personality all its own. Portions can be on the small side and service is quite formal and often a little slow, but that makes Bevanda a good place to linger over coffee and gaze at the sea.

G. Verdia 23, 51410 Opatija. ✆ **051/741-305.** Fax 051/718-354. Reservations recommended. Entrees 52kn–305kn. MC, V. Daily 11am–11pm.

Le Mandrać ★★★ MODERN SEAFOOD   Le Mandrać bills itself as a "fish restaurant for the new millennium." Its ultramodern decor and stylized food presentations certainly follow that theme, but the restaurant is much more. Mandrać's menu is imaginative and changes frequently to take advantage of seasonal ingredients, which the chef combines in unusual pairings. If you have the time (and the money), try the "tasting" menu, which allows diners to sample small servings of a wide range of dishes such as poached egg with Istrian ham and nettle, or fudge with pear ice cream and rosemary.

Obala Frana Supila 10, 51410 Volosko. ✆ **051/701-357.** Fax 051/741-099. www.lemandrac.com. Reservations recommended. Entrees 70kn–290kn. Price of tasting menu varies. AE, DC, MC. V. Free limited parking. Daily 11am–midnight.

Villa Ariston ★★ CROATIAN   There is no finer alfresco dining in Opatija than at the exquisite terraced garden of Villa Ariston. Tables set among trees on terraced cubbies are decorated with pots of lavender and other flowers and each becomes a private bower by the sea. The menu is a blend of traditional Croatian and unbridled adventure, so go for one of the fresh fish dishes, or try the chicken breasts stuffed with truffles and mushrooms. Service at Villa Ariston is efficient but not hovering.

In the Villa Ariston hotel, Maršala Tita 179. ✆ **051/271-379.** Fax 051/271-494. www.villa-arison.hr. Reservations recommended. Entrees 52kn–255kn. AE, DC, MC, V. Daily 8am–11pm.

Moderate

Plavi Podrum ★★ SEAFOOD   Crisp blue awnings and white tablecloths billow in the sea breeze on the waterfront terrace of this fine restaurant, which is just steps away from Mandrać in Volosko. Plavi Podrum offers creative cuisine including green-tea tagliatelle with shrimp, wild asparagus, and nettle without sky-high prices or formality. The wine list is solid, but the bar also pours a wide selection of Scotch and Irish whisky.

Obala F.Supila 4, 51410 Volosko. ✆ **051/701-223.** Fax 051/741-195. Entrees 60kn–120kn. AE, DC, MC, V. Daily noon–midnight.

Slatina ★ Value TRADITIONAL CROATIAN   This restaurant is a local hangout on an enclosed porch across the street from the promenade on Maršala Tita. It dishes up huge portions of Slav specialties. From your table next to large windows that overlook the street and sea, you can see all the action and hear the music from the nearby Palace Hotel, too. Try the *šopse* salad, a mix of chopped cukes, tomatoes, onions, and peppers covered with shaved sheep cheese. The wild mushroom soup is a meal in itself, and the *tavće gravće* (beans in a paprika sauce) will make you turn up your nose at canned pork and beans forever. Heartier appetites will want to try any of the roast meats (lamb, veal, pork, chicken), which can also be had as *mućkalica* (meat with vegetables on top).

Maršala Tita 206, 51410 Opatija. ✆ **051/271-949.** Entrees 30kn–175kn. No credit cards. Daily 11am–1am.

Inexpensive

Opatija is loaded with affordable pizza places and cafes, most of which are along Maršala Tita and the Lungomare.

NIGHTLIFE

Croatia's strict blood alcohol limits for drivers toned-down Opatija's nightlife scene as would-be revelers from Rijeka figured that they could no longer go there to party and risk driving home. But even without Rijeka traffic, the town still rocks until around 11pm, which is closing hour for most Opatija restaurants and bars. Until then, you can sip a glass of wine, have a beer, or get rowdy at **Hemingway's** on the promenade or at any restaurant or cafe along the way.

However, the most nighttime action in Opatija is on the **Lungomare** and **Maršala Tita**—and it is alcohol-free. It seems that on any given evening all of Croatia is out taking a stroll, in-line skating, or pausing to watch break dancers and mimes. An ice-cream cone is the party treat of choice.

LOVRAN ★★ & ENVIRONS

Slower-paced and more casual than Opatija, the picturesque town of Lovran 6km (4 miles) to its north is the choice of tourists who want the Riviera's beaches and recreation opportunities, but not its upscale lifestyle. Lovran is where Opatija's Lungomare ends—or begins—depending on your point of view. Excitement in Lovran (named for its numerous laurel trees) is not limited to toasting on the beach. For 3 weekends every October there, the chestnut is king and you can feast on the celebrated nut in many forms at the annual **Chestnut Festival (Marunada).** There is also a **Wild Asparagus Festival** in April; and **Cherry Days** are in June.

There are reasons other than produce to consider a stay in Lovran, including stunning villas on the town's periphery; a quaint hilltop Old Town complete with a 12th-century church **(St. George's)** with lovely frescoes and Glagolitic inscriptions; a town gate known as **Stubica;** and two municipal beaches.

Getting Around

Buses to and from Rijeka breeze through Lovran every 20 minutes or so, or if you have your own car, you can get to Lovran from Opatija in about 10 minutes. You even can walk there along the Lungomare from Opatija or any point north of town along the 12km (7½-mile) promenade. The tourist office near the harbor can provide maps and other helpful information.

The Lovran Tourist Office's summer hours are 8am to 8pm Monday to Saturday; 8am to noon Sunday. Its winter hours are 9am to 4pm Monday to Friday. For more information, contact ✆ **051/291-740;** or check out www.tz-lovran.hr.

Where to Stay

Bristol ★ **Value** This six-story Belle Epoque building is surrounded by greenery and has a nice view of the sea. Its exterior shows recent maintenance, and the tolerable interior seems geared to vacationers who want a home base from which to get to the beach. Public areas retain touches of yesteryear such as brass sconces and marble staircases. Guest rooms are adequate. Almost all have balconies with views of the water or the Učka massif. If you can't find a sobe for a night, this will do.

Maršala Tita 27, 51415 Lovran. ✆ **051/291-022.** Fax 051/292-049. 102 units. Summer from 570kn double. Rest of year from 280kn double. Rates include breakfast. AE, DC, MC, V. Limited free parking. Closed mid-Nov to Mar except for holidays Dec 22–Jan 10 (varies). **Amenities:** Restaurant; bar; saloon; access to Excelsior's sports facilities. In room: TV, hair dryer.

Hotel Park ★★ The Park is a blue-and-white confection of a hotel next to the historic East Gate that leads to Old Town Lovran. The Park has a long history as a hotel, but its new era began in 2005 after an extensive makeover. Today the Park is a comfortable option away from Opatija's hustle and bustle. Rooms are spacious and equipped with "smart" electricity that operates only when your room key is inserted in a slot at the door. Windows have automated shutters and open to a refreshing sea breeze. Bathrooms are spacious, too, and most have showers only that must have been installed by Paul Bunyan—the fixtures are a good 2m (7 ft.) up the wall.

Šetabšte M. Tita 60, 51415 Lovran. ✆ **051/706-200.** Fax 051/293-791. www.hotelparklovran.hr. 49 units. Doubles from 1,124kn and suites from 1,584kn July–Aug. Other times, doubles from 666kn and suites from 1,022kn. Rates include breakfast. AE, DC, MC, V. Free off-street parking. **Amenities:** Restaurant; coffee shop; bar; pool. In room: A/C, TV, hair dryer, Internet access, minibar.

Where to Dine & Drink

Bellavista ★★ (Finds) CROATIAN There has been a restaurant on this site for 40 years, but this iteration of the atmospheric space just past the historic East Gate entrance to Old Town Lovran opened in 2007 with a new look and a new owner. Ask for one of the tables along the removable windows that look out to sea, but no matter where you sit, you will be rewarded with a fine meal and warm ambience. For a treat, try the salt baked fish, which is sold by the kilo. Or sample any of the homemade pastas like ravioli with spinach and truffles. Bellavista pays special attention to wines, too, and offers tasting plates of food that match select varietals.

Stari Grad 22, 51415 Lovran. ✆ **051/292-123.** www.bellavista.kvarnerinfo.net. Entrees 58kn–122kn. More for fish and meat sold by the kilo. AE, DC, MC, V. Daily 11:30am–11pm.

Gradska Kavana ★ LIGHT FARE This fancy tearoom was restored and redecorated in 2006 and now it's all crystal and flowers in shades of lavender and white. Gradska Kavana is much more than a place to grab a cone: Cocktails, fancy pastries, and American-style breakfasts, including omelets and ham and eggs, are served here, too. Gradska Kavana shares the same real estate as Lovranski Pub, but the Kavana is at street level.

M. Tita 41, 51415 Lovran. No phone. Breakfast 25kn–75kn. AE, DC, MC, V. Daily 7am–midnight.

Kvarner Grill ★ SEAFOOD This covered seaside grill with an extensive fish menu is right on the water and puts its daily catch on display in a refrigerated case at the entrance. Try the calamari any way you like it—the Kvarner Grill serves squid five ways. There are pastas and meats on the menu, too. Finish with sour cherry sorbet made with cherries from the surrounding villages.

Šetalište Maršala Tita 68, 51415 Lovran. ✆ **051/291-118.** Entrees 40kn–255kn. AE, DC, MC, V. Daily 10am–11pm.

Najade ★ SEAFOOD The menu at Najade is in four languages, which usually is code for "tourist trap," but the food at this seaside spot is competently prepared and fresh.

Enjoy a great view of the water from a terrace table while you nibble on grilled squid or risotto Najade, and you'll forget that not many of the guests are locals. Prices are a little higher than they should be, but not high enough to be alarming.

Šetalište M. Tita 60, 51415 Lovran. ☎ **051/291-866.** Fax 051/291-156. Entrees 40kn–90kn. More for fish and meat sold by the kilo. MC, V. Daily 11am–midnight.

4 KRK ISLAND

56km (35 miles) S of Rijeka

Croatia's largest island (pronounced *Kirk* with a strong Scottish burr) is also the country's most developed, especially in the north where the island is connected to the mainland via a mile-long toll bridge that sometimes is congested with commuters who live on Krk but work in Rijeka. Add Rijeka's airport, an oil storage facility, and an oil pipeline to the mix, and you have the ingredients for an industrial region.

Tourism facilities on "The Golden Island" (Krk's official nickname) are mostly on the island's coasts, and they run the gamut from huge package resorts such as **Omišalj, Njivice,** and **Malinska** on the northwest coast, to historic, partially walled **Krk Town** ★★ midway on the island, to the beach with promenade that is **Baška** ★★★ in the south.

Krk Town's settlement followed the familiar Illyrian-Roman-Byzantium-Venetian-Hungarian chain of control that is characteristic of many coastal cities. In the 11th century the city became an important center for the country's Glagolitic script, which was used there until the beginning of the 19th century. At that time, Austria-Hungary took Krk from the Frankopans (the dukes of Krk, a powerful feudal family), who had held it since the 12th century.

As with most of Croatia's islands, tourism is an economic mainstay for Krk, though there is some agriculture (wine and olive production) and industry (the Rijeka airport, pipeline, and a couple of shipyards). There also is an ongoing controversy about a proposal to connect the island's oil pipeline with Russia's.

GETTING THERE & GETTING AROUND

BY CAR   The Krk bridge connects the mainland with the island (13kn one-way). Ferries leave from **Valbiska** on the west side of the island for **Cres** ★★ and **Lošinj** ★★★, while another ferry line makes regular runs between **Lopar** on **Rab** ★★★ and **Baška** ★★★ on Krk's southern end during the summer months. There are several ferries each day from June through September, but ferry schedules are limited the rest of the year. Check the Jadrolinja website, www.jadrolinija.hr, for schedule and price details.

BY BUS   Krk Town is well served by buses from Rijeka and so are the nearby towns of Omišalj, Njivice, Malinska, and **Punat,** which are stops on the same route. Eleven of the 14 daily buses from Rijeka to Krk also go on to Baška in the extreme southern part of the island. You can continue to Cres and Lošinj by bus, but schedules are not firm, so check with Jadrolinja to see what's what.

Even if you don't have your own car, you can see all of Krk's main sites. Buses run regular routes between major towns and connect with less frequent, local lines.

KRK TOWN ★★

Krk Town is the island's largest population center and a tourism magnet. It also is the island's economic, cultural, and religious fulcrum. Krk Town is located in the middle of the Krk's western coast on Krčki Bay. It has an enchanting Old Town complete with sections of the settlement's original city wall; a 13th-century tower; and a narrow, busy shoreline walkway where restaurants, cafes, shops, and bars cater to beachgoers and promenading tourists. On summer nights, this route (**J.J. Strossmayera**) looks like a shopping mall the day after Thanksgiving.

Away from the center and the shore, the island's capital resembles a hilly suburban development that has expanded into every available vacant nook and cranny. In fact, finding your destination away from the center can be challenging as there are houses behind houses and hotels behind those. Krk Town is a popular weekend resort because it is so accessible to the mainland. If you're there just to see the important and interesting sites, you don't need to stay more than a couple of hours.

Tourist Agencies

The private tourist office **Aurea,** at Pupačića 1 (© **051/222-277;** www.aurea-krk.hr), can book private rooms or hotel accommodations as well as arrange excursions. Prices for private rooms are fixed by the tourist board at **Krk-info,** at Nikolića 34 (© **051/222-222;** www.multilink.hr/quanarius). They deal only in first-class properties, which translates to rooms with private bathrooms. Rates are from 275kn per double, breakfast not included. At **Krk Town Tourist Office,** Vela Placa 1 (✆ **051/221-414;** tz@tz-krk. hr; Mon–Fri 8am–3pm, closed weekends), you can get a map of the area and some brochures here, but private agencies have more info on rooms, excursions, and restaurants.

WHAT TO SEE

Katedrala Uznesenja (Cathedral of the Assumption) ★★
The architecture of this impressive house of worship on Trg Vela Placa is like a tangible timeline that spans 13 centuries, as it was built on the site of a 5th-century basilica during the 13th century and fitted with a bell tower in the 18th. The cathedral sits on the site of a 9th-century monastery, which in turn sits on the former site of the city's Roman baths. In fact, a unique feature of the cathedral's design is its utilization of pillars salvaged from a variety of Roman structures. You can see a little of the interior through the vestibule doors if you happen by when the cathedral is closed. However, try to be there when the cathedral is open so you can see the Roman columns, ancient mosaics, interesting paintings, and early stone carvings. The cathedral abuts a square with several examples of Frankopan architecture, where many concerts and cultural events are held.

Trg Sv. Kvinina. No phone. Daily 9:30am–1pm and 5–7pm.

Sveti Kivrin (St. Quirinus) ★
Krk Town's cathedral shares the square with the 11th-century Romanesque church of Sveti Kivrin (St. Quirinus), named after the city's patron saint. The church has an odd, four-section shape on both levels, and holds the town's collection of sacral art. The repository at St. Quirinus contains treasures from other churches in the area as well.

Trg Sv. Kvirina. No phone. Admission 5kn. Daily 9:30am–1pm May to mid-Sept.

WHERE TO STAY

Krk is a popular package destination for nearby European countries, which means that private rooms and accommodations are mostly generic and frequently overpriced. Still, despite the lack of cachet, Krk Town's hotels offer a wide range of services.

Dražica ★
Six floors of guest rooms make the Dražica a target for package tours and family vacations. A plus is that the hotel finished a 4-year renovation in 2003 when its guest rooms were retrofitted to accommodate elderly and people with limited mobility. The facility is close to, but not on, the water, and a 10-minute walk from the center.

Roužmarinska 6. ✆ **051/655-755** or 051/221-022. www.hotelikrk.hr. 127 units. Summer from 128€ double; from 150€ suite. Rest of year from 40€ double; from 50€ suite. MC, V. **Amenities:** Restaurant; bar; children's program; miniature golf; 2 pools; tennis courts; excursions. *In room:* A/C, TV, minibar.

Koralj ★
Located in a pine forest at the edge of a cove, this large hotel was renovated in 2003. It is close to the water and about .5km (¼ mile) from the city center. The Koralj is not a luxury hotel, nor is it spartan, but there is no air-conditioning, which makes for a noisy night because if you keep the windows open, you can hear music from the town center as well as anyone walking into the hotel. Rooms are tight but functional. Eighteen rooms have kitchenettes. Hair dryers are available at reception desk. The restaurant terrace at treetop level is beautiful.

Vlade Tomašića bb, 51500 Krk. ✆ **051/221-063.** www.valamar.hr. 172 units. Summer from 132€ double; from 175€ kitchenette unit. Rest of year from 55€ double; from 80€ kitchenette unit. Rates for kitchenette units do not include breakfast. AE, DC, MC, V. **Amenities:** 2 restaurants; bar; children's program; sauna; tennis courts; excursions. *In room:* TV, Internet access, minibar.

Marina ★★ A 2008 renovation has converted the 1925 Jugoslavia Hotel into the Marina, a quasi-luxury hotel with 10 unique rooms outfitted with modern conveniences and decorator furnishings. All rooms have a view of the sea and four have their own terraces, too.

Obala Hrvatske Mornarice, Krk Town. ⓒ **051/221-128.** Fax 051/221-357. www.hotelikrk.hr. 10 units. Doubles from 220€ July–Aug; from 160€ other times. **Amenities:** Restaurant, bar. *In room:* A/C, TV, hair dryer, Internet access, minibar.

Camping

Autocamp Ježevac There are no campgrounds in Krk Town, but this one is within a reasonable distance, about a quarter of a mile southwest of the town. It's on the coast and the ground is rocky, but if you have a decent air mattress, it's a good place to stay if you want to hit the water.

Plavinća bb. ⓒ **051/221-081.** Fax 051/221-362. jezevac@zlatni-otok.hr. 5.50€ per person plus 7.50€ per tent site.

Politin FKK If you want to try naturist camping (nudist camping), this camp is just southwest of the Koralj Hotel.

Politin bb, 51500, Krk. ⓒ **051/221-351.** Fax 051/221-246. www.zlatni-otok.hr. Closed Oct to mid-Apr.

WHERE TO DINE

There are fish restaurants and pizza places galore along Krk Town's shore. Most have the same offerings and prices. The restaurants listed below are representative of the city's dining options.

Konoba Šime ★★ SEAFOOD With only the Riva between its varnished picnic tables and the water, this casual fish restaurant is always packed with tourists. Service is a bit indifferent, but local cats provide entertainment as they walk up to you and beg for food. There is also an attractive, medieval-looking dining room indoors. Try any of the grilled fish dishes or the local *cevapčići.* The grilled scampi are served with their heads on and are both messy and pricey but delicious.

At the south town gate on the Riva. ⓒ **051/220-042.** Entrees 40kn–150kn. No credit cards. Daily 10am–11pm.

Restaurant Nada ★★★ MEDITERRANEAN It's 11km (7 miles) northeast of Krk Town in Vrbnik, and only two buses a day run there, but if you want a really special meal, this is the place to go. Set in a 100-year-old stone building near the sea, the tiny Nada has been open since 1974. It offers smoked ham, cheese made on Krk, salted fish, Krk lamb, scampi risotto, and Vrbnik's famous Žlahtina wine. You can tour the restaurant's wine cellar under the city walls if you make arrangements ahead of time. ***Warning:*** The only way to access the restaurant is uphill on foot, and it is a good idea to either stay overnight in Vrbnik after a meal with wine or have a designated driver: The roads leading to and from the town are winding and narrow.

Glavača 22, 51516 Vrbnik. ⓒ **051/857-065.** Fax 051/857-205. www.nada-vrbnik.com. Reservations recommended. Entrees 52kn–256kn. AE, DC, MC, V. Mar 15–Nov 1 daily 11am–midnight.

5 BAŠKA & ENVIRONS

70km (44 miles) S of Rijeka

When Croatians hear the word Baška, they immediately think about the 900-year-old tablet that is one of the nation's most important archaeological discoveries. The Baška Tablet is a large stone engraved with the oldest surviving text in Glagolitic script, and it is kept in Zagreb's Academy of Arts and Sciences. Besides its value as a cultural artifact, the Baška stone is also the first record of a Croatian king. It commemorates a gift from the first Croat King, Zvonimir, to the church. The tablet was found in 1851 in the floor of a little church at Baš on Krk and thus its name, but on Krk, the word Baška is also synonymous with sun, surf, and beaches.

The town of Baška is a sun worshipper's paradise with 2,500 hours of rays a year and more than 30 beaches of various sizes. The people who settled here in Roman times wouldn't recognize what this former fishing village has become, partly because it originally was on a hilltop before being relocated closer to the sea following the 16th-century Venetian Wars. Remnants of that era's structures still can be seen in the town's streets and tangled alleyways. Today's Baška retains much of the charm of bygone days, but it is also full of gleaming resorts and offers loads of activities for tourists.

GETTING THERE & GETTING AROUND

Baška is about 72km (45 miles) from Rijeka and less than an hour from Krk Town, but it's a world away from the Catskill atmosphere of Opatija. Buses originating in Rijeka stop at the edge of Baška between the harbor and the beach and it's a short walk to Zvonimirova, the town's main street and the site of the city tourist office, which can provide maps, brochures, and directions. Information about the town and accommodations is also available at a number of private tourist agencies. In addition, summer ferries connect Baška with Lopar on the island of Rab to the south.

Autocamp Zablać, at E. Geistlicha (© **051/856-909;** fax 051/856-604), offers information about camping site, prices, availability, and directions. **Aventura,** at Zvonimira 194 (© **051/856-774;** www.aventura-baska.com), finds private accommodations, changes money, and arranges excursions. **Baška Tourist Office,** at Zvonimirova 114 (© **051/856-817;** fax 051/856-544; www.tz-baska.hr; June–Sept 8am–8pm daily; Oct–May 8am–3pm Mon–Fri), gives maps, brochures, and directions. **Hoteli Baška,** at E. Geistlicha 34 (© **051/656-111;** fax 051/656-801; www.hotelibaska.hr), manages all the big tourist hotels.

WHAT TO SEE & DO

Baška beaches ★★★ Anyone who visits Baška must see the beach even if soaking up the sun isn't on the agenda. By day or night the city's beaches are a center of activity and a great place for people-watching. Baška's long expanse of beach once was a soft sandy strip, but the sand has been covered with pebbles.

Church of St. Lucy ★ The floor of this church in Jurandvor, less than a mile north of Baška, is the place where Croatia's Baška Tablet was found in 1851. As with Egypt's Rosetta Stone, it took years to decipher the Glagolitic script that mentions Zvonimir, Croatia's first king. The church is impossible to miss—it's visible from all over this small town—and is always open.

Stara Baška ★★   It's just a tiny village on a bay to the west of Baška proper, but Stara Baška is a sight worth seeing if you can ignore the nearby weekend homes that seem to be multiplying like rabbits. There are no buses here, so you have to drive or devote a day to hiking in the hills. If you fall in love with the place, there are apartments and rooms available as well as three restaurants. In the summer, you also can catch a cruise to Rab, Cres, and Lošinj, or just stay put and visit the remains of the medieval **St. Jerome Church.**

Wellness Baška ★★★   As Croatian spas go, this is one of the most beautiful in the country. Situated near the Hotel Zvonimir, Wellness Baška opened in June 2005 and was designed to resemble a Mediterranean villa with all the soothing colors and scents associated with that part of the world. In addition to its beautiful environment, Wellness Baška has a list of facilities and holistic services second to none, plus a huge, outdoor pool ringed with exotic plants and flowers.

Emila Geistlicha 38. ✆ **051/656-825.** Fax 051/656-826. www.wellness-baska.info. Daily 9am–9pm.

WHERE TO STAY

Baška is full of hotels, villas, and private accommodations. Hotel rooms for July and August usually are booked well in advance by German and Italian guests who have been coming to Baška for generations. If you must visit during these months, book your rooms by Easter.

Expensive

Atrium Residence ★★★   Atrium is more like a condo complex than a hotel: Most units are suites or studios with mini kitchens and fine appointments, and each has lots of elbow room. Atrium is practically in the water, and its rooms facing the sea are the biggest, the nicest, and the most expensive in town. Some even have saunas en suite and hot tubs on their balconies. Apartments have fridges and cookware. Atrium opened next to the Hotel Zvonimir in 2008, filling a much-need void in Baška's upscale boutique inn category.

Emila Geistlicher 38, Baška. ✆ **051/656-111.** Fax 051/856-880. www.hotelibaska.hr. 64 units. Doubles from 196€; apt from 300€. Rates include breakfast. Closed Nov–Mar. **Amenities:** Restaurant; cafe; bar; access to pools and facilities at nearby Hotel Corinthia. *In room:* A/C, TV, hair dryer, Internet access, minibar.

Moderate

Hotel Zvonimir ★★   You'd never know that the Zvonimir was built in 1906 because the renovation completed in 2005 has turned the hotel into a comfortable contemporary showcase. Guest rooms are furnished in shades of the sea to complement the view out the window. The hotel is steps to the beach and the **Wellness Baška spa** ★★★.

Emila Geistlicha 34 51523 Baška. ✆ **051/656-111.** Fax 051/656-880. www.hotelibaska.hr. 70 units. Summer doubles from 960kn, suites from 2,170kn. Other times doubles from 510kn; suites from 1,270kn. AE, DC, MC, V. Rates include breakfast. **Amenities:** Restaurant; cafe; bar; pool; spa; excursions. *In room:* A/C, TV, Internet access, minibar.

Villa Adria ★★ ⓥ **Value**   Another Hoteli Baška property, this apartment facility down the street from the Zvonimir is spacious and so close to the beach you could throw a rock into the water from your bedroom. The kitchenettes are fully equipped, which is a boon for families and anyone who doesn't want to bother going out for a meal. Guests at Villa Adria also have the option of using any of the Zvonimir facilities. And the two-bedroom units can sleep four or more comfortably.

Emila Geistlicha 34. 51523 Baška. ✆ **051/656-111.** Fax 051/856-880. www.hotelibaška. 12 units. Summer doubles from 763kn; apts from 1,458kn. Other times doubles from 337kn, apts from 641kn. Doubles rates include breakfast; apt rates do not. AE, DC, MC, V. **Amenities:** Access to all Zvonimir Hotel facilities. *In room:* A/C, TV, Internet access.

Camping Zablać ★   Wake up next to the sea at this camp by the water on the south end of the beach. Problem is that when the sun comes up there isn't any shade and everything bakes. But refrigerators are for rent here and there's a surfing school with surfboards for rent about 90m (300 ft.) from the camp.

E. Geistlicha 38. ✆ **051/856-909.** Fax 051/856-604. www.hotelibaska.hr. 220kn for 2 with car and tent site.

FKK Camp Bunculuka   This naturist (nudist) campground has its own beach and is just over the hill east of the harbor. The camp has a restaurant, bar, and sports center, too. It also has washers and dryers so you can wash the clothes you aren't wearing anyway.

E. Geistlicha. ✆ **051/856-806.** Fax 051/856-595. www.hotelibaska.hr. 194kn for 2 with car and tent site.

WHERE TO DINE

Bistro Kvarner ★ CROATIAN   Right on the promenade, this charming tile patio serves up some of the tastiest food around. The menu has pastas, risottos, and the usual complement of grilled meats and fish. You can be adventuresome and order the steak with cherries, but it is the Italian-style pizza with ultrathin crust that stars here. Try the Pizza Pigalo, a concoction with prosciutto, tomatoes, mozzarella, and mushrooms. Service is quick and courteous.

Emila Geistlicha. ✆ **051/856-366.** Entrees 24kn–38kn for a medium pizza and up to 125kn for a fish plate. AE, DC, MC, V. Daily 10am–midnight.

Caffe Mateo GELATO   At least one helping of ice cream is de rigueur for anyone on a beach vacation in Croatia. Some of the best frozen treats are served here along with pastries, coffees, and fancy fruit drinks with or without alcohol.

Emila Geistlicha 22. ✆ **051/856-109.** Drinks and treats less than 20kn. AE, MC, V. Daily 10am–midnight.

Galeb ★★ GRILL   Galeb is tucked into a covered terrace on the Baška promenade along the beach. Grilled meat is featured prominently on the menu, but seafood stars. Try the smoked bass filet with horseradish sauce or the tagliatelle with mixed seafood.

Emila Geistlicher 38. ✆ **051/860-071.** Entrees 60Kn–150kn, more for fish and meat by the kilo. AE, DC, MC, V. Daily 9am–midnight.

Restaurant Cicibela ★★ SEAFOOD   This cute fish restaurant near the tourist office serves well-prepared seafood and meat in a nautical atmosphere. The catch of the day is proudly displayed in an ice case as you enter so you can be sure your dinner is fresh. Try the Baška platter, a mixed grill for two, or the grilled scampi. The *blitva* (potatoes mixed with Swiss chard) is excellent. All seating is indoors, so try to get a window seat.

Emila Geistlicha 22a. ✆ **051/185-013.** www.cicbela.hr. Entrees 54kn–210kn. AE, DC, MC, V. Daily 10am–midnight. Closed Nov 1–Mar 15.

6 RAB ISLAND

Like an actor who insists on being photographed from his "better side," Rab's terrain has two halves that are quite different from each other. If seen from the mainland, Rab resembles a strip-mined mountainside devoid of vegetation and inhospitable to intelligent life. The southwestern side of the island, however, is a very different story. Tranquil beaches and coves, green spaces, and a beautifully kept medieval Old Town belie travelers' first impressions. Rab has been a haven for tourists since the 19th century, but its history goes back even further.

Like Pag to the south, Rab was settled by Illyrians, who were succeeded by a series of conquerors: Romans, Byzantines, Croat-Hungarians, and finally the Venetians, who plundered the timber on Rab and other offshore Kvarner islands to build their ships. This wholesale environmental piracy left a vast swathe of ruined terrain. It wasn't until the late 19th century that tourism began to cross the forlorn-looking east side of the island to get to Rab's verdant southwest side, where hotels began to sprout for aristocrats intent on frolicking in the surf.

Italy and Germany dominated Rab around World War II, and the island finally reverted to Yugoslavia in the late 1940s when Tito took control. Tito converted the barren little island of Goli Otok (btw. Rab's east side and the mainland) into a prison camp where he detained Stalin supporters (though officially the place didn't exist and wasn't mentioned until Tito's death). It is said that men who wound up on **Goli Otok** spent their days carrying rocks from one site to another and back again.

Today Goli Otok is a tour-boat stop and Rab is a mecca for economical family vacations and for visitors who want to combine a beach vacation with a little history. The island's main tourist destinations are Rab Town, with its medieval center and series of Venetian campaniles (bell towers); and Lopar Peninsula at the island's northern tip, with its sandy beach and shallow water. Rab is also becoming a popular overnight stop for luxury yachts, which become tourist attractions themselves when they tie up in Rab Town's horseshoe-shaped harbor.

GETTING THERE

BY CAR AND/OR BOAT Getting to Rab can be tricky if you are anywhere but the mainland because of the vagaries of ferry connections between the islands. The ferry between Baška at the southern end of Krk runs to Lopar only between June and September, and then just five times per day. If you have a car, the efficient Rapska Plovidba car ferries zoom from **Jablanac** on the mainland south of Senj to **Mišnak** on the island's south end every half-hour (or more often) from 5am to 10:30pm during summer, but the schedule is reduced by half in winter. In the summer of 2009 the cost for a car and two people was 120kn one-way. Another Jadrolinja car ferry route runs from Rijeka to Rab and goes on to Mali Lošinj three times a week. At Mali Lošinj you can connect with the Mariner ferry that operates between **Koper** and **Zadar** with stops at **Pula** and **Mali Lošinj.** Lines for the ferry at Jablanac can be excruciatingly long in July and August, but the once-a-day car ferry from Mali Lošinj to Pula or Zadar (depending on the direction) is frequently half-full, so plan accordingly.

BY BUS There are two daily buses from Rijeka to Rab via the Jablanac ferry connection, and two others from Zadar. For other transit options, contact the Rab Tourist Office (p. 214), but in any case, be sure to book ahead. The buses fill up quickly during the summer months.

GETTING AROUND

Moving around the island is no problem as there is frequent bus service between Lopar and Rab Town, and between Rab Town and **Kampor, Barbat,** and **Suha Punta** on the island. A water taxi goes to the tourist complex at Suha Punta on the southwest side of the island four times a day from the Hotel Istra in Rab Town, and another makes the same number of daily trips to the nearby Fraknj FKK compound (nudist camp).

RAB TOWN

Rab Town is a medieval wonder, rich with ancient churches and narrow, cobbled streets that seem to be vertical at points. There also is a wealth of stone buildings with red-tiled roofs, and four Venetian-inspired campaniles that stand sentry at the harbor.

ORIENTATION

Old Town is immediately behind the Riva and marina, and you have a choice of three narrow uphill paths, **Donja, Srednja,** and **Gornja** (lower, middle, upper), to get there. A Merkur store, the bus station, and a few tourist agencies are about a quarter of a mile north of the Old Town and, farther west, you'll find **Komrčar Park** and the **Franciscan Monastery and Cemetery,** with the town's beaches on its south end.

VISITOR INFORMATION

Numerous sources of information are available to visitors on Rab. Many arrange accommodations and excursions. **Rab Tourist Office,** at Trg Municipium Arba 8, Rab Town (✆ **051/771-111;** fax 051/771-110; www.tzg-rab.hr; daily June–Sept 8am–10pm; Oct–May 10am–2pm Mon–Sat), is the official arm of the city's tourist association. There is a satellite tourist office behind the bus station. **Atlas Travel Agency,** at Trg Municipium Arba (✆ **051/724-585;** www.atlas-rab.com; daily June–Sept 8am–10pm; Oct–May Mon–Sat 8am–1pm; closed Sun), can arrange for excursions and private accommodations as well as boat tours of the island. **Kristofor Travel Agency,** at Poslovni Centar Mali Palit 70, Rab Town (✆ **051/775-508;** www.kristofor.hr; daily summer only 8am–9pm), specializes in private accommodations.

WHAT TO SEE & DO
Churches & Bell Towers

Rab Town is a city of churches. Most of these are along the Gornja spur (upper road) that parallels the Riva. Some of the churches are open only for Mass, but most leave vestibule doors open all day so you can peek through a window or iron grate and get a glimpse of the inside. If you are heading uphill from the harbor, be sure to take a look at the **fountain** in **Trg Svetog Kristofora,** which is adorned with sculptures of the mythical figures of **Kalifont** and **Draga.** Between the fountain and the churches are a few 15th-century palaces built by highborn families. **Dominus Palace** and **Nimira Palace** are the most impressive, but both are closed to the public.

There are many strategies for seeing Rab Town's string of churches, but if you are coming from the Nimira Palace and continue on to the top of the hill, you'll run right into **St. Christopher's,** which once was part of the city's highest tower. A small **lapidarium** next door holds ancient tombstones and other artifacts. Turn down Gornja Ulica, and you'll come to **St. John the Evangelist Church (Sveti Ivan Evandelista),** which dates to the 6th or 7th century and is little more than a ruin. The church served as a monastery for various religious orders as well as a bishop's residence, but it was closed in the first third of the 19th century and many of its bricks were used to repair other churches in the city. The 13th-century bell tower next door can be climbed.

Next is **Holy Cross Church (Sveti Križ),** which, according to legend, has a crucifix with a Christ figure that wept because of the townspeople's immoral conduct. **St. Justine Church (Sveti Justina)** is next, with its 16th-century bell tower and collection of sacral items, including the reliquary that supposedly holds the skull of St. Christopher. Continue on past Trg Slobode and you'll come to a third bell tower at **St. Andrew Church (Sveti Andrije),** which dates from the 12th century.

Church Hours

St. Christopher Church: July and August, 9am to noon and 7:30 to 10pm. June and September, 7:30 to 9pm.

St. Christopher Lapidarium: July and August, 9am to 1pm and 6 to 8pm. Admission 5kn.

Holy Cross Church: July and August, 9am to noon and 7:30 to 10pm. June and September, 7:30 to 9pm.

St. Justine: July and August, 9am to noon and 7:30 to 10pm. June and September, 7:30 to 9pm.

St. Mary the Great: Daily 10am to 1pm and 7:30 to 10pm. 5kn to climb the bell tower; kids can go to the first level if accompanied by a parent. Call ✆ 051/724-195.

Just beyond that is the Romanesque **Church of St. Mary the Great (Sveta Marija Velika),** which is not only on the highest hill in town but also has the biggest bell tower. Both the church and its bell tower were built in the 12th century. The *pieta* above the church door dates to the early 16th century. The church itself is full of centuries of history with its 11th-century altar canopy, its 15th-century choir stalls, and its 16th-century architecture. But it is the bell tower that draws the most attention. Situated on Roman ruins, the 23m-tall (75-ft.) tower has four floors and includes a balustraded pyramid on top. You can climb this one for about 5kn. If you look at the four bell towers from the sea, they clearly slope from tallest to shortest. The last church on the route is Baroque **St. Anthony (Sveti Antun),** which has an impressively carved marble altar.

Activities & Celebrations

Besides looking at churches and bell towers, Rab has a wide range of tourist attractions and activities that include watersports, tours, and festivals.

TOURS   Most travel agencies in town offer boat tours of the island as well as day trips to nearby Lošinj or Pag. There are also excursions to Kampor, on the northwest part of the island; and to Barbat, on the south side of Rab.

DIVING   Scuba-diving excursions can be arranged through **Mirko Diving Center** (Barbat 17, 51280 Rab; ✆ **051/721-154;** www.mirkodivingcenter.com); or through **Kron Diving Center** (413a Kampor, 51280 Rab; ✆ **051/776-620;** fax 051/776-630; www.dron-diving.com).

WHERE TO STAY

Very Expensive

Arbiana Hotel ★★ (Finds)   The 1924 building that houses the Arbiana has never looked better. The Art Nouveau boutique hotel reopened in 2007 after decades of neglect and after an almost 4-year renovation. It has been making waves on Rab's waterfront ever since. The owners live in New York, but they took care to incorporate the original building's best features into their plans, and the result is a perfect combination of historic architecture and 21st-century luxury. Guest rooms differ in size and shape because of the building's construction, but all are done in deep jewel colors; and all have ample space, plush upholstered furniture, and several mirrors; all bathrooms have tubs. At turndown time, Arbiana's staff leaves small, wrapped portions of *Rabska torta* on pillows instead of chocolate. The recipe for the delicious cakes is a secret, but they are made by local women and taste like dense pound cake with hints of orange and cherry and a ribbon of marzipan.

Obala Kralja Petra Kresimira 12, 51280 Rab. ⓒ **051/775-900.** Fax 051/775-991. www.arbianahotel.com. 28 units. Double deluxe from 310€; suites from 380€. AE, DC, MC, V. Rates include breakfast and VAT. **Amenities:** Restaurant; grill; 2 bars; babysitting (extra charge); room service; rooms for those w/limited mobility. *In room:* A/C, TV, hair dryer, minibar, Wi-Fi.

Expensive

Rab Hoteli ★   This hotel at the Riva's midpoint is all cool design and elegance that reeks of Euro-chic. Formerly known as the Ros Maris, the hotel lowered its prices when it rebranded in 2008 and changed its name even though services and amenities stayed the same. A rooftop terrace overlooks the bay, and the renovated oversize guest rooms have views of either the sea or Old Town. Bathrooms are sleek; those in suites have their own Jacuzzis. This is a place to be pampered.

Obala Petra Krešimira 4, 51280 Rab. ⓒ **051/778-899.** Fax 051/724-206. www.rabhotel.com. 140 units. Summer and Christmas week from 135€ double. Rest of year from 55€ double. AE, MC, V. **Amenities:** Restaurant; cafe; bar; pool bar; pool; room service, smoke-free rooms available; spa; nightclub. *In room:* A/C, TV w/pay channels, hair dryer, minibar.

Moderate

Hotel Padova   This modern structure isn't much to look at from the outside, but a 2005 update has freshened 65% of the rooms and bathrooms. However, the hotel's public areas still are mired in its former dour socialist persona. The seawater pool is perfect for kids as it is no more than 1m (3 ft.) deep, but a second pool added in 2008 is a knockout. When we visited the single computer in the "Internet Center" was coin operated. The hotel faces Old Town from across the bay, so the view from the small balconies on most rooms is of the skyline. *Tip:* Padova's parking lot is inadequate for the hotel's capacity, and you'll often find lines of cars in throughways blocking legally parked vehicles.

Banjol bb. ⓒ **051/724-444.** www.imperial.hr. 175 units. Summer seaside rooms from 960kn double. Rest of year from 650kn double. Rates include breakfast. AE, DC, MC, V. Limited free parking. **Amenities:** Restaurant; cafe; bar; pool; sun terrace. *In room:* TV, hair dryer, minibar.

WHERE TO EAT

Rab is the land of pizza restaurants and casual konobas that specialize in fresh fish. With a few exceptions, they all dish up roughly the same kind of fare.

Konoba Riva ★ SEAFOOD   The ambience of this casual fish restaurant is definitely rustic, with a decor employing lots of stone and wood. The food, however, is a little better than that of most restaurants in this class. Try any of the grilled fish dishes or the risotto with squid, which is outstanding. There is even something billed "American chicken" on the menu.

Biskupa Draga 3. ⓒ **051/725-887.** www.konoba-riva.hr. Entrees 35kn–135kn. M, V. Daily 10am–11pm.

San Marino ★★ MEDITERRANEAN   San Marino may be the most romantic restaurant on Rab. On nice evenings diners sit at candlelit tables under trees in the park adjacent to the Arbiana with soft music and the sea as background noise. The restaurant's indoor space is also nicely appointed, but it is San Marino's menu that attracts diners. Start with beef and chicken minestrone accessorized with julienned crepes and move on

to Kvarner risotto infused with scampi and garnished with zucchini. For dessert, the **217**
menu lists the usual Croatian suspects—palačinke, flan, ice cream—and the choices are
a letdown after the chef's creative cuisine.

At the Arbiana Hotel, Obala Kralja Petra Kresimira 12, 51280 Rab. © **051/775-900.** Fax 051/775-991.
www.arbianahotel.com. Entrees 86kn–230kn. AE, DC, MC, V. Daily 7:30am–11pm.

Zeko Pizzeria PIZZA   "Zeko" refers to fast food in Croatian and this collection of
bench seat tables along the waterfront sidewalk offers speedy service. Zeko appeals to
families because of its reasonable prices and familiar offerings, but the food, though "fast"
is well prepared and might even be nutritious. Try one of the pizzas—we liked the Nea-
politan with tomatoes and olives—or even a burger and fries.

I Donja bb. No phone. Pizza 37kn–47kn, other choices 28kn–59kn. No credit cards. Daily 11am–9pm
June–Aug only.

---

7 CRES & LOŠINJ ISLANDS

THE KVARNER GULF

Cres and Lošinj are really a single island, separated only by a 48m-wide (30-ft.) man-
made channel that has been bridged by roadway. Despite their proximity and historical
link, these destinations couldn't be more different. Cres stretches 60km (40 miles) from
tip to tip and is twice as long as Lošinj. Both islands are covered with biking and hiking
trails, but it is Cres that is a haven for campers who like to rough it and for hikers who
like a challenge. Lošinj, on the other hand, is the island of choice for yachters and tourists looking for relaxing cafes and beaches.

8

CRES & LOŠINJ ISLANDS

   More than half of Cres is covered with rocks and scrub grass, a landscape interrupted
only by intersecting rock fences and sheep shelters that create a crisscross pattern on the
inhospitable terrain. Osor on Cres is home to the protected griffon vulture. Lošinj is
blanketed with a thick tree cover, well-groomed pebble beaches, lots of shops and restaurants, and several large resort hotels.

   Cres's tourist destinations are the island's main population centers—Cres Town, which
could double as a fishing village in Italy; and Osor, where a tiny bridge spans the narrow
canal separating Cres from Lošinj. Several minuscule, remote villages—**Beli, Lubenice,**
and **Valun**—are worth a detour. Lošinj's main villages are **Mali Lošinj** and **Veli Lošinj.**
Both attract a large number of tourists, but it is Mali Lošinj that is the more developed
center, probably as a result of Lošinj's former status as a shipyard and winter vacation
destination for wealthy Austrians. Today, both islands reap most of their revenue from
tourism, while each retains its character.

   Cres and Lošinj have been inhabited since the Stone Age and followed the familiar
settlement pattern of the rest of Croatia's offshore islands. The islands were home to the
Illyrians more than 3,000 years ago until the Romans came along in the 1st century,
followed by the Byzantines and the Slavs. The Venetians, the Croat-Hungarians, the
Austro-Hungarians, and the Yugoslavs followed until the islands finally came under
Croatian control in 1991. Today, Cres and Lošinj are thriving destinations that cater to
a wide variety of tourism tastes.

GETTING THERE & GETTING AROUND

BY CAR AND/OR BOAT   Getting to Cres and Lošinj is easy if you are driving or taking
the ferry; and a little more complicated if you are traveling some other way. The shortest
ferry crossing is from **Brestova** on the mainland to **Porozina** at the northern end of Cres

and costs about 100kn for a car and two passengers. However, the wait to board there can be brutal in July and August, even though the ferries throw away their schedules and provide nonstop service by crossing as soon as they are full. Sometimes the wait to board is 2 hours long, and except for a small snack kiosk near the ticket booth, there isn't any shade. There is another crossing from **Valbiska** on Krk to **Merag** farther down on Cres. From June to September, a car ferry runs from **Zadar** and **Pula** to **Mali Lošinj,** continuing on to **Koper** across the border in Slovenia. Other routes stop in Mali Lošinj, and some go as far as Venice and Rijeka. Contact Jadrolinja (p. 206) or **Lošinjska Plovidba** (p. 218) for schedules and routes.

BY BUS   There are six daily buses from Veli Lošinj to Cres Town, and all stop at Mali Lošinj on the way. Buses also run to each of the islands' main ferry ports twice a day—Merag, Porozina, and Valbiska—and four buses per day go to Rijeka. In addition, two buses a day go to Zagreb. For details and schedules, contact any tourist agency on the island or the main bus station in Rijeka (p. 190).

LOCAL BUSES   An hourly bus runs from the big hotels on **Čikat Bay** (5kn) to Mali Lošinj, and nine buses a day run between Mali Lošinj and Veli Lošinj (10kn).

VISITOR INFORMATION

Tourist offices are numerous in Mali Lošinj and difficult to find in Cres Town, but offices in either place can help you find accommodations and transport even if it is on another island.

Cres

Cresanka (www.cresanka.hr) provides links to private accommodations on Cres (② 051/ **571-161;** fax 051/571-163; July–Aug, daily 8am–8pm; Sept–June, 8am–4pm Mon–Fri). In summer, double private rooms with bathrooms cost from 280kn, apartments from 715kn. During the rest of the year, double private rooms with bathroom run from 140kn, apartments from 340kn.

Mali Lošlnj

Mali Lošinj Tourist Office   Provides maps, information, and brochures.

Riva Lošinjskih Kapetana 29. ② **051/231-884.** www.tz-malilosinj.hr. June–Sept daily 8am–8pm; Oct–May Mon–Fri 8am–1pm.

Lošinjska Plovidba   This agency specializes in private accommodations on Lošinj. It also arranges sports excursions and sells tickets for the Marinas ferry that runs between Koper and Zadar. Hours here are flexible because the sales agents leave to sell tickets at the marina office half an hour before each sailing.

Riva Lošinjska Plovidba Kapetana 8. ② **051/231-077.** Fax 051/231-611. www.losinjplov.hr.

Manora   This is a friendly agency that specializes in private accommodations, villas, hotels, and excursions. You can also rent a scooter there.

Priko 29, 51550 Mali Losinj. ② **051/520-100.** Fax 051/520-099. www.manora-losinj.hr.

WHAT TO SEE ON CRES

Cres Town ★★

During the day, Cres Town resembles a deserted coastal village somewhere in southern Italy thanks to its complement of small fishing boats, Venetian-style architecture, and relentless sun. When the sun is high, patrons in the cafes are sparse; stores are closed by noon; and even the local dogs curl up in a shady spot to nap. When the sun goes down, families come out to walk around the little harbor with its backdrop of Venetian-style facades.

The sound of Cres's peculiar chatter is a mix of Croatian and Italian that makes you forget that you're in Croatia. In fact, there is a strong Italian influence on Cres and its sister island Lošinj, both of which have been popular vacation destinations for Italian tourists for years, probably because of the islands' proximity to Venice and because both once were under Venetian rule. Everything here—street signs, menus, brochures—is bilingual in Croatian and Italian.

Cres's main square, **Trg F. Petrića,** extends to the harbor. It is home to a lovely 16th-century loggia where public announcements once were posted. It also has an impressive 16th-century clock. From Trg F. Petrića, go through the 16th-century gate to **Pod Urom,** another square where you will find the church of **St. Mary of the Snow.** This little church has a graceful 15th-century portal adorned with a relief of the Virgin and Child. It is open during services only, but it's worth trying to coordinate your visit with Mass so you can see the carved wooden Pieta inside.

At the south end of town, the **Franciscan Monastery** has a small museum. Much of the art inside depicts the order's clerics and is rather boring, but there is a 15th-century Murano of the Virgin and Child that is worth a look if you are an art lover. It can be viewed 10am to noon and 4 to 6:30pm Monday to Saturday, at 10kn per adult.

Beli, Valun & Lubenice

North of Cres Town, the island becomes steep and the road becomes a twisting, narrow ribbon more like a roller-coaster track than a thoroughfare. About 8km (5 miles) past Cres Town, the road forks into **Beli,** a captivatingly rustic village that is practically deserted. **Eco-Centre Caput Insulae** ★★ (Beli 4; © 051/840-525; www.caput-insulae.com; admission 20kn adults, 10kn children; daily 8am–9pm), which was established in 1993 to protect the island's griffon vultures is here, and if you aren't lucky enough to spot one of these endangered birds in the wild, you can take in the center's exhibits.

Valun is just 14km (9 miles) southwest of Cres Town, and it can't be accessed reasonably without private transportation. Buses stop at the main road above the town three times a week, but you have to descend into town on foot from there (and walk back up), which takes nearly 2 hours down and longer for the trip back. Even with a car, you have to hoof it down a long flight of stairs to the harbor. Like Beli, Valun is anything but crowded. There are a few restaurants for those who are attracted by Valun's beaches. For history buffs, Valun is home to the **Valun Tablet,** which is really an 11th-century Glagolitic-inscribed tombstone. The Valun Tablet (with Latin translation in case you can read *that* dead language) can be viewed in the town's parish church. A Cresanka **tourist office** in town can arrange a booking in one of the town's few rooms, but it's better to have a reservation in hand before you go there with the expectation of staying the night. The Valun **tourist office** is near the harbor (© 051/525-050; www.cresanka.hr; July–Aug daily 8am–10pm). **Zdovice Camping** is a small campground (70 sites) with a restaurant and a bar near the beach at Valun. It has accommodations for tents only, and you have to leave your car outside the grounds. Its location is 51557 Valun 9 (© 051/571-161; fax 051/571-163; www.cresanka.hr; 7€).

Lubenice is 4.8km (3 miles) southwest of Valun atop a windy ridge high above a beautiful clear-water cove. You can get bottled water at a small snack bar at the top, and "remote" toilets are available, but that's about all. The **view** ★★★ is breathtaking. You can get to the water below by picking your way down the gravel slope, but invest in a bottle of water and take it with you. Don't forget that you have to climb back up unless someone meets you with a boat in the bay.

There are buses to Valun and the neighboring towns of Lubenice and Beli, but they don't run every day, and schedules are more like suggestions. Buses from Cres Town hit Beli twice a week, for example, but it's best to arrange a tour with Cresenko in Cres Town or rent a car. *Tip:* This trip is not for anyone who is afraid of heights.

Where to Stay

There are few hotel choices on Cres, but plenty of private accommodations. The Cresanka tourist agency in Cres Town is your best bet for these (p. 219).

Moderate

Zlatni-Lav ★   The tiny fishing village of Martinšcica 27km (16 miles) southwest of Cres Town is home to two immaculate stucco buildings that comprise the Zlatni-Lav hotel and restaurant, an oasis of hospitality and Cres's nicest hotel. You'll get a feel for Cres's unspoiled landscape while enjoying modern touches like satellite TV and air-conditioning in the hotel's cheery but utilitarian guest rooms, all of which have balconies and sea views.

Martinšcica 18d, 51556 Martinšcica, Cres. ✆/fax **051/574-020.** www.hotel-zlatni-lav.com. 30 units. Doubles mid-June to mid-Sept from 120€; suites from 225€ double occupancy. Other times, doubles from 63€; suites from 170€. Rates include breakfast. AE, DC, MC, V. **Amenities:** Restaurant; bar; bike and boat tours; hiking; diving; fishing. *In room:* A/C, TV, hair dryer, minibar.

Inexpensive

Autocamp Kovačine   You won't have to go far to get to the water at this campground 1km (½ mile) from Cres Town. Autocamp Kovačine is steps away from the sea and backed by olive and pine trees. It has a restaurant, sports center, and even a diving school for the hearing-impaired. Part of this camp is reserved for nudists.

Melin 1/20, 51557 Cres. ✆ **051/571-423.** Fax 051/571-086. www.camp.kovacine.com. 175kn per day for 2 people, car, and site. Closed Nov–Mar.

Camping Bijar & Preko Mosta   These two campgrounds have 300 sites combined and are close to the tiny town of Osor. They have a playground for kids, a diving center, a boat ramp, and even some mobile homes for rent. Reservations are recommended.

Jazon d.o.o., 51542 Osor 76. ✆ **051/237-027.** Fax 051/237-115. booking@jazon.hr. 160kn per day for 2 people, campsite, and car July–Aug; 105kn other times.

Hotel Kimen ★   Until recently, this housing-development hotel in a wooded area was the only game in or near Cres Town. Kimen's rooms are basic bed-bathroom-balcony affairs without frills, but they are close to the beach and 1km (½ mile) from the town center. *Tip:* Rooms in the main building have undergone a recent renovation that includes air-conditioning, so ask for one of these.

Melin I br. 16, 51557 Cres. ✆ **051/571-161.** Fax 051/571-163. www.hotel-kimen.com. 223 units. MC, V. Summer from 70€ double. Rest of year from 40€ double. Parking lot. **Amenities:** Restaurant; TV lounge; bar; children's program.

Where to Dine

The harbor in Cres Town is ringed with pizza places and a few grills. Most are pretty much the same and can be crowded on summer evenings.

Adria Grill ★ SEAFOOD   Adria's 10 tables are cosseted in a courtyard full of greenery that includes fig and olive trees. Menu mainstays are seafood and grilled meat, but the ambience is pure romance.

Zazid 5, Cres Town. ✆ **051/571-520.** Entrees 30kn–80kn. AE, DC, MC, V. Daily noon–3pm and 5pm–midnight summer only.

Gostionica Riva ★ SEAFOOD   Fish is king at this local hangout, but you can also get omelets and pasta. Try the scampi with pasta or the grilled fish of the day. This place is a little classier than most of the cafes along the harbor.

Šetalište 24. ✆ **051/571-203.** Entrees 20kn–60kn. No credit cards. Daily 10am–11pm.

Pizza Luna Rosa (Value) PIZZA   Adjacent to Pizza Palada, the menu choices are the same, the ambience is the same, the prices are the same, but the decor differs slightly in that Pizza Luna Rosa has better shade during the day.

Palada 6. No phone. Medium pizzas 15kn–60kn. No credit cards. Daily 10am–midnight.

Pizza Palada (Value) PIZZA   This pizza parlor on the marina serves decent food at reasonable prices. It is frequented by families, so tables can be scarce in the evening.

Palada 4. No phone. Medium pizzas 15kn–60kn. No credit cards. Daily 10am–midnight.

Restoran Cres (Kids) ITALIAN   This bright yellow building at the end of the square near the harbor will catch your eye with its huge, bright awning. Restoran Cres serves breakfast, lunch, and dinner with a menu skewed toward Italian fare. Cres offers a kids' menu, vegetarian plates, and some nice-looking salads and tortellini, too.

Riva Creskih Kapetana 10, 51557 Cres. ✆ **051/571-163.** Dinner entrees 27kn–140kn. AE, DC, MC, V. Daily 8am–midnight.

WHAT TO SEE ON MALI LOŠINJ ★★★

Mali Lošinj started building its reputation as a tourist destination at about the same time it stopped building ships for the Austro-Hungarian Empire. Mali Lošinj prospered despite the economic downturn that caused shipbuilding's decline because wealthy Austrians began to winter there as they had in Opatija, though not to the same extent.

Some of the villas built on Losinj in that era still exist, as does the shipyard, which is still working. Despite its annual influx of foreign tourists from all around the globe, Mali Lošinj has retained its charm and character, mostly by keeping the big resort complexes outside of town on Čikat Bay, west of the center. On summer nights, the **Riva Lošinjskih Kapetana** along the harbor can resemble New Orleans at Mardi Gras, and getting a table at a restaurant or a room in a hotel can be impossible. But Mali Lošinj manages to handle the chaos without blinking an eye.

Art Collections ★★   Mali Lošinj isn't flush with vintage buildings and monuments, but it does have a collection of contemporary Croatian artworks and old masters accumulated by the Mihičić and Piperata families that is housed in the former House of Culture behind the harbor.

Vladimira Gortana 35. ✆ **051/231-173.** Admission 9kn. Daily 10am–noon, but hours are flexible.

Church of the Nativity of the Virgin   This 18th-century church off the main square is in the Baroque style, and houses several religious paintings and sculptures of note.

Ulica Sveta Marija. Visit before or after Mass on Sun.

Expensive

Hotel Apoksiomen ★★ Named after a 4th-century-B.C. bronze statue of a legendary Greek athlete found in the waters off Lošinj in 1999, the vintage building that was the Hotel Istra underwent a complete renovation in 2005 and emerged as a comfortable, gleaming hotel with pizazz. Done in sunny shades of yellow and blue, the Apoksiomen may be difficult to pronounce, but it's not hard on the eyes. Rooms are a bit larger than average, with soundproof windows that amazingly block out all noise from the Riva below when they are closed. The marble bathrooms are spacious and well equipped.

Riva Lošinjskih Kapetana 1, 51550 Mali Lošinj. ✆ **051/520-820.** Fax 051/520-830. www.apoksiomen. com. 25 units. Summer from 165€ double; from 220€ suite. Rest of year from 125€ double; from 165€ suite. AE, DC, MC, V. **Amenities:** Restaurant; cafe; room for those w/limited mobility. *In room:* A/C, TV w/ pay stations, hair dryer, Internet access, minibar.

Hotel Aurora ★★ Aurora joined the Apoksiomen in Mali Losinj's luxury hotel category in 2008 when it completed a renovation. It shares woodland territory with the rather dowdy Vespera, but that doesn't take away from its appeal. Aurora now has indoor and outdoor pools and a spa in addition to rooms with modern conveniences and comforts.

Sunčana Uvala, Dražica, Mali Losinj. ✆ **051/231-324.** Fax 051/231-904. www.losinj-hotels.com. 323 units. Doubles from 170€. Rates include breakfast. AE, DC, MC, V. Closed Nov–Apr. **Amenities:** Restaurant; bar; 2 pools; spa. *In room:* A/C, TV, hair dryer, Internet access, minibar.

Moderate

Hotel Vespera ★ Vespera, one of several large package hotels on Čikat Bay, opened the 2009 season sporting a complete renovation. Nonetheless, the hotel still falls into the "generic" category. However, if beach access and staying put are important to you, this is a perfect fit. Vespera's has pleasant rooms, decent bathrooms, balconies, and a host of organized activities and kids' programs. Both Vespera and its twin sister Aurora have the beach at their front door with umbrella attendants and a terrace cafe nearby. There is an FKK (nudist) facility nearby.

Jadranka d.d. Dražica 1, 51550 Mali Lošinj. ✆ **051/661-101.** Fax 051/231-904. 400 units. Summer from 998€ double for minimum of 7 days with half-board; from 555€ double for 7 days. Suite prices do not change. They run from 499€ per person in 2-bedroom suite for 7 days with half-board. Rates include breakfast. AE, DC, MC, V. Closed Nov–Apr. **Amenities:** Restaurant; bar; children's program; Internet access; indoor pool; sauna; excursions. *In room:* TV w/pay stations, minibar.

Hotel Villa Margarita ★ Ⓥ**alue** Just steps from the town center, the Villa Margarita is an immaculate, friendly place convenient to everything. While the 19th-century villa exudes old-world charm, each of the unique guest rooms was updated in 1999, and each has a personality of its own. Bathrooms are generous, with separate rooms for tub and toilet; a few even have little balconies. The huge suites with privacy walls are perfect for family vacations. Be sure to check out the **restaurant** (reviewed below) and the wine bar and garden terrace.

Bočac 64. ✆ **051/233-837.** Fax 051/231-940. www.vud.hr. 10 units. Summer from 700kn double; from 1,010kn suite. Rest of year from 440kn double; from 585kn suite. Suite rates do not include breakfast. 10% discount for stays over 7 days. 5% discount for cash payment. AE, DC, MC, V. **Amenities:** Restaurant; bar; wine bar. *In room:* A/C, TV w/pay stations.

Villa Anna ★★ Tucked away along the bay on the opposite side of the promenade, Villa Anna reeks of exclusivity, but it really is a hotel for anyone who wants to be close to the marina and away from Riva madness. Built in 1999, Villa Anna's rooms have modern but minimalist furnishings with unobstructed views of the sea and the town. There are a lot of extras here, most notably the interesting menu in the hotel's **Villa Anna restaurant** (reviewed below) that avoids the usual resort cuisine. Villa Anna is perfect for families and anyone wanting to stay away from Mali Lošinj's madding crowd but still be close to the beach.

Velopin 31, 51550 Mali Lošinj. ✆ **051/233-223.** Fax 051/233-224. www.vila-ana.hr. 13 units. Summer from 730kn double; from 1,100kn suite. Rest of year from 405kn double; from 655kn suite. Room rates include breakfast. AE, DC, MC, V. Limited free parking. **Amenities:** Restaurant; bar; pool; sauna; solarium. In room: A/C, TV, hair dryer.

Inexpensive

Camping Čikat   Set in a pine forest a little over a mile from Mali Lošinj, this campground is on a small bay and a small beach. The camp has a restaurant and a bar.

Dražica 1, 51550 Mali Lošinj. ✆ **051/232-125.** Fax 051/231-708. www.camp-cikat.com.hr. 110kn for 2 people, car, and site. AE, DC, MC, V. Closed Oct 16–Mar 18.

Where to Dine

The combination of a large contingent of Italian visitors and the availability of fresh fish makes restaurant menus look alike on Lošinj: Most restaurants serve pizza and pasta or fish, or a combination, and prices don't vary much. However, some exceptions try to add surprises. As a general rule, the restaurants and cafes near the harbor are a little higher priced, and the ones inland offer more choices.

Bora Bar Trattoria/Tartufferia ★★ TRATTORIA   Bora Bar's Chef Marco Sasso has Italian roots (Pisa, Italy), U.S. restaurateur experience (Hoboken, New Jersey), and Croatian sensibilities. The result is food that fuses a variety of styles and local ingredients. Try pumpkin soup or tuna Carpaccio with celery root and Istrian truffles to start and follow with sea bass cooked in a salt crust. Bora Bar's pastas and desserts are made fresh daily in the restaurant's kitchen. Most wines are Istrian Quality (IQ) choices.

Rovenska 3, Veli Losinj. ✆ **051/867-544.** www.borabar.com. Entrees 60kn–150kn. AE, DC, MC, V. Daily 10am–midnight Apr–Oct.

Gostonica Baracuda ★★ SEAFOOD   A nautical theme, fishnets, potted palms, and a menu that looks like that of every other fish restaurant in Mali Lošinj might make you think that Baracuda is just another seafood joint on the dock. You'd be wrong. Baracuda grills its fish over charcoal—and that makes all the difference. For a change of pace, try the tuna carpaccio as an appetizer and follow with grilled lobster.

Priko 31. ✆ **051/233-309.** Entrees 70kn–250kn. No credit cards. Daily 10am–11pm.

Grill Konoba Odyssey (Value) GRILL   It's one of those little mom-and-pop grills with a few tables outside on the sidewalk, but this tiny restaurant really packs them in. Besides the usual spaghetti and scampi offerings, the chef mixes in a few Croatian specialties such as *pohani sir* (fried cheese) and goulash.

Velopin 14. ✆ **051/231-893.** Entrees 30kn–116kn. No credit cards. Daily 11am–2pm and 6pm–2:30am.

Restaurant Villa Margarita ★ CROATIAN   As hotel restaurants go, Villa Margarita delivers tasty, well-prepared meals in a delightful setting, whether you choose the indoor dining room or the garden terrace. Margarita's menu is typical Mali Lošinj, so there aren't any surprises, but the fish is fresh, the pasta is al dente, and the price is right. Try the Villa Margarita salad with turkey for a change of pace; or splurge on fresh sea bass.

In the Hotel Villa Margarita, Bočac 64. ✆ **051/233-837.** Fax 051/231-940. www.vud.hr. Entrees 40kn–122kn. AE, DC, MC, V. Daily 7am–11pm.

Restoran Dalmacija ★★ DALMATIAN GRILL   Flowering trees, potted plants, and vines are part of the lovely terraced garden where this Dalmatian-style grill does a brisk business. The waiters are particularly cordial, and everything flows to make your meal an experience. Try the mixed grilled fish for two (which comes with potatoes and vegetables); it includes four whole fish and grilled calamari. It's fascinating to watch the waiters bone whole fish with nothing but a spoon.

Mate Vidulića 19. ✆ **051/232-400.** Entrees 35kn–175kn. AE, DC, MC, V. Daily 10am–11pm.

Villa Anna ★★ MODERN CROATIAN   The classy Villa Anna has a restaurant to match, and that's what keeps tourists returning year after year. Just check the menu outside, and you'll know this is someplace special. But don't stop there. Try the chicken breast with wild berries and Camembert, an exquisite combination. Or go healthy and choose the eggplant stuffed with couscous. Of course Villa Anna serves fish and standards like roast lamb, but why limit yourself?

In the Hotel Villa Anna, Velopin 31. ✆ **051/233-223.** www.vila-ana.hr. Entrees 40kn–110kn. AE, DC, MC, V. Daily 6pm–midnight.

Istria

Istria is bucolic bliss in primary colors: dark red earth, glistening blue sea, and rolling hills that tumble into valleys cloaked in shades of green and gold. It is sensory stimulation packed into a triangular peninsula at the northwestern end of Croatia that dips into the Adriatic just far enough to catch the seductive Mediterranean climate. Most of Istria's pine- and rosemary-scented coastal landscape is lined with beaches and marinas framed by Venetian-style towns that look ready to welcome the tall ships that once anchored in their harbors.

Many nations have occupied Istria over the centuries, and it is remarkable that the peninsula has not become a cultural hodgepodge. Instead the region has embraced the best of every country that contributed to its development through the ages, a philosophy that still informs Istrians' easygoing attitude, tolerance for diversity, love of fine food and wine, and above all, their passion for the land and sea.

Even the most transient tourist will recognize that Istrians have acquired Italian sensibilities without losing their Croatian souls. Istria was Italian until World War II, and many residents still communicate with each other in a local dialect that is a lilting blend of Italian and Croatian. Most towns are known by both their Italian and Croatian names and sometimes fool visitors into wondering if they've made an inadvertent border crossing.

Many of the region's coastal towns are dead ringers for Italian fishing villages, and much of the inland landscape's silvery olive groves and deep green vineyards could double as Tuscan. But when you get the bill for a meal or a hotel room, you'll know you're in Croatia and not Italy—the cost of a week in Istria is well below the cost of the same week just across the Adriatic.

Istria's roots sink deeply into the Adriatic, connecting and separating it from Italy in a sometimes stormy relationship that is responsible for much of Istria's cachet.

All this and a well-developed tourist infrastructure make Istria an ideal destination for anyone looking for a vacation drenched in nature, history, and sybaritic pursuits. Croatia's tourist bureau color-codes Istria into blue (coastal) and green (inland) sectors. Most travelers gravitate to blue Istria, which contributes big numbers to the more than 2.5 million people—mostly Europeans—who visit annually, a number that represents the largest single block of tourism in Croatia.

Istria's past is also rich with heroes, conquerors, states people, and myths, as well as agricultural and commercial tradition. This mélange gives every town an intriguing sense of drama smoothed with Mediterranean *joie de vivre.*

Those who believe in legends say the Greek hero Jason, his Argonauts, and their sailing ship *Argo* took shelter in the Bay of Pula during their quest for the Golden Fleece. Those who believe in miracles say St. Euphemia and her stone sarcophagus somehow washed up on the shores of Rovinj shortly after disappearing from Constantinople in A.D. 800. Historians say Bronze Age tribes built primitive settlements in Istria's verdant hills and that an Illyrian tribe known as Histri gave its name to the land. There is no question that ancient Rome prospered from the trade that flowed through Istria's ports, which were lucrative profit centers coveted at one time or another by Venice, Austria-Hungary, Italy, and others, all of whom vied for control until Marshal Tito declared "game over" and made offshore Brijuni his vacation home.

Istria has been through centuries of unrest, and its turbulent past could have resulted in a legacy of despair. Instead, hard times gave birth to tolerance and acceptance in an enchanting region that is geographically rich, historically significant, and a feast for the senses.

1 ORIENTATION

VISITOR INFORMATION

Tourism is a 2.8-billion-euro industry in Istria, accounting for more than 40% of all tourist overnight stays tourism traffic in Croatia. It's no wonder that Istria County has its own efficient tourist association with information offices in almost every town from Pula on the coast to Oprtalj in the interior highlands. The association maintains an exceptionally helpful and complete website (www.istra.com), where you can find information ranging from maps of the region's olive oil roads to an up-to-date schedule of festivals and events in cities throughout Istria. The county association also publishes a huge number of brochures, maps, CDs, and guides, some for special-interest travelers such as wine aficionados and spelunkers. Local tourist offices in most Istrian towns are staffed with knowledgeable people who will give you maps and brochures or even advice on where to go to dinner.

GETTING THERE

BY PLANE Istria's only major airport is at Pula, about 5km (3 miles) northwest of the center of town, and it is served by Croatia Airlines (www.croatiaairlines.hr). There is a smaller airport for private planes and charters near Vrsar in the middle of the coast. Shuttle buses and taxis (60kn–70kn) run between Pula's airport and the town center, where you can connect to other major Istrian towns via bus or train.

BY BOAT Venezia Lines runs regular catamarans from Venice to Umag, Poreč, Rovinj, Pula, and Rabac; and from Rimini to Pula. Check the website (www.venezialines.com) or call © 041/24-24-000 from 9am to 6pm Venice time to book tickets or for detailed schedule information.

BY BUS Autotrans runs four daily buses from both Rijeka and Zagreb to Pula, and has other lines to major cities such as Umag and Rovinj on the coast. Most interior towns are connected to the coastal cities by at least one bus per day, but travel by bus to inland Istria can be inconvenient and time-consuming. For schedule information and prices, check the Autotrans website (www.autotrans.hr).

BY TRAIN There are train connections between Zagreb and Pula (7 hr.) and Rijeka and Pula (2½ hr.) as well as train connections to other coastal towns and to Pazin, the county seat in the middle of the peninsula. However, if you want to see the remote gems of inland Istria, a car is a necessity. See p. 32 for detail on Croatian Railways (www.hznet.hr).

BY CAR Auto travel is by far the most flexible way to see Istria beyond the coast and the only sensible way to see the interior. There are car-rental agencies in most of the major population centers (see p. 30 for contact information).

GETTING AROUND

BY CAR   Gas prices and parking limitations in larger towns such as Pula notwithstanding, having access to your own car is the only way to explore side roads that lead to tiny wineries, picturesque villages, and hidden treasures (see p. 30 for car-rental information).

BY BUS   Regular and frequent bus service links Istria's coastal cities, but service to inland villages is much less convenient for travelers who want to see a lot in a limited amount of time or who are reluctant to walk a mile or more from the bus stop to get to the sites. For information on bus travel in Istria, the best bus company is **Autotrans** (© **052/741-817;** www.autotrans.hr).

BY TRAIN   Croatian Railways (www.hznet.hr) does have trains that serve the major cities in Istria, and they are fine if you want to get to a destination where you will stay put for a while, but there is no time-efficient way to explore the interior—or even the coast—by train because train schedules are not geared to touring (see p. 32 for more on Croatian Railways).

2 PULA (POLA)

This bustling city of 65,000 at the southern tip of Istria is a working port as well as a repository of some of the best Roman ruins in Europe, including a well-preserved **amphitheater** ★★★ from the 1st century that is Pula's biggest draw. Pula has other vestiges of Roman occupation (**Temple of Augustus, Forum, Arch of the Sergi** ★★★) that are worth seeing, too. Besides its cache of Roman artifacts, the city is home to a graceful Gothic **Franciscan monastery** erected by the monks when they arrived at the end of the 13th century, as well as a 17th-century fortress that now houses Istria's history museum. It was built by the Venetians.

ESSENTIALS

VISITOR INFORMATION   The **Tourist Information Office** is off Forum Square at Forum 2 (© 052/219-197; fax 052/211-855; www.pulainfo.hr), opposite the Temple of Augustus. It provides maps, brochures, and lists of events in Pula and around Istria. The center is open from 9am to 8pm Monday through Saturday and from 10am to 6pm Sunday and holidays.

Private agencies like **Activatravel Istra** at Scalierova 1 (© 052/215-497; fax 052/211-889; info@activa-istra.com) book special-interest tours, including a truffle-hunting excursion and dinner in Livade (in season). Several of the Pula area's hotels, as well as private accommodations, are operated by **Arena Turist;** its offices are in the Riviera Hotel at Splitska 1 (© 052/529-400; www.arenaturist.hr). It is a short walk from the amphitheater and open from 7am to 8pm Monday through Saturday, 8am to 1pm Sunday. **Atlas Travel** at Starih Statuta 1 (© 052/393-040; www.atlas-croatia.com) does business from 7am to 8pm Monday through Saturday; 8am to 1pm Sunday. Atlas books excursions, finds private accommodations, and it is Pula's American Express agent. **Istra Sun-Way** at Kandlerova 34 (© 052/381-329; www.istra-sunway.hr) is open from 8am to midnight and offers accommodations and excursions that range from island tours to land adventures. Istra books tours to the interior, so if you don't want to rent a car, they can take you to some of the smaller inland towns.

You can surf online at **Enigma Computer Center,** one of the better Internet centers in Pula. Enigma, is located at Kandlerova 19 (© 052/381-615) and open daily from 10am to midnight June 1 to September; from 10am to 2pm and 5 to 8pm the rest of the year. The air-conditioned center sits between the cathedral and Augustus's Temple, and management provides users with free music, sweets, and drinks.

GETTING THERE   Pula's busy harbor enjoys healthy shipping and transportation traffic. Tourists can make both regional and international ferry connections between other towns in Croatia and Italy here. For more detailed information, see "Getting There" in "Orientation," earlier in this chapter.

GETTING AROUND   Pula is a very walkable city even outside its center, and its bus system can get you almost anywhere you need to go in town. Beyond that, a large number

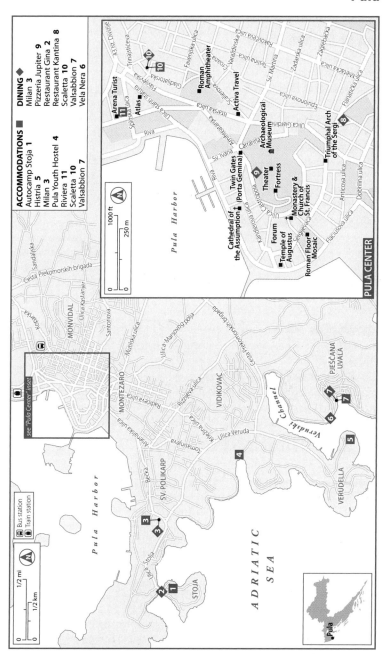

ACCOMMODATIONS ■

Autocamp Stoja **1**
Histria **5**
Milan **3**
Pula Youth Hostel **4**
Riviera **11**
Scaletta **10**
Valsabbion **7**

DINING ◆

Milan **3**
Pizzeria Jupiter **9**
Restaurant Gina **2**
Restaurant Kantina **8**
Scaletta **10**
Valsabbion **7**
Vela Nera **6**

PULA CENTER

1000 ft
250 m

N

Pula Harbor

Arena Turist
Atlas
Riva

Roman
Amphitheater

Activa Travel

Archaeological
Museum

Triumphal Arch
of the Sergi

Cathedral of
the Assumption

Twin Gates
(Porta Gemina)

Theater

Fortress

Monastery &
Church of
St. Francis

Forum

Temple of
Augustus

Roman Floor
Mosaic

see "Pula Center" inset

Bus station
Train station

Pula Harbor

MONVIDAL

MONTEZARO

SV.-POLIKARP

STOJA

VIDIKOVAC

PIEŠĆANA
UVALA

Verudski Channel

VERUDELLA

*ADRIATIC
SEA*

1/2 mi
1/2 km

N

Pula

ISTRIA

9

PULA (POLA)

of bus routes run from Pula to Zagreb to Rijeka, and from the Istrian cities of Rovinj, Vrsar, and Poreč plus the gateway city of Trieste in Italy and coastal towns in Slovenia. If you want to explore the hills and valleys of the Istrian interior, you'll need a car.

WHAT TO SEE & DO

Pula's most interesting sites are its Roman ruins, and of those, the 1st-century amphitheater is the most impressive.

Archaeological Museum ★★   Archaeological finds from all over Istria are displayed in this museum that once was an Austrian secondary school. The emphasis is on artifacts from Old Histri and Roman times, but there are some nice medieval exhibits, too. Be sure to visit the outdoor sculpture garden casually decorated with scattered pieces of history. And note the Roman Twin Gates (above) at the entrance. There is also a Roman Theater in back of the garden. *Tip:* You can access the garden and theater even when the museum is closed.

Carrarina 3. ✆ **052/218-603.** Fax 052/212-415. Admission 12kn adults, 6kn children. Summer Mon–Sat 9am–8pm; Sun and holidays 10am–3pm. Winter Mon–Fri 9am–3pm; closed Sat–Sun.

Cathedral of the Assumption ★   This cathedral has had many makeovers since it was converted from a Roman temple to a church in the 4th century. The current facade and bell tower date from the 17th century. Inside there are a few 5th- and 6th-century mosaic fragments and the cathedral's unusual altar, which is actually a 3rd-century Roman sarcophagus that contains the relics of some 70 saints. The amphitheater's stone seats and other stones were used to build the bell tower.

Kandlerova bb. Daily 8:30am–2pm and 6–8pm. No phone.

Hercules Gate ★★   Walk through the Sergi Arch and bear left until you get to Carrarina, where you will encounter Pula's oldest gate dating from the mid–1st century. It is decorated with a relief of its namesake mythical hero.

Monastery and Church of St. Francis ★   Just behind the tourist information center on Forum Square is the 14th-century complex that includes a single-nave basilica and a tranquil garden framed by Gothic triumphal arches. Stone pieces and mosaic fragments here date from the Roman period on, but they seem randomly strewn about and not well explained.

Castropola (west end of Sergijevaca). No phone. Admission 5kn. June to mid-Sept daily 10am–1pm and 4–7pm.

Roman Amphitheater ★★★   Though smaller than the Coliseum in Rome, the Arena, as it is known by locals, is remarkable because its outer wall is almost entirely intact. Inside, vestiges of the Arena's fittings still are visible, though its stone seats were removed in medieval times to complete other building projects. The facility was designed to host gladiatorial contests and 20,000 people. The Emperor Augustus (31–14 B.C.) started construction of the amphitheater in 2 B.C.; it was finished in A.D. 14, during the rule of Vespasianus. It used a clever system of cloth canopies to shade spectators from the sun and parts of the system still hang from the wall. The chambers under the Arena have been restored and now house a **museum ★★★** whose permanent exhibit, "Olive and Winegrowing of Istria in Antiquity," is beautifully done and captioned in English. During the summer, the Arena is a concert site attracting such big-name stars as Elton John. It is also the site of the prestigious Croatian Film Festival (July). *Tip:* Rent an audio tour the first time you visit the Arena.

For almost a year (Oct 1904–Mar 1905), Irish author James Joyce lived in Pula, where he taught English to Austro-Hungarian naval officers through the Berlitz School. Today, Joyce is immortalized in bronze in the coffee bar Uliks (Ulysses) just steps from the building where he taught. Passersby often do a double-take when they pass the statue of the author, who is portrayed seated at a table as if he were waiting for his afternoon *biela kava.*

Flavijevska bb. ✆ **052/219-028.** Admission 20kn adults, 10kn students. Audio guide 30kn. Daily 8am–9pm. Amphitheater closes early on concert days.

Roman Floor Mosaic ★★ This floor mosaic from the 3rd century represents the mythological punishment of the original wicked stepmother, Circe, who was punished for her evil deeds by being tied to the horns of a bull.

Just past the Monastery and Church of St. Francis, off Sergijevaca.

Temple of Augustus ★★★ Built between 2 B.C. and A.D. 14 on a square that once was the city's Forum, the Temple of Augustus is dedicated to Octavianus Augustus, the first emperor of Rome. The temple was converted to a church after Christianity became the religion of choice in Croatia. It also was used for grain storage, but after being severely damaged during World War II, it was rebuilt. A small museum inside displays artifacts found near Pula; all are captioned in English, Italian, and Croatian.

Trg Republike 3. No phone. Admission 4kn adults, 2kn children. Summer daily 10am–1:30pm and 6–9pm. Closed in winter.

Triumphal Arch of the Sergi ★★★ Farther along Sergijevaca, you'll run right into the Sergi Arch, which opens to Trg Portarata and stands in the middle of a busy shopping area. The privately financed arch was built at the end of the 1st century by Salvia Postuma Sergi to honor three male family members who had fought in the Battle of Actium.

Twin Gates (Porta Gemina) ★★ This double arch is in front of the Archaeological Museum a little beyond the Hercules Gate. According to the literature, the gates date from the beginning of the 2nd century and lead to the amphitheater and beyond.

WHERE TO STAY

There are very few hotels in the center of Pula, though there is a wealth of private accommodations. Inquire at the tourist office in Forum Square. Most hotel and beach options are south of the center in a large resort sector on the **Verudela Peninsula,** at **Pješčana Uvala,** or at **Stoja,** just a few miles from the center. These areas are reachable on the nos. 1, 3, and 7 buses.

Autocamp Stoja ★★ This campground about 3.2km (2 miles) southwest of the center in suburban Stoja is on a peninsula and has 670 spaces for tents plus a bank of mobile homes that sleep up to five people each. Guests have access to a beach, shops, a market, a restaurant, and sports equipment to use on the property or in the waters off the peninsula, which are some of the best around for swimming and watersports.

52110 Pula. 📞 **052/387-144** or 052/529-400. Fax 052/387-748. www.arenaturist.hr. Mobile home with A/C 114€ mid-July to mid-Aug with minimum 7-day stay starting on Sat; from 33€ other times with 3-day minimum stay. AE, DC, MC, V. Closed mid-Oct to mid-Mar.

Histria ★★ **Kids** The Verudela resort area 4km (2½ miles) from the center of Pula is home to the Histria, which has the best position of all the strip's hotels: It's on a hill above the shore. Comfort and elegance are the Histria's watchwords and it has plenty of both. The spacious guest rooms are nicely appointed with sweeping balconies overlooking the sea. Plenty of activities keep kids and even blasé teenagers happy and occupied.

Verudela bb. 📞 **052/590-000.** Fax 052/214-175. www.arenaturist.hr. 240 units. Aug from 318€ double. Rest of year from 180€ double. Add 10% above the double-room price for suite. AE, DC, MC, V. Rates include breakfast. **Amenities:** Restaurant; cafe; bar; disco; casino; 2 pools; sauna; summer activity programs; tennis courts. *In room:* A/C, TV.

Milan ★★ Less than a quarter of a mile from the sea, this 12-room inn is both comfortable and classy. Rooms are furnished in Mediterranean style—soothing colors, smooth woods—and they are above the **Milan Restaurant** ★★★. The only disappointment is that most bathrooms have showers rather than tubs.

Stoja 4. 📞 **052/300-200.** www.milan1967.hr. 12 units. July–Aug from 860kn double. Rest of year from 720kn double. Rates include buffet breakfast. AE, DC, MC, V. Limited free parking. **Amenities:** Restaurant; bar; smoke-free rooms; valet service. *In room:* A/C, TV, Internet.

Pula Youth Hostel ★ This hostel has a beautiful setting, but it is a hike from the town center. The hostel is 4km (2½ miles) south of Pula's center on Valsaline Bay and reachable via the no. 2 bus from Giardini near the Sergi Arch. The hostel is plain, but it's located on a spectacular piece of real estate and it has its own beach and cafeteria; a scuba-diving school is next door. Rooms are dorm-style with four to six beds each, and breakfast is included in the price.

Zaljev Valsaline 4. 📞 **052/391-133.** Fax 052/529-401. pula@hfhs.hr. 152 beds. 98kn per bed per night. Rates include breakfast. MC, V. **Amenities:** Cafe/bar; bike rental; hiking trails; shopping center; luggage storage; free parking. *In room:* Sheets provided.

Riviera The fate of this 1907 Hapsburg-era gem has been in limbo since the hotel changed hands a few years ago. Even so, the Riviera is the choice for economy-minded travelers who want to stay midway between the amphitheater and the train station. Graceful architecture gives the hotel regal curbside appeal, but inside it has been stripped of frills unless you count the amazing views of the amphitheater and harbor from room no. 406 and other corner units. Guest rooms are huge (lots of wasted space) and clean, and breakfast on the terrace is a delight, but the tired condition of the furnishings and the dearth of facilities make the Riviera an overpriced option.

Spliska 1. 📞 **052/211-166.** Fax 052/219-117. www.arenaturist.hr. 76 units. June–Sept from 85€ double. Rest of year 64€ double. Rates include breakfast. AE, DC, MC, V. **Amenities:** Restaurant. *In room:* TV.

Scaletta ★ Book early because rooms go fast at this family-run hotel in central Pula, and it's no wonder: Following a recent renovation, the Scaletta is one of the most convenient hotels in town. Guest rooms are small but bathrooms are roomy and gleaming. There aren't any views, but the Scaletta is within walking distance of the amphitheater and Pula's Old Town. Its **Scaletta Restaurant** ★★ has been recognized as one of the seven best in Istria. The only downside is that access to the reception area requires some stair-climbing and the breakfast room is a tight fit.

Church of St. Fosca (Sveti Foška)

The only directional sign to this unremarkable 7th-century church is a hand-painted sign leading to a gravel strip off the main road to/from Fažana in the direction of Barbaringa. According to locals, the church, which has one interesting fresco, is built on a field of positive energy that allegedly is responsible for healing a wide range of ailments from headaches to arthritis. The first of these healings was noted in the late 17th century, but the Catholic Church has not acknowledged the validity of any claims of miracles at the site. Despite that, people from all over the world visit this tiny church in a meadow to seek their own miracles and to pray to the saint who was betrayed by her father and martyred at 15 because she wouldn't renounce Christianity.

Flavijevska 26. ✆ **052/541-025.** Fax 052/541-599. www.hotel-scaletta.com. 12 units. June 1–Sept 15 99€ double. Rest of year 199€ double. Rates include breakfast. AE, DC, MC, V. **Amenities:** Restaurant; wine cellar. *In room:* A/C, TV, hair dryer, minibar.

Valsabbion ★★★   This chic boutique hotel 5.6km (3½ miles) south of the city center has been around since 1995, but Valsabbion still surprises with its avant-garde thinking. Set above Pješčana Uvala (Sandy Bay), Valsabbion is a stylish blend of comfortable rooms, beach, award-winning restaurant, and select spa services that eliminate stress. Rooms are spacious and exude the same sophistication that extends throughout the hotel, its facilities, and its exceptionally helpful and personable staff. Room prices do not include breakfast, which can be added for 12€ and half-board is pricey, but you'll never forgive yourself if you miss the opportunity to eat as many meals as possible here.

Pješčana Uvala IX/26. ✆ **052/218-033.** www.valsabbion.net. 10 units. July–Aug from 178€ double; from 258€ suite. Rest of year from 150€ double; from 170€ suite. Half-board available (includes welcome drink, fruit Valsabbion basket, buffet breakfast, 4-course dinner). AE, DC, MC, V. 10% discount for cash. **Amenities:** Restaurant; bar; pool; hydro massage pool. *In room:* A/C, TV, hair dryer, minibar.

WHERE TO DINE

There is no shortage of decent restaurants in central Pula, but most of the better (upscale) restaurants are in the suburbs south of the center.

Gina ★★ ISTRIAN   Personal attention to guests and detail makes this family-run restaurant a good place to sample Istrian food and hospitality. Pastas and breads are homemade, which adds a layer of authenticity to every dish. Fish and meat star, but you can't go wrong with crab-stuffed ravioli as a main and lavender semifreddo with fig sauce for dessert. The wine list gives you about 100 choices and includes many Istrian bottles. Note: Gina is a short uphill walk from the seafront promenade near Stoja campground.

Stoja 23. ✆ **052/387-043.** Entrees 50kn–140kn. AE, DC, MC, V. Daily 11am–11pm.

Jupiter ★★ PIZZA   Pizza is the specialty at this popular place near the Forum. Jupiter has several terrace levels of dining and a huge number of pizza toppings to choose from. Pretty good pasta, too.

Castropola 38. ✆ **052/214-333.** www.planetadria.com/Jupiter. Small pizza 15kn–40kn. No credit cards. Daily 9am–11pm.

Kantina ★★ ISTRIAN   The terrace of this former Hapsburg villa behind the city market is a great venue to showcase Kantina's fine regional preparations. The chef has a deft hand with traditional dishes that feature truffles, including *fuži* (Istrian pasta) and dishes with an Italian theme like ravioli filled with pršut and skuta, an Istrian curd cheese. The modest wine list has about 40 offerings.

Flanatička 16. (℘ **052/314-054.** www.kantina.hr. Entrees 110kn–150kn. AE, DC, MC. Daily 7am–10pm.

Milan ★★★ SEAFOOD   This sleek, family-owned restaurant in the hotel of the same name is done in warm woods and has flattering soft lighting. It's in Stoja, less than 3.2km (2 miles) south of Pula. On offer are sublimely fresh fish and an extensive wine list. Try any of the shellfish entrees, which are a specialty, and save room for dessert: The pastry chef is a genius.

Stoja 4. (℘ **052/300-200.** www.milan1967.hr. Entrees 60kn–140kn. AE, DC, MC, V. Mon–Sat 11am–midnight; daily 11am–midnight in summer.

Scaletta ★★ (**Value**) ISTRIAN   The lovely Scaletta is a gastronomic delight with surprisingly well-prepared cuisine that incorporates unusual combinations of ingredients. The dining room up the road from the amphitheater is warm and inviting, with soft lighting, a marble fireplace, and an attractive bar. A smaller dining room in the hotel is much smaller and lacks ambience. The menu is the showstopper, and provides a long list of grilled meats and fish with a lot of twists. Steak with white truffles and lobster with Istrian noodles are especially delicious.

Flavijevska 26. (℘ **053/541-025.** Fax 052/541-599. www.hotel-scaletta.com. Reservations recommended. Entrees 60kn–220kn. AE, DC, MC, V. Daily 11am–midnight.

Valsabbion ★★★ MODERN ISTRIAN   Unique, superb, a don't-miss experience: This is dining at Valsabbion, where Istrian specialties meet artistic sensibilities and expert preparation. Even a simple lunch can be spectacular with the samplers of Istrian cheeses, tapenades, or fish mousses and olives accompanied by house-made breads. Dinner is the *pièce de résistance* here, and if you can't make up your mind between the scampi rolled in Istrian ham or the chicken breast in vermouth sauce with grapes and artichokes, then try the tasting menu with 12 small portions of Valsabbion's best recipes. Don't miss the olive-oil aperitif—three cordial glasses filled with Istrian olive oil, olive tapenade, and olive butter, with crusty bread for dipping. With a bottle of fine wine from Valsabbion's well-chosen cellar, a gentle breeze wafting through the open terrace, and lighting provided by the reflection of the moon on the sea, a meal at Valsabbion is a sensory experience you won't soon forget. Our advice? Book a table on the VIP terrace, a breezy, canopied deck across the street from the hotel that has a view of the bay and a cachet of exclusivity. Splurge on the 12-course tasting menu. You'll feast on tasting portions of such innovative dishes as scallop wrapped in squid ink pasta or potato soup in a ring of spices. There is a 15% surcharge for the terrace, and our tasting menu was 475kn per person (without wine).

Pjescana Uvala IX/26. (℘ **052/218-033.** Fax 052/383-333. www.valsabbion.net. Reservations required. Entrees 90kn–120kn. AE, DC, MC, V. Daily 10am–midnight. Closed Jan.

Vela Nera ★★ SEAFOOD   You can watch your ship come in from Vela Nera's terrace or from the windows of its cozy dining room perched steps away from the Sandy Bay harbor. Either way, you'll be treated to knowledgeable service and inspired cuisine. Vela Nera is a little more casual than Valsabbion, but no less satisfying. Try the risotto Vela Nero for an unusual taste sensation. It's made with peaches, scampi, and sparkling wine. All of the truffle-enhanced entrees are delicious (beefsteak with truffles is especially good). Lighter appetites can try a mixed salad with bacon and freshly baked bread.

Pješčana Uvala bb. ℂ **052/219-209.** Fax 052/215-951. www.velanera.hr. Reservations recommended. Entrees 50kn–150kn. AE, DC, MC, V. Daily 8am–midnight.

3 BRIJUNI ARCHIPELAGO (BRIONI)

The Romans built summer villas on these islands northwest of Pula; the Austro-Hungarians spent their holidays there; and Marshal Tito chose them as the site for his private residence and official retreat. For 30 years Tito spent 6 months of the year receiving world leaders and celebrities amid Brijuni's natural wonders, but before that, the 14 islands and islets were swamplands teeming with malaria carriers. It wasn't until Austrian steel magnate Paul Kupelweiser bought Brijuni in the late 19th century and cleaned it up to build a luxury health resort that the islands became a tourist destination. Today Brijuni is a national park and an official state residence. Consequently, only two of the islands—**Veliki Brijuni** and **Mali Brijuni**—are open to visitors, who must arrive via organized tours unless they are staying at one of Brijuni's hotels.

ESSENTIALS

VISITOR INFORMATION   Almost all tourist agencies on Istria's west coast offer excursions to Brijuni. Once there, your itinerary is limited unless you plan to stay in one of Brijuni's hotels. It is a good idea to check with the national park office to see what's off-limits. The **Brijuni National Park Tourist Office** at Fažana (ℂ **052/525-882;** www. np-brijuni.hr) is open from 8am to 10pm daily in July and August; from 8am to 8pm daily in June and September; and from 8am to 3pm Monday through Saturday other times. Tickets sold at Fažana cost 190kn for adults and 95kn for children.

GETTING THERE & GETTING AROUND   You don't need more than a day to see the accessible parts of Brijuni, and it is easy to book an excursion. Tours leave from the dock at **Fažana** (which is a half-hour drive from Pula) three to five times per day, depending on the season. The trip to Brijuni from Fažana takes about 20 minutes and the guided land tour takes about 4 hours, including breaks and waits for the boat back to shore. (Fažana is also reachable by the no. 6 Pula bus.) *Tip:* Agencies in Pula sell tickets for Brijuni excursions, some of which include bus transportation between your hotel and Fažana. This can be a good choice if you must start and finish your tour at a specific time. But if you don't need that convenience, book at the Brijuni National Park office on the waterfront when you get to Fažana, a choice that saves a considerable amount of money. If you are booking anywhere but the National Park office, be sure you are getting a tour that lets you off on the islands. Some tours merely cruise around Brijuni without docking.

WHAT TO SEE & DO

Once you land on **Veliki Brijuni,** you'll be escorted by an English-speaking guide through the park both on foot and on an environment-friendly tram. The guided tour takes about 4 hours and hits the island's **safari park** (population is down to a few older animals), a 1st-century **Roman villa complex** at **Verige Bay,** the ruins of a **Byzantine fortress,** and the outskirts of Tito's **White Villa.** Other points of interest are the **"Old Lady,"** a 1,600-year-old olive tree in the running for oldest tree in Croatia; a small archaeological museum, **Church of St. Germaine,** with copies of the **Baška**

Tablet and **Dance of the Dead Fresco** from Beram; and **Josip Broz Tito Memorial Museum** ★★★ (📞 **052/525-883** or 052/525-822). The museum is open daily 8am to 7pm in summer; 8am to 2pm at other times, or when excursion boats come in. The Tito is a natural history museum with a collection of **taxidermic** animals on the ground floor, and a photo exhibit titled **"Tito on Brijuni"** on the second floor. The guide will explain that the animals (some endangered species) either died of natural causes on Brijuni's preserve or en route from exotic lands. The photos document Tito's activities on Brijuni and should not be missed, as they give context to Tito and his style of leadership: Each image shows Tito shaking hands or dining with a different head of state or celebrity, proof of his ability to use his strong personality to advantage for his country. There is a small concession outside the museum that serves baguette sandwiches, pastries, and beverages.

4 VODNJAN (DIGNANO)

Vodnjan, as with other Istrian towns, shows evidence of prehistoric settlements and of cultures from the Illyrians through the Italians, who ruled there before the Croatians took over. Vodnjan eventually developed into the most important center of commerce in southern Istria and remained so until 1856, when Pula became Istria's chief port. Today Vodnjan is a sleepy collection of villages known primarily for a large Italian-speaking population and the **Vodnjan mummies** ★★★, a collection of remarkably preserved bodies of holy people that lie in state at **St. Blaise Church** ★★ on the main square.

ESSENTIALS

VISITOR INFORMATION When you arrive at this small town just north of Pula, make your first stop the **tourist office** at Narodni Trg 3 (📞 **052/511-672;** fax 052/511-700; tz-vodnjan-dignano@pu.hinet.hr) on the main square. It is open from 8am to noon and from 5 to 8pm daily in the summer and has variable hours other times. You can pick up a map and brochures that will direct you to Vodnjan's surprisingly rich store of historical sites.

GETTING THERE See "Getting There," in "Orientation," earlier in this chapter.

GETTING AROUND You can drive on most main streets in Vodnjan, but if you do, you'll miss some of the more interesting alleys that twist around the town center.

WHAT TO SEE & DO

When you walk through central Vodnjan, you'll find that the main street is cobblestone and uncharacteristically wide. As you get farther in, you'll notice that the town has a distinct medieval appearance with arched doorways; Gothic, Renaissance, and Baroque architecture; offshoot streets the size of alleys; and a main square where **St. Blaise and its campanile**—the tallest in Istria—stand. Vodnjan is only 6km (4 miles) from the sea and 10km (6½ miles) from Pula. Today, it is not only a tourist stop between Pula and Rovinj, but also a town caught between Istria's agricultural and commercial traditions. Most visitors don't explore Vodnjan in depth, but go straight to St. Blaise Church and its mummies and then head out again.

Church of St. Blaise ★★ To get to St. Blaise, walk through the portal that once was the town gate and that still leads to Vodnjan's oldest sector **(Castelo),** which then opens to the main square and the 18th-century St. Blaise Church and its bell tower. St. Blaise is the largest church in Istria and its bell tower is reputed to be the highest, but the main

(Fun Facts Kažuni

The fields of southwest Istria are dotted with small, dry-stone huts that look like giant gray beehives. Travelers often wonder what they are and what their purpose is. Usually, the huts were built in the corners of fields and served as shelters for shepherds and storage units for tools. Inside, small stone blocks often served as seats around an open hearth. Usually, the door and windows (if any) face away from prevailing winds and are the only openings in the structure. About 3,000 of these mostly intact folk buildings are in the vicinity of Vodnjan, and many still are in use. Many kažuni have been restored and some are even used as summer cottages.

attraction is behind the church's altar. Entrance to the church is free, but there is a charge to view the treasury of sacral art and the mummies. Both are worth the cost.

Trg Sveti Blaz. © **052/511-420.** Daily July–Sept 9am–7pm. Admission during Mass or when the priest is on the premises other times.

St. Blaise Treasury ★★★ St. Blaise's collection of sacral art and relics is in the sacristy off the sanctuary and rather fascinating in a macabre sort of way. It is filled with hundreds of the church's 370 relics (mostly bones) from about 200 saints, as well as vestments and other church objects. Most are displayed in glass reliquaries, one of which reputedly holds the tongue of St. Mary of Egypt. Even if viewing piles of bones is not your thing, consider visiting the treasury to see the **14th-century polyptych of Blessed Leon Bembo ★★**, who had a reputation for healing the sick before and after death, and whose preserved body is on view in the exhibit next door. The panel was painted by Paolo Veneziano in 1321 and was used as the lid to Blessed Leon's coffin. The exhibit is well marked, and both it and the mummies were brought to Vodnjan because they were in danger of being desecrated.

In St. Blaise Church.

The Vodnjan Mummies ★★★ The mummy exhibit is past the gated sanctuary to the rear of the altar in an area that is separated from view by heavy velvet drapes. Pew seats face the display cases, which are dimly lighted and roped off so you can't get too close to the cases. After you enter, the floor attendant will play a tape in English (or a dozen other languages) that gives the history of the exhibit and details about the lives and deaths of the three mummified bodies dressed in period clothing displayed in glass-fronted cases. The cases are topped with more glass cases that contain a foot-high jumble of bones and other body parts, including a bony form reputed to St. Sebastian's torso and a leg bone supposedly belonging to St. Barbara.

In St. Blaise Church at Trg Sveti Blaz. © **052/511-420.** 40kn to view the sacral art and mummies; 30kn mummies only. Daily 9am–7pm.

5 ROVINJ (ROVIGNO)

Rovinj is one of the most photographed cities in Croatia. From the air, its location on a promontory makes it look like a fairy-tale village suspended on a pillow of bright blue sea; at ground level, it looks like the quintessential Italian fishing village. Central Rovinj once was an islet, and it wasn't until the 18th century that the channel separating it from the mainland was filled in. Today, Rovinj's Old Town is a protected monument and one of Istria's most visited sites. Rovinj has preserved the best of its architectural and cultural legacy by allowing development but keeping industry on the mainland, where the Rovinj tobacco factory and cannery still play major roles in the town's economy. Central Rovinj is a tangle of steep pedestrian streets that are paved with sea-salt-polished cobblestones and marked with signs in Italian and Croatian. These narrow, winding streets are lined with galleries, quaint shops, and excellent restaurants. Most lead to the town's highest point, where **St. Euphemia Church** and its campanile dominate the skyline. Add to that Rovinj's strong Italian personality, which includes a thriving fleet of small fishing boats, a smattering of Venetian-style piazzas, numerous restaurants, cafes, and atmospheric rock walls set next to pounding waves, and you have a town that's both vibrant and historical.

ESSENTIALS

VISITOR INFORMATION The **Rovinj Tourist Information Office** is at Pino Budičin 12 (© **052/811-566;** fax 052/816-007; www.tzgrovinj.hr). It is open from 8am to 9pm daily mid-June to mid-September; and from 8am to 3pm Monday to Saturday other times. Located just off the main square at the harbor, it has brochures, maps, and information on accommodations, the town, and Rovinj history.

GETTING THERE Rovinj is just half an hour or 16km (25 miles) north of Pula and linked by well-marked roads if you are traveling by car. There is frequent bus service to and from Pula; service to and from Croatian cities that range from Osijek to Dubrovnik; and international service to select cities in Italy, Germany, and Slovenia. The main bus station is at Trg Na Lokvi 6 (© **052/811-453;** www.tzgrovinj.hr).

GETTING AROUND Rovinj is a wonderful walking city. To visit the Old Town, you'll have to leave your car in the city lot at the north end of town. Fees are a modest 7kn per hour. You can rent a bike at the lot's exit for 100kn per day or 5kn per hour if you don't want to rely on walking or if you want to try Rovinj's picturesque bike trail. Local buses serve areas outside the Old Town area, as do taxis.

WHAT TO SEE & DO

Rovinj is a browser's paradise, with a labyrinth of streets and cubbyholes to explore. Most of the important sites are in the Old Town, but there are a few places of note outside the center. **Zlatni Rt-Punta Corrente Nature Park** ★★ is a fine reason to venture out: It's a densely forested park between the Hotel Park and the Hotel Monte Mulini that is rimmed with rocky beaches and full of hiking paths. **Limska Draga Fjord** ★★★ is a flooded karstic canyon less than 16km (10 miles) north of Rovinj. It looks like a ribbon of clear blue-green water framed with forested walls on two sides. At least two caves with evidence of prehistoric habitation have been discovered there, and several local legends say that pirates used the inlet as a base for ambushing merchant ships. Mussels and oysters are farmed there and you can sample them at any of the restaurants along the road that skirts the area. Excursions to Limska Draga leave from Rovinj and Poreč daily and often can be booked directly at seaside or from any travel agency in town for about 190kn per person.

Balbi Arch ★★ You can enter Old Town from the main square through the 17th-century Balbi Arch, which leads up to Grisia, Rovinj's most interesting street. The arch is on the site where one of the town's seven gates once stood; it is carved with a Turk's head on one side and a Venetian's head on the other.

(Finds) Grisia Street Standout

Rovinj's main street is really a steep, cobbled passageway that runs from the main square all the way up to St. Euphemia Church. It is lined with shops and galleries and buildings that still sport vestiges of the town's medieval roots. **Galerija Peti-Božić** ★★ at no. 22 is one of the most pleasant and most interesting. This tiny shop specializes in Croatian naive art created by Marija Peti-Božić, who has shown her work in galleries and museums in Zagreb and elsewhere in Europe. Most of Peti-Božić's work is oil on glass, typical of the Hlebine School. The shop is run by the artist's jovial husband, who will proudly rattle off his wife's accomplishments as well as wrap your purchases securely for packing.

August is officially the month of Grisia's art celebration; during this month, shops and restaurants remain open as long as there are people in the streets.

Batana House ★★ (**Kids**) Fishing is the focus but multimedia is the catch at this new museum dedicated to the industry that made Rovinj famous. The museum's name refers to the *batana*, wooden fishing boats that still are in use and often moored in Rovinj's harbor. This is no collection of weathered wood and rusty anchors: Instead it is an interactive exhibition that uses film music, and sound to provide a virtual immersion into Rovinj's culture. *Tip:* Kids will love the hands-on experience making fishing nets.

Obala P. Budičina 2. (℃) **052/805-266.** Fax 052/830-650. www.batana.org. Daily 9am–1pm and 7–10pm daily June–Sept; 10am–1pm and 3–5pm Tues–Sun Nov–Dec and Mar–May. Closed Jan–Feb though the museum can be visited by prior arrangement.

Rovinj Aquarium ★ (**Kids**) Founded in 1891, the Aquarium is Rovinj's oldest museum and also one of its best. It is in the same facility as the Ruđer Bošković Center for Maritime Research and has a nice collection of local marine life.

G. Paliaga 5. (℃) **052/804-702.** http://more.cim.irb.hr. Admission 10kn. Summer daily 9am–9pm; rest of year 10am–5pm.

Rovinj Heritage Museum ★ The museum was founded in 1954 to collect and exhibit works of art. Today its collections include old masters, contemporary works, a library, and a cache of local archaeological finds. The museum is housed in a Baroque palace that once belonged to Italian aristocrats.

Trg Maršala Tita 11. (℃) **052/816-720.** Fax 052/830-650. www.muzej-rovinj.com. Admission 15kn adults, 10kn children and students. Summer Tues–Sun 9am–noon and 7–10pm; closed Mon. Winter Tues–Sat 9am–1pm; closed Sun–Mon.

St. Euphemia Church ★★ The Baroque church dedicated to Rovinj's copatron saint is the third iteration of the shrine built in her honor. When the saint and her sarcophagus appeared in Rovinj early in the 9th century, they were housed in a chapel near the Church of St. George. A century and a half later, a larger church dedicated to both saints was built to accommodate pilgrims who steadily streamed into Rovinj to pray to Euphemia. Finally, the present church was built on the same site atop Rovinj's highest hill in the early 18th century. The adjacent **bell tower** ★★ was built 50 years earlier and

The Legend of St. Euphemia

St. Euphemia probably was just a teenager living in 4th-century Chalcedon near Constantinople when she fell victim to Diocletian's campaign to purge the Roman Empire of Christianity. Euphemia was the daughter of a prominent Chalcedon citizen and was imprisoned with 49 other Christians when they refused to worship the town idol and deny their faith. Because of her refusal to deny Christ, the young Euphemia was tortured with fire and snakes and by having her bones broken on a wheel before being thrown to the lions, which miraculously didn't devour her body after they killed her. Christians recovered Euphemia's body and buried it in Chalcedon, but in the 7th century they moved it to Constantinople because they feared the body would be defiled by Persian invaders. In Constantinople, the Christian Emperor Constantine ordered that a church be built in Euphemia's honor. Her sarcophagus remained there until A.D. 800, when the faithful again moved it because they feared that the Emperor Nicefor might remove it to parts unknown.

No one knows for sure how the coffin and its contents got to Rovinj, but one legend says that Christian fishermen probably put it on their boats in an attempt to get it to a safe place, and then somehow lost it in the sea. The legend goes on to attribute Euphemia's arrival on the shores of Rovinj to a miracle. One local legend further states that villagers who found the coffin couldn't budge the heavy stone container from the surf no matter how hard they tried. In the end it was a young boy with a pair of calves who was able to get the coffin out of the water after St. Euphemia appeared to him in a dream and told him what to do. The coffin is now a symbol of Rovinj and rests behind the altar in the right aisle of the church at the top of Rovinj's highest hill. Through the years, large numbers of worshippers come to pray at the site daily, especially on September 16, the day that St. Euphemia died in A.D. 304.

is one of the highest campaniles in Istria. It is topped with a copper statue of St. Euphemia that includes a palm and a wheel, symbols of her martyrdom. The people of Rovinj made St. Euphemia a patron saint of the city along with St. George after the stone sarcophagus containing her body mysteriously showed up on their shores following its disappearance from Constantinople in A.D. 800.

Petro Stankovića. ℂ 052/815-615. Daily summer 10am–3pm; only during Mass other times.

WHERE TO STAY

Rovinj has very few hotels in the city center and not many in the surrounding area either, considering the number of tourists that visit each year. However, that is changing as the Maistra group adds properties and as private accommodations become more abundant and luxurious. Stop at any tourist agency, some of which set up kiosks on the road into town to book a private room on arrival. Not only will these agencies find you a place to sleep, but they also will lead you to it so you can inspect the rooms before paying.

Eden Hotel ★★   Every guest room has a couch and a balcony. The balconies overlook green space or lawn where guests can sunbathe or dine. The lunch buffet is set on a terrace under the hotel eaves where there is often live music at night. Bathrooms, balconies, and public spaces were renovated in 2006 and the Eden promptly won several "Best of" awards (best four-star on the Adriatic, best breakfast in Croatia). *Tip:* The Eden offers more luxuries and sports options than any other hotel in Rovinj.

I Adamovića. ℂ **052/800-250.** Fax 052/800-215. www.maistra.hr. 330 units. Aug from 210€ double. Rest of year from 90€ double. 50% reduction for children 2–11; children 1 and under free. Rates include breakfast and are based on stays exceeding 3 days. 20% surcharge for stays of 3 or fewer days. Half-board available on request. AE, DC, MC, V. **Amenities:** 3 restaurants; coffee shop, 3 bars; babysitting 10am–5pm (included in room rate); 3 pools; spa. *In room:* A/C, TV, hair dryer, minibar, free Wi-Fi.

Hotel Adriatic ★   Reserve your room in this waterfront hotel early because it fills up quickly, especially during July and August. Rooms in the renovated 1912 building are not lavish, but they are comfortable and spacious. However, you'll have to bear some discomfort before you get there. There is no elevator, nor are there any bellhops, so you'll have to get your luggage to your room yourself and that could be up to the fourth floor. Parking is available, but very inconvenient, and night time noise can be a problem, especially if there is a band playing on the square beneath your window. However, the Adriatic's location and views can't be beat and the hotel's Maestral restaurant's modern take on Croatian cuisine is a delight (see review below).

Pino Budačin bb. ℂ **052/500-510.** Fax 052/813-753. www.maistra.hr. 27 units. Aug from 994kn double. Rest of year from 572kn double. 50% reduction for children 2–12; children 1 and under free in parent's room. AE, DC, MC, V. Parking lot (40kn per day). **Amenities:** Restaurant; cafe. *In room:* A/C, TV, hair dryer, minibar, wireless Internet (40kn per hour, 100kn per day).

Hotel Monte Mulini ★★★   When the Monte Mulini took its place as Rovinj's first true luxury hotel during the 2009 season, it was an instant sensation. Built at a cost of 200 million euros on the site of a former Socialist hotel, the Monte Mulini is a completely new structure and signals a commitment to the upscale hotel market for its parent Maistra. When you walk into the Monte Mulini's street level reception area the first thing you see is a dramatic two-story wall of glass that looks out at the Adriatic and down on a terraced pool and sunning area. From then on, everything is a revelation. Corridors are illuminated with lights that subtly change color. Suites are in a separate building ringed with scented gardens that afford privacy. Guest rooms are in the main building, and even the lowest priced room has a large bathroom with a shower that is separate from the tub, an array of Angelo Caroli toiletries, and a sea view. For the ultimate relaxation experience, try the floating bath in the plush spa. It's a 40cm-deep (15½ in.) tub filled with water with such a high concentration of salt that you stay suspended in water.

For a truly memorable meal, don't miss the hotel's **Corsican Wine Vault ★★★** (reviewed below).

A Smareglia bb. ℂ **052/636-000.** Fax 052/636-001. www.maistra.com. 119 units. Doubles from 646€ July–Aug; from 310€ other times. Suites from 807€ July–Aug; from 465€ other times. **Amenities:** Restaurant; buffet; 2 bars; pool; spa; tennis courts; bowling alley; basketball court. *In room:* A/C, TV, hair dryer, minibar, free Wi-Fi.

Hotel Park ★★   From the front, this 1972 structure looks like another big package hotel. The Park might offer packages, but it is surprisingly user-friendly and personal. Rooms are done in yellows and blues in modest but comfortable style. The Park is conveniently located 2 minutes from **Zlatni Rt-Punta Corrente Nature Park** and 5 minutes from Old Town. Despite its size, the hotel fills up from May to October. Call no later than April for reservations during this time. *Tip:* The view of Rovinj and St. Catherine's Island from the balcony off the Park's lobby is spectacular.

IM Ronjigova. ☎ **052/811-077.** Fax 052/816-977. www.maistra.hr. 202 units. Aug from 182€ double. Rest of year from 73€ double. 50% discount for children 2–11. Children 1 and under free. Rates include breakfast and are based on stays exceeding 3 days. 20% surcharge for stays of 3 or fewer days. Half-board available on request. AE, DC, MC, V. Closed 2 months each year, usually mid-Dec to mid-Feb. **Amenities:** Restaurant; bar; ice-cream parlor; babysitting; children's programs; Internet; 3 pools; excursions; exchange office. *In room:* A/C, TV, hair dryer, minibar.

Villa Angelo d'Oro ★★★   This 17th-century bishop's palace in the Old Town was renovated in 2001 and has been kept in superb condition ever since. Each room is unique in size and decor with plush period furniture and fresh colors. Bathrooms have modern fixtures, though most have showers rather than tubs. Guests can treat themselves to one of the best views in the city from the open-air balcony off the third-floor library before or after they dine in the hotel's **Angela d'Oro Restaurant** (reviewed below). Parking is a .5km (¼ mile) away from the hotel, but the staff will pick up and deliver guests and their luggage at their cars.

Via Svalba 38–42. ☎ **052/840-502.** www.rovinj.at. 25 units. Mid-July to mid-Sept from 242€ double. Rest of year from 138€ double. 50% discount for children 3–11. Children 2 and under free. Rates include breakfast. Half-board available on request for 30€ per person per day. AE, DC, MC, V. Limited parking 10€ per day. Closed Sept to mid-Mar. **Amenities:** Restaurant; terrace dining; wine cellar; Jacuzzi; solarium; library. *In room:* A/C, TV, hair dryer, minibar.

Villa Valdibora ★★   The four apartments in this 18th-century town house could not be more unique or more convenient to Old Town Rovinj. Oil paintings, antiques, and old-world service are juxtaposed with ultramodern bathrooms, electronics, and comforts. This is a perfect place to stay to explore Rovinj and environs.

Silvana Chiurca 8. ☎/fax **052/845-040.** www.valdibora.com. 4 apts (2 persons) from 216€ July–Aug; from 100€ other times. AE, DC, MC, V. Rates include breakfast. Pets allowed. **Amenities:** Room service; bike use; laptop rental. *In room:* A/C.

WHERE TO DINE

Restaurants that line the waterfront are touristy and predictable, and prices are inflated. However, all serve respectable seafood and excellent pizza and pasta. Venture uphill into the warren of streets or across the bay for menus that go beyond the expected.

Amfora ★★★ SEAFOOD   The fish is fresh and the ambience cheerful in this beautiful restaurant that overlooks the marina and Old Town. Amfora outshines most Rovinj dining spots on the waterfront both in its cuisine and service—and that is also reflected in its prices. However, if you want first-class seafood, Amfora can't be beat. Try the salted sea bass or one of the risottos and pair it with one of the restaurant's excellent wines. You won't be disappointed.

A. Rismondo 23. ☎ **052/816-663.** Entrees 90kn–175kn. AE, DC, MC, V. Daily 11am–midnight. Closed early Jan to early Mar.

Angelo d'Oro ★★★ ISTRIAN   During the summer, this restaurant is in the hotel's lovely walled garden, and during the winter it moves to an imaginatively styled room inside. Either way, the cuisine is creative yet traditional and beautifully presented. Try the cream of potato soup with truffles or any of the grilled fish dishes. Don't miss a tour of the stone wine cellar, where you can taste Istrian wines and local specialties such as Istrian ham or cheese.

The IQ (Istrian Quality) designation on Malvasia wine is intended for identifying high-quality products made from Istrian Malvasia grapes. It represents the first wine supervision system in Croatia and sets production standards for vintners in all phases of wine production. The 2005 vintage was the first to undergo the system's scrutiny. Since then, the number of producers awarded the designation has grown steadily, as has the number of bottles carrying the IQ mark of quality.

In Villa Angelo d'Oro hotel, Via Svalba 38–42. ✆ **052/840-502.** www.rovinj.at. Reservations recommended. Entrees 90kn–165kn. AE, DC, MC. Daily 7pm–midnight.

Corsican Wine Vault ★★★ MODERN CROATIAN   Chef Tomislav Gretić is a true artist by the looks of the Wine Vault's menu and the dishes that come out of the kitchen in the Monte Mulini Hotel. The bill of fare is illustrated with Gretić's whimsical drawings and the food is as pleasing to the eye as it is to the palate. Bask in the soft glow of faux candle chandeliers while you sip cold pear soup with cinnamon and gorgonzola followed by pheasant for two glazed with beurre noisette and cold port wine sauce. End the meal with lemon crème brûlée and chocolate sorbet and match each course with a selection from the restaurant's incredible 560-bottle wine list, which includes selections from all over the world. This is a restaurant you should not miss. *Tip:* While this restaurant only serves dinner, **Mediterraneo** is the Monte Mulini's casual restaurant for a buffet-style breakfast, lunch, and dinner.

In the Hotel Monte Mulini, A. Smareglia. ✆/fax **052/636-001.** www.maistra.hr. Reservations recommended. Entrees 130kn–204kn. AE, DC, MC, V. Daily 7–11pm.

La Puntulina ★★★ ISTRIAN   La Puntulina gets lots of points for its seaside location, but especially for its terrace, which is suspended above the water. The food is equally impressive as the chef relies on the freshest local produce to deliver dishes that are traditional but with enough creative twist to set them apart from the pack. Try the scallops in brandy, the squid with polenta, or the prawns with olive oil and garlic. *Tip:* You must reserve well in advance to get rights to a table on the terrace. If you can't get a reservation, have an after-dinner drink in the cocktail bar on the terrace below the restaurant.

Sv. Križ 38. ✆ **052/813-186.** Fax 052/815-975. www.videooglasi.com/restoran/puntulina. Entrees 80kn–250kn. MC. Thurs–Tues noon–2pm for lunch and daily 6–11pm for dinner Easter–Nov 1.

Maestral ★★ MODERN CROATIAN   "We try to be a little bit different," our waitress confided as she served us a mint-infused yogurt *amuse bouche* on the waterfront terrace of the 100-year-old Hotel Adriatic (see above). Swiss executive chef Priska Thuring (who happens to be married to Hotel Monte Mulini's Swiss-trained chef Tomislav Gretić) has created a menu for the Adriatic that features the best local ingredients in refined, creative dishes. The result is an oasis of moderately priced fine dining in a sea of cookie-cutter grill mills. We started with carpaccio of sea scallops marinated in lemon juice and accessorized with Granny Smith apple matchsticks and beet vinaigrette and chose herb marinated filet of sea bream poached *sous-vide* as the main. Thuring's food

ISTRIA 9 ROVINJ (ROVIGNO)

emphasizes clear, distinct flavors, and there is a small but well-chosen wine list of mostly Istrian varieties that complements her style.

In the Hotel Adriatic, Pino Budačin bb. ℭ **052/500-510.** Fax 052/813-753. www.maistra.hr. Entrees 75kn–136kn. DC, MC, V. Daily 7–11pm.

Monte ★★★ (**Finds**) MODERN CROATIAN   Monte's location at the foot of stairs leading up to Rovinj's iconic St. Euphemia Church puts the restaurant on the tourist track, but an innovative menu and a classy atmosphere set it apart. Cozy banquettes line the terra-cotta colored walls, and a wine table takes center stage in the room where entrees with names like Duckbread Rosé (duck spring roll with sautéed carrots and orange zest) rule. The wine list emphasizes Istria's best makers, and you should save room for desserts such as four Textures of Lemon (lemon cake, ice cream, jelly, and foam).

Montalbano 75. ℭ **052/830-203.** Fax 053/830-203. www.monte.hr. Reservations recommended. Entrees 179kn–203kn. AE, DC, MC, V. Daily noon–2pm and 6:30–11pm. Closed Nov–Mar.

Piassa Granda ★★ WINE BAR   A commitment to wine in general and Istrian wine in particular is the driving force behind Piassa Granda, which opened in 2008 on a street deep in the heart of Old Town. Tables spill outside from the dark interior but there's nothing to hide when it comes to Piassa Granda's wine list, which features Istrian IQ varieties. Finger food is available to accompany the wine, enough to make a light meal of it. Open daily 10am to 1pm May 1 to October 1.

Veli Trg 1. ℭ **098/824-322.** Snacks less than 50kn. AE, MC, V. Daily 10am–1pm May 1–Oct 1.

Taverna da Baston ★★ SEAFOOD   A warm welcome will make you feel at home at this bustling place next door to Rovinj's fish market. Dark brick walls are hung with fishing nets, and local music provides background. Try any of the super-fresh fish dishes or the handmade gnocchi with truffles.

Svalba 3. ℭ **098/982-63-95.** Entrees 50kn–150kn. AE, DC, MC, V. Prices include tax, *couvert* (cover charge), and service. Daily 6am–midnight.

ROVINJ AFTER DARK

Valentino's ★★ COCKTAILS   Access to Valentino's is down a steep staircase that cuts between two buildings on Križa St. From street level, you can't see anything but huge rocks in the sea with people sitting among them on small blue cushions. That's Valentino's. Drinks are a little pricey, but you get extra salt in your Margarita when the sea breaks on your perch. There is a terrace midway between the sea and street for less adventurous patrons. Open daily 11am to 1am. Sv. Križa 28. ℭ **052/830-683.**

Zanzibar ★ COCKTAILS   People go to Zanzibar to people-watch as often as they go to drink. They practice their sport from the comfort of big wicker chairs on Zanzibar's terrace on the harbor while they sip Zanzibar's pricey (about 60kn) mixed drinks. Open 11am to 1am daily. Obala Pina Budičina. ℭ **052/813-206.**

WHAT TO SEE & DO

Vrsar is a handy stop for those touring the Limska Draga Fjord, and it is noted for its nearby campgrounds, but it isn't a destination. There are a few intriguing restaurants in the area, private accommodations, and some large package resorts. Poreč and Rovinj are better choices as bases for exploring.

Dušan Džamonja's Sculpture Park ★ is another Vrsar site worth a look. Huge metal and stone sculptures scattered about the hills and meadows overlook the sea, creating a

Vrsar (Orsera) & Environs

Vrsar is a beautiful fishing village just north of the mouth of the **Limska Draga Fjord ★★★**, 10km (6¹/₄ miles) south of Poreč and 25km (16 miles) north of Rovinj. Vrsar seems to begin at the hill that is home to the **Church of St. Martin,** its imposing bell tower, and a **12th-century castle,** then spill down the hill to the sea. Away from the harbor and all around its central hill, Vrsar is etched with steep, winding streets dotted with red-tile-roofed houses and restored town gates. The remains of Roman storehouses and a Roman cemetery also are there, as are several churches, some of which date from the 4th century.

Vrsar is well known as a destination for campers or as a day trip from Rovinj or Poreč: It has four campgrounds that can accommodate nearly 20,000 people at sites near the sea. But Vrsar's contemporary claim to fame is its position as a gateway to **Koversada,** one of Croatia's largest naturist colonies. When this huge nudist resort was established on the Adriatic shore in 1960, it was the first in the region. Today, Koversada's villas and campground at 52450 Vrsar (© **052/441-378;** fax 052/441-761; koversada-camp@maistra.hr) are almost always filled to capacity. There are 72 units in the camp's villas. July 30 to mid-August, doubles cost from 52€; during the rest of the year, from 30€. Rates include breakfast. Closed mid-September to May 1.

It's easy to see everything Vrsar has to offer on foot, though some climbing is required. If you want to fully explore the nearby fjord, you'll need a car and a boat.

haunting open-air exhibit. Džamonja's works have been exhibited in the Museum of Modern Art in New York and at museums in London, Paris, Antwerp, and other cities in the world.

6 POREČ (PARENZO)

"Something for everyone" could be Poreč's motto—the seaside resort offers a wide variety of attractions, from a UNESCO World Heritage basilica complex to endless shopping opportunities to slick resort hotels so crammed with activities and services that you think you're in Disney World. Poreč courts tourism, supports tourism, and profits from tourism, but the town and surrounding area still manage to intrigue, perhaps because they are a seamless blend of medieval heritage, a well-oiled service industry, idyllic vineyards and olive groves, and blatant commercialism. Old Town is the epicenter of this mecca, with immaculate cobblestone streets, precisely clipped plantings, multilingual signs explaining all points of interest, and enough jewelry stores and *gelaterias* for every tourist in Croatia.

ESSENTIALS

VISITOR INFORMATION   Poreč knows how to make visitors feel at home and goes out of its way to lay out the welcome mat. People in the tourist offices are knowledgeable

Istria Upsilon

The idea of linking the west and east coasts of Istria with Rijeka via one highway germinated in the mid–19th century but it didn't become concrete until 1981 when the Učka Tunnel was opened, along with the first leg of the project. Today, the expressway through the heart of Istria forms a "Y" or "upsilon" with northern sections radiating from Matulje-in the east and Umag in the west. The two arms of the "Y" meet in Kanafar and merge into a single road to Pula in the south, completing the upsilon. Completion of the Upsilon Project (2008) has made it easier—and safer—to travel to, from, and across the peninsula.

and accommodating, and merchants are welcoming. The **Poreč Tourist Information Office** can provide maps and brochures as well as leads on available accommodations and events. It can be found at Zagrebačka 11 (☎ **052/434-983;** www.istra.com/porec) and is open from 8am to 10pm Monday to Saturday all year. On Sunday during July and August, it is open 9am to 1pm and 6 to 10pm.

Istra Line Travel Agency, located on the outskirts of Old Town at Partizanska 4 (☎ **052/427-062;** fax 052/432-116; www.istraline.hr), is one of several agencies that can book private accommodations. Istra Line specializes in apartment rental but it also can direct you to individual rooms. **Atlas Travel Agency** at Eufrazijeva 63 (☎ **052/434-983;** www.atlas.hr) can arrange excursions, hotels, private accommodations, and airline reservations. It is also the local American Express agent.

Di Tours ★★ at Prvomajska 2 (☎ **052/432-100;** fax 052/431-300; www.di-tours. com) is just one of many private tourist agencies in town, but it has a huge inventory of rooms and apartments in Poreč and the vicinity. In August, it offers doubles with shower from 28€, apartments from 45€. During the rest of the year, doubles cost from 12€, apartments from 16€.

GETTING THERE   See "Getting There" in "Orientation," earlier in this chapter.

GETTING AROUND   Poreč's Old Town is easy to navigate on foot, though its end-to-end shopping opportunities might slow you down. Buses serve the Lanterna complex south of town (the bus station is .5km/¼ mile from the town center) as well as nearby towns, but a car is necessary if you want to stay outside of town or if you want to explore the surrounding area.

WHAT TO SEE & DO

Poreč's Old Town is small, but it is packed with treasures, chief of which is the **Euphrasius Basilica** ★★★ and its stunning **mosaics** ★★★. The rest of Old Town's attractions pale in comparison but are interesting enough to warrant a walk-through.

Baredine Cave ★★★ (Kids)   Excursions to this collection of limestone caverns are among the most popular day trips out of Poreč. Just 7km (4½ miles) northeast of town on the road to Višjan, the caves are breathtaking chambers filled with stalactites and stalagmites. Entry fees cover the services of a guide, who takes you on a 40-minute tour of the underground halls and galleries and talks about the caves' flora, fauna, and minerals. Baredine's guides unfailingly relate the story of the legendary ill-fated lovers who died while looking for each other in the caves.

Euphrasian Basilica Complex ★★★ UNESCO has put this collection of early Christian and early Byzantine architecture on its World Heritage List, and you should put them on your "must-see" agenda, too. Situated near the town center off Eufrazijeva, the basilica is the last of four churches that were built between the 4th and 6th centuries, one on top of the other on this site. Evidence of those earlier churches is still visible, but the current complex originally built by Bishop Euphrasius in the 6th century is the focus. Besides the basilica itself, the complex is home to an atrium, a baptistery, a bell tower, and a bishop's palace. Visitors to the complex enter through the arches of the atrium. The bell tower was built in the 16th century, and the rest of the structures have undergone several renovations. Even if you aren't into visiting churches, make an effort to see the complex's spectacular **gem-studded mosaics ★★★** as well as its symbolic early Christian fish mosaic.

Eufrazijeva Ulica 22. Summer daily 7:30am–8pm. Other times during Mass only. Bell tower 10kn. Daily 10am–7pm.

Poreč Aquarium This is more coffee shop encircled with fish tanks than proper aquarium, though the specimens in those tanks are nice representatives of the area's indigenous marine life. You'll see huge signs and banners all over town advertising the Aquarium, but it is a little tricky to find in its home on a side street off Decumanus. Once there, it takes about 15 minutes to see everything that swims. The exhibit floor plan ends in the middle of the cafe/souvenir shop.

F. Glavinica 4. ✆ **052/428-720.** www.aquarium-porec.com. Admission 10kn. Daily 10am–5pm.

Regional Museum Poreč ★ The 18th-century Sinčić palace is home to this showcase for archaeological finds that include carved Roman tombstones, amphorae from the bottom of the sea, and 17th-century portraits of Venetians. The exhibits chronicle Poreč's history from Paleolithic times to the present.

Dekumanska 9. ✆ **052/431-585.** www.culture-vision.com. Admission 10kn adults; 5kn children. Summer 10am–1pm and 6-9pm; winter 10am–1pm.

St. Nicholas Island ★★★ Porec's better beaches are off this close-in island, which is a short boat taxi ride away from the harbor.

Taxi boats leave the dock every half-hour.

Tar ★★ This quaint Istrian town just 10km (6½ miles) north of Poreč is perched on a plateau 104m (340 ft.) above sea level and the surrounding area. It is said that on a clear day you can see St. Mark's in Venice on one side and the Alps on the other from the town's bell tower. Tar is also known for its summer festival, which includes a donkey race, parades, Istrian music, and lots of food. Tar exudes old-world charm and reputedly produces the best olive oil in Istria.

Tar-Vabriga Tourist Association, Istarska 8/A. ✆ **052/443-250.** www.istra.com/tar-vabriga. Summer daily 8am–9pm; Mon–Fri 8am–3pm other times.

Trg Marafor ★★ The remains of Poreč's Roman Forum and two Roman temples (Mars and Neptune) are the highlight of Trg Marafor, which is on the tip of the peninsula. Today, Trg Marafor is the site of several sleek cocktail bars and jazz clubs such as **Lapidarium ★★★**, which is tucked into a courtyard strewn with stone carvings and

ISTRIA

9

POREČ (PARENZO)

The Legend of Baredine Cave

Baredine's love story is a sad one that originated in the 13th century. According to the legend, a highborn young man named Gabriel fell in love with a beautiful shepherdess named Milka from Nova Vas. Gabriel's mother didn't approve of her son consorting with a mere farm girl and she couldn't dissuade him from the romance, so she hired bandits to kill the girl. Instead of killing her, the robbers took the mother's three pieces of gold and threw Milka into Baredine Cave. When Gabriel discovered the treachery, he supposedly tried to rescue his beloved and disappeared. (Gabriel's horse was found wandering near the cave, so it was presumed he had gone in to find Milka, but neither was heard from again.) The legend goes on to say that Milka's body eventually turned to stone in the cave and is slowly sinking to another chamber where Gabriel has been waiting for her for centuries.

artifacts. Lapidarium is located behind the Regional Museum and hosts jazz concerts in the courtyard nightly during the season.

Lapidarium Caffee/Bar/Gallery. ✆ 052/432-374. www.poup.hr. Daily 9am–2pm and 6pm–2am.

WHERE TO STAY

Poreč is the most visited city in Istria, and as such it has a wide inventory of accommodations. Most hotels in Poreč are managed by a large Croatian chain, but there is a lot of variety available, especially if you opt for a small hotel outside the center. The Poreč area offers everything from luxurious all-inclusive hotels with sophisticated entertainment to rooms in rural homes surrounded by olive groves and vineyards. Nothing within a couple of miles of the center can be classified inexpensive. No matter which option you choose, you'll have to book well in advance if you plan to stay any time during the "season," which runs through July and August.

Dependance Parentino (Value) This former free-standing hotel on the water is now an annex to the Neptun and managed by Riviera hotels. That means the building has guest rooms but not a reception desk and other services, which currently are housed in the Neptun. The Parentino (and its sister hotel, the Jadran) appeals to economy-minded travelers who don't require a lot of frills. All of the Parentino's guest rooms face the sea, a good thing since none have air-conditioning. Hair dryers are available at reception in Hotel Neptun. *Tip:* The Parentino's lobby and terrace have recently been remodeled in shades of gray and white to house a slick bar that is open from 8am to 2pm and 6 to 11pm in summer and that attracts the beautiful people.

Marsala Tita 15. ✆ 052/408-800. Fax 052/451-440. www.valamar.hr. 14 units. July 30 to mid-Aug from 84€ double. Rest of year from 32€ double. Rates include breakfast. AE, DC, MC, V. Annexes Apr–Oct. *In room:* TV.

Diamant ★★ (Value) From the outside, the Diamant looks like another 1970s package hotel, but the interior is a pleasant surprise. Guest rooms are huge and more like suites in this beautifully restored (2003) hotel less than a mile from the center of Poreč. Most guest accommodations have balconies and glass doors that are tinted and shaded, plus two bathrooms, one with a tub. The 10th floor is all suites and most have a refrigerator, dishwasher, and small stove. The Diamant offers every service imaginable, but it is most notable for its effort to make the entire hotel accessible to travelers with limited mobility. The restaurant is cafeteria style, but there are so many food stations and selections that you won't notice. There is also a poolside grill. Service is personal and helpful, more typical of small boutique establishments than huge package hotels. The same is true of the hotel's special bike tour that you can book through Gulliver's Travel. It stops at local wineries, farms, olive groves, and monuments, and features a gourmet picnic.

Brulo. ✆ **052/400-000.** Fax 052/451-206. www.riviera.hr. 244 units. End of July to mid-Aug from 158€ double. Rest of year from 70€ double. Rates include breakfast and are per person daily based on a stay of 4 or more days. 20% surcharge for stays of 3 days or fewer. AE, DC, MC, V. **Amenities:** 2 restaurants; bar; Internet cafe; juice bar; children's program; 2 pools; excursions; hot tub; massage; solarium; whirlpool. *In room:* A/C, TV, hair dryer, minibar.

Hostin Poreč ★★ (Kids)

The Hostin reopened in 2005 after a complete renovation. It is in the middle of a large park and is less than 91m (300 ft.) from the beach, which skirts fairly shallow water, making it perfect for children. However, you don't have to rely on the sea for swimming, thanks to the heated indoor pool. All guest rooms have balconies and all are spacious with bathrooms that are especially nice thanks to the recent renovation.

Rade Končara 4. ✆ **052/432-112.** www.hostin.hr. 60 units. July–Aug from 126€ double. Rest of year from 56€. Rates include breakfast. Half-board available. 20% surcharge for stays fewer than 4 days. AE, DC, MC, V. **Amenities:** Restaurant; cafe; bar; pool; sauna; Turkish bath. *In room:* A/C, TV, Internet.

Hotel Palazzo ★★★ (Finds)

After a 2-year renovation of the Hotel Riviera, which was Poreč's first hotel, built in 1910 on a landfill in the Adriatic, the Hotel Palazzo emerged from the construction debris. The Palazzo opened in July 2009 and it lives up to its new name in every way. Its renovators were careful to keep historic lines in the original building intact while adding a new wing and 21st century amenities throughout both sections. The result is a yellow and cream beauty accented with warm-toned wood and marble that blends classic and modern seamlessly. Each of the Palazzo's 70 rooms and four suites has a unique layout, and most have unobstructed views of the sea. Bathrooms are especially classy and roomy and most have separate showers and tubs. Choose room no. 408 or 314 in the old section for breathtaking views of nearby islands or the Karbola suite, which has windows on three sides and a large arch-framed balcony overlooking the sea. This is *the* place to stay in Poreč.

Obala Maršala Tita 24. ✆ **052/858-800.** Fax 052/858-801. www.hotel-palazzo.hr. 74 units. Superior doubles from 349€ July–Aug; from 179€ other times. Suites from 599€ July–Aug; from 299€ other times. Rates include breakfast, taxes, and parking for superior and suite rooms. AE, DC, MC, V. Parking 20€ per day. **Amenities:** Restaurant; Viennese cafe; bar; cafeteria; pool; spa. In room: A/C, TV, hair dryer, minibar, free Wi-Fi.

Neptun ★

Neptun has a great location facing the sea. It was built in 1968, renovated in 1995, and improved a little every year since. Some rooms have harbor views, as does the rooftop cafe, which is closed during very hot weather. Bathrooms have showers and no tubs. Reception is very helpful and pleasant and also handles details for guests of the hotel's two annexes. Suites have a minibar and hair dryer, but other guests must borrow a hair dryer from the desk. The hotel sometimes closes in January and February or in November and December, depending on reservations, so call ahead.

Maršala Tita 17. ✆ **052/408-800.** Fax 052/431-351. www.valamar.hr. 145 units. July 30 to mid-Aug from 96€ double. Rest of year from 68€ double. Rates include breakfast. AE, DC, MC, V. Half-board available. Discounts for children in parent's room. **Amenities:** Restaurant; bar. *In room:* TV.

Plava Laguna

The bulk of Poreč's hotels—more than a dozen—are in the huge Plava Laguna resort area that sprawls both north and south from Old Town. If you stay in a Plava Laguna property, you can choose from huge package hotels with every imaginable amenity and sports facility to a quiet villa in a residential setting. For information and a description of accommodations, contact Plava Laguna at Rae Končara 12, 52440 Poreč (℃ **052/410-210;** fax 052/451-044; www.plavalaguna.hr).

Camping

Bijela Uvala ★★★ **(Kids)**   Located between Funtana and Poreč, this environment-friendly campground uses solar power and practices ecologically oriented camp management. The campground is partially wooded and blends with nature. Guests are encouraged to use ecologically sound products. The camp also offers a large pebble beach with paved sunning areas and lots of programs to amuse the kids.

52440 Poreč. ℃ **052/410-551.** Fax 052/410-600. www.plavalaguna.hr. July–Aug campsite with tent, car, and 2 people 27€ per day. Rest of year from 14€. AE, DC, MC. Closed Nov–Mar.

Lanternacamp ★★★   If you must stay at a huge campground, Lanternacamp is one of the best. With more than 3,000 spaces for tents and/or campers, Lanterna wisely provides plenty of amenities, such as electricity and water hookups, super-clean bathrooms, supermarkets, a laundry, a pool, and activities for kids. The camp is 13km (8 miles) from Poreč, but you won't mind because the beautifully landscaped, terraced property slopes toward the sea. There is an FKK section for naturists.

52440 Poreč. ℃ **052/405-200.** Fax 052/451-440. www.valamar.com. Campers 4.20€–7.60€ per person; vehicle space 7.80€–26€; mobile home rentals 41€–228€. AE, MC, V. Closed Nov–Mar.

WHERE TO DINE

Dining in Old Town Poreč tends to be a one-note experience with a couple of exceptions: Almost all the restaurants there rely on pizza, pasta, and grilled seafood for their menu mainstays. If you want to taste authentic grilled lamb or more unusual Istrian preparations, your best bet is to get out of (Old) Town.

Bieli San ★ CROATIAN/PIZZA   Big red umbrellas make this restaurant across from the well-known Cardo and Barilla restaurants easy to spot. This is the place to stop for lunch or a substantial snack. We tried the San Remo pizza with artichokes and mushrooms. Bieli San also runs a gelato cafe, so a break for a fancy ice-cream treat works, too.

Trg Matije Gupca 4. ℃ **052/451-819.** Entrees 50kn–120kn; pizzas 30kn–45kn. No credit cards. Daily 7am–midnight.

Cardo ★★ SEAFOOD   Fish is proudly displayed in an outdoor ice case in this classy terrace restaurant. A gnarled old olive tree and soft lights surrounding the terrace create a romantic mood for diners at the outdoor tables, which are always full. Try the salmon piquant or noodles with mussels, either of which is perfect with a glass of Istrian Malvasia. Cardo has the usual assortment of risottos and grilled dishes, too.

Cardo Maximus 6. ℃ **052/255-164.** Entrees 35kn–330kn. AE, DC, MC, V. Daily Apr 1–Nov 1 noon–midnight.

Distinguished Guest ★★ MEDITERRANEAN   High fashion meets the water- front at this stylish restaurant that is dressed up like a French salon with chandeliers and black and cream furniture. DG's broad selection of seafood and meat dishes is complemented by an outstanding wine list. Dine alfresco and enjoy the entertainment of the yacht lineup and the nightly promenade along the wharf. By day, gaze at St. Nicholas Island from DG's terrace tables.

Obala Maršala Tita 20. ✆ **052/433-810.** Entrees 70kn–140kn. AE, DC, MC, V. Daily noon–midnight. Closed Nov–Feb.

Gostonica Istria ★★ SEAFOOD   Locals rave about the seafood at Gostonica Istria, a typical indoor/outdoor coastal place where people-watching from the terrace is a side dish. Istria's multi-language menu makes it easy to order. You'll get expertly prepared authentic Istrian cuisine along with lots of spaghetti options, such as Istrian minestrone, fuži, and spiny lobster with noodles. Service is accommodating even if the prices are a little high.

Msgr. Bože Milanovića 30. ✆ **052/434-63.** Fax 052/451-482. Entrees 65kn–190kn. AE, V. Daily 10am–midnight.

Old Pub Cotton Club ★ PIZZA   This handsome restaurant/cafe under burgundy awnings at the entrance to town looks like a tourist trap, but serious food is prepared here. Try the tortellini *mille voglie* (with clams); or the tortellini with pršut, pumpkin, cream, and truffles. Pasta and pizza are emphasized here, including nine kinds of tagliatelle that include tagliatelle al'Amatriciana (tomato, bacon, onion, olives, hot peppers), plus 20 kinds of pizza and risotto. There are good drink- and ice-cream menus and live music weekend evenings.

Trg Slobode 5. ✆ **052/453-293.** Fax 052/432-074. Entrees 40kn–110kn. No credit cards. Daily 9am–1am.

Parenzo 1910 ★★ REGIONAL CROATIAN   Parenzo is Poreč's Italian name and this restaurant in the Hotel Palazzo (see above) is an homage to Poreč as it was a century ago when Italians comprised the bulk of tourists and Italy owned the peninsula. Parenzo's menu is inspired by the menu guests saw in 1910, but its regional specialties have been updated to today's tastes. Try the salmon with chard crème fraîche and salmon bits, or for more traditional tastes, the sautéed wild boar and venison in red wine sauce with fuži. *Tip:* Ask for a table on the seaside terrace, which is open on three sides.

In the Hotel Palazzo, Obala Maršala Tita 24. ✆ **052/858-800.** Fax 052/858-801. www.hotel-palazzo.hr. Entrees 79kn–199kn. AE, DC, MC, V. Daily noon–midnight.

Peterokutna Kula ★★ SEAFOOD   This place has all the earmarks of another tourist trap—it is built into a pentagonal, 15th-century tower and it is on one of the highest traffic corners in town. The entry is in a tiny room with old stone walls, then up steep steps—but Kula delivers first-rate food. The spectacular view of the city from a rooftop five floors up (no elevator) is the perfect garnish for Kula's fresh food. The seafood assortment platter is a luscious collection of the shrimp, orada, mussels, and calamari at a very reasonable price. Service is friendly and prompt, a wonder since the kitchen is on the first floor. *A word of caution:* No credit cards are accepted and the occasional seagull lands tableside to beg for leftovers.

Decumanus 1. ✆ **052/451-378.** Entrees 55kn–110kn. No credit cards. Daily noon–midnight.

Restaurant Villa Filipini ★★ ISTRIAN   Pastas are handmade and the kitchen is imaginative in this tiny restaurant in one of Istria's delightful **rural small hotels** ★. Seating on the outdoor terrace overlooks a small grove of trees and gives you the impression that you're dining in a forest. There is no written menu: The chef bases his dishes on what is fresh in the market. Choices can include green gnocchi with mixed cheese and walnut sauce, or ravioli filled with fresh cheese in herb butter. Fish dishes and sauces are particularly strengths, as are the excellent wine list and gallant service. Sweet treats such as gelato on fresh cheese with sage honey and chocolate sauce are where the chef really gets creative.

Filipini 1B. ℭ 052/463-200. www.istra.com/filipini. Entrees 40kn–150kn. MC, V. Daily noon–midnight.

Restoran Marconi ★★ ISTRIAN   The delightful, shaded garden area of this bistro next to the cathedral is a great place to enjoy a light afternoon snack or early supper. Its palazzo setting was built by Italian nobles 500 years ago. Pizzas are flavorful, oozing with rich mozzarella; the seafood salad is loaded with squid, shrimp and mussels; and the seafood risotto is just as packed with the same ingredients. Save room for rich homemade ice cream for dessert.

Eufrazijeva 24. ℭ 052/431-922. Entrees 48kn–125kn. Pizzas 30kn–50kn. MC, V. Daily 7am–11pm May–Oct.

Stari Saloon/Bistro/Pizzeria ★★ ⟨Value⟩ PIZZA   It's plopped in a courtyard surrounded by brick buildings, but that doesn't stop people from jamming the place every night. Stari Saloon is primarily a pizza joint, and instead of the usual small, medium, or large designations on the menu, pizza sizes here are listed in centimeters. XXL pizzas a whopping 75 centimeters (29 in.) in diameter are served on a wooden disk the size of a small tabletop and start at 55kn. Crusts are ultrathin and crispy. One of the unusual pizza combos is the Monte Carlo with tomatoes, cheese, salmon, crab, caviar, and scampi.

Ribarski Trg. ℭ 052/453-228. Entrees 35kn–110kn. AE, DC, MC, V. Daily 10am–11pm.

Sveti Nikola ★★★ MODERN ISTRIAN   Nikola is a chic dining spot on the "high style" segment of Poreč's waterfront where large private yachts like to congregate. Food is well prepared and beautifully presented, but pricey. Try the tagliatelle Altijež, ribbons of al dente pasta with scallops, langoustines, and a white wine reduction.

Obala Maršala Tita 23. ℭ 052/423-018. Entrees 80kn–160kn, more for seafood sold by the kilo. MC, V. Daily 11am–1am.

Ulixes ★ ISTRIAN   Located in courtyard set off the main drag, the atmosphere at Ulixes, popular late night, is softened by indirect lighting on the brick walls of surrounding buildings, olive trees, soft background music, and cats that make the rounds looking for handouts. When you order, stick with fish dishes, which are competently prepared, or try a pasta like fuži with pršut or fuži with game. *Tip:* Grilled meat can be overcooked, and portions are on the small side, even for Croatia.

Decumanus 2. ℭ 052/451-132. www.restaurantulixes.com. Entrees 40kn–110kn. No credit cards. Daily noon–midnight. Closed Dec–Feb.

POREČ AFTER DARK
Clubs
Byblos ★★   Byblos is Poreč's only true nightclub with a local vibe and it draws both tourists and residents alike. The interior is a minimalist design in black and white and there is a beach bar, too. Both serve basic and trendy libations and both are nice venues to listen to cutting edge entertainment. Open 5pm to midnight Monday to Saturday. Closed Sundays, and closed October through May. Zelena Laguna. ℭ 091/113 221.

Epoca ★★   Sandwiched between the Hotel Palazzo and Sveti Nickola on the busy waterfront, Epoca has a prime location for excellent cocktails, hot music, and late-night mingling. Open daily 8am to 2am. Obala Maršala Tita 22. No phone.

Lapidarij ★★★   Cosseted in the garden of the city museum, this courtyard bar is worth seeking out. Besides offering a romantic setting for cocktails, Lapidarij hosts concerts, the most notable of which are jazz concerts on Wednesday nights. Open daily noon to midnight. Sveta Maura 10. ✆ 052/431-595.

---

7 NOVIGRAD (CITTANOVA)

You might have a hard time keeping your eyes on the road if you drive the short stretch between Poreč and Novigrad in the early morning when the sun is hitting the water: During this time of day the landscape is bathed in a sheen of gold that gives it a mesmerizing, unearthly beauty. The scenic drive takes you just 18km (11 miles) north of Poreč. Once in Novigrad, you will immediately sense that this town is more relaxed than most coastal tourism destinations.

ESSENTIALS

VISITOR INFORMATION   The **Tourist Office** in Novigrad can provide maps, brochures, and information on area accommodations and events. It is located at Porporella 1 (✆ **052/757-075;** www.istra.com/novigrad) and is open from 9am to 9pm daily (8am–8pm daily spring and summer; 8am–3pm Mon–Sat winter).

GETTING THERE   See "Getting There" in "Orientation," earlier in this chapter.

GETTING AROUND   Novigrad is fairly compact and easy to negotiate on foot. It doesn't take more than an hour to see the entire town unless you can't resist trying out one of the many access points to the sea. Most of the action and attractions are at the waterfront, including Sts. Pelagia and Massima Church.

WHAT TO SEE & DO

Many of Novigrad's Old Town buildings have been replaced or redone, so there is little original architecture there, but the town has a comfortable feel and is a good place to wander around for a few hours, especially the rock walk around the city that takes the place of a beach. The town's breakwater creates a calm swimming area, but access areas for stronger swimmers also are built into the open-seaside.

Be sure to stop in at the **Sts. Pelagia and Massima Church** ★. Built in 1882, it has a beautiful ceiling and unusual elevated gallery behind the ornate marble tabernacle. There is also an intricately carved wooden pulpit inside the church and a soaring bell tower outside. Photographers will want to use the **citi loggia** at the end of Belvedere Street as a frame for images of the sea.

WHERE TO STAY

Novigrad is an unabashed seaside resort, and it is a relatively new town by Istrian standards—its medieval architecture was destroyed by the Turks in the 17th century and rebuilt in the prevailing Venetian style. However, there is something remarkable about accommodations options there. Novigrad does have its share of blah package hotels, but it also has a couple of places that are charmingly boutique and one that is downright decadent, a nice change from the monotonous in-your-face tourist-trap look of Umag to the north and the mind-boggling vacation options in Poreč to the south.

Cittar ★★   At first glance, the Cittar looks as if it's a castle protected by a high wall, but look again. The hotel was built in 1991 behind one of the few sections of the medieval city wall that still stands, and the wall out front was constructed at that time as a grand entryway. Behind it is the lovely Cittar with a leafy terrace and enclosed sunroom off the reception area that give the hotel the air of a Tuscan palazzo. The friendly staff and resident cocker spaniel add to the illusion. Guest rooms are a good size and beautifully decorated in earth tones and wood. They come with comfortably large bathrooms that make the Cittar a fine home away from home.

Prolaz Venecija 1. ℂ **052/757-737.** Fax 052/757-229. www.cittar.hr. 14 units. Aug from 114€ double. Rest of year from 78€. Rates include breakfast. Half-board available. There is a 30% discount for children 7–10; 50% discount for children 2–6; infants 1 and under free. AE, MC, V. Limited free parking. **Amenities:** Restaurant. *In room:* A/C, TV, minibar.

Hotel St. Benedict ★★   Hotel St. Benedict is away from the fray in Dajla, a village on the northwest coast of the Istrian peninsula between Umag and Novigrad. Guest rooms provide peace and quiet, plenty of elbow room, and a comfortable place to kick back after taking in the "bright lights" of Novigrad and Umag.

Dajla bb, Novigrad. ℂ **052/735-513.** Fax 052/735-512. www.sv-benedikt.com/en/home. 27 units. Doubles with balcony and sea view in July–Aug from 119€. Other times, doubles from 83€. AE, DC, MC, V. **Amenities:** Restaurant; pool; beach. *In room:* A/C, TV.

Hotel San Rocco ★★★   A haven for lovers of quiet, relaxation, and fine cuisine, complete with its own swimming pool, this 12-room boutique hotel in Brtonigla caters to guests who want to be near the sea, but not amid the hustle and bustle of the resort towns of Novigrad (5 min. away) or Porec (15 min.). The air-conditioned rooms in this 100-year-old, renovated stone house have sumptuous beds under wood-beamed ceilings, and big bathrooms, some with tubs and turbo-massage showers. In addition, the hotel restaurant **San Rocco** ★★★ has a way with local ingredients. *Tip:* If you can't get to Istria and the San Rocco, you still can get a feel for the hotel and its setting at **Istrian Charms,** a Zagreb boutique that sells San Rocco olive oil and other Istrian products. The store also offers a virtual tour of the hotel and restaurant on a flatscreen TV and you can book a room at the hotel on the spot.

Srednja Ulica 2, Brtonigla, 52474. ℂ **052/725-000.** Fax 052/725-026. www.san-rocco.hr. 12 units. Doubles Apr 1–Oct 1 from 149€. Rest of year, doubles from 133€. Rates include breakfast. 35% discount for singles occupying a double room. **Amenities:** Restaurant; bar; pool; sauna; wine cellar; parking; Wi-Fi in bar area; elevator; access for those w/limited mobility. *In room:* A/C, TV, hair dryer, minibar.

Nautica ★★★   Open since summer 2006, this is Novigrad's nod to luxury lodging—38 rooms and 4 suites dressed in mahogany and brass. Nautica is small enough to be exclusive and large enough to incorporate luxury amenities, all within a reddish-violet-hued building, a color that somehow works against the blue sea. The rooms have huge beds, tons of storage, and immense bathrooms that include tubs, bidets, and German-made toiletries. The hotel's **Restaurant Navigarre** (see below) and bar are sophisticated, spacious exercises in teak and brass with sprawling outdoor seating areas overlooking the marina. There is a free parking lot for guests' cars and 365 berths in the harbor for those who choose to arrive in their multi-million-dollar yachts.

Sv. Antona 15. ℂ **052/600-400.** Fax 052/600490. www.nauticahotels.com. 42 units. Doubles with a sea view from 238€ in summer. Other times, doubles from 143€. Suites from 330€ in summer. Other times, suites from 270€. Rates include buffet breakfast, use of spa and pool, and parking. AE, DC, MC, V. **Amenities:** Restaurant; cafe; bar; fitness center; indoor pool; room service; sauna; ATM; shops; yacht harbor; valet. *In room:* A/C, TV, hair dryer, minibar, Wi-Fi or broadband Internet access.

Torci 18 ★ Torci 18's 12 rooms are simple, clean, and convenient. This is a good option that falls between the moderately priced Cittar and the private accommodations in Novigrad. The Torci does not provide many luxuries, but you're not sharing a bathroom, either. Breakfast prepared in Torci 18's kitchen and served on the terrace is a big plus.

Torci 34. Outside Novigrad. (℃ **052/757-799.** Fax 052/757-174. www.torci18.hr. 12 units. Doubles from 60€ in July–Aug. Other times, doubles from 50€. AE, DC, MC, V. **Amenities:** Restaurant; bar; terrace. *In room:* TV.

WHERE TO DINE

Novigrad has several excellent restaurants, but most are more expensive than the pizza/pasta places in Poreč. The best bars overlook the sea.

Mandrać ★ ISTRIAN The street-level terrace with tables spilling onto the sidewalk is designed to look like it is located within ruined city walls. Inside, beamed ceilings and a blue-and-white color scheme create a pleasant marine ambience. Entrees are mostly variations on grilled fish and pasta dishes, and while preparations and presentation are very good, service can be haughty at times. If you can get past that, try some of Mandrać's specials like the mussels with cheese or the fish baked with potato, for a little twist on tried-and-true Istrian dishes.

Mandrać 6. (℃ **052/757-120.** Entrees 40kn–160kn. AE, DC, V. Daily 10am–midnight.

Restaurant Navigarre ★★★ INTERNATIONAL The signature restaurant of the Hotel Nautica opened in 2006 as a crisp, shipshape venue for serious food. Diners can choose either light meals or "slow" food both inside the brass and teak-fitted dining room and outside on the terrace under huge burgundy umbrellas. The menu, which is in 5 languages including Russian, features creative dishes based on local produce, including lamb, octopus, and veal prepared under the *peka* (with 3-hr. notice). For a lighter meal, try homemade tagliatelle with pršut and peas, or the more complex gnocchi with scallops and truffles. For dessert, the Florentine cream cake is to die for.

Sv. Antona 15, 52466 Novigrad. (℃ **052/600-400.** Fax 052/600-490. www.nauticahotels.com. Reservations recommended. Entrees 75kn–180kn. AE, DC, MC, V. Daily 7am–11pm.

Restoran Torci 18 ★★ (Finds) ISTRIAN It's hard to say if Torci 18 is a restaurant with pansion or a pansion with restaurant because the two are seamlessly blended into a single building with dark wood beams, gardens, and glass under the old walls overlooking the sea. Menu choices are fairly predictable but well prepared. (You know the fish is fresh as can be when you see women cleaning the morning's catch with clamshells on the restaurant's beach side.) Pastas require a two-portion minimum and lobster is sold by the kilo. Atmosphere is gratis. Don't leave without buying a bottle of Torci 18's olive oil made from home-grown olives.

Torci 18. (℃ **052/757-799.** Fax 052/757-174. www.torci18.hr. Entrees 50kn–85kn; more for fish sold by the kilo. AE, DC, MC, V. Daily noon–3pm and 6–10pm.

Vitriol ★★ COFFEE BAR/COCKTAILS Novigrad's bar scene is decidedly low-key, but Vitriol is the center of it all from its seaside perch. The ambience could be classified as Croatian Starbucks in the morning when all the terrace tables are filled with people sipping coffee and reading the newspaper or catching up with e-mail on laptops via Vitriol's free Wi-Fi. Vitriol is behind the breakwater, so the breeze is soft and in tune with the jazz that is always playing softly in the background. In the afternoon, the crowd shifts to the ice cream and cake set and by night the music is hot and the beverages a lot stronger.

Podravska 31. ✆ **052/758-270.** Food items less than 50kn. MC, V. Mon–Fri 7:30am–midnight; until 1am Sat–Sun.

Near Novigrad

Restoran San Rocco ★★★ (Finds) ISTRIAN   The chef at this restaurant in the San Rocco Hotel in Brtonigla, 5 minutes from Novigrad, specializes in three- to five-course tasting menus that rely on local ingredients creatively presented. Typical offerings include octopus salad with olive oil foam and pork breast with pistachios. Pairings with local wines from San Rocco's well-stocked cellar are suggested for each course, but boost the tariff considerably. A la carte options are available, but prices are available only on request.

In the San Rocco Hotel, Srednja Ulica 2, Brtonigla 52474. ✆ **052/725-000.** Fax 052/725-026. www.san-rocco.hr. Tasting menu 290kn–510kn. AE, DC, MC, V. Daily 1–10pm.

8 UMAG (UMAGO) & SAVUDRIJA (SALVORE)

Umag hits visitors in the face with its huge modern hotels, concrete beach, and banners everywhere advertising the city's annual international ATP Croatia Open tennis tournament, festivals, concerts, and even restaurants. The crowded waterfront shops look more like bus station concessions than resort boutiques, and the atmosphere shouts "vacation package deal." Savudrija, on the other hand, is a hard-to-find, lazy, rural village on the sea with nothing but vineyards and farmland at its back. Nonetheless, these two disparate towns have something in common with the opening of the ultraluxurious Kempinski Adriatic in August 2009: sprawling resorts with luxury spas that cater to the well-heeled traveler. The **Sol Umag** in Umag and the **Kempinski Adriatic** in Savudrija target different clientele, but both have spas with endless menus of services and each offers something unique: The Sol Umag hotel is a renovated socialist style hotel with one of the best spas in Croatia, and the splashy Kempinski Adriatic is as exclusive as it gets with the first and only 18-hole golf course in Istria.

ESSENTIALS

VISITOR INFORMATION   Umag's **tourist information office** is at JB Tita 3/2 (✆ **052/741-363;** fax 052/741-649; www.istra.com/umag). They can give you brochures and maps as well as information on sports opportunities and excursions. Nearly two dozen tourist agencies broker thousands of privately owned rooms and apartments in Umag. Umag Renters' Association publishes an exhaustive catalog detailing them. Sol Melia, which manages many of Umag's big hotels and camping services, pumped a significant amount of money into its campgrounds in 2005. Brochures listing facilities and prices for both these types of accommodations are available at the tourist information office in town.

GETTING THERE   See "Getting There" in "Orientation," earlier in this chapter.

GETTING AROUND   Most of Umag's tourist activity is at the waterfront or in Old Town. If you are staying at one of the big hotels on the outskirts or if you want to access

Moments   Lost in Place

We get lost a lot when exploring new territory, but sometimes it pays off. Instead of taking the faster **Istrian Upsilon** (see above) to get to Rovinj from Labin, Sanja and I decided to take the scenic route. On the way, we stumbled across **Svetvincenat** ★★, a surprising little town deep in south central Istria. Svetvincenat has a tongue twister name and a mother lode of sites that surprised us. There's a 12th-century church, a bell tower, a town square with an ancient well *(bunara)*, several vintage houses, and a castle with fortification walls, towers, and a moat. The castle is purported to be the best-preserved keep in Istria.

During a coffee stop at one of the cafes off the square, a waitress told us the castle once belonged to a Venetian family named Grimani and that the tourist office gives tours of the place during working hours (9am–2pm Mon–Fri). We couldn't make it back the next day, but this is a place we will revisit—if we can find it again.

---

the **Stella Maris Sports Complex,** you probably will have to take one of the city buses or drive. Airport transfers to the Kempinski Adriatic can be via air, land, or sea. The Adriatic has its own heliport and it has built access roads through vineyards to the hotel from the main road. While there is no marina as yet, it is possible for boats to dock nearby.

WHAT TO SEE & DO

Umag's beaches are more like concrete slabs in the water and not very appealing, but most of the big hotels have a full slate of activities and sports available as well as programs for children. If you are staying at one of these big hotels—or somewhere else—a few hours at Sol Umag's Istrian-style spa can be a rejuvenating interlude. Savudrija in far northwest Istria is the newest darling among the region's many vacation towns. Perhaps that's because of its proximity to the Slovene border and Italy (2 hr. by catamaran from Venice) or perhaps it's because it is one of the few corners of Croatia as yet undiscovered by mass tourism. That's about to end with the opening of Kempinski's new golf resort.

Kempinski Golf Adriatic ★★★   Istria's first 18-hole golf course is a 7km (4⅓-mile) wonder designed by Austrian landscape architect Diethard Fahrenleitner that sprawls from the sea, through vineyards and into woods as far as the eye can see from the two-story, glass enclosed clubhouse. The course offers a restaurant and four bars. Golf club membership is available or hotel guests can sign up for a single round or more. *Tip:* Northwest Istria can be hot and arid in summer, but Golf Adriatic is using stored rainwater exclusively to keep the course green.

Alberi 300A. ⓒ **052/707-100.** Fax 052/707-101. www.kempinski-adriatic.com. Membership/initiation 10,000€ for year 1 and 2,000€ for year 2 and thereafter. Greens fees for guests are 60€ per round Mon–Thurs and 90€ per round Sat–Sun. Cart rentals are 25€ per day and golfers age 6–17 get a 30% discount on greens fees. Prices include VAT.

Sol Umag Wellness and Beauty ★★★   It's tough to recommend what's essentially a fitness center and salon as a place to seek out on a vacation in a country with almost unlimited natural wonders, but this one is worth a few hours of your time. Designed to look like an Istrian village with arches, mosaics, flowers, waterfalls, and sculptures, the spa takes up three floors of the Sol Umag hotel and doesn't offer mere exercise opportunities and beauty services: It offers *imaginative* exercise opportunities and beauty services. Don't miss the amazing "Blue Cave" relaxation pool, the "Cleopatra" mud room, or the Istrian bio sauna. One- to 7-day beauty packages are available.

Jadranska bb. ℂ **052/714-000.** Fax 052/714-999. www.istra.com/istraturist. Treatments 770kn–4,400kn. AE, MC, V. Daily 8am–9pm.

WHERE TO STAY

Accommodations in Umag range from several large chain hotels to a huge inventory of private accommodations and a string of camping facilities catering to a wide range of tastes. Savudrija has an apartment village on the sea, private accommodations, and now the plush Kempinski Hotel Adriatic.

Hotel Villa Rosetta ★★   Luxury appointments, a spa with exotic baths and treatments, a private beach, and an excellent Mediterranean restaurant draw people to this recent addition (2007) to northwest Istria's accommodations list. Rosetta is on the coast between Savudrija and Umag and while it doesn't have the glamour and posh aura of the nearby over-the-top Kempinski, it is utterly charming.

Crvena Uvala 31, Zambratija. ℂ 052/725-710. www.villarosetta.hr. 24 units. Doubles from 170€ mid-July to late Aug; from 90€ other times. Rates include breakfast and VAT. **Amenities:** Restaurant; bar; spa. *In room:* A/C, TV, hair dryer, Internet, minibar.

Kempinski Hotel Adriatic ★★★   The Adriatic was just days away from its August 1, 2009, opening when we visited, but enough was in place to convince us that the newest addition to Istria's lodging portfolio is something special. The Adriatic is a temple to luxury both inside and out. Landscaping includes mature olive trees, a lavender garden, and an herb garden whose bounty is destined for use in the Adriatic's spa and restaurants. Inside, marble and glass dominate, making every nook and cranny a room with a view. The Carolea Spa (named for a variety of olive) is downright hedonistic with Roman baths, four kinds of saunas and steam baths, and an ice cabin that cools guests down with tiny frozen cubes. Guest rooms are generously sized and all have balconies and glamour bathrooms with separate tubs and showers and TVs integrated into the nonfog mirror. *Tip:* The biggest TV ever produced by Bang & Olufsen is in the Henry Morgan presidential suite. It is a 70×110cm (28×44 in.) flatscreen and cost 100,000€.

Alberi 300A. ℂ 052/707-080. Fax 052/707-081. www.kempinski-adriatic.com. 186 units. Deluxe doubles from 400€; junior sea view suites from 800€; presidential suites from 10,000€. **Amenities:** 2 restaurants; 4 bars; 18-hole golf course; 3 pools; spa; 4 tennis courts; helipad. *In room:* A/C, TV, hair dryer, minibar, Wi-Fi.

Sol Umag ★★   Everything at this big hotel north of the city is in place to fulfill almost any vacation need. Sol Umag underwent a partial renovation in 2004 and its facilities sparkle. Guest rooms are comfortably large and most have balconies that overlook the lovely outdoor pool or the sea. Premier features include a **spa** ★★★ (reviewed above) and access to world-class tennis facilities.

Jadranska bb. ℂ 052/714-000. Fax 052/714-999. hotel.umag@istraturist.hr. 217 units. Aug from 184€ double with balcony, sea view, and half-board. Rest of year from 112€ double with balcony, sea view, and half-board. AE, DC, MC, V. Limited free parking. **Amenities:** Restaurant; poolside snack bar; bar; 3 pools; organized activity programs; wine shop. *In room:* A/C, TV, minibar.

WHERE TO DINE

As you might expect, Umag is full of pizzerias, spaghetterias, and other family friendly dining spots. Most people who stay in the resort hotels take half-board and their meals there, but there are a few upscale options for those who want to go a la carte. So far Savudrija has the Adriatic's **Dijana,** the hotel's main restaurant, and **Slice,** the golf club's restaurant. The hotel plans to add more dining options, including a sushi bar. Neither Kempinski option was open when we visited.

Allegro ★★ CONTINENTAL   Allegro is a fancy hotel restaurant in a fancy hotel (Kristal) where you can choose the attractive dining room or the terrace, which is especially nice in moonlight. If you are tired of traditional Istrian cuisine, choose grilled venison, goat on a spit, or duck in basil sauce, though fish preparations can surprise you, too. Don't miss the huge seafood display on ice on the seaside terrace.

JB Tita 9, Umag. © **052/700-000.** Fax 052/700-499. www.hotel-kristal.com. Reservations recommended. Entrees 70kn–180kn. AE, DC, MC, V. Daily 9am–midnight.

---

9 INLAND ISTRIA

It isn't easy being green in a country where blue is the dominant color, but the Istrian interior's countless hues of vegetation hint at the unspoiled nature and unique experiences that await those who venture into this often overlooked part of Croatia. It hits you as you exit the deep blackness of **Učka Tunnel** in the east or as you drive away from the golden brightness of the **Istrian Coast** in the west: This is territory that feeds the senses—all of them. In **Green Istria** you can take time to breathe the perfumed air, listen to the birds chatter, touch the rough stone of a medieval castle, or savor the taste of local wines.

Inland Istria is a land of discovery where you can climb a hill to listen to cool jazz at **Grožnjan** ★★★, travel the wine road through **Momjan** ★★, watch films under a night sky in **Motovun** ★★★, or soak in hot-spring waters at **Istarske Toplice** ★. Inland Istria is where you can marvel at still-vibrant 15th-century frescoes in a woodland church near tiny **Beram** ★★★, or tramp through the woods outside **Buzet** while following a couple of dogs hunting truffles.

Inland Istria is where you can feast on an elaborate dinner in an award-winning restaurant in **Livade** and wake up the next morning to a breakfast of home-smoked ham, homegrown fruit, and homemade cheese in the kitchen of the rural farmhouse where you spent the night. During the day, you can nose around Glagolitic artifacts in tiny **Hum** ★★ or explore the historic walled city of **Roč** ★★. Inland Istria is the perfect place to immerse you in the land and its people who reside there.

ESSENTIALS

VISITOR INFORMATION   Every town in Green Istria has its own tourist information center, though some offices in smaller towns have limited hours and are difficult to find. To help visitors get the most out of their trip, the **Istria County Tourist Association** has produced some exceptional materials. These include attractive publications on farmhouse stays, cultural itineraries, wine roads, olive-oil roads, and truffle-hunting opportunities. Information on those and many other topics is available through the association, whose main offices are in Poreč at Pionirska 1 (© **052/452-797;** fax 052/452-796; tzzi-po@ pu.hinet.hr), and in Pula at Forum 3 (© **052/215-799;** fax 052/215-722). The association also maintains an excellent website with English-language links to almost every town: **www.istra.com.**

GETTING THERE   No matter how you get to Istria—by plane to Pula, by boat to one of the coastal cities, by bus to Pazin, or by any other method, you will need a car to thoroughly explore the inland area unless you are on a guided excursion.

GETTING AROUND   Most towns in inland Istria are small; one of them, Hum, is known as the smallest town in the world. The main attractions in all of Istria's inland towns can be readily accessed on foot, but many of these are extremely hilly and must be approached by walking over irregular cobblestone streets. To get to Motovun, for example, you have to leave your car at the bottom of a steep street and walk more than a quarter of a mile uphill. In addition, some of the smaller towns are remote, so driving your own car is the only practical way to cover the territory between them.

10 PAZIN (PISINO)

Quiet Pazin in the center of Istria is the antithesis of the touristy coast: Pazin doesn't have glitzy resorts or hordes of tourists, but it does have historic sites worth visiting. Pazin is not a huge transportation hub, but rail and bus service connect it to other parts of the country. While Pazin doesn't have Roman ruins like Pula or a gorgeous coastline like Rovinj, it does have a medieval castle with an interesting history and a deep chasm that inspired author Jules Verne while he was writing *Mathias Sandorf*. In reality, Pazin's personality is similar to that of any small town in America: It's in the middle of nowhere with a strong agricultural base, a little industry, and a neutral location that was a factor in its choice as a regional seat of government. Pazin's central position on the peninsula also makes it an excellent base from which to explore the rest of inland Istria, including the amazing frescoes at St. Mary of the Rock in nearby Beram.

ESSENTIALS

VISITOR INFORMATION   Pazin's **tourist office** is staffed with young, friendly people who speak English and are eager to help. Not only can they tell you about the town's historical treasures and give you tips on how to find them, but they also can direct you to little-known points of interest in the surrounding area. The town's tourist office is at Franine I Jurine 14, P.O. Box 3, 52000 Pazin (© **052/622-460**). Pazin's website (www. tzpazin.hr) is exceptional.

GETTING THERE   Trains and buses serve Pazin from Zagreb, Rijeka, and cities in Istria. See "Getting There" in "Orientation," earlier in this chapter for information.

GETTING AROUND   Pazin is a small town, so its main attractions are best reached on foot.

WHAT TO SEE & DO

It takes half a day to see Pazin. Try to set aside a couple of hours to view the eye-popping frescoes in the tiny Church of St. Mary of the Rock outside the nearby village of Beram, 5.6km (3½ miles) to the west.

Frescoes at the Church of St. Mary of the Rock ★★★   Tiny Beram is a little more than 5.6km (3½ miles) west of Pazin. It's a one-street town with a nice church, but this isn't the church you're looking for. When you get to Beram, ask anyone in town to help you get in touch with the woman who has the key to St. Mary's where the famous frescoes reside. (Two women alternate key possession weekly and don't give out their phone numbers.) The townspeople will call her for you and let you know that you will have to drive her to the church and back to town, which is 1.2km (¾ mile) northwest of the town limits. St. Mary's, a tiny, Gothic-style building in the forest, contains 15th-century frescoes stunning in their brightness and detail. There you will find the walls covered with scenes from the New Testament created by Croatian artist Vincent de Kastav. The main attraction is the almost cartoonish "Dance of the Dead" with skeletons carrying scythes and blowing horns as they lead townspeople to the netherworld. The original, though much older, is far more vibrant than the copy in the Church of St. Germaine on Veliki Brijuni. Explanations are printed in various languages, including English, though your guide probably will speak Croatian only.

Tip: Your guide will tell you that three flash photos total are allowed per visit, so if you are with a large group, this could be a problem. There is no entry charge, but it is customary to offer the woman a gratuity for her time.

In the center of town, Beram.

Istrian Ethnographic Museum ★★★   The display of Istrian cultural artifacts in Pazin's Kaštel museum is one of the best in Croatia. The collection includes traditional Istrian costumes, farm and household items, a model of an old Istrian kitchen with its distinctive traditional hearth, looms, winemaking implements, and much more. Don't miss the display of 14th- through 20th-century bells on the ground floor. The bells were taken from village churches in all parts of Istria during World War II to save them from the fascists, who melted them down to make bullets. The oldest dates from the 15th century. The bells are displayed with photos or drawings that show how they looked in their churches. The bells in this museum are the only ones that survived the war. The displays are well annotated in several languages. *Tip:* Entrance is through Pazin Kaštel.

In Pazin Kaštel. Istarskog Razvoda 1. **052/625-040.** www.tzpazin.hr. Admission 15kn adults, 8kn children. Summer Tues–Sun 10am–6pm. Winter Tues–Thurs 10am–3pm; Fri noon–5pm; Sat–Sun 11am–5pm. Closed Mon.

Pazin Chasm ★★★ (Kids   The 91m-deep (300-ft.) gorge and sheer rock wall next to the Kaštel have inspired science fiction author Jules Verne *(Mathias Sandorf)* and many others to incorporate it into their writing. It also apparently was the site of wartime horrors during World War II and the 1991 civil war. According to one historian, numerous skeletons still wearing military garb (including those of two women) were found at the bottom of the chasm after the last war.

Next to the Pazin Kaštel.

Pazin Kaštel ★   The 9th-century castle is one of the best preserved in Istria thanks to numerous renovations, which altered its appearance. However, the view of the **Pazin Chasm ★★★** from the castle grounds and the **Ethnographic Museum ★★★** inside are the biggest reasons to visit here.

Visitor information same as for the Istrian Ethnographic Museum, above.

St. Nicholas Church ★   This church next to the tourist office originally was built in the 13th century and rebuilt twice—in the 15th century and again in the 18th. The church is notable because of the 14th-century frescoes above the ornate altar depicting the Way of the Cross and scenes from the Old Testament. There are more frescoes under the plaster walls, but they probably won't be restored because it is likely that the process would destroy them. Until the 17th century, many of the church's frescoes were ruined by people who washed them repeatedly in the mistaken belief that plague came out of the walls. The church's late priests are buried under the floor.

Eufrazijeva Ulica 22, across from the tourist office. Admission during Mass and for organized tours.

WHERE TO STAY & DINE

There is only one hotel in Pazin and it is utilitarian at best. However, if you have your own transportation, private accommodations are the best option because rooms are abundant, especially in rural farmhouses. Check with the tourist office (address above) for suggestions.

Boškarin ★ ISTRIAN   The walls of this plain-looking dining room named after the protected Istrian ox display a few farm implements. Tables have bench seats, and the menu covers all the local food groups like fuži, smoked ham, and polenta.

Dubravica 1. ℭ **052/621-327.** Entrees 30kn–90kn. No credit cards. Mon–Sat 10am–11pm; closed Sun.

Laura ★   Private accommodations with two double rooms and four apartments afford a good view of the castle from this position on a rise with a beautiful garden in the town center. All units have balconies and access to fridges and stoves so you can buy and prepare local products from the Puris turkey outlet store in town.

Antuna Kalca 10A. ℭ **052/621-312.** 6 units. For stays of 3 days or fewer from 28€ double; apts 17€ per person. For stays of more than 3 days from 22€ double; 14€ apt. AE, DC, MC, V. Rates do not include breakfast. Limited free parking. *In room:* TV (apts only), access to kitchen facilities.

Lovac   This generic hotel works for an overnight stay or if there are no other options. It's clean but it lacks personality. The a la carte **Restoran Lovac** ★ has a nice terrace and serves interesting fare such as game dishes and truffle pizza.

Šime Kurelića 4. ℭ **052/624-324.** Fax 052/624-384. 27 units. From 50€ double. AE, DC, MC, V. Limited free parking. **Amenities:** Restaurant.

Restoran Lovac ★ ISTRIAN   This restaurant in Pazin's only hotel gets points for variety on its menu. All dishes are prepared with local ingredients, including venison, and others incorporate truffles in unexpected dishes like pizza.

Šime Kurelića 4. ℭ **052/624-324.** Fax 052/624-384. Entrees 40kn–120kn. AE, DC, MC, V. Daily 7am–11pm.

11 GROŽNJAN, BUJE & MOMJAN

The roads that link **Grožnjan** (Grisignana), **Buje** (Buie), and **Momjan** (Momiano) are narrow, steep, and winding, but they snake through some of the most scenic real estate in Istria. Along the way you'll discover a ruined castle (Momjan), a World War II monument dedicated by Tito (Buje), and one of the prettiest hill towns anywhere in Croatia (Grožnjan).

Buje is a short hop from Novigrad and the town itself is fairly uninteresting, except for an 18th-century church (Sv. Servula Mučenika) and a monument and plaque commemorating Tito's 1954 visit to the town. At that time, Tito became an honorary citizen of Buje and dedicated the World War II monument to the freedom fighters from the area. The road out of Buje northeast toward **Momjan** is a jumping-off point for both the wine and olive oil roads of the region as it meanders through vineyards and olive groves past wineries, **Taverna Marino** ★★★, and even the ruins of **Momjan castle** ★. The

On the (Wine & Olive Oil) Road

The best way to explore Istria's wine and olive oil roads is to pick up a map produced by the Istrian Tourist Board (www.istra.hr) that lists about six dozen winemakers and two dozen olive oil producers in the region. Most of Istria's wineries are in the country's north central region, and you will need a car to get from one venue to the next. Roads do have directional signs marking the wine and oil routes, and producers have marked the paths to their doors in some cases. Don't miss the cellars of **Kozlović ★★★**, **Kabola ★★★**, and **Matijašić ★★**, all full-fledged wineries that have expanded their production into microclimate vintages. Kozlović is not set up for unannounced tasters, so call ahead, but Kabola welcomes drop-ins. Matijašić requires reservations for its accommodations. Below, read about how to reach our favorites.

    Kozlović Winery at Vale 78 Momjan (*②* 052/779-177; www.kozlovic.hr) produces 100,000 bottles a year and is open from 8am to noon and 1 to 5pm Monday through Saturday. Closed Sunday.

    Kabola Winery (*②* 052/779-033) is in Kremenje between Buje and Momjan and includes a small winemaking museum and a knock-out restaurant, **Taverna Marino ★★★** (*②* 052/779-047; fax 052/779-047; www.kabola.hr). Open for tasting 10am to 5pm Tuesday through Saturday.

    Matijašić Winery is a working vineyard near Motovun where you can spend the night and perhaps pick a few grapes, too (Pekasi, 52424 Motovun, Istria; *②* 052/682-126).

    Tip: You can stop in at any of the olive oil producers on the map to purchase products, but if you want to see a pressing in action or pick a few olives, reservations are required. Consult Istria's Olive Oil Road Map for details and contact information.

Momjan area is a good place to try the region's outstanding wines, especially those from the Kozlović winery, which has a beautiful tasting room built into the original 100-year-old winery building.

    The tiny hilltop village of **Grožnjan** south of Momjan was almost deserted 45 years ago after most of its Italian population left for economic opportunity. In 1965, the town saw an influx of artists, who took over the town and saved it from extinction by renovating the Old Town core. Since then, Grožnjan has blossomed into a full-fledged artist's colony replete with galleries, shops, restaurants, and a summer jazz festival in July and August that attracts big-name talent and plenty of fans. If you can't get there for a performance, you can stop at one of the village's pleasant restaurants for a bite and listen to the mellow sounds emanating from all corners of the village during daytime practice sessions. It is also fun to poke around the maze of small cobbled streets, a loggia, gates, walls, and a church with good frescoes. In keeping with Grožnjan's title as a "town of artists," numerous shops and ateliers in town sell original paintings, pottery, and jewelry made by local craftspeople.

VISITOR INFORMATION   Facts about this cluster of towns are available at the Istria County Tourist Offices in Pula and Poreč (above) and in each town's local bureau. Buje's visitor center is located at Istarska 2 (© 052/773-353; www.tzg-buje.hr). The staff there can provide you with maps and directions for the area's hiking trails. Grožnjan's tourist office is at Gorjan 3 (© 052/776-131; www.groznjan-grisignana.hr/tz). Any of the offices can provide you with a map of the wine and olive roads complete with the addresses of establishments open to the public for tastings.

GETTING THERE   See "Getting There" in "Orientation," earlier in this chapter.

GETTING AROUND   The important sites in all of these towns can be easily explored on foot, but if you intend to visit wineries or sites in between, a car is a must.

WHAT TO SEE & DO

Besides the old buildings and beautiful views, each of the towns in this group has at least one marquee event during the year and all are worth a few hours of wandering any time. Grožnjan is probably the most accessible because of the large number of venues and restaurants concentrated in a central location.

Grožnjan Musical Summer and Jazz Festival ★★★   If you walk through the streets of Grožnjan anytime during the summer, you will be treated to the sounds of music—all kinds of music. On a random July day in 2009, our stroll through town was accompanied by the sweet sounds of a violin concerto wafting from the practice rooms above our heads. Sometimes the sound is jammin' jazz, and other times it's the voice of a choir—and that's just the free stuff. Grožnjan offers scheduled performances of all kinds almost every evening during July and August. Check www.hgm.hr for full schedules and information.

Momjan Wine Festival ★★   Momjan is surrounded by wine country and the winemakers there are serious about their craft. Every November 9 to 11, the town celebrates the new vintage in honor of St. Martin, patron saint of winemakers, and you can get a preview of the product just by walking around town. Like all Croatian celebrations, tons of food and nonstop music complete the picture. Go to www.momjan.com for more information.

WHERE TO STAY & DINE

Café Bar Arta ★ LIGHT FARE   Arta is a sandwich and drink shop with a nice view of the valley from its balcony.

Trg Cornera 3, Grožnjan. © **052/776-405.** No credit cards. Festival weekends 8am–midnight; 8am–2am other days. Closed Mon.

Konoba Morgan ★★★ ISTRIAN   Morgan is off the beaten track, but it's always busy thanks to locals and foreigners who consider it a destination restaurant. This is a true family enterprise: Chef Marko Morgan uses top-quality local ingredients to create deceptively simple dishes based on Istrian recipes. Sometimes the food incorporates game bagged by his dad, and his mom and sister work in the kitchen and the front of the house. Try any of the game dishes that include wild boar, venison, rabbit, and pheasant, and pair them with a fine Istrian wine. *Tip:* If you make arrangements ahead of time, you can hunt your own entree with Morgan, Sr.

Bracanija 1 btw. Buje and Brtonigla. © **052/774-520.** Entrees 20kn–70kn. AE, DC, MC, V. Daily noon–3pm and 6–10pm mid-Oct to mid-Sept.

Konoba Taverna Marino ★★★ (Finds) ISTRIAN Marino's owner, Marino
Markezić, also directs Kabola, his family's winery. The restaurant is in rural Istria, on the
road between Buje and Momjan. Marino's peach-painted stucco terrace is a perfect setting for the kitchen's heavenly seasonal dishes: In summer it is heavy with hanging red
geraniums and rattan furniture while the dining room is a study in wood, glass, and
Istrian artifacts. If you have time to linger, order Marino's tasting menu, which matches
Kabola vintages to the food. If not, the *sir sa tartufi* (fried cheese with truffles) is a quick
gourmet treat, as is the tender gnocchi with mushrooms. Keep in mind, there are a few
rooms for rent at Marino, which is handy if you sample all of Kabola's wines.

Kremenje 9, btw. Momjan and Buje. ℂ 052/779-047. www.konoba-marino-kremenje.hr. Entrees 14kn–
48kn. AE, DC, MC, V. Feb–Dec Wed–Mon noon–10pm. Closed Tues and Jan.

Restoran Bastia ★★ ISTRIAN Bastia is the fanciest restaurant in Grožnjan, and it
also has the biggest menu in town, helpfully translated into four languages. The nice
range of fish and meat dishes can be enjoyed outside or in the cozy dining room, which
is done in cheery shades of blue and white and which has a wood-burning fireplace.

Svibnia 1, Grožnjan. ℂ 052/776-370. Entrees 30kn–125kn. MC, V. Daily from 8am "until people leave."

Zigante Enoteka ★ (Overrated) WINE BAR One of many Zigante franchises, this
small room is a deli with tables that sells cheeses and other accompaniments to go with
Zigante's wines, which are sold by the glass or bottle. You can take home truffle cheese,
pršut, or truffle-infused olive oil; or you can order a variety plate to go with an overpriced
glass of *vino* from the wine bar.

Gorjan 7, Grožnjan. ℂ 052/721-998. Fax 052/721-999. www.zigantetartufi.com. Wines from 35kn per
glass. No credit cards. Mon–Fri 10am–2pm and 5–11pm; 10am–11pm without a break on weekends.
Store daily 9am–10pm.

12 MOTOVUN, LIVADE & OPRTALJ

Motovun (Montona) is one of Istria's better-known interior towns, perhaps because it
hosts such events as the Motovun Film Festival, hot-air balloon competitions, and a
festival celebrating truffles and wine. It doesn't hurt that this hilltop town is just over
14km (9 miles) north of Pazin or that it is home to the delightful **Kaštel Hotel** ★★.

The village of **Livade** ★ (Levade) is a short distance north of Motovun, and it is fast
becoming a center for gastronomic delights, including the locally venerated truffle. In the
countryside around Livade, you'll see huge tracts of vineyards and olive trees as well as
workers toiling in the fields no matter what the season. There are new vineyards as well
as old, along with lots of hand-painted signs on side roads advertising homemade wine,
olive oil, and grappa for sale.

If you continue on the same road a little farther, you'll reach **Oprtalj** (Portole), a
charming town on a hill high above the Mirna river valley. It is home to the 15th-century
St. Mary's Church and the 16th-century **Church of St. Rock,** both of which have a few
lovely but minor frescoes. However, you'll probably have to be content with looking at
these through the church windows, as they are rarely open.

Despite their remoteness and lack of efficient public transportation, all these tiny
towns are quickly becoming centers of activity for lovers of film, music, fine dining, and
other activities that feed the senses.

VISITOR INFORMATION   Information on all three towns and their festivals is available at the Istria County Tourist Offices in Pula and Poreč (above) and in each town's local bureau. Motovun's tourist office is at Andrea Antico bb (📞 **052/681-642**); and Oprtalj's is at M. Laginje 21 (📞 **052/544-077; tz@oprtalj.hr**).

GETTING THERE   See "Getting There" in "Orientation," earlier in this chapter.

GETTING AROUND   The important sites in each of these towns can be easily explored on foot.

WHAT TO SEE & DO

Besides the Motovun Film Festival in July and ballooning events in October, these towns are ideal places to wander about in search of medieval treasures. They also have excellent restaurants, fine wines and, of course, truffles in abundance.

International Motovun Film Festival ★★   Less than a decade old, the Motovun Film Festival has established itself as a first-class showcase for European art-house films and other cinematic works. Like Aspen's Comedy Festival and Chicago's Film Festival and unlike Cannes, the Motovun event doesn't put barriers between the stars and the public. Instead, everyone comes together for 5 days of nonstop partying.

International Motovun Film Festival. 📞 **052/352-991.** www.motovunfilmfestival.com. Early Aug, but dates are variable.

Truffle Hunting Excursions ★★★   You can arrange truffle-hunting excursions through Restaurant Zigante in Livade or through any of its franchise outlets across Croatia from September to December, though October is the height of truffle season. In addition, Activatravel in Pula arranges truffle excursions in season that include a 1½-hour hunt in the woods with dogs, followed by dinner in Livade.

Activatravel Istra. Scalierova 1, 52100 Pula. 📞 **052/215-497.** Fax 052/211-889. info@activa-istra.com. Minimum 2, maximum 4 people per tour at 60€ per person. AE, DC, MC, V. Tours leave the Livade truffle center at 5pm daily in season only.

Zigante Tartufi ★   Livade is a town with one industry, and that is Zigante. There's nothing much here except a Zigante store selling truffle products and wine, and Restaurant Zigante, though several other restaurants are popping up along the town's main street. Besides selling truffle items and wines with the Zigante label, the store offers recipes for using truffles in seven languages, fresh cheese with truffles, and fresh truffles (at roughly $1,100 per pound). Ask about the truffle that put Zigante in the *Guinness Book of World Records,* and the clerk will show you a plastic model of the giant underground fungus. It looks like a small cantaloupe (a normal truffle is the size of an egg).

Livade 7, Livade. 📞 **052/664-030.** Fax 052/644-031. AE, DC, MC, V. Daily 9am–6pm.

WHERE TO STAY & DINE

Besides the Kaštel Hotel in Motovun, the only accommodations in these villages are in private establishments, making this an ideal opportunity to try a farmhouse stay and to savor the flavors of Istria at one of the area's fine-dining establishments.

Barbacan Enoteque & Restaurant ★★★ ISTRIAN   This tiny restaurant on the main walkway into Motovun pays a lot of attention to detail, from its immaculate interior to its expertly prepared Istrian cuisine. A meal here is pricier than most, but it's also more interesting. Start with the pâté of veal sweetbreads with truffles or the truffled chicken broth. Entrees include filet of beef with black truffle butter; and risotto Montonese with saffron garlic and truffles. Service is delightful and the atmosphere is quite intimate.

Barbakan 1, Motovun. ✆ **052/681-791.** Entrees 85kn–145kn. AE, DC, MC, V. Wed–Sun 12:30–3:30pm and 6:30–10:30pm; Mon–Tues lunch only.

Café-Bar Montana ★ LIGHT FARE   You'll see tables along the wall overlooking the valley immediately after you pass through the first gate that leads into Motovun proper. These belong to Montana, which is across the road and which also contains a nice art gallery. Be aware, this location can be very windy.

Trg Josefa Ressela.2. ✆ **052/681-524.** No credit cards. Daily 8am–midnight. Closed Jan 1–Easter.

Hotel Kaštel ★★   Each room in the Kaštel Hotel has a different view of the terrain, which includes the hotel's park. An excellent **Restoran Kaštel** ★★ serves Istrian home specialties and BošKarin beef and is adept at catering business meetings and other events. A spa center with panoramic views of the Mirna Valley was added in 2008, making the Kaštel the most desirable address in town. The sizeable guest rooms include modern bathrooms that don't destroy the character of the 17th-century former palace. If you call ahead, the hotel will pick you up at the bottom of the street leading into Motovun so you don't have to drag your luggage uphill.

Trg Andrea Antico 7, Motovun. ✆ **052/681-607.** Fax 052/681-652. www.hotel-kastel-motovun.hr. 30 units. July–Aug and Christmas week from 83€ double; from 113€ suite. Rest of year from 67€ double; from 95€ suite. 50% surcharge for a single using a room with twin beds. AE, DC, MC, V. Pets accepted (10€ per day). **Amenities:** Restaurant; excursions. *In room:* TV, Internet.

Matijašić Agrotourism ★   This rustic cottage has been owned by the Matijašić family for 4 centuries. It is a typical Istrian stone house surrounded by nature in the middle of Istria's wine country. The cottage sleeps six, and while no meals are provided, the owner runs a fine konoba 5km (3 miles) away. If you stay here, you also will have the opportunity to walk the vineyard with owner Darko Matijašić, tour his winemaking operation, and even pick a few grapes.

Pekasi, Motovun, 52424 Istria. ✆ **052/682-126.** Fax 052/682-012. www.matijasic.hr. 1 unit. 900kn per day. No credit cards.

Restoran Kaštel ★★ ISTRIAN   The Kaštel's menu offers several unusual Istrian dishes as well as a signature dessert that's not on the menu. Try the *frkanci* with venison goulash, which is what the hotel calls a "forgotten" dish. Frkanci is a pasta that is a cross between gnocchi and noodle and usually only prepared in Istrian homes. In the Kaštel's case, the pasta is handmade by Istrian home cooks just for the hotel. Ask for the restaurant's special truffle for dessert: This one is chocolate, not tuber, and it is the size of an egg. You can dine under a 100-year-old mulberry tree or in the hotel's dining room, where service is not only efficient but friendly, too.

Trg Andrea Antico 7, Motovun. ✆ **052/681-607.** Fax 052/681-652. www.hotel-kastel-motovun.hr. Entrees 45kn–120kn. AE, DC, MC, V. Daily 10am–10pm.

Zigante Restaurant ★★ (Overrated) GOURMET ISTRIAN   Two elegant, formal rooms designed in Istrian style are the setting for Giancarlo Zigante's celebrated cuisine. As expected, most of the dishes (and even some of the desserts) incorporate truffles with spectacular results, but they are not as breathtaking as the prices. Try the medallions of lamb with gooseliver and black truffles as an entree, or the homebred rabbit filled with—what else?—truffles. The wine list is loaded with Croatian wines, including some with the Zigante label, and service is impeccable. There is a cigar area plus another replica of that record-breaking truffle.

Livade 7, Livade. ⓒ **052/664-302.** Fax 052/664-303. www.zigantetartufi.com. Reservations required. Entrees 135kn–205kn. AE, DC, MC, V. Daily summer noon–11pm; winter 11am–10pm.

13 ISTARSKE TOPLICE, ROC, HUM & BUZET

The stretch of road that connects **Istarske Toplice, Roc** (Rozzo), **Hum** (Colmo), and **Buzet** (Pinguente) is as rural as they come. Just below **Oprtalj,** and between **Buje** and Buzet, Istarske Toplice is a health resort nestled in a forested canyon with a spectacular, 91m-high (300-ft.) rock-climbing wall.

ESSENTIALS

VISITOR INFORMATION The **Tourist Information Office** in Buzet serves Roč, Hum, and Istarske Toplice. It is at Trg Fontana 7/1 in Buzet (ⓒ **052/662-343;** www. tzg-buje.hr) and can provide maps, brochures, and information on private accommodations, including farmhouse stays, camping, and events.

GETTING THERE See "Getting There" in "Orientation," earlier in this chapter.

GETTING AROUND Small towns in central Istria are best seen on foot, but travel between them requires a vehicle. Buses do serve the area, but not all routes are covered every day; and in some cases there is only one bus per day. Even then, you'll sometimes have to walk a mile or more from the bus stop to get to the center of town.

WHAT TO SEE & DO

Like many Croatian spas, **Istarske Toplice** was built not as a playground where beautiful, healthy people came to be pampered, but as a place where crippled, infirm people came to be healed. The resort still seems to attract more of the latter than the former, and while you can enjoy a soak in the hot, sulfur-scented water or a rejuvenating mud pack, you could be sharing the pool with a physical therapy session. For those who like rock climbing, the almost vertical granite wall nearby is challenging.

Dubbed the "City of Truffles" because it and nearby **Livade** are prime truffle-hunting territory, **Buzet** is just 10km (6 miles) northeast of Istarske Toplice on top of a 137m (450-ft.) hill. It's worth a visit, especially during **Truffle Day,** usually the second Saturday in September. During this celebration of the earthy delicacy, the whole town throws a block party with music, food, and, of course, truffles. Cars are allowed up the narrow, twisting street into town, but don't try driving up there unless you're sure your brakes are good.

Approaching **Roč** by car or bus, you will see an unusually low **medieval wall** surrounding this fortified town. From that vantage point it doesn't seem as if the tiny town just under 8km (5 miles) southeast of Buzet could possibly have anything worth a detour. Sure, the medieval walls, **town gates,** and a **tower** are nice to see; and interesting **Roman tombstones** are displayed just inside the main gate arch. But one of the most compelling reasons to stop at Roč is its location at one end of the **Glagolitic Alley** ★★. A string of 10 outdoor sculptures that dot the road between Roč and Hum was erected between 1977 and 1981 to celebrate and preserve Glagolitic script. Despite the fact that there aren't any explanations on most of them, the sculptures dedicated to Glagolitic scholars

Black (& White) Gold

Istria is fast becoming as famous as France and Italy for its truffles—pungent, underground tuberous fungi used in many traditional Istrian dishes and sauces. In Istria, specially trained dogs (Istrian Hunters) are used to sniff out the malodorous treasures that grow a foot beneath the floor of the forests around Buzet (France and Italy traditionally use pigs, although dogs are becoming common there, too). True truffle madness takes over the area during Truffle Days, which occur at the start of the season in the area's villages. The most famous of these celebrations is the last Saturday in September in Buzet, where a Veli Jože-size omelet is cooked up with truffles and scarfed down by whomever happens to be merrymaking in town. Truffles' strong, distinctive flavor makes them an acquired taste, but their rarity and astronomical price make them a delicacy. Truffles are less expensive in Croatia than they are in other countries and thus are used more liberally in the cuisine.

are interesting to look at. One of the sculptures, Razvoda, is an arrangement that looks like a Stonehenge garden. Today, Roč is primarily known as a center of Glagolitic literature, and every year the town puts on the **Small Glagolitic Academy** so that Croatia's kids can keep the traditional writing alive. Private rooms are available in Roč (there are signs on the road), and there is a decent konoba.

The strip of road that links Roč and **Hum** is just 6.4km (4 miles) long, but it is a historic corridor because of the commemorative Glagolitic sculptures. Hum's biggest claim to fame is its status as the world's smallest town. However, from the looks of the state of tourism in the present-day village, that could be changing. Tiny Hum has spiffed up recently and is quite appealing. Only about 20 people live within Hum's well-preserved walls, which enclose two small streets and two churches (one dating from the 12th c.).

WHERE TO STAY & DINE

Most accommodations in these small towns are in private apartments, rooms, or farmhouses, which makes this area a center of agro-tourism. Information on private accommodations is available at the tourist office in Buzet. Opportunities to sample authentic Istrian specialties abound in this rural area, which has a nice selection of excellent konobas.

Fontana   Guest rooms in this Buzet establishment are quite worn and basic but larger than most and nicer than you'd expect from looking at the blighted exterior of this three-story hotel near the road into town. The staff is accommodating, and helpful in suggesting area sights and how to reach them.

Trg Fontana 1, Buzet. © **052/662-615.** Fax 052/663-423. hotelfontana@pu.htnet.hr. 57 units. Half-board doubles from 60€. AE, DC, MC. Limited free parking. **Amenities:** Restaurant; bar; disco. *In room:* TV.

Humska Konoba ★★ ISTRIAN   The line was literally out the door when we visited this Hum institution in July 2009 and no wonder. Local flavors are in the food and in the decor and atmosphere, too, in this wood-and-stone building featuring a summer terrace that has a view of the countryside. If you dare, sip home-brewed *biska*, a grape brandy–based aperitif flavored with white mistletoe and other herbs. Nibble on locally produced smoked ham and sheep's cheese. Then dig into such Istrian specialties as fuži with goulash or truffles, and smoked meat and sauerkraut. Have *krostole* (doughnuts) for dessert.

Hum 2, 52425 Roč. ℃ **052/660-005.** Fax 052/660-001. www.hum.hr. Entrees 9kn–35kn. No credit cards. Tues–Sun 11am–10pm. Closed Mon.

Ročka Konoba ★★ ISTRIAN   You'll feel like you're in Mom's kitchen in this rustic dining room with a great view of the rolling countryside. The food is just like home cooking, too—if you live in Istria. Local specials such as fuži, spicy Istrian sausage, hearty soups, and fragrant homemade bread are on the menu.

Roč Center. ℃ **052/666-451.** Entrees 35kn–90kn. AE, DC, MC, V. Hours variable.

Terme Mirna   The sheer granite wall called the **Iron Gate** that is a backdrop for this spa hotel is a spectacular feature of Istarske Toplice, but the facility itself is depressing. The Mirna still is primarily geared to those who need rehab or other medical therapies, though some people might want to stop for the thermal waters, which are rich in sulfur. In fact, sulfur's characteristic rotten-egg odor hits you as soon as you get out of the car in the parking lot. If you do stay, be sure to ask for a Type-A room, which is a little more expensive but which has been updated. Beauty treatments and multiday packages are available, including a 14-day "fit" (aka weight loss) package for 5,000kn that includes the services of a psychologist.

Sv. Stjepan 60, 52427 Livade. ℃ **052/603-000.** www.istarske-toplice.hr. 375 units. From 440kn double (Type-A). Rates include breakfast. AE, DC, MC, V. **Amenities:** Restaurant; coffee bar; 2 pools; spa services. *In room:* TV.

Vrh ★★ ISTRIAN   Technically, Vrh is in Buzet, but it's really in the hills outside town. Get directions at the Buzet tourist office to this oasis of gastronomy on the road between Ponte Porton and Buzet. Vrh's menu is standard Istrian with dishes such as fuži with truffles or gnocchi with game. Sausages are house made, peka-baked meat is a specialty, and nettle pâté is an unusual surprise. Try Vrh's house label wine and if you're staying nearby, a glass of local grappa, which is renowned all over Croatia.

Vrh 2. Buzet. ℃ **052/667-123.** Entrees 42kn–160kn, more for peka meat sold by the kilo. No credit cards. Tues–Sat 1–10pm and Sun 12:30–10pm.

Zagreb

There is a new spirit in Zagreb, a city that travelers once regarded as a stopover rather than a destination as far back as the days of the Orient Express. No more. Zagreb's attractions aren't as famous as Paris's, or as numerous as Rome's, but it's impossible to experience all the city's delights on an overnight stay.

Zagreb always has played a pivotal role in the life of Croatia, mostly because of its location at the crossroads where western and eastern Europe meet.

This is not a glitzy city, but rather one of history, culture, and purpose informed by war and natural disasters. Zagreb still is finding itself after nearly a millennium of foreign domination, but it is changing, growing, and emerging as a destination in its own right.

In the summer of 2009, there was scarcely a square block in central Zagreb that didn't have scaffolding or construction shrouds covering a renovation in progress. The squares were filled with people speaking a variety of languages. New restaurants, attractions, and entrepreneurial ventures were sprouting everywhere. In some ways, contemporary Zagreb's personality is in transition from dour socialist to carefree socialite, and it is subject to being misunderstood. On any rainy Sunday, central Zagreb is deserted: Stores are closed and restaurants and museums are empty. If a visitor has just a day and is forced to see the city from under an umbrella, Zagreb seems a sad, gray place. But if that same visitor is lucky enough to be in the city center on a sunny Saturday, Zagreb is a city pulsating with color and buzzing with energy. On such a day Zagreb hums with chatter as *fashionistas* haggle with wizened old "babushkas" at the colorful Dolac market, and the city becomes a backdrop for friends sipping wine at sidewalk cafes, for curious tourists, and for anyone listening to street musicians who fill Trg Ban Jeličić with beautiful noise.

Weekdays, Zagreb is alive with serious hustle and bustle and what seems like endless hordes carrying briefcases or bags of bread and flowers past a perpetual gallery and sipping coffee at sidewalk cafes. Evenings, Zagreb is all softness and laughter as diners linger over dessert at the newly restored Gradska Kavana, head for jazz clubs, or just stroll the cobblestone streets.

How visitors see Zagreb depends largely on the color of the sky and the day of the week, but the city's blend of old and new, of country and cosmopolitan, is somehow a yin-yang combo that works. This is not a city that instantly takes your breath away, but—given enough time—Zagreb will wiggle its way into your heart and tempt you to stay a while.

1 ESSENTIALS

ARRIVING

BY PLANE   There are no direct flights to Croatia from the U.S., Canada, or Australia, but Croatia Air, the national airline company, connects Zagreb with several major European hubs as well as with other cities in Croatia. **Pleso International Airport** (*©* 01/ **626-52-22**) is about 16km (10 miles) south of the city center, and Zagreb is the entry point for most visitors to Croatia. Croatia Air's shuttle bus runs every 30 minutes from 5:30am to 7:30pm from the airport to and from Zagreb's main bus station for 25kn, and the ride takes half an hour (© **01/615-79-92**). Taxi fares to the city center run between 150kn and 250kn. *Tip:* Croatia Air's weight limits for luggage differ from those of some other international carriers, so if you are not checking your bags directly through to Zagreb from the U.S. on an airline that is not a member of the Star Alliance, you should call Croatia Air for information on this policy, which is subject to seasonal changes. When returning to the U.S., be aware that Croatia Air does not allow any battery-operated devices in checked luggage, so be sure to remove your alarm clock before you get to the ticket counter.

BY BUS Croatia Airlines runs frequent shuttle buses between the airport and Zagreb's main bus station (Autobusni Kolodvor) for 25kn. The bus station is a bright, efficient hub with restaurants, shops, a post office, and connections to the city center. A 24-hour *garderoba* (luggage storage area) charges 1.20kn per hour. ATMs are located near the ticket office, as is an exchange that is open from 6am to 10pm daily. Frequent bus connections link Zagreb and all of Croatia's main cities, which in turn hook up with local lines that run to virtually every village in the country. International connections link Zagreb to an increasing number of European cities.

BY TRAIN The **Zagreb train station (Glavni Kolodvor)** facing Trg Kralja Tomislava on the city's Green Horseshoe was renovated in 2004 and the 19th-century exterior is now bubble-gum pink and adorned with angels and other statuary. It is close to bus and tram connections into the city center, which is a 10-minute walk past several hotels. A 24-hour garderoba is available for 10kn per day. A nice restaurant with terrace overlooks the park. There are ATMs, exchange facilities, and an information center (6–10am, 10:30am–6pm, and 6:30–10pm).

Catch the no. 5, 6, or 13 tram across the street in front of the Kralja Tomislav monument to get to Trg Bana Josip Jeličića. Bus routes may change for construction projects, and when that happens, a handwritten sign with changes is taped up at the bus stop.

BY CAR Driving in Zagreb can be stressful. Most streets are marked by small ornamental signs on plaques affixed to building walls at intersections so you can't see the sign until you're past it. Many buildings in Zagreb do not display street numbers at all, or if they do, they can't be read unless you are on top of them. There also is a tangled network of one-way and pedestrian streets, perpetual street construction, and a parking dearth, all of which add up to a driver's nightmare inside the city limits.

VISITOR INFORMATION

The **Zagreb Tourist Information Center** at Trg Bana Jelačić 11 (© **01/481-40-51;** www.zagreb-touristinfo.hr) is open 8:30am to 8pm Monday to Friday; 9am to 5pm Saturday; and 10am to 2pm Sunday and holidays. The information center provides maps, directions, and brochures, and it has a selection of books about Zagreb and Croatia as well as some souvenirs. It sells the **Zagreb Card** for 90kn, which gives you 72 hours of unlimited city transportation (including the Sljeme cable car), a 50% discount at most museums and galleries, and assorted discounts at participating businesses, including theaters and concert halls. There is a second Tourist Information Center at Trg Nikole Šubića Zrinskog 14 (© **01/492-16-45**).

Zagreb County Tourist Association at Preradovićeva 42 (© **01/487-36-65;** www. tzzz.hr) is invaluable for information about excursions from Zagreb to such places as Samobor and the Žumberak region. Hours are 8am to 4pm Monday to Friday.

Numerous travel agencies in town can book flights, packages, and hotels, but anyone flying out of Zagreb will eventually talk to **Croatia Airlines,** whose main office is at Trg Nikole Šubića Zrinskog 17 (℗ **01/481-96-33**). It is open 8am to 7pm Monday to Friday and 8am to 3pm Saturday.

Tours to sites and cities in Zagreb and all over Croatia can be arranged through various travel agencies. **Atlas Travel** at Zrinjevac 17 (℗ **01/481-39-33**) is Croatia's largest agency and has a huge menu of tours and travel packages. It is also the country's American Express agent. **Generalturist** at Praška 5 (℗ **01/480-55-55;** www.generalturist.com) books flights, excursions, cruises, and other trips.

CITY LAYOUT

The city of Zagreb is nestled between **Mount Medvednica** and the **Sava River.** It is a sprawling metropolis, but almost every attraction of note is within 2.4km (1½ miles) of **Trg Bana Jelačić,** the city's main square commonly known as Trg Jelačić. The area north of the Trg Jelačić includes **Gornji Grad (Upper Town)** and its Gradec and Kaptol neighborhoods, which are perhaps Zagreb's most picturesque areas. **Donji Grad (Lower Town)** south of Trg Jelačić includes Zagreb's famous Green Horseshoe and runs south to the main train station. You can walk to most points of interest from Trg Jelačić, or hop on the public tram system for 7kn per ride. After that, The city's attractions are spread out. **Mount Medvednica Nature Park** ★★★ and its **Sljeme Peak** ★★★ in the hills north of town can be accessed from the square by taking tram no. 14 to the end of the line, and then tram no. 15 to its terminus. From there you can get a cable car to Sljeme's top. **Mirogoj Cemetery** ★★★ is also north of the center and can be reached via the no. 106 bus from the cathedral. **Novi Grad (New City)** is an area of bland apartment towers and industry south of the Sava; except for **Jarun Lake** ★★★ just north of the river and the airport, there isn't much to see here. **Maksimir Park** ★★ is an elegant wooded zone east of the center. It can be reached via tram nos. 4, 7, 11, and 12.

ZAGREB

10

THE NEIGHBORHOODS IN BRIEF

Zagreb is easy to navigate via public transportation if you have a good map and know a few key Croatian terms so you can decipher directional signs on the trams and buses, but you can walk to almost everything of note, too. Most of Zagreb's attractions are in the city center, which is divided into "neighborhoods," each with a distinct character and connected by the city's main square, Trg Jeličića. Gornji Grad (Upper City), the area north of the square, is Zagreb's heart. It is divided along historical lines into Kaptol and Gradec, territory that was halved by a stream that is now Tkalčićeva Street, home to Zagreb's cafe society and increasingly to chic designer shops and artists' ateliers.

THE NEIGHBORHOODS IN BRIEF

Kaptol is both a neighborhood and a street in modern Zagreb. In medieval times, Kaptol was a town and was dominated by the clergy, while neighboring Gradec was a lay settlement. Today, Zagreb's neo-Gothic cathedral and church buildings are still situated in Kaptol. North of the cathedral, Kaptol is quickly becoming a trendy enclave where well-heeled young professionals shop, drink, dine, and mingle. Parts of Kaptol have been converted to a pedestrian mall, though motor scooters rarely pay attention to that legislation. Opatovina Street runs parallel to Kaptol north from the left of the Dolac market; its most interesting feature is the statue of Croatian comedian and social commentator Petrica Kerempuh at the bottom of the street.

Gradec is a hilly residential area dotted with stately mansions and leafy squares as well as some of the city's best galleries and museums. There is a tennis center in the northern section of the neighborhood plus several embassies and consulates and a few upscale restaurants. Gradec is a good place to see ornate homes built by Zagreb's 19th-century aristocrats as well as the only surviving city gate.

Trg Bana Jelačić is Zagreb's fulcrum: It seems that everything begins and ends in this plaza dominated by a statue of Ban Josip Jelačić seated on a proud horse with its tail in the air. Ban Jelačića was a 19th-century governor of Croatia who was much beloved by the people for his bravery (p. 277). His statue is a focal point of the square and the space "under the tail" of the monument is a popular rendezvous spot for the Zagrebačka. The square is a wonderful place to start any city tour because many tram routes crisscross there, and it is within easy walking distance of Kaptol and Gradec, the Dolac market, and Tkalčićeva Street.

Donji Grad (Lower Town) is south of Gradec, and it might seem like a solid block of buildings broken up by a few green spaces. Donji Grad begins at Trg Jelačić and includes Ilica Street, where designer shops are increasing in number every day. It ends at the main train station to the south. Draškovićeva is Donji Grad's eastern border, and Republika Austria the western border. In the middle of this section of the city, a U-shaped series of adjacent parks runs roughly from Trg Bana Jelačić south to the main train station, from there to the western end of the Botanical Gardens, then north to the end of Trg Marsala Tita. Known as the "Green Horseshoe" or Lenuci's Horseshoe, the public green spaces are dotted with galleries, museums, and schools.

ZAGREB

10

ESSENTIALS

GETTING AROUND

BY TRAM OR BUS Zagreb's electric tram system is quick, clean, efficient, and reliable, and it runs 24/7, although the frequency is reduced in the wee hours. New, air-conditioned, Croatian-made cars were added in 2007 on most routes, and they make riding public transportation comfortable. Tram routes cover central Zagreb and connect to buses that run to outlying areas and suburbs. Most lines go to the main train station, Trg Ban Jelačić, or both.

Tickets for both can be purchased at Tisak news kiosks for 7kn or on board for 9kn. Tickets are good for 90 minutes each way and must be validated with a time stamp at the orange machines on board. There are no conductors checking tickets, but there are random control checks. If you are caught without a ticket or with an unstamped ticket, the fine is 150kn on the spot, more if you don't have the money immediately.

There are maps of all tram and bus routes at stops and on most city maps, but if you aren't familiar with the city or the language, it can be difficult to figure out whether a given vehicle goes to your destination because only the final destination and a stop or two are listed on the tram or bus itself. *Tip:* Keep a map of the tram routes and one of Zagreb with you whenever using the system so you can locate the routes' end streets and determine if the tram is going in your direction. Almost none of the tram operators speaks English. *Note:* In the summer of 2009, we spotted newly erected signs pointing the way to museums, churches, and specific tourist attractions all over Zagreb. Some of these were at tram stops to help riders figure out which train to take.

BY TAXI   Taxis are expensive in Zagreb, even for short distances. Taxis charge a 25kn flat fee plus 7kn for every ⅗ mile. A 20% surcharge is added to that on Sunday and at night, which makes taxis a very expensive way to travel. However, if you must use a cab, you can call one at ✆ **01/668-25-05.** It's a good idea to try to negotiate a price for your trip before you hop in.

ON FOOT   Walking is by far the best (and healthiest) way to see Zagreb. Crime in the city is low, and on foot you can safely get to almost any museum or restaurant in the central town within half an hour.

(Fast Facts) Zagreb

American Express   American Express services are available through **Atlas Travel Agency** at Zrinjevac 17, 10000 Zagreb (✆ **01/481-39-33;** fax 01/487-30-49). There is also an American Express office at Lastovska 23, ✆ **01/612-44-22.**

ATMs & Currency Exchange   There are numerous ATMs (Bankomats) in central Zagreb where you can withdraw cash using American Express, Diners Club, Maestro/MasterCard, Cirrus, and Visa. Just be sure the ATM you use is embedded in a building and not free-standing, as the latter have been the sites of fraud in some European cities. You can change money or traveler's checks at most banks, exchange offices, and travel agencies, but you'll be charged a 1.5% or greater fee. Bank hours vary, but most are open from 8am to 7pm weekdays and 8am to noon Saturday. The exchange fee is even higher at hotels. **A-Tours** at the main bus station (✆ **01/600-86-66**) is the exchange office with the longest hours. It is open from 6am to 10pm every day.

Business Hours   Most banks open at 9am and stay open until 7pm or later Monday to Saturday. The airport branch of Zagrebačka Bank is open on Sunday, too. Offices generally are open from 8am to 5pm; some have Saturday hours, usually until 1pm. Store hours vary, with many closing from 2 to 5pm or some other interval during the day, but as a general rule, smaller stores open at 9am, close 8pm Monday to Saturday, and are closed all day Sunday. Stores in larger malls are open 7 days a week, but some don't reopen after the weekend until 2pm on Monday so employees can restock shelves.

Dentists & Doctors   **Dental Emergency** at Perkovčeva 3 (✆ **01/482-84-88**) is open 24/7 and takes walk-ins. For medical emergencies, try the **Emergency Center** at Draškovićeva 19 near the Sheraton. It's open 24 hours. **KB Dubrava** at Avenija Gojka Šuška 6 (✆ **01/290-24-44**) makes house calls to most parts of town.

Embassies & Consulates   The **U.S. Embassy** is at Thomasa Jeffersona ulica 2 (✆ **01/661-22-00;** www.usembassy.hr).

 The **Canadian Embassy** is at Prilaz Gjure Deželića 4 (✆ **01/488-12-00**).

 The **United Kingdom Embassy** is at I. Lučića 4 (✆ **01/600-91-00;** www.british embassy.gov.uk/croatia).

 The **Irish Consulate** is at Turninina 3 (✆ **01/667-44-55**).

 The **Australian Embassy** is at Centar Kaptol, Nova Ves 11/III (✆ **01/489-12-00**).

 The **New Zealand Consulate** is at Trg S. Radića 3 (✆ **01/615-13-82**).

Emergencies For police dial (𝄐 **92;** for an ambulance, (𝄐 **94;** and to report a fire, (𝄐 **93.** For road assistance, dial (𝄐 **987;** for the **Croatian Auto Club,** dial (𝄐 **01/464-08-00.**

Internet Access Croatia has embraced computer technology in a big way, and Internet access is easy to find. Almost all hotels have Internet access in their business centers, but if you are staying someplace that isn't wired, you still can keep in touch. **Sublink Cybercafe** is close to Trg Jelačić at Nikole Tesle 12 ((𝄐 **01/481-13-29**). You can e-mail, print, copy, or scan for.25kn per minute. Sip smoothies at **Cyberfunk** and get 15 minutes of surfing free. Otherwise it's .25kn per minute (Masarykova 26; (𝄐 **01/639-90-70**). Open 8am to 10pm Monday to Saturday. Closed Sunday.

Mail You can mail letters at any yellow Posta box, but if you need to buy stamps or send a package, the Central Post Office is at Jurišićeva 13 near the Jadran Hotel ((𝄐 **01/481-10-90**). Hours are 7am to 9pm Monday to Friday, 8am to 4pm Saturday. The post office will tell you that it takes roughly 2 weeks for regular mail to reach the U.S. from Croatia. Our experience is that mail to the U.S. takes 4 weeks or more. A letter home will cost 8kn per 50gr and a postcard 3.50kn. If you are in a hurry, go to FedEx at Buzinski prilaz 36a near the airport ((𝄐 **01/669-50-00;** www.fedex.com). It's open 8am to 8pm Monday to Friday.

Newspapers & Magazines Very few news kiosks sell English-language newspapers, and those that do sell out quickly. The *International Herald Tribune* is the easiest to find and costs 20kn. Many hotels print faxed copies of U.S. and other English-language newspapers for their guests for a fee. **Algoritam** at Gajeva 1 ((𝄐 **01/481-86-72**), on the ground floor of the Hotel Dubrovnik, has an extensive selection of English-language magazines and books. Hours are 8am to 9pm Monday to Friday; 8am to 3pm Saturday. Closed Sunday.

Parking Croatia is way ahead of the curve when it comes to public parking. There are three parking zones in Zagreb, each with its own rate. When you find a space, you can pay at one of the boxes installed on most corners and display your ticket on the dashboard. Or, you can send an SMS text message to a number displayed on the parking box. Punch your license plate number into your cellphone and you'll get an SMS confirmation. When your time is almost up, you'll get another text asking if you want to add more time or move your car. If you get caught not paying at all, the fine is 250kn; expired time rates a 150kn fine. *Note:* If you don't have a phone with a domestic SIM card, you'll have to dial the international code first.

Pharmacies Need an aspirin? In Zagreb (and all of Croatia) you'll have to go to a pharmacy *(ljekarna)* to buy some. No drugs of any kind are sold anywhere except at a pharmacy. There are several 24-hour ljekarna in Zagreb. Two are at Trg Jelačić ((𝄐 **01/481-61-54**) and at Ilica 301 ((𝄐 **01/375-03-21**).

Safety Zagreb enjoys relatively low crime rates, though there have been some reports that car thefts are on the rise. It's perfectly safe to ride public transportation at night and to walk through high-traffic areas. The police presence on Zagreb streets is subtle and you'll rarely see a uniformed officer, but they're there. Exercise the same precautions you'd take in any big city.

Telephone To call Zagreb from the United States, dial the **international prefix 011,** then Croatia's country code, **385;** and then Zagreb's city code, **1.** Then dial the actual phone number.

To call the U.S. from Zagreb, dial the **international prefix 00,** then the U.S. country code, **1;** then the area code and number. Other country codes are as follows: Canada, **1;** the United Kingdom, **44;** Ireland, **353;** Australia, **61;** New Zealand, **64.**

To call from one city code to another within Croatia: Dial the Croatian city code, including the zero, followed by the phone number.

To make a local call, simply dial the phone number. No codes necessary. Local calls cost about 5kn per minute.

To use a prepaid phone card, call the service, key in the code on the back of the card, and call the number. It's a good idea to have a prepaid phone card with you for emergencies because most pay phones don't take money and you'll need a card to use them. You can buy prepaid cards in denominations of 50, 100, 200, and 500 units at most newspaper kiosks, at post offices, and at some tobacconists. Calls are based on unit-per-minute rates, and the farther away you call, the more each unit costs and the faster you use up your units. You can also buy prepaid cards at **Nexcom,** Zavrtnica 17 (📞 **01/606-03-33**); or at **Voicecom,** Ilica 109 (📞 **01/376-01-23;** www.voicecom.hr). Free 0800 access.

To use a mobile phone, you can buy a SIM card for 400kn to 600kn from **VIP** (📞 **091**) or **T-Mobile** (📞 **098**). Pay-as-you-go SIM cards are available at news kiosks in smaller denominations. If you have a GSM-equipped phone, it will register and readjust to a carrier in Zagreb provided you have activated its international capabilities with your service provider in the U.S. To call the U.S., hold down the zero key until a plus sign appears in the display. Then dial 1 plus the area code and number. Be aware that you will pay for roaming charges besides the call, which are extremely expensive because the call has to bounce from Croatia to the U.S., and back to Croatia again.

Toilets There are no free-standing public toilets in Zagreb. On the other hand, most toilets in restaurants, hotels, and stores are well kept and free, and you usually don't have to be a customer to use them.

2 WHAT TO SEE & DO

The best—and in some cases the only—way to see Zagreb is on foot, with the occasional tram or bus ride. Almost everything in the city center is pedestrian-accessible and so are some of the sites farther afield. Gornji Grad (Upper Town) is flush with historical buildings and churches, restaurants, boutiques, monuments, and entertainment venues. Donji Grad (Lower Town) is strong on museums, parks, historic architecture, and shopping. Other attractions are a short ride from the center of town. Anton Dominik Fernkorn's statue of Ban Josip Jelačić is the centerpiece of **Trg Bana Jelačić (Jelačić Square)** ★★★. It was installed on the square in 1866 and it stood there until World War II, when the square was renamed Republic Square. The statue was removed and stored in pieces because the powers-that-be determined it had become a rallying point for Croatian nationalists, who were seen as a threat to the ruling Communist Party. It wasn't until 1990 that the statue was returned to its original home, and the square to its original name. Today Jelačić Square is ringed by shops and cafes; other, smaller plazas radiate from it.

KAPTOL

Cathedral of the Assumption of the Virgin Mary ★★★   The 105m (345-ft.) twin spires of this magnificent Gothic structure seem perpetually covered with scaffolding. Work began on the cathedral's exterior in 1990 and is ongoing. But despite the dust and mess, the grace and beauty of this Herman Bollé masterpiece shines as a symbol of Zagreb. Inside, the cathedral glows following a refurbishment that was completed in 1988. Note the 18th-century marble pulpit by Slovenian sculptor Mihael Cussal and the sarcophagus of the controversial Blessed Alojzije Stepinac behind the main altar. A Meštrović relief showing Stepanic kneeling before Christ marks the Croatian priest's grave.

Kaptol 31, 10000 Zagreb. 🕿 01/481-47-27. Free admission. Mon–Sat 10am–5pm; Sun 1–5pm. Masses are at 7, 8, and 9am weekdays; and at 7, 8, 9, 10, and 11:30am Sun.

Dolac Market ★★★   Dolac is north of Jelačić Square and starting around 5am daily, vendors pile their stalls with colorful fruits, vegetables, baskets, and other Croatian products. Dolac opened in 1930 and ever since it has been Zagreb's most popular open-air market—some say one of the best in Europe. Fruits, vegetables, plants, and textiles are on the upper level, while meat, olives, and herbs are in the covered area below. Fish and cheese are in separate spaces to avoid olfactory overstimulation.

Dolac bb. Mon–Fri 6am–2pm; Sat 6am–3pm; Sun 6am–noon.

Tkalčićeva ★★★   This cobblestone street to the left of Dolac winds up a fairly steep incline into the belly of the upper city. It is lined with boutiques, bars, restaurants, galleries in rehabbed 19th-century mansions, and renovation projects. Tkalčićeva is also home to Zagreb's cafe society, and every evening the tables along this thoroughfare are full.

To left of the Dolac Market.

GRADEC

Gradec is the second arm of central Zagreb's civic triumvirate. Less commercial than Kaptol, Gradec is packed with some of the city's most interesting museums and monuments.

Atelier-Ivan Meštrović ★★★   The artist's studio and 17th-century house are the setting for a vast array of his sculptures and models. Examples of Croatia's most famous sculptor's renderings of famous people, religious icons, and just plain folks are exhibited inside and outside in the garden. This is a fascinating museum where you can imagine how the artist lived and worked during his years there (1924–42). Not only are finished works on display, but also sketches, models, and photographs, most notably a small study of the Grgur Ninski sculptures in Split and Nin in Dalmatia. Many other Meštrović sculptures are installed in public areas around Zagreb and other parts of Croatia, but

---

ⓕ Fun Facts   Let There Be Light

At night, Zagreb's Gradec neighborhood glows under the light of gas lamps. At 7pm sharp in the summertime, all 267 of the street fixtures are individually lighted by an old-fashioned lamp lighter.

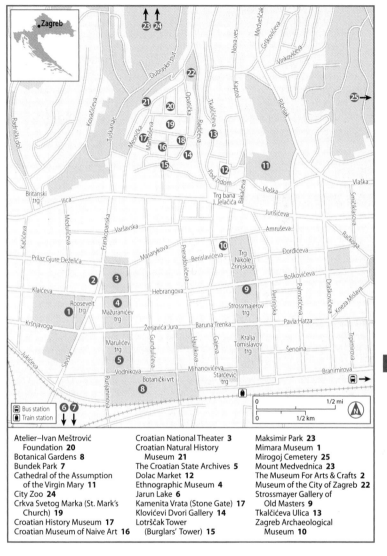

Atelier–Ivan Meštrović
  Foundation **20**
Botanical Gardens **8**
Bundek Park **7**
Cathedral of the Assumption
  of the Virgin Mary **11**
City Zoo **24**
Crkva Svetog Marka (St. Mark's
  Church) **19**
Croatian History Museum **17**
Croatian Museum of Naive Art **16**

Croatian National Theater **3**
Croatian Natural History
  Museum **21**
The Croatian State Archives **5**
Dolac Market **12**
Ethnographic Museum **4**
Jarun Lake **6**
Kamenita Vrata (Stone Gate) **17**
Klovićevi Dvori Gallery **14**
Lotrščak Tower
  (Burglars' Tower) **15**

Maksimir Park **23**
Mimara Museum **1**
Mirogoj Cemetery **25**
Mount Medvednica **23**
The Museum For Arts & Crafts **2**
Museum of the City of Zagreb **22**
Strossmayer Gallery of
  Old Masters **9**
Tkalčićeva Ulica **13**
Zagreb Archaeological
  Museum **10**

currently there is no all-inclusive guide that locates them. In his later life, Meštrović lived in the United States and worked as a professor of sculpture at the University of Notre Dame, which also owns some of his works from that period. A wide array of Meštrović's books, catalogues, and CDs are available in the gallery's small bookstore.

Mletačka 8. ☎ **01/485-11-23.** www.mdc.hr/mestrovic. 20kn adults, 10kn children and seniors. Tues–Sat 10am–6pm; Sun 10am–2pm.

Marija Jurić Zagorka

The bronze statue of a woman in 19th-century dress carrying an umbrella is a showstopper for pedestrians on busy Tkalčićeva Street. The sculpture was created by artist Stejepan Gračan and commemorates Zagorka, who was Croatia's first female journalist. Zagorka was born to a wealthy family in 1873 and was well-educated, but she still had a difficult time breaking into journalism. On the recommendation of Bishop J. J. Strossmayer, she was given a job on a local Zagreb paper, where she started on the editorial board and introduced the first Croatian publication exclusively for women. Zagorka also penned several well-received novels that still are read today. She died in 1957.

Crkva Svetog Marka (St. Mark's Church) The **tile mosaic** ★★★ depicting the Croatian, Dalmatian, and Slavonian coats of arms is St. Mark's best-known feature. Inside, the church is rather ordinary except for some 20th-century frescoes depicting scenes from the Bible and a Meštrović crucifix. Hours are variable and posted on the door, but not always observed by the folks who have the key to the church. Call to be sure it's open. The church is always open for Mass at 6pm Monday through Saturday, and for 7:30, 11am, and 6pm Mass on Sunday and holidays.

Trg Svetog Marka 5. ✆ **01/485-16-11.**

The Croatian Museum of Naive Art ★★ Think Grandma Moses interprets Croatia when you approach the Baroque mansion that houses paintings and drawings by such Croatian masters as Ivan Generalić and Ivan Lacković. This enchanting museum focuses on the Hlebine School. Its 1,500 works are colorful, historical, political, and sometimes politically incorrect, but utterly charming. The imagery depicted by these artists can be bizarre, but it often reflects local customs that still exist in the hinterlands—or in the mind of the artist.

Ćirilometodska 3. ✆ **01/485-19-11.** www.hmnu.org. Admission 10kn adults, 5kn children and retirees. Tues–Fri 10am–6pm; Sat–Sun 10am–1pm.

Croatian Natural History Museum ★ **Kids** This museum should be in a museum because the exhibits look like they haven't been touched since they were installed in the mid–19th century. Here, presentation is as much an artifact as the artifacts themselves. Nonetheless, it is fascinating to view the stuffed mammal collection as well as the endless cabinets filled with animal, vegetable, and mineral specimens. Don't miss the exhibit that showcases **Krapina Man** ★, the remains of a colony of Neanderthals found near Krapina in the Zagorje region north of Zagreb.

Demetrova 1. ✆ **01/485-17-00.** www.hpm.hr. Admission 10kn. Tues–Fri 10am–5pm; Sat–Sun 10am–1pm.

Kamenita Vrata ★★ It's a steep walk up a long flight of stairs to Radićeva from Tkalčićeva and a few minutes more up another steep cobblestone path to Kamenita Vrata, which was one of four entrances to the walled city of Gradec. Kamenita Vrata is the only gate that survived a 1731 fire, which destroyed almost everything wooden in its path. Just inside the gate a small, dark grotto houses the **Chapel of God's Mother** ★★ where a **painting of the Virgin and Child** is ensconced in an alcove behind a Baroque grid. According to legend, the painting survived the fire and it is revered as a miraculous icon. There are a few pews in the urban chapel, where people come to light candles and pray all through the day.

Kamenita bb.

Klovićevi Dvori Gallery ★★ Just down the street from the Croatian Museum of Naive Art, this sister museum in a converted castle houses a huge exhibit of Hlebine (naive art) paintings on loan from galleries or private collections. At any given time, simultaneous exhibits on display here can include neon art, soft sculpture, and other "New European" art forms. There's also a cafe and a surprisingly good gift shop.

Jezuitski Trg 4. ℭ **01/485-19-26.** www.galerijaklovic.hr. Tues–Sun 11am–7pm. Admission 40kn adults, 10kn children.

Kula Lotrščak (Burglars' Tower) ★★ **Kids** A cannon is fired at this vestige of Gradec's fortifications every day at noon to commemorate a Croat victory against the Turks. You can climb the tower to get a fabulous view of the city.

Strossmayerovo Šetalište 9. ℭ **01/485-17-68.** Admission 10kn. Tues–Sun 11am–8pm for climbing. Closed Mon.

Museum of the City of Zagreb ★ Displays in this museum situated in the renovated former convent of the Order of St. Clare illuminate life in Zagreb from medieval times to the present. Attractive presentations of weaponry, religious objects, furniture, ethnic costumes, and an incredible collection of photographs documenting the city through the years are augmented by scale models of Zagreb at various times in its history. Captions are multilingual. There is a nice restaurant (Stara Vura; p. 296) on the premises, too.

Opatička 20. ℭ **01/485-13-64.** www.mdc.hr/mgz. Admission 20kn adults; 10kn children, students, seniors, persons with disabilities, military; free for children 6 and under. Tues–Fri 10am–6pm; Sat–Sun 10am–1pm. Museum personnel will aid those with disabilities.

Lenuci's Horseshoe

The U-shaped block of parks and gardens that runs from Trg Bana Josip Jelačić to the main train station and back is known as Lenuci's Green Horseshoe, a flowing, tree-lined series of grassy areas, fountains, flower beds, monuments, and pavilions dotted with museums and galleries. According to Lenuci's 19th-century plan, the green strips and stately cultural palaces are strategically placed to break up the visual monotony of blocks and blocks of gray apartments and office buildings that characterize this part of town. The horseshoe cuts a green pattern through Lower Town and is home to such landmarks as the neo-Renaissance Academy of Sciences and Art, the neo-Baroque Croatian National Theater, and the Botanical Gardens.

Botanical Gardens ★ Mihanovičeva Street runs west of Tomislavov Trg past Starčevic Trg and the 1925 landmark Regent Esplanade Hotel, one of the best examples of Secessionist architecture in Zagreb. Mihanovic also skirts Zagreb's Botanical Gardens, which opened in 1894 and were supposed to link the two legs of the Green Horseshoe. However, progress and several bland blocks of modern architecture got in the way. The gardens feature an arboretum, ponds, and an ornamental bridge.

Trg Marka Marulića. © **01/484-40-20.** Tues–Sun 9am–6pm. Closed Mon.

Croatian History Museum History buffs will love the 15 collections of 140,000 Croatian artifacts housed in this 18th-century mansion. The artifacts date from medieval times to the present. The sheer volume and minutiae represented here can be overwhelming to all but the most avid fans.

Matoševa 9. © **01/485-19-90.** www.hismus.hr. Admission 10kn adults; 5kn children, students, retirees, military. Daily 10am–5pm.

Croatian National Theater ★★ This neo-Baroque building was designed by Ferdinand Helmer and Hermann Fellner of Vienna. The ostentatious temple to drama opened with lots of fanfare in 1890 when Emperor Franz Josef did the honors. Meštrović's celebrated 1905 **Well of Life** ★★ sculpture is in front of the entrance.

Trg Maršala Tita 15. © **01/482-85-32.** www.hnk.hr.

The Croatian State Archives ★ This Art Nouveau building is UNESCO-listed and one of Zagreb's finest—it's also home to Croatia's most important documents. The Archives' written holdings won't interest most English-speaking visitors, but architecture buffs from any country will be awed by the interior and exterior treasures concentrated in the stately building that opened in 1913. Both the lobby and atrium area one level up are adorned with brilliant mosaics, intricate ironwork, sparkling leaded glass, and lustrous marble. These spaces are also used for art exhibits, all secondary to their dazzling setting. Outside, the symmetrical park landscape is home to an Ivan Meštrović masterpiece. Guided tours are required for admission.

Marulićev Trg 21, Zagreb. © **01/482-90-00.** www.arhiv.hr. 20kn adults; 10kn children. Mon–Fri 8am–noon and 2–4pm (lobby viewing). Tours at noon, 1, and 2pm.

Ethnographic Museum ★★★ (Finds) The Ethnographic Museum south of Trg Maršala Tita is perhaps one of Zagreb's most underrated museums. It is loaded with a dizzying array of traditional aprons and tunics from all parts of Croatia, as well as collections of agricultural artifacts such as olive- and grape-growing and winemaking implements. Most of the museum's items were acquired in the 19th and 20th centuries and cover the full spectrum of how people worked and lived in Croatia through the ages. There is even a gingerbread collection.

Mažuranićev Trg 14. © **01/482-62-20.** www.etnografski-muzej.hr. Free admission Thurs. Other days: 20kn adults, 15kn children and students, free for seniors and Croatian military. Tues–Thurs 10am–6pm; Fri–Sun 10am–1pm.

Mimara Museum ★ (Overrated) The extensive collection of art housed in this neo-Renaissance building west of the city center on Roosevelt Trg is the result of one man's donation: Croatian-born Ante Topić Mimara, an artist himself, was a lifelong collector

Ivan Meštrović (1883–1962)

Ivan Meštrović is Croatia's most famous artist, and he is regarded as the greatest sculptor of religious art since the Renaissance. Meštrović was born in Vrpolje (Slavonia) August 15, 1883, to a peasant family but spent most of his childhood in Otavice, a tiny, impoverished village in the mountainous interior of Dalmatia west of Šibenik. When he was 16, Meštrović was apprenticed to a stone cutter in Split, where he developed his stone cutting skills by reproducing the city's Greek and Roman works of art. After just 9 months in Split, a wealthy Viennese patron sponsored him for a place at the Academy of Fine Arts in the Austrian capital. In Vienna, Meštrović met French sculptor Auguste Rodin, who encouraged him to broaden his artistic vision through travel and who became a strong influence on the young artist. Meštrović took Rodin's advice and spent time working in Paris, Belgrade, and eventually Rome, where he won a first prize for sculpture at the World Exhibition of 1911. In the early 1920s, Meštrović settled in Zagreb, where he transformed a 17th-century house (Meštrović Atelier) into his home and studio. In 1942 he was imprisoned by the Ustashe for his political involvements and released thanks to intervention by Pope Pius XII. Meštrović then moved to Rome, and the next year he left for Switzerland. After World War II, he immigrated to New York where he became a professor of sculpture at Syracuse University. In 1955, he moved to a similar position at the University of Notre Dame in South Bend, Indiana, where he lived until his death in 1962. Throughout his career, Meštrović was a prolific artist. His works are on display in museums, public places (including Chicago's Grant Park), and at Syracuse and Notre Dame universities.

who bequeathed his art inventory to his country. While there has been some controversy about the provenance of some of the works in the collection, the Mimara's vast portfolio still is impressive. Italian, Dutch, and Spanish artists dominate the painting collection, but Renoir and artists from other European schools are also represented. Glass, textiles, and Asian art dominate the ground-floor galleries; sculpture, archaeology, and applied art are in the galleries one flight up; and paintings fill the top floor. The entire collection numbers nearly 4,000 objets d'art, only half of which are on exhibit at any given time. The museum opened in 1987, but displays are surprisingly unsophisticated and the lighting design does not show the collections to advantage. Captions are in Croatian only.

Rooseveltov Trg 5. ℭ **01/482-81-00.** www.mimara.hr. Admission 20kn adults, 15kn children. Tues–Wed and Fri–Sat 10am–5pm; Thurs 10am–7pm; Sun 10am–2pm.

The Museum for Arts and Crafts ★★   The building housing the 160,000 exhibits that chronicle Croatian culture is all German Renaissance. Inside, the exhibits of furniture, textiles, photographs, sculptures, and other vestiges of traditional Croatian life are well done with legends, videos, and computer illustrations.

Trg Maršala Tita 10. ℭ **01/482-69-22.** www.muo.hr. Admission 15kn Tues–Fri 10am–6pm; Sat 10am–1pm.

ZAGREB

10

WHAT TO SEE & DO

Strossmayer Gallery of Old Masters ★★   A huge sculpture of Bishop Josip Juraj Strossmayer dominates the park in front of the academy he founded in 1860 in the middle section of Zrinevac as the Yugoslav Academy of Arts and Sciences. The school occupies the building's ground floor and the gallery is spread out over the rest. Strossmayer began collecting art when he became bishop of Đakovo. He secured funds to build the beige, 19th-century building off Strossmayer Trg, where the gallery opened in 1884 to house his (mostly) religious art. Today it is also home to the fabled **Baška Tablet** ★, which is the oldest known example of Glagolitic script in existence and perhaps Croatia's most important artifact. The tablet is displayed under glass in the ground-floor lobby without any conspicuous sign or fanfare. Entry to the gallery is on the third floor of the building, though no signs direct you there. Fewer than 300 items from the Strossmayer's 4,000-item inventory are displayed at any given time. They include 14th- to 19th-century works from Italian and other European masters.

Trg Nikole Šubića Zrinskog 11. 🕾 **01/489-51-17.** www.mdc.hr/strossmayer. Admission 10kn adults, 5kn children. Wed–Sun 10am–1pm; Tues 10am–1pm and 5–7pm.

Zagreb Archaeological Museum ★   A mixture of Greek, Macedonian, and Croatian artifacts fills glass cases throughout this monument to prehistoric times, but it is the mummies and funerary exhibits that draw the most oohs and ahs. Skeletal remains and the Bronze Age baubles they wore at interment are exhibited as they would have looked in situ. There is no museum map or audioguide available, but occasional English-language histories and titles are available in each exhibition room. The highlight of the collection is the "Zagreb mummy" and its bandages, which are actually a linen book inscribed with Etruscan script.

Trg Nikole Šubića Zrinskog 19. 🕾 **01/487-31-01.** www.amz.hr. Admission 20kn adults, 10kn children and retirees, 30kn family. Tues–Fri 10am–5pm; Sat–Sun 10am–1pm. 100kn English-speaking guide.

Farther Afield

Bundek Park ★★ (**Kids**)   After decades of neglect, a renovated Bundek Park in Novi Zagreb reopened to the public in 2007. The park's gravel-beach lakes, bike paths, gardens, and children's playground all were redone and the result is a serene urban green space that attracts families, joggers, and events such as flower and art shows. Bundek's transformation from overgrown eyesore to city showplace is just the first phase of "Zagreb on the Sava," the city's initiative to develop the banks of the Sava River for recreation and tourism. Bundek is less than a block from the city's new Museum of

---

Rolling Through Zagreb

Take a guided walking tour of the city without the walking on a personal transporter. Segway City Tours offers four itineraries that last from 50 minutes to 2 hours. Choose from a the beginners tour, which includes instruction on how to drive your two-wheeled Segway around the Lenuci Horseshoe (210kn/50 min.), a tour of the lower and upper towns and historical sites by day (350kn/2 hr.) or by night (370kn/90 min.), or a custom tour of the things you want to see most (300kn/70 min.). Meeting place is the Hotel Regent Esplanade. Tours run March 1 to November 30 and December 23 and 26 to 30. Contact 🕾 **01/301-03-90** or www.SegwayCityTourZagreb.com for more information.

(Fun Facts) **Heart of the Matter**

The shiny red hearts on display in nearly every Zagreb souvenir shop are actually *licitar*, honey-dough similar to gingerbread that is shaped in wooden molds, hardened, coated with edible red lacquer, and decorated with flowers, swirls, and other trim. Young men traditionally gave the colorful hearts to their girlfriends as an expression of love. Today, the decorated cookies still are given as a sign of affection, but they also are given as special-occasion gifts or as remembrances. Personalized hearts sometimes are used as wedding favors, toys, and Christmas ornaments. Most recently, they have been used as hospitality tokens by some bureaus of Croatia's tourism board. The hearts have even been immortalized in a ballet, "Licitarsko Srce" ("Gingerbread Hearts"), by Croatian composer Krešimir Baranović. Today, licitar is made in many shapes besides hearts and rarely eaten, but rather saved or displayed as instantly recognizable symbols of Croatia.

Contemporary Art on Avenija Dubrovnik and across from the Zagreb Fairgrounds. The new museum building was not yet finished as we went to print.

Free admission.

Jarun Lake ★★★   This man-made lake 4km (2½ miles) southwest of the center has something for everyone. There are cafes, bars, a white-tablecloth restaurant, a nude beach, sailing, jogging, bike paths, and much more. The beaches are pebble and the lakes are fed by the Sava and have pebble bottoms. In the summer, the city's bars and discos set up shop at Jarun and go well into the night, making it seem like Bourbon Street on the beach. You can get to the lake on tram no. 17 from Jelačić Square and exit at Jarun. *Tip:* You can rent bikes at Jarun's entrance for 20kn per hour.

Entrance to Jarun is free, but there is a 15kn fee for 24 hr. of parking.

Maksimir Park ★★ (Kids)   This lush green oasis about 3.2km (2 miles) east of the center is Zagreb's biggest park and popular among families, dog walkers, and couples going for a stroll. Opened in the late 18th century, it has five lakes and a cafe, and it houses the **Zagreb City Zoo** ★. The park is easily accessible via tram (no. 11 or 12 from Trg Jelačić) and it's free (except for the zoo). Exit the tram at the Bukovacka stop, which is steps from the entrance.

Maksimirirski Perivoj bb. (℃) **01/230-21-98.** Zoo: www.zoo.hr. Admission 20kn ages 7 and up, 10kn children 6 and under, free for everyone on Mon. Daily summer 9am–8pm; winter 9am–4pm.

Mirogoj Cemetery ★★★   Think of Mirogoj as an open-air museum splashed with heavy doses of history and art. Many of Croatia's heroes and common folk are buried here, but this is no Arlington or Shady Lawn. Mirogoj is another Herman Bollé creation, and as such it is a fascinating mix of architecture that includes soaring domes; a neo-Renaissance arcade; and trees, flowers, and gravestones in a riot of shapes, sizes, and colors, all enclosed by a protective wall. Even a short walk-through reveals that this is truly an egalitarian burial place: Christian crosses, Jewish stars, socialist five-pointed stars, and slender five-sided Muslim headstones, mark the resting places of people of all faiths

Zagreb Shopping Malls

Croatians love to shop, and large, Western-style malls are springing up all over Zagreb. Avenue Mall at Avenija Dubrovnik 16 is Zagreb's newest shopping mecca. It's a mix of upscale and moderately priced stores with several coffee bars and dining spots sprinkled in. **Kaptol Center** on Nova Ves in Gornji Grad houses upscale retailers; a multiplex cinema; and an excellent assortment of cafes, restaurants, and bars. **Importanne** runs two malls, one under the park across the street from the main train station, and another at Iblerov Trg just west of the city center. **Branimir Center** on Branimir just east of the train station also has a multiplex plus several decent restaurants, in addition to shops and the Arcotel Allegra Hotel. **King Cross** at Jankomir and City Center southwest of Zagreb are the closest things to an American mall. Each has nearly 100 stores that include brand-name retailers like Benetton, Sisley, and Esprit, plus electronics, sporting goods, and home stores. There are also lots of cafes and a couple of huge supermarkets there. *Tip:* King Cross Mall doesn't open until 2pm on Monday. It opens at 9am Tuesday to Saturday and stays open until 9pm Sunday.

and nationalities. Don't miss President Franjo Tuđjman's tomb, a massive block of black granite perpetually covered with tribute bouquets. To get to Mirogoj, take the no. 106 bus from Kaptol opposite the cathedral for 8kn or the no. 14 tram from Jelačić Square toward Mihaljevac, and exit at the fourth stop.

Mirogoj bb, about 2.4km (1¹/₂ miles) northeast of the city center. Daily 8am–8pm.

Mount Medvednica ★★★ Skiing, hiking, biking—you can do it all on "Bear Mountain" north of the city. There are several cafes, as well as ski rental shops and warming huts. You can even explore the **medieval fortress of Medvedgrad ★★**. By car, the top, Sljeme, is a 20-minute drive from Zagreb's center; and though the uphill turns are rather steep, you don't have to worry about oncoming traffic because the road up is one-way, as is the road down. Be sure you take the correct road down to Zagreb: There is a second route that goes to the other side of the mountain and ends up in the Zagorje region. You can't go wrong by taking the cable car to the top and back.

Cable car: ☏ **01/458-03-94.** www.zet.hr. 11kn up; 17kn down. Daily 8am–8pm. Leaves on the hr. daily.

Organized Tours

There isn't any compelling reason to take a formal tour of Zagreb because almost everything worth seeing is within walking distance of the main square or a short tram or bus ride away. However, if you want to inject some whimsy into your sightseeing, try one of the city's 2-hour-long costumed walking tours. A guide dressed as a famous person from Zagreb history will show you around and perhaps throw in a few little-known facts about the city and its sites. You can buy tickets at the Tourist Information Center on Jelačić Square.

Andrijevićeva 12. ☏ **01/370-35-53** or 01/370-30-88. www.event.hr. 95kn per person. Tours leave from the Tourist Information Center on the square daily at 10am and 4pm.

Exploring Zagreb with children in tow can be challenging on a number of fronts. Ushering little ones across the open tram tracks, up and down steep cobbled streets, and through churches and museums that appeal mainly to interested adults and large groups of students can put a strain on parents and kids alike. Most of Zagreb's hotels and sights don't have any special extras for kids, though most offer a rate reduction for the younger set. Unlike hotels in Croatia's resort towns, Zagreb hotels have no all-day programs to keep younger kids amused, and no special facilities like arcades or Internet rooms for older ones. Very few restaurants have children's menus or highchairs, though most will do what they can for customers with children.

Some of the best bets for keeping kids amused in Zagreb are **Maksimir Park** and the **Zagreb City Zoo** (p. 285). There are a couple of playgrounds with equipment in Maksimir, so kids can let off a little steam before heading back to the hotel. **Bundek Park** (p. 284) is a draw because of its river-fed lakes and a rather elaborate playground set up for kids. **Jarun Lake** (p. 285) south of the center is another option. Besides a beach, Jarun has paddle boats, playground equipment, and often some sports competitions like beach volleyball to keep kids entertained. Children might also enjoy **Zagreb's cinemas.** Most run American movies with English soundtracks and Croatian subtitles, so kids won't have any trouble understanding what's going on.

3 WHERE TO STAY

There are few moderately priced or bargain hotels in Zagreb. In fact, unless you go with private accommodations, most options are at the extreme ends of the price and quality curve. However, special rates at the better hotels are sometimes available on weekends, over the Internet, or for multiday stays, but you have to ask. No matter where you stay, you will find clean, adequate rooms with private bathrooms; but except for top-end hotels, Zagreb accommodations are usually bland. Hotel rates in the city usually are not subject to seasonal changes or cash discounts, and most hotels include breakfast.

VERY EXPENSIVE

Sheraton Zagreb ★★★ The glass-and-metal front of this hotel not far from the train station makes it easy to spot among Zagreb's vintage architecture. With 306 air-conditioned rooms and suites furnished in tasteful shades of apricot, the Sheraton Zagreb reflects Croatia's shift from socialist drab to capitalist chic. Guest rooms and public spaces are bright and airy, and all bathrooms are generously endowed with bathtubs and a selection of toiletries. Most hotel services are available 24/7 and the Fontana Restaurant staff is remarkably adept and knowledgeable. There isn't a thing hotel management hasn't thought of, and everything in the Sheraton Zagreb is superbly executed.

Kneza Borne 2, 10000 Zagreb. ⓒ **01/455-35-35.** Fax 01/455-30-35. www.sheraton.com/zagreb. 306 units. From 235€ double; from 385€ suite. AE, DC, MC, V. **Amenities:** 2 restaurants; pastry cafe; piano bar; casino; concierge; pool; room service; sauna; smoke-free rooms; valet service; rooms for those w/limited mobility. *In room:* A/C, TV, hair dryer, Internet access, minibar.

Westin Zagreb ★★ (Overrated) The former Opera Hotel has gone through several ownership changes in the last few years and is now positioned as a luxury property by its Starwood parent. Situated across the street from the Mimara Museum and its trove of objets d'art, it is too bad the Westin's rooms and amenities are so hotel-generic. Guests checking into a basic room (without breakfast) are offered the chain's Heavenly brand toiletries, bed, and other amenities. However, the room and bathroom are cramped and free of anything that would remind you that you are in Croatia. The Westin has everything you might expect at this level, but the overall impression is "impersonal chain." In addition, some amenities fall short: In-room Internet access is via dial-up and very expensive, but there is free Wi-Fi in the business center. The property itself is well run and staff members seem well trained in guest services. If you need a place for a night that has a full menu of on-site amenities, the Westin is fine, but if you want a place with a little charm and flavor of its home city, there are more convenient, less expensive choices in the city.

Kršnjavoga 1, 10000 Zagreb. ℂ **01/489-20-00.** Fax 01/489-20-02. www.westin.com/Zagreb. 377 units. From 270€ double; from 370€ suite. AE, DC, MC, V. Pets welcome with advance registration. **Amenities:** 2 restaurants; cafe; bar; smoke-free rooms; valet service. *In room:* A/C, TV, hair dryer, minibar.

EXPENSIVE

Arcotel Allegra ★ (Overrated)   The Branimir Center encompasses not only the Allegra, but a multiplex cinema, offices, a fitness studio, and conference rooms. Everything hotel guests need is convenient, which is de rigueur for a hotel in Allegra's price range. But at the Allegra, the little nickel-and-dime things detract, as does the "so-what" attitude of the staff. For example, the hotel's **Radicchio** restaurant (see review below) advertises free parking for patrons, but hotel guests have to pay. The Allegra also advertises wireless connection, but it works only at Joe's Bar in the lobby and to use it, you have to go to the tobacconist next door to buy a code card. Oddly, all hotel signs and instructions are in English and German only, no Croatian. Guest rooms look like Ikea ads with minimalist light-oak furniture, kitschy spreads, and curtains printed with the faces of famous celebrities. Bathrooms are designed for economy and fitted with one-soap-fits-all dispensers in the tub and at the sink; towels feel a bit like sandpaper. If you have kids, note that each room features a prominently displayed ad card (with explicit illustrations) that offers a selection of adult films.

Branimirova 29, 10000 Zagreb. ℂ **01/469-60-00.** Fax 01/469-60-96. www.arcotel.at/allegra.htm. 151 units. From 155€ double; from 250€ suite. AE, DC, MC, V. Parking garage 20kn per day. **Amenities:** Restaurant; bar; free lobby Internet (1 terminal); room service; sauna. *In room:* A/C, TV/DVD player, hair dryer, minibar.

Best Western Astoria ★★   This formerly frayed but now fabulous hotel is situated midway between the train station and Trg Jelačić and is one of the most underrated accommodations in Zagreb. Guest rooms are loaded with modern amenities like heated bathroom floors and French toiletries. Public spaces have a spiffy, polished look, and service is friendly and efficient.

Petrinjska Ulica 71, 10000 Zagreb. ℂ **01/484-12-22.** www.bestwestern.com. 102 units. From 185€ double; from 300€ suite. AE, DC, MC, V. Rates include breakfast. **Amenities:** Restaurant; Internet; smoke-free rooms; rooms for those w/limited mobility. *In room:* A/C, TV, minibar.

(Fun Facts)   Historical Canopy

The huge, stately birch trees that flank Trg Šubića Zrinjskog on the Green Horseshoe were given to the city of Zagreb by the city of Trieste, Italy, 140 years ago.

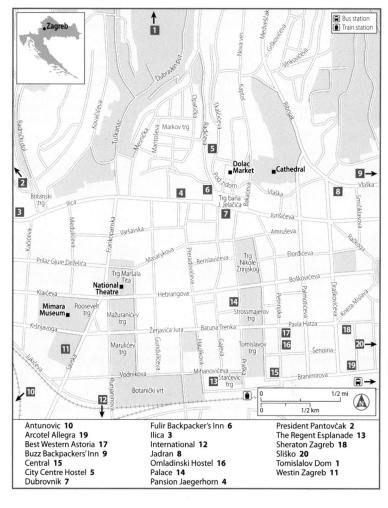

Antunovic **10**
Arcotel Allegra **19**
Best Western Astoria **17**
Buzz Backpackers' Inn **9**
Central **15**
City Centre Hostel **5**
Dubrovnik **7**

Fulir Backpacker's Inn **6**
Ilica **3**
International **12**
Jadran **8**
Omladinski Hostel **16**
Palace **14**
Pansion Jaegerhorn **4**

President Pantovčak **2**
The Regent Esplanade **13**
Sheraton Zagreb **18**
Sliško **20**
Tomislalov Dom **1**
Westin Zagreb **11**

ZAGREB

10

WHERE TO STAY

Hotel Antunovic ★★ This hotel made a splashy entrance to the city's expanding lodging scene when it opened in 2006, and it has been getting better with age. From sumptuous guest rooms, to a Zen-inspired spa to a glass-domed cocktail lounge that offers patrons a spectacular city panorama, the Antunovic has raised the bar for creature comforts in Zagreb hotels. Guest rooms and public spaces are glass-and-steel works of art softened by lots of warm-toned wood. The comfort level is jazzed up with flatscreen TVs, free wireless access everywhere, and strategically placed artwork. Bathrooms are generously endowed with gleaming fixtures, spacious tub-showers, a wide array of toiletries, and showerside phones. For a special treat, book one of the hotel's nine suites: The

Presidential suite has a lavish entertainment area, a powder room, and caterer's staging area, but even the junior suites are well appointed. All suites are in the hotel's glass tower, which makes for dramatic floor plans and views. Antunovic seems to have thought of everything—in-house shopping mall, bank, casino, and on-premises gas station. The only drawback is its location, which is about 6km (3½ miles) from Zagreb's center and 15km (9 miles) from Pleso Airport. To see the city's Old Town, you'll have to catch a cab or bus, which stops 300m (600 ft.) from the front door and requires at least one transfer.

Zagrebačka Avenija 100A, Zagreb. ② **01/204-1-121.** Fax 01/20-41-119. www.hotelantunovic.com. 149 units. Doubles from 187€; suites from 375€. Rates include buffet breakfast, Internet, use of spa facilities. AE, DC, MC, V. **Amenities:** Restaurant; cafeteria; ice cream/pastry cafe; pizzeria; rooftop bar; casino; concierge; pool; room service; sauna; smoke-free rooms; valet service; rooms for those w/limited mobility. *In room:* AC, TV, hair dryer, Internet access, minibar.

Hotel Dubrovnik ★★ "Rms w/vu" should be the motto of this modern-looking glass-and-metal tower off Trg Jelačić where many of the hotel's comfortable rooms look directly down on the Croatian hero's statue in the main square. Opened in 1929 as the Hotel Milinov, the hotel changed its name to Dubrovnik, added more than 150 rooms in a glass-and-aluminum wing in 1982, and completed a total renovation in 2003 to make rooms in the old and new sections equally plush and modern. The hotel is well equipped to handle the needs of business travelers and tourists alike, convenient to just about everything in Zagreb, and staffed with an exceptionally helpful group of people. The Presidential suite (240€) is an eye-popper and includes a rooftop terrace. The indoor tables of the hotel's **Piccolo Mondo** (see below) and outdoor tables of the hotel's ground-floor **Dubrovnik Kavana** comprise a "see and be seen" center of the city, especially on Saturday mornings.

Gajeva 1. P.P. 246, 10000 Zagreb. ② **01/487-35-55.** Fax 01/486-35-06. www.hotel-dubrovnik.hr. 280 units. From 160€ double; from 225€ suite. Rates include breakfast. Special 9-hr. "daily rest" rate 50% the regular room rate. AE, DC, MC, V. Limited free parking. **Amenities:** Restaurant; cafe; bar; room service; smoke-free rooms; valet; rooms for those w/limited mobility. *In room:* A/C, TV, hair dryer, Internet access, minibar.

Palace ★★ Across the street from the Strossmayer Gallery and a section of Zagreb's Green Horseshoe, the Palace is just 5 minutes from Trg Jelačić. The Secessionist-style hotel was built as a private palace in 1891 and converted to a hotel in 1907, which makes it the oldest hotel in the city. So if you're looking for a comfortable, convenient place to stay that has character and a bit of history, then the Palace is the place for you. The restaurant has the ambience of a Viennese tearoom and guest rooms are in tune with the hotel's 19th-century charm. All but 30 of the 123 units have been updated for modern guests. *Tip:* Wi-Fi access is free in guest rooms, but dial-up can be quite costly.

Trg JJ Strossmayera 10, 10000 Zagreb. ② **01/481-46-11,** or 01/492-05-30 reservations. Fax 01/481-13-58. www.palace.hr. 123 units. From 170€ double; from 230€ junior suite; from 315€ suite. 20% discount on weekends. Rates include breakfast. AE, DC, MC, V. Limited free parking. Pets welcome at 15€ per day. **Amenities:** Restaurant; bar; babysitting; room service; smoke-free rooms. *In room:* A/C, TV, hair dryer, Internet, minibar.

The Regent Esplanade ★★★ Nixon slept here. So did Pierce Brosnan, Elizabeth Taylor, and a host of other notables. The elegant Esplanade has attracted well-heeled guests since its opening in 1925, but a painstaking renovation has seamlessly added New World creature comforts to the historic hotel's old-world opulence. Add to that service that is second to none, and the result is one of the most beautiful and best-run hotels in

Croatia. Guests are checked in over a glass of bubbly in the black-and-white marble lobby before being whisked to their richly appointed rooms where fresh fruit, chocolates, and complimentary wireless connections are waiting for them. Amenities are first class and augmented with little luxuries such as fresh flowers, twice-a-day housekeeping, and cushy slippers ideal for padding around on the bathroom's heated marble floor. Liberal use of wood and brass in both private and public areas, a chic modern Croatian restaurant, **Zinfandel** (reviewed below), as well as the modern, French **LeBistro** (also reviewed below), a selection of spa services, and a staff ready to fulfill every need have brought back the landmark hotel's glory days as an indulgent interlude for well-heeled travelers on the Orient Express. This is how it feels to sit in the lap of luxury. *Tip:* The Esplanade offers a menu of scented baths, ranging from a tub full of herbs and oils to a chocolate bath for kids. Staff members draw the bath upon request.

Mihanovićeva 1, 10000 Zagreb. ℭ **800/545-4000** in the U.S., or 01/456-66-66. Fax 01/45-60-50. www. regenthotels.com. 209 units. From 142€ double; from 300€ suite. AE, DC, MC, V. Pets welcome (20€ per day). **Amenities:** 2 restaurants; terrace dining w/live music; bar; casino; club floor; concierge; room service; sauna; smoke-free rooms; 2 rooms for those w/limited mobility; valet service. *In room:* A/C, TV w/pay movies, hair dryer, Internet access, minibar.

MODERATE

Central ★ The Central's location across the street from Zagreb's main train station is a double-edged sword. On one hand, it's convenient to transportation; and on the other, rooms facing the street where trams rumble by day and night can be noisy, so you have to choose between a view and quiet. The quality of the Central's rooms' decor is Wal-Mart, but they are outfitted with a decent number of amenities. Most rooms have showers rather than tubs; some have minibars. The lower-level dining room is bright and cheery. Room prices are moderate rather than bargain-priced (for Zagreb), but you're paying for location.

Branimirova 3, PP 97, 10000 Zagreb. ℭ **01/484-11-22.** Fax 01/484-13-04. www.hotel-central.hr. 76 units. From 900kn double; from 1,400kn suite. AE, DC, MC, V. Rates include breakfast. **Amenities:** Restaurant (breakfast only); adjacent casino. *In room:* A/C, TV, hair dryer, Internet connection.

Hotel President Pantovčak ★★ Christmas 2008 was opening day for this boutique hotel in a private park above Britanski Trg near the epicenter of Zagreb's diplomatic community. Chic Euro design, a restaurant exclusively for guests and their friends, lots of original artwork and global antiques, bathrooms with Jacuzzis, and state-of-the-art electronics make the President Pantovčak a magnet for visiting dignitaries who like creature comforts and their privacy.

Pantovčak 52. ℭ **01/488-14-80.** Fax 01/482-34-75. www.president-zagreb.com. 7 units. Doubles from 109€; junior presidential suite 240€. Breakfast is 15€ per person. Parking (25€ per day). **Amenities:** Restaurant; bar. *In room:* A/C, TV, hair dryer, Internet connection, minibar.

Ilica ★ The Ilica is set back from the far end of Zagreb's main shopping street. It is also priced lower than almost all other hotels in the central city. Guest rooms are simple and adequate, but the suites are over-the-top kitsch that incorporates a lot of gilt and plastic. The staff is polite but reluctant to go beyond niceties without the boss present: The desk clerk refused to reveal the number of rooms in the hotel because his superior was out of the building. The no. 6 tram stops in front of the hotel entrance, and Britanski Trg and its Sunday antiques market are steps away, which makes the Ilica a convenient base for exploring the city.

Ilica 102, 10000 Zagreb. ℭ **01/377-76-22.** Fax 01/377-77-22. www.hotel-ilica.hr. 24 units, including 1 apt. From 68€ double; from 109€ suite and apt. Rates include breakfast. AE, DC, MC, V. Parking 8€ per day. **Amenities:** Restaurant; smoke-free rooms; rooms for those w/limited mobility. *In room:* A/C, TV.

International ★   The shiny glass and steel International soars above the sprawling new business area 3km (2 miles) south of Zagreb's center and the building's new, sleek look belies its plain Jane beginnings as a Socialist tower hotel. The International is outfitted for business, especially the kind done by corporate types. Rooms are serviceable and nicely redone, but the only character that leaks through is that of the place's Socialist roots. Guest rooms are neatly decorated in hotel-bland, but they are equipped with free wireless, coffeemakers, and tubs in the bathrooms. You could do worse.

Miramarska 24. ✆ **01/610-81-00.** www.hotel-international.hr. 270 units. Doubles from 900kn; suites from 1,800kn. AE, DC, MC, V. **Amenities:** Restaurant; bar. *In room:* A/C, TV, minibar, Wi-Fi.

Jadran ★   The Jadran is a pleasant, affordable choice just 5 minutes from the city center. Decor in guest rooms and public areas has been turned up a notch, and both are reasonably modern, though the rooms are not exactly spacious. The Jadran's main advantages are its location and easy access to public transportation.

Vlaška 50, 10000 Zagreb. ✆ **01/455-37-77.** Fax 01/461-21-51. www.hup-zagreb.hr. 48 units. From 98€ double. AE, DC, MC, V. Rates stay the same all year and include breakfast. Limited free parking. **Amenities:** Restaurant. *In room:* A/C, TV, hair dryer.

Pansion Jaegerhorn ★   Jaegerhorn gets points for its convenient location off Ilica, but demerits for being luggage-unfriendly. Getting bags to your room can be difficult: You have to drag them through a mall courtyard mall and up a lot of stairs just to get to the lobby. Jaegerhorn was renovated in 1997, but rates are steep for what amounts to a small air-conditioned space furnished in army-surplus basics and a bed, shower, and TV. If your objective is to roll out of bed and into the action, this is the place for you. Jaegerhorn is .5km (¼ mile) from the main square and opens onto Zagreb's main shopping street.

Ilica 14, 10000 Zagreb. ✆ **01/483-38-77.** Fax 01/483-35-73. www.hotel-pansion-jaegerhorn.hr. 11 units. From 705kn double; from 913kn suite. Rates include breakfast. AE, DC, MC, V. Limited free parking. **Amenities:** Restaurant; terrace; bar. *In room:* A/C, TV.

Sliško ★ (Value)   Located in back of the main bus station, the Sliško Hotel is a solid no-frills hotel a little off the beaten path. Opened in the mid-1990s, the Sliško has just enough amenities to make it comfortable and a pricing scale to prevent wallet welts, too. Rooms are furnished in utilitarian modern and some are small, but all are clean and affordable. Besides its proximity to the bus station, the hotel is an easy 10-minute walk from the main train station. Rooms are priced according to the number of beds used.

Supilova 13, 10000 Zagreb. ✆ **01/619-42-23.** Fax 01/619-42-10. www.slisko.hr. 18 units. From 531kn double; from 776kn suite (4 beds). AE, DC, MC, V. 10% discount for cash. Rates include breakfast. **Amenities:** Restaurant; bar. *In room:* A/C, TV.

Tomislavov Dom ★★   You can't get any better view of Zagreb than from this property set on a rise among trees near the top of Zagreb's Sljeme peak on Mount Medvednica. In the summer it's an idyllic place to return to after a walk in the forest; in the winter, you can't get much closer to the slopes than the Tomislavov. After a 2006 renovation, most guest rooms have a view and simple but modern furniture and bathrooms with showers only. Tomislavov is just a couple of tram rides or a 20-minute drive from the center of town, but compared to most city commutes to the 'burbs, that's nothing.

Sljeme bb, 10000 Zagreb. ✆ **01/456-04-00.** Fax 01/456-04-01. 41 units. From 101€ deluxe double. Rates include breakfast, VAT, and lift tickets during ski season. AE, DC, MC, V. **Amenities:** Restaurant; bar; pool; sauna; solarium; rooms for those w/limited mobility. *In room:* TV, hair dryer, Internet connection, minibar.

Buzz Backpackers ★★ (Finds) Buzz opened in 2008 in the center of Zagreb and it has been a popular addition to the market. Unlike most hostels, which pack guests together in big group-stay rooms, Buzz offers both limited-occupancy dorm-style and private rooms, some of which have balconies. Rates include linens and shelf with reading light for each bed. Take tram no. 9 to Heinzelova.

Babukićeva 1B. 🕐 **01/232-02-67**. www.buzzbackpackers.com. 30 beds. 17€ per bed in 7-bed rooms; 20€ per bed in twin rooms; 46€ per private 2-bed room; 56€ per double-bed private room. MC, V. **Amenities:** Lounge w/plasma TV; computer/Internet; full kitchen; barbecue area; washer/dryer. *In room:* A/C.

Fulir Backpackers' Inn ★ (Value) A couple of large, brightly painted second-floor rooms make up the entirety of the Fulir, but this hostel just off Trg Jelačić is loaded with personality. Its founders are college friends who opened Fulir in 2006 to mimic the kinds of places they like to stay in when they travel. It's clean, safe (someone is always on duty), affordable, and centrally located. The owners explained that Fulir once was owned by one of their grandmothers and that it is in a historic building. There is a kitchen for guests' use and lockers where they can keep their valuables when they are out and about. There is no age limit for guests, and Fulir's doors are open from 8am to 10pm. If you need to leave early or get back late, you can notify the person on duty to let you out or in.

Radiceva 3A. 🕐 **01/483-08-82** or 098/193-05-52. www.fulir-hostel.com or www.myspace.com/fulir hostel. 34 beds. From 16€ per person. **Amenities:** Kitchen; TV room; lockers; bike storage.

Omladinski Hostel ★ The lobby has a cheerful air thanks to a 2008 renovation that replaced all hostel beds and redid all the bathrooms. The Omladinski is one of the few bargain accommodations in Zagreb and even though its amenities are bare bones, it should not be overlooked. Accommodations range from six-bed, dorm-style rooms with shared bathrooms to singles with private bathrooms. There is a computer with Internet access and an ATM in the lobby. The Omladinski is only a 5-minute walk from either the city center or the train station, and the price is right. A satellite hostel opened in July 2009 around the corner at Palmotićeva 59. *Warning:* No one at the Palmotićeva address was able to speak a word of English when we visited.

Petrinjska 77, 10000 Zagreb. 🕐 **01/484-12-61**. Fax 01/484-12-69. www.hfhs.hr. 210 beds. 120kn per person per night except for the 2 rooms with private bathrooms (275kn). Rates include taxes. DC, MC, V. Check-in is 2pm; checkout is 9pm.

Omladinski Hotel Remetinec ★ (Value) This addition to Zagreb's hostel lineup is relatively upscale, but it's in Novi Zagreb, away from most of the action. Each room has a shower and toilet and can accommodate up to three people, though pricing is per person. The Remetinec has a cafeteria, a restaurant, Internet access, and even a meeting room. The Remetinec is run by a Croatian youth organization.

Remetinečki gaj 28. 🕐 **01/614-00-42**. Fax 01/614-00-39. www.nazor.hr. 117 units. From 31€ per bed. DC, MC, V. Free parking. **Amenities:** Restaurant; cafeteria.

PRIVATE ACCOMMODATIONS

City Centre Hostel, at Tkalčićeva 37 (🕐 **01/481-85-42;** no fees for bookings), is an agency that books budget apartments, rooms, hotels, and hostels.

   Evistas ★★, at Šenoina 28 (🕐 **01/483-95-54;** evistas@zg.htnet.hr; Mon–Fri 9am– 1:30pm and 3–8pm, Sat 9:30am–5pm, closed Sun), is low on profile but high on service. Evistas specializes in finding private apartments and *sobes* (rooms) in private homes for frugal travelers staying in Zagreb. It also locates and books city youth hostels, rooms on the coast, and suites in posh hotels if that's your fancy. A couple from Albuquerque waiting in the office for a taxi couldn't hold back their effusive, unsolicited endorsement. "They let us store our luggage here and even found us a place in Dubrovnik. They were an enormous help."

4 WHERE TO DINE

Some say that eating is a Croatian sport and Zagreb is full of places to train. Until recently, the range of cuisine choices in Zagreb was narrow because most restaurants offered nearly identical bills of fare heavy with grilled meat and fish, Italian pastas and risottos, and a few traditional Croatian dishes. That has changed dramatically in the last 3 years as young chefs with a locavore bent create culinary excitement by interpreting traditional recipes with a refined touch. Pizzerias still are the most common types of casual dining spots around the city, and Croatian pizza is remarkably good and inexpensive, but restaurants offering a wide range of ethnic cuisines (Thai, Istrian, Bosnian, Tapas, Mexican, Middle Eastern) are making inroads. These days bar snacks can be as exotic as sea urchin or as familiar as chips. Fast food tends to be pizza by the slice, meat-and cheese-filled *burek* (think phyllo "Hot Pockets") or baguette sandwiches. For sweets, the city's ubiquitous cafes and *slastičarnicas* (ice-cream/pastry shops) provide indulgent treats in a dizzying array of types and flavors.

VERY EXPENSIVE

Marcellino ★★ INTERNATIONAL   Near the top of Jurjevska Street, which is home to embassies and diplomats, Marcellino turns out a portfolio of United Nations cuisines. Try venison with chestnuts, blueberries, and wine sauce or shrimp with orange-olive sauce. Bus no. 105 stops in front of the restaurant. Be sure to ask for a table near the windows: In warm weather they open out into a forest that turns into a beautifully lighted woodland at night. *Tip:* Marcellino recently opened the Hugo dining room, which serves Japanese tempura, Moroccan tagines, Italian pastas, and other international favorites.

Jurjevska 65a. ✆ **01/467-71-11.** Fax 01/467-74-44. www.marcellino.hr. Entrees 45kn–180kn. AE, MC, V. Mon–Sat noon–midnight. Closed Sun.

Paviljon ★★ TRADITIONAL CROATIAN   Paviljon's setting on the Green Horse-shoe flanked by some of Zagreb's best museums gives the restaurant a cultured aura, and its formality and old school decor give it the patina of class. The terrace looks out over a park area toward the main train station and Tomislav Trg and inside, the dining room is all elegance with a cherrywood floor and a fireplace. However, it is the restaurant's well-executed menu featuring Croatian interpretations of classic dishes that steals the show. Start with gooseliver in Cumberland sauce or smoked tuna carpaccio and follow with roast duck with red cabbage and figs for an unusual taste combination. Wines are on the high end, but when you're serving top Croatian names like Grgić, it's understandable.

Trg Kralja Tomislava 22. ✆ **01/455-40-66.** Fax 01/484-10-73. www.restaurant-paviljon.com. Entrees 65kn–125kn. AE, DC, MC, V. Mon–Sat noon–midnight. Bar 10am–midnight. Closed Sun.

Rossini ★★ ITALIAN   "Upscale" defines Rossini, which caters to a crowd that knows Italian food is more than red sauce and noodles. Risottos are especially good in this

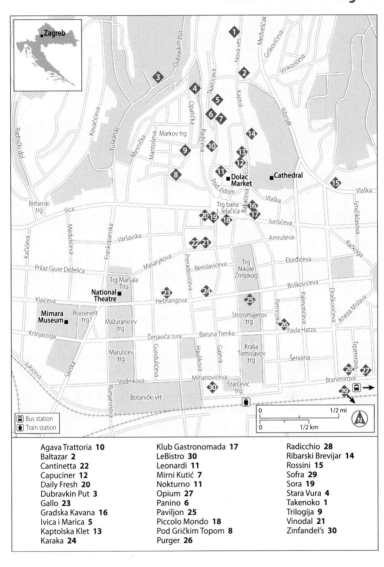

Agava Trattoria **10**	Klub Gastronomada **17**	Radicchio **28**
Baltazar **2**	LeBistro **30**	Ribarski Brevijar **14**
Cantinetta **22**	Leonardi **11**	Rossini **15**
Capuciner **12**	Mirni Kutić **7**	Sofra **29**
Daily Fresh **20**	Nokturno **11**	Sora **19**
Dubravkin Put **3**	Opium **27**	Stara Vura **4**
Gallo **23**	Panino **6**	Takenoko **1**
Gradska Kavana **16**	Paviljon **25**	Trilogija **9**
Ivica i Marica **5**	Piccolo Mondo **18**	Vinodal **21**
Kaptolska Klet **13**	Pod Gričkim Topom **8**	Zinfandel's **30**
Karaka **24**	Purger **26**	

relatively formal dining room; some incorporate asparagus and pancetta, while others blend various kinds of seafood. The wine list is well chosen, but prices seem a little high for Croatia: There aren't any bottles listed under 120kn.

Vlaška 55. ⓒ **01/455-10-60.** Fax 01/455-28-28. Rossini@open.hr. Entrees 60kn–130kn. AE, DC, MC, V. Mon–Fri 11am–midnight; Sat 11am–11pm. Closed Sun.

Sora ★★ SUSHI   Sora means "sky" in Japanese, and considering Sora's wrap-around windows and panoramic views of Zagreb from its perch on the 16th floor of the Ilica Tower in midtown, the name fits. Then there's the food. Try several varieties of Sora's maki and sushi rolls, but don't ignore the beef tenderloin in wasabi sauce or the trout with miso/balsamic glace. Japanese cuisine isn't new to Zagreb, but Sora's inventive interpretation of traditional ingredients and recipes is. **Tip:** Sora opened Sora 2, a summer enterprise, on Hvar Island in 2009.

Ilica 1. ✆ **01/482-89-40.** www.sora.hr. Sushi: 35kn–50kn for 2 pieces; entrees 70kn–280kn. AE, DC, MC, V. 11am–1am Mon–Sat; 1–11pm Sun.

Stara Vura CROATIAN   Entrance to this cute restaurant is in the courtyard that also houses the Zagreb City Museum (p. 281). The menu is typical Croatian with lots of roast meats, but Stara Vura also offers some pastas and game entrees, including boar and deer. The historic courtyard setting is a nice spot for lunch.

Opatička 20. ✆ **01/485-13-68.** www.stara-vura.hr. Entrees 65kn–200kn. AE, DC, MC, V. Mon–Sat noon–midnight. Closed Sun.

Trilogija ★★ MODERN CROATIAN   Restaurants come and go and this food-forward spot next to the Kamenita Vrata (stone gate) is a newcomer that is several steps above Peperocino, which formerly occupied its space. Trilogija's chef likes to interpret old-fashioned Croatian dishes and ingredients through a Mediterranean lens, which makes everyday ingredients like farmer's cheese and pasta interesting. Try the tuna "mojito," tuna flambéed with mint and dark rum and served with spicy vegetable couscous and pear and apple chutney. Like its predecessor, Trilogija pays attention to wine and its list boasts more than 130 choices, 30 by the glass.

Kamenita 5. ✆ **01/485-13-94.** www.trilogija.com. Entrees 65kn–145kn. DC, MC, V. 11am–midnight Mon–Wed, 11am–1am Fri–Sat. Closed Sun.

Zinfandel ★★★ MODERN CROATIAN   By day, diners have a view of the Regent Esplanade's Oleander Terrace through the window-walls of this sophisticated dining room, which is the source of the best breakfast buffet on the planet. A little later, Zinfandel's serves a casual but wonderfully diverse lunch menu. At night, the always exceptional menu has undergone an exquisite update at the hands of Chef Jeffery James Vella. Soft jazz, impeccable service, and fresh flowers provide a sophisticated setting for such appetizers as langoustines with leek flan and asparagus or melon soup with lemon grass and strawberry basil garnish. Such star entrees as veal chop with rosemary and sage or grilled tuna and scallops with lemon-infused pea puree are perfect companions for the breadth and depth of Zinfandel's wine list. For dessert, indulge in the saffron crème brûlée with thyme ice cream and berry brochette.

Mihanovićeva 1. ✆ **01/456-66-66.** www.regenthotels.com. Main courses 125kn–105kn. AE, DC, MC, V. Daily 6–11pm.

EXPENSIVE

Gallo ★★★ ITALIAN   Food is art at this beautiful, unpretentious restaurant behind the facade of an unremarkable building a few blocks from the city center. Homemade pasta in countless shapes and a rainbow of colors dries behind glass near the restaurant entrance. The kitchen, too, is visible behind glass, so diners can watch the chef work his magic. Even the extensive wine cellar is artfully displayed in a corner of the house. The menu is mostly fish with several interesting recipes such as tuna with polenta and red-wine sauce, or beef soup with ravioli. There is a stylish white stone terrace, a cozy casual dining room, and more formal space where crystal and silver set the tone. The waitstaff is congenial and knowledgeable about both the food preparations and complementary wines.

Andrije Hebranga 34. ℂ **01/481-40-14.** Fax 01/481-40-13. www.gallo.castellum.hr. Reservations recommended at dinner. Entrees 60kn–120kn. AE, DC, MC, V. Daily 11:30am–midnight.

Gradska Kavana ★★ CONTINENTAL   When it opened in 1931, Gradska Kavana was an Art Deco coffeehouse and the place to see and be seen in Zagreb. Time and neglect took a toll, but an expensive renovation and a new menu concept have brought this grande dame next to Jelačić Square back to life. Gradska Kavana's dining lineup, including four-, five- and six-course tasting menus, is a perfect complement to the new parquet floors, winding white marble staircase, and black lacquer accents in the dining room. It still is a coffeehouse, too, with a terrace overlooking Jelačić Square and a book-size menu of coffees, juices, cocktails, and other liquid pleasures.

Trg bana Josipa Jelačić 9. ℂ **01/483-23-10.** Fax 01/483-23-13. www.gradskakavana.hr. Dinner reservations recommended. Entrees 60kn–125kn; tasting menu 220kn–280kn. AE, DC, MC, V. Daily 10:30am–11:30pm.

Karaka ★★ SEAFOOD   Anything that lives in the sea is a specialty of this easy-to-miss restaurant named after a medieval sailing ship. Watch for a small, white-sailed sculpture above the doorway of a large dark building on Hebranga. Inside, the nautical theme continues with a decor of sailcloth ceilings and lots of dark wood and fishnets. Preparations are well-seasoned classical Dalmatian, and the menu's fish varieties are based on the day's best available catch. The wine list is respectable.

Andrije Hebranga 12. **01/481-71-50.** Entrees 50kn–150kn. AE, DC, MC, V. Daily noon–11pm. Usually closed first 3 weeks of Aug.

Klub Gastronomada ★★★ (Finds) MODERN CROATIAN   You might be put off by the shabby street-level entrance to this temple of gastronomic creativity that burst onto the Zagreb foodie scene just off Jelačić Square in 2009: Get over it. A singular dining experience awaits on the second floor where chef Gregur Bašic practices sorcery on indigenous Croatian ingredients while co-owner Robert Ripli takes care of the front of the house. The whimsical menu changes often but the emphasis on intense flavors and creative presentation does not. The result is a dining experience that awakens taste buds you didn't know you had. If available, try the pasta triangles filled with snails and nettles topped with spicy tomato sauce and dry curd sheep's milk cheese from Pag. Or sample the color blind soup, a clear tomato broth poured over baked pasta strands, toasted pine nuts, basil, and garlic. Gastronomada's beef is exclusively from Istrian Boškarin cattle and it is aged and marinated, unusual in Croatia. Choose a bottle from the boutique wine list or let Marko match glasses of wine to each course. *Tip:* Save room for the crostada filled with black olive marmalade. It is a taste sensation you won't soon forget.

Jurišićeva 1. ℂ **01/482-02-00.** www.gastronomadi.hr. Entrees 55kn–185kn. DC, MC, V. Noon–midnight Mon–Sat. Closed Sun.

Pod Gričkim Topom ★★★ CROATIAN   Location, location, location is one of the draws at this traditional-style restaurant on the Strossmayerovo Šetalište steps midway between Jelačić Square and Gornji Grad. The atmosphere is intimate and the food superb. Bread and tiny balls of Croatian pâté start the meal, which could be anything from grilled meat to pasta. Try the grilled monkfish, which comes with *blitva,* the Croatian version of chopped spinach; or shrimp risotto, generously laced with juicy, plump pieces of seafood.

Desserts are decadent, but crepes with strawberries and ice cream are just right after the American-size main course. The wine list is loaded with fairly priced Croatian choices.

Zakmardijeve stube 5. ☎ **01/483-36-07.** AE, DC, MC, V. Entrees 65kn–125kn. Daily July–Aug 7am–11pm; 11am–11pm Mon–Sat and 11am–5pm Sun Sept–June.

Radicchio ★ MEDITERRANEAN   Radicchio is a large, modern-looking room that seems a little incongruous for a restaurant in an Austrian hotel (Arcotel Allegra) in the heart of Croatia, but the food here is consistent with Allegra's Mediterranean decor. The menu is just as progressive as the interior, which continues the "famous faces" theme of the Allegra hotel's guest rooms. Try the grilled salmon in port-wine sauce, which is a surprisingly apt pairing. The risotto with pumpkin confit and Marchand de Vin sauce is creamy and complex, and the grilled prawns Provençal conjure visions of olive trees and the sea. However, the view outside the glass wall on the indoor mall is that of shoppers and a perfumery.

In the Arcotel Allegra, Branimirova 29. ☎ **01/469-60-40.** www.arcotel.at/allegra.htm. Entrees 50kn–130kn. Daily 6:30am–3pm and 5:30–10:30pm.

Ribarski Brevijar ★ SEAFOOD   Set back from the street in a courtyard across from the Komedija (Comedy Theater), this restaurant specializes in fish and seafood and offers a large number of choices. Fresh seafood rules, which makes sense because the restaurant is owned by fish merchants. Most preparations are Dalmatian, though there are a few gourmet surprises like scampi soup with saffron. Artisan touches such as house-made bread and pasta add a distinctive flair. The wine list is expensive, though the bottle prices seem a little high. The pleasant terrace is protected from street noise, as is the white-tablecloth dining room. The restaurant is convenient for theatergoers and for those who don't have their own wheels: There is a bus stop outside the entrance.

Kaptol 27. ☎ **01/482-99-99.** Fax 01/482-99-98. Entrees 65kn–100kn or up to 450kn per kilo for lobster. Mon–Sat noon–1am. Closed Sun.

Sofra ★★ BOSNIAN   Sample Bosnian specialties (that aren't entirely unlike Croatian specialties) in this popular restaurant in a residential section of Zagreb. The difference is a touch of Turkish flavor and style that informs the grilled meat and fish dishes. Whatever you order, indulge in Sofra's baklava and Turkish coffee after your meal. *Tip:* It's best to take a taxi to Sofra, which is not at a tram or bus stop.

1.Gardijske brigade Tigrovi 27. ☎ **01/613-10-26.** Entrees 15kn–220kn. AE, DC, MC, V. 9am–midnight Mon–Sat and noon–6pm Sun.

Takenoko ★★★ SUSHI   As beautiful as an origami swan, this restaurant at street level in the Kaptol Center is a no-brainer choice in a city that has access to some of the freshest seafood in Europe. The menu concentrates on sushi and wok preparations and explains the ingredients of each in several languages. There are tables as well as a sushi bar, all done in cool dark wood, wicker, and white cloth upholstery. This is a very sophisticated-looking spot with food to match.

Nova Ves 17. ☎ **01/486-05-30.** Fax 01/486-05-31. Entrees 75kn–100kn. AE, DC, MC, V. Mon–Sat noon–1am; Sun noon–6pm.

MODERATE

Agava ★★ ⓥalue TRATTORIA   Set above Tkalčićeva on a terraced hill, diners at this trendy spot have a bird's-eye view of the action whether they sit on the handsome outdoor deck or in the dining room behind tall glass windows. Agava's food tends to have an Italian influence, but there are some Croatian specialties and salad choices, too. Try

the Coquilles St. Jacques and cashew salad and end with the divine figs and plums in red
wine sauce with vanilla ice cream. *Tip:* There may be RESERVED signs on all the tables.
Don't let that dissuade you. Our waiter quipped that the signs were there "for people who
eat here."

Tkalčićeva 39. ✆ **01/482-98-26.** Entrees 46kn–125kn. AE, DC, MC, V. Daily noon–11pm.

Baltazar ★★ CROATIAN   Grilled meat is the focus of this pleasant dining spot with
a nice terrace, north of the cathedral on Kaptol. It's in what may be the city's trendiest
neighborhood, but the food holds with tradition. This is the place to try Croatian schnitzel and any other national dish you've been curious about. Service is superb.

Nova Ves 4. ✆ **01/466-69-99.** www.morsko-prase.hr. Entrees 55kn–125kn. AE, DC, MC, V. Mon-Sat
noon–midnight. Closed Sun.

Boban ★ ITALIAN   This boisterous cellar restaurant named after a Croatian soccer
star is two flights below the kavana-bar and way below it in noise level. Food is straightforward Italian with a few Croatian-inspired dishes such as venison salami and vegetable-
stuffed pancakes with béchamel. The food here isn't gourmet and you won't be wowed
by creativity either, but the prices won't break your vacation budget. Service can be slow
when all the tables are full—and that's usually all night, every night, as hungry patrons
wander in from nearby Jelačić Square.

Gajeva 9. ✆ **01/481-15-49.** www.boban.hr. Entrees 30kn–80kn. AE, DC, MC, V. Daily 10am–midnight.

Cantinetta ★★ TUSCAN   A warm Tuscan atmosphere envelops patrons who venture into this white-tablecloth spot, and the meal that follows doesn't disappoint. Grilled
anything with an Italian accent is the specialty of the house, so try the calamari or the
ostrich with vegetables and apples. Pastas are cooked to al dente perfection, but there are
very few on the menu. Service is notably professional and friendly, and the chef will
prepare custom dishes if asked.

Nikola Tesle 14. ✆ **01/481-13-15.** Main courses 45kn–120kn. AE, DC, MC, V. Daily 9am–midnight; kitchen
closes at 11pm.

Ivica I Marica ★★ ORGANIC CROATIAN   This kitschy dining spot on busy
Tkalčićeva has introduced a novel concept—Grandma's Croatian preparations made
healthier with whole grains and seasonal local products. The restaurant has lots of wood
and homey touches (servers wear traditional national dress) and what you can see of the
kitchen reveals colorful tole-painted flowers on all the cabinets. The menu at this woodsy
place named after Hansel and Gretel (in Croatian, of course) is no less fascinating. Begin
with whole-grain flatbread accompanied by local fresh cheese or olives and tomatoes. Then
move to *integral sujnudle* (boiled dumplings with hunter sauce or mushroom sauce). Fish
is on the menu, as are moussaka with eggs and soy ham plus four varieties of *štrukli.*

Tkalčićeva 70. ✆ **01/482-89-99.** Fax 098/317-092. ivicaimarica@adriazdravahrana.hr. Entrees 45kn–
125kn. AE, DC, MC, V. Daily noon–11pm.

Kaptolska Klet ★★ TRADITIONAL CROATIAN   A huge array of steaks complements an amazing list of Croatian home recipes such as goulash and roasted lamb or pork
at this attractive spot across from Zagreb's cathedral. There's a menu for dieters (including
ostrich filet) and one for vegetarians, too. The folk-culture ambience on the terrace and
inside seems more touristy than functional, but there's nothing ersatz about the food.

Kaptol 5. ✆ **01/481-48-38.** Fax 01/481-43-30. www.mediacaffe.net/kaptolskaklet. Entrees 35kn–80kn.
AE, DC, MC, V. Daily 11am–11pm.

LeBistro ★★ BISTRO   This glassed-in meet-and-eat place in the Regent Esplanade specializes in classic French preparations such as baked escargot, but there is also a touch of nouveau in simple dishes such as bass with wilted Swiss chard and garlic confit. Le Bistro boasts that it serves the best *zagorski štrukli* (cheese baked in phyllo with cream sauce) in town and even offers a frozen version to take home, but we found the dish rather bland, even with sugar sprinkled on top. Order the crème brûlée with vanilla and ginger stem instead.

In the Regent Esplanade, Mihanovićeva 1. ✆ **01/456-66-66.** www.regenthotels.com. Main courses 40kn–100kn. AE, DC, MC, V. Daily 10am–11pm.

Mirni Kutić ★★ GRILL   Charcoal is what sets Mirni Kutić apart from sister grill restaurants along busy Tkalčićeva Street. Meat and fish are barbecued over the real stuff and pizzas are baked in a stone oven. Mirni Kutić also offers a nice selection of schnitzels and sandwiches.

Tkalčićeva 57. ✆ **01/485-11-63.** Fax 01/485-11-59. Entrees 50kn–165kn. AE, DC, MC, V. Daily 7am–1am.

Opium ★ PAN-ASIAN   Dark as a den, this Asian restaurant/bar is on the lower level of Branimir Center, with tables spilling onto the mall. The menu lists mostly Thai and wok preparations, but there are also teriyaki and curry choices, too. You can't go wrong with Pad Thai, but Phat Wun Sen is more adventurous with glass noodles, seafood, cabbage, eggs, peppers, and onion.

Branimirova 29. ✆ **01/461-56-79.** Fax 01/461-56-80. Entrees 55kn–95kn. AE, DC, MC, V. 11am–midnight Mon–Thurs; 11am–12:30am Fri–Sat; 11am–11:30pm Sun.

Panino ★ MEDITERRANEAN   Panino's menu emphasizes huge, complicated salads, risottos, and pastas, with a few dishes thrown in for meat lovers. Diners get a tasty *amuse bouche* and three kinds of olive oil for bread-dipping in addition to the trendy fare. Try a salad of mixed greens topped with chicken or shrimp and a glass of white wine barrique (oaked) and finish with a plate of fresh fruits and chocolates. *Tip:* There is a 5% discount if you pay for your meal in cash.

Tkalčićeva 43. ✆ **01/209-65-52.** www.panino.hr. Entrees 40kn–100kn. AE, DC, MC, V. Tues–Sun 11am–1am.

Piccolo Mondo ★ ITALIAN   It's kind of a super-storefront restaurant with a street-level view of the action in front of the Hotel Dubrovnik—and there's a lot to see from this attractive dining room. The terrace cafe is always crowded and opens in time for breakfast, but it is the dinner hour that draws the big appetites. Most of the choices are predictable and competently prepared, but there are a few creative surprises served in generous portions. For example, the risotto Bella Casa is a flavorful mix of scampi, tomatoes, wine, cream, cognac, Parmesan and, of course, *al dente arborio,* while *spaghetti aglio e olio ciro* combines anchovies, hot peppers, olive oil, herbs, and Parmesan. There is also a respectable wine list.

In the Hotel Dubrovnik, L. Gaja 1. ✆ **01/481-86-13.** www.hotel-dubrovnik.hr. Entrees 55kn–110kn. AE, DC, MC, V. Daily 6:30am–11pm.

Vinodal ★ TRADITIONAL CROATIAN   Local fare rules at this popular spot in the city center, with grilled meat taking center stage. Try the *janjetina* (lamb), which is grilled to perfection, traditional *sarma* (chopped meat and rice in marinated cabbage), or *vinski gulas* (wine goulash), which is boldly seasoned and melts in your mouth. Diners at Vinodol can enjoy their meals under the stars in the huge outdoor courtyard.

INEXPENSIVE

Capuciner ★ (Value) PIZZA   Endless variations of spaghetti, pizza, and other Italian fare are on the menu at this noisy hangout across the street from the Zagreb Cathedral. Pizza is of the ultrathin-crusted European style, and toppings are mostly fresh ingredients, unless you opt for unusual varieties such as the (untried) Nutella version. Capuciner is a good place to stop if you want a filling meal instead of the coffee/ice cream/beer offerings common in the outdoor cafes in Old Town. The restaurant also has daily blackboard specials for 15kn to 30kn, including a burger made from horsemeat.

Kaptol 6. ℭ **01/481-48-40.** www.capuciner.hr. Entrees including pizza 15kn–60kn. AE, DC, MC, V. Mon–Sat 10am–1am; Sun noon–1am.

Daily Fresh ★ LIGHT FARE   Croatia's version of Panera Bread has five outlets in central Zagreb—off Jelačić Square, at Masarykova 23, at Maksimirska 3, at the Importanne Center, and at Vukovarska 23a. This is the place for espresso and Danish for breakfast and a freshly made salad and deli sandwich for lunch. It is also one of the few places in Croatia where you can get your coffee in a to-go cup.

Frane Petrića 1 at Ilica. ℭ **01/639-71-11.** www.dailyfreshgroup.com. Salads and sandwiches 8kn–50kn. No credit cards. 8am–11pm daily.

Gostionica Purger ★ (Value) TRADITIONAL CROATIAN   It's easy to overlook Purger, a nondescript storefront near the Omladinski Hostel off Zagreb's center, but you shouldn't, especially if you're on a budget. The interior is "cute" but nothing fancy, and the menu is loaded with tantalizing homemade dishes at a fair price.

Petrinjska 33. ℭ **01/481-0713.** Entrees 30kn–92kn. AE, DC, MC, V. Mon–Sat 7am–11pm. Closed Sun.

Nokturno and **Leonardi** ★★ PIZZA   At first glance it's hard to tell where Nokturno ends and its next-door neighbor Leonardi begins. Both are crammed in a space on the side of an alleyway; both have similar menus; and both have the same opening hours. Nokturno is always jammed with patrons, while Leonardi isn't quite so busy, but the pace there is slower, too. Nokturno's pizza attracts crowds with its crispy crust and fresh ingredients. Whichever restaurant you choose, you can't miss.

Nokturno: Skalinska 4. ℭ **01/481-33-94.** Small pizzas 18kn–30kn; other dishes 20kn–45kn. AE, DC, MC, V. Daily 9am–1am.

Leonardi: Skalinska 6. ℭ **01/487-30-05.** Small pizzas 15kn–35kn; other dishes 28kn–65kn. AE, DC, MC, V. Daily 9am–1am.

Pinguin Sandwich Bar ★★★ (Finds) FAST FOOD   Get in line with the locals who mob this tiny made-to-order sandwich shack at all hours. The huge list of sandwiches is entirely in Croatian, but order-takers understand some English, and most sandwiches are illustrated with color photos. Try the Rustico, a tasty combo of mozzarella, pancetta, oregano, olives, tomatoes, herbed mayo, and any of half a dozen condiments between two fresh-made pitalike rectangles of olive bread. American hot dogs and hamburgers are also on the menu. Don't eat these Croatian subs while walking down the street or you'll wear them. Instead, polish them off with a beer at the high tables and stools provided.

Nikola Tesle 7. No phone. Sandwiches 15Kn–30kn. No credit cards. Mon–Sat 9am–5am; Sun 9am–3am.

Slasterčarnica Ivica I Marica ★★ DESSERTS   The ersatz gingerbread house named after an errant brother and sister fairy-tale team serves some of the best sweets on Tkalčićeva, a hot address for Zagreb's cafe society. Stop for a pastry or gelato after dining at Restoran Ivica I Marica next door; or grab a sandwich on whole-grain bread for a light supper or very late lunch.

Tkalčićeva 70. (℃ **01/481-73-21.** Fax 098/317-092. ivicaimarica@adriazdravahrana.hr. Sandwiches 13kn–29kn. No credit cards. Daily 4–11pm.

---

5 ZAGREB AFTER DARK

Nightlife in Zagreb is varied but not obvious: You have to look for the action. Besides the usual complement of bars and cafes, there are casinos, jazz clubs, discos, cinemas, and comedy clubs to occupy even die-hard night owls. Lately, Jarun Lake has become hot year-round with "branches" of almost all of Zagreb's popular bars setting up shop there.

CASINOS

Casino City   This comfortable casino beneath the Regent Esplanade Hotel has roulette tables, card tables, slot machines, and a VIP area for serious gamblers. Free entrance for Esplanade guests. Open daily 8pm to 4am. Mihanovićeva 1. (℃ **01/450-10-00.**

Casino Fortuna   Four floors of keno, poker machines, gambling tables, and live bingo go 24/7 in this temple to chance. Vlaška 9. (℃ **01/481-28-60.**

Club Casino Vega   The stars come out (and dress up) to play at this high-powered casino in the **Sheraton Hotel,** where the games include blackjack, roulette, slot machines, and poker. Open daily 8pm to 7am. Draškovićeva 43. (℃ **01/461-18-61.**

Golden Sun Casino   Electronic gambling is the rule 24/7 with slot machines and electronic roulette. Live entertainment at the cocktail bar. Zagrebačka Avenija 100a (next to the Antunović Hotel). (℃ **01/387-05-30.**

COCKTAIL BARS

Apartman ★   Apartman is a hip club near Flower Square in Zagreb's center. It is frequented by a younger crowd both day and night. Open 9am to midnight Monday through Wednesday and Sunday. Open 9am to 1am Thursday through Saturday. Preradovićeva 7. (℃ **01/487-21-68.**

Boban ★★   This bar/restaurant, owned by one of Croatia's top soccer players, is always packed to the max with a noise level to match. There is also outside seating where promenading in resplendent finery is a sport for both sexes. Hours are daily 7am to midnight. Ljudevita Gaja 9. (℃ **01/481-15-49.**

Hemingway's ★★   The Hemingway opposite the Croatian National Theater is part of a chain of bars that has a presence all over Croatia. This location is one of the chain's busiest, perhaps because it is in the center of Zagreb's culture district or perhaps because of its long work hours. Open 7am to 3am daily. Trg Marsala Tiga. (℃ 098/980-50-00. www. hemingway.hr.

Jackie Brown ★   This cocktail bar at Kaptol Centar is aimed at a sophisticated crowd that enjoys the finer things in life—cool jazz, vintage Armagnac, and classic cars. Open daily 8am to 1am. Nova Ves 17 (Kaptol Center). (℃ **01/486-02-41.**

Joe's Bar   The open-design concept of this slick lounge in the lobby of the Allegra Arcotel lets you watch traffic on Branimirova while you keep tabs on who's checking in. The hotel's lone Internet computer is here and the whole area is wireless, too, so you can use your laptop if you buy wireless minutes from a local provider at the desk or the tobacco shop next door. However, the ventilation system doesn't clear the smoke well despite the room's high ceilings. Open daily 7am to 2am. In the Allegra Arcotel, Branimirova 29. ℂ **01/484-69-48.**

Khala ★★   This hip lounge tends toward Far Eastern harem style, with jeweled lights covered with gauzy fabric and sheer tiebacks hanging from every portal. The effect screams "extremely chic and wealthy," and the clientele does, too: Brown wicker chairs and couches fitted with white linen cushions are always filled with beautiful people sipping exotic drinks while murmuring into cellphones and keeping an eye on their Porsches parked at the curb. Open daily 10am to 2am. Nova Ves 11 (Kaptol Center). ℂ **01/486-02-41.**

Maraschino ★   Named after the famous cherry juice from the coast that is also available in a potent fermented version, Maraschino carries the fruit theme to its drink menu. The crowd here is young and casual, and the music is loud, funky, and occasionally live. Open 8am to 1am Monday through Saturday; 9am to 1am Sunday. Margaretska 1. ℂ **01/481-26-12.**

Oliver Twist ★★   Set against a vine-covered wall on Tkalčićeva Street, Oliver Twist attracts a trendy crowd day and night. Most people sit at the outside tables and move inside after 11pm. Open daily 9am to 4am. Tkalčićeva 60. ℂ **01/481-22-06.**

NIGHTCLUBS

Aquarius   This hoppin' club specializes in theme nights. Live music. In summer, Aquarius opens a waterside franchise at Zrće Beach on the island of Pag. Cafe open from 9am to 9pm daily. Nightclub from 10pm to 6am daily. Matije Ljubeka bb. ℂ **01/364-02-31.**

Bacchus   Redone in 2008, Bacchus is the place to enjoy jazz, sip a glass of wine, and listen to poetry during Wednesday night readings. Open 10pm to midnight Monday to Saturday; noon to midnight Sunday. Trg Kralja Tomislava 16. ℂ **098/32-28-04.**

B.P. Club   B.P. is Zagreb's premiere jazz club. It's managed by internationally acclaimed vibraphonist Boško Petrović, and it attracts notables to both play and listen to the cool sounds emanating from this basement space. Pinguin sandwich shop (p. 301) is just outside the entrance to B.P. (open 24 hr. and a good place to grab a bite after the show). Open 10am to 2am Monday through Saturday and 5pm to 2am Sunday. Nikole Tesle 7. ℂ **01/481-44-44.**

GAY & LESBIAN

Global Club   The most popular gay club/bar in Zagreb, Global has a split personality. By day it is an Internet cafe, but Wednesday, Thursday, and Friday nights it's a dance club for which you need a special club card. The club sponsors boys' nights and girls' nights, and has three bars and a dance floor. Open 11am to 4am Monday to Saturday and 4pm to 1am Sunday. Pavla Hatza 14. ℂ **01/481-48-78.**

Sauna David   This gay-owned bar/sauna is near the Botanical Gardens and main train station. Open 4 to 10pm Monday to Thursday; 2pm to midnight Friday; 4pm to midnight Saturday and Sunday. Maruličev Trg 13. ℂ **01/533-65-07.**

11

Excursions from Zagreb

Most visitors to Croatia know something about the country's stunning Adriatic coastal scenery and its sophisticated capital, Zagreb, but they know little about what lies beyond. In general, there is much less tourism chatter about Croatia's inland towns—both close to Zagreb and farther away—than there is about the coast, even though these inland regions are rich alternatives to the sun-and-fun culture.

Croatia away from Zagreb and the coast dances to a much less frenetic beat than its glamorous siblings. The atmosphere in the cool, green hills is more down to earth and less commercial than it is on the white-hot Adriatic beaches. Inland Croatia is where working towns and farms are juxtaposed with castles and medieval fortresses built long ago to protect the country from foreign invaders. This is where pristine homes stand adjacent to houses bullet-pocked by wounds inflicted during the 1991 war.

The northern regions of the Zagorje and Međimurje are where many of Croatia's heroes were born and where many patriots died fighting for Croatia's freedom. There, hilltop towers stand sentry as if to protect the land against harm and tiny *klets* stand between crop rows to provide shelter for farmers and their tools.

Towns among the rolling hills and flatlands outside Zagreb are beginning to actively court tourists as the capital spreads outward to meet fields of yellow sunflowers waving in the wind. So get out of town and take a trip to the country, where the roads less traveled will lead you to the "real" Croatia and the genuine people who live there.

1 ORIENTATION

You don't have to take a long road trip to sample Croatia's northern heartland: Many of the castles, wineries, historical sites, and natural wonders within a 161km (100-mile) radius of **Zagreb** can be visited on day trips, depending on what you want to see. It takes just a few hours to investigate charming **Samobor** or rustic **Divlje Vode.** Even historic **Karlovač ★** is less than an hour from the capital. Excursions such as a day of hiking the trails at renowned **Plitvice Lakes National Park ★★★** with its waterfalls, karst gorges, and forests; or a day exploring the shops, cafes, and castle at the Baroque town of **Varaždin ★★★**, are within easy reach of Zagreb. Whether you want to spend a few days driving through the Međimurje wine country in extreme northern Croatia, or if you have just half a day to wander around Tito's childhood village at **Kumrovec ★★** in the **Zagorje,** you can do it without spending a lot of time in transit. Check with the **Zagreb County Tourist Association** at Preradovićeva 42 (© **01/487-36-65;** fax 01/487-36-70) for excursion possibilities. The office is open from 8am to 8pm Monday to Friday and from 9am to 1pm Saturday (closed Sun), late June through early September. Other times, office hours are from 8am to 4pm Monday to Friday. The association's website (http://zagzup.tripod.com/turizam/index.html) is handy for tourist contact information in Zagreb's outlying towns and for such statistics as the towns' distances from the capital. To get information on exploring the territory north of Zagreb in the Zagorje or in

Međimurje regions, contact the **Tourist Board of Međimurje County** in Čakovec at R. Boškovića 3 (✆ **040/390-191;** www.tzm.hr).

We've put the sites in Zagreb's orbit into several itineraries according to routes out of the city. Each can be used whole, broken into segments, or combined with other routes to suit individual interests.

GETTING THERE & GETTING AROUND

Once in Zagreb you can book guided excursions from the city in any direction. Multiple itineraries are available and especially useful if you are pressed for time, if you are unfamiliar with the region, if you are without your own transportation, or if you want an overview of the sites that ring Croatia's capital. Some excursions from Zagreb can be reached by train; for schedules, go to **Croatian Railways** (✆ **030/333-444;** www.hznet.hr). Another great way to travel outside Zagreb is by bus. Popular bus companies include **Croatia Bus** (✆ **01/235-23-33;** www.croatiabus.hr) and **Contus** (✆ **023/315-315;** www.contus.hr). No matter how you arrive at your destination, however, your adventure will involve walking, as these destinations are compact and sometimes limited to pedestrians.

2 EXCURSIONS SOUTH OF ZAGREB

Most tourists who set out on the autocesta that stretches southwest from Zagreb toward Rijeka race across the 177km (110-mile) stretch of road as if they were wearing blinders. Usually that's because they are focused on getting to the Adriatic coast and nothing else. If they were to take a short detour onto the Jastrebarsko highway exit, they would find the gateway to a surprising collection of towns and terrains that offer wetlands, castles, upscale accommodations, wineries, and a mind-boggling array of outdoor activities, including river rafting, horseback riding, biking, hiking, and much more. Most of these destinations are within an hour's drive from Zagreb.

ESSENTIALS

VISITOR INFORMATION   Just about every tourist office in every city throughout Croatia offers tours of Plitvice Lakes. Tourist offices in Zagreb in particular have racks of maps, brochures, and information on most attractions and events within 161km (100 miles) of the city. In addition, most towns in Croatia have city tourist offices with more localized information plus commercial tourist agencies that run excursions and handle private accommodations.

GETTING THERE & GETTING AROUND   The area from Zagreb south to **Plitvice Lakes National Park (Plitvička Jezera)** ★★★ can be accessed via the Zagreb-Rijeka autocesta. Each town along the way can be explored on a day trip as well, though the entire itinerary could take several days, especially if you decide to include the **Žumberak** region and Samobor (p. 307) on your list. The same applies if you linger at any destination, or if you are traveling by bus or train and have to wait for connections.

Of all the possible excursions from Zagreb, you need to allot the most time for a trip to Plitvice Lakes National Park, which is 2 hours from Zagreb and a place where most visitors take their time wandering trails and gazing at the countless waterfalls. You might find that overnight stays in **Karlovac** or Plitvice are viable choices to slow the tempo of your travels, or you can speed things up and add itineraries farther afield. Rental cars are handy for such customization, especially if you are interested in visiting tiny hilltop wineries or searching for bird species in the **Crna Mlaka (Black Marsh)** wetlands. But rental cars are not absolutely necessary unless you plan to explore some of the more remote villages deep in the Žumberak region. Public transportation—buses, trains, and private tours from Zagreb, for example—also is available, but that can require some complicated logistical planning.

3 SAMOBOR TO THE ŽUMBERAK

Picturesque, quaint, and full of cafes that serve the delicate but waist-expanding pastry known as *kremšnite,* Samobor is a favorite day trip for Zagrebačka and for tourists who have limited time but want to see a bit of the countryside. Samobor is just 26km (16 miles) west of Zagreb and linked to the capital by frequent bus service, good roads, and lots of tour operators, so it is a convenient destination.

Contemporary Samobor looks like an 18th-century postcard with its flower-bedecked pastel buildings and copper-domed church. During medieval times, the town was a hub for trades- and craftsmen who made a living with their hands. Today, Samobor mostly attracts weekend visitors who want to trek in the hills or stock up on local specialties such as *kremšnite,* a 4-inch-high square of custard meringue between sheets of crispy *mille-feuille* pastry; *samborska muštarda,* mustard made the same way it was made during the French occupation of the region; and Bermet, a distinctive, herb-infused aperitif wine that takes some getting used to. Once in Samobor, you can tour the town's museums, browse in its shops and galleries, or venture into more rural territory such as Zumberak Eko Selo, Divlje Vode, or the Samoborsko Gorje (Samobor Gorge).

Because of its proximity to Zagreb, Samobor is rarely without tourists, but the liveliest time to be in town is during the **Samobor Carnival,** a pre-Lenten celebration that culminates with fireworks and hordes of masked merrymakers swarming the streets. Carnival has been a fixture in Samobor for more than a century, and the town really rocks while it's on.

Samobor has a unique character, but logistically, it is almost a suburb of Zagreb, and its expansive cobbled town square lined with shops, cafes, and crafters could almost classify it as a theme park. You'll want to linger for a while and with good reason. By contrast, the Žumberak is a vast area of forests, hills, rustic villages, and vestiges of the Greek Orthodox culture that once thrived there. There were almost no visible signs of tourism or construction activity there in the summer of 2009, perhaps because there isn't much to see between villages and historic sites, and because this territory isn't easily accessible via public transportation. However, the Žumberak makes for a relaxing drive and lets you get a feel for life in Croatia's hinterlands. The Žumberak is more mountainous in the north than the south, where the landscape gives way to hillside vineyards in the Plešivica wine region.

ESSENTIALS

VISITOR INFORMATION   Samobor's **tourist office** is on the town's spacious main square at Trg Kralja Tomisalva 5 (© **01/33-60-044;** www.samobor.hr). The staff is used to foreign tourists and can help with maps and information about transportation, accommodations, dining, and even area history for Samobor, the Žumberak, and beyond.

GETTING THERE   Buses to Samobor run every half-hour or so from Zagreb's main station (hourly on Sun), which allows for a quick excursion out of the city. (See contacts

Samobor Castle

The ruins of Samobor Castle sit atop a hill right above the town of Samobor, which is only around 25km (16 miles) west of Zagreb. To reach the castle take the Zagreb-Ljubljana highway, get off at the Samobor exit, and follow the road with the concrete surface toward Samobor, taking the left fork into town. Proceed through the town center and walk up from the park on the western edge of town (you can see the ruins immediately above). It is only about a 10- to 15-minute ascent on a switchback trail. As of this writing there was a locked gate at the main entrance to the ruins, but you could still gain access by walking around to the rear.

By the charter of King Bela IV in 1242, the town of Samobor was granted the privileges of a free market town. The castle was built around the same time, and various additions and renovations were made over the next 500 years. The castle was owned by a number of eminent families: the Babonićs, Counts Celjski, the Frankopans, the Ungnads, the Erdodys, the Kulmers, the Kiepachs, and the Allnochs. Samobor Castle was abandoned in the 18th century and gradually fell into ruins.

—*Courtesy of Tocher Mitchell*

for the Zagreb Autobusni Kolodvor, p. 272.) Buses stop north of the main square, but the short walk to the center is easy and pleasant. If you are traveling by car from Zagreb, take A3 south and follow the signs. Parking is outside the center. We clocked our auto trip to Samobor from Zagreb's southern border at 11 minutes using minor roads. Buses to villages in the Žumberak region are infrequent, and some areas are not reasonably reached without a car, though avid cyclists may find the route challenging.

GETTING AROUND   From Samobor, it's easy to get to the Samobor Gorge on foot, where hiking trails abound. If you have your own transport, you can drive past the gorge into the Žumberak to challenging mountain trails in the north or to rustic villages, homes, and churches in the south.

WHAT TO SEE & DO

Samobor was a bustling center of commerce and agriculture during medieval times, but now it's an affluent bedroom community where many city folk from Zagreb have built large, expensive homes. Others flee metropolitan madness for Samobor. Besides excellent access to hiking and cycling trails in the mountains west of town and in the Žumberak region, Samobor has several museums and galleries worth a look.

Anindol ★★   Taking a walk on this wooded promenade in Samobor is reason enough to visit the town. The path is in a park on **Tepec Hill** above the center, which also is where you'll find the **Chapel of St. Anne** and the **Chapel of St. George,** both tucked into greenery. Between the two, there are 14 stone Stations of the Cross with carved reliefs. The ruins of Old Town Samobor and its castle (see below) are farther up the hill above the chapels. Built in the late 13th century, only the defense tower and part of the walls remain.

Liberation Park ★ This green space in the heart of Samobor is dominated by a monument to the victims of the Homeland War. There is a statue of the Blessed Virgin outside St. Anastasia Church on the park and a memorial wall engraved with the names of 51 people from Samobor and environs who died in the fighting.

Museum Marton ★★ Practicality and craftsmanship are the themes at Croatia's first private museum, which has a nice collection of applied art. It's all housed in a restored granary where histories and explanations accompany the fine exhibits of antique crystal, china, furniture, and paintings.

Jurjevska 7, Samobor. ☎ **01/33-64-160.** www.muzej-marton.hr. Admission 20kn adults, 15kn children and seniors. Sat–Sun 10am–1pm. Other days by appointment.

Town Museum ★ Displays in this former 18th-century "palace" chronicle Samobor's history. An ethnographic collection includes rustic farm implements and other vestiges of the area's way of life through the ages.

Livadićeva 7, Samobor. ☎ **01/33-36-214.** Admission 5kn. Tues–Thurs 9am–3pm; Sat–Sun 9am–1pm. Closed Mon and public holidays.

WHERE TO STAY

Samobor has several small hotels and pansions plus a slew of private accommodations that can be booked at any of the tourist agencies in town. For accommodations in Divlje Vode or Žumberačko Eko Selo, make arrangements directly with the facilities or at the Žumberak Nature Park office in Bregana at ☎ **01/33-23-848** or pp.zsg@zg.hinet.hr.

Hotel Lavica The Lavica is the ultimate renovation project: The hotel's history goes back nearly 250 years when it started out as a stable with hayloft on property belonging to a town official. Today, the Lavica is a rustic yet modern inn that combines the ambience of the past with conveniences of the present thanks to a 2003 renovation and ongoing improvements. Guest rooms are tastefully decorated with dark woods and cool colors; bathrooms have updated fixtures, and some have tubs rather than showers. The Lavica is lovely, low-key place to stay.

Ferde Livadićeva 5, Samobor. ☎ **01/332-49-46.** Fax 01/336-66-11. www.lavica-hotel.hr. 22 units. From 314kn double. Rates include breakfast. AE, MC, V. **Amenities:** Restaurant. *In room:* TV, minibar.

Hotel Livadić ★ The Livadić's location on the main square makes it a convenient choice, especially during Carnival, but it is the excellent hotel kavana and friendly atmosphere characteristic of Croatia's family-run hotels that make this a comfortable place to stay. Guest rooms are spacious and done in period decor, but with modern bathrooms. A plus: Guest rooms are off the square behind the restaurant, which minimizes noise from pedestrian traffic.

Trg Kralja Tomislava, Samobor. ☎ **01/336-58-50.** Fax 01/332-55-88. www.hotel-livadic.hr. 17 units. From 465kn double. Rates include breakfast. AE, DC, MC, V. **Amenities:** Restaurant; terrace cafe. *In room:* TV, minibar.

Pansion Divlje Vode There are just seven basic rooms with French beds above the pink stucco trout restaurant on the hill overlooking the biopark below. They come in handy if you don't want to drive back to Zagreb through the forest after dark.

Stojdraga 2, 10432 Bregana. ☎ **01/33-87-623.** 7 units. From 200kn double. AE, DC, MC, V.

Žumberačko Eko Selo ★★ (Kids) Accommodations at this homage to the American Wild West are unique in Croatia. Cabins are log-cabin rustic with touches of class: There are lace curtains on the windows, Indian blankets on the beds, and lots of knotty pine

View from the Top

Many marked trails and several challenging hikes originate in Samobor. Beginners can try a combo ride-walk technique to access a four-story tower and platform erected in 2006. If you aren't afraid to climb this open steel structure (it has stairs), you will be treated to a spectacular 360-degree view of the Zumberak and beyond. From the main square, take the narrow, unmarked road next to the town museum and follow Sv. Ane Ulica to a sign that says "Vidikovac Turanj Tepec" (vantage point). Turn right on the gravel road immediately opposite the sign, park, and walk about 100m (328 ft.) to the tower. There are other marked trails through the woods near the tower. Directions to more challenging routes can be obtained at the tourist office on the main square in Samobor.

on the walls. Guest rooms have the convenience of toilets and showers. Camping facilities are available, too. The "ranch" is open year-round, meals are hearty and delicious, and trail rides through the snow-covered forests are especially beautiful.

Koretići 13, 10456 Kalje. (℃) **01/338-74-73.** Fax 01/336-73-06. www.eko-selo.hr. From 50€ double. MC, V. **Amenities:** Restaurant; stable; excursions.

WHERE TO DINE

Samobor is crammed with pastry cafes that serve its famous *kremšnite* and other guilty pleasures, but it also is known for fine dining and regional specials such as *češnjovke* (spicy sausage). The Žumberak itself is a dining destination with a rustic bent that includes hearty, homey fare. Either way, you won't go hungry in this region where heaping plates of game, freshwater fish, and decadent pastries are devoured with gusto.

Divlje Vode ★★ FISH   A long, almost-finished granite stairway leads up a steep hill to a pale pink mansion that is now part of this rustic restaurant. Divlje Vode serves diners on a terrace in pine trees overlooking the area trout farm where you can watch your dinner swim around before it lands on your plate. Trout is the dish of the day, and for 45kn you can have the fresh catch grilled, deep-fried, pan-fried, poached, or fried in corn flour. For a little more, you can order local specials like Zagorje soup, *štrukli,* or grilled meat, all of which are served in generous portions. Despite its out-of-the-way location, Divlje Vode can get crowded at lunchtime and on weekends. Those who venture to this out-of-the-way spot for a weekday dinner have the option of staying over in one of the restaurant's seven *sobes.*

Stojdraga 2, Žumberak. (℃) **01/33-87-629.** Entrees 35kn–75kn. AE, DC, MC, V. Daily 9am–11pm.

Kavana Lidivać ★★ DESSERTS   Everything in this centrally located hotel coffeehouse/restaurant is bright and welcoming in a meticulously furnished dining room augmented by adjacent garden seating fringed with beautiful container plantings in summer. The *palačinke* (crepes) filled with walnuts are delicious, as are the *kremšnite* and other local specialties.

Trg Kralja Tomislava 1, Samobor. (℃) **01/33-65-850.** www.hotel-lidivac.hr. *Kremšnite* about 10kn. AE, DC, MC, V. Daily 8am–midnight.

Samoborski Slapovi ★★ INTERNATIONAL   Dinner in the woods is one of the attractions in this tiny hotel restaurant about 3.2km (2 miles) northwest of the Samobor center. The food here is substantial but uncomplicated, with grilled meat and regional specials supplemented by Italian and German-leaning choices. You might want to book one of the 12 rooms available for an overnight just so you can enjoy a few more meals in this pastoral setting.

Hamor 16, Samobor. © **01/33-84-063.** Fax 01/33-84-062. Entrees 30kn–65kn. AE, DC, MC, V. Daily 7am–midnight.

4 KARLOVAC

54km (32 miles) SW of Zagreb; 90km (54 miles) N of Plitvice National Park

Leafy Karlovac is 54km (32miles) and less than an hour from Zagreb and it has all the right elements to stand out as a model of Baroque architecture and clever city planning. However, war and neglect have left their marks, and many of Karlovac's treasures are crumbling and in deplorable condition. **Karlovac** was established by the Austro-Hungarians in 1579 as a military installation to defend against the encroaching Turks. Because of its strategic position between the **Kupa** and the **Korana rivers** and its proximity to the **Mrežnica** and **Dobra rivers,** Karlovac has been on the front line of battles spanning 4 centuries.

Many of Karlovac's stately Baroque buildings still bear significant scars from Serbian artillery, and others are towering examples of the former socialist government's indifference to beauty, but the town is showing signs of renewal.

Originally, its medieval footprint was in the form of a six-pointed star set within a system of moats. Today the star-shaped layout still is intact, but it now is a green space that includes the Franjo Tuđman Promenade, a 2.4km-long (1½-mile) path lined with chestnut trees that meanders around the central city.

When you approach Karlovac from any direction, it looks like a blue-collar industrial town ringed by middle-class suburbs. It's easy to miss the Old Town farther in; it once was a wealthy cluster of Baroque homes and businesses. The Old Town is in various stages of dishabille, but it is notable even though damage from the 1991 war still is visible almost everywhere you look. Renovation projects are going on here and there, though they seem inadequate in light of what needs to be done.

Even if some Karlovac residents have not come to terms with the war, there are signs that the town is emerging from hard times. There are two modern hotels in town (**Europa** and **Korana**), name-brand retailers (**Benetton, Levi's),** ubiquitous crowded cafes and pizza places, and even a few tourists taking in the sights before moving on to sun and fun on the coast.

The town's center comprises buildings that still suffer from battle blight, but they are clearly Frankopan or Hapsburg inspired, inspiring anyone wandering past to think of the town's appearance before war left its ugly mark on the facades.

At the west end of town, **Karlovačko Brewery** might be the town's most recognizable brand name, but **Dubovac Castle** ★ on a hill above it is probably its main tourist attraction. It can be reached in 10 minutes from the town center by car (or in 30 min. on foot). It once was possible to stay in one of the castle's 10 *sobes* (rooms), but those have closed and the building is now being renovated. During construction, the defensive tower is home to a permanent exhibition on the history of the castle and the area around it. The banks of the Korana River also are popular and draw crowds at all hours to swim, jog, walk their dogs, or enjoy the scenery.

Dining opportunities in Karlovac range from homey *klets* (rustic restaurants serving local cuisine) on deserted streets to the elegant **Dobra ★★** in the Hotel Korana, which also offers alfresco service on its handsome deck overlooking the river.

About 6km (10 miles) north of Karlovac, the town of **Ozalj** and its imposing hilltop castle offer spectacular views of the Žumberak, a sight that is worth the ride even if the still-under-renovation castle isn't. About 10km (6 miles) northwest of Ozalj, the tiny village of **Krašić** has become a tourist destination because of its church and museum dedicated to the town's favorite son, **Alojzije Stepinac,** who was archbishop of Zagreb during World War II and who is something of a folk hero in Croatia. Stepinac was jailed by Communists after being railroaded on charges of collaboration with the Nazis, and he spent the final years of his life under house arrest in **Krašić,** the town where he was born. There is an imposing statue of Stepinac outside the church, which is open for Mass and tour groups, and for anyone who happens to meet up with the parish priest.

If you continue in the same northerly direction when you leave Krašić, you will see rural villages almost untouched by time (and renovation). You will be in the part of Croatia that is home to a strong Greek Orthodox culture, which is evident in some of the architecture. When you get to **Pribić,** note the **Church of the Annunciation** just outside the village: Its architecture is typical of the Orthodox genre.

From here, you can continue farther north into the Žumberak to **Sočice** to see more churches and a small folk museum displaying farm implements and Greek ethnic garb; then proceed to **Žumberačko Eko Selo** (p. 309). You can then circle back to Samobor and Zagreb.

ESSENTIALS

VISITOR INFORMATION   The **Karlovac Tourist Office** (© **047/615-115;** fax 047/600-602) is located at Petra Zrinskog 3, diagonally across from the **Hotel Carlstadt.** Hours are 8am to 3pm Monday through Friday; 8am to 1pm Saturday; closed Sunday and holidays. A helpful staff, including a few who speak English, can direct visitors to hotels and private accommodations and provide maps and brochures about the city and surrounding areas. Commercial tourist agencies like **Generalturist** at Zrinski Trg 4 (© **047/615-199;** fax 047/615-398) can help you with excursions from Karlovać and can help book rooms for you in town or at other destinations.

GETTING THERE   Karlovac is a little more than an hour from Zagreb by car on the Zagreb-Rieka autocesta (A6). Buses and trains run to and from Zagreb with regularity almost every half-hour. In addition, there is connecting service to Rijeka and some of the Kvarner islands. Train service to and from Zagreb runs with the frequency of a commuter line (18 per day). There also is connecting train service to Rijeka.

GETTING AROUND   Karlovac is a walker's city, especially along the river and in the town center. You can follow the "star," which is lined with trees and a popular promenade, especially after dinner. You can even walk up to the medieval Dubovac Castle by setting out north from the Kupa, but this is a vigorous uphill hike and will take half an hour or more. There is a road for auto traffic to the castle, too.

Besides people-watching from the town's many cafes, exploring the Old Town, tracing the "star," or strolling along the river, there are several notable attractions in Karlovac. Whether passing through or in town for a business meeting, visitors won't lack for things to see during downtime.

City Museum (Gradski Muzej) Currently on Trg Strossmayer, with some exhibits installed in Dubovac Castle, the museum has a large collection of Croatian cultural artifacts and a model of how Karlovac once looked. There also are historic photos of Croatian life and architecture and examples of pottery and other crafts. Descriptions are in Croatian only.

Trg Strossmayerov 7. ℭ **047/615-980.** Admission 10kn for adults, half-price for children 7–18. Mon–Fri 8am–3pm; Sat–Sun 10am–noon. Special appointments available by calling the museum.

Dubovac Castle ★ Originally built in the 13th century, the present castle underwent several redesigns at the hands of the Frankopans and the French, but the exterior has since been restored to some semblance of its former medieval splendor. Inside, the castle has seen better days, and renovation is afoot, but one hotelier says there are plans to eventually turn the building into a youth hostel. You can walk from town to the castle, which is a little over a mile due west of the center, but the steep grade can be challenging. The easiest way to get to Dubovac Castle is by car. Either way, the panoramic view of the city and the rivers that run through it is worth the effort.

2km (1¼ miles) west of the town center. ℭ **047/416-331.** Castle admission 10kn for adults, half-price for children 7–18. Mon–Fri 5–9pm; weekends and holidays 9am–1pm and 5–9pm. For a curator-led tour (free) at other times, call the City Museum at ℭ **047/615-980.**

Holy Trinity Church & the Franciscan Monastery ★ Holy Trinity Church and its attached Franciscan monastery are undergoing renovation, but it is still possible to see the church's interior during Mass. To see the monastery and its museum of sacred art, just knock on the door. Whoever is home will be happy to show you around.

Trg Bana Jelačića 7. ℭ **047/615-950.**

WHERE TO STAY

Karlovač's hotel scene is looking up, thanks to two relatively new hotels and several others that have been updated. Private accommodations are another option (contact the tourist office).

Hotel Carlstadt ★ With the busiest street in town at its doorstep, the Hotel Carlstadt is convenient to sites and transport. The Carlstadt is in a state of ongoing update, though the objective is freshening rather than modernizing, so the guest rooms are still plain. They are, however, within easy reach of stores, cafes, and the city's green periphery with its promenade and public garden. In addition, the busy cafe/bar Carlstadt next door to the hotel at street level is the perfect place to rendezvous with friends or linger over a cup of *kava*.

Vraniczanyeva 1. ℭ **047/611-111.** www.carlstadt.hr. 37 units. June 1–Sept 30 from 455kn double; Oct 1–May 31 from 415kn double. June 1–Sept 30 from 815kn suite; Oct 1–May 31 740kn suite. Rates include breakfast. AE, DC, MC, V. Garage parking. **Amenities:** Coffee/bar; casino. *In room:* A/C, TV, minibar.

Hotel Europa ★ The imposing stucco Hotel Europa is the first thing you see when you head for the Karlovac exit off the Zagreb-Rijeka autocesta. It's painted pink. Opened in 2003, the Europa caters to tourists and businesspeople alike, and it is especially handy as a stopover if you want to visit nearby Plitvice Lakes National Park or if you want to take a leisurely trip to the Adriatic coast. Among the local excursions the hotel can arrange is a picnic along area wine roads, complete with a map and a basket full of locally grown/produced foods.

Banija 161. ☎ **047/609-666.** Fax 047/609-667. www.hotel-europa.com.hr. 32 units. From 650kn double; from 980kn suite. Rates include breakfast. AE, DC, MC, V. Video-monitored parking. **Amenities:** Restaurant; cafe/bar; sauna; solarium; excursions. *In room:* A/C, TV, hair dryer, minibar.

Hotel Korana-Srakovčić ★★★   First-time Korana guests who follow the city's directional signs to this family-run hotel are inevitably taken aback when they approach a war-ravaged structure with broken windows and a burned HOTEL KORANA sign on the roof. Don't gasp and turn around. Instead, keep going about 91m (300 ft.) to the *real* Hotel Korana, a faithful re-creation of a historic 1896 building that was destroyed in the war with Serbia and lovingly rebuilt in 11 months according to the structure's original blueprints. The new Hotel Korana, which opened its doors in 2003, is a true boutique hotel in a park setting. Its personalized guest services sometimes find the staff organizing special events ranging from corporate luncheons to hunts for wild mushrooms. The hotel can even set up a tour of the city's Karlovačko Brewery or rafting on one of the nearby rivers. Guest rooms are spacious and airy, and each is themed to a different flower species, so if you forget your room number, you'll remember that you are in the Petunia Room. The hotel's **Restaurant Dobra** features nouvelle regional dishes that can be served on the wraparound deck, a perfect perch for watching the nightly promenade along the Korana river walk.

Perivoj Josipa Vrbanića 8. ☎ **047/609-090.** Fax 047/609-091. www.hotelkorana.hr. 18 units. From 950kn double with balcony; from 1,350kn suite. Rate includes breakfast. AE, DC, MC, V. **Amenities:** Restaurant; bar; golf; tennis courts; wellness center w/sauna, solarium and massage; room for those w/limited mobility. *In room:* A/C, TV, hair dryer, minibar.

WHERE TO DINE

Karlovač is konoba country. Most of the city's dining spots are casual affairs that specialize in pizza, huge plates of grilled meats, and regional specialties such as platters of mixed grill (meat) and fish. However, a couple of restaurants go beyond the traditional to add a twist to the expected.

Restaurant Dobra ★★ Value MODERN CROATIAN   The Dobra's dining room gleams with crystal, silver, and flowers at every table, but the wide porch overlooking the Korana River provides an even better show. No matter what time it is, diners on the deck can watch the river and an ever-changing kaleidoscope of strollers, dog-walkers, and joggers streaming past their table. The menu includes many Croatian standards such as *cevapči* (meat stew with paprika) and a mixed grill, but the kitchen ventures out of the pantry, too. Try the wild quail chef de cuisine, grilled fresh trout with herbs, or grilled octopus served cold with fresh pineapple. In this area full of hunting enthusiasts, the quail could have been flying and the trout swimming a few hours earlier. Whether you go traditional or modern, you'll get to sample the chef's creativity with an *amuse bouche* before the meal. Ours was a delightful salmon tartar served with homemade whole-grain toast slices. Service is gallant, and menus are in five languages, including English.

In the Hotel Korana, Perivoj Josipa Vrbanića 8. ☎ **047/609-090.** Fax 047/609-091. www.hotelkorana.hr. Entrees 45kn–80kn. AE, DC, MC, V. Daily 8am–10pm.

> **Fun Facts   What's a Konoba?**
>
> A *konoba* is a family-run restaurant that specializes in regional cuisine made with local produce, homegrown and prepared meats, family-caught fish, and even family-made wines. Any dining spot that calls itself a konoba is usually casual and traditional, with family-style service, large portions at low prices, and a lot of regular local customers. Think Irish pub or neighborhood bistro.

Restaurant Žganjer ★★ Finds REGIONAL CROATIAN   This is one of those roadside places where you encounter food that you will remember forever. Grilled lamb and pig, bread from the *krusna pec* (brick stove), capon with olives, turkey baked with *mlinci* (noodles), mouthwatering local pastries, and local Vrbnička Žlahtina wine are among the offerings that will linger in your taste buds for a long time. You might even want to stay the night in the restaurant's 10-room pansion: Each room is nicely equipped with TV and minibar. If you do stay over, you'll have time to try a few more things on the menu.

Jelašl 41 (about 4.8km/3 miles from Karlovač center on State Rd. D-1 toward Split). © **047/641-333.** Fax 047/641-304. Entrees 35kn–75kn. AE, DC, MC, V. Daily 24 hr.

---

5 PLITVICE LAKES NATIONAL PARK

The **Plitvice Lakes National Park ★★★** is Croatia's most touted natural wonder: Its majestic waterfalls, lakes, and forests have earned it a place on the UNESCO register of world natural heritage sites and made it Croatia's second biggest tourist attraction after the Adriatic coast and islands. The park's most compelling features are the waterfalls that interconnect its 16 turquoise lakes, which are set in dense forests of beech, fir, spruce, and soaring rock formations. The park's 4,856-hectares (12,000 acres) include 3,642 hectares (9,000 acres) of forest, 1,133 hectares (2,800 acres) of grassy areas and villages, and 36 hectares (88 acres) of water. Everywhere the water is crystal-clear thanks to deposits of travertine (powdery white limestone rock) under the water. The constant distribution of travertine creates the underwater mounds responsible for the waterfalls. The park is also rich with caves, springs, flowering meadows, the source of the River Korana (a gorge that looks like a green branch of the Grand Canyon), and several animal species including deer, wolves, wild boar, and the increasingly rare brown bear (though these animals rarely make an appearance during the hours when the park is open to visitors).

Plitvice became a national park in 1949. One of the Serb-Croat war's first casualties was a park policeman who was killed in an incident that is sometimes cited as one of the flashpoints for the 1991 war. The park was occupied for most of the war by Serb troops until 1995, and during that time, its offices and hotels were trashed, but the park itself was undamaged. Since then, the hotels and other buildings have been restored, and in the last 10 years visitors have returned to the park in droves. Plitvice now lures nearly a million visitors annually to its acreage, which is crisscrossed with well-marked gravel paths and boardwalks that allow visitors to wander about for anywhere from 2 to 8 hours per outing, depending on how they structure their routes.

Park signs at the trail heads suggest itineraries and the length of time each would take, but in reality, you can make your own path and stay as long or as short a time as you like—provided you don't take a wrong turn and miss one of the bus or ferry stops. The in-park transportation system runs on eco-friendly fuel whisking visitors between sites.

ESSENTIALS

VISITOR INFORMATION   There are two entrances to the park, Ulaz 1 and Ulaz 2, each of which has a tourist info office, gift shop, and snack shop. The tourist office at Ulaz 1 is open daily from 8am to 8pm during July and August, from 9am to 5pm April to June and September, and from 9am to 4pm October to March. The office at Ulaz 2 is open from 8am to 7pm July and August, and from 9am to 5pm April to June and September. You can get brochures and advice about how to approach the park or how to find a hotel, but no decent free maps. The trails and directions to shuttle buses are clearly marked, but having a detailed map is a good idea to avoid detours, which could add hours and extra uphill climbs to your hike. An excellent, though unwieldy, map is available for 20kn at the ticket booth. Tickets are 85kn per day for adults and 40kn for seniors and kids 7 to 18. Children 6 and under are free. Prices listed here are for high season and are lower other times.

GETTING THERE   Plitvice is on the old road (E71) between Split and Zagreb, but you don't need a car to get there from anywhere in Croatia because almost every town and every hotel in the country either runs tours or connects visitors with tours that include Plitvice or focus on it. There is even a separate **Plitvice Tourism Office** in Zagreb at Trg Kralja Komislava 19 (✆ **01/461-35-86**) that will be happy to help you arrange a visit.

By Car   To get to Plitvice by car from Zagreb (trip time about 2 hr.), take the Zagreb-Rieka autocesta to Karlovac. From there, follow the signs to Plitvice via the old road to Split (E71).

By Bus   You can catch a bus from the main bus station in Zagreb (2½ hr.), from 8:20am to 1:45am for 48kn to 70kn one-way, depending on the time of departure, bus line, and other factors. You can check schedules online at www.akz.hr, but you have to call reservations and info (✆ **060/313-333**) or stop at the main office at Avenue Marin Držića 4 in the town center to make a reservation or get a ticket. Make sure your bus stops at Plitvice and that it doesn't take the new highway and bypass the park on the way to Split. This is a possibility because since the Zagreb-Split leg of the A1 autocesta opened in June 2005, it no longer is necessary for anyone going to the coast to take the older road that passes the park.

GETTING AROUND   The delightfully Croatian **Lička Kuča restaurant** (p. 318) is at Ulaz 1, at the north end of the park and close to the bottom of the Lower Lakes, so stop there for lunch. Then hop in the car and drive about 2.4km (1½ miles) south to Ulaz 2 to begin your tour (if you are visiting anytime except Oct–Mar), because that entrance puts you in the middle of the property and gives you more options for exploring the park. Ulaz 2 is also the site of the park's three hotels (Jezero, Plitvice, and Bellevue; p. 317 and p. 318), in case you want to stay near the park and weren't lured by the ubiquitous SOBE signs on the roads leading to and from Plitvice.

WHAT TO SEE & DO

Plitvice is a hikers' paradise, but even couch potatoes can see most of the park's features by combining walking with riding on the Plitvice ferries and buses. Ulaz 2 is roughly in the middle of the park, so if you start there, you can easily get to **Prošćansko,** the

> ### (Fun Facts)   Waterfall Chemistry
>
> Visitors to Plitvice can't help wondering why the water is so clear, why each lake seems to have a different jewel-like color, and what the heck is travertine (park signs forbid visitors from stepping on the stuff). The official park map explains that over thousands of years, super-pure water pouring into Plitvice from the mountains eroded the surrounding limestone rocks, and moss and algae acted as catalysts to turn the dissolved rock (calcium carbonate) into the porous stone known as travertine, which then was deposited in the water. Nature is still "manufacturing" travertine at Plitvice and the dissolve-and-deposit process is responsible for creating the park's waterfalls and for the lakes' vivid blue-green color. (As the travertine sinks to the lake floor, it coats vegetation and the lake's floor in white mineral "dust," which creates a bottom that reflects sunlight and sky. Thus the brilliant colors.) As the travertine accumulates on the bottom, it also builds to the point that it creates barriers between the lakes. These barriers eventually get tall enough to create the waterfalls that are the essence of Plitvice's constantly shifting landscape.

highest and largest lake in the park, which is ringed by a hilly green landscape. No waterfalls here, as you are at the top of the cascade. From Ulaz 2 it is a quick downhill walk to a ferry, which will take you toward paths flanked by waterfalls you can almost reach out and touch. *Tip:* Don't try this. Swimming is forbidden, as is walking on the travertine.

You can also follow the signs here to the foot of **Veliki Slap (Big Waterfall),** where slender streams of water zoom off the vertical granite face into **Korana Gorge.** Veliki Slap is the most dramatic waterfall in the park, and sometimes it seems that everyone is rushing to get there. However, there are smaller falls, series of falls, and clusters of falls in other parts of the park that are impressive, too.

WHERE TO STAY

Hotel Bellevue   Of the three hotels that border park grounds, this is the one with the barest bones. Walls are thin; rooms are small; and service is indifferent where it exists, but the Bellevue is closest to the park's entrance and serves a good breakfast. It's where you stay if you get there late and are going to leave after you visit the lakes the next day.

Plitvička Jezera bb. (©) **053/751-700.** Fax 053/751-165. www.np-plitvicka-jezera.hr. 60 units. July–Aug from 72€ double. June 66€ double. Rest of year 52€ double. AE, DC, MC, V. **Amenities:** Restaurant, bar, room service.

Hotel Jezero ★   This is definitely a hotel for large tour groups: Rooms are small, the restaurant is big, and everything else is generic-looking. However, the restaurant is surprisingly good and the location couldn't be more convenient to the park.

Plitvička Jezera bb. (©) **053/751-400** or 053/751-014. Fax 053/751-600. www.np-plitvicka-jezera.hr. 210 units. July–Aug from 873kn double. May–June, Sept–Oct 799kn double. Rest of year 636kn double. 30% discount for kids 7–12; 50% discount for kids 6 and under. Kids stay free if they sleep in parent's bed. AE, DC, MC, V. **Amenities:** Restaurant; bar; pool; sauna; 5 rooms for those w/limited mobility. *In room:* TV, Internet, minibar.

Hotel Plitvice Farther away from the park than the Jezero or the Bellevue, this smaller hotel is in denser forest. It's the middle-of-the-road choice of the three, all of which were built in the style of Socialist getaways for workers taking their mandated vacations.

Plitvička Jezera bb. © **053/751-100.** Fax 053/751-013. www.np-plitvicka-jezera.hr. 52 units. July–Aug 82€ double. June 74€ double. Rest of year 52€ double. AE, DC, MC, V. Kids stay free in parent's room. **Amenities:** Restaurant. *In room:* TV, Internet, minibar.

WHERE TO DINE

Hundreds of dining spots pepper the road to and from Plitvice, most offering spit-roasted lamb or pig and other local specials. You can stop for a bite or buy your roasted meat by the kilo and picnic in the woods. There are a few sandwich concessions within the park itself as well as hotel restaurants, but there is only one free-standing restaurant within walking distance of the hotels.

Lička Kuča ★★ REGIONAL CROATIAN This large, touristy restaurant is opposite Ulaz 1 and full of folk items, including an open wood-burning stove big enough to roast a whole cow. The restaurant serves regional dishes such as spit-roasted lamb, sausages, and *lička juha* (lamb soup with vegetables).

Ulaz 1, Plitvice National Park. © **053/751-024.** Fax 053/751-026. Entrees 35kn–80kn. AE, DC, MC, V. Daily 11am–11pm. Closed Nov–Apr.

Restoran Degenija ★ Value CROATIAN Head north from Plitvice and you'll run into Degenija, a busy, family-oriented restaurant that is a favorite of vacationers in the area. The flower-bedecked outdoor terrace overlooks the busy highway, but the cozy dining room is a good option, too. Portions are enormous. We ordered the roasted meat platter for two (170kn) and it could have fed four. Menus are in five languages and waiters speak English. Nothing fancy here; just good Croatian home cooking.

Drežničko Selašte bb. © **047/782-060.** Entrees 58kn–85kn. AE, DC, MC, V. Daily 7am–11pm.

6 EXCURSIONS NORTH OF ZAGREB

The green, rolling landscape of the Zagorje and Međimurje regions north of Zagreb could have been patterned on illustrations from *Grimm's Fairy Tales.* This is Croatia's storybook land, where each new vista reveals another gentle swell of green topped with cream-colored hilltop churches and gingerbread-brown brick cottages. In the troughs between these verdant agribreakers, the villages of rural Croatia remain countryside repositories of the nation's early culture and customs, a source of larger-than-life heroes and historic events that helped shape the country and its unique character.

High in the hills, visitors can say a prayer to the Blessed Virgin at **Maria Bistrica** or wander the caves at **Krapina,** where signs of a Neanderthal settlement were discovered in 1899. Farther on, visitors can see the medieval fortresses of **Veliki Tabor** ★ and **Trakošćan** ★★, or marvel at the Baroque town of **Varaždin** ★★★ and its museums and castle. Even casual tourists will see that spas like **Terme Tuhelj** and **St. Martin** are turning their attention to guests looking for luxury rather than rehab, and that the aristocratic "palaces" like **Dvor Desinič** are attracting curious gourmets rather than indolent aristocrats. **Kumrovec** ★★, Tito's rural birthplace, now looks like a Croatian version of Williamsburg, Virginia, with blacksmiths forging iron, costumed guides explaining exhibits, and townspeople selling homemade *rakija* (brandy) and local honey.

At the top of the country, which skirts the Slovenian border, **Međimurje** wine roads curl through the hills near Čakovic, the region's center. There, family vineyards abound, and everyone from Grandma to the smallest of children pitches in to bring in the grapes.

The people of the Zagorje and Međimurje are known throughout Croatia as some of the nation's most industrious and frugal citizens. They also have reputations for generous hospitality, for serving exceptional meals made with local produce, and for loving their land and the fruit of their trees and vines. Just like the winegrowers in France's Beaujolais region who celebrate *le vin nouveau* on the third Thursday in November, the people in northern Croatia also have a designated day (Nov 11, St. Martin's Day) to taste and tout their new vintage. On that day, the wine is blessed and the whole area takes part in a festival of food, wine, and merrymaking, a celebration of a season's work that lasts well into the night, ending only with morning and the beginning of a new cycle of life.

7 MARIJA BISTRICA, KUMROVEC & VELIKI TABOR

11

The route north from Zagreb past Mount Medvednica and through the Stubica Valley leads to the Zagorje region, home to some of Croatia's most beautiful vistas and the best castles, shrines, and historic sites in the country. On the way, you'll be immersed in the Zagorje's appealing rural atmosphere, which hasn't changed much over the centuries. The Catholic faithful will want to stop at **Marija Bistrica** ★★ to see where Pope John II put controversial Croatian Archbishop Alojzije Stepanic on the road to sainthood. History buffs will make a beeline for the ethno village of **Kumrovec (Staro Selo)** ★★, where Josip Brož Tito was born. Anyone game enough to venture into the Croatian countryside should be on the lookout for the lovingly restored 17th-century **Miljana Palace,** which you must admire from afar as it is closed to the public and not completely renovated. However, there's no problem exploring the very public **Veliki Tabor** ★, one of Croatia's oldest castles. This formidable stone keep comes complete with ghosts and a windswept perch on a hill overlooking grasslands and the winding road, and it, too, is undergoing a face-lift.

ESSENTIALS

VISITOR INFORMATION   Marija Bistrica's **tourist office** is at Zagrebač bb (© 049/ 468-380; www.info-marija-bistrica.hr). Hours are 7am to 3pm Tuesday through Friday; and in summer, 8am to 2pm Saturday and Sunday. The office can provide brochures, maps, and information on nearby accommodations. However, you might have to secure a room outside the center or in a farmhouse if any large tours are in town, and to reach them, you'll probably need a car. Try **Zagorje Tourist Agency** at Zagrebačka 88 (© 049/301-580) for that. The **Kumrovec Tourist Board** is at Cesta Lijepe Naša 6A (© 049/502-044; www.kumrovec.hr). You can also try the **Krapina-Zagorje County Tourist Board** at Zagrebačka 2 (© 049/233-653).

GETTING THERE   You can see all three of the above sites in a day if you are driving or taking a guided excursion, but it will take longer if you are using public transport, which is available from Zagreb and other parts of Croatia. Several public buses per day serve Marija Bistrica from Zagreb, and two per day run to Kumrovec. To get to Veliki Tabor, however, you'll have to take one of eight buses to Desinič and walk almost 3.2km (2 miles) to the castle from the bus stop. See "Getting There & Getting Around," in "Orientation," for bus schedule contact information.

GETTING AROUND   Once you reach your destination, walking or biking are the only ways to explore this area. You can drive up to Veliki Tabor, but you must park outside the limits of Staro Selo and explore the village on foot.

WHAT TO SEE & DO

It's possible to fashion a castle tour, a winery tour, or even a Croatian "culture" tour to include the numerous sites in the Zagorje and Međimurje regions in the northwest territory. It's difficult to do justice to these beautiful areas without your own transportation or a focused, organized tour, because while public transportation is available, the time spent in transit and making connections is out of proportion to the time you need to see some of the sites. In this region, some places are destinations, and others are momentary pauses along the way.

Church of the Ascension ★   Go through Sopot on your way out of Veliki Tabor to visit this incongruously large, double-steepled, neoclassical church in the middle of tiny Pregrada; it is known as the Zagorje Cathedral. You'll be even more surprised at the large amount of gilt inside, especially the gold embellishments on the oversize organ, purchased from the Zagreb Cathedral in 1854 when Zagreb decided it was not loud enough for its Herman Bollé church.

In the center of town (Pregrada).

Kumrovec ★★ (Kids)   When you park your car and walk the few steps to Staro Selo, just 40km (25 miles) from Zagreb but deep in the heart of rural Zagorje, you'll think you're going to market: It seems as if half the village is stationed at tables at the entrance selling homemade cakes, wine, rakija, and other foodstuffs with touristy "Tito" labels pasted on them. These entrepreneurs are taking advantage of the heavy traffic flow that leads to the birthplace of the late President Josip Broz Tito, who successfully put his own brand of ad hoc Communism on the former Yugoslavia in the years following World War II until his death in 1980. Staro Selo's main attractions are 19th- and 20th-century cottages and farm buildings that have been restored to look exactly as they did when Tito was born there in 1892 and the effect is that of an open-air ethnographic museum whose centerpiece is an authentic re-creation of the interior and exterior of Tito's childhood home done by the Zagreb Museum of Arts and Crafts. You can walk from building to building, including a memorabilia room, where documents and photographs from Tito's time in office are on display. You can also watch blacksmithing and candle-making demonstrations on weekends. Throughout, docents in period costume can supplement the information in the printed English captions on displays.

Staro Selo. ℭ **049/553-107.** www.mdc.hr/kumrovec. Admission 20kn. Apr–Sept daily 9am–7pm; Oct–Mar daily 9am–4pm.

Marija Bistrica ★★   Just 37km (23 miles) from Zagreb, the little town is a draw for pilgrims on religious tours as well as others who want to see the shrine where a "miraculous" 15th-century statue of the Virgin Mary sits on the main altar of the 19th-century Herman Bollé **Pilgrimage Church of St. Mary ★** off the town center. According to legend, the statue was hidden behind a brick wall in the 17th century to protect it from desecration. It stayed that way until its whereabouts were revealed by a ray of light. The statue survived a fire in the late 19th century, which enhanced its reputed connection with the supernatural. The church itself is less interesting inside than out because of the huge outdoor "altar" and open-air auditorium behind the building. The expansive outdoor facility was built to accommodate John Paul II's visit to Marija Bistrica in 1998, when he beatified favorite son Archbishop Alojzije Stepinac. There is also a **Way of the**

Veronika of Desinić

According to legend, Veronika of Desinić was a beautiful girl who lived in the village at the foot of Veliki Tabor during the 15th century. During that time, the castle was owned by Count Herman II of Celje, a powerful Croatian governor who had a son named Friederich. One day while out riding, Friederich spotted the lovely village maiden and fell madly in love at first sight. However, Herman didn't approve of the liaison and forbade his son to see the low-born Veronika. As the young are wont to do, the couple defied Herman and eloped, but their time together was short. When the count found out what Veronika and his son had done, he had his soldiers hunt them down. Friederich was captured immediately and whisked away to a solitary cell where he was imprisoned for 4 years. Veronika was not so lucky. The count's minions found her and had her brought to Veliki Tabor, where she was jailed and tried as a witch. The judges found Veronika guilty of nothing more sinister than love and ordered her set free. However, Herman was still miffed about being defied and he ordered his servants to drown Veronika in a bucket of water before she left the courtroom. He then had Veronika's body bricked into the walls of the castle's pentagonal tower. In 1982, a female skull was found behind a Veliki Tabor wall during renovation, but there is no proof that it is Veronika's. The skull now resides in the castle's chapel and it is said that on stormy winter nights, a woman's screams can be heard at the castle.

Cross on **Calvary Hill** behind the auditorium, which pilgrims sometimes climb on their knees to do penance. The town itself is quite mundane, but there are several good pizzerias and konobas if you arrive at mealtime.

Marija Bistrica. www.svetiste-mmb.hr. The church is open for Mass and choir practice.

Museum of Peasant Uprisings   This rather dry but significant collection of documents and visuals chronicles the 16th-century revolt organized by the agrarian Catholic population against the Protestant Hapsburg landowners of the time. The landowners took every opportunity to push the labor and financial burdens of their pursuits on the peasant population. The exhibit, located in the former Orsić Palace a mile north of Gornja Stubica, includes a few weapons and other artifacts.

Samci 63–64, Gornja Stubica. Ⓒ **049/587-880.** Fax 049/587-882. www.mdc.hr/msb/seljacka-buna.htm. Admission 20kn. Apr–Sept daily 9am–7pm; Oct–Mar daily 9am–5pm.

Our Lady of the Snows ★   You'll have to negotiate a bumpy, narrow road to get to this church in the tiny village of Belec north of Marija Bistrica, and you might be disappointed when you see the church's unremarkable facade. However, inside, you'll find yourself blinking at the fussy Baroque furnishings and colliding colors that are downright distracting for anyone who wants to pray. The church was built in the 16th century by a noblewoman after she heard about an apparition of the Virgin Mary in a nearby town. The church is enclosed by a wall that provides a more serene courtyard setting.

Belec. Sun 8–11am. No phone.

Veliki Tabor ★   From a distance, Veliki Tabor looks like an impregnable fortress built on the highest point in the area. However, the large crane and blue tarp protruding from the castle's roof signaled the serious repairs going on at this 12th-century behemoth when we visited in the summer of 2007. Veliki Tabor was closed to visitors for 7 months because of the nature of the construction work going on there, but it reopened in October 2007 after a $7-million renovation. The castle is easily accessible because visitors can drive right up to the castle entrance. The interior courtyard with its three floors of colonnades is impressive, as are the restored rooms, among them a wine cellar museum and a first-floor chapel that holds a skull reportedly belonging to the castle's resident ghost. Cosmetic improvements are ongoing

Near Desinic. www.veliki-tabor.hr. Admission 10kn.

WHERE TO STAY

There aren't any big resorts or many hotels (except for those attached to the area's thermal spa centers) in northwest Croatia, and with few exceptions, facilities resemble hospital housing rather than relaxing resort accommodations. Northwest Croatia also has many privately owned castles and mansions and, until recently, most lay unoccupied in disrepair. However, a few entrepreneurs have been restoring some of these mansions and converting them into boutique hotels. Consequently, the list of small hotels, family-run pansions, private accommodations, agritourism opportunities—and even spas retrofitted with luxuries—is growing.

Pansion Zelenjak ★★ (Finds)   You'll feel as if you're in your own castle in the hills in this gorgeous little inn 3.2km (2 miles) south of Kumrovec. The mustard-yellow building, which houses comfortable rooms and the **Zelenjak Restaurant** (see below) that specializes in local fare and fish, is the essence of Zagorje style. The whole effect is one of serenity. A rock garden, a pond and waterfall, and the forest-green backdrop complete the picture from your room's window. The only drawback is that you need your own transportation to reach Zelenjak.

Risvica 1, Kumrovec. ✆ **049/550-747.** www.zelenjak.com. 7 units. From 300kn double. Rates include breakfast. No credit cards. Half-board available. **Amenities:** Restaurant; terrace cafe. In room: TV.

Seljački Turizam Trsek   A farmhouse stay here includes fresh air, locally grown food, long walks in nature, and a lot of farm animals. The restaurant specializes in Zagorje dishes and uses a lot of "found" objects in its decor, including tables made of wine barrels. This is agritourism at its most authentic.

Trnovec Desinièki 23, Desineć. ✆ **049/343-464.** www.trsek.hr. 6 units. From 245kn double. Rates include breakfast. No credit cards. **Amenities:** Restaurant. In room: TV.

Terme Tuhelj ★★ (Kids)   Excellent pool facilities are among the draws for weekenders and day-trippers who patronize this newly renovated spa/hotel about an hour north of Zagreb. As of summer 2007, only 46 of the 136 rooms had been updated to include air-conditioning and satellite TV, so be sure to ask for a "new" room, even though it costs a little more. Since a Slovenian company known for converting aging spas took over in 2005, Tuhelj pool facilities have been transformed to rival those at a water park. Sections of the sprawling pool are connected by a "river current" so swimmers can float from water slide to water guns to covered water effortlessly. Besides a hotel,

spa facilities, and an adrenaline park, Tuhelj has a small restaurant and bar, but swimmers also have the option of walking uphill to the more elaborate **Dvorac Mihanović**
(see below) for meals. Tuhelj is jammed on summer weekends and holidays, and parking can be difficult.

Ljudevita Gaja 4, Tuhelj. ✆ **049/556-224.** Fax 049/556-216. www.terme-tuhelj.hr. 136 units. Renovated
units from 750kn double. Rates include breakfast, children's programs, and use of pools. AE, DC, MC, V.
Amenities: Restaurant; bar; cafe; disco; children's programs; fitness classes; pools; sauna. *In room:* TV,
dial-up Internet connection, minibar.

WHERE TO DINE

There is no shortage of restaurants in the Zagorje area, though most are very small,
family-run affairs. Wherever you stop, it's almost impossible to get a bad meal, especially
if you stick to local specialties.

Dvorac Mihanović ★★ REGIONAL CROATIAN   Dvor means "castle" in Croatian, but the term is often loosely applied to manor houses (many of which are closed to
the public) scattered in the Zagorje Hills. Mihanović is one of the exceptions. Inside this
soft yellow building, the dining room is filled with crystal and dark wood as well as suits
of armor and other doodads typical of the old aristocracy. Mihanović's menu is entirely
in Croatian, and the cuisine is typically Zagorje (grilled meat, turkey *mlincima,* peasant
plate of pork and vegetables), but some dishes are vegetable-driven and designated
"healthy" for those who are at Terme Tuhelj to shape up.

Ljudevita Gaja 6, Tuheljske Toplice. ✆ **049/556-214.** Fax 049/556-216. www.terme-tuhelj.hr. Entrees
40kn–70kn. AE, DC, MC, V. Daily 7am–midnight.

Grešna Gorica ★ (Kids)   REGIONAL CROATIAN   You get more than a meal when
you travel to Grešna Gorica, less than a mile from Veliki Tabor and about 56km (35
miles) from Zagreb. Besides its rustic setting in the woods and its country decor, Grešna
Gorica has a complement of barnyard animals and old farm implements (including
antique winepresses) to add to the rural ambience. The menu continues the theme with
simple Zagorje specials made with local produce and meat. Homemade sausages and
cheeses, house-smoked ham, and Zagorje *štrukli* are among the offerings you can sample
here. If you drive up to the restaurant, be aware that parking there is very limited. Most
people park at the bottom of the hill on the road leading to Grešna Gorica and walk up
a very steep path.

Desinić. ✆ **049/343-001.** Fax 049/343-001. www.gresna-gorica.com. Entrees 42kn–84kn. No credit
cards. Daily (except during snowstorms) 10am to whenever the last guest leaves.

Zelenjak ★★ (Finds) REGIONAL CROATIAN   Serving traditional Zagorje specialties has been a family business since 1936 at Zelenjak. Veal with mushrooms, cream, and
cheese baked in a wooden stove originally used to bake bread *(Odrezak zapecen u Krusnoj
peci)* is the restaurant's signature dish. Local wines are featured. Outside are playground,
sports, and garden areas to keep the kids busy so parents can dine in peace. The restaurant has both a regular dining room with a winter garden and a larger facility that can
accommodate crowds.

Risivica 1, Kumrovec. ✆ **049/550-747.** Fax 049/550-221. www.zelenjak.com. Entrees 40kn–60kn with
signature desserts such as štrukli at 15kn. AE, DC, MC. Daily 8am–11pm.

8 TRAKOŠČAN, KRAPINA, LEPOGLAVA & LUDBREG

There are many interesting side trips possible along the road between Varaždan and Trakošćan. The sights require a few detours and perhaps venturing onto winding back roads, but they help complete the picture of the real Croatia.

ESSENTIALS

VISITOR INFORMATION   Information, maps, and lists of events in these three locations can be obtained at Varaždin's **Tourist Association** (p. 328).

GETTING THERE   Buses and trains serve both Krapina and Lepoglava, but there are no direct public buses from Zagreb to Trakošćan. However, even if you don't have your own transport, you can access Trakošćan by taking a bus to Varaždin and backtracking to Trakošćan.

GETTING AROUND   As with most sites in Croatia, walking is the method of choice for seeing these sites.

WHAT TO SEE

Majestic **Trakošćan Castle** is the main draw in this part of northern Croatia, but there are several towns worth exploring in this region.

Krapina's claim to fame involves the remains of a Neanderthal settlement discovered in the hills between Zagreb and Slovenia in 1899 by Dragutin Gorjanović Kramberger. Kramberger discovered more than 900 fossilized human bones—collectively known as Krapina Man—in caves on Hušnjakovo Hill, just west of the city. According to anthropologists' accounts, these remains belonged to around two dozen Neanderthals, thought to have lived 50,000 to 80,000 years ago. A museum with mock-ups of the famous prehistoric find is located just below the site where the originals were found, but construction of a new facility is under way. Entry is 10kn. The museum is open 9am to 3pm Monday to Friday in summer, 8am to 3pm in winter.

Nineteen kilometers (12 miles) northeast of Krapina on the road between Varaždin and Trakošćan, the town of **Lepoglava** is best known as the site of Croatia's largest prison, and perhaps that single association is unfair. Since its beginning in the late 14th century and until the end of the 19th, Lepoglava was home to a Paulist monastery complex that also was a center of science, culture, education, and art—a reputation it earned when it was home to one of Croatia's first grammar schools and one of its first universities. The Paulist order in Croatia was disbanded by Austrian Emperor Joseph II in the mid–19th century. Shortly after that, the monks' cells were converted to prison cells where many Croatian patriots (Josip Broz Tito, Alojzije Stepinac, Franj Tuđman) were detained, mostly for political reasons. Another, more modern prison was built behind the monastery and still is in use though it is separated from the monastery by a wall. Lepoglava is also known as a center of lace making; its lace once was exported to the affluent European market and used in the fashions of the times. Today, Lepoglava still has a Lace Society, which hosts an International Lace Festival in early October. The Lepoglava Tourist Office is at Trg 1 Hrvatskog Sveučilišta 3 (© **042/791-190;** fax 042/791-389; www. lepoglava.hr).

Hilltop Wonders

Croatia is world renowned for its beautiful Adriatic seacoast. Less known is the treasure trove of mountaintop castles scattered throughout the country. You can find castles in every part of Croatia, from Dalmatia to Istria to Zagorje (area north and west of Zagreb) and Slavonia. Most are in various stages of ruin while some have been restored. All of them are fascinating both historically and architecturally—no two castles are the same—and all have spectacular views of the surrounding countryside.

Most Croatian castles served not only as medieval residences but also as fortresses. They were built in the 12th or 13th centuries to defend against the Tartars (Mongols). In the 16th century they were expanded and refortified as bulwarks against the Ottoman Turk invasions. The Turks succeeded in capturing many of the castles, but some were so inaccessible or impenetrable that they held out. Still others experienced much fighting and changed hands several times. By the 17th century, advances in military technology had rendered castle fortresses obsolete. Besides, by that time noble ladies were refusing to live any longer in isolated, damp, drafty stone castles. So those not destroyed in battle were abandoned in favor of more luxurious, comfortable manor houses in the valleys.

There are approximately 200 visible castle/fortress ruins in Croatia. Unfortunately most of them are rather inaccessible and difficult to find. Usually there are no directional signs. **Medvedgrad** is neither—it's clearly visible from downtown Zagreb about a third of the way up the slopes of Sljeme, the mountain just north of the city. It has been partially restored, some would say not according to historical records. There is a cafe/restaurant and a memorial to fallen Croatian soldiers. Nevertheless, the view of Zagreb to the south and west is very good and the grounds are worth exploring. The castle has a colorful, checkered history. Zagreb's Bishop Filip built the fortress in the 13th century, after King Bela IV granted him a deed authorizing its construction. The fortress had great strategic significance. It could be easily defended during times of war, and it was situated near the western border of the Hungarian-Croatian state. During the 7 centuries after its construction, Medvedgrad had a total of 107 owners.

To reach the castle drive or take bus no. 102, which runs between Britanski Trg and Mihaljevac, and get off at the "Blue Church" in Šestine. Then take the paved road that runs up past the church cemetery toward the mountain. After you pass a restaurant on the right-hand side of the road, if you are walking, look for trail no. 12 going up into the forest on the left side of the road. The hike up from the bus stop takes 35 to 45 minutes and is moderately steep in places. You can also drive to the castle in about 10 minutes on the paved road.

—Courtesy of Tocher Mitchell

Center of the World

The "holy" town of **Ludbreg** in the Drava River Valley near Mount Kalnik is picturesque, but its moniker, *Centrum Mundi* (Center of the World), is dubious. Ludbreg earned the title in ancient times because the great European cities of the world once were described in terms of Ludbreg as the center around which all the cities revolved. To illustrate the point, a series of circles that look like a giant bull's-eye marks the exact "center" of the world on the main square. The monument is embellished with plaques designating cities in Ludbreg's orbit, and every time a new plaque is added, the city celebrates by filling a nearby fountain with sparkling wine. The former Roman town is also known as a pilgrimage site for Catholics because it is one of the few cities founded by papal decree and supposedly where a 15th-century priest saw communion wine change into blood during consecration. Today, the garish pink stucco **Holy Blood Chapel** commemorates that miracle, and on the first Sunday in September thousands of the faithful flock there to do the same.

Trakošćan Castle ★★★   Trakošćan may be one of northern Croatia's most visited sites. As you approach it on the gravel switchback path to the entrance, it looks quite stately. Soaring white-and-yellow stone walls, red-tile capped turrets, a drawbridge, and palatial grounds create a fairy-tale illusion around the fortress, built in the 13th century. Trakošćan has seen hard times and gone through many owners since, the last being Juraj Drašković, who used the castle as a country getaway. Croatia's government took over the property after World War II and, in 1953, Trakošćan was opened to public tours. Today, Trakošćan is still an imposing sight on its hill in Zagorje, but the exterior restoration is far more impressive than the improvements behind its walls. In fact, some of what's inside is downright tacky, though that doesn't mean the displays aren't worth seeing. The first floor is faithful to the 19th century, with period furniture, lots of wood, and portraiture. On higher floors, you'll find crude ancient weaponry, a mishmash of furniture, walls with exposed patches of original wallpaper, and a couple of original tapestries. Note that each room has a unique, fed-from-behind stove, some with very ornate carvings. Also, among the dour, dark, and not particularly well-done portraits, a few by Julijana Erdody stand out as better than average. Unfortunately, that assessment doesn't apply to the painting techniques used on the walls. Heavy-handed *trompe l'oeil* and sponge-painting attempt to re-create period wallpaper designs, and the result is puzzling and bizarre. Trakošćan has much that is worth seeing, and a lot that destroys its restoration credibility.

✆ **042/796-422.** www.trakoscan.hr. Admission 20kn adults, 10kn children. Apr–Sept daily 8am–6pm; Oct–Mar daily 9am–4pm.

Trakošćan Park ★★★   The grounds in the immediate vicinity of Trakošćan Castle offer visitors a variety of activities in addition to Sunday afternoon strolls and picnics. Nearby Rava Gora offers good gusts and jumping-off points for paragliders, while rock climbers find the sheer cliffs challenging. Hikers and cyclers can scramble over miles of trails, and fishing enthusiasts can try their luck in the lake below the castle. Hunting still is a passion in this part of Croatia. The nearby Diana Hunting Grounds and lodge provide opportunities for gun enthusiasts in search of boar, deer, and game birds.

Adjacent to Trakošćan Castle.

WHERE TO STAY & DINE

Hotel Raj ★★ ⓥⓐⓛⓤⓔ   Guest rooms in this pink, flower-bedecked mansion across the road from the Holy Blood Chapel are just like home, with comfy beds and private bathrooms with showers. Situated in the southeast part of town, the hotel is walking distance to Ludbreg's center and its main attractions.

Alojzija Stepinca 2, Ludbreg. ✆ **042/306-377.** Fax 042/306-378. www.hotel-raj.com. 13 units. From 320kn double; from 400kn suite. Rates include breakfast. Half- and full board available. AE, DC, MC, V. **Amenities:** Restaurant. *In room:* A/C, TV, minibar.

Motel Coning ★   This modern (but bland) hotel within walking distance of Trakošćan Castle attracts tour buses and day-trippers who decide to stay over. Guest rooms are fine, though they lack the luxurious touches of a hotel. A gaggle of exercise options helps you get the kinks out after a day of touring medieval towers.

Trakošćan 5, Trakošćan. ✆ **042/796-224.** Fax 042/796-205. www.coning.hr. 80 units. From 92€ double. AE, DC, MC, V. **Amenities:** Restaurant; bar; gym; sauna; tennis courts. *In room:* TV.

Pivnica Mejaši ★ CROATIAN   Loosely translated, Mejaši means "next door neighbor" and the pleasant eatery is next door to St. Joseph Church, where the original Ludbreg medallion resides. You'll find locals filling both the indoor and outdoor tables any time of day enjoying a beer or regional dishes like *suhi govedski jezici* (dried beef tongue), *srneći paprikaš* (venison paprikash), *dimljena prgica* (soft cheese smoked in the attic), or just an ordinary pizza.

Trg Sv. Trojstva 27, Ludbreg. ✆ **042/810-510.** Entrees 19kn–40kn; pizzas 20kn for a small to 60kn for a large. No credit cards. Sun–Fri 8am–11pm and Sat 8am–2am.

9 VARAŽDIN

Eighteenth-century churches, houses, and public buildings are just some of the charms that make Baroque Varaždin a popular excursion from Zagreb. **Stari Grad** ★★★ is Varaždin's magnificent 12th-century castle and the centerpiece of any visit to the former Croatian capital, which today is one of northern Croatia's main cultural and economic centers. Varaždin owes its Baroque character and its title of "Baroque Capital of Croatia" to an unfortunate 1776 fire that destroyed most of the town, though not its historic center—a tragedy the town turned to advantage when the ruined buildings were rebuilt as they appear today.

Trg Kralija Tomislava is Varaždin's main square and lined with the best Baroque facades in town, which are conveniently identified with plaques that explain their lineage. Start at the 15th-century **Town Hall (Gradska Vijećnica),** with its 18th-century clock tower. Go south to the **Cathedral of the Assumption** ★, the town's first Baroque building. The cathedral was built in the mid–18th century by the Jesuits, who also built a monastery and other buildings in Varaždin. Just outside the Cathedral, you'll find **Herzer Palace (Dvor Herzer)** and the **Varaždin Insect Museum (Entomološki Odjel)** ★★, which has especially interesting displays of butterflies. There are other pleasing buildings and museums to visit in Varaždin, but Stari Grad is unquestionably the town's top attraction.

VISITOR INFORMATION   Varaždin's **Tourist Association** is at Ivana Padovca 3 (© **042/210-987** or 049/210-985; www.tourism-varazdin.hr). The office is open April 15 through September 15 from 8am to 6pm Monday through Friday; from 9am to 1pm Saturday; and from 10am to 6pm Sunday. From September 16 through April 14, they are open from 8am to 4pm Monday through Friday; from 10am to 1pm Saturday; closed Sunday.

The very helpful and friendly office not only distributes maps, brochures, and suggestions about dining and accommodations in town, but they also have information about the entire area, including Međimurje to the north.

T-Tours at Ivana Gundulića 2 (© **042/200-991;** fax 042/210-990; www.t-tours.hr) puts together packages for day or overnight tours of Varaždin, Trakošćan, Ludbreg, or Međimurje. Packages include transport, museum tickets, and sometimes meals, rooms, or a wine tasting.

GETTING THERE   Varaždin is about an hour's drive northeast from Zagreb along well-marked highway. The town is also linked to the capital by frequent bus service (26 per day) and train service (14 per day).

GETTING AROUND   Varaždin's central district is a pedestrian area, so you'll have to park on the outskirts of Trg Ban Jelačića north of the sights and walk in. Stari Grad (castle) is a 5-minute walk from the center of town.

WHAT TO SEE & DO

Besides its stunning architecture, Varaždin has several good museums and interesting churches. Restoration is ongoing, but Varaždin is visitor-friendly, with plenty of historical and directional information as well as a large number of cafes, restaurants, and shops. The only drawback is the dearth of accommodations in the center of town.

Cathedral of the Assumption ★★   The cathedral originally was a combination church and gymnasium (school). It was built by the Jesuits in 1647 and its exterior was designed in the Baroque style typical of the Society of Jesus of the time. Inside, you can see an elaborate altar with lots of gilt, statues, and marble columns backed by a painting of the Virgin's Assumption into Heaven as well as frescoes and woodcarvings. Because of its great acoustics, many concerts scheduled during **Varaždin's Baroque Evenings** are held here.

Pavlinska 5. © **042/320-180.** Mon–Sat 9am–6pm; Sun for Mass (9, 11am, 6pm).

Insect Museum (Entomološki Muzej) ★★   You can't visit Varaždin and not investigate the World of Insects display, an unusual collection of bugs and butterflies housed on the main floor of the Baroque **Herczer Palace.** The extensive collection was donated by museum founder Franjo Košćec and dates from 1954. The museum includes 4,500 exhibits of central European insects, nests, habitats, models, and photographs, all of which are well captioned and attractively presented.

Franjevački Trg 6. © **042/210-474.** Admission 10kn. Summer daily 10am–5pm daily. Winter Tues–Fri 10am–3pm; Sat 10am–1pm. Closed Mon.

Stari Grad ★★★   Stari Grad is not only Varaždin's best attraction, but it is also the town's cultural repository. It was designed in the mid–16th century by Domenico Dell'Allio as a defensive complex and it was used as a fortress against invading Turks. The

Gothic/Renaissance compound was privately owned until 1925, when it became a museum. Today Stari Grad is one of the best-designed showcases of Croatian history in the nation, and a must-see for anyone who visits Zagreb and the Croatian interior. From the outside, Stari Grad almost looks like a group of medieval cluster homes, a solid block of white stone walls of various heights and rounded red-roofed towers. Inside the walls, courtyards, and arched walkways give the buildings a softer look and lead to eight rooms that house exhibits of aristocratic interiors and artifacts, all accompanied by marvelous explanations. The Varaždin **Town Museum** is also housed here. Multilingual docents are stationed throughout the building, ready to help anyone who wants further details about what he or she is seeing or who is interested in Varaždin lore.

Šetalište J.J. Strossmayera 7. ℂ **042/212-918.** Fax 049/310-519. Admission 20kn adults, 12kn children and retirees. Tues–Fri 10am–3pm; Sat–Sun 10am–1pm. Closed Mon.

Town Cemetery ★   This arboretum cum cemetery provides cooling respite after a day of touring the city's Baroque treasures. Notable residents are few, but many varieties of the 7,000 cedars, maples, ash trees, red beeches, box trees, magnolias, and birches planted there starting in 1905 are rare.

West of Varaždin Castle (500m/1,500 ft.). No phone. Free admission. May–Sept 7am–9pm; Mar–Apr 7am–8pm; Jan–Feb, Nov 7am–7pm.

Town Hall ★   Varaždin's Town Hall is notable more for its exterior than for what's inside. The building's combination of Gothic and 18th-century stonework occupies a prominent position on the main square and it is a good meeting place or orientation point for visitors. From 10am to noon on Saturdays from May to October there is an added visual element: Guards in bright blue period uniforms stand outside the building.

In the center of town.

WHERE TO STAY

Varaždin accommodations are mostly in pansions and private homes, though there is a fairly modern hotel within a few blocks of the town center and others on the town's periphery.

Hotel Turist   Function triumphs over form in this generic block-style hotel half a mile from the town center. Most guest rooms are small and without personality, but the hotel is undergoing a long-term renovation and not all the rooms have been updated. Ask for one that has been redone. The Turist is increasing its list of amenities and adding excursions that cater to fishermen and hunters. (Kennels for hunting dogs are on the premises.) It will also offer guided mushroom hunts in the fall as well as food and wine events.

Aleja Kralja Zvonimira 1. ℂ **042/395-395.** www.hotel-turist.hr. 104 units. From 500kn double. AE, DC, MC, V. **Amenities:** Restaurant; bar; disco; excursions. *In room:* TV, minibar.

Hotel Varaždin ★★   This new entry (2007) to the Varaždin hotel scene is a welcome addition. Not only does it expand accommodations choices, but it also is the only hotel in Varaždin's center. Guest rooms are comfortably sized and showers all have turbo spray. Hotel Varaždin isn't fancy, but it is a step up in convenience.

Kolodvorska 19. ℂ **042/290-720.** Fax 042/201-916. www.hotelvarazdin.com. 27 units. Doubles from 600kn. Rates include breakfast. **Amenities:** Restaurant; bar; Internet access; pool; tennis court. *In room:* A/C, TV, hair dryer, minibar.

Pansion Garestin ★　Guest rooms are small and spartan in this little guesthouse. The restaurant serves wonderful fish and grilled meat dishes both in its meticulously turned-out dining room and on its lovely covered terrace.

Zagrebačka 34. ☏ **042/214-314.** www.gastrocom.hr. 13 units. From 350kn double. Rates include breakfast. AE, DC, MC, V. **Amenities:** Restaurant. *In room:* A/C, TV, minibar.

WHERE TO DINE

Kavana Korzo ★★ DESSERTS　Elaborate little cakes and coffee provide delightful treats at this Viennese-style cafe where old-world formality is the norm. The rolling pastry cart makes the experience authentic, though when things get crowded in summer, the cafe tosses out the rules and moves tables onto the square.

Trg Kralja Tomislava 2. ☏ **042/390-914.** Pastries 10kn–40kn. AE, DC, MC, V. Daily 8am–11pm.

Park ★★ REGIONAL CROATIAN　As its name suggests, the Park is surrounded by greenery and flowers because its terrace opens to Varaždin's municipal gardens. This is an especially nice restaurant in summer, when you can dine outside on a variety of grilled meats or salads. Try a glass of local Grazevina (white wine) with the Varaždin Salad, a version of Waldorf salad with chicken.

J. Habdelića 6. ☏ **042/211-499.** Fax 042/211-466. www.gastrocom.hr/park.htm. Entrees 35kn–100kn. AE, DC, MC, V. Daily 8am–11pm.

Zlatna Guska ★★ REGIONAL CROATIAN　Heraldry is the theme at Zlatna Guska (Golden Goose) restaurant in what once was the Inquisition Room on the lower level of a Zagorje palace. The stone walls and ceilings are covered with coats of arms belonging to the region's prominent families; dishes are named after them, too. Try the pork medallions St. Hebert, or the Bukan Buccaneers filet (a chicken breast stuffed with shrimp and covered with dill sauce). Service is accommodating. The wine list is filled with Croatian standards. Zlatna Guska is a perennial on Croatia's list of the 100 best restaurants in the country.

Jurija Habdelka 4. ☏ **042/213-393.** Fax 042/200-377. Reservations recommended. Entrees 30kn–90kn. AE, DC, MC, V. Daily 8am–midnight.

10　MEĐIMURJE

Međimurje is sometimes called the "flower garden of Croatia," not just because of its fertile land but because of its cultural, historical, and economic contributions to the nation's heritage. The region lies northeast of Varaždin and makes up the extreme northern part of Croatia where it borders Slovenia and Hungary. Međimurje's western half is characterized by gently rolling hills, vineyards, and orchards; in the east, flat, fertile farmland contributes a large portion of the country's grain and vegetable production.

　　The town of **Čakovec** ★★ is just 92km (55 miles) from Zagreb and it is Međimurje's largest population center. Međimurje's baronial 17th-century castle and exceptional Secessionist-style union building are quickly being eclipsed by a slickly updated town square ringed by lots of stores, restaurants, and bars. The square is enhanced by a conversation-piece fountain that spits arching streams of lighted water at night. But despite the town's new veneer, there still are many treasures waiting for discovery.

ESSENTIALS

VISITOR INFORMATION   The **Tourist Board of Međimurje County** in Čakovec at R. Boškovića 3 (☎ **040/390-191;** www.tzm.hr) can provide you with a well-done map tracing Međimurje's wine road and points of interest. The map also indicates wineries where you can stop to taste or buy local vintages. You can get much of the same information at the **Čakovec Tourist Office** at Trg Kralja Tomislava 2 (☎ **040/313-319;** www. tourism-cakovec.hr).

GETTING THERE   There are frequent bus and train services to Čakovec from Zagreb, plus one daily train to Budapest, but if you want to explore the wine road and areas in rural Međimurje, it is best to have your own transportation. Alternatively, people in the tourism office can arrange wine road tours. *Warning:* Međimurje's wineries are all family operations, so it is best to make arrangements in advance to ensure that vintners will be on premises when you arrive. For bus information, see "Orientation," earlier in this chapter.

GETTING AROUND   Walking is the best way to tour Čakovec, but if you want to see any of rural Međimurje, you'll need a car and a good map.

WHAT TO SEE & DO

The Međimurje region is one of Croatia's most underrated treasures, virtually ignored by tourists and untouched by the 1991 war. In the northwestern corner of Međimurje County, you can meander around hilly, winding roads that end in family wineries of varying sizes. Međimurje is a place where you can walk the land with its owner and taste the wine he made there. This is where you can sit on the deck of a hilltop restaurant and see Slovenia, Hungary, and Austria (and sometimes the hills of the Czech Republic) beyond the restaurant's Croatian vineyard. **Međimurje's wine road** is a relatively new feature in the area, though many of the wineries listed on the vina cesta map have been there for generations. However, the county is now promoting its assets to tourists. You can stop at any of the wineries on the map, and you'll be offered a glass of wine and the opportunity to buy a bottle or two. In some cases, the wine tasting is more formal, but this is like being in Napa, California, before it became popular. (Pick up a map to the wineries at the Čakovec or Štrigova tourist offices.)

There is an order to things in Međimurje that isn't evident anywhere else in Croatia. People follow the tempo of planting and harvest times and they seem more in tune with nature than people in any other part of the country. Once you fall in step with the flow of things, you get it.

Dom Sindikata ★★   As an example of Secessionist architecture, this salmon-and-white building off the town center has no peers. It now houses the offices of the local workers' union and can't be ignored, as it is unlike anything else in Čakovec.

Trg Kralja Tomislava, Čakovec.

Muzej Međimurja Čakovec ★   The original castle on this site at the edge of town was destroyed by a 1738 earthquake. The castle that stands in its place was built in the 18th century by Czech nobles. Many of the "New Castle's" 16th-century walls are still standing. The current Baroque structure houses the Museum of Međimurje, which opened in 1954. Displays include local costumes, paintings, and stone tombstones and sculpture, all from the region. The castle itself is currently undergoing renovation, so access is limited.

Trg Republike 5, Čakovec. ☎ **042/313-499.** Admission 15kn adults, 12kn children. Tues–Fri 10am–3pm; Sat–Sun 10am–noon. Closed Mon.

Dragons & Devils

Dragons *(pozoj)* and devils are synonymous in the Međimurje, where tales of the scary beasts abound. There is one about a green pozoj from Čakovic that causes earthquakes and natural disasters, a black pozoj from Sv. Juraj na Bregu, that supposedly was killed by St. George, and a folk legend about a pit in Donja Dubrava where a pozoj (the devil) supposedly lives. The Donja Dubrava pozoj is closely associated with the mouths of three rivers, the Drava, the Mura, and the Trnava. The legend also mentions *kače,* serpents with nine tails and heads that turn into princes if their wishes are fulfilled.

St. Jerome Church ★★★   Štrigova is home to this Baroque beauty, which was built by Paulist monks in the mid–18th century. The building fell into disuse during Tito's time, and it was roofless and full of chickens as recently as the 1970s. Currently, restoration is under way and access to the church is by appointment only. A visit is worth the phone call to the Štrigova tourist office and the long climb up a steep staircase because inside you'll see the results of modern restoration and at least three partially recovered Ivan Ranger frescoes. There once was a commonly held belief that St. Jerome, a Bible translator, was born in Štrigova, and Pope Nicholas V continued that belief by issuing indulgences to anyone who made a pilgrimage there.

WHERE TO STAY

Accommodations in Međimurje are mostly private, with some hotels attached to spas. This is a wonderful area to try a farmhouse stay.

Pansion Monika ★ Value   This six-room pansion in the Međimurje wine country is the ideal place to use as a base for winery touring or as a place to crash after dinner at Dvorac Terbotz. The rooms above Monika's coffee shop/bar are immaculate. Each has access to a balcony with table and chairs for vineyard gazing. Rooms are available with breakfast, full board, or neither.

Železna Gora 183, Štrigova. ⓒ 040/851-304. www.apartmani-hrvatska.com/osobna.asp?BR=3583. 6 units. From 240kn double. Rates include breakfast. No credit cards. **Amenities:** Restaurant; semiprivate balconies. *In room:* A/C, TV.

Toplice Sveti Martin ★★   The spa's Apartment Village Regina opened to great fanfare in 2005. The complex added a large block of economical condo-type accommodations that look like Colorado ski-country digs with living room, kitchenette, and pullout couch in addition to two beds, though some units are even larger. Think upgraded sports camp. Sveti Martin looks as if it is trying to be a full service resort with a variety of programs geared to weight loss, antiaging, anticellulite, and general fitness. Most spa services are extra and can be purchased a la carte. Available special-interest tours include winery tours, hiking excursions, and hunting trips. Just-plain-relaxation vacations are also available. The complex itself is a village with shops, restaurants, and a market, which is good because most packages here are geared to 5- and 8-day stays, though 1-night rates are available.

Grkaveščak bb, Sveti Martin na Muri. ☎ **040/371-111.** Fax 040/371-171. www.toplicesvetimartin.hr. 84 **333**
units. From 6,600kn double. Rates include buffet breakfast. AE, DC, MC, V. **Amenities:** 2 restaurants; pizzeria; pub; pools; sports facilities; aqua park; excursions. *In room:* A/C, TV, hair dryer.

WHERE TO DINE

Dining in Međimurje is always a treat, especially when you can pair fresh-off-the-farm
foods with fresh-from-the-winery vintages. This is the ideal place to indulge in local
specialties because the odds are they come from the restaurant's backyard.

Dvorac Terbotz ★★ REGIONAL CROATIAN   Just 5km (3 miles) from the Slovenian border, this restaurant is in an elegant, renovated 18th-century mansion. Here you
can sample wines from local producers and eat impeccably prepared local specialties. Try
cigansko pečenje, spicy roast pork with roasted potatoes; or *sarma* with game, cranberries,
and potato purée. Don't miss *Međimurska gebanica* for dessert. That's a cake made of
layers of apples, walnuts, cheese, and poppy seeds. Terbotz is loaded with local dishes like
these. Besides the food and the wine-tasting room, Terbotz has dining on its deck overlooking the restaurant's vineyards. On a clear day you can see Slovenia, Hungary, and
Austria. Terbotz is in the process of adding pansion-style rooms.

Železna Gora 113, Štrigova. ☎ **040/857-444.** Fax 040/857-445. www.terbotz.hr. Entrees 38kn–85kn. AE,
DC, MC, V. Mon–Sat 11am–1am; Sun 11am–1pm.

Katarina ★ REGIONAL CROATIAN   Located in the center of town in a historic
cellar underneath the Millennium Shopping Center, Katarina turns out excellent grilled
meat dishes and local specialties prepared from age-old recipes. The cellar's red-brick
arches and heraldry-inspired decor create a nice backdrop for taste treats such as beef
roulade or poached pears with cherry sauce. The restaurant has a good selection of locally
produced wines.

Matice Hrvatske 6, Čakovec. ☎ **040/311-990.** Entrees 35kn–90kn. AE, DC, MC, V. Daily 10am–11pm.

Mala Hiza ★★★ Ⓕⁱⁿᵈˢ REGIONAL CROATIAN   In our opinion, Mala Hiza (little
house) is one of the finest Croatian restaurants in the country. The building itself is an
1887 structure that once stood outside Zagreb. Thankfully, in 2002 owner Branimir
Tomašić had the vision to dismantle and reassemble it in the village of Mačkovec, 4km
(2½ miles) outside Čakovic. He then surrounded it with a knock-out garden, created a
Croatian interior with lots of wood, stone, and artifacts, and began serving guests a menu
full of creative interpretations of regional Croatian cuisine. You can start with three kinds
of kulen from Slavonia, proceed to turkey roulade with chestnut puree, Dalmatian prsut,
and sour cherry sauce, and complement the lot with thumb-size portions of heavenly
gnocchi stuffed with cheese and spinach. Or you can experiment with ostrich medallions
smothered with mushrooms, green pepper, and cranberries. For dessert, try *zlevanka*, a
special dessert of cornmeal cake topped with walnuts and poppy seed. A huge selection
of off-menu old-time Croatian dishes and *peka*-cooked meats is available with notice,
and the wine list is a showcase for Međimurje vintners. Service is delightfully helpful and
friendly, and there is a well-protected smoke-free section, a rarity in Croatia.

Mačkovec 107, Čakovec. ☎ **040/341-101.** www.mala-hiza.hr. Entrees 35kn–210kn. AE, DC, MC, V. Daily
9am–11pm.

12

Inland Croatia

Tourists planning a trip to Croatia rarely include the regions east of Zagreb in their itineraries. While many of the towns between Zagreb and the country's eastern border on the Danube have not recovered fully from the wounds of the 1991 war, this delightfully relaxed area is flush with attractions steeped in history and tradition.

Inland Croatia offers visitors their best opportunity to become acquainted with the authentic, grassroots culture of the land rather than just the country's glitzy Dalmatian beaches, exotic islands, or romantic ports of call.

It is home to a collection of unique natural wonders, historic sites, and gastronomic delights capable of wowing even the most jaded traveler. Visitors can walk through Čigoć, a village in the Lonjsko Polje Nature Park where whole families of storks nonchalantly regard you from their mammoth nests built atop centuries-old timber cottages. You can visit solemn Jasenovac and its poignant monument to victims of World War II's ethnic violence and feel the sadness in the air. On the road to Đakovo, you can gawk at the horizon where red-brick bell towers of the Cathedral of St. Peter rise in the distance above acres of yellow sunflowers. In Osijek, you can take a turn around the promenade along the mighty Drava, walk the perimeter of the city along the top of what's left of the medieval walls surrounding the Old City, and smile at the ornate gewgaws that decorate the Austro-Hungarian mansions along Europska Avenue. It's almost a certainty that you'll cringe at the devastation still visible in Vukovar, and you'll shake your head at the unspeakable cruelty that the town's citizens suffered when you visit the touching memorial to victims of a 1991 hospital massacre there.

In Ilok, you'll feel exhilaration when you walk 30m (100 ft.) into the Earth to see the second-oldest winery in Europe. Its owners will tell you how they frantically bricked in bottles of the best vintages to save them from invading Serbs during the Homeland war. Then you can taste history in a glass of golden liquid poured from those precious bottles.

Inland Croatia isn't Las Vegas excitement or Disneyland illusion. It isn't an all-inclusive package of hedonistic services or an adrenalin rush of physical tests. Rather, inland Croatia's rewards are more subtle and lasting than frolicking in the sea or playing roulette.

This infrequently traveled region is the sum of all the "ah-ha!" moments that happen as you imagine the horror of war while gazing across the Danube at Serbia from a bluff in Ilok. It is the light bulb that goes off in your head while you stroll through Bjelovar's Norman Rockwell–perfect town square or as you stroke the soft gray muzzle of a horse at Đakovo's Lipizzaner barn and stud farm. It is the amazing sensation that rolls over your tongue when you dig into a bowl of peppery *fiš paprikaš* (fish stew with peppers) in Osijek or when you sip a new vintage from a vineyard in Baranja wine country. It is also the grim realization that overtakes you when you see workers removing land mines along the road to fascinating Kopački Rit Nature Park. The payoff from a trip to inland Croatia isn't a transient thrill, but the total of many experiences that end in the understanding that something important happened there, something that formed Croatia's soul.

1 ORIENTATION

VISITOR INFORMATION

All areas of inland Croatia are served by tourist information offices, though not all have local facilities. For general information about the country's interior, start with the **Croatian National Tourist Office** at 350 Fifth Ave., Ste. 4003, New York, NY 10118 (℗ **212/279-8672;** fax 212/279-8683; www.croatia.hr). Travel agencies and tour operators also are good sources of information. Contact information for local tourist information offices is listed throughout below.

GETTING THERE

Except for the smallest and most remote villages, all the cities and towns of inland Croatia are served by bus and train routes linked to or originating in Zagreb. For bus schedules and ticket information, contact **Autobusni Kolodvor (Main Bus Station)** in Zagreb at Avenija M. Držića bb (℗ **060/313-333;** www.akz.hr). If you are at the station in Zagreb, window no. 14 is the 24-hour information center and is usually staffed by someone who can speak some English. For train information, contact the **Glavni Kolodvor (Main Train Station)** at Trg Kralja Tomislava 12 (℗ **060/333-444;** www.hznet.hr). For anyone with a car, the highway system that runs through inland Croatia is modern and efficient. Expect two-lane secondary roads to the smaller towns and some gravel roads in Lonjsko Polje Nature Park.

GETTING AROUND

Even tiny Čigoć is reachable by public bus, but once there, walking is the only way to see this nature reserve. Larger cities such as Osijek have tram systems that move people around the city efficiently. They also have connections to the rest of Croatia's larger population centers. However, travel to the rural areas of inland Croatia can be tedious and inconvenient on public transport, so it's better to tour the region by car, if possible.

2 SISAK & THE LONJSKO POLJE

The area between **Sisak** and **Jasenovac** is best known for the **Lonjsko Polje Nature Park's** ★★ endangered wildlife and 19th-century villages. The marshland area is also a favorite of bird-watchers, who hoist their binoculars at the **Krapke Dol** bird sanctuary near **Jasenovac.** But it is tiny, rustic **Čigoć** that attracts the most traffic. Čigoć is a designated European Stork Village and a living tribute to 19th-century Croatia.

ESSENTIALS

VISITOR INFORMATION   The **Sisak Tourist Office** can provide maps of the town, and information on reaching Čigoć and Lonjsko Polje. It is at the west edge of the center at Rimska bb (Mali Kaptol; ℗ **044/522-655;** www.sisakturist.com). In Čigoć, the **Tourist Information Center** is at house No. 26 in the village (℗ **044/715-115**). It is open 9am to 4pm daily March through November. The staff there can provide knowledgeable, English-speaking park guides who will tell you about the village and nature park as well as direct you to the village's two ethnographic museums, which hold artifacts from Čigoć's early days. The guides also can direct you to *seoski turizam* (village tourism) houses where guests can stay overnight and share meals with a host family. The 20kn park-entry fee covers exploration of Čigoć; each stub will get you into either of the two museums without charge.

In Jasenovac, the **Jasenovac Tourist Office** is in the city library building (© **044/672-587**). The **Lonjsko Polje Nature Park Administration Office,** where you can get maps and information on the park, is at Trg Kralja Petra Svačića (© **044/672-080;** www.pp-lonjsko-polje.hr).

GETTING THERE   From Sisak, you can take one of four daily buses or drive the 27km (17 miles) of Sisak-Jasenovac road along the Lonja River to Mužilovćica, Lonja, and Krapje. For the next 3.2km (2 miles) along the road past Čigoć, there is a string of villages similar to Čigoć, but without the large stork population. See "Orientation," above.

GETTING AROUND   Sisak, Lonjsko Polje, Čigoć, and Jasenovac all are best explored on foot, though a car is handy to reach the Holocaust Museum from Jasenovac and to thoroughly explore Lonjsko Polje, which covers a huge area between Sisak and Jasenovac.

WHAT TO SEE & DO

Fortresses, storks, and some rural villages are the area's main attractions, and each is spectacular in its own way.

Čigoć ★★★ (Kids   A line of Hansel-and-Gretel Posavina houses made of 200-year-old lowland oak timbers comprise Čigoć, but the entrancing village is best known for the dozens of white storks that descend there in early spring to lay their eggs. Just 30km (19 miles) south of Sisak, Čigoć also is noteworthy as a historic military village where Austro-Hungarian troops set up a frontier against the Turkish invasion in the 17th century. However, it is the storks in their enormous nests atop the village's thatched roofs that entice most visitors to stop here and at a string of similar nearby villages (**Mužilovćica, Lonja,** and **Krapje**). Bird-watching, hiking in the forest, and communing with nature are the primary activities at **Lonsko Polje Nature Park.**

Jasenovac ★★   Jasenovac is a town, but it also is a former concentration camp on the Drava near Bosnia that is now a memorial to the tens of thousands of people who were put to death there during World War II. As you approach Jasenovac's outskirts, you'll see a tall, concrete sculpture that looks like an open tulip rising up from a huge empty field. Go past that and turn left at an unmarked road leading to a low, flat building 180m (600 ft.) ahead. That is the Jasenovac museum and visitor center and well worth a stop.

Jasenovac was the largest concentration camp in the Balkans and many of the more than 70,000 known victims are buried in mass graves on the premises and at the camp's

---

⌐**(Fun Facts**   **Smoke & Mirrors**

If you look carefully at storks nesting on top of the wooden houses in Čigoć, you'll notice that the houses have no chimneys and the birds have built their nests on roofs. Without chimneys, the structures' fireplaces are vented into the attic area, where the smoke collects and seeps out gradually. Because Croats waste nothing—not even smoke. Residents use the area under the roof as a smokehouse where they cure ham, sausages, and some cheeses.

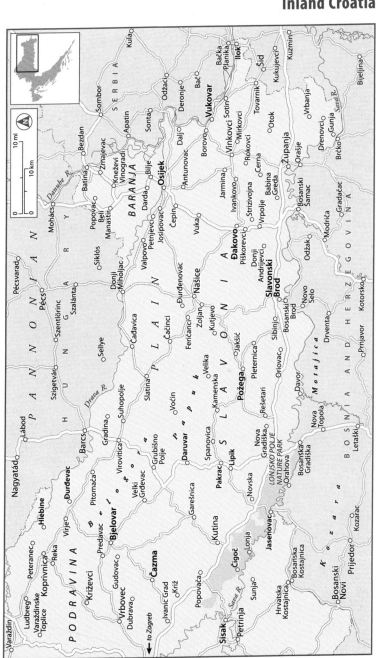

What Happened at Jasenovac?

According to United States Holocaust Memorial Museum records, Jasenovac was not just one big camp but a cluster of five detention centers established by the Ustaša-supported government of the "Independent State of Croatia" during World War II. Collectively, the Jasenovac facility was huge—the third-largest detention camp in Europe—and it was infamous for its deplorable living conditions, unspeakable torture methods, and mass killings. Between 1941 and April 1945, tens of thousands of Jews, Serbs, Roma (Gypsies), Croats, and miscellaneous political prisoners were brought to Jasenovac via trains from communities across Croatia to work if they had skills needed by the Axis regime or to be savagely tortured and/or murdered if they didn't, according to museum research reports. In addition, Jasenovac was especially notorious for its brutal execution methods—strangulation, live burning, live burial, murder by ax, ropes, chains—as well as for the alleged participation of local Catholic clergy in those executions.

Between the summer of 1942 and March 1943, Croatian authorities reportedly emptied the camp of remaining Croatian Jews (about 7,000) and sent them to Auschwitz-Birkenau, leaving only non-Jewish prisoners in the camp. There have been many debates about how many people died at Jasenovac, and there is no agreement on the number that perished here or even who some of them were. In April 1945, the Ustaša guards deliberately destroyed the camp buildings and all records of what went on at Jasenovac when they realized that Tito's Partisan troops were closing in on them. However, most estimates say those killed at Jasenovac's camps number "more than 200,000," including 18,000 Jews.

other four "work sites." The museum and visitor center originally were built in the 1960s, but the facility was occupied by the Serbs during the Homeland War, and it took until November 2006 to recover the items that were stolen during the conflict and to install a permanent exhibit inside.

The current multimedia installation is quite moving, with numerous screens lighting up the dark corners of the black painted space. A continuous slide show of period photos from the camps, footage and audio of survivors talking about their experiences at Jasenovac, and news footage from the 1940s that covers the camps' story are the bulk of the presentation. Three computers are hooked up to the memorial's database and visitors can use them to search family names, events—anything associated with Jasenovac. All captions are in Croatian and English and even the footage of survivor testimony is captioned in English. The ceiling is hung with clear acrylic panels engraved with the names of known Jasenovac victims, and artifacts belonging to them are displayed in glass cases throughout the memorial.

Outside, there is a path that leads to a huge stone memorial sculpture about .5km (¼ mile) from the visitor center. The path meanders past several train cars that were used to transport detainees to the camp. The cars were a gift from Slovenia's railway. Along the way you will see models of what the camp looked like when it was operating between 1941 and 1955. The museum has five curators, including Ms. Ines Sogonić, who speaks English and who will be happy to answer your questions.

Tip: Take a penlight to aid in reading some of the captions. The memorial's database is now online and searchable. More than 75,000 victims have been identified by name.

For more information on the memorial, go to www.jusp-jasenovac.hr. For historical information, on Jasenovac, go to www.ushmm.org/jasenovac, a very impressive website authored and maintained by the U.S. Holocaust Memorial Museum.

Braće Radić 147. 44 324 Jasenovac. © **44/672-319.** Admission to the Jasenovac Memorial Museum is free. Mon–Fri 9am–5pm; Sat–Sun 10am–4pm. Closed holidays.

Lonjsko Polje Nature Park ★★ Kids The **Lonjsko Polje** is Europe's largest wetland nature park, stretching across more than 1,165 sq. km (450 sq. miles) and covering the area southeast from **Sisak** to **Jasenovac,** ending at the border with Bosnia. About 25% of this area is protected. Lonjsko Polje is a combination of forests and flatlands that are flooded half the year (approx. Nov–Apr.) The other half of the year, part of Lonjsko Polje is a pasture that supports a herd of indigenous horses known as **Posavinas** (Posavina is translated as "the area around the Sava River"). The Posavina horses are a protected species of husky wild equines that roam this bio-diverse acreage when the waters recede from the pastureland. Besides Posavina horses, the park is home to 238 bird species and 550 plant species. The area is 40% water and 60% woods and the largest protected wetland in the Danube Basin, Čigoć, is part of this ecological area. If you go, you might run into a member of the environmental group Friends of Lonjsko Polje. They will explain environmental threats to this wetland area to anyone who will listen. The group has launched an initiative promoting rural tourism aimed at allowing area citizens to prosper without ruining Lonjsko Polje's environmental balance.

Sisak ★ is a sleepy river town about 48km (30 miles) southeast of Zagreb and 23km (14 miles) west of the autocesta from the **Popovača** exit. Sisak is a good starting point for a tour of Croatia's eastern and southeastern cities as well as for the **Lonjsko Polje** (translation: field surrounding the Lonja) wetlands. It's worth a short walkabout, though not much more. Situated near the confluence of the **Sava, Odra,** and **Kupa** rivers, Sisak has been a strategic site since Roman times. In fact, the remains of a Roman wall are preserved in front of the **St. Cross** church on Trg Bana Josip Jeličića in the center of town. Sisak has played a long and storied role in Croatian history. It is famous for a June 22, 1593, battle that ended in a Christian victory preventing the Turks from advancing on Zagreb. Besides its war record, Baroque buildings, and St. Cross church, Sisak is known for an annual Knightly Tournament held in June that includes a couple of days of feasting, jousting, and other colorful exhibitions and competitions to commemorate the 1593 victory.

3 PODRAVINA & BJELOVAR-BILOGORA

The north-to-southeast strip of territory from Hlebine to Daruvar runs through the Podravina and Bilogora regions of Croatia, where some of Croatia's richest farmland and most provincial towns and villages lie, each with its own claim to fame. This area is the equivalent of any stretch of small-town America and is just as colorful. You can buy big loaves of still-warm, crusty bread from the back of a bakery truck that makes early morning rounds of village streets. You can watch a twice-daily parade of farmers with metal cans full of fresh milk rushing to the dairy co-op station to have their creamy yields weighed and credited to their accounts. In this part of the country, you still can see elderly goat herders using their staffs to urge their charges toward home. You can fall asleep to off-key group renditions of national songs filling the night air during almost weekly celebrations at the local church, an institution that marks life's defining moments. Here all get up with their roosters and go to bed before the 10pm news; and no one ever completely retires from his or her day job. This is the land of bountiful harvests and the heartbreak of war; of artists who interpret the vagaries of everyday life based on real people, and of men who gather each day to talk about what was and what might still be in Croatia. The towns in Podravina and Bilogora are segments of Croatia's solid backbone, independent but interconnected, and the people who live there are the salt of the earth.

ESSENTIALS

VISITOR INFORMATION   The **Đurđevac Tourist Office** is at S. Radiča 1 (© **048/ 812-046**). Hlebine does not have its own tourist office, but information is readily available from the **Zagreb tourism bureau** (p. 272).

GETTING THERE   See "Getting There" in "Orientation," earlier in this chapter.

GETTING AROUND   Hlebine, Đurđevac, and Čazma are easily explored on foot. Bjelovar and Daruvar are a little larger, so a car is handy for those with limited time and endurance.

4 HLEBINE & ĐURĐEVAC

Hlebine is famous for the naive art movement fostered by a group of 1930s peasant painters collectively known as the Hlebine School. Like the American artist known as Grandma Moses, artists from the Hlebine School portray the landscapes and people of the area in a straightforward, even crude way, depicting everyday activities and relationships with bold humor and even bolder imagery. Much art typical of this movement uses oil on glass as the medium, a technique that produces vivid color and great detail.

The town of Đurđevac, about 24km (15 miles) south of Hlebine, also has galleries dedicated to naive art, but Đurđevac is better known for its Picoki legend, a story about the rooster that saved Đurđevac.

ESSENTIALS

VISITOR INFORMATION   The Đurđevac tourism offices can provide maps, brochures and general information about area attractions. Hlebine does not have a tourist office per se, but personnel at the Hlebine Gallery and other merchants around town will help with directions and with pointing out sights worth a visit.

GETTING THERE   To get to Hlebine via public transportation, you first must go to the provincial town of Koprivnica 13km (8 miles) to the west. Buses and trains from Zagreb stop there. Koprivnica is also where you transfer to one of the six weekday buses that go to Hlebine. However, bus service to Hlebine is infrequent on weekends, so it's best to have your own car if you visit then. See "Getting There" in "Orientation," earlier in this chapter, for contact information for trains and buses to Koprivnica from Zagreb.

> ## (Fun Facts) A Bird in the Hand
>
> During a fabled siege, the Turkish army under the command of Ulama-beg barricaded the people of Đurđevac behind the walls of the Old Town without food or water with the intention of starving them into submission. According to legend, an old woman came up with the idea of shooting a rooster out of a cannon at the invading army to give the impression that the people of Đurđevac had so much food they could outlast the army. In reality, the rooster, or *picok*, was the last bit of food in the compound. The ploy worked and Ulama-beg and his army retreated, believing that the people had a huge store of supplies and that starving them out would be a losing battle. Before he left, Ulama-beg got in one last shot at Đurđevac by putting a curse on the townspeople, saying that from that day on they would be known as Picoki (roosters). Each year during the last week of June, the "Picoki" hold a big festival to commemorate their victory over the Turks. During this celebration, they re-enact the rooster shooting, though they purportedly now use a rubber chicken instead of a live rooster. In 2009, more than 30,000 people descended on Đurđevac for the annual rooster toss.

Đurđevac is connected to Hlebine by infrequent bus service, but it is only 20 minutes away by car.

GETTING AROUND   Once in Hlebine or Đurđevac, walking is the most reasonable way to see the towns' sites.

WHAT TO SEE & DO

In reality, Hlebine is a big artists' colony of more than 200 painters and sculptors who work mostly in the Hlebine School style. Consequently, Hlebine's biggest attractions are its art galleries. Đurđevac, on the other hand, is a one-attraction wonder, and the "rooster castle" is its most visited sight.

Galerija Hlebine ★★   This modern gallery is more like a museum and it is filled with examples of naive art from a variety of painters. Revolving exhibits from the gallery's collection as well as some permanent installations are on display, too. There even is a room with nothing but works from Ivan Generalić, whose sense of humor is evident in his earthy representations of peasant life, especially those works that include demonic-looking roosters. Besides art by Generalić, the gallery has a selection of naive art from various artists for sale.

Trg Ivana Generalića 15, Hlebine. (C) **048/836-075.** Free admission. Mon–Fri 10am–4pm; Sat 10am–2pm. Closed Sun.

Galerija Josip Generalić ★★★   The former atelier of Ivan and Josip Generalić is easy to find because tour buses are usually parked in front of the two modest buildings that hold the artists' work. Ivan Generalić died in 1992 and his son Josip died in 2004. Paintings done by both Generalićes hang on the walls of Josip's workroom and in the small gallery. Some of it is for sale at very reasonable prices. *Tip:* There is a pictorial map

> **(Fun Facts) Cock-a-Doodle-Doo, Ivan**
>
> As the story goes, when Ivan Generalić was a kid, his father would tiptoe into his room when he was sleeping and stick a squawking rooster in his face to wake him up. As a result of this poultry attack, Ivan developed a love-hate relationship with the birds, which usually are portrayed in an unflattering light in his works.

of Hlebine's artists' whereabouts outside the Galerija Hlebine (below) that pinpoints the location of every atelier in town. It is best to make arrangements with individual artists before you arrive, but you can also take your chances finding someone at home. Alternatively, you can ask anyone at Galerija Hlebine to call ahead for you. Be sure to call ahead to make sure someone is on hand to open the gallery.

Gajeva 75—83, Hlebine. ℂ **048/836-071.** galerija.josip.generalic@kc.t-com.hr. Free admission. By appointment only.

5 ČAZMA, BJELOVAR & DARUVAR

Čazma, Bjelovar, and Daruvar are typical towns in north-central Croatia. Not only are they noted as centers of agriculture, they also are the sites of food-processing plants and other industries vital to the entire country's economy. Daruvar also is known for its large Czech population and as one of the towns that was on the front lines during the 1991 war with Serbia.

ESSENTIALS

VISITOR INFORMATION   The **Bjelovarsko-Bilogorska County Tourist Board** is at Trg Eugena Kvaternika 4 (ℂ **043/243-944;** fax 043/241-229; tz.grada-bjelovar@bj. htnet.hr). Čazma's **Tourism Board** is at Milana Novačaća 13 (ℂ **043/772-086;** tz-cazma@bj.htnet.hr). Daruvar's **Tourism Office** is at Julijev Park 1 (ℂ **043/335-499;** fax 043/331-455). Each of these offices can provide maps, brochures, and suggestions about what to see, where to stay, and what to eat.

GETTING THERE   Čazma and Daruvar are linked to Zagreb via bus. Bjelovar has a train stop, but some routes entail multiple stops and transfers. For example, the railroad via Križevci connects Bjelovar with Zagreb, and another one via Virovitica connects it with Osijek. There is no train service to Čazma at this time. See "Getting There" in "Orientation," earlier in this chapter.

GETTING AROUND   Čazma, Bjelovar, and Daruvar all have compact cores, so walking is the best way to explore them.

WHAT TO SEE & DO

Each of the towns listed here is small and readily covered in a couple of hours, even on foot, and each has several pleasing sites worth checking out.

Bjelovar ★★   Picturesque Bjelovar experienced just a few days of fighting during the 1991 civil war in Croatia, but it was a bona fide military town under the Empress Maria Theresa of Austria, who built a fort there in 1756. Today, the town's former army headquarters has been restored and serves as a branch of Zagreb University. Plans include converting the building to a business and cultural center plus galleries and an exhibition hall.

Bjelovar celebrates its military glory days every summer with **Terezijana,** a festival held the last full weekend in June. The celebration commemorates the empress's visit to inspect her city. During the festival, Maria Theresa's "entrance" to the town center is reenacted with carriages, parades, and much fanfare that includes fun, food, and an annual open-air spoof featuring locals portraying the empress and her subjects.

Every September, Bjelovar is the site of one of Croatia's largest livestock exhibitions, an event that draws farmers from all over the country and beyond. The rest of the year, life in Bjelovar, which is just 80km (50 miles) northeast of Zagreb, is fairly quiet and revolves around agriculture. Just about any time, you can stroll Bjelovar's beautiful town square, which twice was voted the best-designed and maintained in Croatia by the Croatian National Tourism Board. You also can take a peek at the town's excellent civic museum, which has a good ethnographic collection. The **Bjelovar City Tourism Board** is at Trg Eugena Kvaternika 4 (℅ **043/243-944**).

Bjelovar Market ★★   Almost every city, town, and village in Croatia has a market where local farmers and merchants sell produce, meat, cheeses, wines, and even household products and clothing. Bjelovar's is better than most, perhaps because of its location in the middle of Croatia's agricultural belt. You'll find colorful fruits and vegetables as well as fresh meats and sausages, cheeses, baked goods, plants, and some textiles. Don't miss the cheese section, where you can buy little pyramid-shaped mounds of cheese—fresh or smoked—called *prgica,* all homemade by vendors who will encourage you to taste their wares before buying.

Tip: Thursday and Saturday are the best days to hit this market. These are the traditional days *(sajmeni dan)* when the market has the most variety and vendors because producers from many parts of Croatia join locals to sell their wares. The practice started centuries ago when farmers brought their livestock to Bjelovar Thursdays and Saturdays each week.

Ivša Lebović. Mon–Sat 7am–4pm; Sun and holidays 7am–1pm.

Čazma ★   This little town in Bjelovar-Bilogora County about 58km (36 miles) east of Zagreb is a sportsman's paradise. Hunters flock to the area for the deer, boar, pheasant, rabbit, and wild duck that freely roam the fields and gentle hills. Anglers are attracted by schools of freshwater fish teeming in the nearby Česma and Glogovnica rivers. For those who are into personal bests, Čazma has a large number of clay tennis courts and other sports venues. It is part of the **"Super-marathon Zagreb-Čazma"** itinerary, a 60km (36-mile) run held the first week of April that has been an annual event since 1976. History buffs can visit the unusually large Romanesque-style, twin-tower **Church of St. Mary Magdalene** built in the 13th century. It was restored with Baroque touches in the 18th. The church is noted for its incredibly ornate altar and pulpit, and for its 18th-century rococo organ decorated with lots of marble and gilt and topped by cherubs. The **Čazma Tourist Board** is at Milana Novačića 13 (℅ **043/772-086**).

Daruvar ★★   In Roman times, Daruvar was the site of baths called Aquae Balissae, which were named for the area's healing waters. Today, Daruvar still attracts tourists who want to soak in the town's mineral springs or who want to explore nearby **Papuk Mountain and National Park.** Daruvar is also a gateway to the county's thriving hunting tourism. Roebuck, wild boar, and game birds are just some of the sought-after prizes that attract outdoorsmen.

Daruvar suffered moderate damage during the 1991 war, most notably at beautiful **Julijev Park** in the heart of town, but it has mostly recovered. Daruvar is also home to a large contingent of Croatia's Czech population, as testified to by the presence of **Staro Česka Brewery.**

Daruvar Tourist Office. Julijev Park 1. ℭ **043/335-499.** Fax 043/331-455. komercialja@daruvarske-toplice.hr.

Papuk Mountain and National Park ★★ Kids

Papuk is the largest mountain in Slavonia. It and the land surrounding it were proclaimed protected areas in 1999. Papuk is geologically and ecologically diverse, and some of its rock formations are estimated to be 350 million years old. Besides of its geological significance, Papuk is home to cultural artifacts from the Iron Age and the remains of seven castles from the Middle Ages. It is also a recreational area frequented by hikers, skiers, and those who want to soak in Papuk's thermal pools and Orahovačko Lake.

S. Radića 46, 34330 Velika. ℭ **034/313-030.** Fax 034/313-027. www.pp-papuk.hr. Year-round.

WHERE TO STAY

Hotels in this part of Croatia are few and far between. Most are pretty basic because they generally cater to visiting farmers and hunters who don't demand much luxury. However, Daruvar's spa hotel is undergoing renovation, and some of the smaller places in town have been fixed up as well.

Hotel Balise ★ If you are passing through sleepy Daruvar, this pansion is a good, economical place in the center of town. The hotel was renovated in 2005 and is within easy reach of Julijev Park, the area's wineries, and Staro Ceška Brewery. From there you can go hiking to nearby **Petrov Peak** in the Papuk National Park or relax in the hotel's pleasant outdoor courtyard. Rooms are small but clean and comfortable, and the breakfast is top-notch.

Trg Kralja Tomislava 22, Daruvar. ℭ **043/440-220.** Fax 043/440-230. 19 units. From 500kn double. Kids 6 and under stay free in parent's room. AE, DC, MC, V. **Amenities:** Restaurant; bar; outdoor patio; excursions. *In room:* TV, hair dryer.

Hotel Termal/Daruvarske Toplice ★ Julijev Park, which is at the doorstep of this therapeutic spa resort, was damaged during the 1991 war, but the hotel was largely untouched. That is a mixed blessing in that the Termal's guest rooms were left intact but remain just as they were in the days when spartan accommodations and socialist drab were in style. However, the hotel still offers thermal waters and a host of fitness activities. The helpful staff will arrange hunting and fishing excursions and other tours for guests. The hotel/spa once was exclusively a rehab/medical center and is still popular among those who book to access health services, but it now caters to tourists.

Julijev Park 8, Daruvar. ℭ **043/623-200.** Fax 043/331-455. www.daruvarske-toplice.hr. 161 units. From 540kn double; from 1,360kn suite. Rates include breakfast and are based on a 7-day stay. Half- and full board are available. AE, DC, MC, V. **Amenities:** Fitness center; indoor/outdoor thermal pools; tennis courts; sauna; bowling alley; hydro massage; room for those w/limited mobility.

WHERE TO DINE

Dining in Čazma, Bjelovar, and Daruvar tends to be casual; most local establishments are pizzerias or ma-and-pa affairs. However, a couple of restaurants offer sit-down food a cut above the rest.

Restoran Terasa ★ REGIONAL CROATIAN   The dining room in this restaurant is just steps away from the Daruvarske Toplice hotel and has plenty of tall windows so diners can enjoy the view of leafy Julijev Park with their meals. The expansive wrap-around terrace provides the best ambience for tasting the restaurant's Slavonian, Czech, and Dalmatian specialties.

Julijev Park 1, Daruvar. ✆ **043/331-705.** Fax 043/331-455. Entrees 40kn–100kn. AE, DC, MC. Daily 9am–1pm.

Slasticarna Zagorje ★★★ COFFEEHOUSE   Peach-colored walls, Biedermeier furniture, and a cheerful garden terrace are the setting for enjoying the best ice cream and cakes in town. There isn't a single local who hasn't had a bowl of the creamy stuff here. This is where men stop to have coffee and read newspapers while their wives shop at the market, where kids beg their parents to take them for a special treat, and where teens take their first dates. In summer, head for the outdoor terrace where you can sit at wrought-iron garden tables with your honey while a delicate scent from the climbing roses creates a romantic cloud.

Ivana Viteza Trnskog 15, Bjelovar. ✆ **043/244-678.** Drinks and snacks less than 50kn. No credit cards. Daily 8am–11pm.

Stara Ura ★ Ⓥalue CROATIAN   This plain-looking restaurant down the street from Bjelovar's military buildings looks like any small-town storefront in America. However, locals regularly choose Stara Ura (old clock) for their nights out because the chef has a reputation for his excellent preparations and adherence to traditional recipes. As at most restaurants in this part of Croatia, grilled meats are the menu mainstays.

V. Nazora 22, Bjelovar. ✆ **043/244-870.** Entrees 40kn–60kn. No credit cards. Mon–Fri 8am–10pm; Sat 8am–midnight; closed Sun.

6 EASTERN SLAVONIA

Venture across the fertile expanse that stretches northeast from Nova Gradiška to Ilok, and you'll eventually see evidence of the violence that affected almost every town and village in the region. Skeletal remains of hothouses once filled with lush greenery, as well as the burned-out Borovo tire plant stand silent witness to the conflict that left Vukovar and other eastern cities bullet pocked and destitute. As of summer 2009 most land-mine warnings had been replaced by red plastic strips on the ground, indicating removal is in progress. But the chilling skull and crossbones signs indicating land-mine danger still confront visitors occasionally, as if to reassert war's horror. Many jagged, more obvious scars from the violence are constant reminders that inland Croatia still is suffering from the effects of the Homeland War. However, there is good news. Besides broken glass and burned-out factories, you'll see new shoots of hope sprouting, growing, even flourishing—proof that the indomitable Croatian spirit is alive and well across the Pannonian plain.

7 SLAVONSKI BROD, ĐAKOVO & NOVA GRADIŠKA

Đakovo ★★   Đakovo is 35km (22 miles) from Osijek and still emerging from damage and a stagnant economy inflicted by the 1991 war. The city is best known for **St. Peter the Apostle Cathedral** ★★★, an imposing red-brick edifice built in 1882 under the sponsorship of Josip Juraj Strossmayer, bishop of Đakovo, who was a patron of sacral art. Besides his attempts to unite the Slavic people, Strossmayer is remembered as the founder of the Yugoslav Academy of Arts and Sciences and its **Strossmayer Gallery of Old Masters** ★★ in Zagreb, to which he generously endowed his personal art collection. In addition to the cathedral, which has become almost synonymous with the city, Đakovo is known for its excellent white wines, a summer embroidery festival, and Državna Ergela Lipicanaca, its 500-year-old **Lipizzaner barn** *(ergela)* ★★★ in town and stud farm in Ivan Dvor where 225 of the majestic horses reside on 400 hectares (about 250 acres) just 5km (3 miles) northwest of town.

Nova Gradiška is a town easily bypassed by tourists. There is no great cathedral, no landmark hotel, no chi-chi gourmet restaurant there. What Nova Gradiška does have is a couple of diamond-in-the-rough attractions. Nova Gradiška's proximity to the Bosnian border made it a shaky place to be during the Homeland War, but the town escaped relatively unscathed. Good thing, too, because that left St. Peter's Church, the church museum, and a 17th-century castle damage-free.

Slavonski Brod Slavonski Brod is Slavonia's second-largest town, and if either Đakovo or Osijek is on your itinerary, the easiest way to get there is to travel south from Požega, where you can rejoin the toll road at Slavonski Brod and continue on. However, you might want to spend an hour or so looking around Slavonski Brod before you hit the highway. Slavonski Brod was heavily damaged during the 1991 war and is slowly being restored. Earlier, it was an 18th-century, fortress-style town made almost entirely of wood. That changed late in the 19th century and in the 20th, when the town acquired some Hapsburg structures and later block-style high-rises to house workers in the local industries. Slavonski Brod isn't worth too much of your time, but the remains of the 18th-century Brod Fortress, which was built to stop the Turks from invading Slavonia, is an interesting pause, especially since an extensive restoration is in progress. Entrance to the buildings was prohibited as of summer 2009, but cycling around the property and imagining the fort in happier times is encouraged.

ESSENTIALS

VISITOR INFORMATION If you stop at Slavonski Brod on your way east, the **tourist bureau** there will provide maps and brochures. That office is at Trg Pobjede 28/1 (☎ 035/447-721; www.tzgsb.hr). The tourist office in Đakovo is staffed by volunteers, but it may be one of the most helpful and welcoming tourist offices in all of Croatia. Besides the cathedral and the museum, the Đakovo tourist rep told us about the Lipizzaner stable, restaurants, hotels, and celebrations in Đakovo, really rolling out the welcome mat. The **Đakovo office** is at Kralja Tomislava 3 (☎ 031/811-233). In Nova Gradiška, head for Slavonskih Graničara 15 (☎ 035/361-495; www.tzgng.hr) for tourist information.

GETTING THERE Both trains and buses stop in Slavonski Brod, Đakovo, and Nova Gradiška. There are 14 buses and 15 trains daily from Zagreb to Slavonski Brod, which is connected to Požega, Nova Gradiška, and Đakovo by local routes. The Slavonski Brod bus station is at Trg Hrvatskog Proljeća (☎ 035/444-300), while the train station (☎ 035/441-082) is across the street from it. In Nova Gradaška, the train station is at Kolodvorska 5 (☎ 035/361-023), and the bus station is almost next door at Kolodvorska 2 (☎ 035/361-219). In Đakovo, the train station is less than a mile east of the center on Kralja Tomislava, and the bus station is less than a mile east of the cathedral

The Treasure of Nova Gradiška

Nova Gradiška is ordinary working-class Croatian town in southeastern Slavonia that was just 3km (1½ miles) from the fighting during the Homeland War. Today Nova Gradiška's citizens can enjoy a beautifully landscaped main square, a couple of decent restaurants, a hotel, and a Franciscan church and a monastery that is home to a trove of fascinating Bible treasures, one of which dates from the 12th century. The church was built by the Franciscans in 1734 and the museum is the result of one priest's passion for all things biblical. Inside you will find artifacts from the Holy Land, texts in various languages, and the marquee attraction, a handwritten, 12th-century Vatican Codex. Rev. Josip Grubišeć is a charming, English-speaking host who delights in sharing the church's treasure with interested tourists. Call ☎ **035/369-043** to arrange a tour at the church at Potočna 4.

on Splitska. See "Getting There," in "Orientation," earlier in this chapter, for transportation contact information.

GETTING AROUND   As with most inland Croatian cities, walking is the best way to navigate Đakovo, but right now Slavonski Brod is a one-attraction town and a car is handy to get to the fort in Slavonski Brod and the monastery in Nova Gradiška.

WHAT TO SEE & DO

Many visitors are drawn to Đakovo because of its awe-inspiring cathedral. Others stop there because Đakovo is the birthplace of Bishop Josip Juraj Strossmayer, who is a historic figure in Croatian politics, and who is especially remembered for his efforts to unite Serbs and Croats in a South Slav (Yugoslav) state. Strossmayer is also responsible for the city's distinctive cathedral, which he commissioned with funds generated by church properties in his see. For most people, however, Đakovo is just a pretty provincial town with a horse farm, a few architectural landmarks, and a nice pedestrian street (Korzo) lined with shops and restaurants.

Cathedral of St. Peter the Apostle ★★★   The neo-Gothic Cathedral of St. Peter the Apostle is enough reason to stop in Đakovo. You'll have to stretch your neck to see the church's 84m (275-ft.) twin spires up close after looking at them for an hour or more while approaching the city on the highway from Zagreb. St. Peter the Apostle is the third iteration of a cathedral on this spot, and this one is magnificent. The enormous building was built between 1862 and 1882 by Viennese architect Baron Frederick Schmidt at the behest of Bishop Josip Juraj Strossmayer. The cathedral's interior is full of fascinating statuary and artistic detail, from frescoes by Alexander and Ludwig Seitz to sculptures by noted Croatian artists of the times. The 19th-century park near the bishop's palace and the Mali (small) park nearby both are protected monuments.

Strossmayer Trg. Daily 7am–noon and 3–7pm.

Đakovo Embroidery ★★★   Đakovački Vezovi is a folklore festival celebrating traditions from the regions of Slavonia and Baranja. Traditional folk costumes, dancing, and singing groups characterize the celebration, which takes place the last weekend in

September. During the festival, the cathedral is the site of choir concerts, operatic performances, and art exhibitions; there is also a horse and wedding wagon. The highlight of the celebration is the show put on by pure white Lipizzaner horses from the city's stud farm, which has been a breeding center since the early 16th century.

Korzo ★ If you turn left after exiting the cathedral past the Strossmayer Museum, you will be on Ulica Papa Ivana Pavli II (Pope John Paul II St.). The pedestrian street is also known as the Korzo. Paved with red bricks, it is alive with shops and a midway that is a solid block of outdoor cafes.

Lipizzaner Stable and Stud Farm ★★★ (Kids) Đakovo's impressive Lipizzaner stable stud farm was founded in the early 16th century by the Hapsburgs, who were charged with providing quality horses for Vienna. Đakovo's is just one of several such farms in central Europe. Lipizzaners are prized for their intelligence and their ability to respond to commands as well as for their agility. The horses are brown when they are born but they turn mostly white in about 3 years. You can visit and even ride these beauties if you call ahead. *Tip:* To get to the stud farm in Ivan Dvor, follow the signs toward Našice for about 5km (3 miles). About 90m (300 ft.) from the road's intersection with Hwy. 7, you'll see a dirt road on the left that seems to go into the woods. Follow that for 2km (1¼ miles) to reach the farm. You will need a four-wheel-drive vehicle for this if the ground is wet. For more details, see the website.

Augusta Šenoe 33. ℂ **031/813-286.** www.ergela-djakovo.hr. Mon–Fri 9am–4pm. Weekend visits by appointment.

Strossmayer Museum ★★ The Strossmayer Museum holds some of the bishop's artifacts and writings. It is immediately north of the cathedral in a pale yellow building.

Admission 5kn. Tues–Fri 8am–7pm; Sat 8am–2pm. Closed Sun–Mon.

WHERE TO STAY

Most accommodations in Slavonski Brod and Đakovo are private, but there are a few small hotels in the region that offer unique experiences.

Hotel Blaža ★★ This relatively new (2002) but smallish hotel offers a higher level of comfort than most. Guest rooms, though not amenity-heavy, are outfitted with good-size modern bathrooms. Furnishings are plain but modern.

Starčević 158, Đakovo. ℂ **031/816-760.** Fax 031/816-764. 20 units. From 470kn double. AE, DC, MC, V. **Amenities:** Restaurant; pool. *In room:* TV.

Vinarija Zdelarević ★★★ This lovely hotel in the middle of a vineyard is just 6km (4 miles) west of Slavonski Brod and 160km (100 miles) from Zagreb, off the A3 east-west autocesta. You'll get an enthusiastic welcome that includes a glass of wine when you arrive. Besides tastefully decorated rooms with modern showers, the Zdelarević has a restaurant that offers tours of its winery, tastes of its vintages, and excellent Slavonian cuisine.

Vinogradska 102, Brodski Stupnik. ℂ **035/427-775.** Fax 035/427-040. www.zdjelarevic.hr. 15 units. From 580kn double; from 750kn suite. Rates include breakfast. Half- and full board available. AE, DC, MC, V. **Amenities:** Restaurant; bar; excursions; paintball; horseback riding; walking tours. *In room:* A/C, TV, hair dryers.

WHERE TO DINE

For the most part, dining is casual and plain in this part of Croatia, but things are looking up as the area's wine industry recovers and cuisine becomes more sophisticated without losing its regional flair.

Gradski Podrum ★ SLAVONIAN Walk a few steps down to access this tidy cellar restaurant off the Korzo in Đakovo. The space has been a restaurant since 1945, but the building is 1880s vintage. The menu is tourist-friendly in that it is written in three languages, including English, and the space is blissfully air-conditioned. Stop for a pizza (10 varieties) or something more substantial like a Đakovo cutlet (veal filled with ham and kulen in a spicy sauce) or savor a mixed grill. The staff is friendly and can also help with directions around town.

H. Velikana 9. *©* **031/813-199.** Entrees 25kn–120kn; pizzas 20kn–28kn. AE, MC, V. Daily 7am–midnight.

Slastica Korzo COFFEEHOUSE The street between Đakovo's cathedral and the rest of town is a solid block of umbrella tables and cafes. It's beyond almost everyone's willpower to navigate the strip without stopping for a "cold one." This little coffee shop serves delicious ice-cream treats as well as more elaborate sweets, and its air-conditioner blows cold air onto the tables outside, a plus.

H. Velikana 18. No phone. Ice cream from 6kn. No credit cards. Daily 7am–9pm.

Zdelarević ★★★ (**Value** SLAVONIAN Slavonian cuisine meets *nouveau* gourmet in this winery restaurant that prides itself on creative cuisine. Whether you eat indoors with a view of the open kitchen or outdoors on the veranda near the vineyard, the experience will be unique and the food superb. Try the *ramstek na vinogradarski,* beef grilled with a frozen "brick" of butter flavored with wine and herbs. Add the *krumpir na Stupnicki,* potatoes baked in the oven with bacon and cream, and you have a very filling meal. The menu is loaded with regional delights, all of them tweaked with expert additions. Pair your food with a bottle of Zdelarević wine from the restaurant winery, which was established in 1985 and is one of the first private wineries in Croatia. It produces chardonnay, Riesling, and other varietals.

In the Vinarija Zdelarević, Vinogradska 102, Brodski Stupnik. *©* **035/427-775.** Fax 035/427-040. www. zdjelarevic.hr. Entrees 35kn–90kn. AE, DC, MC, V. Daily 11am–11pm.

8 OSIJEK

Osijek is just 35km (22 miles) from Đakovo and 29km (18 miles) from the Hungarian border in the northeastern corner of Croatia. It is the largest city in Slavonia and the fourth largest in the country. Osijek finally is recouping some of its former vigor 15 years after the end of the war. At first, Osijek concentrated on repairing damage from the hostilities, but now the city has finished a $10-million face-lift of its main square while rehabbing older properties and building new ones. During the war, all but 15,000 of Osijek's 80,000 citizens fled the city and sought shelter in other parts of Croatia or in foreign countries. Many—but not all—have returned, a sign that the local economy is on the upswing.

Osijek proper is awash with parks and tree-lined streets that link its three centers and shade its stately mansions. Its western skyline, however, is a wall of socialist-era structures that belie the city's beauty. The city comprises three town centers: Tvrđa, Upper Town, and Lower Town, each of which has its own personality. The **Tvrđa** area is Osijek's biggest tourist draw, with its vestiges of Roman culture and Ottoman occupation. These days it looks like a construction zone because its buildings are being renovated. It is also the site of Osijek's summer cultural program, which brings in big-name performers from all over the world.

One of the city's best features is its river walk, a paved path flanking both banks of the Drava that is used by joggers, cyclists, in-line skaters, and people fishing or exercising their dogs. The river walk is quickly becoming a trendy nightlife and shopping spot because of a new adjacent shopping mall. A small bridge leads to Copacabana, the city's most popular beach, and on the river, the marina houses hundreds of powerboats and sculls. Other people-powered crafts can be seen cutting through the water at any time of the day.

ESSENTIALS

VISITOR INFORMATION   Osijek's **tourist office** is located at Županijska 2 (② 031/ **203-755;** fax 031/203-947; www.tzosijek.hr). It can provide maps, brochures, and guidance about the city's sites and surrounding areas.

GETTING THERE   As the largest city in Slavonia, Osijek is served by regular bus and train services that link it to all parts of Croatia. The bus and train stations are adjacent to each other on Trg L. Ružička at the south end of the town center. See "Getting There" in "Orientation," earlier in this chapter.

GETTING AROUND   Osijek has a fast and efficient tram system. Once you're in the center of town, you can walk to the city's most interesting sites.

WHAT TO SEE & DO

There are 15 public squares in Osijek, each with a different personality. Visitors can amble through Gornji Grad's 19th-century splendor in the city's northwestern quadrant to see architectural landmark buildings like the Croatian National Theater or go medieval in Tvrđa, the true center of town, where the fortress created by walls and former barracks is being transformed into a hip university center with trendy restaurants and a vibrant nightlife. Donji Grad is the quietest part of town and the most residential. It is on the northeastern edge of the city along the Drava, where the Baroque pilgrimage church of Our Lady of the Snows draws attention.

Church of Sts. Peter and Paul ★★   This church is often referred to as a cathedral, but it really is a parish church built between 1894 and 1898 according to plans drawn up by architects Franz Langenberg of Germany and Richard Jordan of Vienna. The massive red-brick neo-Gothic building is the biggest structure in town. Its huge footprint now covers the spot first occupied by a wooden chapel (1698) and then a small Baroque church. The current structure covers nearly 1,062 sq. m (3,500 sq. ft.) and includes an 82m-tall (270-ft.) bell tower that is almost as high as the towers in Đakovo. The church on Osijek's main square has five Gothic altars. Its ceilings and walls are covered with sacral paintings.

Trg Marina Držica, Gornji Grad. ② **031/369-626.** Access during Mass; also daily noon–3pm and 5–5:30pm.

The Croatian National Theatre ★★★   The building housing the theater was constructed in 1866, but the theater itself wasn't founded until 1907. The theater is an interesting example of Venetian-Moorish architecture as well as a major cultural institution in Osijek even though it was heavily damaged during Croatia's 1991 war with Serbia. Today it is completely restored to its former glory, though a McDonald's on its street level isn't exactly in keeping with historic fidelity. Many purists resent even the tiny sign advertising the Golden Arches establishment, but in fact McDonald's contributed a

ACCOMMODATIONS■
Hotel Central **3**
Hotel Osijek **8**
Hotel Vila Ariston **9**
Hotel Waldinger **5**
Pansion Strossmayer **2**
Zoo Hotel **10**

Restaurant Kompa **1**
Restoran Osijek **8**
Restoran Strossmayer **2**

ATTRACTIONS●
Church of Sts. Peter & Paul **4**
Croatian National Theater **7**
Holy Trinity Square **13**
Museum of Slavonia **14**
Our Lady of the Snows **18**
Tvrđa **11**
Water Gate **16**

DINING◆
Kod Javora **17**
Kod Ruža **15**
Old Bridge Pub **12**
Restaurant Club Waldinger **6**

significant amount of money to the theater's restoration after the war. The theater stages productions from September to May.

Županijska 9, Osijevk. ℰ **031/220-700.**

Europska Avenue ★★   Osijek's broadest and most interesting street runs between Tvrđa (the Fort) to Gornji Grad (Upper Town) and intersects several city parks in between. Europska Avenue is also the street (from Kapucinska Ulica on the north end) where affluent Austrians built their Art Nouveau mansions between 1904 and 1905. Some of these structures have been repaired and restored, but others are sadly derelict. Note the single-story building at no. 24 (now home to the town's and university's library), as well as the bronze statue in Kralja Državislava Park. The building was a wedding gift from a wealthy citizen to his daughter. The statue was created by Robert Mihanović in 1898 as a memorial to fallen soldiers.

Holy Trinity Square ★★★   Holy Trinity is one of the most attractive town squares in Croatia. Besides the stunning **plague column ★★**, there is a round fountain with two red stone water basins. Restored historic buildings frame the square.

In the center of town. Tvrđa.

Museum of Slavonia ★ A nice collection of archaeological finds from prehistoric to Roman times is exhibited here. Housed in the City Magistrate Building on the southeastern corner of Holy Trinity Square, the 1702 structure is the oldest Baroque building in Osijek. The museum moved there in 1946, and while the building was heavily shelled during the Homeland War, the collections escaped damage.

Trg Svetog Trojstva 6, Tvrđa. © **031/122-505.** Fax 031/120-959. www.mdc.hr/osijek/eng/opci-podaci.
html. Admission 10kn adults, 5kn children. Mon–Fri 7:30am–3:30pm; Sat–Sun 10am–1pm. Closed red-
letter days (holidays).

Our Lady of the Snows ★ Our Lady of the Snows was built in 1895 based on a design of architect Franz Langenberg, who also designed the imposing Sts. Peter and Paul Church in Gornji Grad.

At the south end of Trg Bana Josip Jelačića, Donji Grad.

Tvrđa ★★★ (Kids) The partially walled former fort and center of Osijek is quickly becoming the hippest neighborhood in town. Originally built on the site of a Roman settlement, Tvrđa went through a series of rulers and attacks through the ages. It became the principal city in Pannonia in the 2nd century, was captured by the Avars and rebuilt by the Croats in the Middle Ages, and leveled by Turkish forces in the 16th century. After routing the Turks in the 17th century, the Austrians rid the city of Turkish mosques and minarets and built a fortified compound incorporating the walls left over from Ottoman rule—parts of these ancient fortifications still can be seen today. Even though Tvrđa has changed hands and personalities several times, it has retained its charm and old-world feel. Contemporary Tvrđa is a lovely area with cobblestone streets, lots of restaurants and galleries, and an artists' colony just inside the ramparts and the Water Gate. The Town Hall, Museum of Slavonia, and Osijek University are situated there.

Votive Pillar of the Holy Trinity ★★ This Baroque plague pillar was built in 1729 by the widow of Gen. Maksimilijan Petraš, who died of the disease in 1728. Statuary decoration includes sculptures of Sts. Sebastian, Roch, Rosalia, and Catherine. The plague column was built as a prayer that "God have pity on Osijek and repulse the plague which ravaged the whole of Slavonia."

In the center of town (at Holy Trinity Sq.), Tvrđa.

Water Gate ★★ The Water Gate or Porta Aquatica led toward the Drava from the city fortifications when it was built in 1714. It still stands as an entry to the walled part of the city. There once were five gates into Osijek, but the Water Gate is the only one that remains.

On the north side of the Tvrđa complex, right next to the Waldinger Gallery and near the Franciscan monastery and church.

(Finds) Ernestinovo

Ernestinovo is a little town between Osijek and Đakovo that is known for its fall sculpture festival during which sculptors, most of them Croatian, descend on the town and carve large wooden figures that they place along the side of the road from Ernestinovo to Vinkovci. The rest of the year, a few of these large wooden figures can be seen positioned curbside throughout Ernestinovo.

Osijek's hotel scene is improving, thanks to ambitious renovation projects that have restored or upgraded existing facilities.

Hotel Central   The Central, which was built in 1899, is midway between the Waldinger and Osijek hotels, about a block from the river, and close to the city's tram line. The Central's lobby is frayed around the edges, but the rooms are tidy and fairly priced. There are few room amenities here, but you can walk to the river and the city's best sights in less than 15 minutes.

Trg Ante Starčevića. ☏ **031/283-399.** Fax 031/283-891. www.hotel-central-os.hr. 39 units. From 786kn double; suites from 840kn. AE, DC, MC, V. Rates include breakfast. Half- and full board available. **Amenities:** Restaurant; coffeehouse; bike rentals; solarium; excursions. *In room:* TV, minibar.

Hotel Osijek ★ ⬭**Overrated**   The gleaming metal-and-glass Hotel Osijek soars 14 stories above the town's river walk as if flaunting its 2004 transformation from a Socialist-style ugly duckling into a sleek capitalist swan. It is unabashedly trying to attract a clientele to match its new image and it has succeeded. The Osijek's lobby is minimalist chic and full of designer-clad guests, and its **Zimska Luka Restaurant** seems to attract yuppie corporate types and local celebs doing deals beside a panoramic view of the river. Add to that a lower-level watering hole for hip 20- and 30-somethings, an adjacent ice-cream/coffee shop for families, and a full-service salon, and you have the basics of a trendy hotel. Views from the riverside guest rooms are spectacular, but room size and amenities don't deliver what you'd expect for the expense-account prices charged here. In addition, the staff is cordial and efficient but not exceptionally helpful, and there is an extra charge for the use of bathrobes and slippers strategically placed in the rooms. If you want a hotel on the river, however, this is the only game in town.

Šamačka 4, 31000 Osijek. ☏ **031/230-333.** Fax 031/230-444. www.hotelosijek.hr. 147 units. From 950kn double; from 1,490kn suite. Rates include breakfast. AE, DC, MC, V. 20 free parking spaces and adjacent city parking (free 8pm–7am). **Amenities:** Restaurant; pastry shop; bar; fitness center; valet service. *In room:* A/C, TV, hair dryer, minibar, Wi-Fi (on lower floors).

Hotel Vila Ariston ★   Attention to detail is evident in this butter-yellow hotel 15 minutes from Trg Ante Starčevića, Osijek's main shopping square. The English-speaking staff is eager to please and rooms are oversize with private balconies. Marble shines and parquet wood floors gleam in every corner of the building. The hotel is located around the corner from the train station, which is convenient, but it's a shame that the tram tracks run less than 9m (30 ft.) from the hotel's front door, making noise an issue. It's also too bad that the hotel's location takes it out of the riverfront action, and that the owner didn't think to put in an elevator when he built the three-story Ariston in 2006. But, if you don't mind a little exercise (or a tram ride), and if you want a classy room with comfort and luxury at a moderate price, the Vila Ariston is the place for you.

Zrinjevac, Kačićeva 6. ☏ **031/251-351.** Fax 031/251-350. 8 units. Doubles from 777kn; suites from 999kn. Rates include breakfast. AE, DC, MC, V. Free video-monitored parking. **Amenities:** Restaurant; piano bar; valet service. *In room:* A/C, TV, hair dryer, minibar.

Hotel Waldinger ★★★   The charming Hotel Waldinger is an oasis of elegance in the center of Osijek, a city that still is struggling to recover from the 1991 war. Named after 19th-century painter Adolf Igniat Waldinger and built in the center of town in 1904, this small hotel was completely renovated a century later in 2004. It now offers guests modern conveniences in an elegant, Secessionist-style interior, which is in stark contrast to the ultramodern high-rise Hotel Osijek a block away. Waldinger guest rooms are oversize and distinctive with soft colors, rich fabrics, and luxurious bathrooms. The paintings throughout the public and private spaces communicate the civilized air of a European manor. The English-speaking staff is helpful and courteous. Breakfast for Waldinger guests is in a private first-floor dining room, but the **Kavana Waldinger** at street level is open to the public. Besides its prime location steps away from, Trg Ante Starčevića, one of the city's main squares, the Waldinger has a private lot with video-monitored free parking—a major perk for guests with cars. The elegant **Waldinger Restaurant Club** was added in 2007 just off the parking area.

Županijska 8, 31000 Osijek. ✆ **031/250-450.** Fax 031/250-453. www.waldinger.hr. 23 units. From 950kn double; from 1,200kn suite. Rates include breakfast. AE, DC, MC, V. **Amenities:** Restaurant; cafe; fitness center; Internet; sauna; exchange office; meeting rooms; library; art gallery; valet service. In room: A/C, TV, hair dryer, Jacuzzi tub, minibar.

Pansion Strossmayer ★ (**Finds**) Just seven rooms above Café Strossmayer and Restoran Bischoff comprise Pansion Strossmayer, but you can't beat the location, the price, the extras, or the breakfast crammed into the price of these immaculate units. Units have plasma TV, hydromassage shower, and toiletries—all small touches normally not included at this price.Strossmayerova 133. ✆ **031/375-888.** 7 units. Doubles from 490kn. Rate includes breakfast. AE, DC, MC, V. **Amenities:** Restaurant; bar. In room: A/C, plasma TV, Wi-Fi.

Zoo Hotel ★★ (**Kids**) There aren't any cutesy costumed animal characters walking around in the lobby and no ersatz safari rides either, but there are similarities between the kitschy Zoo Hotel and a themed Disney resort. Zoo Hotel is close to the Osijek City Zoo and it extends the wild animal theme everywhere it can, from imitation animal-skin furnishings to a restaurant that specializes in wild game dishes. Otherwise, it's a hotel built in 2007 that focuses on functionality: Rooms are minimalist, utilitarian, and with enough elbow room to stretch out. You won't need a tram to get to the zoo, either.

Sjevernodravska obala, Tvrdjavica. ✆ **031/229-922.** Fax 031/229-911. www.zoo-hotel.com. 18 units. Doubles from 750kn. AE, DC, MC, V. Free parking. **Amenities:** Restaurant. In room: A/C, TV, minibar.

WHERE TO DINE

Osijek is a Mecca for Slavonian cuisine and no matter where you dine, you won't leave hungry. Many restaurants in this part of Croatia are family style, so don't be surprised when huge platters of food arrive for all to share.

Kod Javora ★★ SLAVONIAN The atmosphere is boisterous at this "dining hall" near the river, but the well-prepared food is authentic Slavonian. Start with grilled pike filets wrapped in local *pršut* and served with a delicate thyme-scented tartar sauce that you'll want to put on everything else you order. Another good choice at this restaurant, whose name means "at the maple tree," is *perkelt,* a ragout variation of fish paprika with a spicy kick. For tamer tastes, *rezanci sa sirom* (noodles with cheese and bacon) is a good choice, though family-style service makes sampling easy. Pair it with a bottle of local Graševina, a crisp white wine that stands up to the intense flavors in most of the dishes here. Seating is available inside or on the river. When it's raining, the restaurant moves its outdoor tables into a big party tent.

Donjodravska obala 14. ✆ **031/506-950.** Reservations recommended. Entrees 50kn–80kn. AE, MC, V. Daily 9am–11pm.

Kod Ruže ★★ SLAVONIAN Slavonia seems to have embraced the "back to our roots" movement in a big way, and Kod Ruže (trans: At Rose's) is no exception. This restaurant housed in a vintage 1758 building near Tvrđa opened in January 2007, and it is full of taxidermed animals, ancient pottery, ancestral photos hanging in hand-carved frames on hand-painted, patterned walls, and other regional antiques. Kod Ruže also tries to duplicate some of the recipes from Grandma's time on the menu. Start with a Slavonian plate for two, generous portions of kulen, local cheese, and crackling "čvanci," or go for a filling bowl of game stew. In winter you can try *sarma,* sour cabbage leaves stuffed with meat and rice, and you can have grilled fish anytime. Kod Ruže makes its own *ajvar,* a Croatian condiment made of red pepper and eggplant, but its pastries have a store-bought taste. The menu changes seasonally, and there is a nice list of Croatian wines.

Kuhačeva 25a. ℂ **031/206-066.** Entrees 25kn–80kn. AE, DC, MC, V. Mon–Sat 9am–11pm and Sun 10am–4pm.

Old Bridge Pub ★ SLAVONIAN   Many levels of dining comprise the Old Bridge experience. Outside-inside, formal-bar-style, and everything in between is possible in this atmospheric spot near Tvrđa named after the 13km-long (8-mile) oak bridge that linked Osijek and its marshy outposts in the 16th century. Try one of the restaurant's excellent pasta dishes—you can choose a pasta and match it with any sauce—or the Big Ben, a huge turkey shish kabob with grilled vegetables. For dessert there is homemade štrukli or *knedle su šlivama,* plum dumplings that resemble sugar-covered jelly donuts filled with whole stewed plums. There is an extensive menu of Irish brews as well as lots of memorabilia from across the channel. Old Bridge offers live music in the downstairs room after 10pm most days.

Kuhačeva 4. ℂ **031/211-611.** www.oldbridgepub.hr. Entrees 34kn–85kn. AE, DC, MC, V. Mon–Thurs 7am–2am; Fri–Sat 7am–4am; Sun 9am–midnight.

Restaurant Strossmayer ★ SLAVONIAN   The dining room is bright and cheerful in this all-purpose restaurant off Osijek's main square. Portions are huge and recipes authentic. Try the turkey shish kabob, which comes with a nice portion of grilled veggies. Or take a chance on the *plat du jour,* in our case, veal roulades in au natural gravy. There is a small outdoor terrace.

Strossmayerova 133. ℂ **031/375-888.** www.pizzastross.com. Entrees 25kn–75kn, more for meat and fish by the kilo. AE, DC, MC, V. Mon–Sat 10am–10pm; Sun 11am–3pm and 7–10pm.

Restoran Kompa ★★ ⓥ**alue** SLAVONIAN   Locals love this family style restaurant where you can dine within feet of the mighty Drava. Very little English is spoken here and you will need your dictionary to figure out the menu, but the authentic Croatian dining experience is worth the effort. Fish is on the menu, but not exclusively, so start with local cheese and sausage and a bottle of the house wine *(Slavonski kulen, sir grbancijaš, vino buteljirano),* and you may not have enough room for dinner. Portions are enormous; do save a little room for the strudel. If you take a table outside after dark, bring along insect repellent.

Splavarska 1. ℂ **031/375-755.** Fax 031/376-358. Entrees from 25kn for *sarma* (chopped meat and rice wrapped in marinated cabbage leaves) to 60kn for *šunka* and *sir* (ham and cheese). AE, DC, MC, V. Daily 9am–10pm.

Waldinger Restaurant Club ★★★ MODERN SLAVONIAN   The level of sophistication evident in the chic design of this restaurant in the middle of sausage-and-paprika Slovenia is as unexpected as Waldinger's inventive menu. Add culinary touches that would be at home in mid-town Manhattan and you have a gastronomic oasis worth a detour from any itinerary. WRC opened in January 2007, and since then diners have been drawn to the softly illuminated space filled with warm cherry floors, gauzy drapes, and lots of glass. Dishes like the "Black Widow," sirloin steak in blackberry-pimento sauce, wild filet of deer, bear, or doe in candied cherry sauce, or duck breast with green pepper and honey-orange sauce are the real draw, though. For dessert, we couldn't resist the restaurant's interpretation of bananas Foster, a beautifully composed dish of flamed fruit, vanilla ice cream, and cinnamon. There is also a wine list deep in Croatian regionals.

Županuska 8. ℰ **031/214-671.** Reservations recommended. Entrees 40kn (for pastas) to 150kn. AE, DC, MC, V. Daily 11am–midnight.

COFFEEHOUSES

Kavana Waldinger ★★ DESSERTS The front of this coffeehouse next to the lobby of the Waldinger Hotel opens to the street. Besides pastries and ice-cream treats, patrons can linger over coffee while pedestrian traffic rolls by.

Županijska 8. ℰ **031/250-470.** AE, DC, MC, V. Daily 8am–11pm.

Mala Kavana ★★ DESSERTS There isn't a more advantageous spot for a coffeehouse than the corner of Gornji Grad's main square, which just underwent a 10-million€ makeover. Besides enjoying some of the best brews and people shows in town, patrons who sit at the outdoor tables can now amuse themselves with the sight of a modern water feature (fountain) and mall entrance.

Županijska 2. No phone. No credit cards. Mon–Sat 6:30am–11pm; Sun 8am–11pm.

OSIJEK AFTER DARK

Clubbing and bar-hopping in Osijek have exploded in the last 2 years thanks to extensive riverfront development and the Tvrđa renovation. It is not unusual to find places for drinking and dancing that stay open until dawn.

Cadillac The acoustic performances from mostly local talent on center stage at Cadillac appeal to all age groups. The dark wood and mirrors give the place a cozy atmosphere that makes everyone feel at home. Open 8am to 3am daily. Kardinala Alozija Stepinca 28. ℰ **031/209-138.**

Gen. Von Becker's ★★ Tvrđa's central square is a prime location for bars and restaurants these days and GVB's is sitting pretty there. The interior is reminiscent of the days when the Hapsburgs set the styles in town, though drinking, not history, is the focus here. Open 7am to midnight Monday through Thursday, 7am to 2am Friday and Saturday, and 10am to midnight Sunday. Franje Kuhača 13. No phone.

K ★ The former Kesten Bar is in a new location near the train station as of 2007, but even with a new identity, the bar's followers have remained loyal. Tame by jet-set standards, the bar usually empties out by 11pm as hard-core partygoers move on to more raucous pastures. Open 9am to 11pm Monday through Friday, 8am to 11pm on Saturday, and 10am to 11pm Sunday. Kardinal Alojzija Stepinca 38a. ℰ **098/843-078.**

St. Patrick's Pub ★★ It's a mystery why Osijek has two Irish pubs, but the attraction of St. Patrick's on the main Tvrđa square is clear. Besides the welcoming interior, St. Pat's has a wonderful outdoor terrace where patrons can hoist a pint to summer—or whatever turns them on. Open 7am to midnight Monday through Wednesday, 7am to 1am Thursday, 7am to 2am Friday and Saturday, and 9:30am to midnight Sunday. Trg Svetog Trojstva. No phone.

Tufna ★ This club opened in 2007 on the site of another club near Tvrđa and it was an instant success. Tufna offers two floors of music from disco to electro beats and it attracts all the beautiful people, provided they can prove that they are over 21. Open 8am

9 BARANJA

Baranja extends beyond Croatia into Serbia and Hungary, but in Croatia, the Baranja land northeast of Osijek and up to Croatia's eastern border is mostly farm and vineyard country, with the **Kopački Rit** wetlands thrown in for good measure. Until recently, tourists avoided Baranja because of land-mine threats, but today almost all hazards have been removed and those that remain are underwater in inaccessible parts of Kopački Rit. Baranja is now coming into its own as a center for farm stays, wine tours, and sustainable tourism.

Baranja Wine Road (Općina Kneževi Vinogradi) ★★★   There are more than 20 wineries listed on the Baranja wine route, and almost all serve food either as a complement to their wines or for those just out for a good meal. Some have lodging. Most of these wineries are family businesses with the owners living on the winery premises. It isn't difficult to arrange to visit any of these Baranja gems, but you should call ahead either to the Baranja Tourism Office or to the individual vintners to make sure they are home and prepared to serve you when you arrive.

Hrvatske Republike 3, Kneževi vinogradi. ℭ 031/730-938. Fax 031/732-106. www.knezevi-vinogradi.hr.

Kopački Rit Nature Park ★★★ (Kids)   Kopački Rit is a 168-sq.-m (65-sq.-mile) flood-plain area of the Danube River, at the river's confluence with the Drava. According to park literature, it is also one of the largest alluvial plains in Europe and extends north into the Republic of Hungary. Kopački Rit was designated a nature park in 1967 to protect the flood-plain ecosystems.

Today, the park is home to many wetland birds from early spring to fall when the Danube overflows its banks. White-tailed eagles, cormorants, great-crested grebes, white storks, and a few black storks can be seen when the plain is flooded and wild boar, deer, and 40 species of fish inhabit the plains and the lakes and ponds that remain when the Danube waters pull back.

Besides wildlife, attractions include Sakadaš and Kopačko lakes where more than 285 species of birds come to fish and nest; the 19th-century Tikveš Hunting Lodge, now home to meeting rooms and a restaurant; and Kopačvo, a traditional Slavonian settlement that has been frozen in time. Zelena Žava is a delightful restaurant that serves traditional specialties. Reservations are necessary if you want to take one of the English-language boat or Jeep tours.

Tip: There is a bicycle path that runs along the Osijek-Bilje road, which means you can stay in Osijek, just 10km (6 miles) southwest from the park, and pedal there. Or you can catch an Osijek-Bilje bus, which runs every half-hour or so, but you will have to walk 4km (2½ miles) from the bus stop to the park's entrance.

Petefi Šandora 33, 31327 Bilje. ℭ **031/752-350.** Fax 031/752-351. www.kopacki-rit.com. 40kn adults, 20kn children Sun. 60kn adults, 45kn children other times. Park-guided boat trip 80kn; guided bird-watching tour 200kn. Daily 9am–5pm.

Restoran Tikveš ★★ (Kids)   You expect to see hunters in camouflage dining in this unpretentious restaurant nestled against Kopački Rit's vegetation. Usually, all you'll see is tourists and a fine meal from the nearby forest and rivers. Pheasant, venison, and boar

A Pair of *Podrumi* (Wine Cellars)

Kolar Wine Cellar ★★★   Produces 80,000 liters from its century-old cellar. The facility includes a restaurant and some of the most immaculate sobes we've seen anywhere in Croatia. Maršala Tita 139, Suza. ✆ **031/733-184.** 3 units. Doubles from 360kn. Rates include breakfast. **Amenities:** A/C; TV. *In room:* Bathroom with shower; one with tub, terrace.

Gerštmajer Wine Cellar ★★★   Four generations of winemakers have worked the land that supplies this 150-year-old winery. Gerštmaijer sells much of his production in bulk to restaurants and for parties, but if you can snag one of his bottles of Rajnski *rizling*, it is sublime. Maršala Tita 152, Zmajevac. ✆ **091/351-55-86.**

are on the menu, as are carp Baranja and the Tikveš sandwich (kulen, cheese, salamiles). Desserts are homey (Grandma's sweet leaves: a concoction of phyllo, poppy seeds and walnuts), and there is a nice selection of Croatian wine.

Konpleks dvorca Tikveš, 31328 Lug. ✆ **031/752-901.** www.restoran-tikves.hr. Entrees 68kn–87kn. AE, DC, MC, V. Daily 9am–10pm.

BARANJA EXPERIENCES ★★★

Baranjska Kuča ★★ SLAVONIAN   Everything is authentic and homemade in this rustic restaurant, which was a Karanac granary 120 years ago. It is just 15km (9 miles) northwest of Kopački Rit but a world away from ordinary. The owner's wife serves *Šapsui sir* (farmers cheese with paprika) with every meal to spread on *lepinja*, little pitalike rolls baked in an oven made hot by burning wood, then removing it. Specialties include *čobanac* (soup with three kinds of meat) and *smud orly* (pike fried in beer). At night, a gypsy band plays everything from rock to traditional Baranja folk music.

Kolodvorska 99, Karanac. ✆ **031/720-180.** www.baranjskakuca.cjb.net or www.baranjskakuca.odmor. org. Entrees 35kn–140kn. AE, MC, V. Mon–Thurs 11am–10pm; Fri–Sat 11am–1am; Sun 11am–9pm.

Sklepić ★★★ **Kids**   Go back in time at this restored Baranja farmhouse complex 8km (5 miles) east of Beli Manastir at the top of Croatia. The owner says the food, activities, and accommodations in the rooms behind a porch decorated with fermenting cherries, geraniums, and drying peppers are as close to authentic as possible. Sklepić is a place where the bathrooms are indoors but TV and A/C are nonexistent. You can walk behind your unit to gather your own eggs and pick your veggies to use in your breakfast omelet and you can even help the family make bread or harvest crops. Lunch and dinner are not offered, but they are available a la carte at nearby Baranjska Kuča.

Kolodvorska 58, Karanac. ✆ **098/739-159.** www.sklepic.hr. 8 units. Doubles from 300kn. Quads from 150kn per person. Rates include breakfast. AE, MC, V.

WHERE TO STAY & DINE

Hotel Patria **Kids**   The Patria is in Beli Manastir, as far as you can go into Baranja County without crossing over into Serbia. In fact, you can see the border from some parts of the property. The hotel opened in November 2006 and it is equipped to handle business travelers, families, even hunters. The hotel aspires to be a miniresort, complete with a petting zoo, barbecue kiosk, dorm facility that sleeps 27, and a kennel for almost two dozen dogs. Most rooms have tubs in the bathroom and a blue plastic elliptical trainer in case you can't make it to the well-equipped fitness center. Did we mention that the hotel's exterior is painted a "can't-miss-it" shade of deep lilac?

The hotel offers an attractive detached hostel with rooms that sleep four to seven guests. Prices are lower than the hotel (150kn per person without breakfast), but the bathroom is down the hall.

Osječka 1C. 31300 Beli Manastir. ⓒ **031/710-710.** Fax 031/710-720. www.hotelpatria.hr. 42 units. Deluxe doubles from 700kn. Rates include breakfast. AE, DC, MC, V. Free parking. **Amenities:** Restaurant; lobby bar; terrace dining; fitness center; children's area. *In room:* A/C, TV, hair dryer, minibar.

---

10 VUKOVAR & ILOK

From a historical point of view, **Vukovar** is an important stop on any tour of Croatia, but until recently there wasn't much for tourists to see except ravaged structures languishing after the Homeland War. That has changed dramatically thanks to an infusion of grant money from the Croatian government in recognition of the area's historical and archaeological significance. Today Vukovar is teeming with archaeologists working to uncover significant vestiges of long-gone civilizations, including Bronze Age settlements on the Danube. Vukovar once was known for its elegance and culture, and until 2006 it looked like a powerful, living antiwar advertisement because of the rubble left over from the almost total devastation it suffered during the war that swept through Slavonia in 1991. Some say the city was offered to the Serbs and the Yugoslav People's Army (JNA) as a sacrificial lamb and left a shambles for years as a reminder of that event.

Before the war, Vukovar was a center of industry and manufacturing in Croatia anchored by the Borovo tire factory and other businesses. The city also enjoyed a modest tourism thanks to its Baroque center, its lovely riverfront location, and its vibrant society. However, Vukovar's large Serbian population (37%) and its position just across the river from Serbia made it a prime target during the war. The result was a 3-month-long siege in 1991 that all but leveled the city and emptied it of people.

Vukovar finally was returned to Croatia in 1998, but not all its citizens have returned, perhaps because there isn't much to return to. Many local businesses and homes lie in ruins, jobs are scarce, and some say the government has been slow to rebuild Vukovar because it wants the ravaged city to remain a physical symbol of the brutal siege.

(Fun Facts) The Vučedol Dove

This ceramic archaeological find was uncovered in the early 20th century about 5km (3 miles) south of Vukovar on the Danube. The little pot made around 2500 B.C. is the most famous and popular artifact of Vučedol culture in southeastern Europe. It has been reproduced and kept in almost every home in Croatia since the 1991 war, when it came to symbolize peace for those fighting for freedom in Croatia. The original is displayed at the Archaeological Museum in Zagreb (p. 284).

About 39km (24 miles) east of Vukovar, **Ilok** is the easternmost city in Croatia and home to a 13th-century fortress and palace that is being excavated. It also has an 18th-century Franciscan monastery that was built inside the walls where St. Ivan Kapestran (St. John Capistrano), a Franciscan warrior monk, successfully defended the banks of the Danube against invading Turks.

St. Ivan died at the monastery after a battle in 1456, but in 1526 another wave of Turks attacked and eventually prevailed. They held Ilok until 1697, when Austria took over. Subsequently, the Hapsburgs gave the entire town—perhaps as a reward—to Livio Odescalchi, an Italian military officer who helped defeat the Ottoman forces.

Ilok's **Fruška Gora** area has been known since Roman times for its microclimate, which supports lush vineyards and robust wine production. Ilok was taken by the Serbs during the Homeland War, but it was not as badly damaged as Vukovar because almost all its citizens were given the opportunity to flee before the attack. Today, several high-powered investors have become interested in Ilok and recently have been acquiring its vineyards and wineries. Ilok's wine industry is approaching prewar production levels.

ESSENTIALS

VISITOR INFORMATION   Vukovar's **tourism office** is at J. J. Strossmayera 15 on the way to the Eltz Palace. You can pick up brochures and maps there, but you need to arrive during weekday office hours 7am to 3pm (© **032/441-762;** fax 032/442-889; turisticka-zajednica-grada-vukovara@vk.htnet.hr)—and you need to know where to look. The **Ilok tourism office** is in the town center at Trg Nikole Iločkog 2 (© **032/590-020;** tz-grada-iloka@vk.htnet.hr).

GETTING THERE   Buses run through flat farmland and vineyards from Osijek and Vinkovci to Vukovar with convenient frequency. There isn't much to see but corn and wheat during the 35km (22-mile) trip. However, the 40km (25-mile) trip from Vukovar is much more scenic whether you take a bus from Vukovar or drive your own car as it follows the Danube through vineyards and the Fruška Gora range.

GETTING AROUND   Both Vukovar and Ilok are best explored on foot, though Vukovar covers a much larger area. If you want to visit Ilok's wineries, you'll need your own transportation.

WHAT TO SEE & DO

Parts of Vukovar have been restored, but except for the remnants of war, there is little to see besides the City Museum in the restored Eltz Palace and the waterfront war monument. Ilok and its vineyards suffered less damage in the war, so that city has much more to offer tourists at this time.

Church and Monastery of Sv. Ivan Kapistran ★★★   This church and monastery are receptacles of history and artifacts from the area thanks to Franciscan monks who booby-trapped the church and monastery with mines during the 1991 war to keep the Serbs out. The head monk stayed inside, though the buildings were damaged. The church also houses St. John Capistrano's relics, which are on display in a glass case. You can see the church's painstaking restoration in progress in a monastery studio, which also holds a large collection of sacral art. Knock on the monastery door, and the church's affable pastor will be happy to show you the church, the monastery, and the treasures hidden there during the war. He might even invite you to lunch.

Ilok. © **032/344-034.** Visits by appointment.

Civic Museum ★★   In 1736, after the Turks had been routed from Vukovar, the city was given to the Eltz nobles, who built churches and an elaborate Baroque palace. The 18th-century Eltz Palace, like many other buildings in Croatia, was nationalized after World War II, after which it became the site of the Vukovar Civic Museum. The building was heavily damaged in 1991 and its treasures whisked away to safety in other parts of Croatia. Today most of the pieces from the collections are back and the damaged areas of the palace are being restored.

Iločki Podrumi Winery ★★★   This winery on the banks of the Danube is one of the region's largest. It also is the second-oldest winery in Europe. The winery was raided by the Serbs in the 1991 war, when most of its barrels were damaged and its stores confiscated, but the owners were able to hide some of the winery's older vintages, which are now for sale. The winery resumed production in 1999 after the 7-year occupation ended in 1998. It now produces more than 4 million liters of traminac, graševina, chardonnay, Rhine riesling, and other varietals annually. It also offers tours, tastings, and meals, and sells retail from the facility. English-speaking guides are available for tours if you make reservations in advance, or you can drop in. The winery also serves Slavonian meals to tour groups or others with advance notice. The Iločki Podrumi winery and its wines are well known and respected throughout Europe. In fact, Ilok wines were served at the coronation of Queen Elizabeth II in 1953.

Dr. Franje Tudmana 72, Ilok. ☏ **032/590-003.** Fax 032/590-047. www.ilocki-podrumi.hr.

Mathias Kulen ★★   *Kulen,* Slavonia's spicy wood-smoked sausage, has many producers in Slavonia, but Mathias is the best there is and available in higher-end grocery stores. This little retail store about 16km (10 miles) southeast of Vukovar is the best place to find the delicacy, which is made only in Slavonia. Kulen production is a fairly complicated and expensive affair; Mathias's kulen sells for about 100kn per pound.

Gustava Krkleca 15, Vinkovci. ☏ **032/367-848.** Fax 032/366-107. mathias@email.htnet.hr. No credit cards. Mon–Fri 8am–3pm; Sat 8am–1pm. Closed Sun.

Sv. Ivan Kapistran

Sv. Ivan Kapistran (St. John Capistrano) was born to a former German knight and his wife in Italy in 1385. John became a lawyer in Perugia and was appointed governor of that Italian city by King Ladislas of Naples. During Perugia's war with another Italian town in 1416, John was taken prisoner, and while confined, he promised God that he would become a priest if he got out alive. John kept his promise to God, then traveled across Italy establishing new Franciscan communities and spreading the word of God. In 1455, at the age of 70, John was asked by Pope Callistus II to lead troops against invading Turks. Thus, he became the leader of 70,000 Crusaders who in 1456 won the Battle of Belgrade against the enemy. John died 3 months later in Ilok, Croatia, where he is buried. The Mission of San Juan Capistrano founded by Franciscan Brother Junípero Serra in 1776 in Orange County, California, is named after this 15th-century hero, who is the patron saint of jurists.

Ovčara Memorial Center ★★★ The memorial 5km (3 miles) south of Vukovar opened November 20, 2006, 15 years to the day when 261 Croat men, women, and children—some hospital patients—were executed in 1991. Ovčara was a series of storage hangars used to keep Croat prisoners en route to Serbian work camps. It is in the same building (restored) where soldiers seeking sanctuary in the Vukovar hospital were taken, then shot and buried in a mass grave northeast of the facility. The memorial's interior is painted black, and photos of the identified dead fade in and out of view. There is an eerie memorial flame in a circular stone frame in the floor, which is "carpeted" with actual bullets found on the property after the massacre. *Tip:* Ovčara does not charge an entrance fee, but there is a small shop at the exit where books and replicas of the Vučedal dove are sold to support the memorial. A TV showing looping news footage of Serb soldiers celebrating the destruction of Vukovar and residents slowly leaving the city carrying their belongings is chilling.

3km (1³/₄ miles) southeast of Vukovar on the Ovčara-Brabovo road. Daily 10am–5pm. Free admission.

WHERE TO STAY

Neither Vukovar nor Ilok merits an overnight stay unless you have business in the area. Until recently there has been a dearth of acceptable accommodations in both cities, but that is changing. Both towns are now regular stops for Danube cruise ships which drop their passengers at the dock in Vukovar to see the town's monument to fallen soldiers. Hotels in both towns are trying hard to respond.

Hotel Dunav ★ The Dunav was built as a package hotel and despite several updates, it still is. Rooms and public spaces still have that dark, Socialist aura and infrastructure like the elevators and bathrooms is very basic. One bright spot: The Dunav has a lovely terrace where you can enjoy drinks and light snacks during the day.

Trg Republike. Hrvratske 1. Ilok. ⓒ **032/441-285.** Fax 032/441-762. 57units. Doubles from 812kn; suites from 904kn. Rates include breakfast. AE, DC, MC, V. **Amenities:** Restaurant; bar.

Hotel Lav ★★ Built on the site a hotel that overlooked the storied river, the Lav's opening in the spring of 2005 is a hopeful sign that Vukovar finally may be on the road to recovery from the Homeland War. The neighborhood around the Lav still shows the effects of the devastating shelling that all but leveled Vukovar, but right now the hotel stands above it like a gleaming promise on the Danube. Guest rooms are comfortably furnished with nice touches like magnifying mirrors and Pascal Morabity toiletries in the bathrooms. Most have great views of the river and Serbia on the opposite bank, especially from the lavishly outfitted suites. The hotel uses environmentally safe operating methods when possible and it is "art friendly" by displaying the work of local artists in its public spaces. *Tip:* Lav management has implemented a "Bike and Bed" initiative to serve an

---

10-Speeds Ahead

Croatia is gradually developing its biking trails and as a result its cycling tourism is growing. Currently there are more than 40 mapped and signed routes from Istria to Dalmatia, including one in Slavonia. Many hotels like the Lav in Vukovar (above) along the way are adding services especially for cyclists. Services like bike storage, bike repair services, and bike rentals are proliferating in places near bike routes. For more information, go to www.cycle-croatia.com.

increasing number of cyclists who take advantage of the area's 100km (60 miles) of bike routes. Besides a hotel room, the Lav provides bike storage.

Try a fine meal at **Restaurant Lav** (reviewed below), or try the adjacent **Tri Vrške** (also reviewed below).

J. J. Strossmayera 18, Vukovar. ✆ **032/297-111.** Fax 032/445-110. www.hotel-lav.hr. 42 units. From 970kn double; from 2,470kn suite. Rates include breakfast. Half- and full board available. AE, DC, MC, V. **Amenities:** Restaurant; bar; cafe; bike storage. *In room:* A/C, TV, Wi-Fi.

WHERE TO DINE

Dining options in Vukovar and Ilok are improving but are almost as thin as hotel options. Casual places serve pizza and simple grilled meat and fish dishes. However, there is a surge in agritourism, which includes home-cooked meals in very small rural wineries and inns. The area's Graševina white wine is excellent.

Restaurant Lav ★★ SLAVONIAN   The Hotel Lav's restaurant serves surprisingly sophisticated cuisine in a space that is bright, tastefully decorated, and generously enhanced with original artwork from local talent. Dig into the Slavonian feast, a platter of grilled pork chops, bacon, and sausage, or go lighter with beef with truffles. There are many local specialties on the menu, a trend that extends to the dessert cart.

In the Hotel Lav, J. J. Strossmayera 18, Vukovar. ✆ **032/297-111.** Fax 032/445-110. www.hotel-lav.hr. Entrees 35kn–130kn. AE, DC, MC, V. Daily 7am–11pm.

Restoran Iločka Kuća ★★ SLAVONIAN   Even though restaurants and cafes almost completely line Dr. F. Tuđmana in Ilok, seek out Restoran Iločka Kuća, because it stands a little taller than its neighbors. Pizza, grilled meat, and home-cooked specialties are the order of the day at this typical Slavonian dining spot, whose servers are very friendly and speak very little English.

Dr. F. Tuđmana 7, Ilok. ✆ **032/590-402.** Entrees 30kn–65kn. No credit cards. Daily 7am–midnight.

Tri Vrške ★ SLAVONIAN   Dining options in Vukovar are mostly limited to cafes and pizzerias, but if you happen to be staying at the Hotel Lav overnight, this casual riverside restaurant, whose name means "Three Fishnets," is just steps away. Besides good Slavonian food, the restaurant has a view of the Serbian landscape from its tables on the banks of the Danube. Most dishes lean toward seafood, but a schnitzel option is served with rice and vegetables. Pike, seafood paprika, grilled calamari, and a fried seafood platter are other possibilities. In the afternoon, you can stop here for a coffee and pastry break.

Parobrodska 3, Vukovar. ✆ **032/441-788.** Entrees 28kn–58kn. AE, DC, MC, V. Daily 8am–10pm.

Fast Facts: Croatia

AREA CODES Croatia's country code is **385.**

BUSINESS HOURS Croatian banks and post offices generally are open from 7am to 7pm Monday to Friday without midday breaks. Public offices are open Monday to Friday from 8am to 4pm. During the tourist season, post offices generally are open until 9pm, including Saturday. Shops and department stores stay open from 8am to 8pm and to 2 or 3pm Saturday without a break. Increasingly, stores in malls are open on Sundays, usually from 10am to 6pm. They then open late on Mondays (2pm). Recently Croatia passed a law requiring stores to remain closed all day on Sunday. That law was rescinded for the 2009 tourist season, then repealed, but many small stores in less populated areas stay closed on Sunday.

DRINKING LAWS The minimum age for purchasing liquor in Croatia is 18, but there is no minimum age for consuming it. Croatia has strict tolerance laws regarding drinking and driving; the legal limit is 0.0% blood alcohol for anyone 24 or under; 0.05% is the limit for those over 24. Package liquor (wine, beer, spirits) can be purchased in markets, wine stores, and some souvenir shops, and at almost every gas station in Croatia.

DRIVING RULES See "Getting There & Getting Around," p. 28.

DRUGSTORES *Ljekarna* are open from 8am to 7pm weekdays and until 2pm on Saturday. In larger cities, one pharmacy in town will be open 24 hours on a rotating basis.

ELECTRICITY Croatian electricity is 220v, 50Hz; the two-prong European plug is standard. Most wall plugs are recessed, however, and in many cases you will need **two two-pronged plugs** to access the outlet.

EMBASSIES & CONSULATES U.S.: Andrije Hebranga 2, Zagreb; © 01/661-22-00. Australia: Krsnjavoga 1, Zagreb; © 01/483-66-00. U.K.: Ivana Lučića 4, Zagreb; © 01/600-91-00. Also U.K.: Obala hrvatskog narodnog preporoda 10, 21000, Split; © 021/341-464.

EMERGENCIES Police © **92.** Fire © **93.** Ambulance © **94.** Roadside assistance © **987.** (When calling from abroad or by cellphone, call © **385 1 987.**) General information © **981.** Information about local and intercity numbers © **988.** Information about international numbers © **902.** Weather forecast and road conditions © **060/520-520.**

ETIQUETTE & CUSTOMS **Appropriate attire:** Croatians, especially Croatian women, take pride in their appearance. In cities, both men and women usually dress in business casual. On the coast and countryside, the "dress code" is more relaxed. You *never* will see Croatians wearing immodest or sloppy clothes in public places. If you plan to visit museums or churches anywhere, plan to wear tops with sleeves and pants that go to at least the knee.

Gestures: *Dobar dan* (good day) is the way Croatians generally greet each other. Handshakes are appropriate for first meetings and between business associates. Good friends will kiss on both cheeks in the European style.

Avoiding offense: Religion and politics are topics to avoid universally. In Croatia, stay away from discussing Croat-Serb relations or anything related to the Homeland War unless you know what you're talking about and have lots of time for debate.

GASOLINE (PETROL) Gasoline and diesel are readily available all over Croatia and almost all stations take credit cards. In the summer of 2009, gas was running about 7.5kn per liter including taxes. One U.S. gallon equals 3.8 liters or .85 imperial gallons. That translates to 29kn or $5.90 per U.S. gallon of gas.

HOLIDAYS Croatian shops and banks are closed on public holidays, which are: January 1, New Year; January 6, Epiphany; March or April, Easter Monday; May 1, Labor Day; May (Thurs after Trinity Sun), Corpus Christi; June 22, Anti-Fascist Day; June 25, Croatian Statehood; August 5, Thanksgiving; August 15, Assumption; October 8, Independence Day; November 1, All Saints Day; December 25 and 26, Christmas. For more information on holidays, see "Calendar of Events," in chapter 3.

HOSPITALS Zagreb: Klinička Bolnica "Sestre Milosrdnice" (Vinogradska cesta 29; ℂ 01/378-71-11). Split: Klinička Bolnica Split (Spinčićeva 1; ℂ 021/556-111). Dubrovnik: Opća Bolnica Dubrovnik (Toka Mišetića bb; ℂ 020/431-777).

INSURANCE Information on traveler's insurance, trip-cancellation insurance, and medical insurance while traveling is at www.frommers.com/planning.

LANGUAGE Most residents of major Croatian cities speak English. Most movie houses and programs on Croatian TV are in English with Croatian subtitles. For basic phrases and words, see the inside front cover of this book. For more specific vocabulary, see the Langenscheidt Universal Croatian Dictionary.

LEGAL AID Consult your embassy if you get into legal trouble in Croatia. See above for contact information.

MAIL It costs 5kn to send a postcard to the U.S., and 11kn to send a letter weighing up to 20 grams (¾ oz.). The post office is fairly reliable, but very slow. It takes about 10 days to 2 weeks for postcards to arrive in the U.S. from Croatia and up to a month for regular mail and packages. Other carriers are available (DHL, FedEx, UPS) in major population centers, but the cost is prohibitive (about 245kn or $50 per pound).

NEWSPAPERS & MAGAZINES English-language newspapers and magazines are a rarity at Croatian newsstands, even in Zagreb. Some of the better hotels supply printed copies of various U.S. publications taken from the Internet. Algorithm bookstores in major population centers are the only common outlets for English-language publications. Look for the *International Herald Tribune* and *USA Today* if you crave English-language news.

PASSPORTS Allow plenty of time before your trip to apply for a passport; processing normally takes 3 weeks but can take longer during busy periods (especially spring). Keep in mind that if you need a passport in a hurry, you'll pay a higher processing fee.

For residents of the United States: Whether you're applying in person or by mail, you can download passport applications from the U.S. State Department website at **http://travel.state.gov**. To find your regional passport office, either check the U.S. State Department website or call the **National Passport Information Center** toll-free number (ℂ **877/487-2778**) for automated information.

For residents of Australia: Applications are available at local post offices or at any branch of Passports Australia, but you must schedule an interview at the passport office to present your application materials. Call the **Australian Passport Information Service** at ℂ **131-232,** or visit the government website at www.passports.gov.au.

13

For residents of Canada: Passport applications are available at travel agencies throughout Canada or from the central **Passport Office,** Department of Foreign Affairs and International Trade, Ottawa, ON K1A 0G3 (✆ **800/567-6868;** www. ppt.gc.ca).

For residents of Ireland: You can apply for a 10-year passport at the **Passport Office,** Setanta Centre, Molesworth Street, Dublin 2 (✆ **01/671-1633;** www. irlgov.ie/iveagh). Those under age 18 and over 65 must apply for a 3-year passport. You also can apply at 1A South Mall, Cork (✆ **021/272-525**), or at most main post offices.

For residents of New Zealand: Pick up a passport application at any New Zealand Passports Office or download it from their website. Contact the **Passports Office** at ✆ **0800/225-050** in New Zealand or 04/474-8100, or log on to www.passports. govt.nz.

For residents of the United Kingdom: To obtain an application for a standard 10-year passport (5-year passport for children under 16), visit the nearest passport office, major post office, or travel agency or contact the **United Kingdom Passport Service** at ✆ **0870/521-0410** or search its website at www.ukpa.gov.uk.

See www.frommers.com/planning for information on how to obtain a passport.

POLICE Call ✆ **92.**

SMOKING In May 2009 Croatia passed a law banning smoking in all public places. However, that was modified 4 months later to give small establishments the option of allowing or not allowing on-premises smoking. The ban still applies to places larger than 200 sq. m (2,153 sq. ft.), but they must confine smokers to separate areas with independent ventilation systems.

TAXES Croatia's VAT was raised to 23% from 22% in August 2009. Refunds of VAT are made to foreign nationals when they leave the country for goods purchased in Croatia for amounts over 500kn with a tax check form. Salespeople will provide this form when you make a purchase over 500kn. There is a 10% nonrefundable tax on excursions and tax on hotel rooms, too. For further information, go to www. carina.hr.

TIME Croatia is 1 hour ahead of Greenwich Mean Time, 6 hours ahead of New York (Eastern Standard Time), and 9 hours ahead of Los Angeles (Pacific Standard Time). Daylight saving time is observed from late March to late September, when clocks are advanced 1 hour.

TIPPING A 10% to 15% gratuity is expected in upscale restaurants. Otherwise, it is considered polite to leave any coins from your change on the table in cafes and restaurants. A 10% tip for other service providers (taxi drivers, hotel personnel, and others) is the norm, as is a tip for anyone who helps you carry your luggage or conducts a tour.

TOILETS There are no free-standing public restrooms in Croatia, but most restaurants and public buildings have them and will let you use them if you make a purchase.

WATER Tap water is potable throughout Croatia.

INDEX

Accommodations, 47–48
  best, 3–4
  eco-conscious, 41
Adriatica.net, 44
Adriatic Dolphin Project, 41
Adriatic Tours, 46
Adventure and wellness
  trips, 45
Air travel, 28–31
American Express
  Dubrovnik, 61
  Split, 104
  traveler's checks, 33–34
  Zagreb, 275
Amphitheater, Salona, 120
Anindol (Samobor), 308
Annunciation, Church of the
  Pribić, 312
  Supetar, 130
Apartman (Zagreb), 302
Apparition Hill (Međugorje),
  100
Aquarium
  Dubrovnik, 66
  Poreč, 247
  Rovinj, 239
Aquarius (Zagreb), 303
Aquarius Bar (Vis), 154
Archaeological Museum
  Brijuni, 235–236
  Pula, 230
  Split, 110
  Vis, 151
  Zadar, 169
  Zagreb, 284
Area codes, 364
Art and architecture, 17–19
Art Collections (Mali Lošinj),
  221
Ascension, Church of the
  (Zagorje Cathedral;
  Pregrada), 320
Assumption, Church of the
  (Dubrovnik Cathedral), 66
Atelier-Ivan Meštrović
  (Zagreb), 278

ATMs (automated teller
  machines), 33
Austro-Hungarian rule, 14

Bacchus (Zagreb), 303
Balbi Arch (Rovinj), 238
Banje (Dubrovnik), 73
Baranja, 357–359
  cuisine, 22
Baranja Wine Road (Općina
  Kneževi Vinogradi), 357
Baredine Cave (Poreč),
  246–248
Baška, 210–212
Baška Tablet (Zagreb), 284
Batana House (Rovinj), 239
Beaches. *See also specific
  beaches*
  Baška, 210
  best, 5
  Blue Flag, 40
  Dubrovnik, 73–74
  Hvar, 137
  Orebić, 95
Beli, 219
Benedictine Convent (Zadar),
  170
Biennale (Zagreb), 24
Big Blue (Bol), 131
Biking and mountain biking,
  45
Biograd na moru, 182–183
Biokovo Nature Park, 127
Biševo Island, 150
Bishop Grgur Ninski
  (Gregorius of Nin)
  Memorial, 179
Bjelovar, 342–345
Bjelovar-Bilogora, 339–340
  cuisine, 21
Bjelovar Market, 343
Black Marsh (Crna Mlaka)
  wetlands, 307
Blaise, St., 69
Blato (Korčula), 148
Blue Cave (Modra Špilja), 150

Blue Flag beaches, 40
Blue Line International, 31
Blue Planet (Dubrovnik), 74
Boating (boat rentals), 45
Boban (Zagreb), 302
Bokar Fortress (Dubrovnik),
  64, 71
Bol, 129, 130
Bonj les Bains beach club
  (Hvar), 142
Bonj Les Bains (Hvar), 137
Books, Croatia in, 19
Botanical Gardens (Zagreb),
  282
Bottle collection, 40
B.P. Club (Zagreb), 303
Brač, 129–133
Braće Radić Trg (Voćni Trg or
  Fruit Square; Split), 106
Branimir Center (Zagreb),
  286
Branislav-Desković Modern
  Art Gallery (Bol), 131
Brela, 126
Bridge Gate (Zadar), 170
Brijuni Archipelago (Brioni),
  235–236
British naval cemetery (Vis),
  150
Bronze Gate (Split), 108
Broz, Josip ("Tito"), 15
  Memorial Museum
  (Brijuni), 236
Brsalje Square (Dubrovnik),
  71
Buje (Buie), 262
Bunari Secrets of Šibenik,
  185–186
Bundek Park (Zagreb),
  284–285
Burglars' Tower (Kula
  Lotršćak; Zagreb), 281
Business hours, 364
Bus travel, 31–32
Buža I (Dubrovnik), 88
Buzet (Pinguente), 268, 269
Byblos (Poreč), 252

368 Cadillac (Osijek), 356
Caesarea Gate (Salona), 119
Caffe Bar Biliba (Vis), 154
Čakovec, 330–333
Calendar of events, 24–26
Camping, 48
  Baška, 210, 212
  Borik, 173
  Cres, 219, 220
  Korčula, 146
  Krk, 209
  Mali Lošinj, 223
  Pag, 164
  Poreč, 250
Capitano (Dubrovnik), 88
Caput Insulae Ecology Center
  (Cres), 41
Carpe Diem (Hvar), 142
Car rentals, 30, 32–33
Car travel, 30, 32
Casablanca (Dubrovnik), 88
Casinos, Zagreb, 302
Castles, best, 6–7
Cathedral of St. Peter the
  Apostle (Đakovo), 347
Cathedral of the Assumption
  Krk, 208
  Pula, 230
  Varaždin, 327, 328
Cathedral of the Assumption
  of the Virgin Mary
  (Zagreb), 278
Cavtat, 92–94
Čazma, 342–345
Cemetery, Cavtat, 93
Chapel of God's Mother
  (Zagreb), 281
Churches. See also under first
  significant word (e.g., Holy
  Ghost, Church of the)
  best, 6
Čigoć, 41, 335, 336, 339
Čiovo, 120
Čipiko Palace (Trogir), 121
City Museum (Gradski Muzej;
  Karlovac), 313
City Museum (Split), 109–110
City Tower (Gradski Toranj;
  Rijeka), 193
City Wall (Dubrovnik), 64
Civic Museum (Vukovar), 361
Classic Journeys, 44
Climate, 23
Clock Tower
  Dubrovnik, 72
  Hvar, 137
  Trogir, 122

Coffee, 20–21
Colonnade Beach Bar (Hvar),
  142
Comic Book Festival
  (Zagreb), 26
Connex Diving (Pag), 162
Contemporary Dance Week
  (Zagreb), 24–25
Copacabana Beach
  (Dubrovnik), 73–74
Country code, 364
Credit cards, 34–35
Cres, 217–224
Cres Town, 218–219
Crikvenica, 195–197
Crkva Svetog Marka
  (St. Mark's Church; Zagreb),
  280
Crna Mlaka (Black Marsh)
  wetlands, 307
Croatia Air, 28
Croatian History Museum
  (Zagreb), 282
Croatian Museum of Naive
  Art (Zagreb), 280
Croatian National Theater
  Osijek, 350–351
  Split, 106–107
  Zagreb, 282
Croatian Natural History
  Museum (Zagreb), 280
Croatian State Archives
  (Zagreb), 282
Croatia Travel Agency, 46
Cuisine, 20–22
Currency and currency
  exchange, 33
Customs regulations, 26–28

Đakovo, 345–349
Đakovo Embroidery,
  347–348
Dalmatian Coast, 49,
  101–155
Dalmatian cuisine, 22
Daruvar, 343–344
Delicium Nostrum (Trogir),
  122
Dietary red flags, 35
Dinga wine district, 97
Diocletian's Palace (Split),
  107
Disabilities, travelers with,
  37–38
Dive Center Jurgavan (Hvar),
  137
Dolac Market (Zagreb), 278

Dominican Monastery and
  Museum (Dubrovnik), 64,
  72
Dominican Monastery (Hvar),
  141
Dom Sindikata (Čakovec),
  331
Donat, Bishop, 165
Dragons (pozoj), 332
Drinking laws, 364
Drniš, 185
Drugstores, 364
Dubovac Castle (Karlovac),
  311–313
Dubrovnik, 59–100
  accommodations, 74–83
  American Express, 61
  arriving in, 60
  ATMs, 61
  banks, 61
  bars and nightlife, 88–89
  beaches, 73–74
  business hours, 61
  day trips from, 89–100
  emergencies, 61
  getting around, 63–64
  Internet access, 62
  neighborhoods, 62–63
  orientation, 59–61
  pharmacies, 62
  restaurants, 83–88
  sights and attractions,
    64–73
  suggested itinerary, 56–58
  travel agencies, 61
  visitor information, 60–62
  walking tours
    escorted, 73
    self-guided, 70–72
  weather, 62
Dubrovnik Aquarium and
  Maritime Museum, 66
Dubrovnik Cathedral (Church
  of the Assumption), 66, 72
Dubrovnik International Film
  Festival, 24
Dubrovnik River, 71
Dubrovnik Summer Festival,
  25
Dubrovnik Walking Tours, 73
Dugi Otok, 181
Đurđevac, 340–342
Đurovic Cave (Dubrovnik), 63
Dušan Džamonja's Sculpture
  Park (Vrsar), 244–245
D'vino (Dubrovnik), 88
Dvor Herczer (Herzer Palace;
  Varaždin), 327, 328

Eastern Slavonia, 345
Eastwest Beach Club
(Dubrovnik), 74
East-West (Dubrovnik), 88
Eco-Centre Caput Insulae
(Beli), 219
Elafiti Islands, 89–90
Electricity, 364
Embassies and consulates,
275, 364
Emergencies, 364
England (Šibenik), 187
Enigma Computer Center
(Pula), 228
Entomološki Muzej (Insect
Museum; Varaždin), 328
Entry requirements, 26–28
Ernestinovo, 352
Escorted tours, 46
Ethnographic Museum
(Split), 107
Ethnographic Museum
(Zagreb), 282
Etiquette and customs,
364–365
Euphemia, St., legend of, 240
Euphrasian Basilica Complex
(Poreč), 247
Europska Avenue (Osijek),
351
Extreme Sports Festival
(Brač), 25

Families with children, 38
Ferries, 31, 32
Festivals and special events,
24–26
Five Wells Square (Trg 5
Bunara; Zadar), 170
Food and cuisine, 20–22
Food and wine tours, 45–46
Fort Lovrijenac (Dubrovnik),
71
Fortress (Fortica; Hvar), 136
Forum (Zadar), 170
Franciscan Monastery
Cavtat, 93
Cres, 219
Hvar, 136
Karlovac, 313
Orebić, 95
Trsat, 194
Vis, 150
Franciscan Monastery/
Museum (Dubrovnik),
66–67, 71

Fruška Gora (Ilok), 360
Full Moon Festival (Zadar),
172

Gaga (Split), 117
Galerija Hlebine, 341
Galerija Josip Generalí,
341–342
Galerija Peti-Boži (Rovinj),
239
Gasoline, 365
Gay and lesbian travelers,
36–37
Zagreb, 303
Gen. Von Becker's (Osijek),
356
Gerštmajer Wine Cellar
(Baranja), 358
Ghetto (Split), 117
Glagolitic Alley, 268–269
Global Club (Zagreb), 303
The Gold and Silver of Zadar,
170
Golden Cape (Zlatni Rat),
129, 130
Golden Gate (Split), 109
Golf, Umag, 257
Goli Otok, 213
Gradec (Zagreb), 278
Gradska Kavana (Dubrovnik),
72
Gradska Vijećnica (Town Hall;
Varaždin), 327, 329
Gradski Muzej (City Museum;
Karlovac), 313
Gradski Toranj (City Tower;
Rijeka), 193
Green Cave (Zelena Špilja),
150
Gregorius of Nin, Bishop, 179
Grgić Vina, 97
Grisia Street Art Festival
(Rovinj), 25
Grožnjan (Grisignana),
262–265
Grožnjan Musical Summer
and Jazz Festival, 264

Hapsburg Empire, 13
Health concerns, 35–36
Hektorović, Petar, 138, 141
Hemingway's (Zagreb), 302
Hercules Gate (Pula), 230
Herczer Palace (Dvor Herzer;
Varaždin), 327, 328

Hiking
Brela, 127
Samobor, 310
History of Croatia, 9–17
Hlebine, 340–342
Holidays, 365
Holy Blood Chapel (Ludbreg),
326
Holy Cross Church (Nin),
179–180
Holy Cross Church (Sveti Križ;
Rab), 214
Holy Trinity Church
(Karlovac), 313
Holy Trinity Square (Osijek),
351
Homeric Tours, 46
Hospitals, 365
Hotels, 47–48
best, 3–4
eco-conscious, 41
Hula Hula Beach Bar (Hvar),
142
Hvar, 134–142

Ilyrians, 11, 13
art and architecture, 18
Iločki Podrumi Winery, 361
Ilok, 359–363
Indijan Winery (Grgić Vina),
97
Inland Croatia, 49, 334–363
Insect Museum (Entomološki
Muzej; Varaždin), 328
Insurance, 365
International Children's
Festival (Šibenik), 24
International Folklore
Festival, 25
International Jazz Days
(Zagreb), 26
International Motovun Film
Festival, 266
International Puppet Festival
(Zagreb), 25
Internet access, 44
IQ (Istrian Quality)
designation, 243
Istarske Toplice, 268
Istria, 52–53, 225–270
cuisine, 22
getting around, 227–228
inland, 259–333
traveling to, 226
visitor information, 226
Istrian Ethnographic
Museum (Pazin), 261
Istria Upsilon, 246

Itineraries, suggested, 53–58
Ivan Kapistran, Sv., 361

Jabuka Island, 149
Jackie Brown (Zagreb), 302
Jadrolinija, 31
Jarun Lake, 285
Jasenovac, 336, 338–339
Jelačić Square (Trg Bana Jelačića; Zagreb), 274, 277
Jelsa, 141
Jesuit Church of St. Ignatius of Loyola (Dubrovnik), 67
Jewish Synagogue (Dubrovnik), 67
Joe's Bar (Zagreb), 303
Josip Broz Tito Memorial Museum (Brijuni), 236
Joyce, James, 231
Julijev Park (Daruvar), 344

K(bar; Osijek), 356
Kabola Winery, 263
Kamenita Vrata (Zagreb), 280–281
Kamerlengo Castle (Trogir), 122
Kaptol Center (Zagreb), 286
Karlovac, 311–315
Karlovačko Brewery (Karlovac), 311
Katedrala Sv. Marka (Korčula), 144–145
Katedrala Uznesenja (Cathedral of the Assumption; Krk), 208
Kažuni (Vodnjan), 237
Khala (Zagreb), 303
King Cross Mall (Zagreb), 286
Klovićevi Dvori Gallery (Zagreb), 281
Kolar Wine Cellar (Baranja), 358
Koločep, 89
Komiža (Vis), 150
The Konavle, 92
Kopački Rit Nature Park, 41, 357
Kopački Rit wetlands, 357
Korana Gorge, 317
Korčula, 143–148
Kornati National Park, 183–184
Korzo (Đakovo), 348
Korzo (Rijeka), 193
Koversada, 245
Kozlović Winery, 263
Krapina, 324

Krapina Man (Zagreb), 280
Krašić, 312
Krizevac (Cross Hill; Međugorje), 100
Krka National Park, 186
Krk Island, 206–209
Krk Town, 206–208
Kula Lotršćak (Burglars' Tower; Zagreb), 281
Kumrovec (Staro Selo), 318–320
Kvarner Gulf, 53, 189–224
    cuisine, 22

Lace Museum, Pag, 162
Land Gate
    Korčula, 145
    Trogir, 122
    Zadar, 169
Language, 365
Latino Club Fuego (Dubrovnik), 88
Lavender, Hvar, 139
Legal aid, 365
Lenuci's Green Horseshoe (Zagreb), 281
Lepoglava, 324
Liberation Park (Samobor), 309
Licitar, 285
Limska Draga Fjord, 238, 245
Lipizzaner Stable and Stud Farm (Đakovo), 346, 348
Livade (Levade), 265, 266
Loggia (Trogir), 122
Lokrum, 90
Lonjsko Polje Nature Park, 41, 335, 336, 339
Lopud, 89–90
Lošinj, 217–224
Lovran, 204–206
Lovrijenac Fortress (Dubrovnik), 64
Lubenice, 219–220
Ludbreg, 326
Lumbarda (Korčula), 148
Lungomare (Šetalište Franza Josefa; Opatija), 198
Luža Square (Dubrovnik), 67–68

Mail, 365
Makarska, 126–128
Makarska Riviera, 126–128
Maksimir Park (Zagreb), 285
Mali Brijuni, 235

Mali Lošinj, 217, 218, 221–224
Mali Ston, 97–99
Manastirine Necropolis (Salona), 119–120
Maraschino (Zagreb), 303
Marco Polo, 144
Marija Bistrica, 320–321
Maritime Museum (Orebić), 95
Marjan (Meštrović Gallery; Split), 107–108
Markets
    best, 3
    Bjelovar, 343
    Rijeka, 194
    Split, 108–109
    Zagreb, 278
Marmontova Street (Split), 106
Martinje (St. Martin's Day), 26
Marunada (Chestnut Festival; Lovran), 26
Mary, Statue of (Međugorje), 100
Mathias Kulen, 361
Matijašić Winery, 263
Meals and dining customs, 20
Međimurje, 319, 320
    cuisine, 21
Međimurje region, 330–333
Mediterranean Experience Ltd. (Dubrovnik), 73
Međugorje (Bosnia-Hercegovina), 99–100
Medvedgrad, 325
Medvednica, Mount, 286
Memorial Room of the Dubrovnik Defenders (Dubrovnik), 72
Meštrović, Ivan, 122
    Atelier-Ivan Meštrović (Zagreb), 278–279
    biographical sketch of, 283
    Bishop Grgur Ninski Memorial (Nin), 179
    Cavtat, 92, 93
    Gallery (Marjan; Split), 107–108
    Mausoleum (Cavtat), 92
    Otavice, 185
    statue of Bishop Grgur Ninski (Split), 109
    statue of John the Baptist (Split), 110
    Well of Life (Zagreb), 282

Meštrović Gallery (Marjan; Split), 107–108
Meštrovi family mausoleum (Drniš), 185
Milna, 130
Mimara Museum (Zagreb), 282–283
Minčeta Tower (Dubrovnik), 64, 71
Mirogoj Cemetery (Zagreb), 285–286
Mljet, 90–92
Mljet National Park, 91
Modra Špilja (Blue Cave), 150
Momjan (Momiano), 262
Momjan Wine Festival (Grožnjan), 264
Monastery and Church of St. Francis (Pula), 230
Morčićl (Moretto, Moro; Rijeka), 190
Moreška Sword Dance (Korčula), 143, 147
Mosquitoes, 35
Motovun (Montona), 265
Motovun Film Festival, 25
Murter, 181
Museum for Arts and Crafts (Zagreb), 283
Museum Marton (Samobor), 309
Museum of Peasant Uprisings (near Gornja Stubica), 321
Museum of Slavonia (Osijek), 352
Museum of the City of Zagreb, 281
Muzej Međimurja Čakovec, 331

Narodni Trg (People's Sq.; Split), 109
Nativity of the Virgin, Church of the (Mali Lošinj), 221
Nehaj Fortress (Senj), 156, 157–158
Newspapers and magazines, 365
Night Club Revelin (Dubrovnik), 88–89
Nin, 177–181
Nova Gradiška, 346, 347
Novalja, 161
Novigrad (Cittanova), 253–256
Novi Vinodolski, 195–196

Old Christmas, 24
Oliver Twist (Zagreb), 303
One-Minute Film Festival (Požega), 24
1001 Delights, 24
Onofrio's Fountains (Dubrovnik), 68
Onofrio's Large Fountain (Dubrovnik), 71
Onofrio's Small Fountain (Dubrovnik), 72
Opatija, 197–204
Opatija Riviera, 197–206
Općina Kneževi Vinogradi (Baranja Wine Road), 357
Operetta (Opatija), 198
Oprtalj (Portole), 265
Orebić, 94–97
Orlando's Column (Dubrovnik), 68, 72
Osijek, 349–357
Otavice, 185
Ottoman Turks, 12–13
Our Lady of the Snows
   Belec, 321
   Cavtat, 93
   Osijek, 352
Our Lady of Trsat Church, 194
Our Saviour, Church of (Dubrovnik), 71
Ovčara Memorial Center (near Vukovar), 362
Ozalj, 312

Pag Carnival, 162
Pag Island, 158–164
Pag Lace Museum, 162
Paklenica National Park, 177–178
Pakleni Otoci (Hvar), 137
Papalić Palace (Split), 109–110
Papuk Mountain and National Park, 343, 344
Park Angiolina (Opatija), 198
Pašman, 181
Passports, 26, 365–366
Pazin (Pisino), 260–262
Pazin Chasm, 261
Pazin Kaštel, 261
Pelješac Peninsula, 94–99
People's Sq. (Narodni Trg; Split), 109
Petkovi, Marija, 148

Petrinović Mausoleum (Supetar), 130
Petrol, 365
Pile Gate (Dubrovnik), 64, 68, 71
Pinakoteka-Galerija (Cavtat), 92
Planning your trip, 23–48
Plava Laguna, 250
Plitvice Lakes National Park (Plitvička Jezera), 306–307, 315–318
Ploče Gate (Dubrovnik), 68–69, 71, 72
Podobuče, 94
Podravina, 339–340
   cuisine, 21
Police, 366
Poreč (Parenzo), 245–253
Poreč Aquarium, 247
Porta Gemina (Twin Gates; Pula), 231
Posavinas, 339
Prehistory, 10, 18
Prescription medications, 36
Pribić, 312
Prošćansko, 316–317
Pula (Pola), 228–235
Pupnat Harbor (Korčula), 148

Quasimodo (Split), 117–118

Rab Festival, 25
Rab Island, 212–217
Rector's Palace
   Cavtat, 93
   Dubrovnik, 68–69, 72
Regional Museum Poreč, 247
Regions in brief, 49–53
Restaurants, 20–21
   best, 7–8
Revelin Fort (Dubrovnik), 64
Ribarnica (Split), 109
Rijeka, 189–195
Rijeka Carnival, 24
Riva
   Split, 104
   Zadar, 170–171, 176
Riva Lošinjskih Kapetana (Mali Lošinj), 221
Roč (Rozzo), 268–269
Roman Amphitheater (Pula), 230–231
Roman Floor Mosaic (Pula), 231

Roman Forum (Zadar), 170
Roman Gate (Stara Vrata;
Rijeka), 193–194
Romans (ruins and
antiquities), 11
art and architecture, 18
best ruins, 5
Brijuni, 235
Pag, 161
Poreč, 247–248
Pula, 230–231
Roč, 268
Zadar, 165
Rovinj (Rovigno), 237–245
Rovinj Aquarium, 239
Rovinj Heritage Museum,
239

St. Anastasia Cathedral and
Bell Tower (Zadar), 171
St. Andrew Church (Sveti
Andrije; Rab), 214
St. Anne's Fortress (Šibenik),
187
St. Anselmo, Church of, and
Treasury (Nin), 179
St. Anthony (Sveti Antun;
Rab), 215
St. Blaise Church
Dubrovnik, 69, 72
Vodnjan, 236–237
St. Blaise Treasury (Vodnjan),
237
St. Chrysogonus Church
(Zadar), 171
St. Dominic, Church of
Split, 109
Trogir, 122
St. Domnius, Cathedral of
(Split), 106
St. Donatus (Zadar), 171
St. Euphemia Church
(Rovinj), 238–240
St. Fosca, Church of (Sveti
Foška; Pula), 233
St. Francis, Monastery and
Church of (Pula), 230
St. Germaine, Church of
(Brijuni), 235–236
St. Ignatius of Loyola
(Dubrovnik), 67
St. Ivan, Church of (Hvar),
141
St. James, Cathedral of
(Šibenik), 186
St. Jerome Church (Čakovec),
332

St. John the Evangelist
Church (Rab), 214
St. Justine Church (Sveti
Justina; Rab), 214
St. Lawrence, Cathedral of
(Trogir), 121
St. Lawrence, Church of
(Hvar), 141
St. Lucy, Church of (Baška),
210
St. Mark, Cathedral of
(Korčula), 144–145
St. Mark's Church (Crkva
Svetog Marka; Zagreb),
280
St. Mark's Tower (Trogir), 122
St. Martin, Church of
Split, 109
Vrsar, 245
St. Martin's Day (Martinje),
26
St. Mary, Church of
Mljet, 90–91
Oprtalj, 265
Pag, 162
Vrboska, 141
Zadar, 169
St. Mary, Pilgrimage Church
of, 320
St. Mary Magdalene, Church
of (Čazma), 343
St. Mary of the Rock, Church
of (near Pazin), 260–261
St. Mary of the Snow (Cres),
219
St. Mary the Great, Church of
(Sveta Marija Velika; Rab),
215
St. Nicholas Church (Cavtat),
92, 93
St. Nicholas Church (Pazin),
261–262
St. Nicholas Day (Komiža), 26
St. Nicholas Island, 247
St. Patrick's Pub (Osijek), 356
St. Peter's Church (Korčula),
145
St. Peter the Apostle
Cathedral (Đakovo),
347
St. Quirinus (Sveti Kivrin;
Krk), 208
St. Rock, Church of (Oprtalj),
265
St. Saviour Church
(Dubrovnik), 66, 70
St. Simeon, Church of
(Zadar), 169

St. Stephen's Cathedral
(Hvar), 136
St. Stephen's Square (Trg
Sveti Stjepan; Hvar), 136
Salona, 118–120
Salona Amphitheater, 120
Samobor, 307–311
Samobor Carnival, 307
Samobor Castle, 308
Sauna David (Zagreb), 303
Savudrija (Salvore), 256–259
Scuba diving, 52
Brela, 127
Dubrovnik, 74
Hvar, 137
Rab, 215
Vis, 151
Zadar, 172
Sea Gate (Zadar), 169–170
The Sea Organ (Zadar), 171
Seasons, 23
Sea urchins, 35
Segway Tours (Zagreb), 284
Senior travel, 39
Senj, 156–158
Senj Town Museum, 156, 158
Šetalište Franza Josefa
(Lungomare; Opatija), 198
Shipwreck diving, 52
Šibenik, 184–188
Single travelers, 39
Šipan, 90
Sisak, 335–339
Škrip, 130
Slavonia
cuisine, 22
eastern, 345
Slavonski Brod, 346
Smart phones, 43–44
Smithsonian Journeys, 44
Smoking, 41, 366
Smokvica (Korčula), 148
SNAV, 31
Sobes, 48
Sočice, 312
Special events and festivals,
24–26
Special-interest trips, 44–46
Split, 101–118
accommodations, 111–114
American Express/Atlas
Travel, 104
banks, 104
getting around, 104
holidays, 104
layout of, 104
nightlife, 117
post office, 104

restaurants, 114–117
sights and attractions, 104–110
traveling to, 102–103
visitor information, 102
walking tours, 110
Split Archaeological Museum, 110
Split Card, 117
Split Summer Festival, 25
Sponza Palace (Dubrovnik), 70, 71–72
Stara Baška, 211
Stara Vrata (Roman Gate; Rijeka), 193–194
Stari Grad (Hvar), 141
Stari Grad (Varaždin), 327, 328–329
Stepinac, Alojzije, 312
Stiniva Beach (Vis), 151
Ston, 97–99
Ston Wall and Fortifications, 98
Stradun (Dubrovnik), 70, 71
Street Art Festival Poreč, 25
Strossmayer Gallery of Old Masters (Zagreb), 284
Strossmayer Museum (Đakovo), 348
Sts. Pelagia and Massima Church (Novigrad), 253
Sts. Peter and Paul, Church of (Osijek), 350
Student travel, 39
Summer Festival
Dubrovnik, 71
Split, 106, 110
Sunčani Hvar Hotels, 137
Sun exposure, 36
Sunset Lounge (Dubrovnik), 89
Supetar, 129–130
Sustainable tourism, 40–42
Sveta Marija Velika (St. Mary the Great; Rab), 215
Sveti Andrije (St. Andrew Church; Rab), 214
Sveti Antun (St. Anthony; Rab), 215
Sveti Ivan Evandelista (Rab), 214
Sveti Justina (St. Justine Church; Rab), 214
Sveti Kivrin (St. Quirinus; Krk), 208
Svetvincenat, 257
Sv. Ivan Kapistran, Church and Monastery of, 360

Tar, 247
Tarsatica (Rijeka), 194
Taxes, 366
Telephones, 43–44
Temperatures, average, 24
Temple of Augustus (Pula), 231
Temple of Jupiter (Baptistery; Split), 110
Time zone, 366
Tipping, 21, 366
Tkalčićeva Ulica (Zagreb), 278
Toilets, 366
Top Sky Bar & Terrace (Hvar), 142
Toreta, fortress of, 183
Town Cemetery (Varaždin), 329
Town Hall (Gradska Vijećnica; Varaždin), 327, 329
Town Museum
Korčula, 145
Samobor, 309
Varaždin, 329
Town Treasury/Abbey Treasury (Korčula), 145
Train travel, 30–32
Trakošćan, 324–327
Trakošćan Castle, 326
Trakošćan Park, 326–327
Transportation Security Administration (TSA), 29
Transportation within Croatia, 31–32
Traveler's checks, 33–34
Traveling to Croatia, 28–31
Trg Bana Jelačića (Jelačić Square; Zagreb), 274, 277
Trg 5 Bunara (Five Wells Square; Zadar), 170
Trg F. Petrića (Cres), 219
Trg Marafor (Poreč), 247
Trg Sveti Stjepan (St. Stephen's Square; Hvar), 136
Triumphal Arch of the Sergi (Pula), 231
Trogir, 120–126
Troubadour (Dubrovnik), 89
Trsat, 194–195
Trsat Castle, 194–195
Trsteno (Dubrovnik), 73
Truffle Days, 268, 269
Truffle Hunting Excursions (Livade), 266
Truffles, 268, 269
Tufna (Osijek), 356–357
Tusculum (Salona), 120

Tvrđa (Osijek), 352
Tvrdalj (Hvar), 141
Twin Gates (Porta Gemina; Pula), 231

Učka Tunnel, 246
Ugljan, 181
Umag (Umago), 256–259
Upper Dalmatia, 155–188

Valentino's (Rovinj), 244
Valun, 219
Valun Tablet, 219
Vanilla (Split), 118
Varaždin, 327–330
Varaždin Festival of Baroque Music, 25–26
Vela Luka (Korčula), 148
Veliki Brijuni, 235
Veliki Slap (Big Waterfall), 317
Veliki Tabor (near Desinić), 322
Venetian Loggia (Hvar), 137
Venezia Lines, 31
Veronika of Desinić, 321
Viking Diving Center (Hvar), 137
Villa Angiolina (Opatija), 197, 198
Vinarija Lipanović (Vis), 153
Vinarija Toreta (Korčula), 148
Vis, 148–154
Vis Archaeological Museum, 151
Visas, 26
Vis Town, 150
Vodnjan, 236
The Vodnjan Mummies, 237
Volosko, 198
Votive Pillar of the Holy Trinity (Osijek), 352
Vrboska, 141
Vrsar (Orsera), 244–245
Vučedol Dove, 359
Vukovar, 359–363
Vukovar Puppet Festival, 24

Water, drinking, 366
Waterfalls, Plitvice, 317
Water Gate (Osijek), 352
Watersports
Bol, 131
Hvar, 137
Pag, 162
Zadar, 172

374 Way of the Cross (Marija Bis-
trica), 320
Weather, 23
Wellness Baška, 211
Western Slavonia, 345–347
Wildlife, 41
Wildlife concerns, 35–36
Wind farms, 41
Windsurfing, 45
Bol, 131
Hvar, 137
Wineries
Baranja, 358
Iločki Podrumi Winery, 361
Istria, 263
Međimurje's wine road,
331
Women travelers, 38
World War I, 14
World War II, 15

Youth hostels, 48
Yugoslavia, history of, 15–17

Zadar, 165–177
getting around, 167
traveling to, 166–167
visitor information, 166
The Zadar Archipelago, 181
Zadar Dreams Festival, 25
Zadruga (Vis), 154
Zagorje, cuisine, 21

Zagorka, Marija Jurić, statue
of (Zagreb), 280
Zagreb, 271–303
accommodations, 287–294
American Express, 275
arriving in, 271–272
ATMs and currency
exchange, 275
business hours, 275
cuisine, 21
doctors and dentists, 275
embassies and consulates,
275
emergencies, 276
excursions from, 304–333
north of Zagreb,
318–319
orientation, 304–306
Samobor to the
Žumberak, 307–311
south of Zagreb,
306–307
getting around, 274–275
Internet access, 276
for kids, 287
layout of, 273
mail, 276
neighborhoods, 273–274
newspapers and maga-
zines, 276
nightlife, 302–333
organized tours, 286
parking, 276
pharmacies, 276

restaurants, 294–302
safety, 276
shopping malls, 286
sights and attractions,
277–287
suggested itineraries,
53–54
telephone, 277
toilets, 277
visitor information,
272–273
Zagreb Archaeological
Museum, 284
Zagreb Baroque Festival, 25
Zagreb City Zoo, 285
Zagreb International Trade
Fair, 26
Zanzibar (Rovinj), 244
Zaton Mali (near Dubrovnik),
82
Zelena Špilja (Green Cave),
150
Zigante Tartufi (Livade), 266
Zimmer Frei (Hvar), 142
Zlatna Luka Diving Center
(Zadar), 172
Zlatni Rat (Golden Cape),
129, 130
Zlatni Rt-Punta Corrente
Nature Park, 238
Zrće Beach (Pag), 161–162
Žumberak, 307
Žumberak region, 306–312